THE ROUTLEDGE HANDBOOK ON THE MIDDLE EAST ECONOMY

AF755493

This *Handbook* captures the salient features of Middle Eastern economies and critically examines the public policy responses required to address the challenges and opportunities across the region. Bringing together wide-ranging perspectives from carefully selected and renowned subject specialists, the collection fills a gap in this relatively young and growing academic field.

Combining discussion of theory and empirical evidence, the book maps out the evolution of Middle East economics as a field within area studies and applied development economics. Presented in six thematic sections, the book enables the reader to gain an in-depth understanding of the region's main economic themes and issues:

- Growth and development in comparative perspectives
- Labour force and human development
- Natural resources, resource curse and trade
- Poverty, inequality and social policy
- Institutions and transition to democracy
- Corruption, conflict and refugees

Providing an overview of the principal economic problems, policies and performances relating to the countries in the Middle East and North Africa region, this collection will be a key resource for upper-level undergraduates, graduates and scholars with an interest in Middle East economics, applied development economics, development studies and area studies.

Hassan Hakimian is Professor of Economics and Director of the Middle Eastern Studies Department (MESD) at Hamad Bin Khalifa University in Qatar and at SOAS University of London. During 2010–19, he was Director of the London Middle East Institute (LMEI) and Reader in the Economics Department at SOAS University of London. Dr Hakimian is a Founding Member and a past President of the International Iranian Economic Association (IIEA), a Research Fellow and Chair of the Advisory Committee of the Economic Research Forum (ERF) in Cairo. In 2003 he launched the *Routledge Political Economy of the Middle East and North Africa* series.

THE ROUTLEDGE HANDBOOK ON THE MIDDLE EAST ECONOMY

Edited by
Hassan Hakimian

Routledge
Taylor & Francis Group
LONDON AND NEW YORK

First published 2021
by Routledge
2 Park Square, Milton Park, Abingdon, Oxon OX14 4RN

and by Routledge
605 Third Avenue, New York, NY 10158

Routledge is an imprint of the Taylor & Francis Group, an informa business

© 2021 selection and editorial matter, Hassan Hakimian; individual chapters, the contributors

The right of Hassan Hakimian to be identified as the author of the editorial material, and of the authors for their individual chapters, has been asserted in accordance with sections 77 and 78 of the Copyright, Designs and Patents Act 1988.

All rights reserved. No part of this book may be reprinted or reproduced or utilised in any form or by any electronic, mechanical, or other means, now known or hereafter invented, including photocopying and recording, or in any information storage or retrieval system, without permission in writing from the publishers.

Trademark notice: Product or corporate names may be trademarks or registered trademarks, and are used only for identification and explanation without intent to infringe.

British Library Cataloguing-in-Publication Data
A catalogue record for this book is available from the British Library

Library of Congress Cataloging-in-Publication Data
A catalog record has been requested for this book

ISBN: 978-1-138-09977-7 (hbk)
ISBN: 978-1-032-02137-9 (pbk)
ISBN: 978-1-315-10396-9 (ebk)

Typeset in Bembo
by Deanta Global Publishing Services, Chennai, India

To Mitra for her grace and wisdom

CONTENTS

FIGURES

TABLES

CONTRIBUTORS

Khalid Abu-Ismail is the Chief of the Economic Development and Poverty Section at UN-ESCWA. He has been the lead author and co-author of several UN Flagship publications, including "Arab Vision 2030" (ESCWA, 2015), "Arab Middle Class" (ESCWA, 2015), "Arab Multi-Dimensional Poverty" (LAS, OPHI, UNICEF and ESCWA, 2017), and the co-lead author of the joint ESCWA ERF report on "Rethinking Inequality in Arab States" (2019). He is a Policy Affiliate at the Economic Research Forum (ERF).

Facundo Alvaredo is Professor at the Paris School of Economics and Research Fellow at IIEP-UBA-CONICET. He is also Senior Research Fellow of INET at Oxford University. He is Co-Director of the World Inequality Database and the World Inequality Lab.

Lydia Assouad is a PhD Candidate at the Paris School of Economics and a visiting student at Harvard University, specialising in political economy, development and economic history. She is also the El-Erian Fellow at the Carnegie Middle East Center and a Research Fellow at the World Inequality Lab. She is the author of "Rethinking the Lebanese Economic Miracle: The Extreme Concentration of Income and Wealth in Lebanon" and "Measuring Inequality in the Middle East 1990–2016: The World's Most Unequal Region?" with Facundo Alvaredo and Thomas Piketty.

Izak Atiyas is Associate Professor of Economics at Sabanci University, Istanbul, Turkey. He has worked as a senior economist at the World Bank in the Private Sector Development Department and at Bilkent University as Visiting Assistant Professor of Economics. He has been with Sabanci University since 1998, and is also the Director of TUSiAD-Sabanci University Competitiveness Forum. His research areas include productivity, industrial policy, policy, political economy, regulation of network industries and privatisation.

David Cobham is Professor of Economics at Heriot-Watt University, Edinburgh. His research concentrates on monetary policy, in the UK and in other countries, but he also has a special interest in the MENA region.

Julia Devlin is Lecturer at the University of Virginia where she teaches a course on the Economics of the Middle East. She was previously at the World Bank (1999–2011) and a Nonresident Senior Fellow in the Center for Global Economy and Development at the

Brookings Institution (2012–2015). Her academic activities include teaching classes on the economics of the Middle East at Harvard University, the School of Advanced International Studies at Johns Hopkins University as well as the University of Virginia.

Ishac Diwan holds the Chair Monde Arabe at Paris Sciences et Letters, and has held teaching positions at Harvard Kennedy School, Dauphine University and New York University. He worked at the Work Bank for many years in the Research Complex, the Middle East and Africa Departments and the World Bank Institute. Professor Diwan directs the Political Economy program of the Economic Research Forum (ERF), an association of Middle East social scientists and economists based in Cairo.

Safaa El Tayeb El-Kogali is the Education Manager for east and southern Africa at the World Bank. She has worked in numerous departments and regions at the World Bank and was also the Regional Director for West Asia and North Africa at the Population Council. El-Kogali is a Policy Affiliate with the Economic Research Forum. Her latest publications include: *Expectations and Aspirations: A New Framework for Education in the Middle East and North Africa* (2020) edited jointly with Caroline Krafft.

Hassan Hakimian is Director of the Middle Eastern Studies Department at the College of Humanities and Social Sciences (CHSS) in Hamad Bin Khalifa University (HBKU) in Doha. He is also an Emeritus Professor in Economics at SOAS University of London, where he was Director of The London Middle East Institute (2010–2019). He is a Research Fellow of the Economic Research Forum (ERF) and a Founding member, past President and a Board member of the International Iranian Economic Association (IIEA).

Hatem Jemmali is an Associate Professor at the University of Manouba and a Senior Research Fellow at the Laboratory for Research on Quantitative Development Economics in Tunisia. His research concentrates mainly on water poverty, climate change, internal migration, poverty and inequality in the MENA region. He has carried out a number of research projects and consultancies related to inequality of opportunity, wage disparities and climate change impacts.

Fida Karam is Associate Professor of Economics in the Department of Economics and Finance at Gulf University for Science and Technology (Kuwait) and a Research Fellow at ERF and EMNES. Her research focuses on international trade and trade policy in the MENA Region, international and internal migration, computable general equilibrium models and microfinance.

Massoud Karshenas is an Emeritus Professor of Economics at the Department of Economics at SOAS University of London. He is Research Fellow of the Economic Research Forum for Arab Countries, Iran and Turkey (ERF), and a founding member and current President of the International Iranian Economic Association (IIEA).

Caroline Krafft is Associate Professor in the Department of Economics and Political Science at St. Catherine University. As a development economist, her research focuses on labour, education, health and inequality in the MENA region. Among recent projects are work on refugees, early childhood development, labour market dynamics, life course transitions, human capital accumulation and fertility.

Samir Makdisi is Professor Emeritus of Economics and Founding Director of the Institute of Financial Economics, the American University of Beirut (AUB). He has served as Minister of Economy and Trade, Lebanon, 1992; Deputy President of AUB, 1992–1998; Chair of the Board of Trustees, Economic Research Forum for the Arab Countries, Iran and Turkey, 1993–2001.

He is the author of *The Lessons of Lebanon, the Economics of War and Development* (2004, 2016), co-editor of *Democracy in the Arab World: Explaining the Deficit* (Routledge 2011) and co-editor *of Democratic Transitions in the Arab World* (2017).

Adeel Malik is Associate Professor at the University of Oxford's Department of International Development and holds the Globe Fellowship in Economies of Muslim Societies at the Oxford Centre for Islamic Studies. He teaches and researches issues of Middle Eastern political economy. He recently co-edited a volume titled *Crony Capitalism in the Middle East: Business and Politics from Liberalization to the Arab Spring* (2019).

Mahmood Messkoub has thought and researched at the International Institute of Social Studies (ISS, the Hague, Erasmus University of Rotterdam) and Universities of London and Leeds. His current research interests are in the areas of economics of social policy (e.g. cash transfers and universal versus targeted social provisioning), population ageing and migration. He has published in areas such as social policy in MENA, population ageing, cash transfers and migration. He has acted as consultant to ESCWA, ILO and the UN (DESA, UNFPA).

Valentine M. Moghadam is Professor of Sociology and International Affairs, past director of Middle East and Mediterranean Studies and co-founder of the Gender and Development Initiative. She served as a senior researcher at UNU/WIDER (Helsinki, 1990–1995) and a section chief at UNESCO (Paris, 2004–06), and is the author of *Modernizing Women: Gender and Social Change in the Middle East* (1993, 2003, 2013).

Jeffrey B. Nugent is Professor of Economics at USC. As a development economist, he has worked on a wide variety of issues, problems and analytical techniques and in and on a variety of countries in Latin America, Africa, South and East Asia and especially the Middle East and North Africa. In recent years, much of it has made use of new institutional economics and political economy perspectives. His affiliations include Economic Research Forum (ERF), IZA, MEEA, AEA.

Jennifer C. Olmsted grew up in Beirut, Lebanon and is Professor of Economics and Director of the Social Entrepreneurship Semester and the Arabic and Middle East Studies programs at Drew University, Madison, NJ, USA. Her research focuses on gender and economic well-being in the Middle East/armed conflict contexts. She has published in *Feminist Economics*, *Journal of Development Studies*, *Journal of Middle East Women's Studies*, *Women's Studies International Forum* and *World Development*.

Thomas Piketty is Professor at EHESS and at the Paris School of Economics, and co-director of the World Inequality Lab. His work focuses on wealth and income inequality. He is the author of the international best-seller *Capital in the 21st Century* (2013) and of *Capital and Ideology* (2020).

Jared Rubin is a Professor of Economics at Chapman University. He is an economic historian interested in the role that Islam and Christianity played in the long-run "reversal of fortunes" between the economies of the Middle East and Western Europe. His book, *Rulers, Religion, and Riches: Why the West got Rich and the Middle East Did Not* (2017), which addresses these issues, has won multiple book awards.

Niranjan Sarangi is an Economic Affairs Officer and Project Leader on "Public Finance and Inclusive Fiscal Policy" at UN-ESCWA. He has published in journals and UN publications on issues of fiscal policy, growth, poverty and inequality. He is the lead author of UN publications

"Rethinking Fiscal Policy for the Arab Region" (2017) and "Social Expenditure Monitor for Arab States" (2019). His work focuses on connecting macroeconomics to human development policies and actions in Asia and in the Arab states over the past 15 years in the UN system.

Raimundo Soto is Associate Professor of Economics, Pontificia Universidad Católica de Chile. He specialises in macroeconomic theory and econometrics and has published extensively in international journals covering long-run growth, exchange rate misalignment and monetary policy, as well as corruption, resource curse, institutions and fiscal policy. His most recent book is *The Economy of Dubai* published in 2016.

Caroline Sullivan is Professor of Environmental Economics and Policy at the School of Environment, Science and Engineering, Southern Cross University, Australia. She specialises in water management and policy, climate adaptation and valuation of ecosystem services.

Aysit Tansel is Professor of Economics and teaches part-time at the Middle East Technical University (METU), Ankara. She is a Research Fellow of the Institute of Labor Economics (IZA) in Bonn and the Economic Research Forum (ERF) in Cairo. Her publications have appeared in journals such as *Economics of Education Review*, *Economic Development and Cultural Change*, *Journal of Development Economics*, *Public Choice*, *International Migration*, *Applied Economics* and *Weltwirtschaftliches Archiv*.

Zafiris Tzannatos is an independent Consultant for Development Strategy and Social Policy based in Jordan having previously served in senior positions at the World Bank, ILO and academia, including as Professor and Chair of the Economics Department at the American University of Beirut. He was the lead author of the ILO/UNDP flagship publication "*Rethinking Economic Growth: Towards Productive and Inclusive Arab Societies*" (2012). His other publications include more than 15 books and 250 papers and reports.

Chahir Zaki is Associate Professor of Economics, Faculty of Economics and Political Science, Cairo University, and Director of EMNES Egypt and Senior Economist at ERF. He is also a consultant for several international organisations including the World Bank, the International Labour Office and the International Trade Centre. He has published on international trade, trade policy, trade in services, applied economics and macroeconomic modelling.

Abdallah Zouache is University Professor of Economics at Sciences Po Lille. His research relates to the economic challenges of MENA countries and is focused on the following areas: growth and development, the colonial legacy, the foundations and practices of economic policy and the political economy of conflicts and reforms.

ACKNOWLEDGEMENTS

Editing a handbook on one of the world's key regional economies such as the Middle East is no small task and without the help and inspiration of many colleagues and friends over the years, it would have been even more daunting to contemplate, let alone undertake.

As I explain in the Introduction to this volume, Middle East economics has come a long way over the past decades to evolve into a specialist field within applied development economics, area studies and development studies. The availability of relevant and appropriate references and teaching materials, although growing over time and reflecting this process of maturation, has at times been a constraint for those engaged in teaching the subject.

Soon after the initial invitation from Routledge, my initial hesitation quickly gave way to the compelling logic of the need for a new text – as distinct from a textbook – to take stock of the latest state of thinking and research on the subject, whilst being widely accessible to a large learner community. Just over four years later, the current volume reflects extensive collaboration with nearly 40 contributors and many others whose footprint is in the subject but who do not make a direct appearance in the book.

I owe the belief in, and commitment to, this volume to many of my students over the years during my years at SOAS both as a member of the Department of Economics (beginning in 1993) and more recently as Director of the London Middle East Institute (2010–19). The intellectual environment of the Department of Economics as well as the wider and vibrant community of Middle East specialists at SOAS were essential for helping me shape my ideas in broader political economy terms and avoid the entrapments of a narrow area studies approach. I am particularly in debt to my long-time friend and colleague, Professor Massoud Karshenas, with whom I taught the course over several years.

Several Routledge editors were very helpful at different stages of the book's preparations. Among these are James Whiting who first approached me, Emma Tyce who followed up before moving on and Titanilla Panczel who steered the manuscript through in its final stages. I am also grateful to the Routledge production team, which saw the publication through its final stages with exemplary professionalism.

While the initial stages of this book overlapped with my last two years at SOAS (before my retirement in 2019), the final two benefited from my new position as Director of the Middle Eastern Studies Department at HBKU in Qatar. Here, I am indebted to our Masters students as well as all my colleagues for another vibrant and collegiate environment in which I saw the project through whilst getting to terms with work and life in a new environment after more than four decades in London! I am especially grateful to our Dean, Dr Amal Al-Malki, who inspired and energised us to go about our daily routines especially during the uncertainties brought about by the pandemic crisis.

Being an active member of important international research and scholarly networks on the Middle East has also been an important element in the formation of the ideas behind the book and has offered me the contacts and the networks I could draw from to bring it to fruition. Chief among these is the Economic Research Forum (ERF), the Cairo-based network of economic researchers dedicated to the study of the Arab countries, Iran and Turkey. Regular and extensive interactions with ERF colleagues – many of whom feature in the book – no doubt facilitated my task of soliciting contributions for a wide range of topics.

I am grateful to all contributors for their cooperation and especially for their patience while different parts of the book were shaping up at an uneven pace!

The final word goes to my wonderful family, who continue to give me the space and inspiration to devote myself to my professional undertakings, knowing I could always draw from their support and wisdom. My sons, Bijan and Babak, and my wife, Mitra, whom the book is dedicated to, are also present for me in the book in ways that they would not directly recognise. Without their friendship, I would have lacked the energy or inspiration to undertake it.

The usual disclaimer of course applies and any errors or omissions contained in any chapter or part are the sole responsibility of the authors and not of their institutions or other individuals.

Hassan Hakimian
2 April 2021, Doha

1
INTRODUCTION

Hassan Hakimian[1]

Knowledge of Middle Eastern economies as a field within development economics is arguably of recent origins and has evolved in uneven ways. Unlike some other regions which have played a more notable role in the genesis or evolution of development theory and practice, the contribution of Middle Eastern economies has been more limited and to a large extent confined to more recent decades.[2] Despite this, Middle East economics has grown steadily and diversified enough over the last fifty years to warrant this brief and selective review as an introduction to the present volume.

By contrast, preoccupations with regional development challenges in Latin America go back to the 1930s, predating – 'albeit slightly' – the early formulation of development economics in the writings of a group of economists in Britain and North America in the 1940s and 1950s (Hunt, 1989: 47).[3] The declining prices for primary commodity exports during the Great Depression in the 1930s, and the subsequent disruption to international trade caused by World War II which curtailed imports of manufactures, acted as a boost for domestic industries, raising new and challenging questions for the development trajectory in the Latin American context. A generation of economists led by Raúl Prebisch began to question the benefits of adhering to conventional comparative advantage trade theory (Prebisch, 1950). The establishment of the UN's Economic Commission for Latin America (ECLA) – of which Prebisch was the first Director – paved the ground for the emergence of the structuralist school in development economics (Love, 1980). The theorists and practitioners associated with ECLA formulated the case for Import Substitution Industrialisation (ISI) supported by active state intervention in the course of economic development. Even the subsequent disillusionment with the ISI strategy which led to another influential development school – the Dependency School – originated in Latin America. Borrowing from the structuralists the notion of 'unequal exchange', the proponents of this school conceptualised the asymmetrical relationship inherent in the international division of labour between the developed 'core' and underdeveloped 'periphery'.[4]

South Asia, too, was home to – and arguably served as a testing ground for – some of the nascent development theories and debates in the 1950s. Although perhaps more under the influence of Soviet planning, India's independence in 1947 instigated a long tradition of five-year development plans that were to last until recently.[5] The first two Plans focused on boosting long-run economic growth. The First (1951–6) was based on the Harrod–Domar growth model and focused on the development of the primary sector. The Second (1956–61) was based on the model developed by Mahalanobis (1955), the Indian statistician who extended the growth model to two sectors in which the development of the capital goods industry received priority attention.[6]

The early period: 1940s–60s

To suggest that big ideas in development theory did not originate in the Middle East and North Africa (MENA) region does not mean that they did not reach the region. An interesting, yet perhaps little known, case is found in Arthur Lewis's seminal paper in 1954 ('Economic Development with Unlimited Supplies of Labour') in which he mentions Egypt along with India and Jamaica, where he considers the 'unlimited supply of labour' as 'obviously the relevant assumption' (Lewis, 1954: 140).[7] Lewis, who was the first development economist to receive a Nobel Prize in economics (jointly in 1979), stated later that the initial idea behind his two-sector model of economic development came to him in 1952 when he was 'walking down the road in Bangkok' (Tignor, 2006: 88). His visit, however, to Egypt in the spring of 1953, where he delivered three lectures on industrialisation, led Tignor to suggest that 'in many ways, the Egyptian lectures previewed the main ideas in Lewis's 1954 article' (2006: 87).[8]

It would be incorrect, therefore, to suggest that development economics or policy debates escaped the MENA region altogether. A number of seminal works covered this early period. Some of these focused on individual country experiences (Bharier, 1971, on Iran; Mabro and Radwan, 1976, on Egypt); others addressed the agrarian and land reform aspects in the region (Lambton, 1953; Warriner, 1948); and yet others provided invaluable contributions to the economic history of the Middle East (Cook, 1970; Issawi, 1952, 1949).[9]

The 1960s and 1970s were, in fact, periods of rapid growth and transformation in the region. Between 1960 and 1985, the annual GDP growth rate in MENA was 3.7%, only surpassed by that of East Asia and the Pacific at 4.3% per annum. Productivity growth in MENA too was the highest in the world, with output per worker rising at 6% annually in the 1960s (Page, 1998: 133; Yousef, 2004: 95–96). These improvements were matched by increases in a wide range of social indicators, such as falling infant mortality and rising life expectancy and literacy.

In this 'golden' period, many states followed an import substitution model of industrialisation, embarked on land reform programmes and initiated large-scale public investment projects to boost their physical infrastructure (Richards and Waterbury, 1996; Yousef, 2004: 93). Overall, the development model of this period has been described as 'interventionist-redistributive' (Ayubi, 1995) with the state viewed as the primary provider of welfare (subsidising education, health care and food). Gradually rising oil revenues, a strong nation-building ideology in the newly independent states and the prevailing Keynesian macroeconomic paradigm at the time provided the justifications for active state intervention in the economy throughout this period (Yousef, 2004).

The oil boom era: 1970s

The formation of OPEC in September 1960 was, however, to prove a turning point in the contemporary economic history of the region as seen in the meteoric rise in its importance on the world energy and financial scenes especially after the 1970s.[10] The first oil boom, which saw crude prices quadruple in 1973–4, and the subsequent change of ownership from foreign to national oil companies catapulted the region into the international spotlight transforming its position within the wider international political economy. This occurred at two levels: the hugely shifting economic landscape of the region and within it the group of oil-exporting nations which were now recipients of significant oil windfalls, as well as the rising importance of MENA as a whole in the international economy after the mid-1970s. Not unsurprisingly, these developments attracted the attention of economists who began to highlight the opportunities and challenges which these vast energy riches posed for the region's long-term development.

Interestingly, however, one of the earliest and most notable contributions to the political economy of oil and development in MENA predated – albeit slightly – the mentioned developments in the oil sector and the subsequent emergent literature. Although Hossein Mahdavy's seminal paper in 1970 on the 'Rentier States' was with reference to one of the larger producers in the region (Iran), it did not attract the attention it merited at the time. Over time, however, with increased importance of oil revenues, a copious literature emerged which correlated oil rents with poor economic outcomes in resource-rich economies. That burgeoning literature – known as the 'resource curse' theory – embraced a wider notion of natural resources beyond oil and energy in the Middle East, but it had a special resonance in MENA with lasting influence to date.[11]

The drawbacks of over-dependence on natural resources were clearly highlighted in Mahdavy's early contribution:

> The danger that faces the Rentier States is that while some of the natural resources of these countries are being fully developed by foreign concerns and considerable government expenditures (usually in a few cities) are creating an impression of prosperity and growth, the mass of the population may remain in a backward state and the most important factors for long-run growth may receive little or no attention at all.
>
> *(Mahdavy, 1970: 437)*

The foundation stone for the emergent resource curse literature was thus arguably laid out in the MENA region. Along with its various strands,[12] this approach came to constitute perhaps the most influential approach to MENA economics since the 1970s and is arguably one of the few theoretical contributions that seems to have originated in the region and subsequently moved outwards. This appears in contrast to most debates and issues that were borrowed from elsewhere and applied to the Middle Eastern context.

The growth crisis in MENA and push for reforms: 1980s and 1990s

By the 1980s, the region's fortunes had begun to take a turn for the worse in both oil- and non-oil economies. The oil price crash of the 1980s and open discord and disunity within OPEC choked off the oil bounty and with it the flow of remittances within the region.[13] Elsewhere, deteriorating public finances, rising debt and shrinking public investment programmes were common experiences. Struck by a deep economic crisis, MENA was now struggling to keep pace with both its past growth record and with other regions as its GDP growth rate sank to 1% per annum during the period 1986–2001 (Shafik, 1998; Yousef, 2004: 99).

The deterioration in MENA's economic outcomes inevitably impacted the development discourse within the region, shifting its focus openly to the 'growth crisis' of the 1980s (Page, 1998).[14] If the region's natural riches and the oil bounty had put it in the academic and policy spotlight a decade earlier, now it became a curiosity to explain its inferior comparative performance that shaped these debates. This period saw the proliferation of a rich and multi-faceted literature devoted to MENA economies fuelled by a desire to shed light on the region's apparently distinct problems. The spotlight was now on why MENA lagged behind other parts of the world and how this could be rectified.

At one level, this period's experience seemingly confirmed the premonitions of the resource curse literature. The mineral riches and the oil boom had not only failed to benefit the region in a sustained way, they had seemingly dented its prospects for growth and development. While the resource curse theory and its various forms and applications in the region continued to flourish, interest in MENA's economies and their challenges nevertheless diversified and extended to encompass a broader set of topics (see below).

One important characteristic of this period was the rising influence and growing prominence of the International Financial Institutions (IFIs) and donor agencies in articulating the region's policy discourse. MENA countries' growth crisis and their need for external assistance now gave the Washington Consensus institutions an opportunity to advocate market-friendly economic reforms as part of an overarching plan to resuscitate MENA's growth and to avoid further costs of delaying their implementation. Thus, a considerable amount of the intellectual output and energy of these institutions in this period focused on making the case for a transition to market-oriented regimes founded on domestic economic liberalisation and privatisation on the one hand, and a more open approach to the international economy on the other (Shafik, 1998; Handoussa, 1997).

According to this approach, MENA states were characterised as 'laggards' since they seemed to be reluctant and lacked the capacity to capitalise on the benefits of the pervasive globalisation trends and a rolling back of the state (Cammett et al., 2015: Chapter 7; Hakimian and Moshaver, 2001: Chapter 1; Karshenas and Moghadam, 2001). As elsewhere, in MENA too, the push for reforms now featured as an integral part of the Structural Adjustment Programmes (SAPs) which some states in the region – led by Morocco, Tunisia, Jordan and Egypt – turned to, albeit in varying degrees, to redress their ailing economies.

In this era and from this perspective, the imperative to adopt appropriate (read neoliberal) economic policies moved centre-stage and was considered pertinent for success. However, equally important was institutional reform since evidence suggested a 'virtuous cycle' between the quality and capacity of institutions in the course of economic development on one hand, and policy reforms and growth on the other. Hence, the quality of public administration in MENA was seen as 'the missing' link between policy reform and growth (Page and Van Gelder, 2001).

Another manifestation of the MENA region's poor, yet distinct, economic performance in this period – and one matching its growth crisis – was the incidence of high unemployment rates and a persistent lack of success in job creation across the region. After years of experiencing some of the highest population growth rates on a global scale, MENA's expected 'demographic transition' seemed to be delayed or disrupted. For many this apparent 'demographic puzzle' – persistently high fertility rates incommensurate with the region's high per capita GDP standards – presented itself as another symptom of a perceived 'Middle Eastern exceptionalism' (Courbage, 1999; Fargues, 2008; Tabutin and Schoumaker, 2005; Roudi-Fahimi, 2001).

Unsurprisingly, the stalled demographic transition had important consequences for the labour market with wider population pyramids, a growing 'youth bulge' and persistently high unemployment rates in many countries: double-digit national rates along with some of the highest youth unemployment rates in the world were now common experiences in many MENA countries (ILO, 2000; see also Chapters 6 and 18 of this volume).

This led to a burgeoning of the literature in this period, which focused on various labour force issues and the dynamics of the labour market. But opinion was divided as to whether the explanation for high unemployment rates was rooted in supply-side factors (the demographics of the region) or on the demand side reflecting the incapacity of the private sector to absorb new labour market entrants and an over-reliance on the public sector to generate the required jobs (see Chapter 18 in this volume for more on this).

By now, Middle East economics was in full swing with debates and controversies proliferating and the literature extending well beyond the growth and jobs crises. Concerns now extended to diverse issues encompassing 'structural economic imbalances … deficient political systems, conditions of war and conflict and even culture and religion' (Yousef, 2004: 92).

Other notable features of this period, which indicated growing interest in the economies of the Middle East, were the rise in intellectual output and publications on one hand, and the expansion of research capacity in the region on the other. The number of economists and policy advisors who specialised in the region rose, at least partially aided by the IFIs and their capacity-building and training programmes, but also due to the rise in the number of professionally trained economists working in the MENA region itself, now estimated to reach 'perhaps two thousand' (Pfeifer, 2016: 8).[15]

The bumpy road to and through the 'Arab Spring': 2000s

In this period, interest in Middle Eastern economies continued its upward trajectory although important qualitative changes were also to follow.[16]

During the opening decade of the 2000s, debates over the supposed benefits of international integration and economic reforms intensified. This was part of a global backlash against the one-size-fits-all model of globalisation advocated by IFIs and indicated a pushback against the supposed benefits of the Washington Consensus-type policies globally (Stiglitz, 2002). This process was principally driven by concerns about the wider socioeconomic and welfare impacts of these policies in developing countries but was fanned also by the Asian Financial Crisis in 1997 which swept across the highly successful Asian economies (Hakimian, 2001).

In the MENA region itself, in several countries that had been undergoing SAPs and the austerity packages that accompanied them, the impetus for such rethink was gathering pace. Street protests and riots had arisen as early as 1977 in Egypt, 1984 in Tunisia, 1988 in both Algeria and Jordan and 1993 in Morocco. These were emblematic of the growing dissatisfaction with the promised 'trickle down' in these policies and highlighted the uneven distribution of their perceived benefits. Just as state-led development of the previous era had made way for market-friendly policies, the pendulum began to swing back in the opposite direction with the welfare consequences and social impacts of the neoliberal reforms coming under increased scrutiny.[17]

The biggest shock to economic thinking in the Middle East context, however, came from the tumultuous uprisings and political unrest that swept across the Arab world after 2010 – the so-called Arab Spring. Like any landmark event, these posed new and difficult questions for the economies of the region. Some of these related to understanding and explaining the root causes of these events and some to their consequences.

An important question raised by these uprisings was why economists had failed to anticipate upheavals of such enormity in the first instance (Hakimian, 2017).[18] In the decade prior to the onset of these upheavals, the region in general had experienced respectable annual average growth rates of about 4.5–5% between 2001 and 2010 (Hakimian, 2011). Poverty, too, at least judged by conventional criteria and on a comparative basis, was moderate in the region and in some countries like Egypt appeared to be declining (see Chapters 8 and 12 of this volume). These gains were somewhat diluted by the population growth that accompanied them, with real per capita GDP growth rates hovering at around 2–2.5% and continued high unemployment rates, especially among the youth. It is, however, fair to suggest that the growth crisis of the previous decades had been reversed and the region experienced a significant improvement in its performance compared to the 1980s and 1990s, when it lagged behind other regions as seen above.

Whether a pay-off to the Washington Consensus policies in the region or fuelled by the global commodity price boom in the first decade of the 2000s, the advocates of these policies felt justified enough to attribute the dividends to the adoption of their policies, even leading some IFIs to laud the Arab autocrats on their economic performance on the eve of the uprisings (Harrigan and El Said, 2014; Mossallam, 2015).[19] The World Bank's subsequent stark and sincere *mea culpa* , however, indicated that not all had gone according to plan (World Bank, 2015).[20]

Although arguably of political and social nature, these upheavals raised a raft of questions for economists dealing with the MENA region. For instance, were they misled by using wrong indicators? Or rather did weak analysis or faulty inferences let them down? Should they have paid more attention to potential pitfalls? Or even more simply put, was data quality to blame? (Hakimian, 2017).

At one level, one could argue that mainstream economics, and its *marginalist* framework in particular, is ill-equipped for dealing with social and political upheavals on such scale, given its focus on equilibrium-seeking behaviour of *homo economicus*, guided by rational choice.

Viewed from a broader perspective, MENA countries were experiencing improvements in relative prosperity, not economic downturns or stagnation in the period before the Arab Spring uprisings. This goes against conventional thinking, which generally links mass revolts to economic hardship, contending that periods of relative prosperity are correlated with mass political quiescence.[21] This is also borne out by history. The Iranian Revolution in 1979, like the Arab uprisings in the 2000s, followed unparalleled economic growth, driven by highly favourable international oil prices (which had quadrupled in 1973–4).[22] This is of course not to deny that popular grievances abounded and there were plenty of reasons for ordinary people, especially the young and the educated middle classes, to feel politically and economically alienated under the Arab autocratic regimes, especially after years of pursuing austerity programmes.

Whatever the causes, the Arab uprisings, however, made both a quantitative and qualitative impact on MENA economics. This period saw not only greater interest in the economies of the region and an associated quantitative growth of the literature, it also brought a lateral expansion in the scope and coverage of the political economy of MENA. Among economists now there is arguably greater and more explicit recognition of the importance of political and social factors. This has in turn helped enrich the scope and diversity of topics covered including poverty and inequality, human development, the role of religion and Islam in development, crony capitalism, governance and transition to democracy, gender, impacts of conflict and forced displacements (refugees), to mention some. These themes and the associated literature are addressed in different sections of the present volume (especially Sections IV–VI).

Contours of Middle East economics

It can be argued that regional economics in general sits uncomfortably between two distinct and disparate disciplines: area studies, which is geared towards humanities and social sciences, and mainstream economics, which is dominated by technical or quantitative approaches. Seen from this perspective, Middle East economics is arguably no exception (Olmsted, 2005).

This brief review has brought out a number of notable issues about the growth and evolution of Middle East economics since the middle of the last century. We have seen that a study of these economies as a specialised sub-discipline started late and progressed slowly within the domain of applied development economics, especially compared to other regions (Latin America and South Asia).

Moreover, the subject evolved over three phases after the 1950s, each one reflecting the economic circumstances and the associated challenges and opportunities encountered by the region at the time. In the 1970s, academic interest in MENA's economies galvanised around its oil riches and the region's changing contribution to the international political economy after the oil booms of the 1970s. This led to the resource curse theory moving centre-stage, dominating the debates, analysis and empirical evidence presented on oil-exporting economies. What is perhaps significant about this broad approach – and one that possibly sets it apart from most other debates and applications – is that it had its roots in the region and travelled outwards to contribute to the wider development economics literature on a global scale.

The second wave came in the 1980s, when the region's weak performance opened up a plethora of questions for development economists and practitioners focused on explaining a record of inferior performance and outcomes (jobs and growth). The perceived limits of the interventionist-redistributive model in this period gave the IFIs a platform for advocating neoliberal policies for ailing economies such as Tunisia, Morocco, Jordan, Yemen and Egypt. This period saw a strong push for institutional reform and structural adjustments of the MENA economies.

In the third and current phase, the Arab countries in the region were rocked by significant political and social upheavals with a lasting impact to date. Two inter-related considerations have made these stand out: the fact that they occurred somewhat unexpectedly, as well as that they ran against the prevailing economic orthodoxy which saw the region's economies to be on the right policy paths. Inevitably these events led to hard questions being asked among the region's observers and helped shift the research agenda of Middle East economists, too. As a result, the boundaries of the economics of the region have been stretched to accommodate political economy and inter- or cross-disciplinary topics, hence broadening the research agenda to encompass novel topics.

The choice of topics and the range of subjects covered in the ensuing chapters in this book in many ways reflect both the contours of the Middle East economics as discussed above, and the open nature of many of the recent topics and debates unfolding especially after the 2010–11 upheavals.

Below, I offer an overview of these chapters and the different sections in which they appear in this volume.

Book structure and chapters

In Section I of the book, two chapters are devoted to the theme of MENA's growth and development in comparative perspective. Chapter 2 by Jeffrey B. Nugent addresses how to explain growth in the Middle East. Nugent argues that the MENA countries are sufficiently distinctive as a group to justify their study and analysis as a region and to be compared with other regions. Yet, at the same time, they are sufficiently different from one another in resource endowments, structure, size, governance and behavioural patterns to justify comparisons among them. Nugent focuses on different factors which can help explain both the commonalities and differences in these various respects (including their volatility) and especially in their economic growth rates over time.

In Chapter 3, Julia C. Devlin follows on the same topic by addressing the overarching question of whether the MENA region is indeed exceptional in terms of its growth pattern and experiences. She points out that, despite achieving higher growth rates, significant gains in living standards and deeper integration with global markets for much of the 2000s, MENA countries' experience, nevertheless, suffered from underlying patterns of weak total factor productivity growth, high fiscal and current account deficits and a lingering import 'bias', raising questions about the sustainability of their economic performance in this period. Devlin explores the structural features of MENA countries relative to their comparators and proposes several unique aspects of these economies. Among the problems and challenges she highlights are high levels of public sector employment and economic activity; weak growth prospects and lack of access to finance for many private firms; concentrated markets and low exports; limited labour market opportunities for youth, particularly female workers; inefficient social transfers; and lacklustre agricultural productivity growth together with rising freshwater scarcity.

Section II in the book takes up the theme of labour force and human development in the region.

In Chapter 4, Khalid Abu-Ismail and Niranjan Sarangi provide a review of the main human development stylised facts for the Arab states compared to other developing regions based on the global Human Development Index (HDI). The results indicate the region has scored many impressive development achievements since 1990. However, notable differences can be observed at the sub-regional level and some countries are regressing after 2010 due to ongoing conflicts. There are also major inequality deficits, particularly in gender and education. The chapter then discusses what is missing from this index and discusses the impact on the HDI for Arab countries when one of the missing dimensions, good governance, is included. It argues that these findings may lead us to rethink the conventional wisdom on human development in Arab states and to do more work on human development measurement from a regional perspective.

In Chapter 5, Aysit Tansel picks up an important theme central to the HDI by examining private returns to investment in education across the region. Here, she reviews the trends and patterns of the estimates of the private returns to investment in education in MENA countries. The overall regional average for MENA is observed to be rather low compared to the other regions of the world. Explanations for this observation are provided. Where possible, private returns to education by gender and by levels of schooling over time are also presented and discussed.

The last chapter in this section – Chapter 6 by Massoud Karshenas and Valentine M. Moghadam – is devoted to women's employment and female labour force participation (FLFP). It examines the supply- and demand-side factors and forces behind the problem and puzzle of low FLFP and low female employment in MENA. It addresses several related questions: Why are women with basic or secondary schooling less likely to be in the workforce than those with a university education?; What explains the high rates of female unemployment? To address these two puzzles, Karshenas and Moghadam provide first an overview of various explanatory frameworks: culturalist, supply-and-demand, and institutionalist approaches. They find merit in all three explanations, which they argue create a kind of 'vicious cycle' of low female labour force participation, conservative social norms and the absence of institutional support. They end with some suggestions for further research and highlight the need for more institutional support structures to incentivise maternal employment.

Section III is devoted to the theme of natural resources, the resource curse and trade.

In Chapter 7, Raimundo Soto asks whether the GCC economies can escape the oil curse. An abundance of natural resources has shaped the development of GCC economies. While hydrocarbon exports have allowed high welfare for the national population, symptoms of an oil curse are present in the dependence on resource wealth for fiscal revenues, chronically low productivity growth and a perennial inability to cope with the volatility of oil prices. This chapter aims at answering three key questions. First, is there hard evidence of a resource curse in the GCC economies? Second, if so, can GCC economies escape the curse? And third, what can be learned from success stories in dealing with the resource curse?

In Chapter 8, Hassan Hakimian re-examines the oil curse from the perspective of possibilities oil-exporters have to potentially transform their oil rents into inclusive growth. A copious literature on the resource curse correlates these rents with poor economic outcomes in resource-rich economies. The common yardstick for evaluating economic performance is generally GDP growth rates. This chapter focuses on the broader question of whether the experience of MENA oil-exporters has been conducive to inclusive growth both over time and in a comparative context. To find out if these countries have been successful in turning their hydrocarbon wealth into wider benefits for their population, Hakimian computes a novel Inclusive Growth Index and associated rankings for 154 countries during three five-year periods between 2001 and 2015. The results show a marked deterioration in the case of MENA's oil-exporting countries over the periods of 2001–05 and 2006–10, particularly marred by a poor record in job creation especially for the young population.

In Chapter 9, Hatem Jemmali and Caroline A. Sullivan address water conflicts in MENA through a comparative analysis which uses a restructured Water Poverty Index. Under the premise that water scarcity is inherently multidimensional, integrated composite indices have been developed to go beyond traditional deterministic approaches to water poverty assessment. In this chapter, an enhanced methodology, to overcome weaknesses in existing indices, is used to develop a *restructured* Water Poverty Index (*r*WPI). This approach is applied to provide a multidimensional assessment of water poverty in the MENA region. Findings reveal a clear distinction between oil-rich yet water-poor countries and water-rich yet money-poor countries. They highlight the likely utility of the *r*WPI approach to ultimately guide appropriate action towards sustainable water management and transparent allocation of shared resources.

Chapter 10 by Fida Karam and Chahir Zaki considers trade and economic growth, asking if trade in goods and trade in services differ in their impact on growth in MENA. It highlights the findings of Karam and Zaki (2015) regarding the macroeconomic and sectoral effects of goods and services trade on the economic performance of MENA countries. Their findings indicate, first, that a positive association exists between real GDP growth and both services and goods trade. Second, that, as goods trade increases, the marginal effect of services trade on real GDP growth decreases. However, the overall effect of services trade on real GDP is positive. Third, a decomposition of GDP growth reveals a greater contribution of goods trade than services trade to growth.

Section IV is devoted to poverty, inequality and social policy themes.

In Chapter 11 Khalid Abu-Ismail offers a study of poverty and vulnerability in Arab states. Here, he provides a critical review of the main poverty stylised facts for MENA and other developing regions based on the commonly applied global indicators of money metric and multidimensional poverty compared to an alternative set of stylised facts based on nationally defined and regionally sensitive money metric and multidimensional poverty indicators using results from household income and expenditure surveys and the Arab Multidimensional Poverty Report. When poverty measures tailored to MENA middle-income countries are applied, the region appears to have significantly higher poverty and vulnerability. The global money metric and multidimensional poverty indices are more suitable for Less Developed Countries. This calls for rethinking the conventional wisdom on poverty and economic policy in the MENA.

Chapter 12 by Facundo Alvaredo, Lydia Assouad and Thomas Piketty is concerned with measuring inequality in the Middle East. Here, the authors reference and combine all income data existing in the region – household surveys, national accounts, income tax data and wealth data – in order to estimate income concentration in the region for the period 1990–2016. According to their benchmark series, the Middle East appears to be the most unequal region in the world, with a top decile income share as large as 64%, compared to 37% in Western Europe, 47% in the US and 55% in Brazil. This is due both to enormous inequality between countries (particularly between oil-rich and population-rich countries) and to large inequality within countries (which is probably under-estimated, given limited access to accurate fiscal data). The authors stress the importance of increasing transparency on income and wealth in the Middle East and hope more research can shed light on the dynamics of income concentration, within-country inequality as well as the drivers of such extreme levels.

Chapter 13 takes a different look at inequality from the perspective of early childhood development. Looking at childhood as the most important phase of human development, Caroline Krafft and Safaa El-Kogali argue that deficits in early childhood development have lasting impacts on subsequent human development and economic outcomes. Inequalities in this early stage therefore contribute to the intergenerational transmission of poverty and socioeconomic status. Despite their importance, early childhood development and inequalities in this stage have only recently become the focus of research in the Middle East and North Africa. This chapter reviews the growing literature on inequality of opportunity in early childhood development in the region and discusses next steps for this field of research.

In Chapter 14, Mahmood Messkoub considers MENA's social policy track record and challenges. He points out that, despite a long history of social programmes in the region, these have mostly covered formal sector employees including those in the civil service. Large numbers of informal sector workers, rural residents and agricultural workers, however, have had to rely on poor, publicly provided services or have fallen back on meagre family resources and charitable handouts of the non-state providers in an informal security regime. All in all, the various social policy programmes of health, education, old-age pension and social protection fall below the needs and aspirations of their respective populations. State expenditure on social policy programmes are constrained by expenditure on generalised indirect subsidies such as, *inter alia*, fuel, public utilities, water and staple food. The higher income groups in general benefit most from these indirect subsidies. This has led to debates increasingly focusing on the need for social policy reform and reduction of indirect subsidies, and on moving away from a universal rights-based approach to social provisioning and towards targeting poverty and improving social protection.

Section V is dedicated to the all-important topic of institutions and transition to democracy in MENA.

In Chapter 15, Jared Rubin examines the relationship between religion and politics, asking: 'Why did the West get rich and the Middle East not?' More specifically, why did the modern economy emerge in Western Europe and not in the Middle East? The answer to this question is not obvious: for centuries following the spread of Islam, Middle Eastern economies were far ahead of those in Europe. In this chapter, Rubin argues that the greater capacity of Muslim religious authorities to legitimate political rule played a key role in the reversal of fortunes. While European rulers eventually relied less on religious legitimation – turning instead to the economic elites of their parliaments – religious legitimation has remained a potent force in the Middle East to the present day. This has a number of consequences for the types of laws and policies that emerge from Middle Eastern governments, many of which are not amenable (although not necessarily contradictory) to modern economic growth.

Chapter 16 by David Cobham and Abdallah Zouache examines the relationship between Islam and economic development in the economic literature. First, it considers the rise of Islamic economics, with particular reference to Islamic banking and finance, arguing that Islamic economics has failed to provide an alternative paradigm in most areas or to provide a truly distinctive set of practices in the finance area. Second, it considers the neo-institutionalist view that Islam has held back the development of the Muslim world, and here it argues that the case has not been made and suffers from a significant degree of prejudice. It concludes by calling for an economic analysis of the relation between Islam and economic development without religious or ideological preconceptions.

In Chapter 17, the same authors look at the all-important topic of the 'Arab Spring', its economic features, consequences and policy challenges. Here, the long-term failure of economic policies in the Arab world to generate significant domestically based growth is reviewed as a determinant of the Arab Spring and as a background to a more detailed focus on economic policies. An examination of the economic programmes of three Islamist political parties shows that they are relatively moderate and centrist, but suffer from important, though not surprising, gaps. The economic policies that might have been expected from any reformist (non-Islamist and non-authoritarian) governments which emerged from the uprisings are considered. While these two sets of policies have much in common (and coalitions could be envisaged), Cobham and Zouache argue that neither can successfully address the failures of the pre-Spring economic policy in the Arab countries and that new economic policies are needed. For example, the crony capitalism which developed out of the liberalisation process needs to be confronted and the associated corruption needs to be eliminated. In conclusion, an appeal is made for the development of more specific economic policy proposals in these and other areas, proposals which reformist governments could implement and which could be used to challenge authoritarian governments that are reluctant to reform.

Chapter 18, by Zafiris Tzannatos, also examines the Arab Spring but from a different perspective. These tumultuous uprisings are often ascribed in the literature to the role played by the youth bulge in the demographic structure of the Arab countries. Tzannatos juxtaposes the case of the demographic youth bulge and high youth unemployment *versus* structural reasons as causes for these uprisings. He argues that the youth bulge was practically over at least a decade before the uprisings, youth unemployment had been reduced more than adult unemployment during the preceding two decades and discontent arising from the liberalising economic reforms pursued since the 1990s was generalised across the population, not just among the youth. This despite the fact that the reforms reduced the deficit, debt and inflation while economic and employment rates accelerated from their low rates during the 'lost' decade of the 1980s. However, the reforms were implemented in a way that their benefits were captured by a few insiders. Overall, evidence lends support to more complex economic, institutional and political explanations for the uprisings than demographic ones, especially those centring on the youth. Tzannatos argues that for policy purposes, future approaches should first focus on improving the functioning of the macroeconomy and its ability to create inclusive growth. Hence, youth *and* adult issues should be examined together, rather than routinely attributing the underperformance of labour markets to the low quality and relevance of education or school-to-work transition issues, both of which can always be improved and not only in the Arab countries.

In Chapter 19, Samir Makdisi takes up the topic of Arab development and the transition to democracy. He starts with the observation that genuine democratic governance in the Arab world – with the exception of Lebanon post-independence and Tunisia after the 2011 uprisings – remains a largely unfulfilled reality. The chapter highlights three major features in Arab countries in this regard: (a) overall, a socioeconomic record that shows the Arab countries to be generally in line with other developing regions; (b) the prevalence of a highly conflictual environment; and (c) the persistence of varying forms of autocracies or what is referred to as the 'democracy deficit'. Makdisi argues that these three features of Arab development are interconnected and his aim is to explore this interconnectedness. He looks at several themes such as the non-correlation between development and democracy in the Arab region; factors that explain the region's lagging steps towards democracy; and the uprisings and the transition to peace-building and inclusive development.

And finally, Section VI is dedicated to the theme of corruption, conflict and refugees in the region.

Chapter 20 by Izak Atiyas, Ishac Diwan and Adeel Malik takes up the theme of cronyism which has already emerged in several preceding chapters and especially in the post-Arab Spring literature. It summarises recent empirical evidence emanating from a multi-country project on business–state relationships in the Middle East. Combining qualitative databases on the presence of politically connected businesses in individual sectors of the economy with firm- and sector-level data, it offers, for the first time, highly fine-grained information on the nature, extent and mechanisms of crony capitalism in the Middle East.

The last two chapters address important aspects of conflict, which is of special significance in the MENA context. In Chapter 21, Jeffrey B. Nugent addresses the effects and challenges posed by refugees. He examines the impacts of war and refugee status on both refugee and host populations in the MENA region. In view of the enormous magnitude of the problems emanating from these effects and the danger of their further escalation, Nugent also attempts to identify some policy initiatives that may help deal with these problems.

And finally, Chapter 22 by Jennifer C. Olmsted looks at the gendered socioeconomic impacts of conflict in the Middle East. It is commonly recognised that armed conflicts have had devastating effects on the region. War and externally imposed sanctions have adversely impacted a range of socioeconomic outcomes, often in gendered ways. Olmsted examines the impacts of health (mental and physical), education, household formation, control of income and wealth and gender norms on coping strategies and outcomes. Gendered intergenerational impacts of armed conflict require policies that take into account intersectionality in order to break the intergenerational cycle of poverty through a focus on the different impact conflict can have on individuals not only based on gender, but also on marital status, age, sexual orientation, race and location, which is what the chapter addresses.

In all, these chapters provide an overview, and confirm the diversity and richness, of Middle East economics as we know it today. They bring home the fact that whilst the economies in the MENA region are diverse and each country confronts specific challenges of its own, there is a lot that unites them, hence justifying their collective study as an important sub-field within a broad range of subject areas: applied development economics, development studies, regional studies and Middle Eastern studies.

I hope the careful selection of these topics and contributions from scholars and subject specialists in the book will help advance our understanding of the subject further.

Notes

1 This chapter has benefited from comments and feedback from Jennifer Olmsted, Jeff Nugent and Valentine Moghadam. I am grateful to them for their help and advice, which helped me improve the final draft. The usual disclaimer applies and only I am responsible for the views expressed, and any remaining errors or omissions.

2 As Karen Pfeifer observes, 'Economics in the Middle East grew from the 1980s to the 2000s in terms of the number of economists working in the region and the magnitude of published output' (2016: 8).

3 Chief among these were Rosenstein-Rodan (1943), Nurkse (1953), Hirschman (1958) and Lewis (1954) to name only a few.

4 See Palma (1978) for a review of the Dependency School.

5 Between 1951 and 2017, India had 12 Five-Year Plans. In 2014, the administration of Prime Minister Narendra Modi announced the abolition of India's Planning Commission thus making the Twelfth Plan, which had got under way in 2012, the last one.

6 This is often referred to as the Feldman–Mahalanobis model though the Feldman model dated back to the 1920s.

7 Lewis defined an unlimited supply of labour 'to exist in those countries where population is so large relatively to capital and natural resources, that there are large sectors of the economy where the marginal productivity of labour is negligible, zero, or even negative' (1954: 141).

8 This was at the invitation of the Egyptian Society of Political Economy, Statistics, and Legislation. Tignor has further opined that although Lewis was invited to deliver three lectures on industrialisation in Cairo, he started by focusing on the importance of agriculture, remarking: 'To industrialize without promoting agricultural improvement "is to ruin the industrialists (who won't have enough workers or consumers) and to improve agriculture without industrialization will ruin farmers (who will live in a society with vast hordes of unemployed)"' (Lewis, 1953: 7; quoted in Tignor, 2006: 86–87).

9 The latter (Issawi, 1949) provides a review of some of the earliest titles on Middle East Economics mainly published in the 1940s. See Issawi (1982) and Owen (1981) for later publications offering more comprehensive treatments of the region's economic history.

10 OPEC was formed in a secret meeting in Baghdad in September 1960 at the instigation of Venezuela and involved Iran, Saudi Arabia, Kuwait and Iraq (Sampson, 1975). Income from oil exports rose moderately but steadily throughout the 1960s and OPEC membership doubled reaching ten nations by the end of this decade. However, it was not until the 1970s when the organisation began to flex its muscles on the international oil scene and had to be contended with by importing nations.

11 As noted by Sachs and Warner (1999), emerging countries have been incapable of turning the returns of oil discoveries or commodity price booms into engines of industrialisation and sustained growth (see Chapter 7 in this book).

12 This comprises a vast literature which spans the economics and politics of the region. The political resource curse contributions have focused on the 'governance gap' in the region and the impact of oil rents on authoritarianism, corruption and conflict (Ross, 2015 and 2012; World Bank, 2003). The literature on economic resource curse has instead focused on the correlation between oil rents and observed instability and poor growth performance. This includes diverse approaches such as the Dutch disease (Corden and Neary, 1982) at one end and the Rentier State (Beblawi and Luciani, 1987) at the other. More recent approaches have stressed the challenge in terms of oil revenue volatility (Mohaddes and Pesaran, 2014). See Chapter 7 of this volume for a thorough review of the resource curse theories.

13 By the mid-1980s, oil prices had crashed to below $10 per barrel and OPEC was riddled with deep internal discord. Two members – Iran and Iraq – were openly engaged in war with each other and the organisation was broadly divided between the 'hawks' (Iran, Iraq and Libya) and 'doves' (Saudi Arabia, Kuwait and UAE) with conflicting pricing strategies and objectives (Dorraj, 1993).

14 See Cammett et al. (2015: Chapter 7) for a discussion of the contradictions of state-led growth in MENA.

15 Pfeifer remarks that 'The emergence of this cohort is due partly to students from the region studying economics at the graduate level in the United States, in the United Kingdom, and in Europe' (2016: 8).

16 See Pfeifer for an idea on the magnitude of published output on the Middle East from the 1980s to the 2000s. Accordingly three specialist journals were established and the number of publications steadily rose. Despite this, judged by EconLit entries on 'journal articles, edited volumes, and dissertations', it would appear that as of 2013 the MENA region appeared to be 'relatively less well studied' compared to other regions such as sub-Saharan Africa and Latin America (2016: 9–11).

17 One notable, early contribution came with the first edition of the Arab Human Development Report in 2002 which focused attention on the welfare aspects of economic policy (UNDP, 2002). Others articulated the idea of a social contract between the state and society in the search for a viable economic development in Arab countries (World Bank, 2004).

18 Gause (2011) and Hounshell (2011) pose similar questions to Middle East specialists at large.

19 According to Mossallam, 'In fact just a few months before the revolution erupted in 2011, the IMF was praising Egypt's economic performance, as well as its sound macroeconomic management and structural reforms' (2015: 12, referring to IMF, 2009). Similarly, Tunisia's liberalisation policies (1987–2011) under Ben Ali were praised by the World Bank as 'the Arab model' to follow (Cammett et al., 2015).

20 In a 2015 report, the World Bank reflected: The Arab Spring events caught the world by surprise. Standard development indicators failed to capture or predict the outburst of popular anger during the spring of 2011. What could explain this conundrum, which we refer to as the 'Arab inequality puzzle'? Was economic inequality much higher than suggested by household expenditure data? Or were the grievances linked to factors other than economic inequality, such as decline in the overall quality of life, growing corruption, and lack of freedom, among others? (World Bank, 2015: 11)

21 Aristotle's *Politics* offers a radically different interpretation of the relationship between economic performance and political stability: 'In order to secure his power, a tyrant must keep the population in poverty, so that the preoccupation with daily bread leaves them no leisure to conspire against the tyrant'.

22 Even in cases when revolutions have been preceded by economic downturns, prior improvements in prosperity may have played a role. According to the American sociologist James C. Davies's so-called *J-curve theory*, revolutions – such as the Russian Revolution of 1917 and Egypt's Revolution of 1952 – occur when periods of prolonged economic and social development are sharply and suddenly reversed (Davies, 1962). In other words, it is not straightforward economic hardship, but frustration with the disparity between expectations and reality that awakens the masses.

References

Ayubi, Nazih (1995), *Over-Stating the Arab State*, London: I. B. Tauris.

Beblawi, Hazem and Giacomo Luciani, eds. (1987), *The Rentier State*, London: Croom Helm.

Bharier, Julian (1971), *Economic Development in Iran 1900–1970*, London: Oxford University Press.

Cammett, Melani, Diwan, I., Richards, A. and John Waterbury (2015), *A Political Economy of the Middle East*, Fourth edition, Boulder: Westview Press.

Cook, M.A., ed. (1970), *Studies in the Economic History of the Middle East*, London: Oxford University Press.

Corden, W.M. and J.P. Neary (1982), "Booming Sector and De-industrialisation in a Small Open Economy", *The Economic Journal*, Vol. 92, December: 825–848.

Courbage, Youssef (1999), *New Demographic Scenarios in the Mediterranean Region*, Paris: INED; available from: https://cahier-youssef-courbage.site.ined.fr/en/

Davies, James C., (1962), "Toward a Theory of Revolution", *American Sociological Review*, Vol. 27, No. 1, February: 5–19.

Dorraj, M. (1993), "Will OPEC Survive?", *Arab Studies Quarterly*, Vol. 15, No. 4: 19–32; available from: www.jstor.org/stable/41858061

Fargues, P. (2008), *Emerging Demographic Patterns across the Mediterranean and Their Implications for Migration through 2030*, Washington DC: Migration Policy Institute; available from: http://mait.camins.cat/ET2050_library/docs/med/migration.pdf

Gause, F. Gregory (2011), "Why Middle East Studies Missed the Arab Spring: The Myth of Authoritarian Stability", *Foreign Affairs*, July/August: 81–90; available from: https://www.foreignaffairs.com/articles/middle-east/2011-07-01/why-middle-east-studies-missed-arab-spring

Hakimian, Hassan (2001), "From MENA to East Asia and Back: Lessons of Globalization, Crisis and Economic Reform", Chapter 4 in Hakimian and Moshaver, eds. (2001).

Hakimian, Hassan (2011), "The Economic Prospects of the 'Arab Spring': A Bumpy Road Ahead", *CDPR Development ViewPoint*, Vol. 63: 1–2; available from: https://eprints.soas.ac.uk/12032/

Hakimian, Hassan (2017), "Why Economists Missed the Arab Spring," *Project Syndicate*, Op-Ed, 20 March; available from: https://www.project-syndicate.org/commentary/arab-spring-economic-forecasting-failure-by-hassan-hakimian-2017-03.

Hakimian, Hassan and Ziba Moshaver, eds. (2001), *The State and Global Change: The Political Economy of Transition in the Middle East & North Africa*, London: Curzon Press.

Handoussa H., ed. (1997), *Economic Transition in the Middle East – Global Challenges and Adjustment Strategies*, Cairo: The American University in Cairo Press.

Harrigan, Jane and Hamed El Said (2014), "Economic Reform, Social Welfare, and Instability: Jordan, Egypt, Morocco, and Tunisia, 1983–2004", *The Middle East Journal*, Vol. 68, No. 1: 99–121.

Hirschman, Albert O. (1958), *The Strategy of Economic Development*, New Haven: Yale University Press.

Hounshell, Blake (2011), "Dark Crystal: Why Didn't Anyone Predict the Arab Revolutions?", July/August; available from: www.foreignpolicy.com/articles/2011/06/20/dark_crystal

Hunt, D. (1989), *Economic Theories of Development: An Analysis of Competing Paradigms*, London: Harvester Wheatsheaf.

ILO (2000), *World Labour Report 2000*, Geneva: International Labour Organization.

IMF (2009), "Arab Republic of Egypt: 2008 Article IV Consultation", *Egypt Country Report Number 09/25*, Washington, DC: International Monetary Fund; available from: https://www.imf.org/external/pubs/ft/scr/2009/cr0925.pdf

Issawi, Charles (1949), "Recent Books on Middle East Economics", *Pakistan Horizon*, Vol. 2, No. 3: 156–165. Retrieved September 19, 2020, from https://www.jstor.org/stable/41392432?seq=1

Issawi, Charles (1952), "Prospects for Economic Development in the Middle East", *Proceedings of the Academy of Political Science*, Vol. 24, No. 4: 27–42; https://doi.org/10.2307/1173502

Issawi, Charles (1982), *An Economic History of the Middle East and North Africa*, Columbia Economic History of the Modern World Series, New York: Columbia University Press.

Karam, F. and C. Zaki (2015), "Trade Volume and Economic Growth in the MENA Region: Goods or Services?", *Economic Modelling*, Vol. 45: 22–37.

Karsehnas, M. and Valentine M. Moghadam (2001), "Female Labor Force Participation and Economic Adjustment in the MENA Region", in Cinar, E. Mine, ed. (2001), *The Economics of Women and Work in the Middle East and North Africa*, Amsterdam: JAI: 51–74.

Lambton, A.K.S. (1953), *Landlord and Peasant in Persia*, London: Oxford University Press.

Lewis, W. Arthur (1953), *Aspects of Industrialization: National Bank of Egypt, Fiftieth Anniversary Commemoration Lecture*, Cairo.

Lewis, W. Arthur (1954), "Economic Development with Unlimited Supplies of Labour", *Manchester School*, Vol. 22, No. 2, May: 139–91.

Love, J. (1980), "Raúl Prebisch and the Origins of the Doctrine of Unequal Exchange", *Latin American Research Review*, Vol. 15, No. 3: 45–72.

Mabro, Robert and Samir Radwan (1976), *The Industrialization of Egypt 1939–1973. Policy and Performance*, Oxford: Clarendon Press, Oxford University Press.

Mahalanobis, P. C. (1955), "The Approach of Operational Research to Planning in India", *Sankhya*, 16 (1–2): 3–130.

Mahdavy, Hossein (1970), "The Patterns and Problems of Economic Development in Rentier States: The Case of Iran", in Cook, ed. (1970).

Mohaddes, Kamiar and M. Hashem Pesaran (2014), "One Hundred Years of Oil Income and the Iranian Economy: A Curse or a Blessing?", Chapter 1 in Alizadeh, Parvin and Hassan Hakimian, eds. *Iran and the Global Economy: Petro Populism, Islam and Economic Sanctions*, London: Routledge.

Mossallam, Mohammed (2015), "The IMF in the Arab World: Lessons Unlearnt", *Bretton Woods Project*, November; available from: https://papers.ssrn.com/sol3/papers.cfm?abstract_id=2705927

Nurkse, R. (1953), *Problems of Capital Formation in Underdeveloped Countries*, Oxford: Basil Blackwell.

Olmsted, Jennifer C. (2005), "Does/Should Geography Matter for the Discipline of Economics?", paper presented at the Sixth Mediterranean Social and Political Research Meeting, Montecatini Terme, 16–20 March 2005.

Owen, Roger (1981), *The Middle East in the World Economy, 1800–1914*, London: Methuen.

Page, John (1998), "From Boom to Bust – and Back? The Crisis of Growth in the Middle East and North Africa", in Shafik (1998): 133–158.

Page, John and Linda Van Gelder (2001), "Missing Links: Institutional Capability, Policy Reform, and Growth in the Middle East and North Africa", in Hakimian and Moshaver (2001): 16–49.

Palma, G. (1978), "Dependency: A Formal Theory of Underdevelopment or a Methodology for the Analysis of Concrete Situations of Underdevelopment", *World Development*, Vol. 6: 881–924.

Pfeifer, Karen (2016), "Oil on the Waters? Middle East Studies and Economics of the Middle East", Chapter 3 in Seteny Shami and Cynthia Miller-Idriss, eds. (2016) *Middle East Studies for the New Millennium, Infrastructures of Knowledge*, New York: Social Science Research Council and New York University Press: 112–151.

Prebisch, Raúl (1950), *The Economic Development of Latin America and its Principal Problems*, New York: United Nations.

Richards, Alan and John Waterbury (1996), *A Political Economy of the Middle East*, Boulder: Westview Press.

Rosenstein-Rodan, P., (1943), "Problems of Industrialisation of Eastern and South-eastern Europe", *Economic Journal*, Vol. 53, No. 210/211, June-September: 202–211; reprinted in Agarwala, A. and Singh, S., eds. (1958), *The Economics of Underdevelopment*, Oxford University Press.

Ross, M. (2012), *The Oil Curse: How Petroleum Wealth Shapes the Development of Nations*, Princeton: Princeton University Press.

Ross, M. (2015), "What Have We Learned about the Resource Curse?", *Annual Review of Political Science*, Vol. 18: 239–259.

Roudi-Fahimi, Farzaneh (2001), *Population Trends and Challenges in the Middle East and North Africa*, New York: Population Reference Bureau; available from: https://www.prb.org/populationtrendsand challengesinthemiddleeastandnorthafrica/183/

Sachs, J.D. and A.M. Warner (1999), "The Big Push, Natural Resource Booms and Growth", *Journal of Development Economics*, Vol. 59: 43–76.

Sampson, Anthony (1975), *The Seven Sisters: The Great Oil Companies and the World They Shaped*, New York: Viking Press.

Shafik, Nemat, ed. (1998), *Prospects for Middle Eastern and North African Economies: From Boom to Bust and Back?* London: Macmillan Press.
Stiglitz, Joseph E. (2002), *Globalization and its Discontents*, New York: W. W. Norton.
Tabutin, Dominique and Bruno Schoumaker (2005), "The Demography of the Arab World and the Middle East from the 1950s to the 2000s: A Survey of Changes and a Statistical Assessment", *Population*, Vol. 60, Issue 5-6: 505–615; doi:10.3917/popu.505.0611
Tignor, Robert L. (2006), "Unlimited Supplies of Labor", Chapter 3 in Tignor, Robert L. (2006), *W. Arthur Lewis and the Birth of Development Economics*, Princeton: Princeton University Press.
UNDP (2002), *Arab Human Development Report 2002*, United Nations Development Programme; available from: http://arabstates.undp.org/content/rbas/en/home/library/huma_development/arab-human-development-report-2003-building-a-knowledge-society.html.
Warriner, Doreen (1948), *Land and Poverty in the Middle East*, London: Royal Institute of International Affairs.
World Bank (2003), *Better Governance for Development in the Middle East and North Africa: Enhancing Inclusiveness and Accountability*, Washington, DC: World Bank.
World Bank (2004), "Unlocking the Employment Potential in the Middle East and North Africa: Toward a New Social Contract", *Lead Author Tarik Yousef*, Washington, DC: World Bank.
World Bank (2015), "Inequality, Uprisings, and Conflict in the Arab World", *MEA Economic Monitor*, October, Washington, DC: World Bank; available from: http://documents1.worldbank.org/curated/en/303441467992017147/pdf/Inequality-uprisings-and-conflict-in-the-Arab-World.pdf
Yousef, Tarik M. (2004), "Development, Growth and Policy Reform in the Middle East and North Africa since 1950", *Journal of Economic Perspectives*, Vol. 18, No. 3: 91–116.

SECTION I

Growth and development in comparative perspectives

2

EXPLAINING GROWTH IN THE MIDDLE EAST

Jeffrey B. Nugent

2.1 Introduction

Different international agencies and scholars identify the countries in the Middle East (MENA) region in different ways. For the purposes of this chapter, MENA is defined in its most common form as stretching geographically from Morocco in the western part of North Africa to Iran in the east and from Turkey in the north to Yemen in the south. This makes up 20 countries, which are listed at the top section of Table 2.1. Israel is another country in the region but is generally not included in MENA because of the European background of most of its inhabitants.

In what follows, we aim to illustrate the several ways in which countries of the region differ from one another but also ways in which they are similar with respect to the critical ingredients of economic development, namely, capital and human capital formation, technological change and institutions. Given the importance of oil and other natural resources in the MENA region, we pay considerable attention to how such resources may help or hurt the development process.

The remainder of the chapter is organised as follows: Section 2.2 points to the wide variation both in current levels of per capita GDP and in growth rates over time among MENA countries, and how they compare with other countries and regions. Section 2.3 goes on to examine each of the key factors contributing to GDP growth over time, such as physical capital, human capital and productivity. Section 2.4 turns to structural and institutional changes in MENA countries and to the long-run environmental challenges they face. Finally, Section 2.5 presents our conclusions, including suggestions for dealing with the long-run economic and environmental challenges.

2.2 MENA growth rates: across countries and over time

Of the 20 MENA countries listed in Table 2.1, most are regarded as resource-rich (RR), a few (like Morocco, Jordan and Turkey) for minerals but most (Algeria, Bahrain, Egypt, Iran, Iraq, Kuwait, Libya, Oman, Qatar, Saudi Arabia, Sudan, Syria, Tunisia, United Arab Emirates (UAE) and Yemen) for their oil and gas. Only Lebanon and the West Bank and Gaza (the latter still not a nation state, but two slightly separated territories occupied by Israel) are without significant natural resource endowments.

Table 2.1 Levels of GDP per capita and growth rates of real GDP and population

	GDP per capita in 2017 in $US of 2010	*Average annual growth rates of real GDP by decade*						*Average annual growth rates of population*
	1	*2*	*3*	*4*	*5*	*6*	*7*	*8*
Country	*2017*	*1960s*	*1970s*	*1980s*	*1990s*	*2000s*	*2010–16*	*2000–17*
Algeria	4123	2.2	6.9	2.5	1.1	2.9	3.6	1.7
Bahrain	23,655	..	7.9	0.2	4.5	4.8	3.3	4.8
Egypt, Arab Rep.	2413	5.0	6.5	6.6	4.6	3.9	3	2
Iran, Islamic Rep.	5415	5.1	6.2	1.1	3.6	3.8	1.8	1.2
Iraq	5166	..	10.2	-1.6	1.1	3.6	8.7	2.9
Jordan	4130	6.2	5.8	0.6	5.4	6.4	2.8	3.8
Kuwait	29,040	..	7.2	3	8.4	5.6	3.9	4.1
Lebanon	8524	..	-3.2	-1.2	7.1	5.2	1.4	3.7
Libya	7998	4.7	7.9	-2.5	1.7	5.6	-2.7	1
Morocco	3007	7.0	5.1	4.1	2.7	6.2	4.3	1.3
Oman	15,668	..	7	8.4	5.7	3.8	3.9	4.2
Qatar	63,506	..	6.2	1.5	5.7	11.6	5.3	8.8
Saudi Arabia	20,761	..	7.9	-1.4	2.68	3.2	4.1	2.7
Sudan	2,998	..	2.2	3.9	5.6	6.7	2.1	2.3
Syrian Arab Republic	1,700	1.4	10.6	1	5	5.4	-1.45	0.6
Tunisia	3,491	6.9	7.9	4.2	4.9	4.5	1.3	1
Turkey	10,541	4.7	4.5	5.3	3.6	4.3	6.5	1.4
United Arab Emirates	40,699	..	16.5	0.8	5.7	4.6	4.5	6.4
West Bank and Gaza	3,095	..	6.1	4.1	5.8	4.1	3.9	2.8
Yemen, Rep.	1,402	..	7.3	5.8	7.4	5.2	-5.5	2.7
Israel	40,270	4.1	4.8	4.5	6.6	3.5	3.5	1.9
World	**10,714**	**2.1**	**4.6**	**3.6**	**3.2**	**3.2**	**2.9**	**1.2**
Sub-Saharan Africa	1,647	2.0	3.3	2.2	2	5.5	4	2.7
South Asia	1,779	2.6	2.8	3.3	5	6.1	6.1	1.5
East Asia	6,138	3.6	3.7	5.3	3.7	4.2	4.9	0.8
Latin America & Caribbean	8,879	3.5	6.2	2.1	2.7	3	2.1	1.3

Sources: Columns 1 and 7 from World Bank, World Development Indicators; columns 2–6 computed from United Nations Statistical Office, National Account Statistics.

Column 1 of Table 2.1 presents official estimates of per capita GDP in $US for 2017 (except for Syria and Yemen where such estimates for 2017 were not yet available and had to be constructed from such estimates from earlier years as well as from non-official sources). As can be seen, there is extremely wide variation within the region ranging from Qatar with the highest GDP per capita in the world to Yemen among the world's poorest, even though it has oil in at least modest amounts. Sudan is also a poor oil country but one which lost most of its oil when South Sudan seceded from Sudan in the last decade. MENA also includes Tunisia and Egypt where oil and gas have been developed but not in sufficiently large amounts to have become important exports. Note also that Lebanon and the West Bank and Gaza, the two MENA countries without any significant natural resources, have higher GDP per capita than some RR MENA countries.

In columns 2–6 of Table 2.1 are the average annual GDP growth rates for particular decades, starting with 1960–69 and finishing with the still incomplete decade, 2010–16. For RR countries, the price of their natural resource is understandably an important determinant of their economic growth rates. The three most positive cycles for oil prices were the 1970s, 2000–08 and 2010–13. Since rising export prices typically generate higher export revenues and in turn higher government revenues, the higher oil prices can be expected to trigger large increases in government expenditures and other spending, whereas during the adjacent periods of low or falling oil prices the opposite consequences are expected.

As indicated in the table, the 1970s and the 2000s were indeed the decades with the highest or second highest GDP growth rates out of all the decades for almost all RR MENA countries (Algeria, Bahrain, Iran, Iraq, Kuwait, Libya, Oman, Qatar, Saudi Arabia, Syria, Tunisia, UAE and Yemen). Even non-oil-exporting countries like Jordan, Egypt, Morocco and to a lesser extent Tunisia also had relatively high growth rates in these decades, in part because they gained substantially from exports to these oil-exporting countries, and the flows of FDI and worker remittances received from them. There were, however, some exceptions to this pattern of high growth rates by oil exporters during periods of high and rising oil prices, such as Algeria and Iraq in the 2000s, and especially Libya, Syria and Yemen in the 2010–16 period. In each case, however, these exceptions can be attributed to rather severe national security breakdowns occurring at these times.

The comparisons in growth rates across decades show that the growth rates of MENA countries have been much more volatile than those of either Israel or the world as a whole or other regions (shown in the last six rows in the table). This extreme volatility in growth can reduce long-term development in a number of ways, such as by increasing investment risks and reducing the efficiency of capital spending over time. Yet, even maintaining an average growth rate of over 7 percent per annum, as did Bahrain, Iran, Iraq, Jordan, Kuwait, Saudi Arabia, Syria, UAE and Yemen during the 1970s, Oman during the 1980s (when oil was just coming into much larger production) and Qatar in the 2000–09 period, has been quite a remarkable achievement, rarely surpassed elsewhere in the world. A few MENA countries, however, experienced negative growth rates sustained over periods of up to a decade as did Iraq, Lebanon, Libya and Saudi Arabia in the 1980s, and Libya, Syria and Yemen between 2010 and 2016. Even of those countries and periods with high GDP growth rates, considering the often unusually high population growth rates recorded in the last column of Table 2.1, it is clear that in per capita terms their growth rates would have been much smaller than those indicated in columns 2–6, and as a result not that much higher than those in other regions.

2.3 Determinants of growth across MENA countries and over time

According to virtually all economic growth theories ranging from those of Adam Smith to Karl Marx, David Ricardo and Robert Solow, the major determinants of long-run economic growth are believed to be the growth of capital, labour and human capital, and technological change and efficiency.[1] Many other factors such as trade, international capital flows, and institutional development may lie behind these factors and many of these factors may be closely interrelated. Nevertheless, to identify the most important differences and begin to explain the differences in growth rates across countries and over time, we proceed by presenting measures of each of these, one at a time.

We begin in Table 2.2 with physical capital, presenting two different measures of capital growth for each of the 20 MENA countries, and for Israel, the world as a whole and the four other regions identified in Table 2.1. The first of these measures is the average annual growth rates of capital stock and the second is the average share of gross capital formation in GDP computed from annual data on both gross capital formation and GDP in constant $US of 2010. In each case, we provide these measures for different periods. For average annual growth rates of capital stock, in columns 1 and 2 we present these growth rates for 1990–2000 and 2000–17.

Table 2.2 Indicators of the growth of physical capital

	Average annual growth rates of capital stock by period		*Average shares of gross capital formation in gross domestic product overall and by decade*					
	1	*2*	*3*	*4*	*5*	*6*	*7*	*8*
Country	*1990–2000*	*2000–17*	*1970–2016*	*1970s*	*1980s*	*1990s*	*2000s*	*2010–16*
Algeria	0.1	7.9	35.9	40.3	34.1	28.3	32.6	44.1
Bahrain		2.3	29	32.5	35	24.6	25.5	26.4
Egypt, Arab Rep.	5.4	5.2	21.4	21.3	30.1	21.2	18.5	15.8
Iran, Islamic Rep.	-0.4	3.1	36.7	38.4	29.1	34.7	40.2	37.6
Iraq			17.8	8.4	20.1	17.6	24.5	18.3
Jordan	0.3	4.9	26.8	26.1	31.1	29.4	26.1	21.5
Kuwait			17.1	13.4	18.5	18.5	16.6	17.9
Lebanon	-5.8*	6.7	23.9	19.5	22.3	32.7	22.8	24.6
Libya			23.8	23.9	22.2	14	33.2	25.8
Morocco	4.2	6	29.7	27.4	29.8	26.8	30.9	33.7
Oman		12.8*	27.7	32	30.1	23.1	25	29.3
Qatar		15.5*	27.3	23.1	18.3	26.1	35.8	33
Saudi Arabia		9.8	23.7	22.5	23.5	20.6	22.6	29.4
Sudan	23.7	2.2	19.1[d]	16.7	14.1	18	20.5	26.2
Syrian Arab Republic			24.7	23.9	21.8	22.5	22.5	28.4
Tunisia	3.1	5.5*	24.2	24.2	25.9	24.6	24.1	22.9
Turkey	4.1	7.1	24.6	19.4	21.5	23.8	24.8	28.8
United Arab Emirates		7.2	27.2	33.9	30.5	25.5	22.8	23.2
West Bank and Gaza	7.8*	3.3	31.6[d]	32.4	40.7	38.9	25.5	20.5
Yemen, Rep.		-12.6*	19.2	18.7	18.8	15.6	23.6	15.5
Israel	6.5	3.8	23	29.8	21.7	25	20.6	20.1
World	0.8	4.3	16.7	16.5	17	16.6	16.8	16.8
Latin America & Caribbean			20.6	23.3	20.5	20.1	20.1	21.4
Sub-Saharan Africa			17	...	15.6	15.7	16.9	21.1
South Asia			20.1	13.4	15.9	19.9	26.3	27.1
East Asia			38.2	41.3	36.7	36.3	35.1	43

Notes: * indicates computed over a slightly shorter period due to missing data.

Sources: Columns 1–3 taken from World Bank World Development Indicators Database; columns 4–8 computed from annual figures for gross capital formation and gross domestic product both in current US dollars taken from United Nations Statistical Office, National Account Statistics, then averaged over the period indicated.

Consistent with the expectations for different oil price periods and the findings on GDP growth rates in Table 2.1, the growth rates of capital were generally lower during the low oil price 1990s than during the higher oil price period after 2000. Exceptions are Sudan and the West Bank and Gaza which had relatively high capital growth rates during the low oil price period of the 1990s. For Sudan this was when oil was being developed, and for the West Bank and Gaza this was when peace negotiations with Israel seemed promising and considerable international financial support was being attracted.

In column 3, we present the average shares of gross capital formation in GDP over the entire period of 1970–2016. The data show that the large oil-exporting countries, especially Algeria, Iran, Libya and all six GCC countries, have had average capital formation shares in GDP exceeding Israel's of 23 percent, and hence well above the world average and all regions listed except East Asia. At the same time, several non-oil-exporting MENA countries like Jordan, Lebanon, Morocco, Tunisia, Turkey and the West Bank and Gaza also had average shares of gross capital formation in GDP at least exceeding the world average and in many cases also Israel's 23 percent benchmark. Yet, two oil-exporting countries in MENA, namely, Iraq and Kuwait, sustained such shares well below the Israeli benchmark. The remaining columns in the table present these same average investment shares for each of the same different decades as in Table 2.1. For the most part the differences across decades reflect the same oil price, oil development, and conflict and other crisis years discussed above for Table 2.1.

In general, the data presented in Table 2.2 reveal, as for GDP growth rates in Table 2.1, that there is considerable variation in the average shares of gross capital formation in GDP from one decade to another. Indeed, each MENA country, except Kuwait, Morocco, Tunisia and Turkey, had a gap of over 9 percent between decades with the largest and smallest such shares, which is about the maximum gap experienced by Israel and is far greater than that of the world as a whole, or any of the regions listed, no doubt contributing to the large differences in growth rates between decades in Tables 2.1 and 2.2. This also shows that, for many MENA countries, the average capital formation shares over the whole period are remarkably high compared to those in the world as a whole and even higher than relatively rapidly growing Israel. The growth rates of capital stock, however, are somewhat lower than one would expect given the unusually large investment shares in GDP, suggesting the possibility of inefficiency in investment.

Columns 1–9 of Table 2.3 provide snapshots of five different aspects of human capital wherever possible in two quite different years for which comparable measures of the different measures are available for the largest number of countries. It does so for the same set of countries and regions as in the previous tables. In columns 1 and 2 are the measures whenever available for a commonly used measure of the *educational* component of human capital, namely, secondary school enrolment rates as gross percent of the relevant population age group. Normally, these rates should be no more than 100 percent, but with enrolments of immigrants and/or children outside the normal age range per grade, they can exceed 100 percent. We see sharply increasing secondary school enrolment rates between the two years for Bahrain, Egypt, Iran, Kuwait, Oman, Qatar, Saudi Arabia and UAE, and at least fairly substantial increases in these rates for most non-RR countries as well. The two exceptions in which these enrolment rates were not rising are Syria and Lebanon, the former due to the civil war which broke out after 2011 in virtually all parts of Syria, and the latter in part because it got inundated with refugee children from Syria. Yet, notice that, even in 2016, the enrolment rates of Egypt, Iraq, Sudan, Syria and Yemen were still below the world average, and for some others, the increases were also below those in the world as a whole.

The next four columns (3–6) present country-specific data on two measures of human capital in the form of health, namely, life expectancy and under-five mortality rates as a percent of

Table 2.3 Growth in human capital quality and relevance

	Education		*Health indicators*				*Test scores*			*Female labour force participation rate age 15 and over*		*Average annual growth rates of the labour force*
	Secondary school enrolment rates (% gross)		*Life expectancy at birth*		*Under-five mortality per 100 live births*		*Index of financial literacy*	*PISA*	*TIMSS*			
	1	*2*	*3*	*4*	*5*	*6*	*7*	*8*	*9*	*10*	*11*	*12*
Country	*1990*	*2016*	*1990*	*2016*	*1990*	*2016*	*2014*	*2015*	*2015*	*1990*	*2017*	*1970–2014*
Algeria	66[ab]	99[a]	67	76	49	25	33	362	378	12	15	3.62
Bahrain	87	102	73	77	23	8	40		451	29	44	6.16
Egypt, Arab Rep.	75	86	65	71	86	23	27		392	21	22	2.73
Iran, Islamic Rep.	68	89	64	76	57	16	20		431	10	17	2.97
Iraq	47	53	66	70	54	31	27			8	19	3.26
Jordan	76	82	70	74	37	18	24	399	388	11	14	4.19
Kuwait	78	95	72	75	18	8	44		353	39	47	5
Lebanon	69	61	70	77	33	8	44	376		19	23	3.42
Libya			69	72	42	13				20	26	2.43
Morocco	37	63	65	76	80	27			377	24	25	3.2
Oman	42	104	67	77	39	11			425	20	30	5.23
Qatar	80	91	75	78	21	9		407	439	40	58	8.38
Saudi Arabia	66[ab]	108	69	75	45	13	31		383	14	22	5.04

Sudan	73[ab]	74[a]	56	64	131	65	21			23	24	2.63
Syrian Arab Republic	51	50	71	70	37	18				22	12	3.12
Tunisia	45	93	69	76	57	14	45	371		22	24	2.31
Turkey	88	103	64	76	74	13	24	424	483	34	32	1.73
United Arab Emirates	62	96	72	77	17	8	38	433	452	29	41	9.81
West Bank and Gaza	70	83	68	73	45	19	25			10	20	4.48
Yemen, Rep.	42[ab]	49	58	65	126	55	13		248	17	6	4.62
Israel	89[ab]	104	77	82	12	4	68	472	511	46	59	2.92
World	51	76	65	72	93	41	37	500	500	51	49	1.47
Sub-Saharan Africa	23	43	50	60	181	78						
South Asia	36	71	58	69	129	48						
East Asia	39	86	68	74	60	17						
Latin America & Caribbean	76	94	67	75	57	18						

Sources: Unless otherwise indicated, columns 1–6 World Bank, World Development Indicators; column 7 from Standard and Poor's Ratings Services Global Financial Literacy Survey; columns 8–9 from websites of PISA and TIMSS; columns 10–11 from International Labor Office ILOSTAT database; and column 12 from Penn World Tables except where this source is incomplete for the period 1990–2017 from World Development Indicators.

Notes: Blanks imply missing data. [a] indicates that the source is United Nations UNESCO; [b] indicates that it is for a year between 2004 and 2008.

live births for 1990 and 2016. Naturally, on the first such index a higher score signifies a higher quantity or quality of human capital, but a higher one on the second index signifies worse health and weaker human capital.

As in the case of education, the figures show that most MENA countries also made considerable improvements in human capital in the form of health between 1990 and 2016 by both measures. The leading exception was again Syria where life expectancy actually fell slightly, from being six years above the world average in 1990 to two years below it by 2016. Even in 2016, Egypt, Iraq, Sudan, Syria and Yemen remained below the world average in life expectancy, and Sudan and Yemen above the world average in under-five mortality. Notice, also, that for all three of the aforementioned indicators, by 2016 Israel scored better on these human capital indicators than any of the MENA countries and in most cases by substantial margins.

While the data in columns 1 and 2 of Table 2.3 show that more children were receiving education in 2016 than in 1990,[2] this index says nothing about the quality of that education. In columns 7–9 we present three alternative measures of the quality of that education relevant to economic growth in a recent year. The first is a very specific index of financial literacy deemed relevant to the ability of individuals to make appropriate investment and financial decisions throughout their lives. It was constructed by Standard and Poor's Rating Services based on a 2014 survey. Note that even countries with secondary school enrolment rates in 2016 far above the world average, such as Algeria, Jordan, Saudi Arabia, Turkey and the West Bank and Gaza, had scores well below the world average on financial literacy. Even worse, for test scores on the mathematics components of the standardised international tests PISA and TIMSS, shown in columns 8 and 9, not a single MENA country exceeded either the world average or the Israeli average on these tests. Hence, to the extent that these kinds of tests may be deemed relevant to measuring the quality and relevance of education to economic growth, they would seem to indicate serious shortcomings in these relevant educational quality measures despite enormous improvements in access to education.

In columns 10 and 11 of Table 2.3, we present estimates for 1990 and 2017, respectively, of labour force participation rates of women over 15 years of age. Note that there has been some progress in raising these rates between 1990 and 2017 for all MENA countries except Syria and Yemen, both of which have been disrupted by civil wars in recent years. Yet, even in 2017, the female labour force participation rates of all MENA countries except Qatar (where most of the female workers are foreign) remain well below the world average. These low labour force participation rates of women in almost all MENA countries imply that much (though certainly not all) of the benefits of the investments in the form of human capital do not contribute directly to their economic growth. Finally, and even despite the often low rates of female labour force participation, in column 12 we see that the average annual growth rates of labour force in MENA countries have been unusually high. They range from 1.73 percent for Turkey (well above the world average) to almost 10 percent for the UAE, although the quality of that labour force has been less than sensational.

It should be clear from Tables 2.2 and 2.3, therefore, that in general MENA countries were experiencing relatively rapid growth of human and especially physical capital. But what about technological change? A common measure of technological efficiency is total factor productivity (TFP). Extremely accurate measures of TFP growth require data on labour, capital and human capital, shares of labour and capital in GDP, all quality adjusted on a consistent basis over time, a requirement which probably exceeds the quality of such data available for most MENA countries. Nevertheless, in 2015, the Penn World Table database came out with a set of estimates of TFP of pioneering quality (Feenstra et al., 2015) over time for most countries in the world, including MENA countries, over the period 1970–2014.

In columns 1 and 2 of Table 2.4, we present the resulting indexes of TFP at constant national prices for 1970 and 2014, wherein for each country the value of that index was set equal to 1.0 in 2011. Even if not perfect, these estimates are, to our knowledge, the best available for all countries for which such information is available. For comparison purposes, at the bottom of the table we include the same TFP estimates for a few other countries (both developing and developed) besides Israel. Comparing the estimates of the two different years, one can see that in general TFP increased over time not only in Israel but also in each of the other non-MENA countries included in the table. In China and India, these increases in TFP were quite substantial. Yet, among MENA countries, the only ones where there was even modest TFP growth over the period were Tunisia, Turkey and Iraq. The Iraqi case is explained in part by the fact that because of its wars the capital stock experienced no real growth over the 1983–2005 period. The positive TFP growth in Tunisia and Turkey can be partly attributed to the fact that they were the two MENA countries with the lowest rates of labour force growth (Table 2.3) yet maintained relatively high and quite steady rates of GDP growth over all decades from 1970 (as shown in Table 2.1).

In columns 3–5 of Table 2.4 we present country-specific values for the most recent year available on three different technology-related indexes, the Global Innovation Index, the Global Competitiveness Index and R&D Expenditures as a share of GDP, respectively. On the Global Competitiveness Index, only Qatar and the UAE have scores slightly above those of Israel and several MENA countries received scores that were but small fractions of Israel's. On the other two indexes, not a single MENA country obtained scores anywhere near those of Israel or above the world average. Thus, the TFP and different technology-related measures presented in this table indicate quite clearly that technological change has contributed little to overall growth in MENA countries. While comparable TFP estimates are unavailable in the Penn World Tables for several MENA countries, there is little reason to believe that any of those countries performed better in TFP growth than the countries for which such estimates are presented.[3]

2.4 The oil curse and other growth theories: productive structure, environmental concerns and institutions

Given the high proportion of MENA countries which are NR-rich, this section turns to some more specific variants of growth theory suggested as being especially relevant for such countries. The principal component of these is the so-called oil curse or Dutch disease coming from Corden (1984) and others who showed that oil discovery in a country is likely to divert much of its labour force from its "traditional" locus, typically agriculture and manufacturing, into non-traded goods and services, potentially hurting long-term development. Sachs and Warner (2001) subsequently showed that countries with greater *dependence* on oil (measured by the share of natural resource exports in total exports), though not greater *abundance* (measured by oil rents as a share of GDP), grew more slowly over time. Hence, productive structure came to be seen as playing a large role in this.[4]

To ascertain the applicability of this mechanism, in columns 1 and 2 of Table 2.5 we present corresponding estimates in different years of the shares of manufacturing in GDP for 1970 and 2016 and in columns 5–8 we do the same for agriculture, though separately for men and women as shares of total employment for 2000 and 2016. Given the well-known trend toward services in the world as a whole, and that jobs in agriculture are rural and usually have lower wages than manufacturing in urban areas, both agriculture and manufacturing shares would be expected to decline over time, but agriculture more so than manufacturing. Indeed, comparing these shares for the world as a whole for early and recent years shows that this has been happening at the

Table 2.4 Technology and technological change measures

	Index of TFP at constant national prices, 2011=1		*Global Innovation Index*	*Global Competitiveness Index*	*R&D expenditures as share of GDP*
	1970	*2014*	*2017*	*2017*	*2015*
Country	*1*	*2*	*3*	*4*	*6*
Algeria			23.9	4.07	0.1
Bahrain	2.75	1.05	36.1	4.54	0.11
Egypt, Arab Rep.	1.05	0.938	27.2	3.9	0.72
Iran, Islamic Rep.	2.526	0.894	33.4	4.27	0.32
Iraq	0.696	0.909			0.04
Jordan	1.701	0.948	30.81	4.29	0.43
Kuwait	3.373	0.877	34.4	4.43	0.3
Lebanon			28.21	3.84	
Libya					
Morocco	1.243	1.003	31.11	4.24	0.71
Oman			32.8	4.31	0.25
Qatar	1.515	0.881	36.6	5.11	0.48
Saudi Arabia	1.263	0.926	34.3	4.83	0.82
Sudan	1.11	0.933	19.8		0.3
Syrian Arab Republic			23.7		
Tunisia	0.765	0.96	32.9	3.93	0.63
Turkey	0.886	0.962	37.4	4.42	1.01
United Arab Emirates			42.96	5.34	0.87
West Bank and Gaza					0.49
Yemen, Rep.			15.01	2.87	
Israel	0.886	0.981	56.8	5.31	4.27
China	0.593	1.042	53.1	5	2.07
Finland	0.626	0.996	59.6	5.44	2.9
France	0.69	0.988	54.4	5.22	2.23
Germany	0.602	0.996	58	5.65	2.88
India	0.669	1.022	35.2	4.59	0.63
United Kingdom	0.664	1.01	60.1	5.51	1.7
United States	0.713	1.01	59.8	5.85	2.79
World					**2.23**
Sub-Saharan Africa					..
South Asia					0.58
East Asia					1.99
Latin America & Caribbean					..

Sources: Columns 1 and 2: *Penn World Tables Database*; column 3: *Global Innovation Index 2017*, World Economic Forum; column 4: *Global Competitive Report 2017–2018*, S. Dutta, B. Lunsin and S. Wunsch-Vincent, eds.; and column 5: World Bank, World Development Indicators.

world level. What is most striking in this table, however, is not the difference between oil and non-oil MENA countries, but rather the large differences between MENA countries of the two types and the world as a whole.

For two oil exporters, Algeria and Syria, the declines in manufacturing and agriculture have been much sharper than in the world as a whole, indicating that they may indeed have suffered from this particular form of oil curse. Iraq has also suffered a very sharp reduction in manufacturing but largely due to wars, and Bahrain, Sudan, UAE and Yemen have experienced especially sharp declines in agriculture. For Syria its decline in manufacturing is largely due to the civil war it has experienced since 2011. The West Bank and Gaza also have had sharp reductions in their manufacturing sectors, but in this case due to the severe limitations on their ability to export imposed by Israeli occupation. On the other hand, especially for Bahrain, Qatar, Tunisia and the UAE, their shares of manufacturing in GDP have increased very substantially, reflecting their ability to use their oil in such a way as to avoid the oil curse, allowing the countries to diversify their economies away from oil and non-traded goods. This is an important accomplishment, suggesting that this version of oil curse theory can be overcome under certain conditions. Non-oil Jordan also increased its manufacturing share in GDP quite significantly, thanks in part to its trade agreements with both the EU and USA. Even so, however, many MENA countries had manufacturing shares in GDP in 2016 that were only a small fraction of the overall average for East Asia.

Note from columns 5–8 that all MENA countries except Iraq and Libya experienced declines in the shares of employment in agriculture. Those exceptions were attributable in large part to war-caused disruption in the years preceding 2016 which left agriculture as one of the last resorts for employment. The declines were largest in Algeria, Morocco (although only for men), Tunisia, Turkey and Yemen. Of these only Algeria and Yemen can be attributed to oil as opposed to declining water availability and urbanisation.

Columns 3 and 4 reflect the levels of still another aspect of labour force structure in 1999 and 2013, respectively, namely, the percentages of labour force deemed to be in the shadow or informal sector, i.e. in activities not registered with the relevant authorities especially for labour and tax regulations. As Hassan and Schneider (2016) show, the reason for this is largely to avoid the costs that abiding by these regulations would entail. Since these shares of the labour force have been declining among all oil-exporting countries except UAE, in some cases rather sharply like in Algeria, Bahrain, Kuwait and Qatar, but rising in several of the non-oil MENA countries, clearly high and rising informality cannot be attributed to oil.

Another variant on the oil curse is air pollution. The country's exploitation of its oil, either for export or especially for use in production, is bound to increase air and water pollution and contribute to other environmental problems, unless efficiency in energy use is increased significantly. This can be exacerbated by a political economy hypothesis of relevance to oil countries like the GCC where, by law, the oil is owned by the state which is in the hands of monarchs who may feel the need to satisfy an 'authoritarian bargain' (Desai et al., 2009). According to this, oil-rich monarchs are likely to satisfy their authoritarian bargain by offering fuel and other subsidies to the citizens in return for the willingness of the citizens to allow the monarchs exclusive control over policies. Fuel subsidies, of course, greatly increase fuel use in automobiles, desalination of water and air conditioning, contributing to larger CO2 and other emissions.

To this end, note from columns 11 and 12 of Table 2.5 that by 2014 CO2 emissions per capita of all six GCC monarchies were at least three times as high as those of the world as a whole and as high as all other MENA countries except Iran and Libya, where substantial fuel subsidies were also provided. Indeed, that of Qatar was, to the best of our knowledge, the highest in the world in 2014. Although the somewhat lower oil prices since 2014 have forced several of these

Table 2.5 Production structure, energy efficiency and environment

Country	*Share of manufacturing in GDP*		*Size of the shadow (or informal) economy*		*Shares of labour force in agriculture*				*GDP per unit of energy use*		*CO^2 emissions in metric tons per capita*	
					Males		*Females*					
	1	*2*	*3*	*4*	*5*	*6*	*7*	*8*	*9*	*10*	*11*	*12*
	1970	*2016*	*1999*	*2013*	*2000*	*2016*	*2000*	*2016*	*1990*	*2014*	*1990*	*2014*
Algeria	13.3	4.41	34.2	27.24	22.8	13.4	11.9	9.6	12	10.2	3	3.7
Bahrain	10.12	18.13	18.6	13.59	2	1.2	0.2	0	3.3	4.1	25.1	23.4
Egypt	18.7	16.85	35.5	39.35	27.4	22.4	39.4	38.4	10.4	12.1	1.3	2.2
Iran	12.4	11.89	19.1	16.71	23.9	17.1	25.3	22	9.2	5.8	3.7	8.3
Iraq	14.2	1.97			15.1	12.6	34.8	43.7	10	10.5	2.7	4.8
Jordan	9.9	16.02	19.4	16.14	4.5	4.1	3.7	1.2	6.8	9.3	2.9	3
Kuwait	4.19	5.88	20.1	12.58	3.9	4.8	0.1	0.1	9.7	7.9	24.3	25.2
Lebanon	9.58	4.66	34.1	32.16	4.3	4.2	0	0	10.9	10.3	3	4.3
Libya	1.73	3.42			10.5	17.6	7.8	13.9		5.7	8.3	9.2
Morocco	17.02	15.79	36.5	40.72	40.7	30.9	53.4	57.2	12.9	13	0.9	1.7
Oman	0.39	10.1	19.1	16.07	6.5	6.9	5.3	0.6	15.1	6.6	6.3	15.4
Qatar	3.12	9.04	18.7	10.45	3	1.4	0	0		6.5	24.7	45.4
Saudi Arabia	8.25	12.58	18.7	17.73	6.7	6.9	2.3	0.6	12	7.2	11.4	19.5
Sudan	8.85	8.35			61.6	54.5	49.5	45.9	4.3	10.5	0.2	0.3
Syria	19.16	4.68			25.5	22.9	58.9	22.1			3	1.6
Tunisia	8.32	15.05	38.7	39.45	22.5	14.2	25	12.1	9.3	11.4	1.6	2.6
Turkey	17.62	16.6	32.7	32.7	26.7	15.4	60.2	28.6	11.7	14.1	2.7	4.5
UAE	1.64	9.25	26.3	28.41	6.7	0.2	0.1	0	10.1	8.2	28	23.3
West Bank, Gaza	16.59	11.8			10.3	7.3	35.5	12.6				0.6
Yemen, Rep.	4.65	8.89	27.7	38.92	39.3	34.4	82.5	57.2	16	12	0.8	0.9
Israel	22.7	11.68	22.7	20.45	3.1	1.5	0.8	0.6	6.1	11.5	7.8	7.9
World	19.88	15. 58	33.02	35.45	38	26.3	40.6	27.6	6.6	7.9	4.2	5
South Asia	14.35	15.03	33.65	31.92	54.0	38.5	74.3	59.9	5.6	8.8	0.6	1.5
East Asia	..	27.20	25.79	35.12	44.1	22.3	48.5	25.2	5.0	7.0	1.8	5.8
Latin America & Caribbean	21.94	12.50	40.16	45.51	27.7	20.3	14.5	8.2	9.5	10.8	2.1	2.8

Sources: Columns 3 and 4 from Hassan and Schneider (2016); all other columns from World Bank, World Development Indicators.

oil exporters to reduce their fuel and other subsidies, these emissions data provide strong support for this environmental variant of oil curse theory. Note also that between 1990 and 2014 CO2 emissions per capita were rising considerably faster in most MENA countries (and especially its oil countries) than in the world as a whole. Part of the reason for this is the declining efficiency of energy use shown in columns 9 and 10 in several oil-rich MENA countries (Algeria, Iran, Kuwait, Oman, Saudi Arabia and UAE) despite the fact that such efficiency was on the rise in Israel and the world as a whole. The effects of heavy fuel use and CO2 emissions are not limited to air pollution but also include desalination and increasing salinity of the ocean, both lowering sustainable growth in the long run.[5]

Aside from subsidies to fuel consumers, another important connection between NR-richness and CO2 emissions is that coming through natural resource-based manufacturing. Note that the largest CO2 emissions per capita in 2014 were in Bahrain, Kuwait, Qatar, Saudi Arabia and UAE which were among the relatively few MENA countries with increasing shares of manufacturing since 1970 (as shown in columns 1 and 2).

Still another variant of the oil curse hypothesis derives from the link between oil dependence and lower institutional quality. As Haber and Menaldo (2011) suggested, and further elaborated by many others (e.g., van der Ploeg, 2011; Mohaddes et al.,2019), the leader of any state (monarch or otherwise) that is well endowed with natural resources need not go to the trouble to develop institutions like tax systems, property rights, efficient budgetary systems and other institutions designed to promote the production of public goods and stimulate private businesses.

While there are perhaps thousands of institutions whose development could be inhibited by oil or other natural resource rents, for illustrative purposes in Table 2.6 we identify eight commonly cited ones, beginning with bureaucratic quality and concluding with ease of doing business, that could increase risks and transactions costs to firms and households. The first seven of these indexes are all ones in which a higher score signifies higher institutional quality. The last, the country's rank on ease of doing business, however, is an inverse measure with 1 the highest possible and 190 the lowest.

For each of the first seven indicators (bureaucratic quality, government stability, law and order, socioeconomic conditions, investment profile, control of corruption and democratic accountability) we present the country scores for both 1984 (the first year for which these indexes were constructed) and 2015. Each country's score on that indicator is constructed on the basis of several sub-indicators to capture the different governance risks of importance to business development and greater efficiency in resource allocation.[6]

From the different country scores for MENA countries in all columns of the table it can be seen that there is considerable variability both across MENA countries and over time on each of these eight indicators. From columns 1–14, it is clear that there were more MENA countries which showed improvement than those which showed declines in these scores between 1984 and 2015. Indeed, for government stability, law and order and investment profile, 17 MENA countries showed improvements and only one or two reflected declines. Yet, on control of corruption, the scores improved in only four MENA countries, while declining in twelve. While, overall, this performance may have been fairly satisfactory, it should be noted that non-oil Israel improved on all seven of these indicators over the period indicated and in most cases, only a few MENA countries did as well as Israel, and on both control of corruption and democratic accountability not a single one did as well. Relative to the oil curse theory, however, there would not seem to be much difference between RR and non-RR MENA countries in either levels or changes. In the latest year available, MENA as a whole fell especially far below the high ranked countries in bureaucratic quality, control of corruption and democratic accountability. Notably, however, the one MENA country which managed to improve in every institutional index

Table 2.6 Institutional indicators

Country	*Bureaucratic quality*		*Government stability*		*Law and order*		*Socio-economic conditions*		*Investment profile*		*Control of corruption*		*Democratic accountability*		*Rank on ease of doing business*
	1	*2*	*3*	*4*	*5*	*6*	*7*	*8*	*9*	*10*	*11*	*12*	*13*	*14*	*15*
	1984	*2015*	*1984*	*2016*	*1984*	*2016*	*1984*	*2015*	*1984*	*2015*	*1984*	*2015*	*1984*	*2015*	*2017*
Algeria	1	2	7.4	7.3	2	3	7.3	5.5	7.4	8.5	3	2	2	3.5	156
Bahrain	3	2	5	7.8	4	4.5	6	6.5	6.8	9.5	3	2.6	2	3.5	63
Egypt	1	2	7.8	8.1	2.7	3	6	4	6.2	6.9	1.7	2	3.8	2	122
Iran	1	2	5.3	7.2	1.7	4	4.7	6.2	5	6.2	3	1.5	1.6	3	120
Iraq	0.6	1.5	3.5	7	1	1.5	4	0.5	3.4	6.5	2.7	1	1.9	4	165
Jordan	2	2	7.1	8	2	5	7.8	4	8	9	3	3	1.8	3	118
Kuwait	2	2	6	6.6	2	4	7	8.9	8	9	3	3	2	3	102
Lebanon	1	2	2.5	6.7	1	4	3.8	5	3.8	7.9	3	1.9	2	5	126
Libya	0.6	1.5	4.8	5.6	1	4	5.7	4	4.7	6.5	3	1	1.7	2	188
Morocco	2.4	2	6.7	7.1	2	4.5	5	5.5	6	8	2	2.5	2	4.5	68
Oman	2	2	6	9.5	3	5	6	6.5	8.4	11	3	3	3	2	66
Qatar	1	2	6	10.5	3	5	7.6	8	6	10	2	4	2	2	83
Saudi Arabia	2.8	2	7.3	8.4	3.7	5	8.6	6.2	8.7	10.3	3.3	3	1.8	1.1	94
Sudan	0	1	3.1	6	2	2.5	5.3	1	5.1	6.8	1.4	0.5	1.3	2	168
Syria	0.4	1.5	5.7	6	1.6	4.5	5	3.5	4.4	4	1.4	1	1.2	1	173
Tunisia	2	2	4.3	6.2	2	5	5	5	5.3	7.6	3	2.5	2.5	4.5	77
Turkey	2	2	8	6.9	3	3	7.4	6	8	6	3	2.5	3.8	4	69
UAE	2	3	7	10	2.7	4	5.7	9.5	7.7	11.5	3	4	1.6	2.5	26
West Bank, Gaza															140
Yemen, Rep.	2	1	3.8	4.6	3	2	3.2	3.1	4	4.8	3	1	3.5	2.8	179
Israel	2.3	4	6.2	7.5	2	5	5.8	8.5	5.5	10	5	5.5	5.3	6	52
Highest Value Assigned in the Year Indicated	4	4	11	10.5	6	6	11	10.4	11	12	6	5.5	6	6	1

Sources: Columns 1–14 governance indicators of the International Country Risk Guide; column 15 World Bank, Doing Business (2017).

between 1984 and 2015 was UAE, which was also ranked 26th out of 190 on ease of doing business, considerably higher even than Israel. Other MENA countries which scored relatively high on several of these indicators and recorded some of the greatest improvements over time were Bahrain and Oman among oil-exporting countries, and Morocco and Tunisia among non-oil-exporting countries. If, as many governance analysts would suggest, bureaucratic quality, control of corruption and democratic accountability are in fact the most important institutions for achieving efficient institutions and long-term economic growth and development, weakness in these institutions may be holding back growth and development in MENA countries.

2.5 Conclusions and alternative policies for dealing with some of the major challenges facing MENA countries

In the preceding sections we have compared MENA countries in several dimensions relevant to their overall economic growth, GDP and population growth in Table 2.1, capital and human capital growth in Tables 2.2 and 2.3 and technology and institutions in Tables 2.5 and 2.6. In Table 2.4, we also called attention to changes in structure, with generally declining shares of tradable goods and especially manufacturing in most MENA countries.

Several characteristics of growth in MENA countries stand out in the above analysis.

(1) Growth rates of GDP over the 1970–2016 period have generally exceeded the world average.

(2) The growth rates of GDP have varied considerably from one decade to another, being large in periods of high and rising oil prices such as during the 1970s and 2000s, and low or even non-existent during the falling oil price period of the 1980s.

(3) As suggested above, there may be important reasons why this volatility in growth and in rates of investment over time may have lowered long-run growth, such as by decreasing the efficiency of investment, raising credit failures and bankruptcy rates, and causing undesirable delays in infrastructural completion. As a very modest attempt to test for this, we ran a simple panel regression of the growth rates of country i over decade t (GY_{it}) on both the average capital growth rates GK_{it} and the volatility in those capital rates in that same period (measured by the coefficient of variation) V_{it} in such rates.

$$GY_{it} = \alpha + \beta_1 GK_{it} + \beta_2 V_{it} \quad (1)$$

When this is done by decade for the sample of 20 MENA countries, the sample size is 111 and the estimate of β_1 is 0.948 with standard error 0.037 and that of β_2 is -7.453 with standard error 2.727; α is 0.209 with standard error 0.653 and adjusted $R^2 = 0.876$. This result provides at least tentative and preliminary support for the hypothesis that economic growth across countries and decades over the 1970–2016 period has been significantly and substantially reduced by the unusually high volatility in their capital growth rates.

(4) Most MENA countries have had unusually large shares of gross capital formation in GDP and for the most part these high shares have been converted into high rates of capital growth, thereby contributing to the high GDP growth rates as supported also by the aforementioned regression result. The most important exceptions have been cases like Libya, Sudan and Syria in which violence or financial instabilities have been sufficiently great to allow much of the existing capital to depreciate.

(5) With their relatively young and rapidly growing populations, and in most cases also rising investment in education and health, human capital has also been rising quite satisfactorily,

but in quality-adjusted terms not to the same extent as physical capital. Factors curtailing the increases in human capital have been: (a) serious internal conflicts that have caused sharp reductions in the quality and quantity of the labour force in some countries and decades; (b) the low quality of education (as measured by the various test scores); and (c) their extremely low female labour force participation rates.

(6) The most serious shortcoming has been in productivity growth, which, in considerable contrast to most other countries, has been negligible or even negative. Among the factors lying behind this are: (a) the extreme pro-cyclicality of growth in relation to oil prices which can lower the efficiency of investment allocations, and lead to bankruptcies; (b) the authoritarian bargain whereby so much of their oil revenues has been used for government consumption, often taking the form of cushy but low productivity jobs for nationals in the public sector and various subsidies; and (c) their weak institutions which tend to lower the efficiency of government and investment spending, and fail to control corruption and ensure the supply of services that people want.

(7) Of the several outcomes considered to be possible consequences of the so-called 'natural resource curse', the three links which would seem most important are (a) the institutional curse (including the failure to reduce corruption, to raise bureaucratic quality and to develop democratic institutions, and other means of either raising revenues to offset sharp reductions in revenues and expenditures when oil prices are low; (b) the 'authoritarian bargain' that prioritises the cushy government jobs, overdevelops non-tradables and provides too much in the way of fuel subsidies that worsen environmental problems and reduce competitiveness; and (c) the conflict trap which came to Libya, Sudan and Yemen after the development of oil, and to Syria as that country set about repressing efforts to provide greater democratic accountability.

Finally, we identify some of the countries which have been most successful in overcoming these problems, in some cases offering possible explanations. Notably, the three oil countries that have succeeded most in growing their capital and human capital stocks and GDP levels, diversifying their economies by raising their shares of manufacturing in GDP and obtaining very respectable scores on the Global Competitiveness Index (all at the same time) are UAE, Bahrain and Oman. Saudi Arabia and Qatar have also done quite well in these respects, much better than other oil countries have. Probably, the two most important things that the more successful countries have done are (a) to have opened up their economies to foreign workers, thus avoiding the Dutch disease effect and quite sharply increasing female labour force participation rates, and (b) to have improved the various institutional indexes identified in Table 2.6. Note that in this respect the UAE increased all of them, and by 2017 was ranked 26th on the ease of doing business index among all countries in the world. Bahrain, Iran, Kuwait and Oman have also done quite well on each of these counts, in the case of Bahrain and Oman contributing substantially to their comparative success in economic diversification. While there is no evidence of positive TFP growth in any of these countries, Bahrain and UAE have done better than Kuwait and Iran in this respect and because of their phenomenal growth rates in capital, labour and human capital, they have still managed to grow quite rapidly.

Among non-oil MENA countries, the greatest challenges are maintaining steady but relatively high rates of capital and human capital growth and achieving at least somewhat more favourable TFP and other productivity indicators. The two countries with positive TFP growth are Tunisia and Turkey which have done relatively well on R&D, global innovation and human capital. Jordan has also done very well in increasing its labour force, raising human capital quality and increasing the relative importance of its manufacturing sector. Jordan and Tunisia have also done well on the institutional indexes, increasing four of the seven between 1984 and 2015. All these countries have managed to keep their growth rates more stable from one decade to another than most other countries listed.

Notes

1 Mention should also be made of Ibn Khaldun, the pre-classical growth scholar from the MENA region itself, as explained by Boulakia (1971). Although agreeing on the basic pillars of growth, these scholars differed considerably on their relative importance, Smith devoting considerable attention to trade and technology growth, Marx to labour, Solow to technology growth and Ibn Khaldun to trade and institutions.
2 Although not shown here, data on tertiary gross enrolment rates in tertiary education from the same source as for secondary education show that enrolment rates in tertiary education were also rising rapidly in all countries.
3 Indeed, one effort to come up with TFP estimates for UAE (Soto, 2019) shows TFP growth to have been negative for that country.
4 One of the relevant mechanisms for this to happen would be an increase in the real exchange rate which would serve to lower the country's ability to export traditional sector goods, and increase dependence on imports in that sector.
5 The most technically advanced projections (e.g., Bucchignani et al., 2018) predict that temperatures in MENA will rise by another 2–6 degrees centigrade over the century and induce still more resources to be allocated to treating the consequences thereof, and quite conceivably reducing efficiency and the quality of human capital.
6 The governance indicators of the World Bank provide an alternative source for quite similar indexes but we concentrate on the ICRG indexes since these are available for a slightly longer time horizon. We deliberately exclude five other sources of risk constructed by the ICRG itself since they would seem more attributable to exogenous influences like ethnic and religious differences and external or internal conflicts and on which MENA countries are known to score very poorly for reasons not especially relevant to oil curse links.

References

Boulakia, J.D.C. (1971), "Ibn Khaldun a 14th Century Economist", *Journal of Political Economy*, 79 (5): 1105–1118.

Bucchignani, Eduado, Paola Mercugliano, Han-Jurgen Panitz and Myriam Montesarchio (2018), "Climate Change Projection for the Middle East-North Africa Domain with COSMO-CLM at Different Spatial Resolutions", *Advances in Climate Change Research*, 9 (1): 66–80.

Corden, W. M. (1984), "Booming Sector and Dutch Disease Economics: Survey and Consolidation", *Oxford Economic Papers*, 36 (3): 359–380.

Desai, Raj M., Anders Olofsgard and Tarik M. Yousef (2009), "The Logic of Authoritarian Bargain", *Economics and Politics*, 21 (1): 93–125.

Feenstra, Robert C., Robert Inklaar and Marcel P. Timmer (2015), "The Next Generation of the Penn World Table", *American Economic Review*, 105 (10): 3150–3182.

Global Innovation Index (2017), available from: https://www.wipo.int.

Haber, Stephen and Victor Menaldo (2011), "Do Natural Resources Fuel Authoritarianism? A Reappraisal of the Resource Curse", *American Political Science Review*, 105 (1): 1–26.

Hassan, Mai and Friederich Schneider (2016), "Size and Development of the Shadow Economies of 157 Countries: Update and New Measures 1999–2013", *Journal of Global Economics* 4 (3); doi:10.4172/2375-4389.1000218.

International Labour Office (ILO), ILOSTAT Database.

Mohaddes, Kamiar, Jeffrey B. Nugent and Hoda Selim, eds. (2019), *Institutions and Macroeconomic Policies in Resource-Rich Arab Economies*, Oxford: Oxford University Press.

Penn World Tables Database (PWT); available from: https://www.rug.nl/ggdc/productivity/pwt/

PISA Scores: PISA; available from: https://oecd.org>pisa

Sachs, Jeffrey D. and Andrew M. Warner (2001), "Natural Resource and Economic Development: The Curse of Natural Resources", *European Economic Review*, 45: 827–838.
Soto, Raimundo (2019), "Fiscal Institutions and Macroeconomic Management in the United Arab Emirates", Chapter 12 in Mohaddes, Nugent and Selim (2019).
Standard and Poor's Ratings Services, Global Financial Literacy Survey, available from: gflec.org/initiative/sp-global-finlit-survey/.
TIMSS Scores: IEA; available from: https://iea.nl
United Nations Statistical Office, National Account Statistics; available from: https://unstats.un.org/unsd/snaama/
United Nations UNESCO; available from: https://en.unesco.org>themes>education>database
van der Ploeg, Frederick (2011), "Natural Resources: Curse or Blessing?", *Journal of Economic Literature*, 49(2): 366–420.
World Bank, Doing Business (2017), available from: https://www.doingbusiness.org/.
World Bank, World Development Indicators; available from: https://datacatalog.worldbank.org/dataset/world-development-indicators
World Economic Forum, *Global Competitiveness Report (2017–2018)*; available from: https://www.weforum.org

3

IS MENA EXCEPTIONAL?

Julia C. Devlin

3.1 Introduction

The MENA region is home to small, relatively open economies and policymakers thus face the ubiquitous challenge of balancing domestic priorities with external economic pressures.[1] Today, with more than a decade of relatively strong growth performance and rising per capita consumption after 2003, there are looming challenges to sustaining gains in living standards in the face of underlying structural vulnerabilities and a more uncertain global outlook.

MENA economies are generally characterised by volatile growth performance coupled with weak underlying total factor productivity growth, persistent fiscal and current account deficits and high import dependence. Expansion in private investment tends to go hand in hand with low rates of small firm growth and the inability of many small firms to achieve sustained increases in employment and sales. There are wide gaps in productivity across firms. Export capacity remains highly concentrated and dualistic labour and capital markets inhibit social and economic mobility for young, particularly female, workers and small and medium enterprises, respectively. Rapid aggregate gains in poverty reduction have coincided with underlying gaps in social and economic opportunity and welfare. A fragile natural environment and in some cases, low productivity of agriculture and water use relative to per capita income levels heighten exposure to risks in global food commodity markets.

According to the perspective of old and "new" structuralist approaches to economic development, structure matters for growth and economic performance.[2] In this view, economic structure is in fact a determining feature of growth performance and structural change – the transfer of resources from less to more productive firms – alongside growth in factor productivity. Structural features of MENA economies therefore have important implications for securing recent gains in per capita consumption and future development policy efforts.

This chapter examines such distinguishing features in MENA countries from the vantage point of structuralist approaches to economic development and comparisons with other middle-income regions. Section 3.2 briefly reviews the region's growth performance in light of the enduring challenges of weak total factor productivity growth and persistent fiscal and current account deficits. Section 3.3 discusses forces both inhibiting and promoting private sector development and exports. Section 3.4 reviews the functioning of labour and financial markets and identifies factors contributing to the region's high youth unemployment and lacklustre social mobility. Section 3.5 discusses social welfare trends and poverty incidence and Section 3.6 identifies challenges in current approaches to use of water resources. Section 3.7 concludes.

3.2 Growth and the macroeconomy

Since the 1970s, levels of real GDP in MENA countries have demonstrated modest and, in some cases, volatile growth (Figure 3.1). Relative to countries in East Asia and the Pacific, for example, levels of per capita real GDP were higher in Iran and Saudi Arabia in the early 1970s but increases have largely flatlined since the 1986 oil price shock.

Relative to per capita real GDP, measures of real household consumption appear to be converging more rapidly to high income levels over the 2000s, particularly in the case of Tunisia, for example and in comparison with other middle-income regions such as East Asia and the Pacific (Figure 3.2).

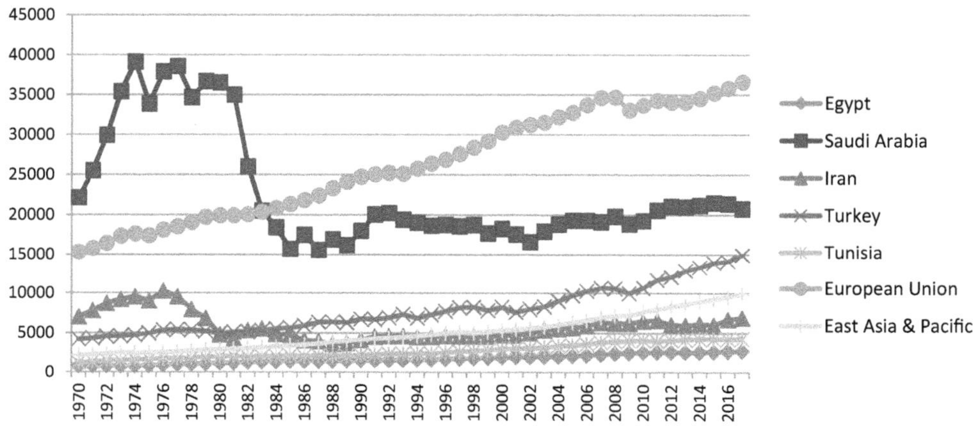

Figure 3.1 Real per capita GDP (constant 2010 US$). *Source:* World Development Indicators, World Bank.

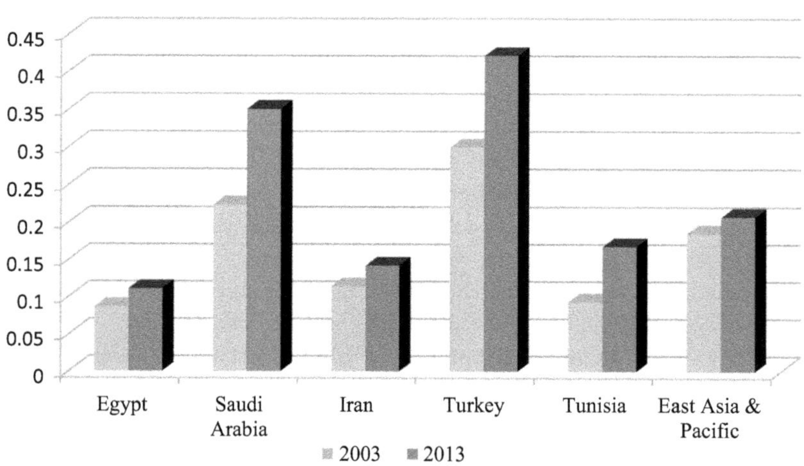

Figure 3.2 Real per capita household (HH) consumption relative to the European Union (% HH real per capita consumption as % EU level of HH real pc consumption). *Source:* World Development Indicators, World Bank.

3.2.1 Weak total factor productivity growth

Are these gains sustainable? It is widely acknowledged that raising per capita income over time is generally achieved in part by increasing the overall effectiveness with which capital and labor are used or total factor productivity. For most MENA countries, total factor productivity over the longer term does not appear to be increasing (Figure 3.3). A number of studies explain the region's weak performance in productivity in terms of significant levels of public investment relative to private investment; limited progress on structural reforms, particularly the need to create a more competitive business environment including financial market development; gaps in the adoption of competitive production methods; and levels of worker talent (Sala-i-Martin and Artadi, 2002; Keller and Nabli, 2007; Mitra et al., 2016).

This pattern is particularly acute in oil-exporting MENA countries such as Iran and Saudi Arabia where total factor productivity has generally not achieved the levels attained in the 1970s. Limited prospects for economic diversification and institutional weaknesses have played an important role (Fasano-Filho and Iqbal, 2003; Hakimian, 2008).

Much of the growth resurgence in the 2000s is linked with higher oil prices and increased infrastructure commitments, particularly physical capital accumulation (Mitra et al., 2016). Relative to Brazil, for example, shares of investment in GDP are relatively high but lower than in South Korea (Figure 3.4).

3.2.2 Structural transformation

In comparison with countries in East Asia such as South Korea, MENA countries tend to exhibit somewhat idiosyncratic patterns of structural change (Figure 3.5). In general, declining shares of GDP in agriculture and rising shares of industry and manufacturing accompany shifts in sector productivity and changing patterns of demand. In the case of MENA countries, particularly oil exporters, sectoral shifts away from agriculture have occurred primarily in the direction of oil and mining sectors (included in industry) and services as opposed to non-oil

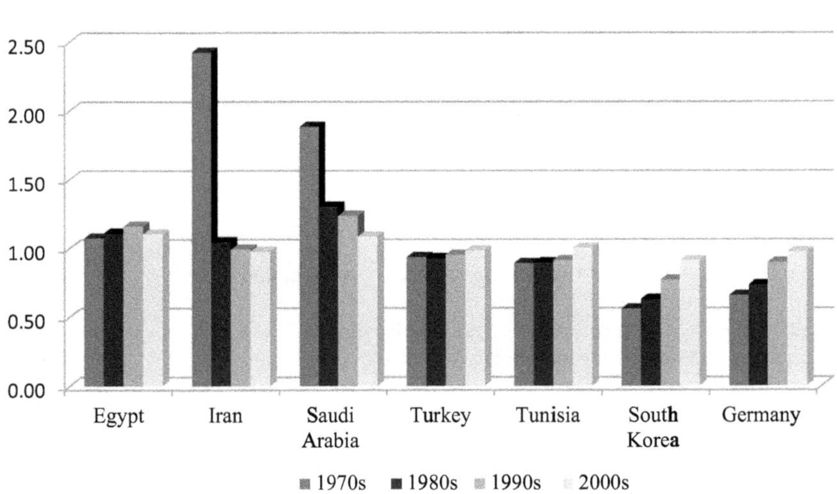

Figure 3.3 Average annual total factor productivity. *Note*: indicator is total factor productivity at constant national prices, base year 2011, annual, not seasonally adjusted. *Source*: University of Groningen and University of California, Davis, Total Factor Productivity at Constant National Prices for Turkey [RTFPNATRA632NRUG], retrieved from FRED, Federal Reserve Bank of St. Louis; https://fred.stlouisfed.org/series/RTFPNATRA632NRUG.

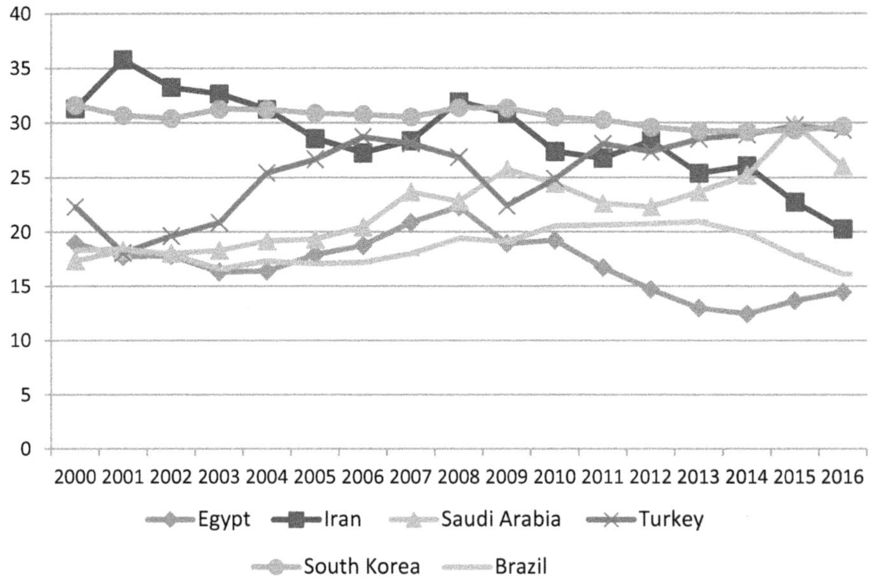

Figure 3.4 Investment share of GDP (gross fixed capital formation % GDP). *Source:* World Development Indicators, World Bank.

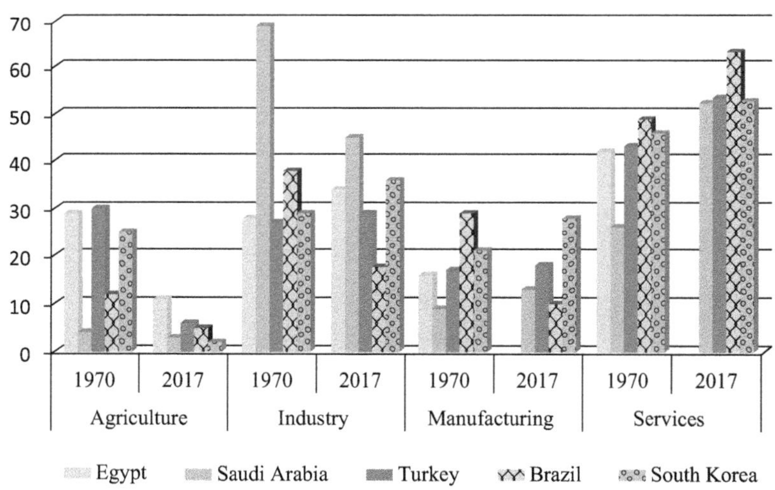

Figure 3.5 Structural change in MENA countries (value added by sector as % of GDP). *Source:* World Bank (1995) and World Development Indicators, World Bank.

industries and manufacturing. This suggests room for accelerated structural transformation, particularly with respect to non-oil industry and manufacturing activities.

3.2.3 Macroeconomic imbalances

Government spending is an important component of GDP growth in MENA countries and net borrowing by the government as a share of GDP is high relative to other middle-income com-

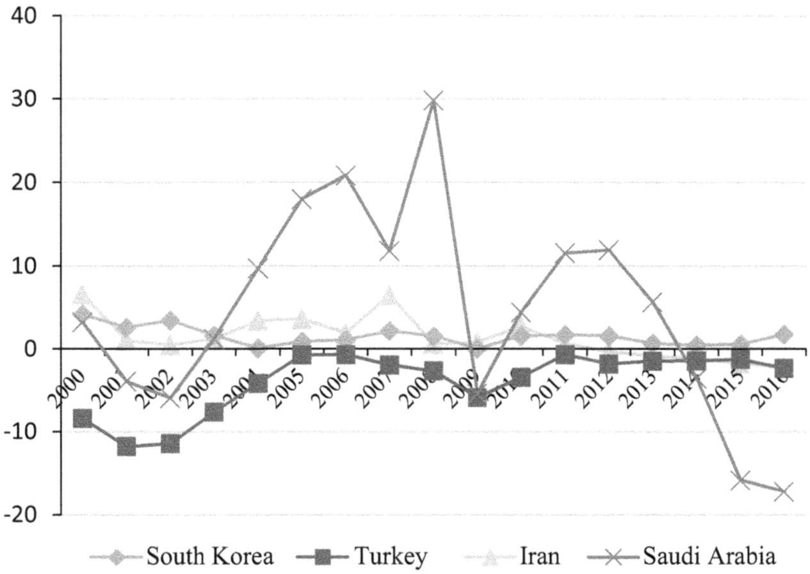

Figure 3.6 Government net lending/borrowing (% of GDP), annual, not seasonally adjusted. *Source*: University of Groningen and University of California, Davis, Total Factor Productivity at Constant National Prices for Turkey [RTFPNATRA632NRUG], retrieved from FRED, Federal Reserve Bank of St. Louis; https://fred.stlouisfed.org/series/RTFPNATRA632NRUG.

parators (Figure 3.6). In Turkey for example, the correlation between government spending and GDP is estimated at 0.61, significantly higher than in "resilient" emerging market economies, which is estimated at 0.06 (IMF, 2013).

This is coupled with a large and persistent "import bias" (high % of imports in GDP), a structural feature which has not received much attention in recent analysis of MENA countries (Figure 3.7). In comparison with other middle-income and high-income regions, MENA countries exhibit high import dependence, associated in some cases with a legacy of import substitution industrialisation (ISI) policies and trade protectionism. In the case of Turkey, high levels of dependence on imports relate to the country's role as an early pioneer in ISI together with its support of infant industries beginning in the 1930s. Following unsustainable growth in fiscal and current account deficits, among others, the government adopted wide-ranging reforms to curb growth in government expenditure, temper public sector interventionism and promote foreign investment and exports beginning in the 1980s.

Thus, a long-term dynamic of growth in MENA countries – expansionary fiscal policy, structural rigidities and external resource inflows which work together to provide a growth stimulus and forge a national consensus– remains intact (Onis and Riedel, 1993; Devlin, 2010, 2016). Given the region's weak factor productivity growth, promoting internal drivers of the growth process and pro-productivity measures are paramount. An important complement to this approach is a concerted focus on underlying patterns of reallocation in productive resources and high import dependence.

3.3 Firms and the global economy

Growth dynamics from the structuralist perspective are closely linked with firm behaviour in high productivity sectors and upstream and downstream linkages with other activities. This is an

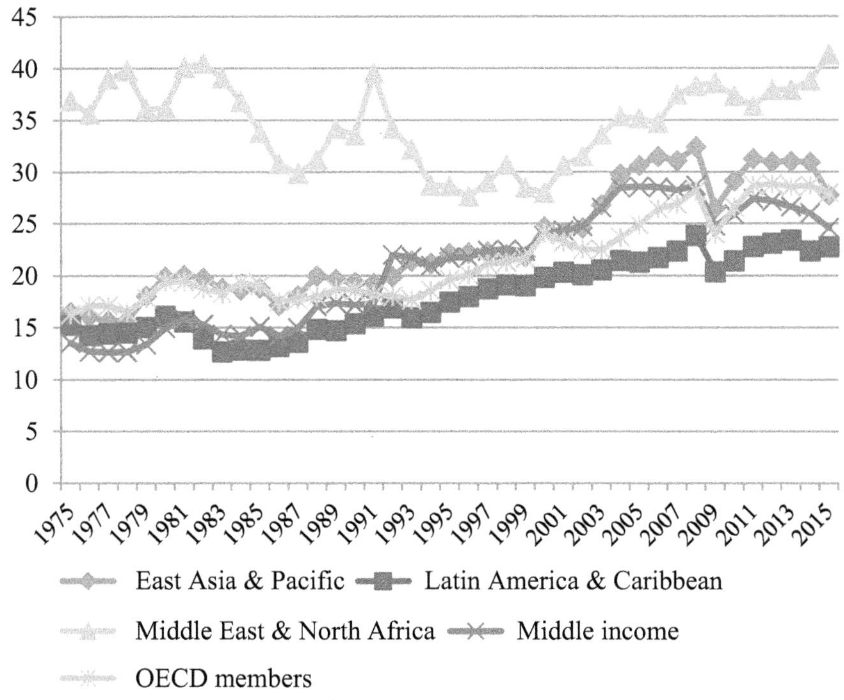

Figure 3.7 Import dependence (imports as % of GDP). *Source:* World Development Indicators, World Bank.

ongoing challenge in the MENA context. Over the 2000s, growth in private investment among MENA countries significantly outpaced levels in the 1990s, averaging nearly 10% of GDP in countries such as Egypt. Nevertheless, at the microeconomic level, growth and innovation remain relatively concentrated among firms.

3.3.1 A prevalence of small firms and limited growth potential

Similar to other developing regions, MENA economies tend to be characterised by a large number of small firms and a handful of large firms, including state-owned enterprises. In Egypt and the West Bank and Gaza for example, micro-establishments with fewer than five employees dominate the private sector – accounting for 60% of firms (Schiffbauer et al., 2015). Moreover, this trend is increasing over time. Between 1996 and 2006, for example, the share of employment in large firms declined by seven percentage points in Egypt whereas it increased over the same period in micro-establishments.

From an employment and growth perspective, the shortage of medium- and large-sized young firms is a particular challenge in the MENA region. The probability that medium-sized firms grow to become large firms is low. Of all SMEs in Tunisia in 2007, for example, 4% became large firms by 2011 (Schiffbauer et al., 2015).

3.3.2 Productivity gaps across firms

There are also wide gaps in productivity and growth across firms active in rural and urban sectors, domestic and export markets, the formal and informal economy and within the manufac-

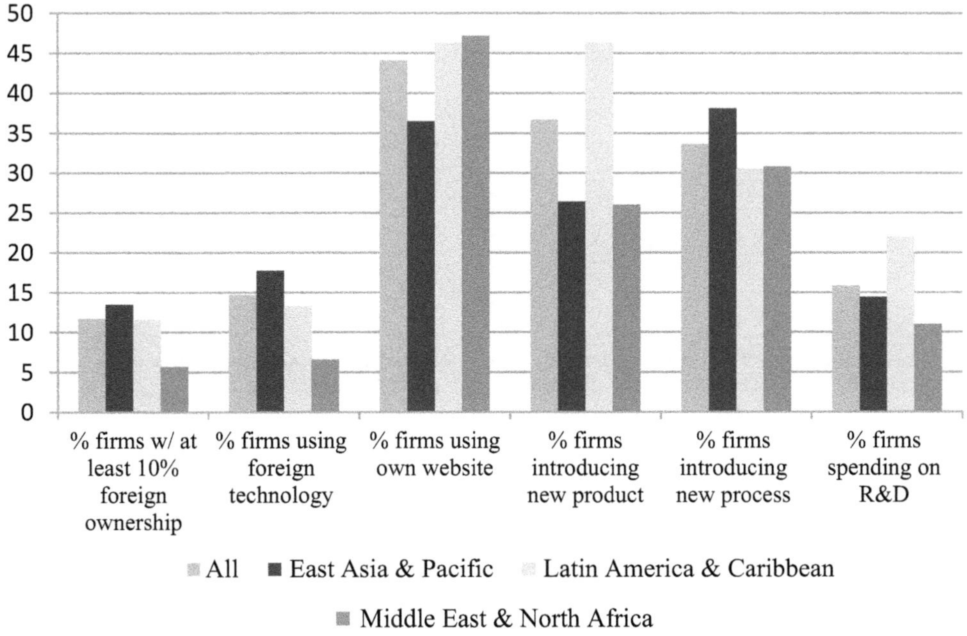

Figure 3.8 Firm characteristics in MENA countries (2013). *Source:* World Bank Enterprise Surveys.

turing sector itself. This is consistent with characteristics of "dualism" in developing economies as exemplified by the Lewis (1954) two-sector growth model and more recent analysis which finds wide gaps in productivity within manufacturing itself.[3]

In MENA countries, high-growth firms in manufacturing provide formal training to employees, using email or a company website, securing an international quality certificate such as ISO 9000 and maintaining a workforce in which 5% or more of workers have a university education (Stone and Badawy, 2011). Many of these characteristics are also capacities in which a number of MENA firms tend to perform well relative to middle-income comparators (Figure 3.8). Today, a handful of high-growth firms in particular accounts for a large share of job creation – an estimated 64% and 42% of total net job creation in Jordan and Tunisia (respectively) and many are young firms (Schiffbauer et al., 2015).

3.3.3 *Weak market dynamism*

External factors also play an important role in firm performance for MENA economies. Growth in factor productivity requires physical and capital accumulation but also the right regulations and institutions to ensure that this capital is used productively. Conditions in the business environment, particularly the degree to which they promote competition and firm growth, are thus vital foundations for productivity gains. In this regard, MENA countries continue to face challenges, particularly with regard to entry (Figure 3.9). Even in countries with a relatively robust private sector, entry rates are well below comparators.

Recent surveys of obstacles among MENA firms point to high levels of political instability and corruption as being challenges in the business environment relative to comparators (EBRD et al., 2016). Other difficulties include lack of adequate access to electricity, particularly for firms in Egypt, the West Bank and Gaza, Yemen and Lebanon.

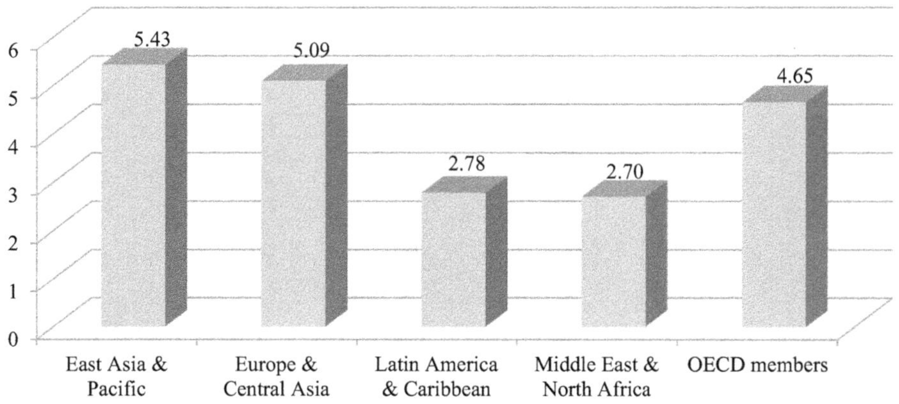

Figure 3.9 New business entry (new registrations per 1,000 people ages 15–64). *Source*: World Development Indicators, World Bank.

With respect to access to finance, the majority of firms in Egypt resort to internal financing of investment and in larger percentages than other middle-income economies. This suggests that access to formal financing mechanisms may be concentrated among a handful of firms and/or that firms may be risk-averse with respect to prospects for market growth. The latter factor may also play a role in explaining the relatively low incidence of formal training among firms. Relative to businesses in other middle-income regions, for example, an estimated 10% of firms report offering formal training to workers as opposed to 32% in other middle-income regions (World Bank, 2016a).

Financial markets tend to be dominated by banks to a greater extent than in comparator countries and credit has typically been more concentrated than in other middle-income regions. In the first decade of the 2000s, for example, the ratio of the top 20 loan exposures to total equity was 242%, the highest in the world (Rocha et al., 2011). Equity markets are characterised by relatively low turnover of shares and high concentration among finance and infrastructure sectors (Rocha et al., EBRD et al., 2016). There are gaps in insurance, leasing and nonbanking financial services relative to per capita income levels.

3.3.4 Concentrated FDI and export potential

For the MENA region as a whole, foreign direct investment lags considerably behind other middle-income regions. In 2016, for example, levels of foreign direct investment (net inflows) were 10% of levels in East Asia and the Pacific and 20% of levels in Latin America and the Caribbean (World Bank, 2017). Moreover, net FDI inflows to MENA countries are concentrated in a handful of activities. From 2003 to 2010, Jordan experienced one of the highest net inflows of FDI among emerging market economies, but more than half of that investment was concentrated in real estate. Such patterns also tend to prevail in other MENA countries and contrast with high shares of FDI inflows into manufacturing and ICT services in India, Indonesia, China and Brazil (Schiffbauer et al., 2015).

Similarly, the region's export capacity is concentrated in a small number of firms and products. Algeria for example has one of the highest levels of export concentration globally, with hydrocarbons generating 98% of export revenues (African Development Bank, 2012).

About half of total exports across the MENA region are generated by large firms accounting for the bulk (52%) of total exports; furthermore, the top-exporting firms face few competitors.

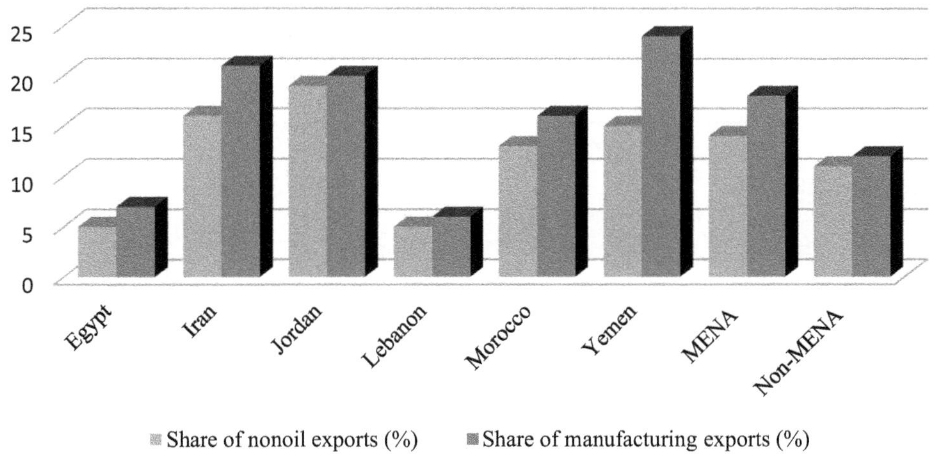

Figure 3.10 Export shares of top one exporting firm in select MENA countries (2006–11). *Source*: Data from Freund and Jaud (2015: Table 2.2, p. 15) based on Freund and Pierola (2014).

In Iran, Jordan and Yemen, for example, the top exporting firm accounts for over one-fifth of manufacturing exports (Freund and Pierola, 2014; Freund and Jaud, 2015) (Figure 3.10).

In terms of products, export big "hits" can play an outsized role in generating export earnings. Egypt, for example, earned nearly one-quarter of its total manufacturing export revenues from one product – ceramic bathroom and kitchen items to one destination – Italy, capturing 94% of the Italian import market for that product in the 2000s (Easterly et al., 2009).

Moreover, a number of studies point to the concentration of MENA firms in "sparse" areas of the product space in which export products such as phosphates and crude oil have few natural "spillovers" in terms of firm "capabilities" for exporting related products (with revealed comparative advantage), inhibiting the potential for export diversification. In the case of Morocco, for example, while the country has developed a comparative advantage in medium- and high-tech manufactures representing around 40% of exports in 2010, the number of products involved is relatively small and has not generated sufficient growth for the economy to attain middle-income averages in growth in per capita income (African Development Bank 2012; Osorio Rodarte and Lofgren, 2015).

Thus, high levels of concentration in firm size and "capability" together with weak market dynamism are underlying factors in helping to explain patterns of concentrated production and specialisation in MENA countries. This suggests the need for strengthened policy efforts in the areas of competition and innovation along with more targeted measures to address gaps in growth dynamics across sectors and firms. Addressing such obstacles will also be critical for generating productive employment and wage growth for rising cohorts of educated, young workers.

3.4 Labour markets and unemployment

Well-functioning labour markets are integral to the growth and entry of firms and the process of reallocating resources to more productive uses economy-wide. In this regard, the MENA countries face distinctive challenges. High youth unemployment combined with large-scale public sector employment and the growing informalisation of work, among other factors, help to create barriers to entry into the workforce as well as worker mobility.

Table 3.1 Youth unemployment (aged 15–24) and gender employment gaps (2017)

Region	*Total (%)*	*Male (%)*	*Female (%)*	*Gender gap in employment rate (% points, male–female)*
Arab states	29.7	24.0	51.0	28.2
Latin America & Caribbean	17.1	13.9	21.8	19.6
Eastern Europe	16.2	15.8	16.8	7.9
Central and Western Asia	17.5	16.8	18.7	18.2
South-Eastern Asia & Pacific	13.6	13.4	13.9	12.8
Northern, Southern and Western Europe	18.9	19.5	18.2	3.3

Source: International Labour Organization (2016), World Employment Social Outlook: Trends for Youth.

3.4.1 High rates of unemployment

Region-wide, estimates of youth unemployment outpace most other developing regions and among the 15–24 age group in Arab states rates were nearly 30% in 2017 (Table 3.1). Moreover, rates of unemployment are significantly higher for women at 51% in 2017 and gender gaps in male–female employment rates are well above those in middle-income and industrialised country averages.

A number of studies explain the high incidence of youth unemployment in terms of the region's legacy of demographic dynamism, slowing public sector employment and gaps in private sector job creation (Gatti et al., 2013). More recent studies point to the role of search frictions and prestige factors. The evidence for "reservation prestige" or the phenomenon in which graduates reject jobs they consider unsuitable appears to be particularly relevant in explaining unemployment among educated youth in Jordan (Groh et al., 2014).

3.4.2 The role of the public sector

A particular challenge facing MENA economies is the large share of government employment and its associated impact on the functioning of labour markets (Figure 3.11) (Said, 2001; Assaad, 2013). Public administration shares of employment are among the highest in the world and the majority of young people would prefer to work for the public sector as suggested by job search and educational choices (Behar and Mok, 2013; World Bank, 2012).

The structure of remuneration and labour protection characteristic of public sector employment are also linked with segmentation features of labour markets in the MENA region (Assaad, 2002; Pissarides, 1993). For example, wage differentials between public and private sectors for workers with similar characteristics in Egypt are particularly high for women and estimated at 33% in 2006 (Said, 2009; Assaad, 2013).

Entry into public sector employment in countries such as Egypt is also becoming more concentrated. For example, although public sector employment opportunities declined significantly between 1998 and 2006, the decrease mainly affected children of industry, service and agricultural workers as opposed to white collar workers (World Bank, 2012).

High levels of public sector employment and barriers to entry for public sector jobs have been paralleled by the growth of an expansive informal labour market (Figure 3.12). A typical MENA country for example produces about one-third of its GDP and employs nearly 65% of its labour force informally (Gatti et al., 2014).[4] Informality rates are particularly high among youth.

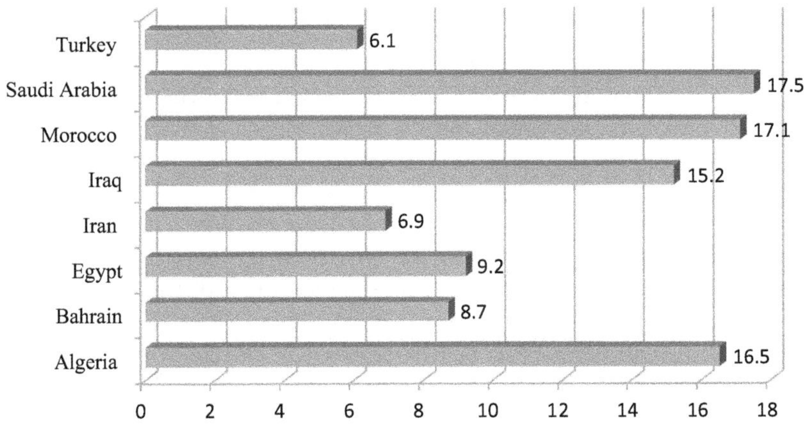

Figure 3.11 Ratio of public to private sector employment (most recent year). *Note*: public sector employment is defined narrowly as public administration employees. Data is based on most recent year available and is as follows: Algeria (2004), Bahrain (2010), Iran (2008), Iraq (15.2), Morocco (2006), Saudi Arabia (2009) and Turkey (2010). *Source*: based on data from Behar and Mok (2013: Table 1, p. 13).

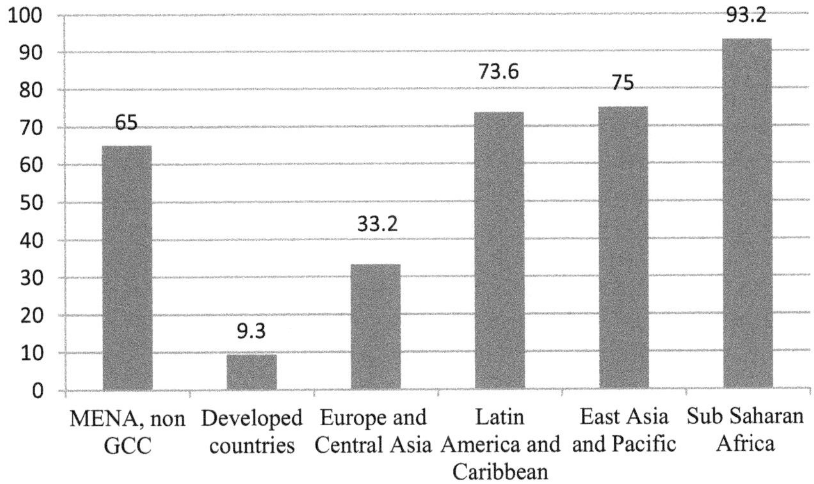

Figure 3.12 Informality of employment in MENA countries (% of total employment). *Note*: workers characterised as "informal" are those lacking access to health insurance and/or are not contributing to a pension system. *Source*: based on data from Gatti et al. (2014: Figure O.2, p. 7).

Studies at the microeconomic level suggest that factors such as age and education tend to be negatively associated with informality and being female is associated with higher informality rates in countries such as Yemen. Moreover, informal workers tend to move into public sector jobs suggesting that queuing in the informal sector is common for those seeking employment in the public sector (Angel-Urdinola and Tanabe, 2012). Such trends tend to differ from other middle-income countries in Latin America for example where transitions tend to occur between informality and self-employment (Perry et al., 2007; Angel-Urdinola and Tanabe, 2012).

3.4.3 Female labour force participation

MENA countries continue to maintain the lowest level of female labour force participation globally and numerous studies point to social and economic factors underlying this phenomenon including legal and social restrictions on mobility, lack of employment opportunities, educational preferences and others (Nabli and Chamlou, 2004; World Bank, 2013). A study of young female community college graduates in Jordan for example revealed that, while 93% said they wanted to work after graduation, only 23% were employed 16 months after graduation (Groh et al., 2012). For policymakers this places a premium on identifying the right combination of policies to support successful transitions from school into the labour market for the region's youth, particularly women.

Thus, from the labour market perspective, high rates of youth unemployment and low levels of labour force participation among women together with rising levels of informality pose significant challenges for a more efficient allocation of productive resources across MENA countries. Moreover, shrinking avenues for social and economic mobility in the form of declining public employment prospects together with weak growth potential among small- and medium-sized firms have implications for sustaining the region's gains in social welfare and living standards.

3.5 Poverty and social welfare

For most MENA countries, poverty reduction and improved social welfare have generally gone hand in hand with accelerating growth. However, unlike other middle-income regions, poverty incidence did not necessarily increase during periods of slower growth and adjustment in the 1980s and 1990s. High levels of public sector employment and external capital flows in the form of international remittances appear to have played an important role (Adams and Page, 2003).

Poverty incidence in the MENA region is low in comparison with other middle-income regions. In 1990, for example, the percentage of population living on US$ 1.90 per day (2011 PPP) was 6.3% or about 44% of levels in Latin America and the Caribbean and 10% of levels in East Asia and the Pacific (World Bank, 2017). However, using broader measures of poverty (US$ 3.20 2011 PPP), the data suggest that rates of poverty reduction have lagged behind other middle-income regions raising questions about the extent to which recent growth in per capita income has translated into broad-based gains in welfare (Figures 3.13 and 3.14).

Who are the poor in the MENA region? In general, the poor are characterised as young, rural, uneducated and employed in the private, informal economy (Silva et al., 2013; Gatti et al., 2014). Cash transfer programs across MENA countries have historically been targeted categorically (i.e. widows) rather than using income or means-based testing and have tended to be small. Moreover, surveys of public opinion suggest that conditional cash transfers are not viewed as positively as in other developing regions (Silva et al., 2013). Consumer subsidies on the other hand are significantly more important than in other developing countries – petroleum subsidies have accounted for nearly half of global energy subsidies (Sdralevich et al., 2014; Clements et al., 2013; Araar and Verme, 2016).

In contrast to consumer subsidies and expenditures on education, social expenditure linked with health is relatively modest. Average health expenditure as a share of GDP in 2015 was 5.5% compared to 6.8% in East Asia and the Pacific and 7.4% in Latin American and the Caribbean (World Bank, 2017). MENA countries also have some of the highest levels of out-of-pocket spending for healthcare among middle-income regions, estimated at 31% of total current health expenditure in 2015 (World Bank, 2017).

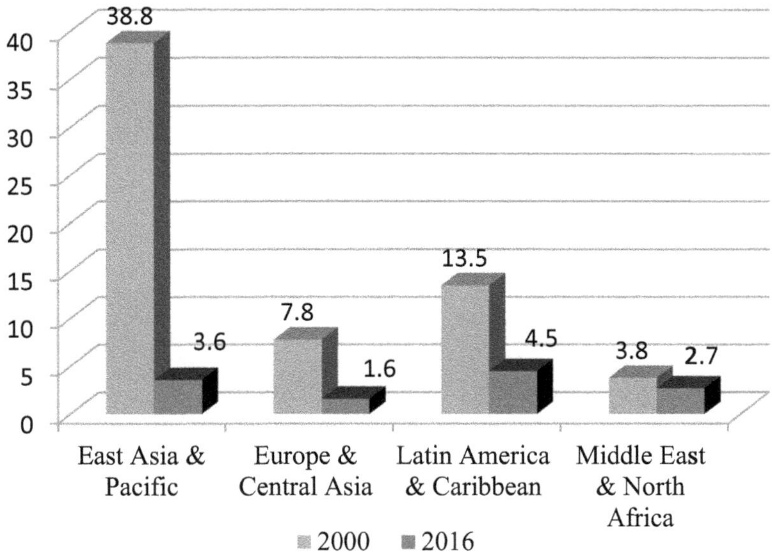

Figure 3.13 Poverty incidence (% population at $ 1.90 per day 2011 PPP). *Source*: World Development Indicators, World Bank.

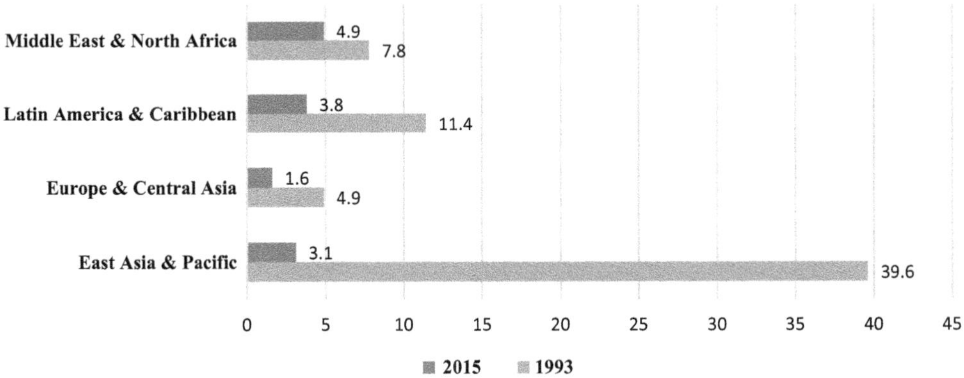

Figure 3.14 Poverty incidence (% population at $ 3.20 per day 2011 PPP). *Source*: Poverty and inequality Database, World Bank.

Evidence suggests that patterns and levels of government expenditure have been important drivers of social well-being as well as growth in MENA countries. Whether or not existing approaches can protect per capita consumption to the same extent is an issue, given the apparent slowdown in poverty reduction over the 2000s and patterns of distribution in consumption. This is particularly critical in light of structural inefficiencies in labour and product markets. Moreover, there may be room for more concerted efforts to improve social welfare through an asset-driven and/or human capital-focused approach.

3.6 Water scarcity and food security

Through the process of growth and structural transformation, gains in agricultural productivity have been an important driver of overall productivity gains and the movement of resources to

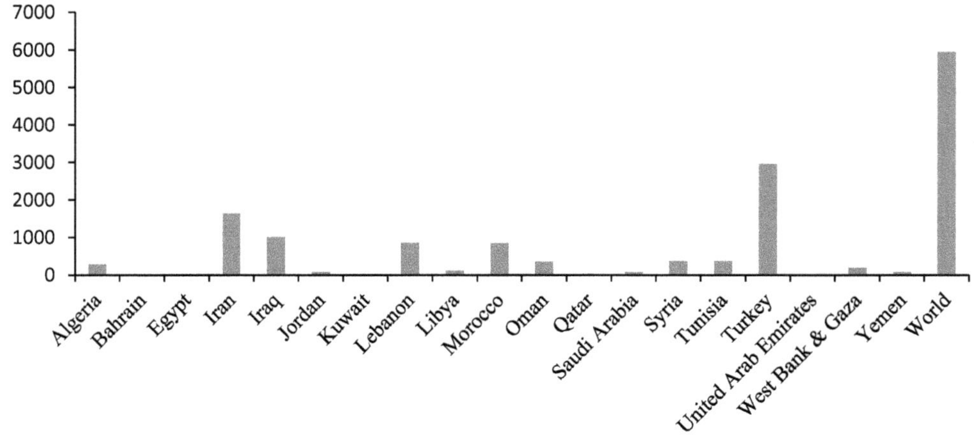

Figure 3.15 Freshwater resources per capita (cu. m) (2014). *Note*: data are internal renewable freshwater resources. *Source*: World Development Indicators, World Bank.

higher-valued activities. In water-constrained regions such as the Middle East and North Africa, however, maximum rates of output allocated to boost water supplies, for example, do not necessarily guarantee higher growth prospects. What matters is that the net marginal productivity of capital exceeds the higher output costs of water supply provision and that there are sufficient freshwater resources available (Barbier, 2004; Devlin, 2014).

Today, MENA countries have the lowest levels of freshwater resources globally (Figure 3.15). Additionally, projections for the impact of climate change on water availability are challenging, with some estimates suggesting that water-related losses in agriculture, health, income and poverty could detract 6% or more of MENA GDP by 2050 (World Bank, 2016b).

Policy biases also constrain agricultural productivity. Relative to other middle-income economies, levels and growth in agricultural productivity have been modest over the 2000s (Figure 3.16). A number of MENA countries lag behind in the intensity of input use in agriculture (Figure 3.17). At the same time, agriculture remains the dominant user of water in the MENA region as elsewhere and inhibits more efficient use of the region's scarce water resources (World Bank, 2007, 2018).

As an important economic and employment sector in MENA countries, agriculture benefits from relatively high levels of trade protection – in countries such as Morocco and Tunisia average applied trade protection in the early 2000s was more than twice as high as developing country averages (Breisinger et al., 2010). Striking a balance between trade liberalisation and domestic reforms in the agricultural sector remains a challenge for policymakers, particularly in light of the region's high level of food import dependence and poverty incidence in some rural areas.

3.6.1 Food security

MENA countries are the most food import-dependent countries globally and during the 2000s, net food imports accounted for 25–20% of national consumption (Breisinger et al., 2010). Arab countries in particular imported more than 30% of globally traded wheat in 2010 and more than 50% of cereal calories consumed (World Bank and FAO, 2009). Two global price shocks and high levels of commodity price volatility in wheat and other agricultural commodities

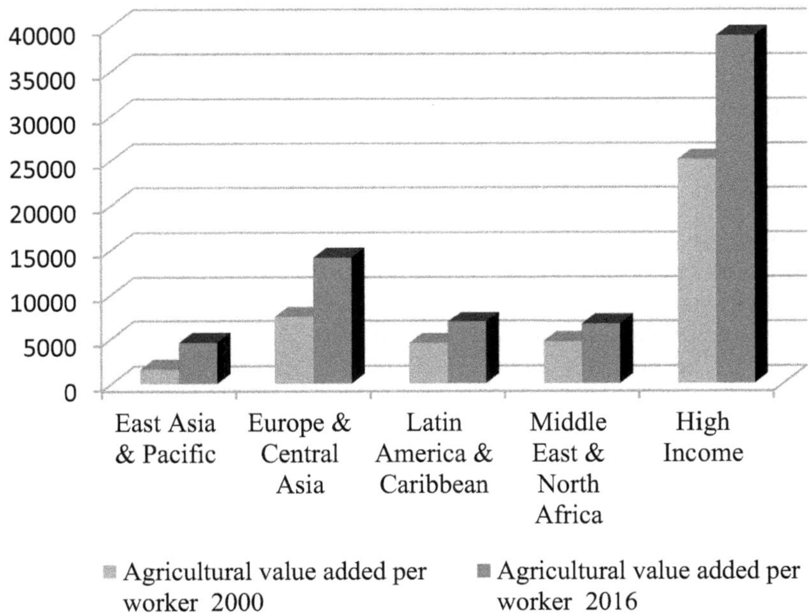

Figure 3.16 Agricultural productivity (US$ 2010). *Source:* World Development Indicators, World Bank.

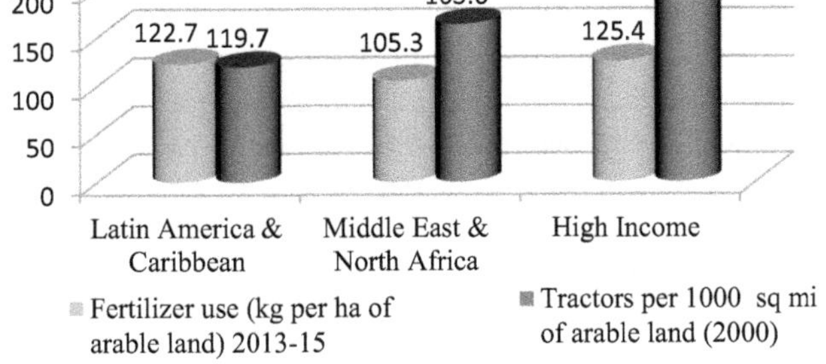

Figure 3.17 Intensity of input use in agriculture. *Source:* World Development Indicators, World Bank.

during the 2000s compounded the risks. Thus policymakers face an ongoing challenge somewhat unique to middle-income countries – balancing food imports, supply chains and strategic reserves of high risk commodities, together with domestic agriculture. Assessing existing levels of consumer food subsidies is of paramount importance. Innovation and technologies related to advanced water technologies, drought stress and salinity tolerance can also play a role. This could include for example using crop breeding, biotechnology and genetic modification to adapt existing varieties of agricultural products to stresses related to climate change, including drought, heat and salinity – all of which are set to spread and intensify under climate change in the region. These technologies can be combined with the tapping of traditional knowledge in crop varieties and adaptation (Breisinger et al., 2010).

3.7 Conclusion

The observation that structure matters for growth is not a novel insight for practitioners working in developing country contexts. From a theoretical standpoint, recognition of the need to adapt conventional frameworks and neoclassical modelling of the growth process to structural realities in developing countries is also increasingly commonplace (Agenor and Montiel, 1999). Many of the characteristics of developing countries and "stylised" facts identified appear evident in the case of MENA countries: high openness to global markets and reliance on capital inflows, dependence on imported intermediate inputs and capital goods, concentration of market power in some cases, gaps in financial market development and a degree of informalisation in wage determination and employment.

In the MENA context, it is apparent that external capital inflows together with adjustments in government expenditure and investment have worked to stimulate growth but at the cost of volatility and persistent fiscal and current account imbalances over the longer term. An intrinsic import bias, low levels of nonoil export capacity, idiosyncratic patterns of structural transformation and gaps in dynamism in the domestic market work to compound the issue. From social welfare perspectives, high levels of public employment in particular and consumer subsidies have worked to smooth consumption and lower poverty in the face of external shocks and growth deceleration. At the same time, inefficient forms of social transfers, together with distortions in trade and production structures, play a role in limiting economic and social mobility and the informalisation of employment. Economic reforms and social expenditures aimed at improving asset ownership through expansion of financial market access and the promotion of human capital through more and better focused health expenditure among others, remain a challenge. The region continues to be highly exposed to conditions in global food commodity markets.

Understanding the full impact of such structural features of MENA economies on their growth and development remains an important area for future research, given the imperative needs for targeted policies to achieve macroeconomic stability, market-oriented price adjustments and regulatory reforms. Well-designed and targeted social expenditure policies, for example, can work to reduce inequalities while also improving allocative efficiency and enhancing endogenous growth prospects. Moreover, it is clear from the MENA context that production and distribution occur within a framework of social and political goals and relations that are important for understanding emerging trends and transitions. Events and developments surrounding the "Arab Spring" for example are framing social relations, policy directions and economic structures in ways that are significant and as yet little understood.

Notes

1 See Devlin (2010) for a more complete discussion.
2 For an exposition of "new" structuralist approaches to development, see Taylor (1979, 1990) and Lin (2010).
3 See Syverson (2011) for a review of the literature.
4 In this study, workers characterised as "informal" are those lacking access to health insurance and/or are not contributing to a pension system.

References

Adams, R. and J. Page (2003), Poverty, Inequality and Growth in Selected Middle East and North Africa Countries, 1980–2000, *World Development* 31(12): 2027–2048.

African Development Bank (2012), *Comparative Study on Export Policies in Egypt*, Morocco: Tunisia and South Korea.

Agenor, P. and P. Montiel (1999), *Development Macroeconomics*; Second Edition, Princeton: Princeton University Press.

Angel-Urdinola, D. and K. Tanabe (2012), *Micro-Determinants of Informal Employment in the Middle East and North Africa Region*; SP Discussion Paper No. 1201, Washington, DC: World Bank.

Araar, A. and P. Verme (2016), *A Comparative Analysis of Subsidy Reforms in the Middle East and North Africa*; Policy Research Working Paper No. 7755, Washington, DC: World Bank

Assaad, R. (2002), *The Egyptian Labor Market in an Era of Reform*, Cairo, Egypt: The American University in Cairo Press.

Assaad, R. (2013), *Making Sense of Arab Labor Markets: The Enduring Legacy of Dualism*; Institute for the Study of Labor Discussion Paper No. 7573, Bonn: Forschungsinstitut zur Zukunft der Arbeit GmbH (IZA).

Barbier, E. (2004), *Water and Economic Growth Economic Record*; Vol. 80, March: 1–16.

Behar, A. and J. Mok. (2013), *Does Public Sector Employment Fully Crowd Out Private Sector Employment*; Working Paper 13/146, Washington, DC: International Monetary Fund.

Breisinger, C., T. van Rheenen, C. Ringler, A. Nin-Pratt, N. Minot, C. Aragon, B. Yu, O, Ecker and T. Zhu (2010), *Food Security and Economic Development in the Middle East and North Africa; Food Policy Research Institute*; Discussion Paper 00985, Washington, DC: International Food Policy Research Institute.

Clements, B., D. Coady, S. Farbizio, S. Gupta, T. Alleyne and C. Sdralevich (2013), *Energy Subsidy Reform: Lessons and Implications*, Washington, DC: International Monetary Fund.

Devlin, J. (2010), *Challenges of Economic Development in the Middle East and North Africa Region*; Studies in International Economics No. 8, Singapore: World Scientific Press.

Devlin, J. (2014), *Is Water Scarcity Dampening Growth Prospects in the Middle East and North Africa? Op-Ed*, Brookings Institution, June 24.

Devlin, J. (2016), *Economics of the Middle East. Lecture Notes in Economics*; Vol. 2, Singapore: World Scientific Press.

Easterly, W., A. Reshef and J. Schwenkenberg (2009), *The Power of Exports*; Policy Research Working Paper 5081, Washington, DC: World Bank.

European Bank for Reconstruction and Development, European Investment Bank, and International Bank for Reconstruction and Development (2016), *What's Holding Back the Private Sector in MENA?* London: EBRD, EIB and World Bank.

Fasano-Filho, U. and Z. Iqbal (2003), *GCC Countries: From Oil Dependence to Diversification*, Washington, DC: International Monetary Fund.

Freund, C. and M. Jaud (2015), *Champions Wanted: Promoting Exports in the Middle East and North Africa*, Washington, DC: World Bank.

Freund, C. and Pierola (2014), *Export Superstars*; Mimeo, Washington, DC: World Bank.

Gatti, R., D. Angel-Urdinola, J. Silva, and A. Bodor (2014), *Striving for Better Jobs: The Challenge of Informality in the Middle East and North Africa*, Washington, DC: World Bank.

Gatti, R., M. Morgandi, R. Grun, S. Brodmann, D. Angel-Urdinola, J. Moreno, D. Marotta, M. Schiffbauer and E. Mata Lorenzo (2013), *Jobs for Shared Prosperity: Time for Action in the Middle East and North Africa*, Washington, DC: World Bank.

Groh, M., N. Krishman, D. McKenzie and T. Vishwanath (2012), *Soft Skills or Hard Cash? The Impact of Training and Wage Subsidy Programs on Female Youth Employment in Jordan*; Impact Evaluation Series No. 62, World Bank.

Groh, M., D. McKenzie, N. Shammout and T. Vishwanath (2014), *Testing the Importance of Search Frictions, Matching and Reservation Prestige Through Randomized Experiments in Jordan*; Policy Research Working Paper No. 7030, Washington, DC: World Bank.

Hakimian, H. (2008), *Institutional Change, Policy Challenges, and Macroeconomic Performance: Case Study of the Islamic Republic of Iran (1979–2004)*; Commission on Growth and Development Working Paper No. 26, Washington, DC: World Bank

International Labour Organization (2016), *World Employment Social Outlook. Trends for Youth*, Geneva: International Labour Organization.

International Monetary Fund (2013), *Turkey: Selected Issues Paper*, December, Washington, DC.
Keller, J. and M. Nabli (2007), *Breaking The Barriers To Higher Economic Growth: Better Governance and Deeper Reform in the Middle East and North Africa*, Washington, DC: World Bank.
Lewis, A. (1954), Economic Development with Unlimited Supplies of Labour, *Manchester School of Economics and Social Studies* 22: 139–191.
Lin, J.Y. (2010), *New Structural Economics: A Framework for Rethinking Development. Policy*; Research Working Paper No. 5197, Washington, DC: World Bank.
Mitra, P., A. Hosny, G. Minasyan, M. Fischer and G. Abajyan (2016), *Avoiding the New Mediocre: Raising Long-Term Growth in the Middle East and Central Asia; Middle East and Central Asia Department*, Washington, DC: International Monetary Fund.
Nabli, M. and N. Chamlou (2004), *Gender and Development in the Middle East and North Africa: Women in the Public Sphere; Middle East Development Report*, Washington, DC: World Bank.
Onis, Z. and J. Riedel (1993), *Economic Crises and Long Term Growth in Turkey*, Washington, DC: World Bank.
Osorio Rodarte, I. and H. Lofgren (2015), *A Product Space Perspective on Structural Change in Morocco*; Policy Research Working Paper No. 7438, Washington, DC: World Bank.
Perry, G., W. Maloney, O. Arias, P. Fajnzylber, A. Mason and J. Saavedra-Chanduvi (2007), *Informality: Exit and Exclusion; Latin American and Caribbean Studies*, Washington, DC: World Bank.
Pissarides, C.A (1993), *Labor Markets in the Middle East and North Africa; Middle East and North Africa*; Working Paper Series No. 5, Washington, DC: World Bank.
Rocha, R., Z. Arvai and S. Farazi (2011), *Financial Access and Stability: A Road Map for the Middle East and North Africa*; Middle East Development Report; Washington, DC: World Bank.
Said, M. (2001), Public Sector Employment and Labor Markets in Arab Countries: Recent Developments and Policy Implications, *Labor and Human Capital in the Middle East*; ed. D. Salehi-Ishfahani, Reading: Ithaca Press and Economic Research Forum: 91–145.
Said, M. (2009), The Fall and Rise of Earnings and Inequality in Egypt: New Evidence from the Egypt Labor Market Panel Survey 2006, *The Egyptian Labor Market Revisited*; ed. R. Assaad, Cairo: American University in Cairo Press: 53–85.
Sala-i-Martin, X and E. Artadi (2002), *Economic Growth and Investment in the Arab World*; Columbia University Department of Economics Discussion Paper, 0203–08.
Schiffbauer, M., H. Abdoulaye, S. Hussain, H. Sahnoun and P. Keefer (2015), *Jobs or Privileges: Unleashing the Employment Potential of the Middle East and North Africa*; MENA Development Report; Washington, DC: World Bank.
Sdralevich, C., R. Sab, Y. Zouhar and G. Albertin (2014), *Subsidy Reform in the Middle East and North Africa: Recent Progress and Challenges Ahead*, Middle East and Central Asia Department, International Monetary Fund.
Silva, J., V. Levin and M. Morgandi (2013), *Inclusion and Resilience: The Way Forward for Social Safety Nets in the Middle East and North Africa*; Middle East Development Report, Washington, DC: World Bank.
Stone, A. and L. Badawy (2011), *SME Innovators and Gazelles in MENA: Educate, Train, Certify*; Compete! MENA Knowledge and Learning Quick Notes Series. No. 43, Washington, DC: World Bank.
Syverson, C. (2011), What Determines Productivity? *Journal of Economic Literature* 49(2): 326–365.
Taylor, L. (1979), *Macro Models for Developing Countries*, New York: McGraw Hill.
Taylor, L. (1990), *Socially Relevant Policy Analysis*, Cambridge, MA: MIT Press.
World Bank (1995), *Workers in an Integrating World*, New York: Oxford University Press.
World Bank (2007), *Making the Most of Scarcity: Accountability for Better Water Management in the Middle East and North Africa*; Middle East Development Report, Washington, DC: World Bank.
World Bank (2012), *Arab Republic of Egypt: Inequality of Opportunity in the Labor Market*, Washington, DC: World Bank.
World Bank (2013), *Opening Doors: Gender Equality and Development in the Middle East and North Africa*; MENA Development Report, Washington, DC: World Bank.
World Bank (2016a), *Arab Republic of Egypt Enterprise Surveys Country Profile*, Washington, DC: World Bank.
World Bank (2016b), *High and Dry: Climate Change, Water and the Economy*, Washington, DC: World Bank.
World Bank (2017), *World Development Indicators*, Washington, DC: World Bank.
World Bank (2018), *Beyond Scarcity: Water Security in the Middle East and North Africa Region*, Washington, DC: World Bank.
World Bank and FAO (2009), *The Grain Chain: Food Security and Managing Wheat Imports In Arab Countries*, Washington, DC: World Bank.

SECTION II

Labour force and human development

4
ARAB HUMAN DEVELOPMENT IN COMPARATIVE CONTEXT

Khalid Abu-Ismail and Niranjan Sarangi[1]

4.1 Introduction

The human development approach, developed by the economist Mahbub Ul Haq, is anchored in the Nobel laureate Amartya Sen's work on human capabilities.[2] The theoretical underpinnings of the human development concept are framed around the range of things that people can *do* or *be* in life – about enlarging people's choices to lead lives that they value. It is a multidimensional concept and it broadly encompasses crucial aspects of human lives, such as dignity, freedom, equity, sustainability and opportunities, which are ignored in any unidimensional measure of development such as the gross national product.

Human development is too broad a concept to be measured accurately by social and economic statistics. Since the development of the first HDI in the 1990 Human Development Report, it has gone through a long evolution via debates and discussions of Nobel laureates, eminent scholars, philosophers and development practitioners. The aim of the HDI is to capture the essence of human development concept, i.e., people's achievements on well-being through their acquired capabilities to function.

The formulation of the HDI has gone through several methodological changes. However, the three basic dimensions of the HDI remain the same as they were construed in 1990. These are: to have access to resources for a decent standard of living (income), to acquire knowledge (achievements in education) and to lead a long and healthy life (health), which are essential enablers for enlarging people's choices and opportunities. It tells a broader story of development achievements than that of the GDP, despite the fact that the HDI as a quantitative measure suffers from several limitations to capturing the concept of human development fully. According to Amartya Sen, HDI is a crude measure of human development, but it is a better crude measure that comes closer to people's lives in multiple ways than the GDP index does as the sole measure of development.

The HDI challenged the notion that economic growth is a sole prerequisite for improvements in human well-being. Cross-country evidence during 1970–2010 shows that improvements in health and education are possible without high income growth (UNDP, 2010b). Amartya Sen provided strong arguments in favour of this by examining achievements in health and education against the GDP per capita in 1980 in several countries such as Brazil, Mexico, South Korea, China and Sri Lanka. He concluded that

> if the Government of a poor developing country is keen to raise the level of health and the expectation of life, then it would be pretty daft to try to achieve this through raising its income per head, rather than going directly for these objectives through public policy and social change, as China and Sri Lanka have both done.
>
> *(Sen, 1983: 753)*

In general, human development and economic growth are interdependent (UNDP, 1990). Historical data show that HDI improvements and income growth across countries have a strong positive association. It may be noted that income is part of the HDI itself, but it is used as a necessary means, not an end in itself (Sen, 2003). A conceptual two-way link between human development and economic growth is presented by Boozer et al. (2003) and Ranis and Stewart (2005). Increased human development for any person is connected with consumption growth on core human development items such as nutrition, education and so on. This is possible only if economic growth is distributed so that it reaches and benefits the poor. The dynamic effect of high human development to high growth has been well documented. For example, increases in earnings are associated with additional years of education, with the rate of return varying with the level of education, and it plays a key role in contributing to productivity growth (Roemer, 1990; Behrman, 1990a, 1990b). The stronger the links between human development and economic growth, the more pronounced the virtuous cycle, with growth feeding into human development, which, in turn, promotes further growth (Ranis and Stewart, 2005). Conversely, the weaker the link, the stronger the propensity to enter a vicious downward cycle where growth may not be sustainable.

Human development is also tied to the concept of inequality and social justice. According to ESCWA, social justice means equal rights and access to resources and opportunities for all, men and women, paying particular attention to the removal of barriers that hinder the empowerment of disadvantaged groups to fulfil their potential to participate in decisions that govern their lives. In the Arab region, social injustices have undermined human development through discrimination, social exclusion, conflict, occupation and corruption. Social justice must therefore be an integral part of any analysis of Arab human development (see Box 4.1).

Against this backdrop, this chapter has two main objectives. First, it provides a review of the main human development stylised facts for the Arab states and other developing regions based on the global HDI. Second, it questions what is missing from this index and provides an alternative perspective when one of the missing dimensions, good governance, is included in the global HDI. The chapter ends with a few concluding remarks on how these findings may lead us to rethink the conventional wisdom on human development in Arab states.

Box 4.1 HDI – concept and measurement

The Human Development Index (HDI) was introduced in the first publication of the Human Development Report in 1990. Its indicators reflected 'longevity, knowledge and basic income for a decent living standard' (UNDP, 1990). The initial corresponding indicators were life expectancy at birth, adult literacy rate and the logarithm of real GDP per capita. Real GDP per capita was in purchasing power parity terms and was not given any weight beyond a global 'poverty' threshold.

The second iteration of the Human Development Report in 1991 saw the addition of an indicator of mean years of schooling to the adult literacy rate to create a broader measure of 'knowledge' (UNDP, 1991). After 1995, the indicator for mean years of schooling was replaced by the combined gross primary, secondary and tertiary enrolment ratio.

In the 2010 Human Development Report, two education indicators replaced the combined gross enrolment ratio: *attained* mean years of schooling and *expected* mean years of schooling. Also, a natural logarithmic transformation was imposed on real GNI per capita, instead of GDP per capita, and the cap on the income level was removed (Klugman et al., 2011).

These changes were designed to make the Human Development Index more comprehensive, enabling it to reflect human development across a broad spectrum of achievements. One of the HDI's initial weaknesses was that both the education and income indicators were designed to focus on *basic* levels of human capability.

This is an important point to consider while searching for an appropriate measure of human development for the Arab region. Has the HDI highlighted human development shortfalls from a level that is relevant for the region? In other words, has the HDI so far been too focused on *basic* human capabilities and achievements, so that only severe deprivations have been considered?

Another important issue is that the HDI is not a stand-alone index. Over time, it has been supplemented by various other indices designed to respond to critical issues, such as poverty and gender inequality.

For example, in the *2013* Human Development Report, three indices were presented as supplements to the HDI: an Inequality-Adjusted HDI (IHDI), a Gender Inequality Index (GII) and a Multidimensional Poverty Index (MPI) (UNDP, 2013).

The last index, the MPI, is a refinement of the original Human Poverty Index that was introduced in the *1997* Human Development Report. The MPI is a more complex aggregation of various indicators than the HPI. The MPI is not relevant in this discussion, since, like the indicator for extreme income poverty (for example the one based on $1.25 income per day per person), the MPI is not adept at identifying broader forms of deprivation in the Arab region. In contrast, both the Inequality-Adjusted HDI and the Gender Inequality Index deal with specific issues that are important for the Arab region.

The Inequality-Adjusted HDI was introduced in the 2010 Human Development Report. It discounts average achievement in each of the three dimensions of the HDI by inequality in actual achievement levels across the population. In this sense, while the HDI reflects *potential* human development (assuming, unrealistically, equality of achievement across the population), the IHDI reflects *actual* varying achievement levels (UNDP, 2010).

The 1995 Human Development Report introduced the first global indices that considered gender inequalities in human development. These were the Gender-Related Development Index and the Gender Empowerment Measure (UNDP, 1995). In the 2010 Human Development Report, the two indices were replaced by the Gender Inequality Index (GII), which covers three critical dimensions for women: labour market participation, empowerment and reproductive health (UNDP, 2010).

Adapted from: Terry McKinley (2016).

4.2 Human development from the lens of the Human Development Index

4.2.1 Where does the region stand?

The region's HDI is below the world average and almost on a par with the average for developing countries. What separates the Arab region is its relatively higher GNI per capita. Arab states are the richest among developing regions, but their health and education profiles still lag behind. For example, life expectancy and schooling levels in Arab states are only slightly above those in South Asia despite having almost two and half times more GNI per capita. Latin America, which has a GNI per capita that is slightly below Arab states, has a significantly higher HDI due to its far higher health and education achievements. It appears therefore that compared to other developing regions, Arab countries are richer than they are humanly developed.

Still, there are major differences within the region. Table 4.1 reports the HDI and its components for 21 Arab countries for which most recent data is available. The United Arab Emirates,

Table 4.1 Human Development Index and its components for Arab states (2017)

HDI rank	*Country/ HDI group*	*Human Development Index (HDI)*	*Life expectancy at birth*	*Expected years of schooling*	*Mean years of schooling*	*GNI per capita*
		Value	*(years)*	*(years)*	*(years)*	*(2011 PPP $, 000s)*
34	United Arab Emirates	0.863	77.4	13.6	10.8	67.8
37	Qatar	0.856	78.3	13.4	9.8	116.8
39	Saudi Arabia	0.853	74.7	16.9	9.5	49.7
43	Bahrain	0.846	77.0	16.0	9.4	41.6
48	Oman	0.821	77.3	13.9	9.5	36.3
56	Kuwait	0.803	74.8	13.6	7.3	70.5
	Very high HDI	0.894	79.5	16.4	12.2	40.0
80	Lebanon	0.757	79.8	12.5	8.7	13.4
85	Algeria	0.754	76.3	14.4	8.0	13.8
95	Jordan	0.735	74.5	13.1	10.4	8.3
95	Tunisia	0.735	75.9	15.1	7.2	10.3
108	Libya	0.706	72.1	13.4	7.3	11.1
	High HDI	0.757	76.0	14.1	8.2	15.0
115	Egypt	0.696	71.7	13.1	7.2	10.4
119	Palestine	0.686	73.6	12.8	9.1	5.1
120	Iraq	0.685	70.0	11.0	6.8	17.8
123	Morocco	0.667	76.1	12.4	5.5	7.3
	Medium HDI	0.645	69.1	12.0	6.7	6.8
155	Syrian Arab Republic	0.536	71.0	8.8	5.1	2.3
159	Mauritania	0.520	63.4	8.6	4.5	3.6
165	Comoros	0.503	63.9	11.2	4.8	1.4
167	Sudan	0.502	64.7	7.4	3.7	4.1
172	Djibouti	0.476	62.6	6.2	4.1	3.4
178	Yemen	0.452	65.2	9.0	3.0	1.2
	Low HDI	0.504	60.8	9.4	4.7	2.5

Source: UNDP, Human Development Report Office (2019).

(1) Human Development Index (HDI): A composite index measuring average achievement in three basic dimensions of human development: a long and healthy life, knowledge and a decent standard of living.[3]
(2) Life expectancy at birth: Number of years a new-born infant could expect to live if prevailing patterns of age-specific mortality rates at the time of birth stay the same throughout the infant's life.
(3) Expected years of schooling: Number of years of schooling that a child of school entrance age can expect to receive if prevailing patterns of age-specific enrolment rates persist throughout the child's life.
(4) Mean years of schooling: Average number of years of education received by people ages 25 and older, converted from education attainment levels using official durations of each level.
(5) Gross national income (GNI) per capita: Aggregate income of an economy generated by its production and its ownership of factors of production, less the incomes paid for the use of factors of production owned by the rest of the world, converted to international dollars using PPP rates, divided by midyear population.

which has the highest HDI ranking among Arab countries, has an GNI per capita of 67,800$ (in 2011 PPP), nearly 50 times that of Comoros. The average GNI per capita for the six Gulf Cooperation Countries which all have a very high HDI score (above 0.8) is significantly higher than that for the OECD but life expectancy in the latter is four years higher. Conversely, Egypt, Palestine, Iraq and Morocco, the four countries which belong to the medium HDI category (0.55–0.7 HDI score) have a GNI per capita that is close to the average for developing countries but have scored better education and health outcomes despite the conditions of occupation, political instability and conflict conditions affecting some of these countries. The first stylised fact does not apply therefore if the resource-rich and very high-income group of GCC States are excluded. The remaining 15 states have health and education outcomes close to other developing regions with the same income per capita.

The nexus between social outcomes as manifested in health and education levels and economic growth outcomes as manifested in the level of GNI per capita income can be easily evaluated by comparing the difference in ranking by GNI per capita and by HDI value. The Human Development Report has been reporting consistently negative values for the majority of resource-rich Arab countries, meaning that these countries are better ranked by their GNI than by their HDI value. All GCC countries showed losses in their ranks in 2017. However, two resource-poor Arab countries recorded a gain in their ranks (Lebanon, Tunisia).

To summarise, with an HDI score of 0.698 in 2017, the region has a comparatively medium to high level of human development, which is also exemplified in the fact that eleven of the region's 21 countries' HDI scores placed them in the 'high' and 'very high' human development category. However, it would be misleading to think there is only one human development narrative for the region as a whole. The level of human development is strongly affected by a variety of factors, especially resource richness and conflict. In 2010 Syria's HDI fitted it into the medium HDI group and was on track to join the high HDI group within a decade. The country's on-going conflict has instead resulted in it slipping into the rank of low-human development countries. Slower human development progress, as we shall see in the following section, has also characterised many other countries in the region in recent years.

4.2.2 Human development progress

Since the 1960s, the Arab region has seen consistent improvements in literacy and school enrolment of boys and girls. The average years of schooling for adults (15 years and above) rose from 1.3 years in 1960 to 5.4 years in the 2000s, and illiteracy rates were halved (United Nations and League of Arab States, 2013). There have also been significant improvements in higher education. In 1940, only ten universities existed in the Arab region; in 2018, there were more than 1,000 higher education institutions.[4] Child mortality has declined significantly, and health outcomes have improved since the 1970s (Kuhn, 2011). Per capita income has also increased (Sarangi and Abu-Ismail, 2015). Better education, increased life expectancy and higher income have led to improved capabilities and greater socioeconomic mobility, reflected in a rising HDI score between the 1970s and 2010. In fact, five Arab countries were among the top ten global achievers in human development progress over the period 1970–2010 (UNDP, 2010a). However, some of these top performers witnessed uprisings in 2010–2011, indicating that human development assessments as seen through the lens of the HDI have ignored significant deficits and injustices. These gaps shall be covered in the following sections.

The rate of HDI progress, however, has slowed significantly since 1990 and even more so since 2010 (see Abu-Ismail et al., 2011). The average annual percentage change in the HDI score shown in Figure 4.1 indicates that the region has the slowest progress among developing

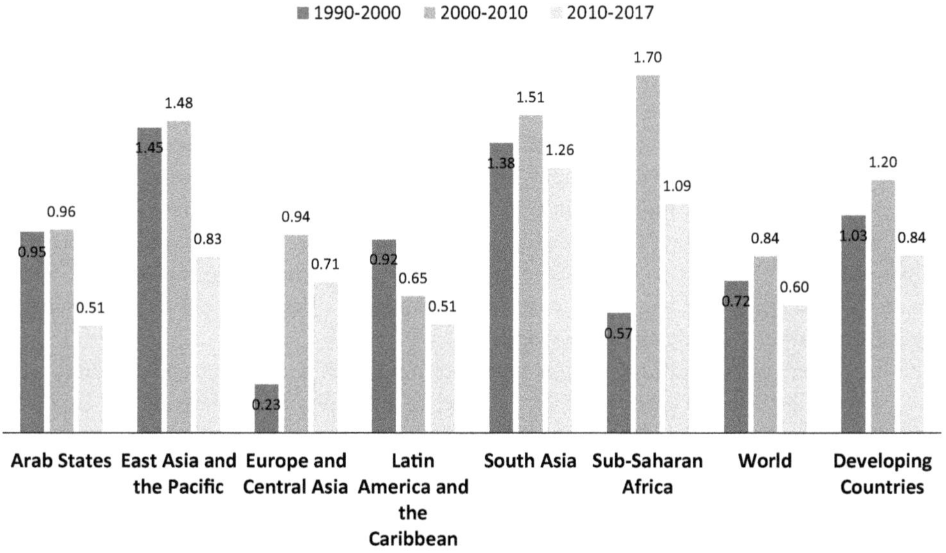

Figure 4.1 Average annual change in HDI for Arab states and other regions, 1990s, 2000s and 2010-2017 (percentage). *Source*: Authors' calculations based on data from the United Nations Development Programme, Human Development Reports Data

	Morocco	Sudan	Mauritania	Bahrain	Saudi Arabia	Iraq	Egypt	Qatar	Algeria	United Arab Emirates	Tunisia	Kuwait	Jordan	Libya	Yemen
1990-2000	1.47	1.96	1.69	0.60	0.64	0.60	1.12	0.72	1.10	0.94	1.39	0.99	1.31	0.72	1.03
2000-2010	1.51	1.58	0.96	0.06	0.84	0.67	0.86	0.19	1.24	0.47	0.91	0.07	0.36	0.38	1.18
2010-2017	1.13	0.95	0.95	0.87	0.78	0.77	0.64	0.52	0.49	0.45	0.38	0.20	0.14	-0.97	-1.37

Figure 4.2 Average annual change in HDI for selected Arab states, 1990s, 2000s and 2010-2017 (percentage). *Source*: Ibid.

regions at 0.51 percent, which is almost half the average for developing countries and less than half that of sub-Saharan Africa. This is not difficult to explain given the country performance levels in Figure 4.2. During the most recent period, 2010–2017, HDI growth was marginal for most countries and zero or negative for conflict-affected countries, such as Libya and Yemen. Morocco is the only country that achieved progress rates of above 1 percent in the period from 2010 to 2017. It is also interesting to note that, excluding the conflict-affected states, the decline in HDI progress has affected both resource-rich and resource-poor countries.

These findings should not underestimate the enormous social progress achieved in most Arab countries. The region has scored some major positive advancements on education and other basic human capabilities since the 1970s. However, the declining rate of progress of the HDI since 1990 significantly changes the human development narrative for the region. What lies behind this slowdown? Figure 4.3, which examines the trends in three of the component indicators of the HDI, offers a clear explanation. Clearly, progress in life expectancy and educational achievements continued at a relatively high pace for most countries despite a slight reversal for the mean years of schooling for the low HDI group (from approximately 4.2 years in 2013 to 4 years in 2017). The problem lies with the growth in income which remained sluggish in all groups, and thus did not match the progress in these social indicators. As argued in the ESCWA Vision 2030 Report, the Arab economic development model had reached its limits by the 1990s and could not deliver on growth or decent employment thus failing to meet the expectations of an increasingly educated youth and middle class (ESCWA, 2015).

4.2.3 Inequalities in human development

As we have seen, the HDI summarises achievements or progress in terms of life expectancy, education and income. These measures, however, do not take into account the inequality of access, within the population of a country, to these three measures of well-being. Despite their HDI rankings, whether very high, high, medium or low, countries do not provide all their citizens with equal access to the measures of human development improving their well-being. Thus, the HDI, in itself, does not give an indication of the well-being of the whole population of a country. There are a lot of reasons behind inequalities, as they can be related to ethnicity, race, gender and class.

In order to able to assess the impact of inequality on the HDI, it is advised to have a look at the Inequality-Adjusted Human Development Index (IHDI), which in addition to the HDI, provides an indication on the distribution of health, education and income in a population by 'discounting' the dimensions of the HDI depending on the level of inequality. Having a look at the HDI and IHDI, regionally, shows that all regions are subject to inequality, but the levels of inequalities are different between regions. Arab states come in third place after South Asia and Sub-Saharan Africa in terms of inequalities, as the adjustment from HDI to IHDI reflects a decrease of around 25 percent in the Arab states, 26 percent in South Asia and 31 percent in Sub-Saharan Africa (Figure 4.4). Even very high HDI regions are subject to inequalities, to a lesser extent as there is a decrease of 12 percent between HDI and IHDI in Europe and Central Asia. The Arab region's loss in HDI due to inequality is higher than that of the world which is around 20 percent.

Looking at the difference between the levels of HDI and IHDI in selected Arab countries in Figure 4.5, despite their HDI level, all of these countries face considerable losses when taking into consideration the impact of inequality on human development levels. Tunisia, belonging to the group of high HDI countries, is highly impacted by inequality, losing 22 percent between the levels of HDI and IHDI due to inequality.

The Arab region's loss in HDI due to inequality is higher than that of the world which is around 22 percent. If we have a closer look at the inequality measurements, compared to the other regions the Arab region has a high rate of inequality in education of 33 percent, compared to 25 percent in developing countries (Figure 4.6). The progress of HDI as a whole in the Arab region is misleading as to the increase in well-being of the Arab population, as the region is highly affected by inequality and does not provide equal access to all the citizens to pursue

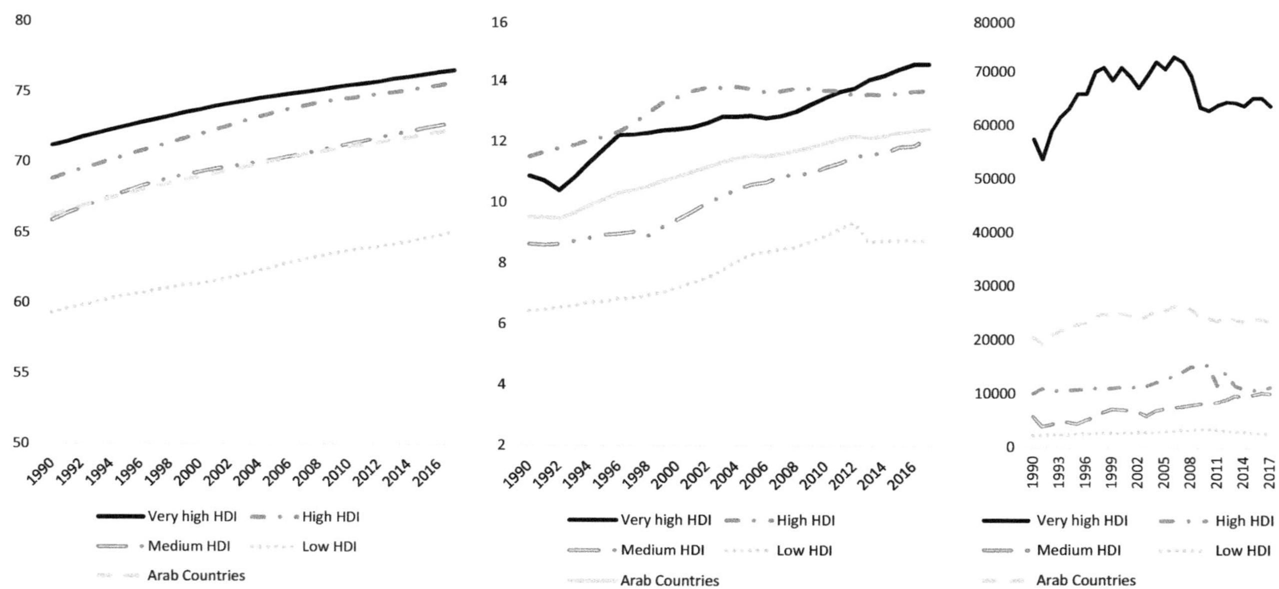

Figure 4.3 Life expectancy at birth (a), mean years of schooling (b) and gross national income (in 2011 PPPs) (c) for selected Arab states, 1990-2017. *Source*: Ibid.

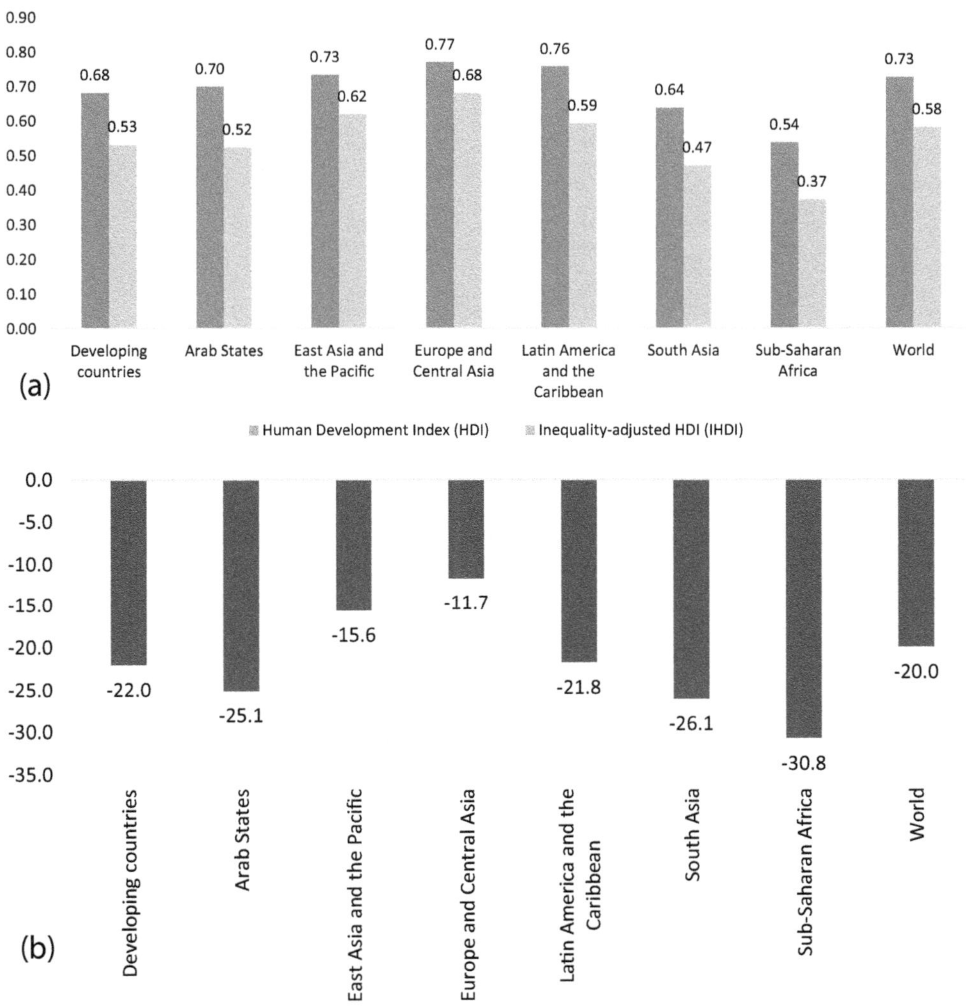

Figure 4.4 Levels of HDI and IHDI (a) and percentage loss between HDI and IHDI (b) by region (2017).
Source: Ibid.

their education. The Arab region is in fact subject to conflict, violence, security threats, lack of good governance, scarce resources and imbalance in political participation which are all drivers of inequality and will hinder the improvements in human development in the region (UNDP AHDR, 2016).

One of the main reasons for inequality in the Arab region is gender inequality which is lagging behind due to several reasons among which are discrimination against women, social values that tolerate inequality between men and women in politics, the labour market and education, in addition to laws which undermine any possible improvements towards gender equity, i.e. women's right to marry, divorce, obtain child custody and inherit (*Ibid.*).

The Gender Inequality Index (GII) was developed in order to measure gender inequalities in Human Development, specifically in the areas of reproductive health, maternal mortality, adolescent birth rates, empowerment, labour participation. The Arab region has the second highest GII

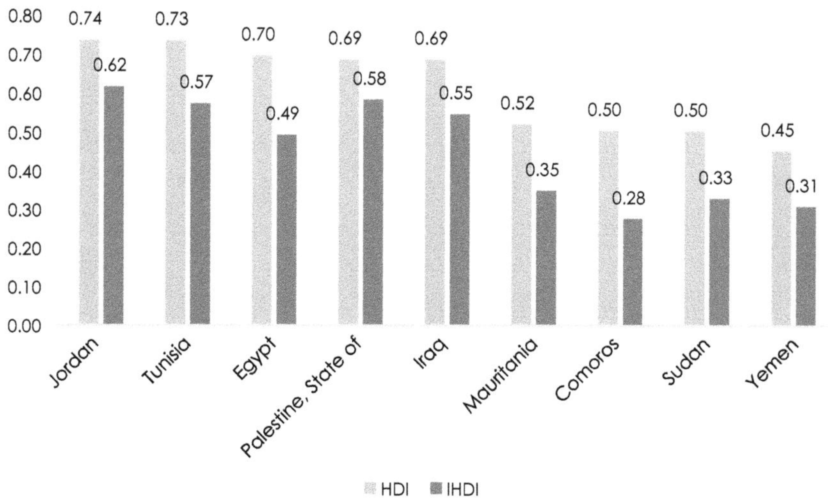

Figure 4.5 Levels of HDI and IHDI in selected Arab countries 2017. *Source*: Ibid.

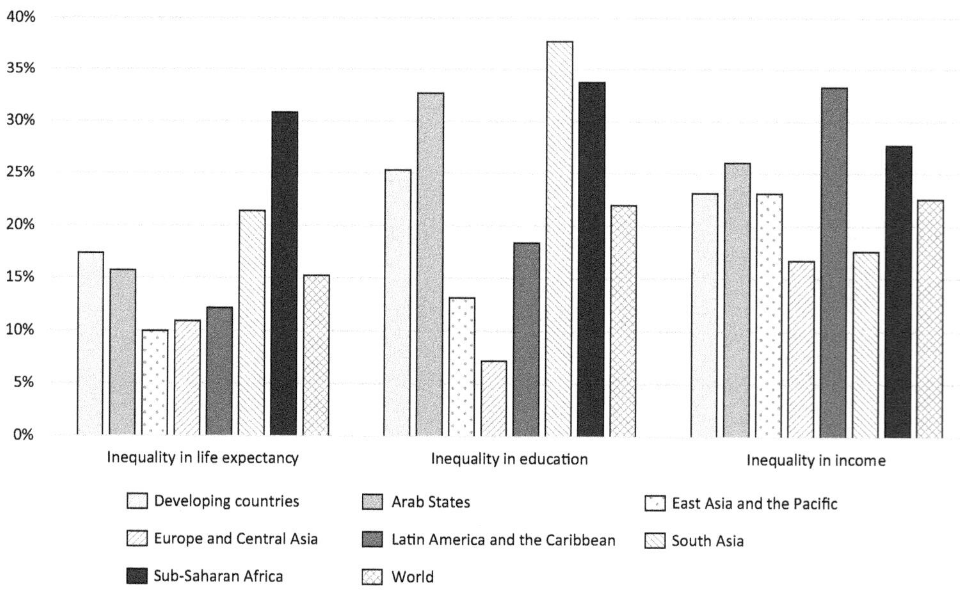

Figure 4.6 Percentage of inequality in human development measures by region in 2017. *Source*: Ibid.

after Sub-Saharan Africa, with the participation of only 22 percent of women in the labour force and only 17.5 percent of women holding parliamentary seats, which are the lowest rates among all the other compared regions in 2017, making Arab women among the most disadvantaged in the world (Figure 4.7).

Since 1995, the Arab region GII has been decreasing, showing a relative improvement in the status of women in Arab societies. Despite the improvements in maternal mortality, education

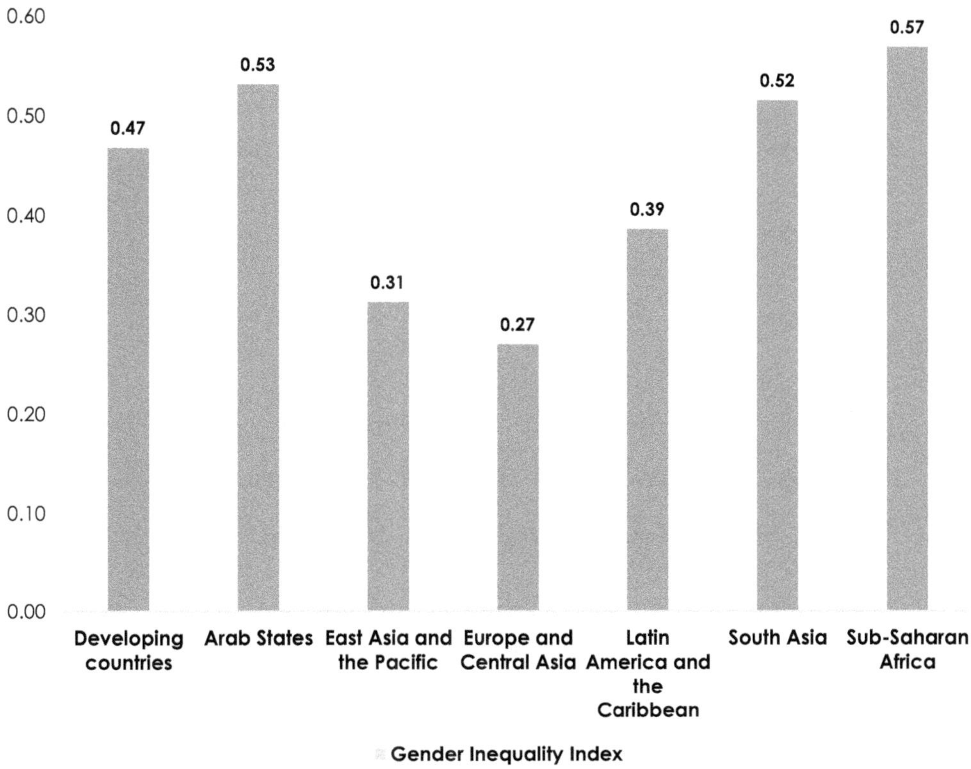

Figure 4.7 Levels of GII by region in 2017. *Source*: Ibid.

and parliamentary seats, the region is still lagging in terms of gender equity as can be seen from the trend of the GII in Arab countries (Figure 4.8).

Amelioration of the GII in the Arab region will unsurprisingly require a slow transition as the factors hindering the improvements in gender equality are imbedded in the social norms of Arab societies. Additionally, most Arab countries share a set of common challenges which are standing in the way of stagnating inequality faced by women such as conflicts, gender-based violence, a low rate of women in the labour market, low political participation and discriminative laws against women (ESCWA, 2016).

4.3 Human development and Human Development Index: what is missing?

4.3.1 Missing dimensions of the HDI

As noted in the introduction, the HDI is narrower than the concept of human development. Translating some of the capabilities into functionalities and quantifying them as indicators to be included in the HDI is often difficult, such as for human freedom. Related to freedom, some capabilities listed by Martha Nussbaum (2000) such as the possibility to move freely, interact socially in various forms and participate in politics, as well as the absence of discrimination, are not explicitly captured by the HDI. Similarly, the capabilities that relate to the state of governance, intergenerational equity and the collective dimension of capability such as social integration and sustainability have also not been explicitly captured by the HDI. The unavailability of

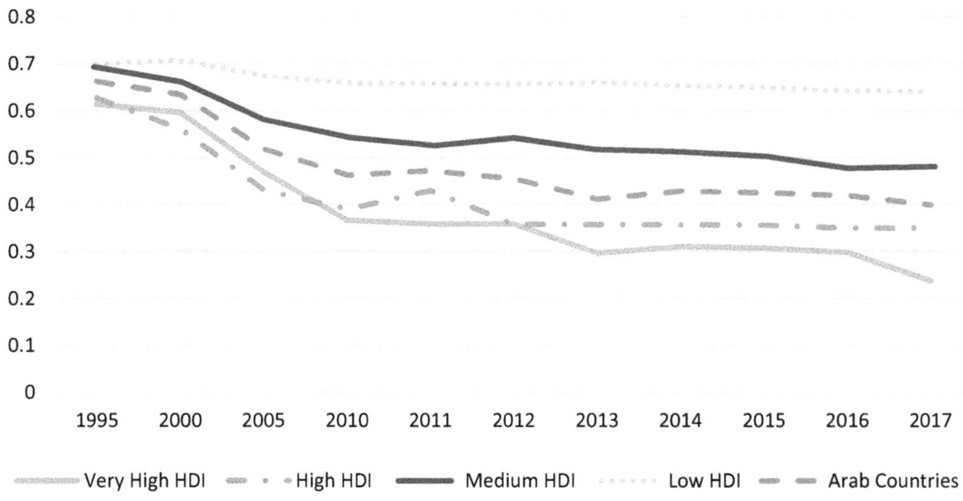

Figure 4.8 GII Trends in Arab countries by HDI groups (1995-2017). *Source*: Ibid.

good data, data quality and the complexity of the indicators often hinder the quantifying of the capabilities. However, it is worth discussing some of the fundamental missing dimensions that influence choices and opportunities in human lives.

4.3.1.1 Human freedom

The first Human Development Report in 1990 stated that 'human development is incomplete without human freedom'. It is acknowledged in the first work of the HDI construction that any index of human development should give adequate weight to a society's human freedom in pursuit of material and social goals. Two countries having similar human development levels (as indicated by the HDI) could be quite different depending on how these capabilities are acquired. In 2002, the first Arab Human Development Report identified three priorities for overcoming the human development crisis in the Arab region: full respect for human rights and human freedoms; complete empowerment of Arab women by building their capabilities; and knowledge acquisition and its effective use. These challenges still persist in the Arab countries, which are not adequately reflected in the HDI. Some argue that *process* indicators, which are *means* to influence outcomes, should be added to the HDI formula as well, but it would actually miss the point that the achievement of those capabilities has to be executed a certain way. They assume that those freedoms are not capabilities but contribute to the promotion of other capabilities (Comim, 2016). In any case, quantifying human freedom is difficult given its complex and multifaceted manifestations in human lives.

4.3.1.2 Governance

Governance systems are at the root of human development deficits, a fact which the HDI, being an outcome indicator, does not capture. For instance, the global Human Development Report 2010 stated that five Arab countries (Oman, Saudi Arabia, Tunisia, Algeria and Morocco) were among the ten 'top movers', countries that have seen the greatest improvements in the HDI since 1970. Only a few months after the publication of the 2010 HDR, the Arab spring commenced from Sidi Bouzaid, a city in the centre of Tunisia, not because of abject poverty or lack of education and health services, but because of the lack of economic opportunities, social injustices and infringements on basic human rights. These were arguably also the root causes of uprisings in other Arab countries such as Egypt and Syria where progress in basic education and health goals was quite remarkable but failed to translate into broader human development gains.[5] The HDI did not consider this possibility since it does not include a measure of good governance.

Hunger is also an outcome of governance failures, as argued in Sen's *Poverty and Famines* (1981). He established that food production is actually independent from its availability. Famine is thus not a matter of production or economic development but structural justice and politicisation. Studies show that the famines in Bengal (1943), Ethiopia (1973) and Bangladesh (1974) occurred without any decline in food production (Dreze and Sen, 1989).

4.3.1.3 Environmental sustainability

The idea of sustainability needs to be better understood in its entirety with human freedom. According to Sen (2013: 6),

> human beings are reflective creatures and are able to reason about and decide what they would like to happen, rather than being compellingly led by their own needs – biological or social. A fuller concept of sustainability has to aim at sustaining human freedoms, rather than only at our ability to fulfil our felt needs.

The 1994 Human Development Report points out that sustainable development and human development have to be built jointly, as 'both are based on the universalism of life claims' that people are of equal worth (Kant, 1791), the ones of today and tomorrow. Sustainable development is defined as 'development that meets the needs of the present without compromising the ability of future generations to meet their own needs' (United Nations, 1987). Today's progress and development should not hamper tomorrow's, revealing the inherent sustainability of human development (Fitoussy and Malik, 2013). Hence, the adaptation of the HDI to these new concerns is all the more necessary as Sen (2013) underlines that the definition of sustainable development has to be broadened. Sustainable development is, according to him, development that promotes the capabilities of present people without compromising the capabilities of future generations. This is not about needs but capability. The future generations should be able to live the lives they value.

Studies argue that human development, measured by the HDI, would be terribly affected by environmental constraints, which will either slow or reverse its path (Hugues et al. 2011). Environmental degradation, caused by human agency, will hamper or even erode human capability. The Sustainable Development Goals (SDG) shed light on the fact that environmental degradation is destroying human capabilities, 'eroding biodiversity, land and food security and impacting a range of socially oriented goals from poverty reduction and women's empowerment to inequality and peace' (Khoday, 2011). Hence, human capability alone cannot define by itself human development but has to be linked with the capability of the planet to support human development. Thus, HDI has to take into account environmental concerns as the capability of the future generations will be impacted by the development process of the current generation.

'Greening' human development underlines the idea that environmental protection does not hamper human and economic development. Some countries have achieved high levels of human development with low or moderate environmental degradation (UNDP, 2011). Developing countries can choose a green path of human development as did New Zealand and Sweden instead of developing regardless of any environmental concerns. However, 'greening' human development has remained debatable due to the complexity and political sensitivity of the indicators of environmental degradation and their accounting.

4.3.1.4 Security

Sen (1999) defines 'capability' through instrumental freedoms as pillars of human development, namely *political freedoms, economic facilities, social opportunities, transparency guarantees* and *protective security*. The latter means a 'social safety net for preventing the vulnerable sections of society from being reduced to abject misery and in some cases even starvation and death' and this aspect of human development through capability is not included in the HDI. Narayan (2000) defined capability as necessary to human development through the concepts of civil peace, physically safe environments, lawfulness, rule of law, personal physical security and security in old age. Stewart (2013) sheds light on how social institutions affect capability. Regarding the security aspect of capability, he argues that community associations have a positive impact on capability whereas warring groups and criminal gangs have a negative impact. Societal norms, as well as institutions, also impact security. Those elements bind individual and collective choices and may hamper people in living the lives they value. Obtaining reliable information on quantitative measures of security for most countries, however, has remained a challenge. National human development reports, such as in Thailand in 2011, incorporated human security as a dimension of the Human Development Index.

4.3.1.5 Happiness

The subjective perception of development and well-being is also not captured in the HDI. The 2016 World Happiness Report reveals huge differences between itself and the HDI in rankings of happiness versus human development. This suggests that people from different countries or regions rank and value their well-being differently. There are therefore differences between subjective and objective evaluations of development and well-being. This indicator of happiness includes for instance the variable 'healthy life expectancy' instead of the standard 'life expectancy' variable used in the HDI (Comim, 2016; Helliwell et al., 2016).

4.4 A governance-adjusted HDI: how does it impact the HDI of Arab countries?

A recent study of human development in the Arab states introduced a governance dimension to the HDI as a proxy for empowerment to complement the economic and social dimensions of the HDI. Arguably, good governance leads to better systems of justice, reduces spatial and gender inequalities, which reduces political instability and ceteris paribus, and induces inclusive economic growth. This in turn leads to better social development outcomes, further enhancing the individual capabilities required for maintaining these systems of good governance and so forth.[6]

The governance dimension was introduced as the Governance Index (GI).[7] The GI was constructed by using the same HDI methodology, taking into account voice and accountability and the rule of law indicators from the Worldwide Governance Indicators database.[8] Figure 4.9 (A) plots the human development index (HDI), which measures health, education and income, against the GI, showing a generally positive relationship across 160 countries. The clustering of countries at the top end of the line suggests that synergies between good governance and human development are maximised, thus yielding a more straightforward relationship between the two. Figure 4.9 (B) plots the values of gross national income (GNI) and the GI. It is quite

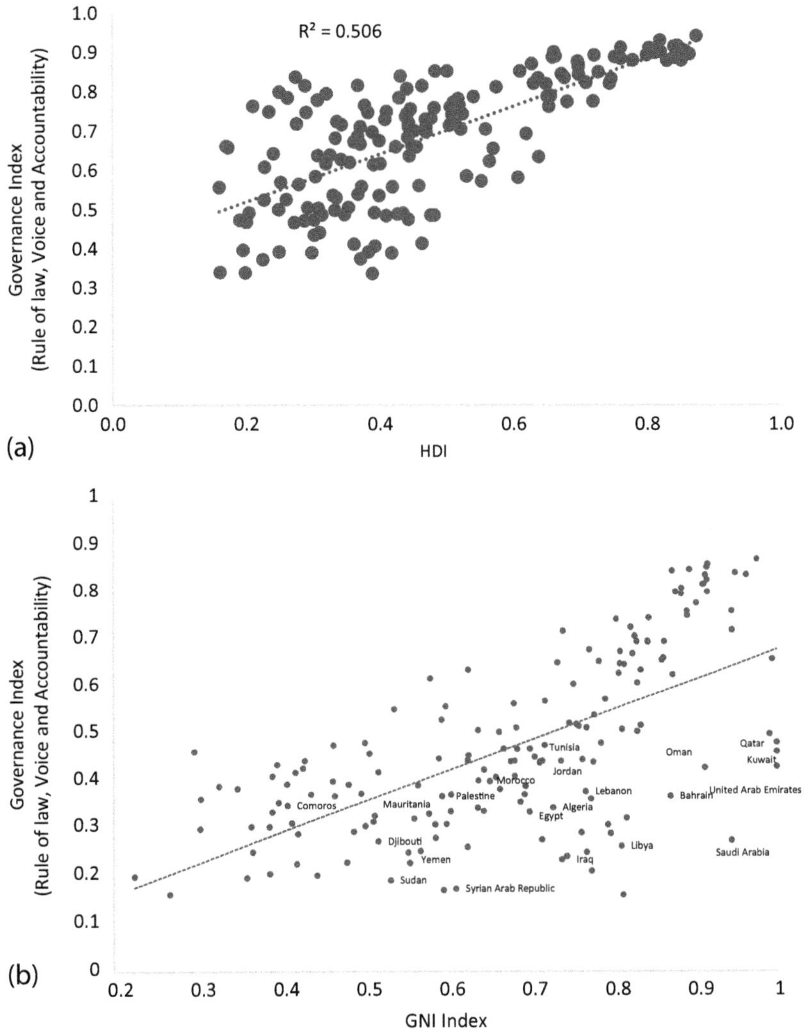

Figure 4.9 Association between HDI, income and GI is generally positive (all countries, 2013). *Source*: Abu-Ismail et al. (2016), based on data from UNDP (2016) and World Bank (2016).

clear that the governance performance for several countries in the Arab region are far below what would be expected of them, given their level of income, against the global average.

The average GI score for the Arab states is below 0.400, implying that Arab countries have low governance quality despite their income levels. As such, the popular notion that as countries get richer their governance improves does not seem to hold for the region. By including GI as a human development dimension, all Arab countries suffer losses to their HDI score, albeit to varying percentages between 10 to 30 percent (Figure 4.10).

4.5 Conclusion

Since its introduction to the development discourse, the HDI has remained an important monitoring tool for countries around the world to measure human well-being, and countries tend to see the HDI as an indicator to maximise. Regional and national efforts in monitoring human

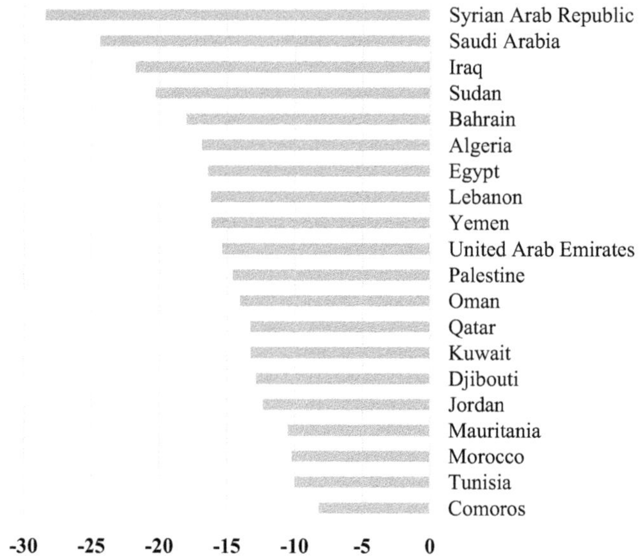

Figure 4.10 Impact on HDI scores when the GI is factored in (% loss to HDI by including GI as a HD dimension). *Source*: Calculation based on Abu-Ismail et al. (2016).

development have led to revisions of the HDI, taking into account region- and country-specific dimensions. The novelty of the measure is such that it provides the scope to tailor the measure to national, sub-national or regional levels. The evolution of the HDI is a continuous process and everyone is encouraged to rethink the HDI as long as it contributes to the idea of better measuring capability and achieves higher rates of human development. For instance, the introduction of the Inequality-Adjusted HDI and the Gender Inequality Index as part of the HDI family provides a more comprehensive picture of human development in a national context.

Nevertheless, 'What we measure affects what we do' (Stiglitz et al., 2010). What we measure leads to political decisions and policies and those lacks underlined in the computation of the HDI might lead to certain decisions that undermine people's empowerment as well as the collective and sustainable character of human development. The missing dimensions of the HDI, such as freedom, governance and sustainability, would send the message that these aspects do not count, or do not count as much as the others, despite the fact that these are acknowledged as important determinants of human well-being in the rich description of human development reports. These are all important dimensions that influence the human capability to function and there is significant effort at the global level to quantify these important dimensions in the HDI. In this chapter we have seen how the inclusion of one of these missing dimensions, governance, can dramatically alter the Human Development Index narrative for Arab countries. The governance deficit in the region is not new, neither is the stylised fact that the region has achieved major gains in education and health over the span of the past three decades. What is new is the importance of viewing these dimensions from a unified perspective that is consistent with the tenets of the human development approach.

Notes

1 This chapter is a contribution by the Economic and Social Commission for Western Asia (ESCWA). It builds on several technical papers and a report (Arab Vision, 2030, ESCWA, 2015) produced by

the Economic Development and Integration Division of the Economic and Social Commission for Western Asia.

2 See UNDP 'About Human Development' (http://hdr.undp.org/en/humandev).
3 See *Technical note 1 at* http://hdr.undp.org/sites/default/files/hdr2018_technical_notes.pdf for details on how the HDI is calculated.
4 See http://www.webometrics.info/en/world.
5 United Nations and League of Arab states (2013).
6 See Arab Vision 2030 Report (ESCWA, 2015)
7 See detailed methodology in Abu-Ismail et al. (2016).
8 The voice and accountability index captures perceptions of the extent to which a country's citizens are able to participate in selecting their government, as well as freedom of expression, freedom of association and a free media. The rule of law index captures perceptions of the extent to which agents have confidence in and abide by the rules of society, and in particular the quality of contract enforcement, property rights, police and courts, as well as the likelihood of crime and violence.

Bibliography

Abu-Ismail, K., Abo Taleb, G., Olmsted, J., and M. Mohiedin (2011). *The ADCR 2011: Employment, Vulnerability, Social Protection and the Crisis of Arab Economic Reforms.* Arab Development Challenges Background Paper, No. 2011/05. Cairo: United Nations Development Programme.

Abu-Ismail, K., Kunčič, A. and N. Sarangi (2016). *Governance-Adjusted Human Development Index, The Case for a Broader Index and its Implications for Arab States.* Beirut: United Nations, available from: https://www.unescwa.org/publications/governance-adjusted-human-development-index.

Behrman, J.R. (1990a). *The Action of Human Resources and Poverty on One Another: What We Have Yet to Learn.* Living Standards Measurement Study (LSMS) Working Paper, No. 74. Washington, DC: World Bank.

Behrman, J.R. (1990b). *Human Resource Led Development? Review of Issues and Evidence.* New Delhi: Asian Regional Team for Employment Promotion and International Labour Organization.

Boozer, M., Ranis, G., Stewart, F., and Suri, T. (2003). *Paths to Success: The Relationship between Human Development and Economic Growth.* Economic Growth Center Yale University, Center Discussion Paper No. 874, available from: https://www.econstor.eu/handle/10419/98362.

Comim, Flavio (2016). *Human Development Report Background Paper, Beyond the HDI? Assessing Alternative Measures of Human Development from a Capability Perspective.* New York: United Nations Development Programme.

Dreze, J., and A.K. Sen (1989). *Hunger and Public Action.* Oxford: Clarendon Press.

Economic and Social Commission for Western Asia (2015). *Arab Development Outlook: Vision 2030.* E/ESCWA/EDID/2015/3.

Economic and Social Commission for Western Asia (2016). *Against Wind and Tides: A Review of the Status of Women and Gender Equality in the Arab Region.* New York, available from: https://www.unescwa.org/sites/www.unescwa.org/files/publications/files/women-gender-equality-arab-region.pdf.

Hughes, B. B., Irfan, M. T., Moyer, J. D., Dale, Rothman, S., and J. R. Solórzano (2011). *Human Development Research Paper, 2011/08, Forecasting the Impacts of Environmental Constraints on Human Development,* United Nations Development Programme, Human Development Reports Research Paper, November.

Khoday, K. (2011). *Rethinking Human Development in an Era of Planetary Transformation.* Human Development Report Office, Discussion Paper. New York: UNDP.

Kant, I. (1781). *Critique of Pure Reason.*

Klugman, J., Rodríguez, F., and Hyung-Jin Choi. (2011). *The HDI 2010: New Controversies, Old Critiques.* United Nations Development Programme, Human Development Reports, Research Paper, April 2011.

Kuhn R. (2011). On the Role of Human Development in the Arab Spring. *Population and Development Review,* Vol. 38, No. 4, pp. 649–683.

Morse, S. (2003). Greening the United Nations Human Development Index? *Sustainable Development,* Vol. 11, pp. 183–198.

Narayan, D. et al. (2000). *Voices of the Poor: Can Anyone Hear Us?* Oxford: Oxford University Press.

Nussbaum, M. (2000). *Women and Human Development: The Capabilities Approach.* Cambridge: Cambridge University Press.

Ranis, G., and F. Stewart (2005). *Dynamic Links between the Economy and Human Development.* United Nations Department of Economic and Social Affairs Working Paper, No. 8. ST/ESA/2005/DWP/8.

Sarangi, N., and K. Abu-Ismail (2015). *Economic Growth, Inequality and Poverty in the Arab Region.* Issues Brief for the Arab Sustainability Development Report, available from: http://css.escwa.org.lb/SDPD/3572/Goal1.pdf.

Sen, A. (1981). *Poverty and Famines: An Essay on Entitlement and Deprivation.* Oxford: Oxford University Press; New York: Clarendon Press.

Sen, A. (1983). Development: Which Way Now? *The Economic Journal*, Vol. 93, No. 372, pp. 745–762.

Sen, A. (1999). *Development as Freedom.* Oxford: Oxford University Press.

Sen, A. (2003). Development as Capability Expansion. In *Readings in Human Development*, S. Fukuda-Parr and A.K. Shiva Kumar, eds. New Delhi and New York: Oxford University Press.

Sen, A. (2013). The Ends and Means of Sustainability. *Journal of Human Development and Capabilities*, Vol. 14, No. 1, pp. 6–20.

Stiglitz, J., Sen, A., and J.P. Fitoussi (2009). *The Measurement of Economic Performance and Social Progress Revisited: Reflections and Overview.* Paris: Commission on the Measurement of Economic Performance and Social Progress.

Stiglitz, J., Sen, A., and J.P. Fitoussi. (2010). *Mismeasuring Our Lives: Why GDP Doesn't Add Up.* New York: The New Press.

Terry, McKinley (2016). *The Need for a Framework for Defining a Development Measure for Arab Countries.* Beirut: United Nations.

United Nations (1987). *Our Common Future. Report of the World Commission on Environment and Development*, available from: https://www.are.admin.ch/are/en/home/sustainable-development/international-cooperation/2030agenda/un-_-milestones-in-sustainable-development/1987--brundtland-report.html

United Nations and League of Arab States (2013). *The Arab Millennium Development Goals Report: Facing Challenges and Looking beyond 2015.* E/ESCWA/EDGD/2013/1. United Nations, and League of Arab States (LAS), available from: https://www.unescwa.org/publications/millennium-development-goals-arab-region-2013

United Nations Development Programme (1990). *Human Development Report.* UNDP. New York: Oxford University Press.

United Nations Development Programme (2010a). *Human Development Report 2010 – The Real Wealth of Nations: Pathways to Human Development.* New York: UNDP.

United Nations Development Programme (2010b). *What Will it Take to Achieve the Millennium Development Goals? An International Assessment.* New York.

United Nations Development Programme (2011). *Greening Human Development: Capturing Wins in Equity and Environmental Sustainability.* By Subhra Bhattacharjee and Usman Ali Iftikhar.

United Nations Development Programme (2013). *Human Development Report Office, Occasional Paper, Choices, Capabilities and Sustainability.* Jean-Paul Fitoussi and Khalid Malik.

United Nations Development Programme, Human Development Reports Research Paper, November 2011. *Human Development Research Paper, 2011/08, Forecasting the Impacts of Environmental Constraints on Human Development,* Barry B. Hughes, Mohammod T. Irfan, Jonathan D. Moyer, Dale S. Rothman, and José R. Solórzano.

5
PRIVATE RETURNS TO INVESTMENT IN EDUCATION IN MENA COUNTRIES

Aysit Tansel

5.1 Introduction

The decision to invest in education involves costs and benefits. The costs include current expenditures such as tuition and fees, books, transportation; incidental expenditures; and the opportunity cost of the time spent acquiring the education. The benefits include higher expected future income. Education could be viewed as a desirable consumption good as well as an investment that could increase the future productivity of the individual. The consumption good aspect of education is not much investigated due to the difficulties of observing it. The human capital theory considers education as an investment good (Schultz, 1961; Becker, 1964). In principle, therefore, individuals invest in education until the private return for them from an additional year of schooling equals the private cost of capital.

This chapter surveys the recent estimates of the returns to education in the Middle East and North Africa (MENA).[1] Some MENA countries such as Libya and Syria are not covered due to lack of estimates for them. I consider only the private returns to education and not the social returns to education. I present and discuss the overall returns to education and whenever possible the estimates for men and women as well as the estimates by level of education. Details such as public versus private returns to education, and returns by programme types such as general versus vocational schools, estimates with Heckman sample selection correction and estimates using instrumental variables, are not included in this review since such estimates are not available for most of the MENA countries. I mostly focus on the returns estimates based on OLS estimates of the Mincerian earnings function in order to maintain comparability among the countries.

This chapter is organised as follows. Section 5.2 defines the rate of returns to education and discusses the various computational procedures. Section 5.3 summarises the general pattern observed in the private returns to education in the world. Section 5.4 discusses the average returns to education in the MENA region. The MENA country estimates are presented and discussed in Section 5.5. Section 5.6 provides concluding remarks.

5.2 The rate of returns to education

5.2.1 Definition and computation

As with investments in general, investment in education is also evaluated by its rate of return. Rising returns give signals to individuals and governments to invest more in education. Estimates of the private rates of returns to education according to levels of education, programme types, gender and sector of the economy determine the individual's investment priorities. Similarly, estimates of the social rates of returns to education by different education levels and programme types determine public investment priorities. Estimating returns to education has important equity, efficiency and financing implications. A comparison of the returns to education with alternative investments can guide both individuals and policymakers in their investment decisions. A comparison of the returns to education at different levels of schooling can guide investment decisions. In most parts of the world, the share of public educational expenditures in GDP is increasing. At the same, time private education at all levels is flourishing. People who have access to education benefit from this expansion.

Estimates of returns to education are based on human capital theory. The human capital theory posits that investment in education increases future productivity. The private rate of returns to education is defined as follows. It is the internal rate of return which equates the present value of the real and opportunity cost of education to the present value of the (after tax) earnings. On the other hand, the social rate of return includes the social costs and benefits in addition to the private costs and benefits. In practice, the social rate of return is obtained by the addition of private returns and the per capita public cost of education. For this reason, the social rates of returns to education are always less than the private rates of returns to education due to high social costs. In this sense the difference between the private and social returns could be taken as a measure of public subsidisation of education. The difference between the private and the social rates of return is in particular large at the higher education level in developing countries. The estimates of the social rates of return do not take into account the monetary value of the external benefits of education. Such external benefits include reduced crime rates, lower fertility for women, reduced child mortality rates, improved health and nutrition and civic participation. Therefore, estimates of the social rates of return must be considered only a lower bound of the true social rates of return. Refer to Munich and Psacharopoulos (2018) for a discussion of the external benefits of education.

The first estimate of returns to education dates back to the 1950s. There have been several reviews of this literature in an effort to set up patterns (see Psacharopoulos, 1972, 1973, 1985, 1994; Psacharopoulos and Patrinos, 2004, 2018). There are three main methods of estimating the rates of returns to education: (a) the short-cut method, (b) the full discounting method and (c) the Mincerian earnings function approach. These methods are explained in Psacharopoulos (1995), Psacharopoulos and Mattson (1998) and Patrinos et al. (2019) in detail.

The short-cut method is the easiest and the least data-intensive method. The full discounting method is the most data-intensive method and can provide private as well as social returns while the Mincer earnings function method gives only private returns. Psacharopoulos and Mattson (1998) compared the different methods of estimation with the Venezuelan data. They find that the short-cut method, full discounting method and Mincerian method all give similar estimates. They also find that the full discounting method is superior to all other methods and should be used when sample size allows. The short-cut method is inferior to the other methods but could be used for easy and quick estimation. The earnings function method is also relatively simple to apply. In the discussion of the methods below we follow the notation and explanations in Psacharopoulos and Mattson (1998) closely.

(a) The short-cut method

The short-cut method is based on the following simple formula which illustrates the private and the social returns at the university level (r_u).

$$\text{Private } r_u = \left(\bar{W}_u - \bar{W}_s\right)/S\left(\bar{W}_s\right)$$

$$\text{Social } r_u = \left(\bar{W}_u - \bar{W}_s\right)/S\left(\bar{W}_s + C_u\right)$$

$\bar{W}_u$ and $\bar{W}_s$ are the mean earnings of university and secondary school graduates, respectively. C_u is the direct cost of university education. It includes the annual cost of providing schooling which is usually incurred by the state such as personnel salaries and rental of buildings. S is the number of years of university education, in other words years of foregone earnings due to schooling.

The short-cut method assumes a flat age-earnings profile. Computation using the short-cut method is easy but rather crude. It requires only the average earnings by education level.

(b) The full discounting method

One of the very first estimates of returns to education was performed by Becker (1964) using the full discounting method. He made use of tables where costs and earnings are grouped by age and education. This is called an age-earnings profile by education matrix. Using this matrix and the formula below we can estimate the private and social returns to different levels of education. The private costs of education include tuitions, fees and incidental expenditures plus the earnings foregone while studying. The private benefits of education (for example at the university level) are the extra earnings (after taxes) (W_u) of a university-educated individual compared to that of an individual with less education (W_s). The private rate of return (r) is then the rate of discount (r) that equates the stream of discounted benefits to the stream of costs at the university education lasting five years. This can be expressed by the following formula.

$$\sum_{t=1}^{42} \frac{\left(W_u - W_s\right)_t}{\left(1+r\right)^t} = \sum_{t=1}^{5} \left(W_s + C_u\right)_t \left(1+r\right)^t$$

C_u denotes the direct costs of university education (tuition, fees, books). W_s represents the student's foregone earnings. In the computation of the social rates of return the social costs include the state's spending on education such as the rental of buildings and personnel salaries plus foregone taxes. Similar computations apply for the other levels of education.

The full discounting method requires a sample of individual observations. For this method we need a well-behaved age-earnings profile matrix by level of education. If it is not well-behaved (some cells do not have enough observations) different procedures can be used to smooth the profile. These procedures include three-year moving averages or exponential smoothing or others. Psacharopoulos and Mattson (1998) compared these smoothing procedures. They suggest that when smoothing is required the moving average procedure should be preferred.

(c) The Mincerian earnings function method

In recent studies individual survey data are often used to estimate the logarithmic earnings function of the Mincerian method (Mincer, 1974). These earnings functions include years of schooling, experience and a quadratic term in experience as explanatory variables. The coefficient estimate of the years of schooling provides an approximate estimate of the internal rate of return to a year of extra education. In order to estimate the returns to different levels of education (such as primary, secondary and tertiary), different programmes (such as general and vocational) or different sectors of the economy (such as public and private), a log-earnings function is estimated by including dummy variables for different education levels, different programmes or different sectors of the economy. The basic Mincerian earnings function of Mincer (1974) is a semi-logarithmic specification as follows.

$$\ln \mathrm{W_i} = \alpha + \beta \mathrm{S_i} + \gamma_1 \mathrm{EX_i} + \gamma_2 \mathrm{EX_i^2} + \varepsilon_\mathrm{i}$$

i indicates the individual, *W* is the individual's earnings, *S* is the number of years of schooling and *EX* is the number of years of labour market experience. It is defined as equal to *age minus years of schooling minus the school starting age*. The β coefficient on years of schooling (S) is interpreted as the average rate of return to one additional year of schooling. Here, the schooling spans all educational levels. This method assumes that only cost of education is the foregone earnings. Therefore, it estimates only the private rate of return. As shown in detail by Psacharopoulos (1995) this is equivalent to the private rate of return by the short-cut method (see also Patrinos, 2016).

In order to estimate the rates of return for different levels of schooling we use the extended earnings function as follows.

$$\ln \mathrm{W_i} = \alpha + \beta_\mathrm{p} \mathrm{D_p} + \beta_\mathrm{s} \mathrm{D_s} + \beta_\mathrm{u} \mathrm{D_u} + \delta_1 \mathrm{EX_i} + \delta_2 \mathrm{EX_i^2} + \varepsilon_\mathrm{i}$$

D_p, D_s and D_u represent the dummy variables for primary, secondary and university levels of schooling respectively. There is no dummy variable for those with no schooling. This is the base (omitted) category. As can be seen in the extended earnings function, the continuous variable S is replaced by the discrete dummy variables. After estimating the extended earnings function the private rates of retun to investment in different levels of education can be computed as follows. They are indicated by r_p, r_s and r_u for the private rates of return at the primary, secondary and university levels of education.

$$r_p = \beta_p / S_p$$

$$r_s = (\beta_s - \beta_p) / (S_s - S_p)$$

$$r_u = (\beta_u - \beta_s) / (S_u - S_s)$$

S_p, S_s and S_u are the number of years of schooling for the primary, secondary and university levels of education, respectively. The empirical works assume that the primary school children forgo only two or three years of earnings.

We can estimate the basic earnings function or the extended earnings function by using different subsamples of the data such as women and men, the public sector and the private sector or vocational and general secondary schools in order to obtain the returns to schooling at such divisions. Such estimations typically indicate higher returns for women than for men. Further, typically, higher returns are obtained in the competitive private sector than in the non-competitive public sector and the returns to general secondary school are higher than those of vocational schools. Psacharopoulos and Patrinos (2018) establish these results as a general pattern in most countries.

5.2.2 Estimation issues

Most studies employ samples of employees only. Although self-employed and unpaid family labour make up a large portion of the labour force in developing countries they are not studied often. Further, the earnings of the self-employed include the return to their capital as well as their labour. Since it is difficult to impute the earnings of these two groups most studies estimate the returns to education only for the employees.

Using the sample of wage earners to estimate the returns to education creates an important problem. If the selection of the sample of wage earners is related to the earnings–education relation this will result in biased estimates of returns to education. Heckman (1979) address the sample selection issue when subsamples split by gender or sector are used. Recent studies consider this situation by estimating the selection process into the sample in addition to the Mincer earnings function. In such studies the Mincer earnings function is often estimated separately for men and women. Sample selectivity bias is in particular important for women since in most developing countries women's labour force participation is low. Not taking this into account gives rise to biased estimates. Most studies such as Schultz (1988) indicate that the sample selection bias affects women's returns to education more so than that of men's. Dubos and Psacharopoulos (1991) estimated the returns by splitting the Brazilian men's data across various labour market states including self-employment and rural areas. They addressed the sample selection bias in each subsample of the labour market.

It is well known that an individual's earnings are also related to that individual's ability, the quality of the schools he or she attended and the past savings of his or her parents. In practice these factors are not handled mainly due to lack of data. This could result in biases in unknown directions when estimating the returns to education. Schultz (1988) investigates the problems in relation to the estimation of the Mincer function and the likely sources of biases in estimating the returns to education. The issue of ability bias, namely, the omission of the ability variable from the Mincer equation as well as of causality, has had considerable attention recently (Card, 1999). Angrist and Krueger (1991) found that returns estimates were similar to the conventional ones while Angrist and Krueger (1992) found returns 10% higher than the conventional ones when using identical twins' data to control for ability differences. The instrumental variable estimation method is used to address the issues of causality (Heckman et al., 2006). Compulsory schooling laws, birth dates and distances from schools are extensively used for generating exogenous variation in schooling. Measurement errors in self-reported schooling is another issue that has been widely considered. Glewwe (1991) in Ghana, Psacharopoulos and Velez (1992) in Colombia and Ashenfelter and Krueger (1994) in the US found that when measurement errors in self-reported schooling are taken into account returns estimates are lower than the conventional ones.

Another issue revolves around human capital hypothesis versus screening hypothesis in the interpretation of the returns to education (Layard and Psacharopoulos, 1974). The human capital hypothesis suggests that individuals' productivity increases as they acquire additional schooling resulting in an earnings premium. The screening hypothesis argues that the earnings premium is the result of credential effects. In this view additional schooling does not necessarily raise productivity but signals to the employer a better potential performance by the worker. Card (2001) and Clark and Martorell (2014) found no or little evidence for the screening hypothesis. Ashenfelter and Krueger (1994) found no bias in the returns to education estimates while testing the screening hypothesis using pairs of identical twins in the US.

The effect of the socioeconomic background on educational returns is addressed by Neuman (1991) in Israel and Card and Krueger (1992) in the US and they find contradictory results.

5.3 The patterns of private returns to education

Estimating the returns to education has attracted the attention of many researchers. As remarked earlier, Psacharopoulos has conducted and updated several reviews since the early 1970s. Harmon, Oosterbeek and Walker (2003) have conducted another recent review. The most recent review is by Psacharopoulos and Patrinos (2018). Some researchers such as Montenegro and Patrinos (2014) and Peet et al. (2015) have created databases to generate comparable estimates of the returns to education around the world.

Psacharopoulos and Patrinos (2018) based their review on 1,120 estimates in 139 countries over the last decade. They reached several global conclusions summarised as follows. First, private average global returns to education are about 9% a year and have been stable over the last decades. Second, returns to tertiary education have increased over time. This makes the issues of equity in and financing of higher education important topics to debate. Third, average rates of returns to education for women are higher than those for men. This implies that the education of girls should be a priority across the world. Fourth, the average rates of return are higher in low-income countries compared to high-income countries. Fifth, the average rates of return in the (competitive) private sector of an economy is higher than in the (non-competitive) public sector. This result supports the productive value of education in contrast to the signalling value of education.

5.4 Average returns to education in the MENA region

Economic theory predicts and empirical evidence confirms that the rates of returns to education will decline as schooling increases over time. Access to education has increased over recent decades in the MENA region. In MENA the average years of schooling for the population aged 15 and over has increased from 0.76 years in 1950 to 7.25 years in 2010 while that of world has increased from 3.12 to 7.89 during the same period (Barro and Lee, 2013).

Pritchett (1999, 2006) notes that the MENA region has experienced an increase in educational attainment but that this has not translated into increased productivity. Several studies note the low returns to education in the MENA region (see Psacharopoulos and Patrinos, 2004: 112, 2018; and Tzannatos et al., 2016). Table 5.1 presents the regional averages for world regions including MENA. In Panel A, the first two columns are taken from Psacharopoulos and Patrinos (2018). They indicate that although the mean years of schooling in MENA (7.5 years) is not the lowest among the world regions, the overall average returns to education is the lowest with 5.7% among the regions of the world. It is also lower than the world average of 8.8%. The rest of the columns in Panel A are taken from Montenegro and Patrinos (2014). Observations in these columns indicate the following. The overall rate of returns to education for MENA is 7.3% which is the lowest compared to all other regions. It is also lower than the world which is 9.7%. Considering the returns for men, MENA has the lowest rate with 6.5% which is again lower than the world average while the returns for women with 11.1% is similar to the world average

Table 5.1 Rates of returns to education by region, gender and education level (%)

Panel A	*Mean years of schooling*[a]	*Total*[a]	*Total*	*Male*	*Female*	*N*
High-income economies	9.5	8.0	10.0	9.5	11.1	33
East Asia and Pacific	6.9	8.7	9.4	9.2	10.1	13
Europe–Central Asia	9.1	7.3	7.4	6.9	9.4	20
Latin America–Caribbean	7.3	11.0	9.2	8.8	10.7	23
South Asia	4.9	8.1	7.7	6.9	10.2	7
Sub-Saharan Africa	5.2	10.5	12.4	11.3	14.5	33
Middle East–North Africa	7.5	5.7	7.3	6.5	11.1	10
World	8.0	8.8	9.7	9.1	11.4	139
Middle East–North Africa[1]			5.6	5.1	8.0	23

Panel B	*Total* *P/S/T*	*Male* *P/S/T*	*Female* *P/S/T*
High–Income economies	4.9/6.6/11.1	3.3/7.5/10.7	7.2/5.2/12.3
East Asia and Pacific	13.6/5.3/14.8	12.6/5.8/15.0	9.5/6.4/15.8
East Europe–Central Asia	13.9/4.7/10.3	12.1/4.2/9.8	11.9/6.4/12.2
Latin America–Caribbean	7.8/5.4/15.9	7.9/5.3/15.7	8.7/6.5/17.4
South Asia	6.0/5.0/17.3	4.7/3.9/16.6	4.8/6.2/23.3
Sub-Saharan Africa	14.4/10.6/21.0	12.5/10.1/21.0	17.5/12.7/21.3
Middle East–North Africa	16.0/4.5/10.5	12.7/4.3/10.2	21.4/7.4/13.5
World	11.5/6.8/14.6	10.1/6.7/14.4	13.2/8.2/16.1

Sources:
a: Psacharopoulos and Patrinos (2018) Table 3. The rest of the columns in panels A and B are from Patrinos and Montenegro (2014) Tables 3a and 3b.
Notes:
N is the number of countries. P/S/T are primary/secondary/tertiary respectively.
1: This row is taken from King et al. (2010).

of 11.4%. Further, the returns for women in MENA are higher than in all other regions except in Sub-Saharan Africa. The last row in Panel A gives the MENA averages from yet another source: King et al. (2010). All these sources indicate low returns to education in the MENA region.

Panel B of Table 5.1 gives the returns for primary, secondary and tertiary levels for the various world regions. There are two points to note. First, the MENA average at the primary level is higher than at the secondary and tertiary levels. Second, the MENA average for primary education is the highest (16.0%) among the other regions and is higher than the world average (11.5%). The returns for the secondary level are very low (4.5%). It is the lowest of all regions and lower than the world average. The returns for the tertiary level of education (10.5%) is also lower than the world average (16.6%). Third, Panel B also shows the returns for men and women at different levels of education. The returns for women are higher than those of men at all levels of education. This is also the case for the averages of the other regions and also for the world average. These are similar to those reported by King et al. (2010). Tzannatos et al. (2016) also confirm the low overall and low secondary and tertiary returns in the Arab countries which includes the MENA region as a subset. Tzannatos et al. focus exclusively on Arab countries which differs from MENA but has similar overall characteristics.

The reasons for the low returns to education in MENA must be sought in the labour markets in the region. Education affects both the supply of and the demand for labour. The supply and demand considerations are both responsible for the observed low returns to education. These considerations are discussed by Tzannatos et al. (2016) and Kingsbury (2018). Higher returns to primary education compared to secondary and tertiary levels imply higher relative demand for the less educated. The low overall returns to education in the MENA region is in agreement with those economies where production is typically of low capital-intensity and low value-added type. Previous literature ascribes the low returns to low-quality education and possibly to teaching subjects not relevant to the labour market. The low quality of education is confirmed by the poor performance of the region's students in the international tests such as PISA. The adult, youth and the educated youth unemployment rates in the region are very high and they are the highest in the world. Tzannatos et al. (2016) conclude that the problems in the region's labour markets are macroeconomic in nature and related to the demand for labour. More clearly, not enough jobs are created for adults and the youth in the region's labour markets. According to Tzannatos et al. the policies responsible for this are weak governance, cronyism and lack of accountability. These issues started to be discussed in the region's labour market studies only after the Arab Spring.

Low demand for labour has two aspects. It pushes the wages down and at the same time diminishes the motivation to invest in education. However, the anticipation of a job in the public sector or abroad may stimulate investment in education. In accordance with this observation, public sector predominates the labour market in the region and the region's skilled emigration rate is one of the highest in the world. High-skilled emigration lowers the returns for the remaining population while at the same time low returns encourage emigration as stressed by Tzannatos et al. (2016).

Researchers have identified government repression, corruption and limited opportunity for upward mobility as the main political and economic factors for the Arab Spring. Kingsbury (2018) noted the low returns to education as the cause of the unrest in the MENA region. Conversely research on the causes of low returns to education in the region is limited. Kingsbury empirically examines the relationship between returns to education and the characteristics of the political economy of the region. He relates the rate of returns to education to factors that might explain the region's low returns, namely, religiosity, poor economic performance, reliance on natural resources, corruption and property rights. He finds plausible evidence that religious orthodoxy, poor educational quality, reliance on natural resource exports, corruption, nepotism and non-meritocratic government policy may reduce returns to education.

5.4.1 Returns for women exceed those of men

The reviews by Schultz (1993), Psacharopoulos and Patrinos (2018) and earlier reviews report that returns to education for women exceed those of men as a generic pattern. This pattern is also observed in the MENA region except in Tunisia as discussed below in Section 5.5.4. This pattern can be explained with the low rate of labour force participation of women which is attributed to the traditional patriarchal gender roles in the region. Further, educated women are a select group of high-ability or high-motivation individuals. It is also suggested that women may have high-quality teachers (Kingsbury, 2018). Dougherty (2005) attributes higher returns to women than men to discrimination, tastes and circumstances. High returns for women imply that priority should be given to girls' education.

5.5 MENA country results

The country estimates of the private returns to education are presented in Tables 5.2–5.5. These tables report the returns obtained from the OLS estimates of the Mincer wage equations so as

Table 5.2 Private returns to education, Egypt (%)

Year	*Years of schooling*	*Overall*	*Male*	*Female*	*P/S/T total*	*P/S/T male*	*P/S/T female*	*GDP per capita*[3]	*Source*
1988	5.5	7.8			4.7/7.7/14.2			1480	Wahba (2000)
1988			4.0	3.5				1480	Nugent and Saleh (2009)
1997	5.9	5.2						1772	Psacharopoulos and Patrinos (2004)
1998			3.3	4.0				1810	Nugent and Saleh (2009)
1998					2.7/19.4/3.0			1810	Herrera and Badr (2011)
1998		2.3	2.1	3.0				1810	King, Montegenro and Orazem (2010)
2001	5.2		9.7					1982	Arbak (2012)
2006	11.1		5.4					2217	Salehi et al. (2009)
2006					1.8/4.5/8.4			2217	Herrera and Badr (2011)
2006					1.0/3.0/8.0	8.0/15.0/17.0	9.0/26.0/28.0	2217	Barouni and Broecke (2014)
2006					2.2/4.7[2]/10.9			2217	Said (2007)
2011	8.8	3.4	2.9	4.8	2.1/3/9.2	1.9/2.1/9.1	4.1/5/8	2594	Rizk (2016)
2012					1.1/5.6[3]/9.4			2594	Said (2007)

Notes:
P/S/T stand for primary/secondary/tertiary levels of schooling respectively.
1: Unless otherwise stated, the entries in the table are obtained from OLS estimates of the Mincerian equation.
2:Vocational Secondary School.
3: GDP per capita figures are taken from World Development Indicators. They are in constant 2010 US $.

to ensure comparability. There may still be differences due to variations in the samples and age groups covered or control variables used, etc.[2] Private returns decline as the per capita level of income of the country increases. Similarly, private returns decline as the level of economic development improves and the years of schooling increase. Therefore, in the tables in this section I provide the years of schooling and the gross domestic product (GDP) per capita of the countries in order to be able to observe changes over time in relation to these factors.

I first discuss Egypt, Palestine and Turkey and provide separate tables for these countries due to the availability of substantially more estimation points for these countries than for the others. The rest of the MENA countries are discussed together in Section 5.5.4.

5.5.1 Private returns to education in Egypt

Table 5.2 presents the estimates of private returns to education in Egypt. Years of schooling increased from 5.5 in 1988 to 11.1 in 2006 but decreased to 8.8 in 2011. GDP per capita increased by about 75% during the period 1988–2012. Overall returns to education have declined over time by about half from 7.8% in 1988 to 3.4% in 2011. Women's returns are

Table 5.3 Private rates of returns to education, Palestine (%)

Year	*Years of schooling*	*Overall*	*Male*	*Female*	*P/S/T total*	*P/S/Tmale*	*P/S/T female*	*GDP per capita*[2]	*Source*
1981	7.8		4.0						Angrist (1995)
1983	8.0		3.2						Angrist (1995)
1984	8.1		3.9						Angrist (1995)
1985	8.2		3.1						Angrist (1995)
1986	8.4		2.1						Angrist (1995)
1987	8.4		2.6						Angrist (1995)
1988	8.4		1.1						Angrist (1995)
1989	8.5		0.3						Angrist (1995)
1990	8.5		1.4						Angrist (1995)
1991	8.7		1.7						Angrist (1995)
1998		1.4			7.9/0.7/0.1			2334	Montenegro and Patrinos (2014)
1999		1.8			6.1/1.2/0.2			2683	Montenegro and Patrinos (2014)
1999	8.4	2.8	1.4	0.6		na/7.4/23.7	na/2.6/40.0	2683	Daoud (2005)
2000		1.6			5.8/0.5/0.7			2356	Montenegro and Patrinos (2014)
2001		0.7			1.5/na/1.6			2148	Montenegro and Patrinos (2014)
2001	8.7	2.6	2.7	0.0		na/8.8/20.3	na/13.1/23.1	2148	Daoud (2005)
2002		2.8			11.6/na/5.1			2064	Montenegro and Patrinos (2014)
2003		3.0			10.5/0.4/4.2			2205	Montenegro and Patrinos (2014)
2004		4.3			11/1.0/5.6			2334	Montenegro and Patrinos (2014)
2004	11.7	5.4	5.0	11.1	2.9/1.0/10.2	2.3/0.6/9.6	4.9/5.8/17.3	2334	Tansel and Daoud (2014)
2005		4.0			17/1.1/5.0			2524	Montenegro and Patrinos (2014)
2006		5.0			13.4/1.7/5.8			2348	Montenegro and Patrinos (2014)
2007		5.0			8.4/1.6/5.9			2249	Montenegro and Patrinos (2014)
2008		3.8			28.7/0.2/5.5			2025	Montenegro and Patrinos (2014)
2008	11.6	4.1	3.6	10.5	1.9/1.2/8.0	1.7/1.2/7.2	-0.2/7.0/18.3	2025	Tansel and Daoud (2014)
2011	11.2	5.1	7.0	7.3	4.1/6.5/7.0	3.5/5.2/6.4	4.7/15.4/6.6	2442	Rizk (2016)

Notes:
P/S/T stand for primary/secondary/tertiary levels of schooling respectively.
1: Unless otherwise stated, the entries in the table are obtained from OLS estimates of the Mincerian equation.
2: GDP per capita figures are taken from World Development Indicators. They are in constant 2010 US $.
3: na stands for not available.

Table 5.4 Private returns to education, Turkey (%)

Year	*Years of schooling*	*Overall*	*Male*	*Female*	*P/S/T total*	*P/S/Tmale*	*P/S/T female*	*GDP per capita*[3]	*Source*[2]
1968						17.5/17.0/4.7	20.4/14.8/8.9	4120	Kara (2008)
1987						5.5/16.4/11.0	6.5/12.4/12.1	6375	Kara (2008)
1987	4.9	6.5						6375	Salehi et al. (2009)
1987						1.8/8.2/16.0	3.7/8.8/13.4	6375	Tansel (1994)
1989						1.7/10.1/16.9	4.2/11.7/14.7	6890	Tansel (2001)[4]
1994						6.0/12.0/10.8	8.0/14.6/14.8	6890	Kara (2008)
1994	7.5	12.4	17.6					6890	Tansel (2010)
1994	7		7.7			4.9/8.5/14.0		6890	Tansel and Bodur (2012)
2001		19.7						7632	Arbak (2012)
2002	8		7.6			3.6/7.4/13.1		8004	Tansel and Bodur (2012)
2002	8.4	11.8	11.5	13.1		4.3/15.2/16.0	1.4/14.9/20.3	8004	Tansel (2010)
2003	8.4	12.2	11.7	13.4		6.8/11.1/18.3	2.1/13.0/21.6	8332	Tansel (2010)
2004	8.4							9010	Tansel (2010)
2004	11.7	11.7	10.9	13.7	8.6/12.0/16.6	8.9/11.5/16.1	2.8/14.6/18.0	9010	Tansel and Daoud (2014)
2005	8.3	10.9	10.1	12.5		8.6/11.7/16.2	4.4/9.5/22.5	9692	Tansel (2010)
2008	11.6	11.8	10.9	14.1	4.8/9.4/20.0	5.4/9.3/18.7	-1.0/11.4/22.6	10600	Tansel and Daoud (2014)

Notes:
P/S/T stand for primary/secondary/tertiary levels of schooling respectively.
1: Unless otherwise stated, the entries in the table are obtained from OLS estimates of the Mincerian equation.
2: Montenegro and Patrinos (2014) have extensive estimates for Turkey, 2002–2010. However, they are not included here since there is double presentation.
3: GDP per capita figures are taken from World Development Indicators. They are in constant 2010 US $.
4: Heckman two-step estimation.

Table 5.5 Private returns to education, other MENA countries (%)

Country	*Year*	*Years of schooling*	*Overall*	*Male*	*Female*	*P/S/T total*	*P/S/T male*	*P/S/T female*	*GDP per capita*[2]	*Source*
Algeria	2002	6.4		2.2					3755	Arbak (2012)
Algeria	2016	11.2	9.5	9.2	13.5	9.6/15.6/8.4			4828	Boutayeba (2017)
Iran	1975	2.7		11.6		10.6/15.3/19.3			9026	Psacharopoulos (1985)
Iran	1987	4.4		6.9					3989	Salehi et al. (2009)
Iran	2001	7.3		8.8					4750	Salehi et al. (2009)
Iran	2006	9.0		7.6					5902	Salehi et al. (2009)
Iraq	2006	6.2	0.7	0.5	3.0	2.2/1.5/0.9			4144	Peet et al. (2015)
Iraq	2006		3.4			7.7/1.2/3.2			4144	Montenegro and Pantrinos (2014)
Iraq	2006		1.8	1.4	6.0				4144	King et al. (2010)
Jordan	2001	7.7	6.7						2907	Arbak (2012)
Jordan	2002		8.9			10.3/4.2/8.4			3020	Montenegro and Pantrinos (2014)
Jordan	2002		7.3	6.9	10.1				3020	King et al. (2010)
Lebanon	2002					5.6/2.6/-1.6			6657	Dah and Hammami (2002)
Lebanon	2011		5.5			na/na/9.8	na/na/7.7	na/na/16.6	8450	Montenegro and Pantrinos (2014)
Morocco	1970	2.9	15.8						1020	Psacharopoulos (1994)
Morocco	1991		10			6.6/8.7/14.6			1811	Montenegro and Pantrinos (2014)
Morocco	1991		6.9	6.2	10.0				1811	King et al. (2010)
Morocco	1998		10			11.6/6.2/16.1			1962	Montenegro and Pantrinos (2014)
Morocco	1998		7.2	6.3	10.3				1962	King et al. (2010)
Morocco	2000	3.9	4.3						1972	Müller and Nordman (2004)
Morocco	2001	3.9	2.8						2091	Arbak (2012)
Tunisia	1980	4.8	8						2029	Psacharopoulos (1994)
Tunisia	2001		8.5			12.3/8.1/17.4			3091	Montenegro and Pantrinos(2014)
Tunisia	2001		6.5	6.4	6.4				3091	King et al. (2010)
Tunisia	2010					3.0/12.0/27.0	3.0/11.0/27.0	1.0/13.0/28.0	4140	Barouni and Broecke (2014)
Tunisia	2011	11.1	7	7	7.3	4.7/1.2/9.7			4015	Rizk (2016)
Yemen	1985		10	41	56					Psacharopoulos (1994)[2]
Yemen	2005		2.9	2.7	6.1				1215	King et al. (2010)
Yemen	2005		5.4			na/3.8/na	na/3.7/na	na/8.0/na	1215	Montenegro and Pantrinos (2014)

Notes:
P/S/T stand for primary/secondary/tertiary levels of schooling respectively.
1: Unless otherwise stated, the entries in the table are obtained from OLS estimates of the Mincerian equation.
2: GDP per capita figures are taken from World Development Indicators. They are in constant 2010 US $.
3: na stands for not available.

slightly higher than men's. Returns at the primary level are the lowest and returns at the tertiary level the highest for all of the years except for 1998 where secondary level returns are the highest. One of the main characteristics of the Egyptian labour market is the predominance of public sector employment (Assaad, 1997). In the early 1960s guaranteed public employment for secondary and university graduates was introduced. This led to a rapid expansion of the number of graduates at all levels of education. The public sector hires on the basis of credentials and pays on the basis of seniority rather than productivity. These rules extend to the private sector of the economy leading to distortions.

5.5.2 Private returns to education in Palestine

Table 5.3 presents the private returns to education in Palestine. The average schooling level rose from 7.8 in 1981 to 11.2 in 2011. GDP per capita did not change much over the years. The tertiary education system expanded rapidly during this period. According to Angrist (1995) the returns to schooling of men declined from 4.0% in 1981 to 2.6% in 1987 which is the beginning of the first Intifada. It was 0.3% in 1989 and rose to 1.7% in 1991. In the following years the overall returns rose somewhat but dropped again to 1.6% in 2000 during the second intifada and to 0.7% in 2001. Israel closed its doors to Palestinian workers after the second Intifada. Enrolment in tertiary education increased during this period. Unemployment increased, capital inflow from abroad diminished (Daoud, 2005). The increase in the supply of tertiary-educated graduates resulted in a decline in the returns of the tertiary level of schooling. The overall returns increased to about 4% in 2004 and remained in the range of 4.0–5.0% over the period 2004–2011. According to estimates by Daoud (2005), returns for women were higher than those for men except during the two years of 1999 and 2001. Higher returns for women than for men were due to women's low participation rates and their employment mostly in NGOs and international organisations. During the period of 1998–2001 the returns to secondary and tertiary levels were very low and close to zero in some years. In the following years the returns to secondary level remained low but at the tertiary level rose above 5.0%. It was 10.2% in 2004 and 8.0% in 2008.

5.5.3 Private returns to education in Turkey

A recent extensive review of returns to education in Turkey is provided in Patrinos, Psacharopoulos and Tansel (2020). The returns estimates in Turkey dates back to the 1970s. These studies used the full discounting method. There are studies that provide estimates for general and vocational secondary schools and public and private sectors. More recent studies report selectivity corrected returns estimates, instrumental variable returns estimates and pseudo-panel data estimates. Di Paolo and Tansel (2017) estimate wage differentials to different college majors. A review of such studies and their references can be found in Patrinos, Psacharopoulos and Tansel; we do not dwell on them here as they are outside the scope of this study.

Table 5.4 presents the estimates of private returns to education in Turkey. Years of schooling increased from 4.9 in 1987 to 11.6 in 2008. GDP per capita more than doubled over the 40 years from 1968 to 2008. The returns were high in 1968 as is observable in the male and female columns of primary/secondary/tertiary (P/S/T). After that date the returns declined and remained at around 11.0–12.0% except in 2001 where it was about 20.0%. Women's returns were higher than those of men's. Returns were lowest at the primary level and highest at the tertiary level. Similar patterns are also observed for males and females by level of schooling. There was an expansion of tertiary education in 1992 with the establishment of 22 new universities and again a new wave of expansion in 2006. GDP per capita increased substantially over the years. In spite of these observations the returns remained buoyant during the latter part of the period.

5.5.4 Private returns to education in other MENA countries

Table 5.5 presents the estimates of private returns to education in the rest of the MENA countries in alphabetical order.

Algeria: Years of schooling increased substantially from 6.4 in 2002 to 11.2 in 2016. GDP per capita increased by about 30% during the same period. Men's returns increased considerably from 2.2% in 2002 to 9.2% in 2016. Women's returns were larger than those of men's. The highest return is observed at the secondary level of schooling.

Iran: Years of schooling increased substantially from 4.4 years in 1987 to 9.0 years in 2006. GDP per capita also increased by almost 50%. Returns figures are only available for men. The returns for men first increased by about two percentage points from 1987 to 2001 and then decreased by about one percentage point from 2001 to 2006.

Iraq: Years of schooling was 6.2 in 2006. Returns estimates are available only for 2006 from three different sources. Overall returns and those of men were very low due to the US occupation and the ensuing civil war. Women's returns were higher than those of men's. The lowest returns were at the secondary and the tertiary levels.

Jordan: Only figures for 2001 and 2002 are observed. Years of schooling was 7.7 in 2001. There was a slight increase in GDP per capita during this period. Returns increased somewhat from 2001 to 2002. Women's returns were higher than those of men's. The lowest returns are observed at the secondary level of schooling.

Lebanon: There are figures for only two years: 2002 and 2011. GDP per capita increased substantially. In 2002 the lowest returns were at the tertiary level and the highest at the primary level. Returns at the tertiary level increased in 2011 to a substantial 10%. Women's tertiary level returns were higher than those of men's.

Morocco: The increase in years of schooling was slow from 2.9 years in 1970 to 3.9 years in 2001. GDP per capita remained stagnant for most of the latter part of the period. The overall returns in Morocco seem to have declined substantially from about 16% in 1970 to about 3% in 2001. The returns to women's schooling were substantially larger than those of men's. The lowest returns were at the secondary level and the highest at the tertiary level.

Tunisia: Years of schooling increased substantially from 4.8 in 1980 to 11.1 in 2011. GDP per capita more than doubled during this period. Returns declined from 8% in 1980 to 6.5% in 2001 and to 7.0% in 2011. In 2010 the lowest returns were at the primary level and the highest returns were at the tertiary level. The Higher Education Act was introduced in 2008 which resulted in an increase in enrolments especially of female students. Unemployment increased as a result among the tertiary-educated. There was a high supply of female workers with secondary and tertiary degrees compared to male workers. This possibly caused lower returns for women than for men in Tunisia in contrast to the pattern in other MENA countries and the MENA regional averages.

Yemen: Returns declined substantially from 1985 to 2005 from 10% to about 5%. The decline in men's and women's returns was also substantial. Women's returns were higher than those of men. Evidence for this country is scanty due to internal strife.

5.6 Conclusions

The average returns to education are relatively low in the MENA region although the mean years of schooling is not the lowest among the world regions. The World Bank (2008) reports that educational systems have low quality in the region due to inadequate funding. The public sector has a large role in employment. This introduces distortions in the signals that guide investment in human capital in the MENA region (World Bank, 2004). The highest returns to education are observed for Turkey and the lowest for Egypt and Palestine. In Lebanon, the returns are highest at the primary level, while in Iraq, Jordan and Morocco the returns are lowest at the secondary level. They are highest at the tertiary level in some countries for example Egypt, Morocco, Tunisia and Turkey. Years of schooling and GDP per capita have increased in all countries. Accordingly, in most countries the returns have declined over time except in Turkey where they have remained about the same. Returns for women are higher than those for men. However, women's returns are lower than those of men's in Tunisia and they are about the same in Egypt and were for some years in Turkey. The case for continued investment in education throughout MENA is supported.

Notes

1 The World Bank definition of MENA includes the following 19 countries: Algeria, Bahrain, Djibouti, Egypt, Iran, Iraq, Jordan Kuwait, Lebanon, Libya, Morocco, Oman, Qatar, Saudi Arabia, Syria, Tunisia, United Arab Emirates, Palestine (West Bank and Gaza), Yemen. In this study, I exclude the Gulf Cooperation Countries since they are high-income countries compared to the rest of the region. I also include Turkey in my review due to its importance for the region. Palestine refers to the Israeli-occupied Palestinian territories of the West Bank and Gaza Strip.

2 The tables in this study include countries for which there are estimates in the published sources including working papers. Unpublished processed papers or conference papers are not included in this survey or in the tables.

References

Angrist, J.D. (1995). The Economic Returns to Schooling in the West Bank and Gaza Strip. *American Economic Review*, 85(5), pp. 1065–1087.

Angrist, J.D. and Krueger, A.B. (1991). Does Compulsory School Attendance Affect Schooling and Earnings? *The Quarterly Journal of Economics*, 106(4), pp. 979–1014.

Angrist, J.D. and Krueger, A.B. (1992). *Estimating the Payoff to Schooling Using the Vietnam Era Draft Lottery*. Working Paper No. 4067. National Bureau of Economic Research (NEBR), New York.

Arbak, E. (2012). *Measuring Returns to Education and Human Capital in the Southern Mediterranean*. MEDPRO Technical Report, 17. Mediterranean Prospects European Commission, Brussels.

Ashenfelter, O. and Krueger, A.B. (1994). Estimates of the Economic Return of Schooling from a New Sample of Twins. *American Economic Review*, 84(5), pp. 1157–1173.

Assaad, R. (1997). The Effects of Public Sector Hiring and Compensation Policies on the Egyptian Labor Market. *World Bank Economic Review*, 11(1), pp. 85–118.

Barouni, M. and Broecke, S. (2014). The Returns to Education in Africa: Some New Estimates. *Journal of Development Studies*, 50(12), pp. 1593–1613.

Barro, J.B. and Lee, J.W. (2013). A New Data Set of Educational Attainment in the World 1950–2010. *Journal of Development Economics*, 104, pp. 184–198.

Becker, G.S. (1964). *Human Capital: A Theoretical and Empirical Analysis with Special Reference to Education*. New York: Columbia University Press.

Boutayeba, F. (2017). Estimating the Returns to Education in Algeria. *Asian Journal of Economic Modelling*, 5(2), pp. 147–153.

Card, D. (1999). The Causal Effect of Education on Earnings. In O. Ashenfelter and D. Card (eds.), *Handbook of Labor Economics*, Amsterdam: Elsevier, Volume 3, Chapter 30, pp. 1802–2863.

Card, D. (2001). Estimating the Return to Schooling: Progress on Some Persistent Econometric Problems. *Econometrica*, 69(5), pp. 1127–1160.

Card, D. and Krueger, A.B. (1992). Does School Quality Matter? Returns to Education and the Characteristics of Public Schools in the United States. *Journal of Political Economy*, 100(1), pp. 1–39.

Clark, D. and Martorell, P. (2014). The Signaling Value of a High School Diploma. *Journal of Political Economy*, 122(2), pp. 282–318

Dabos, M. and Psacharopoulos, G. (1991). An Analysis of the Sources of Earnings Variation among Brazilian Males. *Economics of Education Review*, 10(4), pp. 359–377.

Dah, A.M. and Hammami, S.C. (2002). Returns to Education in Lebanon. In *Economic Research Forum Seventh Annual Conference*. Lebanon.

Daoud, Y. (2005). Gender Gap in Returns to Schooling in Palestine. *Economics of Education Review*, 24(6), pp. 633–649.

Di Paolo, A. and A. Tansel. 2017. *Analyzing Wage Differentials by Fields of Study: Evidence from Turkey*. July 2017, IZA Discussion Paper No. 10915.

Doughtery, C. (2005). Why are the Returns to Schooling Higher for Women Than for Men? *Journal of Human Resources*, 40(4), pp. 969–988.

Glewwe, P. (1991). *Schooling Skills and the Returns to Government Investment in Education*. LSMS Working Paper No. 76. The World Bank, Washington DC.

Harmon, C., Oosterbeek, H. and Walker, I. (2003). The Returns to Education: Microeconomics. *Journal of Economic Surveys*, 17(2), pp. 115–156.

Heckman, J.J. (1979). Sample Selection as a Specification Error. *Econometrica*, 47(1), pp. 153–161.

Heckman, J.J., Lochner, L.J. and Todd, P.E. (2006). Earnings Functions, Rates of Return and Treatment Effects: The Mincer Equation and Beyond. In E. Hanushek and F. Welch (eds.), *Handbook of the Economics of Education*, Amsterdam: Elsevier, Volume 1, pp. 307–458.

Herrera, S, and Badr, K. (2011). *Why Does the Productivity of Education Vary Across Individuals in Egypt? Firm Size, Gender and Access to Technology as Sources of Heterogeneity in Returns to Education*. Policy Research Working Papers No.5740. The World Bank, Washington, DC.

Kara, O. (2008). Comparing Two Approaches to the Rate of Return to Investment in Education. *Education Economics*, 18(2), pp. 153–165.

King, E.M., Montenegro, C.E. and Orazem, P.F. (2010). *Economic Freedom, Human Rights, and the Returns to Human Capital: An Evaluation of the Schultz Hypothesis*. Policy Research Working Paper No.5405. The World Bank, Washington, DC.

Kingsbury, I. (2018). Making Sense of Low Private Returns in MENA: A Human Capital Approach. *International Journal of Educational Development*, 61, pp. 173–183.

Layard, R. and Psacharopoulos, G. (1974). The Screening Hypothesis and the Returns to Education. *Journal of Political Economy*, 82(5), pp. 985–998.

Mincer, J. (1974), *Schooling Experience and Earnings*. New York: National Bureau of Economic Research, Columbia University Press.

Montenegro, C.E. and Patrinos, H.A. (2014). *Comparable Estimates of Returns to Schooling Around the World*. Policy Research Working Paper Series, No. 7020. The World Bank, Washington, DC.

Muller, C. and Nordman, C. (2004). *Wages and Human Capital in Exporting Firms in Morocco*. CREDIT Research Paper, No. 06 (04).

Munich, D. and Psacharopoulos, G. (2018). The External and Non-Market Benefits of Education: A Review. *EENEE, Analytical Report*, 2017(3).

Neuman, S. (1991). Parental Background, Educational Attainments and Returns to Schooling and Marriage: The Case of Israel. *Applied Economics*, 23, pp. 1325–1334.

Nugent, J.B. and Saleh, M. (2009). *Intergenerational Transmission of, and Returns to Human Capital and Changes Therein Over Time: Empirical Evidence from Egypt*. Working Paper No. 468. Economic Research, Cairo.

Patrinos, H.A. (2016). *Estimating the Return to Schooling Using the Mincer Equation*. Bonn: IZA World of Labor 2016.

Patrinos, Harry A., Psacharopoulos, George. and Aysit, Tansel. (2020). Private and Social Returns to Investment in Education: The Case of Turkey with Alternative Methods. *Applied Economics*, 53(14), pp. 1638–1658.

Peet, E.D., Fink, G. and Fawzi, W. (2015). Returns to Education in Developing Countries: Evidence from the Living Standards and Measurement Study Surveys. *Economics of Education Review*, 49, pp. 69–90.

Pritchett, L. (1999). *Has Education Had a Growth Pay-Off in The MENA Region? Middle East and North Africa*. Working Paper No: 18. Washington DC, The World Bank.

Pritchett, L. (2006). Does Learning to Add Up Add Up? The Returns to Schooling in Aggregate Data. In E. Hanushek and F. Welch, (eds.), *Handbook of the Economics of Education*, Volume 1. Amsterdam: Elsevier: pp. 635–695.

Psacharopoulos, G. (1972). Rates of Return on Investment in Education around the World. *Comparative Education*, 16(1), pp. 54–67.

Psacharopoulos, G. (1973). *Returns to Education an International Comparison*. San Francisco: Elsevier.

Psacharopoulos, G. (1985). Return to Education: A Further International Update and Implications. *The Journal of Human Resources*, 20(4), pp. 583–597.

Psacharopoulos, G. (1994). Returns to Investment in Education: A Global Update. *World Development*, 22(9), pp. 1325–1343.

Psacharopoulos, G. (1995). *The Profitability of Investment in Education: Concepts and Methods*. Human Capital Development and Operations Policy, Working Papers No. 63. Washington DC, The World Bank.

Psacharopoulos, G. and Mattson, R. (1998). Estimating the Returns to Education: A Sensitivity Analysis of Concepts and Methods. *Journal of Educational Planning and Administration*, 12(3), pp. 271–287.

Psacharopoulos, G. and Patrinos, H.A. (2004). Returns to Investment in Education: A Further Update. *Education Economics*, 12(2), pp. 111–134.

Psacharopoulos, G. and Patrinos, H.A., (2018). *Returns to Investment in Education: A Decennial Review of the Global Literature*. Policy Research Working Paper. Washington DC, The World Bank.

Psacharopoulos, G. and Velez, E. (1992). Schooling, Ability and Earnings in Colombia, 1988. *Economic Development and Cultural Change*, 40(3), pp. 629–643.

Rizk, R. (2016). *Returns to Education: An Updated Comparison of Arab Countries*. Forum Working Paper, No. 986. Economic Research, Cairo.

Said, M. 2007. *The Fall and Rise of Earnings and Inequality in Egypt: New Evidence from the ELMPS, 2006*. Forum Working Paper No. 0708. Economic Research, Cairo.

Salehi-Isfahani, D., Tunali, I. and Assaad, R. (2009). A Comparative Study of Returns to Education of Urban Men in Egypt, Iran, and Turkey. *Middle East Development Journal*, 1(2), pp. 145–187.

Schultz, T.P. (1988). Educational Investments and Returns. In H. Chenery and T.N. Srinivasan (eds.), *Handbook of Development Economics*, Amsterdam: North Holland and Co, Volume 1, Chapter 13, pp. 543–630.

Schultz, T.P. (1993). Returns to Women's Education. In E.M. King and M.A. Hill (eds.), *Women's Education in Developing Countries: Barriers, Benefits and Policies*. Baltimore: The John Hopkins University Press, Chapter 2, pp. 51–99.

Schultz, T.W. (1961). Investments in Human Capital. *American Economic Review*, 51(1), pp. 1–17.

Tansel, A. (1994). Wage Employment, Earnings and Returns to Schooling for Men and Women in Turkey. *Economics of Education Review*, 13(4), pp. 305–320.

Tansel, A. (2001). Self-Employment, Wage-Employment, and Returns to Schooling by Gender in Turkey. In D. Salehi-Isfahani (ed.), *Labor and Human Capital in the Middle East: Studies of Markets and Household Behavior*, Reading: Ithaca Press, pp. 637–667.

Tansel, A. (2010). Changing Returns to Education for Men and Women in a Developing Country: Turkey, 1994, 2002–2005. In ESPE 2008 Conference, June 18-21, 2008, London, United Kingdom and ECOMOD 2008 Conference, July 2-4, 2008, Berlin, Germany, MEEA Conference, March 2009, Nice, France, and ICE-TEA Conference, September 1–3, 2010, Girne, Republic of Northern Cyprus.

Tansel, A. and Bodur, F.B. (2012). Wage Inequality and Returns to Education in Turkey: A Quantile Regression Analysis. *Review of Development Economics*, 16(1), pp. 107–121.

Tansel, A. and Daoud, Y. (2014). Comparative Essay for Returns to Education in Palestine and Turkey. *Perspectives on Global Development and Technology*, 13, pp. 347–378.

Tzannatos, Z., Diwan, I. and Ahad, J.A. (2016). *Rates of Return to Education in Twenty Two Arab Countries: An Update and Comparison between MENA and the Rest of The World*. Working Paper, No.1007. Economic Research Forum, Cairo.

Wahba, J. (2000). *Returns to Education and Regional Earnings Differentials in Egypt*. Discussion Papers in Economics and Econometrics, No. 33062. University of Southampton, Southampton.

World Bank (2004). *Gender and Development in the Middle East and North Africa: Women in the Public Sphere*. MENA Development Report. The World Bank, Washington, DC.

World Bank (2008). *The Road Not Travelled: Education Reform in The Middle East and North Africa*. MENA Development Report. The World Bank, Washington, DC.

6

WOMEN'S EMPLOYMENT AND LABOUR FORCE PARTICIPATION

Puzzles, problems and research needs

Massoud Karshenas and Valentine M. Moghadam

6.1 Introduction: the problem and the puzzle

In the Middle East and North Africa (MENA) region, female labour force participation (FLFP) increased between 1990 and 2018, but the regional average remains just over 19 per cent, less than the rate for any other world region (Figure 6.1). On the supply side, women's educational attainment has been expanding and fertility declining, and as economic theory would predict, educated women and those with fewer children do tend to gravitate toward the labour market. However, the female labour force still constitutes a small proportion of the overall labour force in any given MENA country. As shown in Figure 6.2, the MENA countries at all levels of female educational attainment have the lowest female labour force participation rates compared to other developing countries. This applies equally to countries such as Yemen and Morocco with the lowest female educational levels and Lebanon and Palestine with female literacy rates of over 90 per cent (Figure 6.2). The same pattern is also observed in relation to other relevant variables such as fertility rates, per capita GDP, etc., where the MENA countries show the lowest female labour force participation compared to other countries conditional on any of these variables.

These realities raise several questions. Given women's rising educational attainment, lowered fertility, households' economic needs, and international advocacy for women's economic participation and empowerment, what accounts for the persistence of low FLFP and women's small share of paid employment?

One specificity of FLFP in some of the countries in the MENA region is that the participation of women with tertiary education is at a par with comparator countries, but the low participation rates amongst women with intermediate and lower education push down the overall female participation rates in the region (see Figure 6.3). This is a particularly important observation, as the vast majority of working-age women in both the MENA region and other countries have education levels at or below the 'intermediate' or secondary school level (see Figure 6.4). Furthermore, high participation rates amongst university-educated women are accompanied by high levels of unemployment – between 20 and 35 per cent across different countries (ILO, 2016). Why are women with basic or secondary schooling less likely to be in the work force than those with university education? What explains the high female unemployment rates? What supply- and demand-side factors and forces might be behind the problem and the puzzle of low FLFP and low employment in MENA?

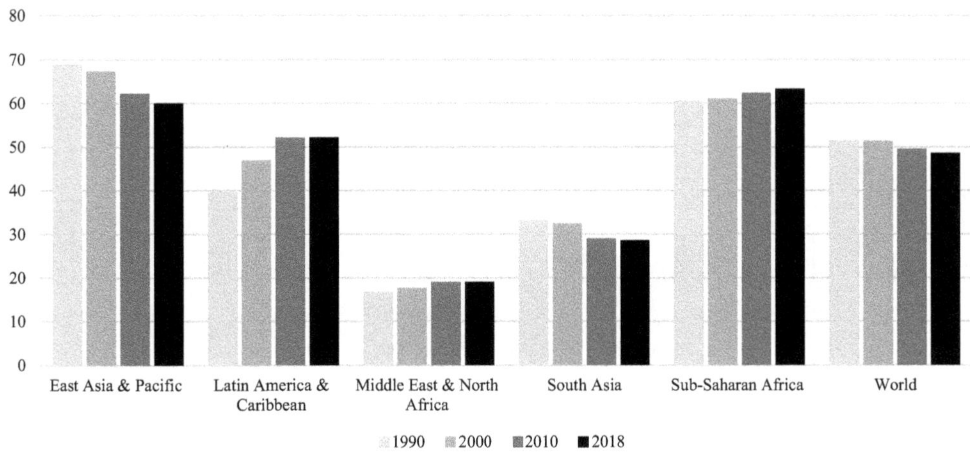

Figure 6.1 Female labour force participation rates in the MENA region compared to other developing world regions, 1990–2018 (%). *Notes*: FLFP is defined as female labour force, both employed and unemployed, as % of female population aged 15 plus. Only developing countries in each region are included. *Source*: World Bank World Development Indicators, February 2019.

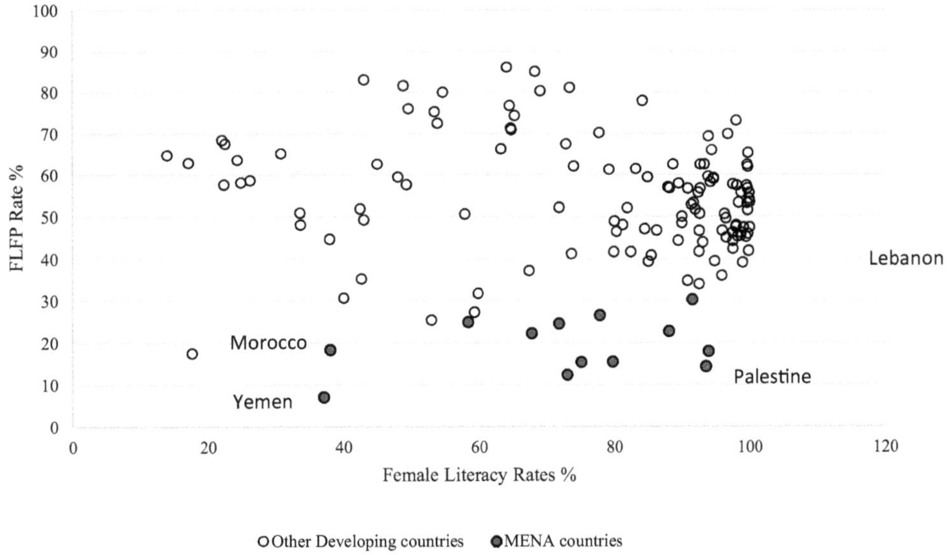

Figure 6.2 Female labour force participation rates against educational attainments in MENA countries and other developing countries (2010–18 averages). *Notes*: Adult literacy rates relate to women in age groups of 15 years and above. The MENA countries shown in the graph are Algeria, Egypt, Iran, Iraq, Jordan, Lebanon, Libya, Morocco, Palestine, Syria, Tunisia, Turkey, and Yemen. *Source*: World Bank World Development Indicators, February 2019.

Let's begin with why attention to female economic participation matters. Feminist economists and sociologists have long argued that women's economic participation and income control – and especially access to remunerative work in the formal sector of the economy – are key to their equality and empowerment. Employment and income-earning provide women with voice, agency, and resources to make decisions within the household and community, join

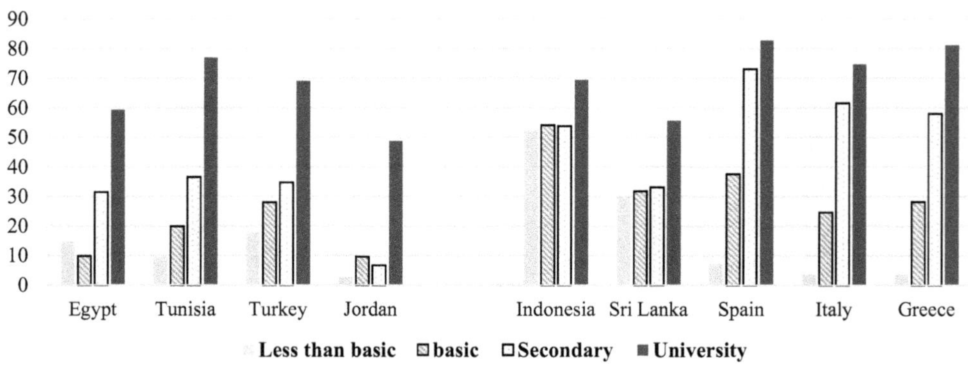

Figure 6.3 Female labour force participation rates by education levels, 25+ (2016). *Source*: International Labour Office, Geneva, ILOSTAT, 2018.

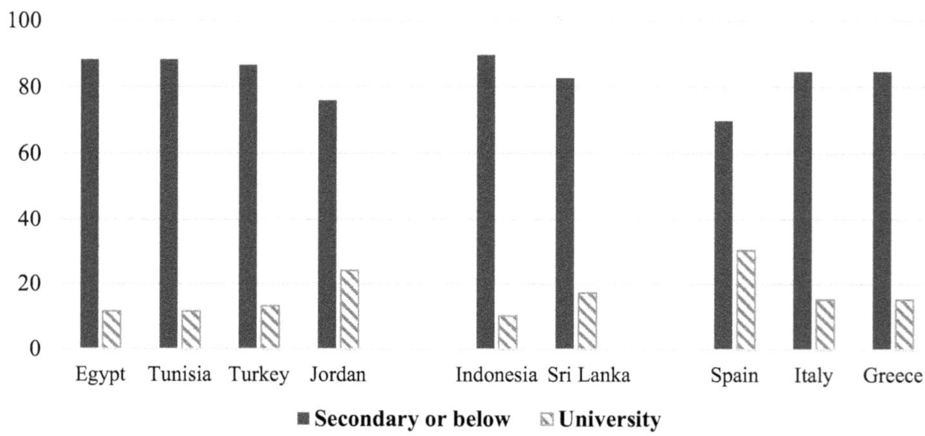

Figure 6.4 Female population by education levels, 25+ (2016). *Source*: International Labour Office, Geneva, ILOSTAT, 2018.

associations and unions, avoid domestic violence or leave an abusive domicile, join political parties and run for office, and contribute to overall economic growth and development. Employed women tend to have greater control over decision-making within the family; households also benefit when women control income and spending, and the well-being of children is increasingly linked to female education and income (Blumberg, 1984, 1989, 1995; Chafetz, 1990; Moghadam, 1998; World Bank, 2012, 2014).

Women's employment has other benefits. Research shows that women's participation in productive labour has been the entrée to their participation in political society; FLFP correlates with women's parliamentary representation (Walby, 2009), which in turn leads to women's 'interest legislation'. Studies have found positive correlations between women's economic participation and their political rights and representation (Besamusca et al., 2015; Iversen and Rosenbluth, 2008;). Wyndow et al. (2013) find that empowering women through education and employment may have a causal effect on democratic development by raising the benefits of political participation and expanding the broad base of support for democracy. Walby (2009) has argued that increased female employment could raise the likelihood of support for social democracy, echoing Iversen and Rosenbluth (2006: 17) in their analysis of OECD countries: 'paid employment makes women more "left-leaning"'. Conversely, studies have found that non-employed women are less likely to hold egalitarian or emancipatory attitudes and more likely to support fundamentalist movements or ideologies (Blaydes and Linzer, 2008; Iversen and Rosenbluth, 2006, 2008). Turkish scholars have found a greater propensity for homemakers to vote conservative and specifically for the ruling party AKP (Bozkurt, 2013; Elveren, 2018; Ilkkaracan, 2012, 2017). Thus, as more women seek employment and as more find their way into parliament and other decision-making and professional careers, it is believed that the attitudes of the wider society could change in a more egalitarian direction.

It is therefore not surprising that enhancing and improving women's gainful employment has become a mantra within mainstream international policy circles and agencies. The World Bank, the IMF, the McKinsey Global Institute, and other such entities offer economic arguments or a 'business case' for women's economic participation and empowerment, arguing that investing in women's education and especially employment is integral to building the national human resource and tax base and increasing national income and growth (Revenga and Shetty, 2012; World Bank, 2012; see also Chamlou and Karshenas, 2016).[1] They also draw attention to productivity and growth losses due to women's exclusion from paid labour. In a 2012 report, the United Nations Economic and Social Commission for Asia and the Pacific (which includes Iran), estimated that the Asia-Pacific region lost $42–47 billion annually due to women's limited access to employment, compared to $16–30 billion lost per year due to inequality in education (UN-ESCAP, 2012: 103). According to World Bank President Jim Yong Kim, women's low economic participation rates created income losses of 27 per cent in the Middle East and North Africa (cited in Cuberes and Teignier, 2012). Estimates by Karshenas et al. (2016) indicate that on average for each country in MENA, there was a net GDP loss of about 32 per cent during the 1980–2010 period, due to low female labour force participation rates.

There has been much discussion in development literature and international policy circles on women's entrepreneurship as a way out of poverty as well as a pathway to their economic empowerment (Atlan-Okay, 2014; Yetim, 2008). A distinction is made between subsistence micro-enterprises and productive businesses, while acknowledging that women's difficulty in obtaining credit, loans, and training is further complicated by the absence of a transparent and accessible legal and regulatory environment, and business and industry networks. Over the years, many programmes have been initiated across MENA countries to support women's entrepreneurship, but women entrepreneurs are concentrated in services, particularly retail, and their activities are less diversified and less capital-intensive than those of men (CAWTAR, 2007; Chamlou and Karshenas, 2016). The focus on economic gains through women's entrepreneurship and other forms of economic participation, however, does not seem to have made much difference in the MENA region. Thus, the puzzle and the problem remain in this region.

In the sections that follow, we survey the literature on women and work in MENA, with a focus on explanations for the low rates of FLFP and employment. We offer three categories of explanation that appear in the literature:

a) 'culturalist' arguments that put the spotlight on conservative cultural norms and the influence of religion and religiosity;
b) economic arguments based on supply- and demand-side factors; and
c) institutionalist arguments that focus on institutional barriers and supports.

We end with suggestions for future research.

6.2 Culturalist arguments

There is a long history of culturalist arguments about MENA women's status in general and low FLFP rates in particular (see, e.g., Youssef, 1971; Clark et al., 1991). Such a perspective fell out of favour for a while, but with the growing popularity and use of the World Values Survey and the Arab Barometer, a new wave of empirical studies has proliferated that emphasises cultural norms. Many of the second-generation 'culturalist' studies hold that patriarchal values dominate in Muslim-majority countries and especially in Arab societies (Alexander and Welzel, 2011; Donno and Russett, 2004; Fish, 2002; Inglehart and Norris, 2013; Lussier and Fish, 2016). Hayo and Caris (2013) and Diwan and Vartanova (2017) agree and show that measures of patriarchal culture are negatively correlated with FLFP. Other research reveals that religious women enter the labour market less than non-religious women (Besamusca et al., 2015; Dildar, 2015: Pastore and Tenaglia, 2013: 9) and that women in Muslim-majority MENA countries (especially Arab countries) and Muslim communities in Europe and the US are less represented in the labour force, compared with women from other religions (Korotayev et al., 2015; Pastore and Tenaglia, 2013; Read, 2004). The Pew Research Center (2016) has found that women who participate in the labour force tend to show lower levels of religious commitment than women who do not work outside the home for pay.[2]

Much of the debate within, and innovations of, the second-generation culturalist literature has centred around constructing appropriate measures of cultural attributes based on value surveys. Studies show that subjective measures of cultural attributes, such as religiosity or conservative belief systems (variables constructed from the various subjective questions in value surveys), whether at the individual or overall societal level, are correlated with FLFP. This contrasts with some of the older culturalist literature where culture was sometimes reduced to specific religions, through nominal overgeneralisations about Islam, Hinduism, Catholicism, and so on. Surveys find that attitudes toward women, work, and family remain conservative in many countries, leading to the continued association of women with family roles or to discriminatory practices within enterprises. Even in Switzerland, and despite the 1981 equal-rights constitutional amendment, a study found that gender pay gaps within firms correlated with discriminatory social attitudes (Janssen et al., 2016).

In their analysis of six MENA countries, Spierings et al. (2010) focused on economic need, job opportunities, and values, and found that the presence of traditional values was equally salient in explaining low FLFP.[3] Using individual-level data, Chamlou et al. (2016) show that conservative attitudes about gender deter women's employment in Cairo, Amman, and Sana'a. Through data on patriarchal norms and religiosity from Turkey's 2008 Demographic and Health Survey, Dildar (2015) found that women who had 'internalized patriarchal gender norms' and were more religious had a lower probability of joining the work force. In their study of Egypt, Nazier and Ramdan (2018: 145) find that in patriarchal societies, 'non-economic factors' play a significant role in labour division both inside and outside the home in these countries, and that social norms linking women to the home need to be targeted. In addressing the problem and puzzle of low FLFP, Soltani (2017) constructs a multi-dimensional patriarchy index and finds that the MENA region, and the oil-dependent Muslim-majority economies in particular, have the most entrenched levels of patriarchy, which in turn reduce women's economic participation. A conjoint survey experiment on earned income applied to Jordan finds that while higher wages would make a job more desirable, mixed-sex workspaces remain a strong deterrent (Barnett, Jamal, Monroe, 2020).

In writing about the constraints faced by Israeli-Palestinian women in both an 'unwelcoming Jewish-dominated economy' and the enclave Palestinian labour market, anthropologist Sa'ar

(2016) argues for a 'non-culturalist cultural analysis' that combines structure and social norms. Noting that Palestinian women 'are tied to their communities by poor public transportation and insufficient childcare facilities', she adds that

> jobs perceived as right for women – part-time, close-to-home, clerical jobs – are rare and poorly paid. Women, particularly those employed in the Palestinian private sector, report precarious employment, including salaries lower than the sum written on their pay slips, harassment, overtime without pay, and arbitrary redundancies. (Sa'ar, 2016: 57)

What is encouraging is that in some cases, attitudes and values have been evolving. Reviewing World Values Survey results for Morocco, Benstead (2016) reports that men who hold egalitarian values tend to be married to employed wives. Reviewing 2011 survey results for Algeria, Ennaji (2018) finds some egalitarian attitudes toward women, work, and political representation:

> An Arab Barometer poll carried out in 2011 revealed that the majority of respondents, 55.7%, said that they were against the election of a woman as head of state or prime minister, while 41.4% did not mind that a woman could hold such high posts. Fully 54.5% of women agreed or strongly agreed. Over a third of judges in Algeria are women. Concerning married women and work, the majority of all respondents were in favor.

And yet the 2016 survey results (Arab Barometer Wave IV) found more conservative attitudes, with just 36 per cent of Algerian respondents agreeing or strongly agreeing that a woman can become president or prime minister and that a married woman can work outside the home if she wished, although once again, women's agreement on both questions was higher. In 2016, Algerian women's labour force participation rate was just 16.6 per cent (Lassassi and Tansel, 2020: 8).

The correspondence between objective human action such as labour force participation and subjective value systems through which individuals and societies perceive and justify such action has not been in dispute. The main criticism of the culturalist position has been its inability to explain the varied transformation experiences during the 20th century across different countries that started from similar patriarchal norms and FLFP rates. That is, why did FLFP rates and subjective norms regarding female labour change in some countries, while in others such transformation did not take place (Karshenas, 1997)? Low FLFP may very well be linked to patriarchal attitudes, values, and norms, as Spierings (2014) and others have argued. But this begs the question of why such conservative attitudes and values persist. In addressing this question, a much broader set of variables related to economic development and structural change, as well as socio-economic institutions and policies, have been discussed in the literature.

In theory, the economic environment is expected to play an important role – with influences from both the supply and demand sides and links with the prevailing labour market institutions and wage-setting procedures. In addition, conservative cultural norms may be reinforced by certain formal institutions codified in law (such as family laws) or by the absence of support structures for working mothers (such as statutory paid maternity leave and quality and affordable crèches and pre-school facilities) – which in turn may prevent women's labour force attachment. The following two sections provide an overview of the literature with regard to those issues.

6.3 Economic explanations: labour supply and demand

The economic theories of FLFP were developed to explain the lack of women's labour market participation in the early decades of the 20th century, followed by the rapid increase in married women's labour market participation rates in industrialised countries after the mid-20th century. The standard theory is based on changes in gender-based comparative advantages in home production versus market-based work (Becker, 1981). Increased productivity and wages in advanced capitalist economies during the 20th century, it is argued, increased the opportunity cost of time allocated by women to home production, thus encouraging women to divert their time increasingly to market-based activities. Concomitantly, the substitution of home production with purchased goods and greater engagement of women in labour markets helped reduce fertility. Where fertility declined, accompanied by exogenous factors such as improved health and falling mortality, women's labour force participation intensified. With the gradual increase in female labour market participation, women began to invest in human capital more congruent with market type activities, which in turn narrowed the gender gap in comparative advantages between home production and labour market engagement. In this theory there is a close association between female labour force participation, female educational attainment, and fertility. It is in this context that the stylised facts regarding the MENA region, summarised at the start of this chapter, pose a puzzle.

In this theory there are complex interactions between supply-side and demand-side factors. The empirical literature in the MENA region has been mainly focused on the supply-side interactions. Even at that level, identification of the interactions between female labour supply, fertility, and human capital indicators such as educational attainment and experience remains a daunting task. Still, establishing these interactions forms the basic architecture of the various empirical models used in the MENA literature. Depending on the focus of analysis, various authors add other variables to this basic model to test certain hypotheses. For example, the MENA literature is not usually focused on the labour supply of married women; rather it includes the whole of the female working-age population, with marital status included as an additional variable in the model. Various culturalist studies reviewed in the previous section also test the influence of cultural variables by using this basic architecture and adding the cultural variables to the human capital and fertility variables. In this section we focus on the ways that the basic economic model can be used to shed light on the female labour force participation puzzle in the MENA region.

There is a proliferation of supply-side models using micro-survey data covering individual country case studies or groups of countries. Here we focus on the salient findings of this literature, supported by most of the available studies, with regard to the impact of fertility and especially human capital in MENA women's labour force participation.

In most studies the fertility rate as measured by the number of young children has a statistically significant relationship with FLFP (see, e.g., Assaad and Zouari, 2003 for Morocco; Dayıoğlu and Kirdar, 2010 on Turkey; Spierings and Smits, 2007 for Egypt, Jordan, Morocco, Syria, and Tunisia; on Iran see Salehi-Isfahani, 2001; Esfahani and Shajari, 2012). However, since the decisions to participate in the labour force, get married, and have children are joint decisions, the correlation between the number of young children and non-participation does not necessarily imply a one-way causality from fertility to labour force participation. In a recent study Majbouri (2018) shows that once the problem of the endogeneity of fertility is accounted for there remains no evidence of direct effect of fertility on FLFP in four Arab countries: Egypt, Jordan, Morocco, and Tunisia. It appears that in all the countries in the region, university-educated women working in public sectors do not change their labour market participation status upon marriage or child birth. But women with lower educational attainments and those working in the private sector do (see, e.g., Assaad et al., 2017; Spierings et al., 2010).

As to the human capital effect, all the studies using micro-survey data for various countries find a significant effect of women's education on female labour force participation. This may appear contradictory to the observed fact of rising female educational attainment combined with stagnant and in some cases declining FLFP in the MENA region. Various economic explanations have been put forward in the literature to explain this apparent puzzle. The World Bank (2019) amongst others suggests that the educational system does not provide women with the skills necessary to enhance their productivity in market-based activities, as women are mainly enrolled in the so-called 'soft subjects'. This however does not tally with the fact that education has a significant effect on women's labour force participation. Furthermore, studies have found that returns to education are much higher amongst women than men in most MENA countries (e.g., Tansel and Daoud, 2016). A UN report shows that women's enrolments in the sciences in Morocco, Oman, and Tunisia exceed those for women in Latin America, Europe, and the US (UNWomen, 2015: 263).

A closer inspection of micro-studies on the role of education in female labour market participation in the MENA region indicates that in all countries post-secondary education and particularly tertiary education significantly increases the probability of FLFP, while educational attainments at or below secondary level do not significantly increase the probability of participation. This is in fact the marginal counterpart of one of the stylised facts mentioned at the beginning of this chapter, which is that low female labour force participation in the MENA region is largely confined to women with secondary schooling or less. The implication of these estimation results is the absurd conclusion that only when all women attain tertiary education in MENA countries can the FLFP rates reach the normal levels as in other countries in East Asia or Latin America. The high unemployment rates amongst the university-educated women in the MENA countries show the impracticality of this scenario, and it could indeed be a negative signal for women to stop seeking tertiary education. This hypothetical disincentive could in turn lead to a growing mass of working-age women with secondary schooling only or even less, and low labour force participation rates – resulting in a flattening of the participation curve in relation to educational attainments as observed in recent studies (see, e.g., Assaad et al., 2020). The upshot of all the econometric studies estimating female participation functions finally boils down to the question of why women with secondary schooling or less – who we can assume to be from working-class or lower-income households – have such low labour force participation rates. Addressing this issue more directly would explain the low levels and adverse trends of female participation rates.

Various economic arguments, from both supply and demand sides, have been put forward to explain this phenomenon in the literature. Moghadam (1993, 1998) proposed that the regional oil economy suppressed the demand for female labour and reinforced the 'patriarchal gender contract' (see also Ross, 2008). Karshenas (1997) and Karshenas and Moghadam (2001) pointed to fast rates of urbanisation in a period where resource endowments could enable high urban wages and hence the maintenance of patriarchal norms and one-breadwinner families in urban economies. Ilkkaracan (2012) confirms this for Turkey. Another component of this process was the industrialisation strategies and government provision of household subsidies. Kocabicak (2018) extends this line of argument by linking forms of agricultural production and women's exclusion from landownership to low levels of FLFP.

A recent demand-side hypothesis (Assaad et al., 2020) posits that the inability of the private sector to create appropriate jobs for women, combined with the contraction of good public sector employment, keeps FLFP low and female employment limited. Presumably, it also keeps female unemployment high. Some of such demand-side factors may arise from the effect of social norms on employers' attitudes in employing women, but unsuitable work conditions in small workshops and lack of flexibility in working hours or long commutes and unsafe modes of transport can be additional demand-side factors (Assaad and Arntz, 2005).

What has been missing in the various demand- and supply-side arguments in the literature so far is the absence of formal models to integrate the supply- and demand-side factors by introducing wage-setting processes. After all, in economic theory wages are supposed to equilibrate the supply and demand for labour. Could wage-setting institutions and wage discrimination play a role in FLFP? Existing studies of wage discrimination in the MENA region find that there appears to be no gender-based wage discrimination in the public sector, but there is evidence of large wage discrimination in the private sector (Assaad, 1996; Said 2003, 2014). A recent study on wage discrimination along the educational divide in Jordan finds that while there appears to be no wage discrimination against women at post-secondary educational levels, there is an immense gap in wages of women with secondary schooling and less when compared to men with the same observed characteristics (Boustati, 2019). Such significant wage discrimination in the case of working-class women needs to be substantiated in the case of other MENA countries, and explained. As highlighted in the introductory section of this article, the main deficit in female labour force participation in MENA countries is due to low participation of this lower educated category. Gender wage differentials are also likely to play a key role in bringing together the supply- and demand-side models in the existing literature.

Finally, there is the issue of the lack of institutional supports for working women or policies and structures to encourage maternal employment, which is suggested in a number of studies. This absence, along with other institutional impediments, is discussed in the section that follows.

6.4 Institutionalist explanations: barriers and supports

Women's employment by itself does not emancipate women, especially if the jobs do not pull women and their households out of poverty or provide what the ILO calls 'decent work', which includes the enjoyment of a work–family balance.[4] As feminist economists have noted, women's involvement in the work force requires institutional supports, notably an adequate social infrastructure (Elson, 1999; Razavi, 2007). Governments that have been responsive to this reality have adopted measures such as ILO Convention 183 on maternity protection, the UN's Convention on the Elimination of All Forms of Discrimination against Women (CEDAW), and the Beijing Declaration and Platform for Action, as well as many domestic legislations prohibiting employment discrimination, sexual harassment, and domestic violence. Labour codes may stipulate the presence of workplace crèches above a certain number of female employees. However, enforcement and monitoring are absent in many countries, labour codes may pertain only to the public sector and the largest private enterprises, and paid maternity leave may devolve on the employer only. Many labour laws in the region still discriminate against women, prohibiting them from working in certain industries or partaking in night work. In instances where discriminatory laws have been amended, weak implementation has impeded tangible progress.

Whether by law or custom, women's unequal inheritance and lack of property ownership, especially of land, has profound implications for labour force participation, employment, and entrepreneurship. Kocabicak (2018) maintains that uneven gender relations in agriculture have contributed to the gender gap in economic well-being, social status, and empowerment. In turn, this has knock-on effects for the economy and society. In addressing the "oil curse" hypothesis, Alice Kang (2009) raises the importance of gender quotas as institutional enablers for wider female participation; Liou and Musgrave (2016) underscore "anti-social policies" as obstacles.

Family laws that place women under the supervision of male kin may constitute a special type of impediment to enhanced female labour force participation. Feminist scholars have long examined the discriminatory nature of family laws in MENA (Joseph and contributors, 2000; Welchman, 2004) but Moghadam (2006) has drawn attention to how such laws may implicitly or explicitly inhibit women's access to paid employment (see also Gonzales et al., 2015). Family laws – also known as personal status laws – place female kin in a subordinate position within the family, emphasise men's breadwinning and women's family roles, establish unequal inheritance, grant men easy access to divorce, and codify male guardianship over women. The practice of unequal inheritance leaves women at a disadvantage when they seek to set up a small business, given that family wealth is often the basis of start-up capital. Male guardianship requires a woman to obtain the permission of father, husband, brother, or other male kin to work or travel. Related cultural practices, such as the *mahr* (dower), may reinforce the traditional sexual division of labour and women's marital and family roles. In some cases, women are barred from certain fields of study or professions (notably that of judge), cannot take substantive part in the political process, or are denied leadership roles. Women may have unequal or limited access to resources and assets, including landownership. This reality may be a historical legacy, the result of cultural practices (e.g., women transferring their inheritance to brothers) or the result of codified laws.

Such practices, norms, and laws often are justified as religiously mandated or culturally embedded. In truth, they are characteristic of a patriarchal social order (Ennaji, 2011; Moghadam, 2003; Sa'ar, 2016; Soltani, 2017; Walby, 1990) in that they reinforce notions of men's and women's absolute 'difference' and of their 'complementary roles'. Such norms and laws are doubtlessly experienced differently by women of different social classes, although a recent survey of Egypt, Lebanon, Morocco, and Palestine sponsored by Promundo and UN Women (El Feki et al., 2017) found that two-thirds to more than three-quarters of men support the notion that a woman's most important role is to care for the household. Formal institutions such as family law, therefore, may reinforce conservative social norms.

In Algeria, the women's organisations continue to protest Article 11 of the 1984 family law, which stipulates that the woman conclude her marriage contract in the presence of her *wali*, or guardian, as witness (Ennaji, 2018). The practice of guardianship continues to place Algerian women in a subordinate role in the family – even though one-third of judges and members of parliament are women. However, as noted, only about 17 per cent of Algeria's measured labour force is female.

Family law and conservative social norms, including women's exclusive responsibility for childcare, household, and elder care, make it difficult for those women who *are* employed to take part in worker protest actions. Sara Ababneh (2016) shows how Jordanian women day workers – a feature of Jordan's 'flexible' labour market – were able to join, and in some ways lead, a campaign in 2010–11 to improve working conditions, but this was possible because of the horizontal and informal nature of the campaign, and because it entailed the cooperation of family members. A more structured and formal worker organisation, notably a trade union, might have difficulty providing women workers with leadership opportunities because of the entrenched nature of the household sexual division of labour.

Even where a formal institution is reformed, a cultural lag may take time to overcome. Morocco's much-lauded family law reform of 2004 and its 2011 constitution have vastly improved women's legal status, but Fatima Sadiqi (2018) reports that women's economic empowerment has not improved, especially for working-class, poor, and rural women, along with female-headed households. Social norms, she notes, appear to constitute 'the biggest hurdle in the implementation of the Moudawana' (Morocco's family law). Sadiqi explains that although some changes were made to the inheritance law, rural women often give up their already unequal share to male relatives. In the countryside, she adds, women still face difficulty in securing loans because they often do not have bank accounts or assets in their names. Sadiqi's observations align with studies that find a cultural lag between legal reform on the one hand, and normative and behavioural changes on the other (Seguino, 2007). On the positive side, Morocco very recently opened to women the profession of *adoul* – marriage officers under Muslim law, authorised to write legal acts, for example of marriage or inheritance. Could women's access to a previously male-dominated occupation help change social norms?

6.4.1 Violence against women

Women's employment may be impeded in another way. Violence against women is pervasive, cross-cultural, and trans-historical, but discriminatory practices, laws, and norms may contribute to the persistence of domestic violence, 'honour crimes', street harassment, and workplace sexual harassment (Arfaoui and Moghadam, 2016; Chaudhry, 2016; Ennaji, 2011; Ennaji and Sadiqi, 2011; Moghadam, 2003) – all of which may deter women from seeking work or staying in jobs. The Promundo/UNWomen survey found that 10–45 per cent of ever-married men in the four countries surveyed reported having used physical violence against a female partner. The findings for Egypt are especially disturbing:

> Support for female genital mutilation is high. Some 70 per cent of men, and more than half of women, approve of the practice. ... Men and women alike reported high rates of men's use of violence against women. ... More than 70 per cent of men and women said they believe that wives should tolerate violence to keep the family together. Street sexual harassment is commonly perpetrated by men and frequently experienced by urban women. More than 60 per cent of men reported ever having sexually harassed a woman or girl, and a similar proportion of women reported such unwanted attentions. More women than men blame the victim for having been harassed.
>
> *(El Feki et al., 2017, Executive Summary: 14)*

Whether at home, on the streets, or at workplaces, violence against women is a form of patriarchal control that not only punishes women for being women but also may prevent them from joining the labour force, remaining employed, or even leaving the house. The absence of women's physical security prevents their agency, occupational choices, and social mobility. Stronger laws, enforcement, and prosecutions are needed to create an institutional environment more conducive to women's physical security and thus their increased labour force participation.

6.4.2 Supports for maternal employment

The absence or presence of institutional supports for working mothers has been identified as a key driver of FLFP. In his study of OECD countries, Thévenon (2013) finds that women's employment rates respond to changes in tax rates and leave policies, but he underscores the significance of the provision of formal childcare services to working parents with children under age three. Besamusca et al. (2015) studied families and gender ideologies in 117 countries and found that women are more likely to participate economically when paid maternity leave schemes exist and enrolment in pre-primary education is higher. In MENA, school starts at age six and public pre-school facilities are rare. In interviews conducted in 1996, Moghadam found that an Egyptian human-resources manager blamed women workers for taking too many maternity leaves, while Jordanian women employees stressed the need for institutionalised and affordable 'baby care' (Moghadam, 1998: 111, 137). Ilkkaracan (2012) stresses the lack of work–family reconciliation measures as an important part of the explanation for low FLFP in Turkey (and elsewhere). Although all MENA countries require some degree of paid maternity leave, it remains the financial responsibility of the employer and in some countries is of very short duration. This may also explain the observed wage discrimination against women in the private sector in MENA countries (see, for instance, Moaven Razavi and Habibi, 2014; Said, 2014, 2015). Moreover, paternity leave hardly exists in the region.

Do conservative family laws correlate with the absence of statutory paid maternity leave, paternity leave, and a network of subsidised, good-quality childcare and pre-school facilities? If so, they also may be preventing female labour market attachment, especially on the part of women from working-class and low-income households. And they reinforce conservative social norms.[5]

6.5 Conclusions and directions for future research

The above discussion has shown that the causes of low FLFP rates in MENA could not be found in a single variable but can be found – as a recent research project has shown – in a broader explanatory framework taking into account the macroeconomic environment, labour market institutions and wage-setting processes, employer recruitment practices and biases, and social institutions.[6] More research is needed into the interaction of those factors, how they operate to form a kind of vicious cycle in MENA, and how it may be possible to turn that cycle into a virtuous one. Data and information gaps too need to be filled. For example, what do we know about the role of unions and the women's sections within them? How do wage-setting processes operate to incentivise female supply and demand? Is there widespread demand for paid maternity leave of a decent duration, along with affordable childcare, and if so, could this help strengthen women's labour force participation, especially among lower-middle-class, working-class, and poor women? Would the expansion of pre-school facilities improve women's employment prospects? Could the introduction of paid leave for fathers help change the household division of labour? Enterprise and institutional surveys, along with in-depth interviews with employers, policy-makers, union officials, and advocates for women's economic participation and rights, could shed light on these complex and interlinked questions and ultimately help resolve the problem and puzzle of low FLFP in MENA.

Notes

1 See also *The Economist*, 'Forget China, India and the Internet: Economic Growth is Driven by Women' (April 5, 2006: 16), which analysed the strongest factors promoting global GDP growth from 1985 to 2005.

2 Certain international organisations now include data and information on social norms. See, for example, www.oecd-ilibrary.org/development/atlas-of-gender-and-development_9789264077478-en; and ESRC/DFiD, available at http://www.theimpactinitiative.net/resources/key-issues-guide-women-work-understanding-social-norms-restrict-womens-access-paid-work.

3 See also Gündüz-Hoşgör and Smits (2008) on the role of 'the strong patriarchal ideology' on Turkey's married women's labour force participation, and Göksel (2013) on the effects of conservatism on female employment in urban areas.

4 See http://www.ilo.org/global/topics/decent-work/lang--en/index.htm.

5 In recent years, international organisations have constructed databases and indices of gender inequality that include social institutions. See the OECD's SIGI index (available at https://data.oecd.org/inequality/social-institutions-and-gender.htm; the World Bank's *Women, Business, and the Law* website (http://wbl.worldbank.org/); IMF paper on legal rights and women's LFP (http://www.imf.org/external/pubs/ft/sdn/2015/sdn1502.pdf).

6 This was confirmed by studies conducted under 'Female Employment and Dynamics of Inequality (FEDI) Network' focused on the Middle East, North Africa, and South Asia, PI Massoud Karshenas, funded by ESRC/GCRF, SOAS, University of London, January 2017-September 2018; see: https://www.soas.ac.uk/fedi/network-members/.

References

Ababneh, Sara (2016). "Troubling the Political: Women in the Jordanian Day-Waged Labor Movement." *International Journal of Middle East Studies*, 48: 87–112.

Alexander, Amy C. and Christian Welzel (2011). "Islam and Patriarchy: How Robust is Muslim Support for Patriarchal Values?" *International Review of Sociology*, 21: 249–276.

Altan-Okay, Ozlem (2014). "Entrepreneurial Subjectivities and Gendered Complexities: Vignettes from Neo-Liberal Citizenship in Turkey." *Feminist Economics*, 20 (2): 235–259.

Arfaoui, Khedija and Valentine M. Moghadam (2016). "Violence against Women and Tunisian Feminism: Advocacy, Policy, and Politics in an Arab Context." *Current Sociology*, 64 (4): 637–653.

Assaad, Ragui (1996). "'Do Workers Pay for Social Protection? An Analysis of Wage Differentials in the Egyptian Labour Market." ERF Working Paper Series No. 610, Economic Research Forum, Cairo, Egypt.

Assaad, Ragui and M. Arntz (2005). "Constrained Geographical Mobility and Gendered Labor Market Outcomes Under Structural Adjustment: Evidence from Egypt." *World Development*, 33 (3): 431–454.

Assaad, R. and S. Zouari (2003). "Estimating the Impact of Marriage and Fertility on Female Labour Force Participation When Decisions Are Interrelated: Evidence from Urban Morocco." *Topics in Middle Eastern and North African Economies*, vol. 5 (September), *http://www.luc.edu/publications/academic/*

Assaad, R., C. Krafft and I. Selwaness (2017). "The Impact of Marriage on Women's Employment in the Middle East and North Africa." ERF Working Paper Series No. 1086, Economic Research Forum, Cairo, Egypt.

Assaad, R., Rana Hendy, Moundir Lassassi and Shaimaa Yassin (2020). "Explaining the MENA Paradox." *Demographic Research,* 43 (July–December): 817–850. doi: 10.4054/DemRes.2020.43.28

Barnett, Caroline, Amaney Jamal and Steve Monroe (2020). "Earned Income and Women's Segmented Empowerment: Experimental Evidence from Jordan." *American Journal of Political Science* (October). doi: 10.1111/ajps.12561

Becker, Gary (1981). *A Treatise on the Family*. Cambridge, MA: Harvard University Press.

Benstead, Lindsey (2016). "Explaining Egalitarian Attitudes: The Role of Interests and Exposure." In Marwa Shalaby and Valentine M. Moghadam (eds.), *Women's Empowerment after the Arab Spring*. London: Palgrave Macmillan: 119–146.

Besamusca, J., K. Tijdens, M. Keune and S. Steinmetz (2015). "Working Women Worldwide: Age Effects in Female Labor Force Participation in 117 Countries." *World Development*, 74: 123–141.

Blaydes, Lisa and Drew Linzer (2008). "The Political Economy of Women's Support for Fundamentalist Islam." *World Politics*, 4: 576–609.

Blumberg, Rae Lesser. (1984). "A General Theory of Gender Stratification." *Sociological Theory*, 2: 23–101.

Blumberg, Rae Lesser (1989). *Making the Case for the Gender Variable*. Washington, DC: USAID.

Blumberg, Rae Lesser (1995). "Introduction: Engendering Wealth and Well-Being in an Era of Economic Transformation." In Blumberg et al. (eds.), *Engendering Wealth and Well-Being: Empowerment for Global Change*. Boulder CO: Westview Press: 1–14

Boustati, Alma (2019). *An Economic Analysis of Female Labour Force Participation in Jordan*. PhD dissertation, Department of Economics, SOAS University of London, September.

Bozkurt, U. (2013). "Neoliberalism with a Human Face: Making Sense of the Justice and Development Party's Neoliberal Populism in Turkey." *Science & Society*, 77(3): 372–396.

CAWTAR (2007). *Women Entrepreneurs in the Middle East: Characteristics, Contributions and Challenges*. Tunis: CAWTAR and International Finance Corporation.

Chafetz, Janet Saltzman (1990). *Gender Equality: An Integrated Theory of Stability and Change*. Thousand Oaks CA: SAGE.

Chamlou, Nadereh and Massoud Karshenas, (eds.) (2016). *Women, Work, and Welfare in the Middle East and North Africa*. London: Imperial College Press.

Chamlou, Nadereh, Silvia Muzi and Hanane Ahmed (2016). "The Determinants of Female Labour Force Participation in the Middle East and North Africa Region: The Role of Education and Social Norms in Amman, Cairo, and Sana'a." In Chamlou and Karshenas (eds.), *Women, Work, and Welfare in the Middle East and North Africa*. London: Imperial College Press: 323–382.

Chaudhry, Ayesha S. (2016). "Interrogating the 'Sharia' Excuse: Religious Reasoning, International Law, and the Struggle for Gender Equality in the Middle East." In Marwa Shalaby and V.M. Moghadam (eds.), *Empowering Women after the Arab Spring*. London: Palgrave Macmillan: 21–44.

Clark, Roger, Thomas W. Ramsbey and Emily Stier Adler (1991). "Culture, Gender, and Labor Force Participation: A Cross-National Study." *Gender & Society*, 5 (1): 47–66.

Cuberes, David and Marc Teignier (2012). "Gender Gaps in the Labour Market and Aggregate Productivity." University of Sheffield Economic Research Papers, available at: http://www.shef.ac.uk/economics/research/serps/articles/2012_017.html.

Dayıoğlu, Meltem and Murat G. Kirdar (2010). "Determinants of and Trends in Labor Force Participation of Women in Turkey." Working Paper No. 5. Ankara: State Planning Organization of the Republic of Turkey and the World Bank.

Dildar, Yasemen (2015). "Patriarchal Norms, Religion, and Female Labor Supply: Evidence from Turkey." *World Development*, 76: 40–61.

Diwan, Ishac and Irina Vartanova (2017). "The Effect of Patriarchal Culture on Women's Labor Force Participation." ERF working Paper No. 1101, June.

Donno, Daniela and Bruce Russett.(2004). "Islam, Authoritarianism, and Female Empowerment: What are the Linkages?" *World Politics*, 56 (July): 582–607.

El Feki, S., B. Heilman and G. Barker (eds.) (2017). *Understanding Masculinities: Results from the International Men and Gender Equality Survey (IMAGES) – Middle East and North Africa.* Cairo: UN Women and Promundo-US.

Elson, D. (1999). *Gender-Neutral, Gender-Blind, or Gender-Sensitive Budgets? Changing the Conceptual Framework to Include Women's Empowerment and the Economy of Care.* London: Commonwealth Secretariat, available at: https://gsdrc.org/document-library/gender-neutral-gender-blind-or-gender-sensitive-budgets/.

Elveren, Adem Y. (2018). "The Pious Predator State: The New Regime in Turkey." *Challenge*, 61 (1): 85–91.

Ennaji, Moha (2011). "Violence against Women in Morocco: Advances, Contentions, and Strategies to Combat it." In Moha Ennahi and Fatima Sadiqi (eds.), *Gender and Violence in the Middle East.* London: Routledge: 199–220.

Ennaji, Moha (2018). "Update on Women and Work in Algeria." Paper prepared for the ESRC/GCRF Workshop, London, May.

Ennaji, Moha and Fatima Sadiqi. (2011). "Introduction: Contextualizing Gender and Violence in the Middle East." In Moha Ennaji and Fatima Sadiqi (eds.), *Gender and Violence in the Middle East.* London: Routledge: 1–9.

Esfahani, Hadi and Shajari Parastoo (2012). "Gender, Education, Family Structure, and the Allocation of Labour in Iran." *Middle East Economic Development Journal*, December, 4 (2): 1250008-1–1250008-40.

Fish, Steven (2002). "Islam and Authoritarianism." *World Politics*, 55 (1): 4–37.

Göksel, İdil (2013). "Female Labor Force Participation in Turkey: The Role of Conservatism." *Women's Studies International Forum*, 41: 45–54.

Gonzales, Christian, Sonali Jain-Chandra, Kalpana Kochhar and Monique Newiak (2015). *Fair Play: More Equal Laws Boost Female Labor Force Participation.* Washington, DC: IMF Staff Working Note, February, available at: https://www.imf.org/external/pubs/ft/sdn/2015/sdn1502.pdf

Gündüz-Hoşgör, Ayşe and Jeroen Smits (2008). "Variation in Labor Market Participation of Married Women in Turkey." *Women s Studies International Forum*, 31 (2): 104–117.

Hayo, Bernd and Tobias Caris (2013). "Female Labour Force Participation in the MENA Region: The Role of Identity." *Review of Middle East Economics and Finance*, 9 (3): 271–292.

Ilkkaracan, Ipek (2012). "Why So Few Women in the Labor Market in Turkey?" *Feminist Economics*, 18 (1): 1–37.

Ilkkaracan, Ipek (2017). "The Economic Gender Gap and the Political Gender Gap: Implications for Path Dependency in Gender Inequalities and Sustainable Growth." Paper presented at the 26th Annual Conference of the IAFFE, Seoul, Korea, June 29–1 July.

ILO (2016). *Women at Work: Trends 2016.* Geneva: International Labour Office.

ILO (2018). *ILOSTAT.* Geneva: International Labour Office.

Inglehart, Ronald and Pippa Norris (2013). "The True Clash of Civilizations." *Foreign Policy*, March-April.

Iversen, Torben and Frances Rosenbluth (2006). "The Political Economy of Gender: Explaining Cross-National Variation in the Gender Division of Labor and the Gender Voting Gap." *American Journal of Political Science*, 50 (1): 1–19.

Iversen, Torben and Frances Rosenbluth (2008). "Work and Power: The Connection between Female Labor Force Participation and Female Political Representation." *Annual Review of Political Science*, 11: 479–495.

Janssen, Simon, Simone Tuor Sartore and Uschi Backes-Gellner (2016). "Discriminatory Social Attitudes and Varying Gender Pay Gaps within Firms." *ILR Review*, 69 (1): 253–279.

Joseph, Suad (ed.) (2000). *Gender and Citizenship in the Middle East.* Syracuse, NY: Syracuse University Press.

Kang, Alice (2009). "Studying Oil, Islam and Women as if Political Institutions Mattered." *Politics & Gender*, 5 (4): 560–568.

Karshenas, Massoud (1997). "Macroeconomic Policy, Structural Change, and Employment in the Middle East and North Africa." In Azizur Rahman Khan and M. Muqtada (eds.), *Overcoming Unemployment*. London: Macmillan: 320–396.

Karshenas, Massoud and Valentine M. Moghadam (2001). "Female Labor Force Participation and Economic Adjustment in the MENA Region." In Mine Cinar (ed.), *The Economics of Women and Work in the Middle East and North Africa*. Amsterdam: JAI: 93–116.

Karshenas, Massoud, Valentine M. Moghadam and Nadereh Chamlou (2016). "Women, Work and Welfare in the Middle East and North Africa: Introduction and Overview." In Nadereh Chamlou and Massoud Karshenas (eds.), *Women, Work and Welfare in the Middle East and North Africa: The Role of Socio-Demographics, Entrepreneurship, and Public Policies*. London: Imperial College Press: 1–30.

Kocabicak, Ece (2018). "What Role Does Agriculture Play in Reducing Female Paid Employment: The Case of Turkey." Paper prepared for the ESRC/GCRF workshop, London, May.

Korotayev, Andrey V., Leonid M. Issaev and Alisa R. Shishkina (2015). "Female Labor Force Participation Rate, Islam, and Arab Culture in Cross-Cultural Perspective." *Cross-Cultural Research*, 49 (1): 3–19.

Lassassi, Moundir and Aysit Tansel (2020). "Female Labor Force Participation in Five Selected Mensa Countries: an Age-Period-Cohort Analysis (Algeria, Egypt, Jordan, Palestine and Tunisia). MPRA Paper No. 103774 (October), available at: https://mpra.ub.uni-muenchen.de/103774/1/MPRA_paper_103774.pdf.

Liou, Yu-Ming and Paul Musgrave (2016). "Oil, Autocratic Survival, and the Gendered Resource Curse: When Inefficient Policy is Politically Expedient." *International Studies Quarterly*, 60 (3) (September): 440–456.

Lussier, Danielle N. and M. Steven Fish (2016). "Men, Muslims, and Attitudes toward Gender Inequality." *Politics and Religion*, 9 (1): 29–60.

Majbouri, Mahdi. 2018. "Fertility and the Puzzle of Female Employment in the Middle East." IZA DP No. 11322, February.

Moaven Razavi, Seyed and Nader Habibi (2014). "Decomposition of Gender Wage Differentials in Iran: An Empirical Study Based on Household Survey Data." *Journal of Developing Areas*, 48 (2): 185–204.

Moghadam, Valentine M. (1998). *Women, Work, and Economic Reform in the Middle East and North Africa*. Boulder, CO: Lynne Rienner Publishers.

Moghadam, Valentine M. (1993, 2003). *Modernizing Women: Gender and Social Change in the Middle East*. 1st and 2nd eds. Boulder, CO: Lynne Rienner Publishers.

Moghadam, Valentine M. (2006). "Maternalist Policies vs Economic Citizenship? Gendered Social Policy in Iran." In Shahra Razavi and Shireen Hassim (eds), *Gender and Social Policy in a Global Context: Uncovering the Gendered Structure of 'the Social'*. Basingstoke: Palgrave: 87–108.

Nazier, Hanan and Racha Ramadan. 2018. "Ever Married Women's Participation in Labor Market in Egypt: Constraints and Opportunities." *Middle East Development Journal*, 10 (1): 119–151.

Pastore, Francesco and Simona Tenaglia (2013). "Ora et non Labora? A Test of the Impact of Religion on Female Labor Supply." IZA Discussion Paper No. 7356, April.

Pew Research Center (2016). *The Gender Gap in Religion Around the World*, available at: http://www.pewforum.org/2016/03/22/the-gender-gap-in-religion-around-the-world/

Razavi, Shahra (2007). "The Political and Social Economy of Care in a Development Context: Conceptual Issues, Research Questions and Policy Options." Gender and Development Working Paper no. 3. Geneva: UNRISD.

Read, Jen'nan Ghazal (2004). "Cultural Influences on Immigrant Women's Labor Force Participation: The Arab-American Case." *International Migration Review*, 38 (1): 52–77.

Revenga, Ana and Sudhir Shetty (2012). "Empowering Women is Smart Economics." *Finance & Development*, March: 40–43, available at: http://www.imf.org/external/pubs/ft/fandd/2012/03/pdf/revenga.pdf

Ross, Michael (2008). "Oil, Islam, and Women." *American Political Science Review*, 102: 107–123.

Sa'ar, Amalia (2016). "The Gender Contract under Neoliberalism: Palestinian-Israeli Women's Labor Force Participation." *Feminist Economics*, 23 (1): 54–76.

Sadiqi, Fatima (2018). "Update on the Family Law, Women and Work in Morocco." Paper prepared for the ESRC/GCRF workshop, London, May.

Said, Mona (2003). "Distribution of Gender and Public Sector Pay Premia: Evidence from the Egyptian Organized Sector." SOAS Economics Department Working Paper No. 132, School of Oriental and African Studies, University of London.

Said, M. (2014). "Wage Formation and Earnings Inequality in the Jordanian Labor Market." In R. Assaad (ed.), *The Jordanian Labour Market in the New Millennium*. Oxford: Oxford University Press: 144–171.

Said, M. (2015). "Wages and Inequality in the Egyptian Labor Market in an Era of Financial Crisis and Revolution." In R. Assaad and C. Krafft (eds.), *The Egyptian Labor Market in an Era of Revolution*. Oxford: Oxford University Press: 52–69.

Salehi-Isfahani, Djavad (2001). "Fertility, Education, and Household Resources in Iran, 1987–1992." *Research in Middle East Economics*, 4, Wlsevier/JAI Press.

Seguino, Stephanie (2007). "Plus ça Change? Evidence on Global Trends in Gender Norms and Stereotypes." *Feminist Economics*, 13 (2): 211–232.

Soltani, Fariba (2017). *Women, Work, and Patriarchy in the Middle East and North Africa*. Cham: Palgrave Macmillan.

Spierings, Niels (2014). "The Influence of Patriarchal Norms, Institutions, and Household Structures on Women's Employment in 28 Muslim Countries." *Feminist Economics*, 20 (4): 87–112.

Spierings, Niels, Jeroen Smits and Mieke Verloo (2010). "Micro- and Macrolevel Determinants of Women's Employment in Six Arab Countries." *Journal of Marriage and Family*, 72 (5): 1391–1407.

Tansel, Aysit and Yousef Daoud (2016). "Returns to Education in Palestine and Turkey: A Comparative Analysis." In Chamlou and Karshenas (eds.), *Women, Work and Welfare in the Middle East and North Africa*. London: Imperial College Press: 33–56.

Thévenon, Olivier (2013). "Drivers of Female Labour Force Participation in the OECD." Social, Employment and Migration Working Paper No. 145. Paris: OECD.

UN-ESCAP(2012). *Economic and Social Survey of Asia and the Pacific: Surging Ahead in Uncertain Times*. New York: UN Economic and Social Commission for Asia-Pacific.

UN Women (2015). *Progress of the World's Women 2015–2016: Transforming Economies, Realizing Rights*. New York: United Nations.

Walby, Sylvia (1990). *Theorizing Patriarchy*. Oxford: Blackwell.

Walby, Sylvia (2009). *Globalization and Inequalities: Complexity and Contested Modernities*. London: SAGE.

Welchman, Lynne (ed.) (2004). *Women's Rights and Family Law: Perspectives on Reform*. London: Zed.

World Bank (2012). *World Development Report 2012: Gender Equality and Development*. Washington, DC: World Bank.

World Bank (2014). *Voice and Agency: Empowering Women and Girls for Shared Prosperity*. Washington, DC: World Bank.

World Bank (2019). *World Development Indicators, February 2019*. Washington, DC: World Bank.

Wyndow, Paula, Jianghong Li, and Eugen Mattes (2013). "Female Empowerment as a Core Driver of Democratic Development: A Dynamic Panel Model from 1980 to 2005." *World Development*, 52: 34–54.

Yetim, Nalan (2008). "Social Capital in Female Entrepreneurship." *International Sociology*, 23 (6): 864–885.

Youssef, Nadia H. (1971). "Social Structure and the Female Labor Force: The Case of Women Workers in Muslim Middle Eastern Countries." *Demography*, 8 (4): 427–439.

SECTION III

Natural resources, resource curse and trade

7

CAN THE GCC ECONOMIES ESCAPE THE OIL CURSE?

Raimundo Soto[1]

7.1 Introduction

For many countries, an abundance of natural resources has not led to economic growth and sustained development, high welfare for their population with lower inequality, and real participation in political life. Paradoxically, such abundance has fuelled unending political conflicts and civil wars, government corruption, and patronage networks that consolidate the power of entrenched elites and regime supporters, sharpening income inequality and stifling political reform. Energy exporting is, perhaps, the most emblematic case for the resource curse, a *malaise* that shows in both economic and political areas (Gelb, 1988).

The *political resource curse* occurs when hydrocarbon wealth tends to adversely affect a country's governance. Robust evidence suggests that oil tends to make authoritarian regimes more durable, to increase corruption, and to help trigger violent conflict in low- and middle-income countries (Ross, 2015). Typically, a negative correlation is found between oil riches and democracy. One possible explanation, applicable to Middle Eastern economies, is that lucrative oil reserves provide strong incentives for dictators to remain in power and to deter political opponents (Tsui, 2009). In fact, none of the 12 MENA countries that accounted for over 40% of all crude oil exports in 2018 have democratic governments. Econometric studies confirm that the risk of civil war greatly increases when countries depend on the export of primary commodities, particularly fossil fuels (Elbadawi and Soto, 2014). This correlation could be due to the prospect that resource rents may be an incentive to rebel, that wealth from resources may enable rebel groups to finance their operations, or that the high levels of corruption and poor governance that accompany resource wealth often generate grievances leading to rebellion. Findley and Marineau (2015) show that lootable natural resources motivate third parties to intervene in civil conflicts.

The *economic resource curse* occurs when economies develop an extreme dependence on resource wealth for fiscal revenues, export sales, or both; display low saving rates; and, as a consequence of their inability to cope with highly volatile resource revenues, tend to display instability and poor growth performance. There is ample evidence that nations with abundant natural capital have less trade and foreign investment, more corruption, less education, and less domestic investment than other nations that are less well endowed with, or less dependent on, natural resources (Gylfason, 2001a). GCC countries have long viewed oil riches as a source for the "big push" that would allow them a swift transition to full development. As noted by Sachs and Warner (1999), however, emerging countries have been incapable of turning the returns of oil discoveries or commodity price booms into engines of industrialisation and sustained growth.

While the experience of most resource-rich economies is disappointing, some economies have escaped this gloomy fate. Australia, Canada, and Norway have been immune to both the political and economic maladies usually associated with oil exporting. This is not surprising since all three countries were already industrialised economies when hydrocarbons became prominent. A few non-oil, resource-rich emerging economies have also avoided the curse—such as Botswana, Malaysia, and Chile—showing a possible path to escape the curse. In Malaysia and Chile exports of natural resources are quite significant but both economies have been able to grow systematically since the 1990s, achieving an income per capita similar to that of Greece or Portugal in PPP terms. Botswana, one of the very few success stories in Africa, has wisely managed its natural wealth—diamonds and nickel—to consolidate as an upper-middle-income country. As discussed below, incentives and institutions are key components of success.

High income per capita, nevertheless, does not signal sustainable development or identify countries that have escaped the resource curse. Income per capita in the oil-rich GCC economies is, by any standard, exceedingly high. But the symptoms of the curse are present in the extreme dependence on resource wealth for fiscal revenues, slow growth in productivity, and a chronic inability to cope with the highly volatile oil price (Kakanov et al., 2018). Beyond oil-related industries, trade in the GCC is limited and foreign investors cannot be lured into developing new businesses unless governments provide generous subsidies. On the political front, all GCC countries are absolute monarchies and political participation is typically restricted to a few members of the elite. Yet, political instability has been largely avoided and there is wide respect for a social contract whereby the rulers transfer resources to the population in exchange for political support (Desai et al., 2009; Soto, 2019a).

In what follows, I study the resource curse in the GCC economies, aiming at answering three questions. First, is there hard evidence of a resource curse in the GCC economies? Second, if so, can GCC economies escape the curse? And third, what can be learned from success stories in dealing with the resource curse?

7.2 The oil-curse in the GCC economies

Several theories have been advanced as explanations for the oil curse, i.e., the shocking fact that countries endowed with abundant natural resources often suffer from long-standing economic malaises that inhibit their economic and social development. I review the different rationales proposed for the resource curse and its most common symptoms, evaluating their relevance for the GCC countries.

Natural resources by themselves are not a problem; all countries in the world are endowed with varying quantities and qualities of them. The *size of natural resource rents*—defined as the difference between selling price and production costs—and the *few hands in which they are frequently concentrated* are what largely determine their mismanagement and the unveiling of the resource curse. In some economies—particularly those based on agriculture—the resource curse is not an issue because rents are small and property is spread among a large number of atomistic producers. On the contrary, rents in minerals and hydrocarbons can be sizable—due to the geographical concentration of deposits and the presence of significant scale economies—and are usually concentrated in the hands of the government. This provides an environment where the resource curse can develop.

These two conditions are present in the GCC countries. Table 7.1 provides a snapshot of resource rents in the world in the last 50 years, the longest period for which reliable statistics are available. Taking the world average as reference, we conclude that resource rents are significant—and the curse most likely to appear—in the Arab world, particularly in the GCC economies, and in Sub-Saharan Africa. Elsewhere rents tend to be small. Of course, individual countries can enjoy significant rents within these geographical areas (e.g., Norway in Europe or Indonesia in Asia).

Further scrutiny suggests that high resource rents are not always linked to high incomes: in fact, European economies have the lowest share of resource rents in aggregate income. Second, abundance of natural resources requires good management but countries often fail to achieve it: on average the highly indebted, poor countries of Sub-Saharan Africa have significant resource rents, yet their economies are so distressed that international organisations have made them the focus of special debt and reforms assistance under the HIPC initiative. Third, resource rents can provide high income levels but not necessarily high development levels: hydrocarbon exporters

Table 7.1 Average natural resource rents (as share of GDP)

	1970s	*1980s*	*1990s*	*2000s*	*2010s*
GCC economies	54.8	33.3	26.5	32.7	29.8
Petroleum rents	54.6	32.7	25.8	30.7	27.3
Natural gas rents	0.2	0.6	0.7	1.9	2.5
Arab world	32.7	26.3	19.7	29.2	26.3
Petroleum rents	32.2	25.8	19.2	27.8	24.4
Natural gas rents	0.1	0.3	0.4	1.2	1.5
Sub-Saharan Africa	8.9	8.4	9.0	12.4	12.0
Petroleum rents	5.1	3.1	3.5	7.3	6.0
Natural gas rents	0.0	0.0	0.0	0.2	0.4
Latin America	3.8	5.9	2.9	5.5	4.9
Petroleum rents	2.6	4.6	2.2	4.0	2.8
Natural gas rents	0.0	0.1	0.1	0.2	0.1
South Asia	1.8	2.6	2.1	3.1	2.9
Petroleum rents	0.3	1.1	0.8	1.0	0.7
Natural gas rents	0.0	0.0	0.1	0.2	0.2
East Asia & Pacific	2.3	2.5	0.9	2.2	2.6
Petroleum rents	1.0	1.3	0.4	0.8	0.6
Natural gas rents	0.0	0.0	0.0	0.1	0.2
Europe & Central Asia	0.4	0.8	0.7	1.6	1.9
Petroleum rents	0.1	0.4	0.4	0.9	1.1
Natural gas rents	0.1	0.1	0.1	0.4	0.5
World	2.9	3.2	1.5	2.9	3.3
Petroleum rents	1.9	2.2	1.0	1.8	1.9
Natural gas rents	0.3	0.3	0.2	0.4	0.3

Source: Author's own estimations based on data from World Economic Indicators 2019 (World Bank, 2019a). Annual resource rents are computed by commodity as the difference between international prices and extraction costs multiplied by the volume of resources extracted and divided by total GDP.

are usually among the highest-income countries but do not typically belong to the group of developed economies.

Figure 7.1 displays three fundamental characteristics of the GCC economies. First, per capita income levels in these economies are exceedingly high. During the last 40 years, GDP per capita in real terms in GCC economies has been significantly higher than the (weighted) average for all economies in the world. This attests also to high welfare levels for the population. Second, income per capita in these countries is volatile. Because hydrocarbons are the main contributor to exports and GDP, income per capita tends to follow the oil-price cycle (El Anshasy et al., 2019). Third, the most striking feature of the evolution of the GCC countries is that in the two decades ending in 2018, real GDP per capita has contracted significantly in the region. According to IMF data, real GDP grew on average at above 4% per year in the period 1985–2018, but in per capita terms it declined by 0.1% per year. This, naturally, indicates that population growth has been extremely fast in the GCC, a result of the massive inflows of workers—to the tune of 28 million—observed since the mid-1980s.

While resource rents in the region have allowed the attaining of high income levels (if not for the entire population, at least for the local population),[2] several of the resource-curse symptoms are present indicating that the GCC countries have not been immune to the disease.

Gylfason (2011) describes four main channels of transmission from natural resource abundance to slow economic growth. These explanations centre on the notion that natural capital crowds out other types of capital (physical, human, social, or institutional), thereby inhibiting sustainable economic growth.

First, the ample supply of foreign currency derived from exports of natural resources could induce the so-called Dutch disease (Corden and Neary, 1982). Foreign currency inflows—particularly when they occur in a short period of time—can induce a swift appreciation of the local

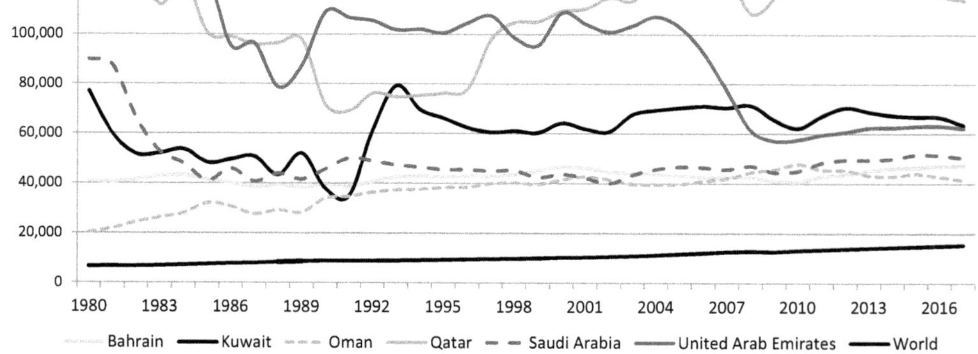

Figure 7.1 Real GDP per capita (in US dollars of 2010). *Source*: Author's own estimations based on data from World Economic Indicators 2019 (World Bank, 2019a).

currency, thereby reducing the profitability of exporting sectors and shrinking the productive basis of the economy. While part of the currency appreciation reflects an equilibrium adjustment subsequent to the fact that the economy is now richer than it was before, the currency overvaluation often exceeds any long-term equilibrium appreciation. Appreciation also shows in rising real wages and the costs of capital and land.

Second, significant resource rents in conjunction with institutional weakness (e.g., ill-defined property rights, imperfect or missing markets, and lax legal structures) may lead to rent-seeking (Krueger, 1974). Rent-seeking refers to the efforts undertaken by economic agents to increase their share of existing wealth without creating net new wealth. This diverts resources away from socially profitable economic activities. In extreme cases, civil wars break out for the control of such rents; in less extreme cases, the struggle for resource rents may lead to the hoarding of economic and political power in the hands of elites that, once in power, would use the rents to placate their political supporters and secure their hold on power. Elbadawi and Soto (2016) show that power hoarding results in slow growth. Rent-seeking also breeds corruption, distorts the allocation of resources, and reduces both economic efficiency and social equity (Gelb, 1988).

Third, resource rents may distort incentives to accumulate human capital, due to a high level of non-wage income or when wages are disconnected from the effort of workers. Resource-rich nations seem to underestimate the long-run value of education. Empirical evidence shows that, across countries, natural resource abundance is inversely related to public expenditures on education, expected years of schooling, and school enrolment (Gylfason, 2001b). Abundant natural capital appears to crowd out human capital which forms the basis of sustained economic growth. Human capital scores in education and health in the GCC countries are higher than their regional peers but much lower than their economic peers (World Bank, 2019b).

Fourth, high resource rents usually fuel consumption booms and tend to depress national saving. In turn, this leads to a lower than optimal accumulation of private capital, in particular in non-oil sectors (Arezki et al., 2011), and of public capital (Bhattacharyya and Collier, 2011). Furthermore, financial funds are frequently provided directly from the government on a non-competitive basis leading often to low-return investments thus retarding the development of financial institutions which ought to identify and fund the most productive projects on a social basis. Unproductive investments may seem unproblematic to governments when they are flush with oil cash.

A key question is to what extent these phenomena are present in the GCC countries. Table 7.2 displays key macroeconomic variables of GCC economies and a comparison with a group comprising the other 19 main oil exporters.[3] The evidence suggests that the Dutch disease has not been important in the GCC. RER misalignment has been present in all GCC economies but to a significantly lesser extent than in other oil-exporting economies, as shown in columns (1) and (2). A key element that has sheltered Gulf economies is the exchange regime: the GCC countries have historically pegged their currencies to strong currencies (the British pound or the US dollar) and therefore do not suffer from nominal appreciation. Another key element is the massive inflow of migrant workers that has prevented real wages from rising. In non-GCC oil exporters misalignment has been dealt with using sovereign wealth funds. These funds have not played a role in avoiding the currency misalignment in the GCC countries, but they have been important contributors in bringing security to foreign and domestic investors vis-à-vis the sustainability of the currency.

While the Dutch disease has been largely absent from the GCC, other symptoms of the resource curse are present. One symptom relates to economic fluctuations. Data indicates that business cycles are much more pronounced in hydrocarbon exporters than in the rest of the countries: in the period 1980–2017, growth volatility in oil exporters was 40% larger than

Table 7.2 Key macroeconomic indicators for the GCC and other oil exporters 1980–2017

Country	*Misalignment of the real exchange rate*		*Correlation of business cycles with natural resource rents*	*Exports concentration Herfindahl index*	*Correlation of natural resource rents with government expenditure*
	Before the adoption of SWF	*After the adoption of SWF*			
	(1)	*(2)*	*(3)*	*(4)*	*(5)*
Bahrain	3.7%	2.6%	13.1%	0.33	4.4%
Kuwait		2.8%	61.5%	0.76	5.3%
Oman		3.2%	13.9%	0.72	14.2%
Qatar	3.1%	3.8%	36.3%	0.60	14.7%
Saudi Arabia		3.0%	36.5%	0.72	27.4%
UAE		3.5%	71.5%	0.49	37.3%
Other oil exporters	*10.70%*	*4.00%*	*22.20%*	*0.47*	*11.30%*

Source: Author's elaboration based on Soto (2019b) and World Bank (2019a). Cycles are computed as deviations from long-run trend computed using the Hodrick and Prescott (1997) filter.

elsewhere in the world (World Bank, 2019b). GCC economies, nevertheless, fared slightly better with only 16% extra volatility in growth levels, largely because they avoided RER misalignments.

But where does volatility come from? As shown in column (3), the main source of volatility comes from shocks to the rents of natural resources, resulting from the instability of oil prices. The correlation between the business cycle and shocks to the rents of natural resources is very high in four GCC economies (Kuwait, Qatar, Saudi Arabia, and the UAE) but it is negligible in Bahrain—where natural resources are not significant—and Oman. The linkage between oil-price volatility and business cycles is notoriously higher in the GCC than in other oil producers because exports are not well diversified. Export concentration amplifies the pervasive effects of oil-price volatility. As shown in column (4), the Herfindahl[4] index of export concentration in the GCC is much higher than in other oil exporters, with the only exceptions being Bahrain and the UAE. Relatively low export concentration in the latter is largely due to Dubai's diversified economy, a phenomenon I discuss below as a possible strategy to escape the resource curse.

Export volatility transforms into government revenue instability, both through fluctuating tax revenues levied on oil production and/or exports, as well as through unstable profits and dividends of public oil companies. In principle, revenue instability should not pass through to expenditures and, thereby, to GDP because governments can use planning tools and fiscal policies to avoid inducing economic instability. Such policies include value-added and income taxes, multiyear fiscal budgeting and fiscal frameworks, stabilising sovereign wealth funds, external borrowing, and fiscal rules with independent fiscal councils. Most of these instruments are noticeably absent in GCC economies (Soto, 2019a). Income taxes are non-existent and VAT was only introduced in Saudi Arabia and the UAE in 2018. No country has implemented any form of fiscal rules or multiannual budgeting procedures, so that fiscal policies continue to operate with substantial opaqueness. Sovereign wealth funds are typically structured as investment vehicles but not as stabilising funds.

It is therefore not surprising to find that governments are relatively unable to isolate the budget from oil-price shocks, a phenomenon labelled "fiscal policy procyclicality". As shown in column (5) of Table 7.2, only in two GCC economies—Bahrain and Kuwait—do government expenditures not respond to oil prices. In the other economies and with varying intensity, oil-price shocks filter through to the economy via the government budget.

On the other hand, the GCC governments have made significant efforts to develop institutions, infrastructure, and other public goods to secure the competitiveness of their economies. As shown in Table 7.3, in terms of overall competitiveness GCC economies rank in advanced positions vis-à-vis other 140 economies in the world. Nevertheless, they are quite heterogeneous. Whilst there are minor differences in terms of the quality of institutions and infrastructure, differences in terms of technology adoption are much larger, with three countries lagging behind (Kuwait, Oman, and Saudi Arabia). The fourth index, macroeconomic stability, provides a somewhat misleading viewpoint of the situation as it concentrates only on inflation and public debt. These, in the case of GCC economies, do not capture the essence of instability which arises from fiscal procyclicality, as discussed.

Finally, while existent in the GCC countries, rent-seeking does not seem to be rampant or capable of interfering massively with the market allocation of resources. In Table 7.4 I present indicators that can be linked to rent-seeking behaviour. The GCC economies rank relatively high in having well-defined and protected property rights, thus reducing the incentives for

Table 7.3 Competitiveness indicators (2018–2019) as compared to 140 economies

Country	*Overall ranking*	*Pillar 1: Institutions*	*Pillar 2: Infrastructure*	*Pillar 3: ICT adoption*	*Pillar 4: Macroeconomic stability*
Bahrain	50th	42nd	30th	38th	119th
Kuwait	54th	57th	61st	62nd	1st
Oman	47th	36th	24th	61st	58th
Qatar	30th	31st	26th	9th	40th
Saudi Arabia	39th	39th	40th	54th	1st
UAE	27th	19th	15th	6th	1st

Source: Author's elaboration based on WEF (2019).

Table 7.4 Rent-seeking indicators (2018–2019) as compared to 140 economies

	Bahrain	*Kuwait*	*Oman*	*Qatar*	*Saudi Arabia*	*UAE*
Efficiency of legal framework in settling disputes	23	42	13	14	21	12
Efficiency of legal framework in challenging regulations	14	33	19	9	29	13
Incidence of corruption	87	73	59	26	50	21
Property rights	27	54	20	30	29	26
Shareholder governance	90	76	106	124	5	15
Extent of market dominance	36	78	31	23	26	18
Distortive effect of taxes and subsidies on competition	13	49	9	6	17	3
Conflict of interest regulation	84	65	84	139	23	16
Strength of auditing and reporting standards	29	86	37	25	33	38

Source: Author's elaboration based on WEF (2019).

abusive behaviour. Likewise, they have adopted high standards of auditing and reporting for the private sector, thus providing investors and authorities with timely information regarding the stance of firms and businesses. On the contrary, most GCC economies have done very little to inhibit the deleterious effects of conflicts of interest on the working of their economies, with the sole exceptions of Saudi Arabia and the UAE. Bahrain, Kuwait, Oman, and Qatar lag significantly behind in this regard, opening space for rent-seeking behaviour. This problem is compounded with the inability of some economies to control corruption, i.e., the use of public power positions for illicit personal enrichment, and to instil accountability in the public sector. Alshehabi (2017) studies the accountability in public budgets in the GCC and concludes that, with the exception of Kuwait, there is strong evidence to suggest that significant amounts of oil revenues are undeclared, which go either into private hands or into undisclosed government transactions.

A subtler form of rent-seeking behaviour is encouraged when minority investors and individuals are limited in defending their interests. In advanced economies, shareholder governance regulation protects minority investors from being abused by large investors or controllers. Only two economies in the GCC are at the forefront in this regard (Saudi Arabia and the UAE), whilst the other economies exhibit regulatory frameworks that are among the worst in the world. Some counterbalance is provided by the legal system. In all GCC economies, the legal system seems to be efficient in settling disputes (i.e., swiftly and at a low cost), thus reducing the space for rent seekers. Finally, although taxes and subsidies do not pose a heavy burden on competition, the extent of market dominance in the region is worrying, particularly in Kuwait. Protection for local producers in the form of exclusivity rights and trade licensing allow for rent extraction from consumers, particularly in industries facing limited competition from abroad (services, real estate, etc.).

In summary, the empirical evidence indicates that three of the four explanations for the resource curse (Dutch disease, institutional weakness, and rent-seeking) cannot account for the protracted stagnation of GCC economies in terms of GDP per capita. While symptoms of these explanations do occur in all GCC economies, they are not strong enough to explain this phenomenon. In the following section I focus on the last channel of transmission of the resource curse, i.e., the case where resource rents hamper physical and/or human capital accumulation or induce an inefficient use of such resources.

7.3 Economic growth, productivity, and the resource curse

As mentioned, while real GDP grew vigorously in all GCC economies in the period 1985–2018, per capita GDP stagnated in Bahrain, increased only very modestly in four of them (Kuwait, Oman, Qatar, and Saudi Arabia), and declined systematically in the UAE. The explanation, naturally, lies in the exceptional expansion in population in the GCC economies: however, and in contrast to most emerging countries, the massive inflow of workers observed since the mid-1980s is an endogenous phenomenon, as discussed below, resulting from the development strategy embedded in government policies.

7.3.1 The sources of economic growth in the GCC economies

In order to understand what lies behind this apparent paradox, I decompose real GDP growth in each country according to its "sources". The sources of economic growth are a combination of physical capital accumulation, expansion in employment and its capacities, and improvements in the way in which these factors are employed, i.e., changes in total factor productivity (Barro and Lee, 1994). When computing the sources of growth, I follow Solow (1956) and use a simple, aggregate production function of the form:

$$\text{GDP}_t = f(A_t, K_t, HK_t, L_t)$$

where K_t is the stock of physical capital, L_t is the use of the labour force, and HK_t is the stock of knowledge or human capital. Variable A_t is an indicator of the efficiency in the use of factors, usually labelled total factor productivity (TFP). TFP is not measured directly; rather, it is obtained as a residual after accounting for the contributions of all other factors of production to growth in output. TFP encompasses not only technological capacity but also the efficiency in the use of production factors. Accordingly, several elements could affect factor productivity beyond the technical ability to mix inputs and generate goods and services. For example, poor government regulation leading to lower use of capital and, thus, lower production is interpreted as declining TFP. On the other hand, reforms that reduce bureaucracy and corruption are interpreted as increasing TFP.

Real GDP growth can be decomposed as follows:

$$\widehat{GDP} = \theta_K \hat{K} + \theta_L \hat{L} + \theta_{HK} \widehat{HK} + \widehat{TFP}$$

where $\hat{X}$ indicates the growth rate (measured in log changes) of any given variable X. Parameters θ_K, θ_L, and θ_{HK} are constants.

I use the data provided by the Total Economy Database on the growth rates of GDP, capital, human capital, and labour to compute changes in TFP. Table 7.5 provides the results of the sources of growth decomposition for the GCC economies in the period 1990–2018, setting θ_K=0.34 and θ_L=θ_{HK}=0.33.[5]

The evidence of the resource curse in the GCC is clear. First, while the GCC grew roughly at the same pace of emerging economies, growth relied heavily on accumulating physical capital

Table 7.5 Sources of economic growth in GCC economies and other regions of the world

	Average growth rate between 1990 and 2018				
	GDP	*Quantity of labour*	*Quality of labour*	*Capital*	*Total factor productivity*
Bahrain	4.3	5.2	0.7	5.1	-1.3
Kuwait	3.4	3.6	0.0	4.8	-0.6
Oman	3.6	6.0	0.0	4.3	-1.8
Qatar	7.7	7.7	0.2	8.0	-0.2
Saudi Arabia	3.4	3.5	1.7	5.9	-2.0
United Arab Emirates	4.4	7.0	0.6	3.9	-1.9
GCC unweighted average	***4.5***	***5.5***	***0.5***	***5.3***	***-1.3***
Other oil exporters	***2.8***	***2.0***	***0.7***	***3.3***	***-0.1***
Middle East & North Africa	*3.6*	*4.3*	*0.7*	*4.3*	*-1.0*
Emerging economies	*4.3*	*1.8*	*0.6*	*4.2*	*0.4*
OECD economies	*2.2*	*0.7*	*0.4*	*3.7*	*0.3*
World	*4.3*	*1.6*	*0.6*	*4.1*	*0.1*

Source: Author's elaboration based on the Total Economy Database.

and raw labour, while human capital lagged and TFP significantly declined. Second, in all but one GCC country, employment has grown faster than GDP and much faster than elsewhere in the world. The increasing reliance on employment as a source of growth has led to a massive immigration of workers, largely from the Indian subcontinent. GDP per worker—and thereby GDP per capita—has declined steadily. This is a remarkable phenomenon: despite their huge natural-resource capital, these economies have become increasingly labour-intensive. Third, in all GCC economies physical capital has grown faster than GDP, with the only exception being the UAE, indicating that growth has also been driven by high levels of investment. Fourth, human capital has remained stagnant in four of these economies (Kuwait, Oman, Qatar, and the United Arab Emirates). Fifth, the most worrisome result is that TFP has declined systematically in the past 30 years, at around 1.3% per year in the region. The cumulative effect of this phenomenon indicates that nowadays the average GCC economy uses its resources with 30% less efficiency than in the early 1990s. The decline in TFP accounts for around 80% of the decline in output per worker in the GCC area. Other oil exporters have not suffered from the same problem.

Figure 7.2 shows the evolution of TFP in the region as well as in other country groups. TFP in the OECD countries grew slowly but steadily until the global recession of 2008–2010. Afterwards, it slightly dropped and stagnated. A similar trend is observed at the world level but with more pronounced fluctuations driven by the performance of the emerging economies. Again, after the global recession, TFP remained stagnant. The evolution in the Middle East and in the GCC is quite different: TFP did not expand in the Middle East prior to the global recession as elsewhere and it has declined steadily since the mid-2000s. TFP in the GCC fared better before the global downturn but afterwards it dropped dramatically; as of 2018, there are no indications of a recovery.

The evidence suggests that the resource curse in the GCC shows up in countries sustaining economic growth on the basis of accumulating physical capital and labour and being unable to

Figure 7.2 Total factor productivity indices. *Source*: Author's elaboration based on the Total Economy Database.

reverse the secular decline in efficiency that started in the mid-2000s. The evidence also begs the question of why all GCC economies behave in a similar fashion for such a long period of time. While the origin of shocks may be related to hydrocarbon prices and demand, the declining productivity path is more suggestive of structural and institutional constraints than to transient phenomena.

7.3.2 Segmented labour markets

As noted, the notable expansion in employment has been largely in the form of a massive immigration of workers, principally from the Indian subcontinent. Data on migrants is presented in Figure 7.3. One can identify two phases in the arrival of migrants to GCC economies. The first phase occurs between 1985 and 2005 when migrants increased at around 4.5% per year and the second phase, between 2005 and 2018, when migrants grew at 6.0% per year. As of 2018, expatriates represented over 85% of the population in Qatar and the UAE, 70% in Kuwait, and 55% in Bahrain. In Saudi Arabia, expatriates comprise 38% of the population but amount to a massive immigration wave of around 12 million workers.

Expatriates in the GCC represent a much larger share of the labour force than that of population, because most if not all migrants are employed while the local population include those that do not participate in the labour market (mainly underage, students, and the inactive). Furthermore, participation rates for GCC nationals are noticeably low: in 2016 only 47% of nationals participated in the labour market vis-à-vis 85% of expatriates. Most immigrants have low educational levels and are generally employed in low-skilled positions, in which the highly paid nationals are not interested in (e.g., construction workers).

This massive accumulation of workers is puzzling: why would entrepreneurs prefer to employ labour-intensive production techniques when they have unrestricted access to the highly sophisticated capital goods and top-notch technologies that the world economy offers?

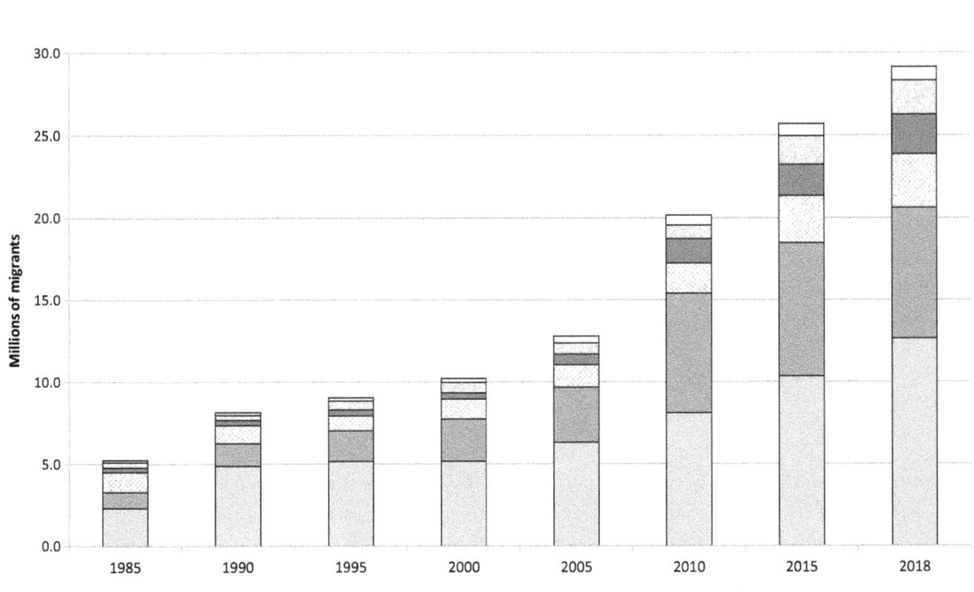

Figure 7.3 Migrants in GCC economies. *Sources*: World Bank (2019a) for 1990–2015; Migration Data Portal (2019).

As discussed in Soto and Vazquez-Alvarez (2011) and Diop et al. (2018) the peculiar institutional framework of the labour market under the sponsorship system or *kafala* provides a compelling explanation. Under the *kafala*, employers have significant market power derived from the fact that the expatriates are restricted to working only for the sponsor and are forbidden to change occupations while the contract is in force without the assent of the sponsor. This effectively limits horizontal mobility and allows employers to extract economic rents, even if the worker is paid above his/her reservation wage in his/her country of origin. When choosing production technologies, therefore, employers would tend to focus on labour-intensive techniques that, in addition to the normal profit obtained from selling goods and services in the market, would allow them to extract the highest rents from the worker. Moreover, the *kafala* biases the choice of technology towards low-skilled workers that are easily replaceable. High-skilled workers are relatively scarcer and better equipped to counterbalance the market power of employers.

The preference of entrepreneurs for labour-intensive technologies is visible in many activities in the GCC countries, particularly in industries that do not feel the pressure of international competition (e.g., non-tradable goods and non-financial services). But there is a more subtle dynamic implication of the preference for labour-intensive technologies: it goes against the trend in advanced economies whereby new and more efficient technologies are labour-saving and knowledge-intensive (Acemoglu, 2010). In advanced economies rising wages induce the adoption of labour-saving technologies. The massive inflow of workers to the GCC countries has kept unskilled expatriate wages relatively low, thereby inhibiting the adoption of more productive technologies.

In rapidly growing emerging economies, TFP gains largely determine the evolution of productivity levels and, in so doing, the path of real wages (Syverson, 2011). In the GCC, the connection between productivity gains and wages is feeble in the case of expatriates and almost non-existent in the case of nationals. The main reason for the latter is that GCC governments have chosen to pass on some of the natural resource riches to the citizens through the labour market; in particular, by setting exorbitantly high public-sector wages and extremely protective regulations for nationals working in the private sector. For nationals, favourable treatment effectively disconnects effort from reward and disincentivises training, upgrading, and human capital formation.[6]

Evidence indicates, for example, that Saudi nationals earned on average around 2.6 times more than migrants in 2007 (Hertog, 2012) and that these large differences remain even after controlling for education levels and productivity. Differences increase significantly when public wages are included in the analysis, to an estimate of 4.6 times higher (Ramady, 2013). Tamirisa and Duenwald (2018) found that the average wage gap between the public and private sectors in Kuwait and Bahrain was over 200% in 2016, while those for Qatar and Saudi Arabia were over 150%.

7.3.3 Labour quotas

During the late 1990s, it became apparent that GCC nationals were becoming progressively less employable by the private sector and that unemployment was chronically high. Instead of eliminating distortions, GCC governments embarked in job-nationalisation reforms, pompously labelled Emiratisation, Saudisation, Omanisation, etc. These reforms aimed at forcing private-sector firms to hire growing quotas of nationals or reserving altogether certain jobs for the local population. As is often the case with non-market-based interventions, reforms were not successful in reducing unemployment among nationals (Hertog, 2014).

More importantly, reforms did little to improve—and most likely were instrumental in damaging—productivity. Replacing well-trained and relatively inexpensive expatriates by inexperienced and highly expensive nationals proved to be very costly, particularly for small- and medium-sized firms. Overly ambitious targets for nationalisation were met with resistance by firm managers and owners, and governments had to reluctantly agree to slow the pace of reforms in view of their high cost (Alfarhan and Al-Busaidi, 2018). Peck (2017) and Abdulkarim (2018) find that Saudisation increased the ratio of Saudis in total employment, but at a significant cost to firms, since it raised exit rates and reduced total employment in surviving firms. In addition, there was a negative short-term impact of the policy on labour productivity which forced the exit of the less productive firms from the market.

Labour quota systems as those in vogue in the GCC miss the mark altogether by targeting employment rather than productivity: indeed, forcing firms to hire costly nationals not only reduces profitability in the short run but, more importantly, does nothing to improve on the incentives for nationals to become more employable by the private sector. Employability depends on having high productivity and displaying healthy work habits, trademarks of high levels of human capital formation.

7.3.4 Foreign investment

The *kafala* has a second component with pervasive effects on productivity growth and efficiency: the limitations imposed on foreigners to own property and engage in foreign direct investment (FDI). Between 2015 and 2017, FDI to GCC economies amounted to around 1% of GDP, well below the average level for emerging economies which stand at 4% of GDP (World Bank, 2019b). The monetary value of FDI is irrelevant given the massive resources that Gulf economies receive from oil exports and the substantial reserves they hold in sovereign wealth funds. The main reason to attract FDI is the potential benefits these flows may have on the efficiency, productivity, and international competitiveness of the GCC countries.

Evidence indicates that foreign firms tend to have higher productivity, more capital intensity and know-how, better technology and risk management, a larger supply of internal finance, and easier access to international goods and capital markets (Arnold and Javorcik, 2009). Local firms are thus widely thought to benefit from attracting FDI. Spillover effects arise when FDI fosters the creation of local firms, thus leading to more active domestic markets in which locals learn from foreign firms and subsequently implement this knowledge in their newly opened firms.

Historically, the GCC economies limited the participation of foreign investors using: (a) restrictions on land access, (b) prohibitions on entering certain industries, and (c) limitations on the ownership and control of businesses. Until the most recent wave of reforms, land property in most GCC economies was reserved to nationals and locally owned businesses. Long-term leasing was thus the only mode of access to land for non-nationals. Foreign investors have also been forbidden from entering sectors traditionally reserved for national firms (oil exploration and production; fishing, real estate; wholesale and retail distribution; telecommunications; and transport). These sectors are dominated by state-owned enterprises which, more often than not, do not show high productivity levels. The most pervasive limitation has nevertheless been on ownership. GCC economies have limited foreign participation using property rules that invariably gave more than 50% of ownership to nationals or local firms fully owned by nationals.

The adverse effects of the *kafala* on FDI have been tacitly acknowledged by governments in their fostering of free-trade and other special development zones (SDZ). Saudi Arabia and the UAE started their SDZ in the mid-1980s, while the rest of the regional economies followed suit in the 1990s and 2000s. Elsewhere, SDZ typically offer investors preferential treatment in terms of invariability of taxes and improved access to physical infrastructure. Tax benefits are not necessary in the GCC given the generalised absence of income taxes. Likewise, physical infrastructure is among the best in the world. The main attractions of SDZ in the GCC rely on (a) offering 100% ownership of firms, (b) access to land, and (c) higher labour flexibility and less demanding labour quota requirements (Soto, 2017). These areas, free from the constraints of the *kafala*, have become magnets for FDI and hubs of economic activity in the region.

Measuring how costly the restrictions on FDI have been in terms of productivity sacrifice is very difficult. Elbadawi (2016) compares efficiency levels in Dubai vis-à-vis their counterparts in SDZ. The main results indicate that firms located in SDZ outperform their counterparts in Dubai in terms of productivity in light and heavy manufacturing, financial services, and non-financial services. Firms in SDZ accumulate higher levels of physical and human capital, which contribute to their better performance. The observed differences in average labour productivity are largely shaped by total factor productivity (TFP). Soto and Vazquez-Alvarez (2011) estimate that, on average, technical inefficiency resulting from the *Kafala* amounted to 6.6% of total costs (or 11% of profits) and that it is significant in all economic sectors of the Dubai economy.

7.4 Escaping the resource curse: economic policies and political challenges

The above discussion indicates that the resource curse in the GCC shows up in declining TFP and concomitant low levels of labour productivity. It also shows as a protracted phenomenon that can be linked to the distorted incentives in the labour market imposed by the sponsorship system and the restrictions levied by the governments on FDI. Evidence indicates government interventions in the form of administrative, non-market-based policies have largely failed (labour market quotas, government subsidies to innovation, etc.).

Successful reforms rely on achieving two sets of goals. First, they must change incentives, i.e., the set of rewards and penalties that guide the decisions of economic agents (individuals, firms, and the government). While altruistic behaviour exists, economic agents largely behave in self-interest by weighing the benefits and costs of the decisions they make. Reforms that do not affect incentives are but dead letter. Affecting incentives implies that some economic agents may lose while others, hopefully the majority, benefit. Second, reforms must build the institutions that would implement and sustain the desired change in incentives. Without institutions, affected economic agents will bypass reforms and the potential benefits will never accrue for those for which the reforms are intended. Institutional building is slow and expensive, but a necessary condition for success.

Timing is also a key consideration on two regards. First, there is an important asymmetry in the costs and benefit of reforms: the cost of reforms is customarily significant in the short run and the benefits are usually received in the long run. In the short run, there will be losers and they are likely to voice their discontent. But in the long run, higher productivity means better real wages and higher and better employment. The medium-term gains for society as a whole might offset the short-terms costs for certain groups. Policies aimed at reducing the adjustment costs are therefore important for both economic and political reasons. But perseverance with reforms is even more important. Second, confidence and support for the reforms require setting an agenda of realistic, attainable goals with a clearly defined timeline. In the past, reforms in the GCC set unrealistic goals vis-à-vis the nationalisation in the labour market, only to be scaled down when targets proved unattainable, with unavoidable reputation costs.

The governments of GCC economies have long attempted to change matters and reforms have been either announced or implemented, aiming at awakening investment and jump-starting innovation and technology adoption. Their overarching goal was to diversify away from oil and, hopefully, into a knowledge-based type of development path. However, the past record of diversification has yielded only meagre results. Hvidt (2013) notes that the policy response to pre-empt the Arab Spring uprising indicates that GCC authorities easily give up their well-argued and planned policies when under pressure and fall back on established ways of doing business, namely through patronage and the predominant role of the public sector. Kumar and van Welsum (2013) are also sceptical of the abilities of the GCC countries to transform into knowledge-based economies. They acknowledge that while the GCC countries have performed well in providing a physical ICT infrastructure, without sufficient local human capital and an appropriate business environment in place to take advantage of adopted technologies, their potential is unlikely to be realised.

A number of the ongoing, pro-market reforms in GCC economies aim at dealing with the issues discussed in this chapter. Some of the costly consequences of the *kafala* are being dealt with by a combination of increased labour market flexibility and a lessening of FDI restrictions. Reforms have been implemented to reduce red-tape and administrative burdens placed on domestic and foreign firms.[7] Increasing labour market flexibility and/or making more it expensive to hire low-skilled expatriates is being discussed by GCC authorities. While it is too early to assess their success, Mina (2018) points to evidence that these reforms may strongly reinforce each other; using data for the period 2007–2016, he found that second-generation, market-oriented labour policies implemented already in the mid-2010s in the GCC have had a positive and significant impact on inward FDI flows.

Reforms have also been discussed or implemented to improve on isolating the GCC economies from the oil-price cycle. Fiscal reforms are making strides towards such a goal. The implementation of value-added tax will provide the UAE and Saudi Arabia with an important automatic stabiliser for the economic cycle. Likewise, the adoption of better practices in budgeting and fiscal management—as those reviewed by Soto (2019a)—should enhance the fiscal stabilisation of oil-price cycles. Mohaddes et al. (2019), nevertheless, identify a number of fiscal institutions missing from GCC and that would require implementing if diversification is to be successful. These include budgetary information and transparency; improvements on the mandate, financial management, and governance of the sovereign wealth funds; adoption of fiscal rules (see Schmidt-Hebbel and Soto, 2017) and project and programme evaluations with effective external control and auditing; and the establishment of an independent fiscal council.

Will these reforms be sufficient? Most certainly not, many other reforms (particularly in education, technology, and innovation adoption) are also much needed and could prove as decisive as those currently in effect. But the above recommendations are among those identified by Schmidt-Hebbel (2016) as the key components in the success of Chile and Norway in dealing with the natural resource richness and avoiding the curse. Likewise, Doraisami (2015) identifies similar elements in the success story of Malaysia, but warns us of two important challenges. First, the eventual setbacks brought upon by oil bonanzas, which soften the resolve of governments towards structural reforms. Second, the political costs to governments embarked on reforms as they will inevitably hurt their supporters that benefit from *status quo*. For example, it seems obvious that economic diversification requires the government's ability to incentivise nationals to leave the public sector and increase labour productivity in the private sector.

In fact, these economic reforms will have important political effects and will raise the key question for GCC authorities of how to transfer oil rents to the population to keep political support without destroying the incentives for efficiency, productivity, and competitiveness. If reforms succeed it is easy to anticipate the emergence of a new social contract whereby political inclusion and participation arises from a more decisive entry of nationals to the private sector, particularly medium-to-high skilled women. The transition to a scenario in which the majority of GCC nationals work in the private sector will not be easy: abandoning the government job guarantee historically provided to male citizens will be politically challenging. The policies to facilitate such a transition might have to go beyond labour fees and subsidies.

Notes

1 The opinions in this chapter are the author's sole responsibility and do not reflect those of his institutional affiliation. I am grateful to Hassan Hakimian for his constructive comments and suggestions on an earlier draft.
2 Nationals are usually a tiny fraction of the expatriate population in the GCC economies but enjoy preferential treatment in the form of higher salaries, access to restricted residential land, and massive subsidies in health, education, and utilities.
3 The group of "Other oil exporters" comprises Algeria, Azerbaijan, Colombia, Congo, Ecuador, Gabon, Indonesia, Iran, Iraq, Kazakhstan, Mexico, Nigeria, Norway, Russia, Sudan, Trinidad-Tobago, Turkmenistan, Venezuela, and Yemen.
4 The Herfindahl index measures the concentration of exported goods between 0 and 1. A higher number indicates a more concentrated export bundle. A mono-exporter country would yield a value of 1 in the index.
5 Results remain qualitatively unchanged if parameters θ_K, θ_L, and θ_{HK} are adjusted to match national accounts.
6 Forstenlechner and Rutledge (2010) found that over 60% of the youth (15–29 years old) in Qatar, Saudi Arabia, and the UAE preferred to work for the government. Figures rose above 70% in Kuwait and Bahrain.
7 Strict restrictions on foreign ownership of land may also continue to be a potential impediment to FDI: such ownership is strictly limited to zones designated by the government (Bahrain), tourist areas (Oman), or areas for housing purposes (Qatar). Non-GCC citizens may not own land in Kuwait.

References

Acemoglu, D. (2010), "When Does Labor Scarcity Encourage Innovation?", *Journal of Political Economy*, 118(6): 1037–1078.

Alabdulkarim, M. (2018), "Labour Demand, Firm Survival & Productivity in Dual Labour Markets: The Case of the Nitaqat Policy in Saudi Arabia", A thesis submitted to King's College London, For the degree of Doctor of Philosophy, King's Business School, February.

Alfarhan, U. and S. Al-Busaidi (2018), "A 'Catch-22', Self-inflicted Failure of GCC Nationalization Policies", *International Journal of Manpower*, 39(4): 637–655.

Alshehabi, O. (2017), "Show Us the Money: Oil Revenues, Undisclosed Allocations and Accountability in Budgets of the GCC States", LSE Kuwait Programme Paper Series No 44, September.

Arezki, R., Hamilton, K. and K. Kazimov (2011), "Resource Windfalls, Macroeconomic Stability and Growth: The Role of Political Institutions", IMF Working Paper No. 11/142.

Arnold, J. and B. Javorcik (2009), "Gifted Kids or Pushy Parents? Foreign Direct Investment and Plant Productivity in Indonesia", *Journal of International Economics*, 79(1): 42–53.

Barro, R.J. and J.W. Lee (1994), "Sources of Economic Growth", *Carnegie-Rochester Series on Public Policy*, 40: 1–57.

Bhattacharyya, S. and P. Collier (2011), "Public Capital in Resource-Rich Countries: Is There a Curse?", Centre for the Study of African Economies Working Paper 2011/14, Department of Economics, Oxford University.

Corden, W.M. and J.P. Neary (1982), "Booming Sector and De-industrialisation in a Small Open Economy", *The Economic Journal*, 92 (December): 825–848.

Desai, R., Olofsgard, A. and T. Yousef (2009), "The Logic of Authoritarian Bargains", *Economics & Politics*, 21(1): 93–125.

Diop, A., Johnston, T. and K.T. Le (2018), "Migration Policies across the GCC: Challenges in Reforming the Kafala", in *Migration to the Gulf: Policies in Sending and Receiving Countries*, edited by Philippe Fargues and Nasra M. Shah, Gulf Research Center, pp. 33–60.

Doraisami, A. (2015), "Has Malaysia Really Escaped the Resource Curse? A Closer Look at the Political Economy of Oil Revenue Management and Expenditures", *Resources Policy*, 45(C): 98–108.

El Anshasy, A., Mohaddes, K. and J.B. Nugent (2019), "Oil, Volatility and Institutions: Cross-country Evidence from Major Oil Producers", in *Macroeconomic Institutions and Management in Resource-Rich Arab Economies*, edited by K. Mohaddes, J.B. Nugent and H. Selim, Cambridge University Press, pp. 52–72.

Elbadawi, I.A. (2016), "Productivity, Efficiency, and Sustainability of Economic Growth", in *The Economy of Dubai*, edited by A. Alfaris and R. Soto, Oxford University Press, pp. 311–329.

Elbadawi, I.A. and R. Soto (2014), "Resource Rents, Institutions and Civil Wars", *Defence and Peace Economics*, 26(1): 89–113.

Elbadawi, I.A. and R. Soto (2016), "Resource Rents, Political Institutions and Economic Growth", in *Understanding and Avoiding the Oil Curse in the Arab World, I*, edited by A. Elbadawi and H. Selim, Cambridge University Press, pp. 187–224.

Findley, M.G. and J.F. Marineau (2015), "Lootable Resources and Third-Party Intervention into Civil Wars", *Conflict Management and Peace Science*, 32(5): 465–486.

Forstenlechner, I. and E. Rutledge (2010), "Unemployment in the Gulf: Time to Update the"Social Contract", *Middle East Policy*, 17(2): 38–51.

Gelb, A. (1988), *Oil Windfalls: Blessing or Curse?* World Bank: Oxford University Press.

Gylfason, T. (2001a), "Natural Resources and Economic Growth: What Is the Connection?", CESifo Working Paper No. 530.

Gylfason, T. (2001b), "Natural Resources, Education and Economic Development", *European Economic Review*, 45: 847–59.

Gylfason, T. (2011), "Natural Resource Endowment: A Mixed Blessing?", CESIFO Working Paper 3353.

Hertog, S. (2012), "A Comparative Assessment of Labor Market Nationalization Policies in the GCC", in *National Employment, Migration and Education in the GCC. The Gulf Region: Economic Development and Diversification*, edited by S. Hertog, 4 Gerlach Press, pp. 65–105.

Hertog, S. (2014), "Arab Gulf States: An Assessment of Nationalisation Policies", GLMM Research Paper, 1. Gulf Labour Markets and Migration Programme, Badia Fiesolana, Italy.

Hodrick, R. and E.C. Prescott (1997), "Postwar U.S. Business Cycles: An Empirical Investigation", *Journal of Money, Credit, and Banking*, 29 (1): 1–16.

Hvidt, M., (2013), "Economic Diversification in GCC Countries: Past Record and Future Trends", Working Paper 27, Kuwait Programme on Development, Governance and Globalisation in the Gulf States.

Kakanov, E., Blöchliger, H. and L. Demmou (2018), "Resource Curse in Oil Exporting Countries", Economics Department Working Papers No. 1511, OECD.

Krueger, A.O. (1974), "The Political Economy of the Rent-Seeking Society", *The American Economic Review*, 64(3): 291–303.

Kumar, K. and D. van Welsum (2013), *Knowledge-Based Economies and Basing Economies on Knowledge. Skills a Missing Link in GCC Countries*, Santa Monica, CA: RAND Corporation.

Migration Data Portal (2019), https://migrationdataportal.org/?i=stock_abs_&t=2017, accessed July 24, 2019.

Mina, W. (2018), "Labor Market Policies and FDI Flows to GCC Countries", ERF Working Paper Series 1201, Economic Research Forum, Cairo.

Mohaddes, K., Nugent, J. and H. Selim (2019), "Reforming Fiscal Institutions in Resource-Rich Arab Economies: Policy Proposals", in *Institutions and Macroeconomic Policies in Resource-Rich Arab Economies*, edited by K. Mohaddes, J.B. Nugent, and H. Selim, Oxford University Press, pp. 237–274.

Peck, J.R. (2017), "Can Hiring Quotas Work? The Effect of The Nitaqat Program On The Saudi Private Sector", *American Economic Journal: Economic Policy*, 8(1): 316–347.

Ramady, M. (2013), "Gulf Unemployment and Government Policies: Prospects For The Saudi Labour Quota or Nitaqat System", *International Journal of Economics and Business Research*, 5(4): 476–498.

Ross, M. (2015), "What Have We Learned about the Resource Curse?", *Annual Review of Political Science*, 18: 239–259.

Sachs, J.D. and A.M. Warner (1999), "The Big Push, Natural Resource Booms and Growth", *Journal of Development Economics*, 59: 43–76.

Schmidt-Hebbel, K. (2016), "Fiscal Institutions in Resource-Rich Economies: Lessons from Chile and Norway", in *Understanding and Avoiding the Oil Curse in the Arab World*, edited by I.A. Elbadawi and H. Selim, Cambridge University Press, pp. 187–224.

Schmidt-Hebbel, K. and R. Soto (2017), "Fiscal Rules in the World", in *Rethinking Fiscal Policy After the Crisis*, edited by Ľudovít Ódor, Cambridge University Press, pp.103–138.

Solow, R. (1956), "Technical Change and The Aggregate Production Function", *Review of Economic and Statistics*, 39: 312–320.

Soto, R. (2017), "Foreign Direct Investment Restrictions in Special Development Zones in Honduras", mimeo, Inter American Development Bank (in Spanish).

Soto, R. (2019a), "Policy Goals, Fiscal Institutions and Macroeconomic Management in the United Arab Emirates", in *Macroeconomic Institutions and Management in Resource-Rich Arab Economies*, edited by K. Mohaddes, J.B. Nugent and H. Selim, Cambridge University Press, pp. 356–425.

Soto, R. (2019b), "Herfindahl's Indices for Exports and Imports: 1962–2017", mimeo, Pontificia Universidad Católica de Chile.

Soto, R. and R. Vazquez-Alvarez (2011), "The Efficiency Cost of the Kafala in Dubai: A Stochastic Frontier Analysis", Working Paper IE-PUC, No. 399.

Syverson, C. (2011), "What Determines Productivity?", *Journal of Economic Literature*, 49(2): 326–365.

Tamirisa, N.T. and C. Duenwald (2018), *Public Wage Bills in the Middle East and Central Asia*, Washington, DC: International Monetary Fund.

Tsui, K. (2009), "More Oil, Less Democracy", *The Economic Journal*, 121(551): 89–115.

World Bank (2019a). *World Development Indicators*, Washington, DC: The World Bank.

World Bank (2019b), "Building the Foundations for Economic Sustainability: Human Capital and Growth in the GCC", Gulf Economic Monitor #4 (April), Washington, DC.

World Economic Forum (2019), *The Global Competitiveness Report 2018–2019*, Geneva.

8

FROM OIL RENTS TO INCLUSIVE GROWTH

Lessons from the MENA region

Hassan Hakimian[1]

8.1 Introduction

The burgeoning resource curse literature is focused on the link between oil rents and poor economic performance in resource-rich countries.[2] The yardstick for evaluating economic performance in oil-exporting countries, such as those in the MENA region, has largely been GDP growth. Little attention has been devoted to whether the experience of economic development in these countries has been inclusive and, if not, why not? This is at odds with the fact that the relationship between growth and equity has a long tradition and deep roots in economics thinking and development policy.

Inclusive growth can be broadly conceived of as policies that benefit 'the widest' social and economic groupings. However, there is no universally agreed definition of this concept, which has also complicated attempts at operationalising it.

Despite this, recent interest in ensuring that growth is inclusive has been on the rise bolstered by a desire to understand the economic performance of the Arab countries in the period leading up to the uprisings that brought down several autocratic regimes after 2010/11 (Hakimian, 2011, 2013). The fact that the decade before these uprisings also coincided with unprecedentedly buoyant international oil prices and highly favourable oil incomes for oil-exporters has extended the habitual curiosity about the relationship between richness in oil endowments and performance in this period.

This chapter focuses on the experience of economic development in oil-exporting countries in the MENA region in the period 2001–2015 and addresses whether their experience in this period has been 'inclusive' in the sense of socially and economically benefitting 'the widest' sections of the population.

We construct a single composite index for measuring inclusive growth for a dataset comprising 154 countries drawing from a wide range of indicators (15 in all). These pertain to such broad components of inclusive growth as economic, social, political and environmental aspects. We use a comparative approach to rank all countries for which consistent and reliable data are available grouped in three five-year sub-periods: 2001–05, 2006–10 and 2011–15. The choice of the period – and sub-periods within it – reflects an interest in the period before and soon after the Arab uprisings. The results, in particular for oil-exporting economies, offer new insights to the resource curse debates and literature as well.

In the next section, we discuss the meaning and significance of inclusive growth and examine its broader implications before turning to its measurement and application in the MENA region.

8.2 What is inclusive growth?

Recent interest in inclusive growth has led to a flourishing literature addressing a wide range of issues from conceptual and analytical complexities of the subject to its measurement difficulties and specific country experiences.[3] To a large extent, this reflects the fact that growth is deemed as a necessary, but not sufficient, condition for a country's ability to improve the welfare of its population. The quality of growth, its sustainability as well as the degree to which its benefits may extend to the widest sections of the society have also attracted increasing attention (Hakimian, 2013). This interest has permeated recent policy debates with equal vigour and inclusive growth has been adopted as a common objective for international development agencies as well.[4]

Despite growing calls for growth to be made more inclusive, there is not yet a universally agreed notion of 'inclusive growth'. While growth is easier to define and measure, specifying what makes it 'inclusive' is much more contentious. There is broad agreement that inclusive growth is growth for 'the benefit of most and not just the poor', but ambiguities and disagreements abound beyond this general idea.

Taking a somewhat narrow approach, for instance, Rauniyar and Kanbur (2010) characterise inclusive growth as 'growth plus declining income disparities'. In this formulation, inclusive growth stretches the pro-poor-growth (PPG) approach by adopting a wider notion of who constitutes the poor. This definition, it must be noted, excludes non-income considerations and, therefore, lends itself much more easily to measurement (Klasen, 2010: 10).

At the opposite extreme, inclusive growth is also sometimes loosely referred to as 'growth that benefits everyone'. But as Klasen points out, in this and its broadest sense, the concept seems to imply that growth should 'benefit all stripes of society, including the poor, the near-poor, the middle-income groups, and even the rich' (*Ibid.*: 2). This is equally problematic and highlights the fact that it is not just *who* is to benefit from growth but that the *extent* and *distribution* of such benefits (any implicit trade-offs) should not be overlooked.

Both the narrow and broad definitions, however, focus on income and are concerned with outcomes only. By contrast, more recent formulations of inclusive growth seek to incorporate non-income elements and depict it as a *process* and not just an *outcome*.

For instance, some contributors have stressed the role of *opportunities* in generating inclusive growth.[5] But there is some ambiguity over the main drivers that would oversee or bring about improved access to opportunities, particularly in relation to the role of state and public policy. For instance, are we to rely on market forces to bring about the desired improvements in opportunities for all or is state intervention justified to improve access to these? The former approach, which is arguably a 'trickle down' version of the inclusive growth approach, is seen in the World Bank's 2006 Development Report on 'Equity and Development', which defines equity broadly as 'equal opportunities to pursue a life of one's choosing'. In a similar light, Ianchovichina and Lundstrom emphasise that inclusive growth is about 'raising the pace of growth and enlarging the size of the economy' and not about 'redistributing resources' (2009: 3).

Safety nets and social protection as well as the provision of public and social goods are also considered important elements of the inclusive growth package. Ali and Son (2007) refer to the provision of social opportunities (such as access to health and education) and how these may vary with income levels. Similarly, the World Bank's Commission on Growth and Development talks of inclusiveness as encompassing 'equity, equality of opportunity, and protection in market and employment' (World Bank, 2008).

Focus on *process* helps to broaden the scope of the debate to include social and institutional aspects of growth and development. But it also throws up new challenges. One of these is how to deal with a trade-off between processes and outcomes (Hakimian, 2013). For instance, is growth more – or less – inclusive when improved processes result in poorer economic outcomes? This can happen, for instance, when improvements in civil rights and greater mass participation in social and political affairs (such as following a revolution or popular uprising) lead to short-term setbacks to economic outcomes by stoking greater instability and turmoil. A converse scenario is equally conceivable: if better outcomes are secured in the absence of any commensurate improvements in inclusivity as a process, does that make the experience of overall growth less desirable? This can happen, for instance, with an economic boom under an autocratic regime in the absence of any real reforms or improvements in governance.

Such issues could be better addressed if we had a commonly agreed indicator for measuring inclusive growth. Unsurprisingly, some of the conceptual challenges discussed above are also mirrored in measurement difficulties and problems (McKinley, 2010). Measurement is generally easier if our focus is on material outcomes alone (for instance, better income and/or access to social goods and safety nets), since such outcomes are more readily quantifiable. However, when access to, and benefits from, growth are envisaged in terms of *processes*, measurement becomes harder and more complex. According to Klasen the absence of a universally agreed notion of inclusive growth has led to a wide range of measurement indicators which varies from 'unclear' to 'straightforward' to 'technically difficult' (2010: 9).

It can thus be seen that growing interest in the subject has not been matched by success over a universal definition of inclusive growth that can help both implement and monitor relevant policies. A variety of approaches have emerged with emphases on different aspects of the concept. Narrower concepts stress outcomes (e.g., growth plus equity) and are easier to measure and monitor. Wider concepts are multi-dimensional and hence more ambitious in scope: they stress improved opportunities for achieving better outcomes; they differentiate between processes and outcomes; and they widen outcomes to include non-income aspects (social goods and safety nets). An implicit risk is that an overambitious notion of inclusive growth becomes both meaningless and impractical if it comes close to advocating 'everything for everyone' (Hakimian, 2013: 8).

We now proceed to a proposed measurement of the concept and examine its application in the MENA context.

8.3 Measuring inclusive growth

A composite index synthesises information conveyed by a large number of indictors into a single number or score, which allows ready comparisons of performance for each country across multiple dimensions. A wide range of these indices is now used to measure performance in such disparate areas as human development, environmental sustainability, social progress, gender inequality, water poverty and governance, to name but a few (Hakimian, 2015; Barr, 2013).

Reflecting this interest, a number of methodological manuals have sought to guide the construction and use of these indicators (OECD, 2008; Nardo et al., 2005). Key challenges relate to (a) the need for conceptual clarity in constructing an index (this relates to the broad dimensions or 'pillars' of the phenomenon being measured); (b) choice of indicators (common concerns are measurability, country coverage and availability, relevance and relationship to each other); (c) missing values (these need to be considered and addressed as they can affect the aggregation methodology); (d) weighting and aggregation methods (these need to be clearly stated);

and (e) normalisation (this would be required to make a ranking of indicators comparable, for instance, when country data coverage is not uniform for different indicators).

The choice of a single measure or indicator for inclusive growth is still in its infancy stages (McKinley, 2010; Barr, 2013; Ncube et al., 2013; ADB, 2011; and Hakimian, 2013, 2015). In what follows, we offer a methodology for measuring a composite index for inclusive growth (IG) and use the results to compare the performance of oil-exporting nations both over time and in comparative terms.[6]

8.3.1 Data and methodology

The first issue one encounters in constructing an index is the choice of the broad categories, components or 'pillars' that define the phenomenon being measured. From this then follows the choice of specific sub-indicators that are used to capture each dimension.

In the African Development Bank's (AfDB) formulation, inclusive growth is defined in terms of four broad components: economic, social, spatial and political (AfDB, 2013). Similarly, the Asian Development Bank (ADB) (2014: 22) has classified its inclusive growth concept within the following thematic construct or pillars: (a) income and non-income poverty and inequality; (b) creation-of-opportunities; (c) access-to-opportunities; (d) social protection; and (e) good governance and institutions.

In our approach, we have adopted eight components and used fourteen sub-indicators to construct our index. The choice of these indicators reflects both relevance to the task at hand as well as considerations of data availability.

Macroeconomic Performance: To take account of economic performance, we include two macro indicators: Real Per Capita GDP Growth and Inflation. The choice of the former implies we do not control for GDP size as such but consider its growth performance net of population growth instead. The inclusion of inflation (measured by annual % change in consumer prices) reflects a belief that inflation is a tax on future generations (it favours long-term borrowers) as well as its regressive distributional effects on the current generation (distributes purchasing power against those with fixed incomes). This is why – along with unemployment rate – it is banded together as one of the two elements of what is commonly referred to as the 'Misery Index'.

Health & Demographics: Here three indicators are included. Life Expectancy at Birth, Under-Five Mortality and Public Health Expenditure as % of GDP. Unlike the other indicators which are outcome or output indicators, the latter is an input indicator. Its inclusion is, however, justified as a proxy for access to public health. This rests on the assumption that increased public health expenditure is likely to improve access to health facilities in general.

Labour Force & Employment: Three indicators are included here. Wage & Salaried as % of Total Employment and Employment-to-Population Ratios both for adults (% of those aged 15+) and youth (% of those aged 15–24). The first one of these reflects on the structure of the labour market and the extent to which formal – subject-to-contracts – employment is prevalent in each country's labour market, and the latter two reflect the extent of job creation (or indirectly the prevalence of unemployment) across different age cohorts in each.

Education: Two indicators are used. The first – the Educational Parity Index – is the deviation from parity in gender access to secondary education. Here we take the ratio of female students as % of male students in secondary enrolments, reflecting the extent to which girls and boys progress past primary education in public and private schools (a figure of one indicates complete parity). The second indicator – public spending on education as % of total spending on education – is again an input indicator which is included as a proxy for efforts to widen public access to education.

Gender: To capture the gender aspects of inclusivity, we rely on a composite index – the Gender Inequality Index (GII) provided by the United Nations Development Programme (UNDP). This index shows 'the loss to potential achievement in a country due to gender inequality'. It uses a number of carefully chosen indicators to 'reflect women's reproductive health status, their empowerment and labour market participation relative to men's' (GII, 2017).[7]

Environment: Here too we use a composite index – the Environmental Performance Index (EPI) – to capture the various and multi-faceted aspects of a country's environmental performance. The EPI is preferred to other composite indicators available due to its focus on performance (rather than selected aspects of climatic change or environmental risk) and concern with outcomes rather than policies or inputs.[8]

Inequality and Poverty: Inequality is here measured by the Gini Index and poverty by the Poverty Gap at $3.2 a day (2011 PPP). The latter reflects the depth as well as incidence of poverty and is measured as the mean shortfall in income or consumption from the poverty line, expressed as % of the poverty line (the nonpoor are counted as having zero shortfall). Both measures are available from the World Bank's Development Indicators although coverage is limited to 115–121 countries only in our dataset (see Table 8.1).

Governance: Finally, governance is also represented through a composite index – the Corruption Perception Index (CPI) – which is produced annually by Transparency International. This index ranks countries according to perception of corruption in the public sector based on different assessments and business opinion surveys relating to the administrative and political aspects of corruption.[9]

8.3.1.1 Missing values

The selection of indicators as well as countries included in our dataset (154 in total)[10] reflects careful consideration of data availability. As shown in Table 8.1, most indicators are readily available from standard sources (such as the World Bank's Development Indicators). However, availability decreases noticeably for some indicators such as the Gini Index and Poverty Gap (and for the Education Parity Index to a lesser extent).

Availability also varies over time with data missing for certain periods for different countries. This applies in the case of some MENA countries. For oil-exporting countries, gaps are most serious for the UAE followed by Oman, Iraq and Saudi Arabia. By contrast, Egypt, Tunisia and Morocco have full datasets in this regard.[11] In general, missing data reduce the estimation's accuracy. This is specially an issue for the Inclusive Growth Index since the gaps for 'Inequality and Poverty' indicators seem widest, which are very important for any such computations. The results therefore must be interpreted carefully.

8.3.1.2 Aggregation

Additive or multiplicative aggregation methods have been much discussed in the literature and are widely used (Garriga and Foguet, 2010; Sullivan and Jemmali, 2014). A multiplicative method computes an overall inclusive score for each country (IG_i) as a geometric mean of all its different indicators rescaled into standardised values.[12] This method is, however, less intuitive than the arithmetic mean approach especially when many indicators are involved.

An arithmetic mean can be more simply computed by averaging the sum of the normalised values for each indicator s_j for country i as follows:

$$IGi = \sum_{i=1}^{m} w_j \cdot s_{ji} \tag{1}$$

Table 8.1 Selected indicators for computing the Inclusive Growth Index

Components (C_K)	*Individual indicators* (s_j)	*No. of countries for which data are available* (m_j)			*Datasource*
		2001–05	*2006–10*	*2011–15*	
Macroeconomic Performance	1. Real Per Capita GDP Growth	154	154	153	WDI
	2. Inflation	138	146	147	WDI
Health & Demographics	3. Life Expectancy at Birth	154	154	154	WDI
	4. Mortality Rate Under-5 (per 1,000)	154	154	154	WDI
	5. Public Health Expenditure (% GDP)	152	153	153	WDI
Labour Force & Employment	6. Wage & Salaried (% of Total Employment)	154	154	154	WDI
	7. Employment-to-Population Ratios (% of 15+)	154	154	154	WDI
	8. Employment-to-Population Ratios (% of 15–24)	153	154	154	WDI
Education	9. Educational Parity Index	134	137	133	WDI
	10. Public Spending on Education (% of total)	127	139	127	WDI
Gender	11. Gender Inequality Index (GII)	139	145	148	GII
Environment	12. Environmental Performance Index (EPI)	153	153	154	EPI
Inequality & Poverty	13. Gini Index	115	121	119	WDI
	14. Poverty Gap at $3.2 a day	115	120	118	WDI
Governance	15. Corruption Perception Index (CPI)	145	153	151	CPI
Total number of countries in the dataset		**154**	**154**	**154**	

Sources: World Bank, World Development Indicators; the Gender Inequality Index (GII); the Environmental Performance Index (EPI); and Transparency International for the Corruption Perception Index (CPI).

where:

(i = 1,... m: country i included in the dataset),

(j = 1,... n: indicator j included in the dataset).

As stated above and shown in Table 8.1, we have m=154 countries and n=15 indicators in our dataset.

s_j is a standardised score for the rankings obtained in respect of indicator j for country i. Standardised scores are obtained using the following formula:

$$s_{ji} = 100 \cdot \left(\frac{m_j - r_j}{m_j - 1} \right)_i \tag{2}$$

where r_j is a country's rank (ordered in descending order) with respect to indicator j and m_j is the total number of countries for which data for indicator s_j is available (the maximum number of countries here is 154). This takes into account the variable number of countries for which data is available for specific indicators. The standardised values thus obtained lie between a minimum of 0 and a maximum of 100 (lower values indicate lower rank).

In our estimation, we apply equal weights to all indicators. This yields an equal weight of $w_j = \frac{1}{15} = 0.0666$ for all 15 indicators used. It is important to realise that under this assumption, un-weighted (or more accurately equally weighted) indicators assign greater weight to some 'components'. For instance, this is the case with 'Health and Demographics' and 'Labour Force and Employment' which receive a total weight of 20% each followed by 'Education' and 'Inequality and Poverty' with a weight of 13.3% (this is because weights *de facto* depend on the number of indicators within each component).[13]

8.3.2 Results

Table 8.2 presents a summary of our estimated scores for the 'Inclusive Growth Index' (IG_i) for MENA countries for the three periods of 2001–05, 2006–10 and 2011–15 along the lines explained above. It also shows the results for the MENA oil-exporters and compares them with other oil-exporting peers outside the region. A number of interesting patterns emerge here.

First, among oil-exporting countries in the Middle East, the smaller GCC states (Bahrain, Kuwait, Qatar, the UAE and to a lesser extent Oman) attain the highest IG indices. With scores around or exceeding 60 (on a scale of 0–100) they appear in the top median globally (only Israel surpasses them in the MENA region with an IG score over 70). Saudi Arabia, by contrast, appears to be the least inclusive in all three periods with an IG index which is on par with other more populous oil-exporters such as Algeria: with IG scores of around 47 in 2011–15, both are in the bottom median globally.

Second, among the wider MENA nations, only Tunisia scores in the top half (with an IG index exceeding the 50-score mark). Jordan and Lebanon show a sharp contrast in behaviour: Jordan starts in the top median in 2001–05, but moves down (from 55.8 to 43.7) by 2011–15, whereas Lebanon starts lower and ends much higher (from 40.6 up to 49.2 in the same period). All other MENA countries are typically bunched in the 40–45 range indicating that as a group they underperform internationally (see Appendix Table 8.1 for the global comparisons of the IG indices calculated across all the 154 countries in our dataset). At the bottom end, however, Yemen and Iraq stand out as serious underperformers with the lowest scores both regionally and internationally (Yemen among the bottom five worldwide and Iraq ranked around 120; see Table 8.2 and Appendix Table 8.1).[14]

Table 8.2 Estimated inclusive growth scores, 2001–2005, 2006–2010 and 2011–15, normalised ranks (min=0; max=100)[(a)]

	2001–05	*2006–10*	*2011–15*	*Change, % 2006–10/2001–05*	*Change, % 2011–15/2006–10*
Oil exporters					
GCC countries					
Bahrain	64.4	59.3	64.5	**-8.0**	8.8
Kuwait	67.3	53.6	52.2	**-20.4**	**-2.5**
Oman	56.9	56.1	59.1	**-1.4**	5.3
Qatar	66.5	60.8	56.2	**-8.5**	**-7.6**
Saudi Arabia	55.2	47.1	47.8	**-14.7**	1.4
UAE	62.1	65.7	73.8	5.8	12.4
Other MENA oil exporters					
Algeria	40.8	39.3	46.9	**-3.6**	19.5
Iran	41.2	38.0	34.6	**-7.7**	**-9.1**
Iraq	24.9	33.8	35.7	35.5	5.7
Libya	45.6	43.6	41.6	**-4.4**	**-4.5**
Other oil exporters					
Angola	23.9	27.7	26.4	15.9	**-4.7**
Ecuador	48.7	50.0	49.9	2.7	-0.2
Gabon	31.5	28.2	29.8	**-10.3**	5.6
Indonesia	49.6	54.7	55.9	10.3	2.2
Kazakhstan	49.6	54.7	55.9	10.3	2.2
Mexico	49.6	50.3	48.9	1.5	**-2.8**
Nigeria	23.9	21.7	17.7	**-9.1**	**-18.5**
Russia	55.9	53.0	52.7	**-5.2**	**-0.4**
Venezuela	40.6	41.0	36.9	1.0	**-9.9**
Other Middle East					
Egypt	42.4	42.1	36.0	**-0.5**	**-14.7**
Israel	73.1	74.1	72.8	1.4	**-1.8**
Jordan	55.8	51.9	43.7	**-7.0**	**-15.8**
Lebanon	40.6	53.1	49.2	30.9	**-7.3**
Morocco	39.3	44.7	43.0	13.7	**-3.8**
Syria	49.7	42.9	30.9	**-13.6**	**-27.9**
Tunisia	55.9	53.5	52.1	**-4.2**	**-2.7**
Turkey	39.2	42.8	49.4	9.3	15.2
Yemen	30.7	21.7	14.3	**-29.4**	**-33.9**

Top 5 countries	**2001–05**	**2006–10**	**2011–15**
1	Iceland	Norway	Iceland
2	Norway	Denmark	Norway
3	Denmark	Netherlands	Denmark
4	Sweden	Sweden	Netherlands
5	Switzerland	Iceland	Sweden
Bottom 5 countries	**2001–05**	**2006–10**	**2011–15**
154	Liberia	Congo, Dem. Rep.	Yemen, Rep.
153	Congo, Dem. Rep.	Guinea	Central African Republic
152	Guinea	Sierra Leone	Nigeria
151	Gambia	Yemen, Rep.	Congo, Dem. Rep.
150	Congo, Rep.	Nigeria	Afghanistan

Source: Author's estimates based on data indicated in Appendix Table 8.1.
Note: [(a)] Based on Normalised Country Rankings for indicators specified in Table 8.1. Mean values are arithmetic means with equal weights used for each of the 15 indicators used in Table 8.1.

At the high end of the IG index, Table 8.2 also indicates that the Nordic countries (Iceland, Norway, Denmark and Sweden) and the Netherlands dominated the top five positions. At the bottom end of rankings, African countries dominated along with Yemen in 2006–10 and 2011–15. Remarkably, perhaps, one big oil exporter – Nigeria – too had joined the ranks of the bottom five after 2006.

Examining performance over time also reveals interesting patterns especially in the periods before and after 2010 (a threshold level capturing changes before and after the global financial crisis and the Arab uprisings). With the exception of the UAE, the GCC oil-exporters indicate a deterioration in their IG performance before 2010: Kuwait, Saudi Arabia, Qatar and Bahrain (in that order) show the biggest deterioration followed by Oman (-1.4%). After 2010, however, with the exception of Qatar (-7.6%) all others follow an improved trajectory (with the UAE's improvement consolidating significantly).

For other MENA oil-exporters – Algeria, Iran and Libya – too the period before 2010 is marked with a similar deterioration. After 2010, Algeria reversed the trend (with a significant improvement of almost 20%), but both Iran and Libya progressed further along a declining trajectory. Only Iraq showed a marked and consistent improvement in both periods: a more serious improvement in 2006–10 over 2001–05 (35.5%) followed by a more modest one in 2011–15 over 2006–10 (in both cases indicating perhaps a low base pertaining to the aftermath of the 2003 invasion of the country).

Beyond the region, the experience of other oil-exporters seems mixed: in the first period Gabon, Nigeria and Russia seem to have followed the experience of the small GCC states exhibiting deterioration during 2001–10. This contrasts with Angola, Ecuador, Indonesia, Kazakhstan and – to a much smaller extent – Mexico and Venezuela, which improved their indices over the same period. After 2010, the picture outside MENA is mixed again with four countries deteriorating: Nigeria, Venezuela, Angola and Mexico (in that order); and three improving (Gabon, Indonesia, Kazakhstan); and two almost stationary (Ecuador and Russia). Amongst this group, the biggest decline belongs to Nigeria followed by Venezuela.

The poor performance of oil exporters in the pre-2010 period has to be seen in the context of generally buoyant international oil prices during much of this period: between the Iraq invasion in March 2003 and July 2008 when average monthly oil prices hit an all-time high of $132 per barrel, oil prices doubled with an average of around $60 per barrel. This trend was reversed after the onset of the international financial crisis though by 2011 a recovery phase had begun which continued until June 2014: oil prices averaged $110.3 per barrel between January 2011 and June 2014. After this, the downward trend set in with a monthly average price of almost half to the end of 2015.[15] The point here is that those countries with less diversified economies, which are more dependent on oil rents, the poor IG index performance has reflected the wider impact of the oil price trends beyond GDP alone.

Turning to non-oil-exporters in the MENA region, the deteriorating trends for Syria and Yemen stand out: both record some of the heaviest declines over the five-year periods before and after 2010. By contrast, consistent improvers in MENA are: Turkey, Iraq and the UAE (they record improvements both before and after 2010).

Another interesting pattern emerging from Table 8.2 is that both Tunisia and Egypt – the two countries that led the 'Arab Spring' in 2010–11 – show a modest deterioration in their IG index in the two quinquennial periods before their uprisings. Prior to 2010, Egypt did better than Tunisia with an IG contraction of only -0.5% in contrast to the latter's -4.2%. After 2010, the order was reversed with Tunisia suffering a deterioration of -2.7% in contrast to Egypt's -14.7% loss.

More significantly, perhaps, it is hard to detect a simple and one-to-one relationship between IG performance and the incidence of political uprisings. On one hand, countries such as Bahrain, Libya, Syria and Yemen, all of which experienced a deterioration in their IG, were rocked by uprisings. On the other hand, there were countries – such as Kuwait, Saudi Arabia, Qatar, Jordan and Algeria – that suffered a deterioration in their IG scores but had no major uprisings. Even more interestingly perhaps and by contrast, a country like Morocco saw an improvement in its IG score before 2010 (by nearly 14%) and was still rocked by similar uprisings (although no regime change followed).

To sum up: two important findings follow our study. First, we find evidence in support of the oil curse thesis in the context of inclusive growth: as we have seen, during the buoyant oil price period (2001–10), several oil economies experienced a deterioration in their IG scores (more specifically over the periods of 2001–05 and 2006–10). The most notable among these were: Algeria, Iran, Libya, Bahrain, Kuwait and Iran in MENA followed by Angola, Gabon and Nigeria in Africa.

Second, our analysis points to the absence of an unequivocal relationship between inclusive growth and experiencing political upheaval during the so-called Arab Spring. As we have seen, some countries improved their IG score and experienced upheavals yet others suffered from a deterioration but did not experience such upheavals. Thus, whether in respect of the resource curse theory or shedding light on the forces underlying the Arab uprisings our finding seems to offer interesting and novel perspectives.

8.3.2.1 Sensitivity analysis

To ascertain the relative influence of each of the specific indicators used in the last section on the overall IG performance of countries, we offer sensitivity analysis below for a selection of the oil-exporting countries. Figures 8.1(a), 8.1(b) and 8.1(c) offer sensitivity analysis for the 15 indicators we have used in the construction and estimation of the IG indices for each of the three sub-periods, respectively 2001–05, 2006–10 and 2011–15. In these figures, a baseline of 100% indicates no change and each data point shows the re-estimated IG if a particular indicator were to be excluded from the calculations (as if they were given a weight of zero). Figures above 100% (baseline) indicate the indicator has a negative effect on the overall index since its elimination (as shown in these figures) improves the index. The opposite is true of figures below 100% (i.e., they have an overall positive effect in the IG index makeup since their elimination lowers the IG score).

The results here are reported for four large MENA oil-exporters, all OPEC members: Algeria, Iran, Libya and Saudi Arabia (the smaller GCC states are left out as they are in many ways untypical in general). Each figure also highlights the indicator which has the largest sensitivity impact (see the % figures shown on each figure).

This analysis shows unemployment and youth unemployment have the largest negative impact on the IG index in all four countries. These are measured by 'employment-to-population ratios 15+' and 'employment-to-population ratios 15–24' in our dataset. It can be seen that in all three periods, employment creation was a challenge for these four countries. In the case of Libya and Saudi Arabia youth employment creation (15–24) proved to be the most significant factor impacting on the final IG index. In the case of Saudi Arabia (2001–10), the Gender Inequality Index (GII) too has a big negative influence, an influence similar to that of inflation in the case of Iran.[16]

While employment challenges of the populous oil economies are well known, the policy implications of these results should be drawn with care. As we shall see below, critics of com-

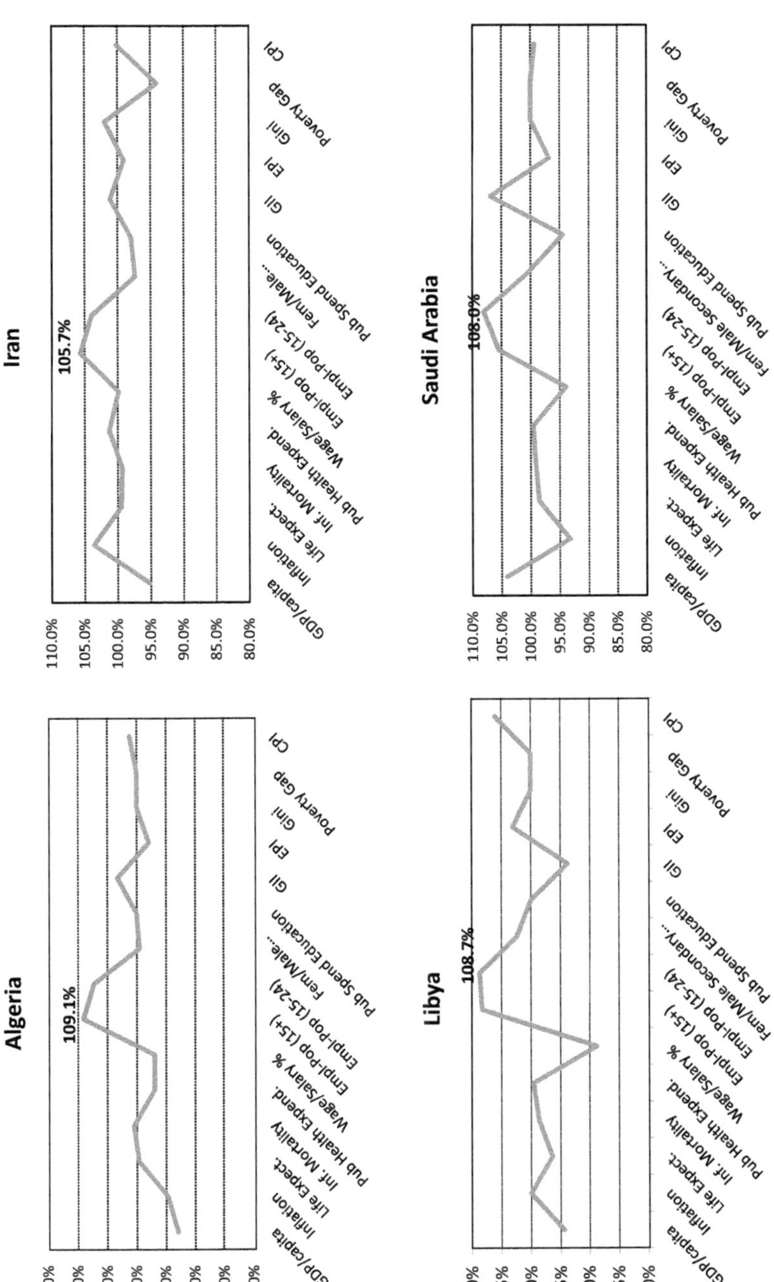

Figure 8.1 (a) Inclusive growth sensitivity analysis (2001–05)

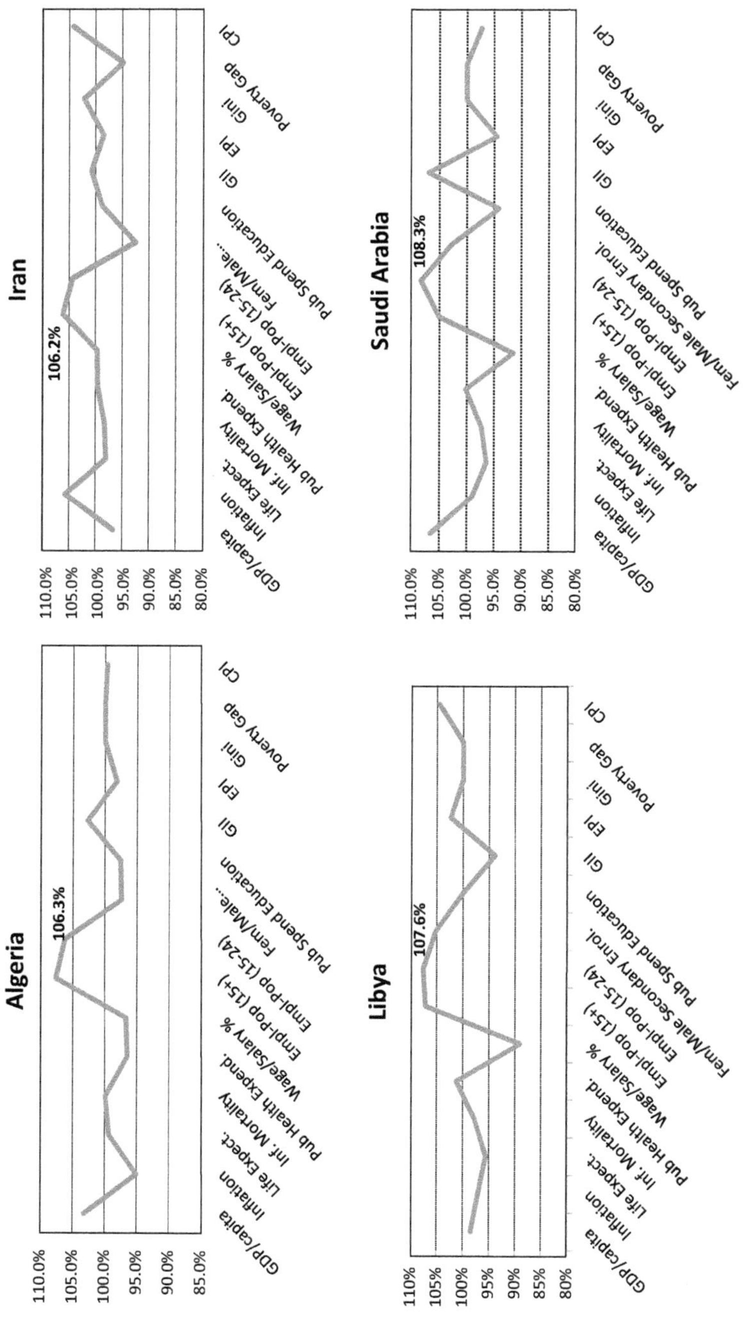

Figure 8.1 (b) Inclusive growth sensitivity analysis (2006–10)

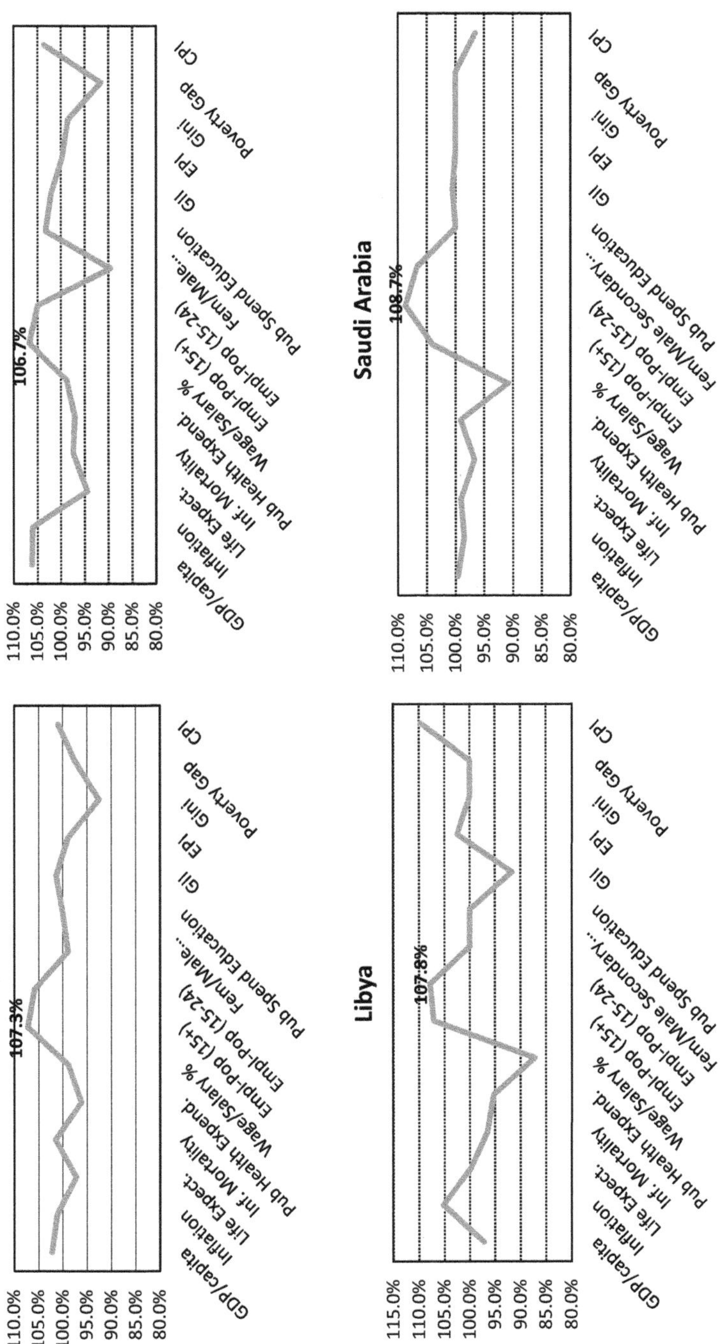

Figure 8.1 (c) Inclusive growth sensitivity analysis (2011–15). *Source:* Author's calculations.

posite indicators are wary of hasty conclusions based on 'mechanically constructed' composite indices, as they can be misleading for policy purposes. The value-added of such composite indicators is, ultimately, in their ability to capture real performances. With regards to our findings above, two points stand out with policy implications for oil-exporting countries.

First, as is widely known, labour market issues (job creation and lowering, especially youth, unemployment) remain a key challenge and the principal route to achieving inclusive growth. Second, the performance of these countries (with the exception of the smaller GCC states) is consistently lack-lustre across a wide range of dimensions and it would require a concerted effort to improve their inclusive growth record. A focus on one or two selective dimensions will not be sufficient to improve their comparative ranks.

8.3.3 Limitations

We should recall that our methodology for computing a single composite index for IG is based on an aggregate average ranking of 154 countries in 15 selected areas over the three periods of 2001–05, 2006–10 and 2011–15.

The perceived advantages of a composite index are mainly to do with the parsimony in the use of data and its presentation: they help summarise complex data by providing a shortcut to many separate indicators. Moreover, they make the task of assessing and monitoring performance, across countries and/or over time, easier. They can thus be used for setting targets and communicating easily and effectively with the public over holistic topics. But there are limitations too.

On one hand, there is concern with the near-obsession with country rankings (the so-called 'tyranny of international index rankings') that emanates from the estimation and use of composite indicators in a wide range of fields. From this perspective, too much faith should not be placed on the accuracy of these rankings. Allowing for uncertainty, for instance, Høyland et al. (2012) have shown that the link between rankings and indicators on one hand and real performance on the other might in fact be quite 'fuzzy' (2012: 2).[17]

Another line of criticism has been articulated by those concerned with the value-added of these 'mashed up' indices in offering real policy insight. Ravallion warns that their 'meaning, interpretation and robustness are often unclear' (2010: 2) especially compared to monitoring the components of what has been termed 'a large and eclectic dashboard' of separate indicators (Stiglitz et al., 2009: 62).[18]

Despite these legitimate concerns, however, even the hardest critics of composite indicators do not favour their complete abandonment. As articulated by Ravallion, the main lesson is probably 'that the current enthusiasm for new mashup indices needs to be balanced by clearer warnings for, and more critical scrutiny from, users' (2010: 30). This applies with equal vigour to our exercise here in estimating the Inclusive Growth Index for MENA countries and using it to reflect on the performance of the oil-exporting economies in the region.

8.4 Conclusion

This chapter has addressed whether the recent growth experience of MENA countries in the one and a half decades between 2001 and 2015 has been 'inclusive' in the sense of benefitting 'the widest' sections of the society.

To address this, we constructed a single composite index for measuring inclusive growth for each country based on a wide range of indicators (15 in all) pertaining to such broad components as economic, social, political and environmental. We used a comparative approach to rank all 154 countries in our database for which consistent and reliable data were available in the three five-year periods of 2001–05, 2006–10 and 2011–15.

Two interesting results emerge from our study: first, we find support for the resource curse theory in the case of oil-exporting economies in the region before 2010, and second, we cast doubt on the supposed relationship between the Arab uprisings and inclusive growth prior to 2010.

Regarding oil-exporters, we found that despite the generally buoyant international oil prices during 2002–08, both large and small oil exporters – Algeria and Iran, on one hand, and Libya, Bahrain and Kuwait (Qatar to a lesser extent) on the other – suffered a deterioration in their experience of inclusive growth before 2010. Moreover and on further examination, we also showed that the IG index for the four largest oil-exporters (Algeria, Iran, Libya and Saudi Arabia) was highly sensitive to these countries' (in)ability to create sufficient jobs to check unemployment. This seems to confirm that labour market issues remain key to achieving inclusive growth for these economies. This aspect is reflected in their alarmingly low rankings for unemployment in general and youth unemployment in particular.[19] Our analysis also shows that other development indicators such as gender and environment drag down their performance (data on poverty and inequality unfortunately are patchy).

Second, our analysis points to the absence of an unequivocal relationship between inclusive growth and political upheavals during the so-called Arab Spring. As we have seen, some countries improved their IG score and experienced upheavals yet others suffered from a deterioration but did not experience such upheavals.

Finally, our study underscores perhaps one overriding economic lesson of the last decade and half: the need to examine outcomes not just in terms of growth but also the quality of that growth, its sustainability as well as the degree to which its benefits may extend to the wider sections of the society. To achieve this, a concerted effort is required to improve their inclusive growth track record. A focus on one or two selective dimensions – important though they may be – is not sufficient to improve their experience or comparative ranks.

Appendix Table 8.1 Inclusive growth index and overall rankings: 2001–15

	IG (2001–05)	*Rank*	*IG (2006–10)*	*Rank*	*IG (2011–15)*	*Rank*
1. Afghanistan	24.0	146	27.0	143	21.6	150
2. Albania	53.3	65	56.8	52	48.2	80
3. Algeria	40.8	98	39.3	104	46.9	85
4. Angola	23.9	149	27.7	141	26.4	143
5. Argentina	47.0	83	52.0	70	52.6	65
6. Armenia	46.3	87	50.4	76	47.1	84
7. Australia	77.2	13	77.0	14	71.0	24
8. Austria	79.1	11	78.4	9	74.9	17
9. Azerbaijan	47.5	80	39.2	106	38.4	109
10. Bahrain	64.4	42	59.3	45	64.5	37
11. Bangladesh	30.9	135	31.5	132	27.5	139
12. Barbados	67.9	29	61.9	37	55.9	53
13. Belarus	65.7	39	67.1	32	63.1	38
14. Belgium	69.9	25	69.8	26	68.6	29
15. Belize	54.3	63	51.7	73	52.3	66
16. Benin	31.0	134	31.8	129	28.6	136
17. Bhutan	50.5	69	52.2	69	46.1	88
18. Bolivia	43.3	91	47.7	81	49.9	73
19. Bosnia & Herzegovina	56.4	55	56.7	54	59.5	46
20. Botswana	41.1	95	40.9	99	41.6	102
21. Brazil	47.0	82	52.0	71	48.8	78
22. Bulgaria	56.9	53	57.3	49	55.8	54
23. Burkina Faso	36.5	117	35.6	118	35.5	121
24. Burundi	28.5	140	33.2	123	28.6	137
25. Cabo Verde	53.7	64	51.4	74	47.7	82
26. Cambodia	40.1	104	38.1	110	42.7	100
27. Cameroon	32.0	126	28.6	137	28.9	135
28. Canada	79.2	10	77.6	12	78.8	7
29. Central African Rep.	24.9	145	23.1	148	15.4	153
30. Chad	31.3	130	26.2	144	21.7	149
31. Chile	59.5	47	57.0	51	59.4	47
32. China	57.4	51	59.2	46	59.8	45
33. Colombia	46.8	84	47.6	82	49.5	74
34. Congo, Dem. Rep.	19.0	153	17.0	154	20.2	151
35. Congo, Rep.	22.6	150	31.3	135	26.9	141
36. Costa Rica	57.9	50	60.0	42	60.5	42
37. Cote d'Ivoire	27.7	141	25.8	145	28.5	138
38. Croatia	62.7	43	60.4	40	59.9	44
39. Cuba	72.4	23	74.2	18	69.5	26
40. Cyprus	73.8	20	74.2	19	69.3	28
41. Czech Republic	74.9	18	72.7	23	72.6	21
42. Denmark	84.1	3	84.5	2	82.7	3
43. Dominican Republic	36.0	118	39.6	102	42.7	99
44. Ecuador	48.7	76	50.0	78	49.9	72
45. Egypt	42.4	93	42.1	95	36.0	119

(*Continued*)

Appendix Table 8.1 Continued

	IG (2001–05)	*Rank*	*IG (2006–10)*	*Rank*	*IG (2011–15)*	*Rank*
46. El Salvador	46.1	88	49.5	80	52.2	67
47. Eritrea	30.8	136	27.1	142	36.0	117
48. Estonia	65.9	38	66.5	33	72.9	19
49. Eswatini (Swaziland)	37.3	114	34.2	119	38.8	108
50. Ethiopia	41.1	96	38.4	109	37.2	112
51. Fiji	52.0	67	44.4	88	45.6	90
52. Finland	80.2	7	79.3	7	77.5	9
53. France	76.4	14	77.1	13	75.3	14
54. Gabon	31.5	128	28.2	139	29.8	133
55. Gambia, The	20.2	151	28.0	140	25.1	145
56. Georgia	43.2	92	44.4	89	45.2	92
57. Germany	79.2	9	78.4	8	77.4	10
58. Ghana	37.3	115	39.9	101	39.8	106
59. Greece	66.2	36	59.6	43	56.5	50
60. Guatemala	39.5	107	39.5	103	38.8	107
61. Guinea	19.4	152	18.5	153	23.7	147
62. Guyana	40.1	103	36.6	116	41.2	104
63. Honduras	41.0	97	38.6	108	41.2	103
64. Hungary	67.6	30	63.7	36	65.3	36
65. Iceland	87.0	1	81.6	5	86.6	1
66. India	33.9	122	31.8	128	34.2	126
67. Indonesia	39.6	106	41.9	96	43.0	97
68. Iran	41.2	94	38.0	112	34.6	125
69. Iraq	24.9	144	33.8	120	35.7	120
70. Ireland	74.8	19	74.4	17	77.2	11
71. Israel	73.1	21	74.1	21	72.8	20
72. Italy	66.8	34	65.3	35	60.9	41
73. Jamaica	48.4	78	45.0	86	45.3	91
74. Japan	76.0	16	75.4	15	75.3	15
75. Jordan	55.8	59	51.9	72	43.7	94
76. Kazakhstan	49.6	72	54.7	59	55.9	52
77. Kenya	31.2	131	31.3	134	32.3	128
78. Korea, Rep.	66.1	37	69.5	29	70.2	25
79. Kuwait	67.3	31	53.6	61	52.2	68
80. Kyrgyz Republic	46.7	85	46.7	84	52.8	63
81. Lao PDR	39.3	108	37.5	113	35.1	122
82. Latvia	64.4	41	60.1	41	67.1	31
83. Lebanon	40.6	102	53.1	65	49.2	76
84. Lesotho	31.0	133	31.7	130	32.3	129
85. Liberia	13.8	154	22.6	149	24.3	146
86. Libya	45.6	89	43.6	91	41.6	101
87. Lithuania	66.9	32	61.7	38	65.5	35
88. Luxembourg	72.2	24	75.0	16	69.4	27
89. Madagascar	33.2	123	33.7	121	31.1	130

(*Continued*)

Appendix Table 8.1 Continued

	IG (2001–05)	*Rank*	*IG (2006–10)*	*Rank*	*IG (2011–15)*	*Rank*
90. Malawi	28.8	139	32.9	126	34.6	124
91. Malaysia	61.5	45	56.8	53	60.0	43
92. Maldives	48.8	75	57.1	50	53.4	58
93. Mali	32.2	125	28.3	138	26.7	142
94. Malta	68.6	28	71.8	24	76.7	12
95. Mauritania	24.0	147	25.7	146	25.3	144
96. Mauritius	54.8	62	53.2	63	53.1	61
97. Mexico	49.6	73	50.3	77	48.9	77
98. Moldova	49.9	70	52.8	68	56.9	49
99. Mongolia	47.3	81	42.4	94	46.6	87
100. Montenegro	57.9	49	59.5	44	61.0	40
101. Morocco	39.3	109	44.7	87	43.0	98
102. Mozambique	35.7	119	31.5	133	33.0	127
103. Namibia	40.7	99	37.2	114	36.1	116
104. Nepal	34.6	121	39.2	105	40.7	105
105. Netherlands	80.9	6	84.3	3	81.2	4
106. New Zealand	79.2	8	77.9	11	78.5	8
107. Nicaragua	37.4	113	40.5	100	45.7	89
108. Niger	26.1	142	33.0	125	38.4	110
109. Nigeria	23.9	148	21.7	150	17.7	152
110. North Macedonia	48.1	79	49.5	79	53.1	60
111. Norway	86.1	2	85.0	1	84.7	2
112. Oman	56.9	52	56.1	56	59.1	48
113. Pakistan	31.4	129	25.5	147	27.0	140
114. Panama	56.7	54	54.4	60	51.9	71
115. Paraguay	40.0	105	43.7	90	46.9	86
116. Peru	51.4	68	55.7	57	54.1	57
117. Philippines	38.8	112	37.1	115	43.5	96
118. Poland	65.0	40	69.5	28	68.1	30
119. Portugal	66.9	33	68.6	30	67.0	32
120. Qatar	66.5	35	60.8	39	56.2	51
121. Romania	49.6	74	52.8	67	52.2	69
122. Russia	55.9	58	53.0	66	52.7	64
123. Rwanda	40.6	100	41.0	97	44.4	93
124. Saudi Arabia	55.2	61	47.1	83	47.8	81
125. Senegal	33.0	124	33.1	124	38.3	111
126. Serbia	56.4	56	59.2	47	54.5	56
127. Sierra Leone	25.5	143	19.6	152	22.0	148
128. Singapore	72.9	22	71.2	25	71.1	23
129. Slovak Republic	68.7	27	69.5	27	66.3	33
130. Slovenia	76.2	15	78.1	10	75.7	13
131. South Africa	38.8	111	38.6	107	36.9	113
132. Spain	69.2	26	67.6	31	65.8	34
133. Sri Lanka	46.6	86	46.2	85	43.5	95
134. Sweden	81.6	4	83.2	4	80.9	5
135. Switzerland	81.1	5	81.4	6	80.5	6

(*Continued*)

Appendix Table 8.1 Continued

	IG (2001–05)	*Rank*	*IG (2006–10)*	*Rank*	*IG (2011–15)*	*Rank*
136. Syria	49.7	71	42.9	92	30.9	131
137. Tajikistan	30.0	138	31.7	131	36.5	115
138. Tanzania	43.5	90	35.9	117	34.8	123
139. Thailand	60.0	46	56.4	55	55.7	55
140. Togo	31.6	127	31.9	127	36.0	118
141. Trinidad & Tobago	55.8	60	53.2	64	47.5	83
142. Tunisia	55.9	57	53.5	62	52.1	70
143. Turkey	39.2	110	42.8	93	49.4	75
144. Uganda	35.1	120	33.2	122	29.1	134
145. Ukraine	58.3	48	55.3	58	52.9	62
146. UAE	62.1	44	65.7	34	73.8	18
147. UK	77.2	12	74.1	20	75.1	16
148. USA	75.1	17	73.0	22	71.3	22
149. Uruguay	48.5	77	57.7	48	61.4	39
150. Venezuela	40.6	101	41.0	98	36.9	114
151. Vietnam	52.7	66	50.9	75	53.3	59
152. Yemen	30.7	137	21.7	151	14.3	154
153. Zambia	31.2	132	29.1	136	30.4	132
154. Zimbabwe	36.6	116	38.1	111	48.6	79
Max	**87.0**		**85.0**		**86.6**	
Min	**13.8**		**17.0**		**14.3**	
Average	**50.2**		**50.0**		**49.8**	

Source: Author's estimations.

Notes

1 This chapter was published as a Working Paper by the Economic Research Forum (ERF) in December 2019 (see Hakimian, 2019). I am grateful for helpful feedback and comments I received in several international conferences and workshops, where I presented my work. It draws from my earlier research on inclusive growth for the African Development Bank's Regional Department for North Africa (ORNA). An earlier version of this appeared in Spanish in *Revista Awraq* (no. 15), published by Casa Árabe (Madrid: February 2019). The usual disclaimer applies.

2 See, for instance, Sachs and Warner (1995); Ross (1999).

3 See, *inter alia*: Ali (2007), Rauniyar and Kanbur (2010), Klasen (2010), Felipe (2010) and Ianchovichina and Lundstrom (2009).

4 In 2008, the Asian Development Bank's *Strategy 2020* adopted inclusive growth as one part of its strategic development agenda (the other two being environmentally sustainable growth and regional integration; ADB, 2008). The African Development Bank too has adopted it as one of its two strategic objectives for 2013–22 to broaden access 'to economic opportunities for more people, countries and regions, while protecting the vulnerable' (the other strategic priority being green growth 'to make growth sustainable'; AfDB, 2013: 10).

5 The ADB's Eminent Persons Group refers to inclusive growth as 'economic opportunities' that are 'available to all – particularly the poor – to the maximum possible extent' (ADB, 2007: 13–14). Others have been equally specific in stating 'inclusive growth focuses on both creating opportunities and making the opportunities accessible to all' (Ali and Zhuang, 2007: 10).

6 The discussion here draws from the approach developed in Hakimian (2013, 2015).

7 Due to data limitations, we have used back-casted data for the years 2000 and 2005 to obtain an average for the period 2001–05 and data for 2005 and 2010 to get an average for the period 2006–10, respectively.

8 The EPI uses a number of detailed indicators to measure performance across the two broad categories of *Environmental Health* (with a weight of 40%) and *Ecosystem Vitality* (with a weight of 60%); see Hsu et al. (2013) for methodology and weights used. Due to data limitations, we have used an average for the period 2002–05 for the first sub-period. Data for the period 2002–10 are from the 2014 back-casted data and those for 2011–15 are from the 2016 back-casted data (EPI, 2014, 2016).
9 In earlier years, scores were assigned on a scale from 10 (very clean) to 0 (highly corrupt). In 2012, Transparency International revised the methodology used to construct the index to allow for comparison of scores from one year to the next. Period averages for 2001–05 and 2006–10 use historical data available from earlier estimations and for 2012–15 from the new dataset. For 2011, figures are not available (Transparency International, 2019).
10 See Appendix Table 8.1 for a full list of the countries included in the dataset.
11 For a detailed discussion of this and its application, see Hakimian (2105).
12 The Human Development Indicator (HDI), for instance, switched to geometric mean in 2010. For another example of this method, see Hakimian (2013).
13 Hakimian (2015) considers an alternative weighting method, where each *component* is given equal weight.
14 The West Bank and Gaza are not included in this dataset due to data limitations.
15 Oil prices refer to average monthly Brent crude prices and are derived from data provided by the US Energy Information Administration (EIA) available online from: https://www.eia.gov/dnav/pet/hist/LeafHandler.ashx?n=PET&s=RBRTE&f=M.
16 Given the low coverage of the poverty and inequality indicators in the dataset, the results for these indicators have to be used with caution (see Section 8.3.1.1 on 'Missing Values' above).
17 Their discussion of three common and widely used composite indicators (Doing Business, the Human Development Index and Freedom House) shows that the rankings in the top and bottom ends are more stable but the middle 80% are subject to considerable uncertainty (Høyland et al., 2012: 8).
18 To use a familiar analogy, each one of the key indicators on a car's dashboard (for instance, fuel level, oil pressure and battery level) convey important data about the car's roadworthiness and safety in their own right. Hence, mashing up all of these into a single index as a general indication of a car's 'well-being' would not be helpful (Ncube et al., 2013: 14).
19 Saudi Arabia, for instance, ranked last for youth unemployment among 154 countries in the dataset in the 2006–10 period and rose only slightly to rank 151st during 2011–15.

References

ADB (2007), *Toward a New Asian Development Bank in a New Asia: Report of the Eminent Persons Group*, Manila: Asian Development Bank.

ADB (2008), *Strategy 2020 – The Long-Term Strategic Framework of the Asian Development Bank 2008–2020*, Manila: Asian Development Bank.

ADB (2011), *The Framework of Inclusive Growth Indicators 2011: Key Indicators for Asia and the Pacific*, Manila: Asian Development Bank.

ADB (2014), *ADB's Support for Inclusive Growth – Thematic Evaluation Study*, Manila: Asian Development Bank.

AfDB (2013), *At the Center of Africa's Transformation, Strategy for 2013–2022*, Tunis: African Development Bank.

Ali, Ifzal (2007), *Pro-Poor to Inclusive Growth: Asian Prescriptions*, ERD Policy Brief, No. 48; Manila: Asian Development Bank, May.

Ali, Ifzal and Hyun Hwa Son (2007), "Measuring Inclusive Growth", *Asian Development Review*, Vol. 24, No. 1.

Ali, Ifzal and Juzhong Zhuang (2007), "Inclusive Growth Toward a Prosperous Asia: Policy Implications", ERD Working Paper Series, No. 97, July, Manila: Asian Development Bank.

Barr, Jane (2013), "Exploring the Feasibility of an Inclusive Green Economy Index", Background paper for the 'UNEP Workshop on Developing an Inclusive Green Economy Index', 6-7 November, Geneva.

EPI (2014 and 2016), *Environmental Performance Index*; available from: http://epi.yale.edu/; backcasted data for 2002–10 are available from: http://epi.yale.edu/files/2014epi_backcasted_scores_0.xls; and for 2011–2015 available from: http://epi2016.yale.edu/downloads.

Garriga, R.G. and A.P. Foguet (2010), "Improved Method to Calculate a Water Poverty Index at Local Scale", *Journal of Environmental Engineering*, Vol. 136, No. 11.
GII (2017), "Table 5: Gender Inequality Index", Data from the site of 'Human Development Reports', New York: United Nations Development Programme; available from: http://hdr.undp.org/en/composite/GII.
Hakimian, Hassan (2011), "The Economic Prospects of the 'Arab Spring': A Bumpy Road Ahead", Development Viewpoint, No. 63, Centre for Development Policy and Research, London: SOAS.
Hakimian, Hassan (2013), "The Search for Inclusive Growth in North Africa: A Comparative Approach", Economic Brief, Tunis: African Development Bank.
Hakimian, Hassan (2015), "Measuring Inclusive Growth: From Theory to Applications in North Africa", mimeo, Regional Department for North Africa (ORNA), Tunis: African Development Bank.
Hakimian, Hassan (2019), "From Oil Rents to Inclusive Growth: Lessons from the MENA Region", Working Paper No. 1380, Cairo: Economic Research Forum, December; available from: https://erf.org.eg/publications/from-oil-rents-to-inclusive-growth-lessons-from-the-mena-region/.
Høyland, Bjørn, Karl, Moene and Fredrik Willumsen (2012), "The Tyranny of International Index Rankings", *Journal of Development Economics*, Vol. 97, No. 1.
Hsu, A., L.A. Johnson and A. Lloyd (2013), *Measuring Progress: A Practical Guide from the Developers of the Environmental Performance Index (EPI)*, New Haven: Yale Center for Environmental Law & Policy.
Ianchovichina, Elena and Susanna Lundstrom (2009), "Inclusive Growth Analytics", Policy Research Working Paper, No. 4851, Economic Policy and Debt Department, Washington DC: The World Bank, March.
Jesus Felipe (2010), *Inclusive Growth, Full Employment, and Structural Change: Implications and Policies for Developing Asia*, Manila: Anthem Press.
Klasen, Stephan (2010), "Measuring and Monitoring Inclusive Growth: Multiple Definitions, Open Questions, and Some Constructive Proposals", ADB Sustainable Development Working Paper Series, No. 12, June.
McKinley, Terry (2010), "Inclusive Growth Criteria and Chief Indicators: An Inclusive Growth Index for Diagnosis of Country Progress", ADB Sustainable Development Working Paper Series, No. 14, June.
Nardo, M., Saisana, M., Saltelli, A., Tarantola, S., Hoffman, A. and E. Giovannini (2005), "Handbook on Constructing Composite Indicators: Methodology and User Guide", OECD Statistics Working Paper, STD/DOC(2005)3, Paris: OECD.
Ncube, Mthuli, Shimeles, Abebe and Stephen Younger (2013), "Inclusive Growth Index for Africa: Methods and Application", mimeo, Tunis: African Development Bank.
OECD (2008), *Handbook on Constructing Composite Indicators: Methodology and User Guide*, Paris: OECD; available from: http://www.oecd.org/std/42495745.pdf
Rauniyar, Ganesh and Ravi Kanbur (2010), "Inclusive Development: Two Papers on Conceptualization, Application, and the ADB Perspective", January draft; Independent Evaluation Department, Manila: Asian Development Bank.
Ravallion, M. (2010), "Mashup Indices of Development", Policy Research Working Paper 5432, Washington, DC: The World Bank.
Ross, M.L. (1999), "The Political Economy of the Resource Curse", *World Politics*, Vol. 51, No. 2.
Sachs, J.D. and A.M. Warner (1995), "Natural Resource Abundance and Economic Growth", National Bureau of Economic Research Working Paper 5398.
Stiglitz Joseph, E., Jean-Paul, Fitoussi and Amartya Sen (2009), *Report by the Commission on Measurement of Economic Performance and Social Progress*, Paris: OFCE - Centre de recherche en économie de Sciences Po; available from: https://www.ofce.sciences-po.fr/pdf/dtravail/WP2009-33.pdf.
Sullivan, Caroline A. and Hatem Jemmali (2014), "Toward Understanding Water Conflicts in the MENA Region: A Comparative Analysis Using Water Poverty Index", Working Paper, No. 859, Cairo: Economic Research Forum (ERF), November.
Transparency International (2019); available from: https://www.transparency.org/research/cpi/overview.
World Bank, *World Development Indicators*, Washington, DC: The World Bank; available from: http://data.worldbank.org/data-catalog/world-development-indicators
World Bank (2006), *World Development Report 2006: Equity and Development*, Washington, DC: The World Bank.
World Bank (2008), *The Growth Report: Strategies for Sustained Growth and Inclusive Development, Commission on Growth and Development*, Washington, DC: The World Bank.

9

UNDERSTANDING WATER CONFLICTS IN THE MENA REGION

A comparative analysis using a restructured Water Poverty Index

Hatem Jemmali and Caroline A. Sullivan

9.1 Introduction

During the last three decades, the experience of water scarcity has become more widespread across the world, and much effort has gone into the development of suitable indicators to represent this phenomenon. Water availability itself is defined, according to the well-known Falkenmark approach (Falkenmark et al., 1989), as the *annual runoff available for human use.* Hydrological modelling and the measurement of physical water availability and shortages have long been considered the most important aspect, with few efforts made to recognise the socio-political, economic, and ecological drivers of water scarcity, more reflective of our current understanding of the Earth system. In more recent years, water scarcity has been progressively recognised as an inherently multidimensional phenomenon, highlighting the need to move to a wider perspective, where multiple dimensions are both instrumentally and intrinsically important (Salameh, 2000; Sullivan, 2001; Sullivan et al., 2003; Jemmali & Matoussi, 2013; Johnson & Wilk, 2014; Jemmali & Sullivan, 2014). Such approaches try to link the biophysical and social worlds to produce a more meaningful assessment of what it means, in reality, to be water-poor.

The Middle East and North Africa (MENA) region is known as one of the most water-scarce regions of the world; ten of the 15 most water-poor countries in the world are located in this region (Alterman & Dziuban, 2010). In the last few years, some countries in the region have experienced a crisis of water and sanitation, and in many areas, there is a concern that the water situation is rapidly deteriorating from bad to worse. In addition to dramatic ecological effects on groundwater and river systems, the water shortages in these countries are a major burden to society, causing waterborne diseases, hygiene problems and a constraint to human development.

The objective of this study is twofold. First, it aims to adopt a methodological framework for a multidimensional assessment of water poverty that overcomes the limitations of traditional indices. In this regard, a *restructured* Water Poverty Index (*r*WPI) is proposed as an alternative to the *initial* Water Poverty Index (*i*WPI), originally developed by Sullivan (2000, 2002). Principal component analysis (PCA) and a weighted multiplicative function are employed in the construction of this *r*WPI, strengthening the theoretical framework and statistical foundation of this measure of water poverty. Secondly, this research demonstrates the suitability of the index to address the main drivers of current and potential water conflicts in the key river basins of the MENA region (the Jordan, Tigris–Euphrates, and Nile River basins). The holistic approach developed here to assess water stress in these basins could fill a key role in implementing a fairer, more equitable and transparent decision-making process for the allocation of shared resources. Overall, this chapter aims to demonstrate an effective and improved index of water poverty that will practically help policymakers to alleviate conflicts over water allocation and use.

This chapter is structured as follows: in the next section we provide a brief overview of the water situation in the MENA region, and subsequently, we discuss the methodology and data used for our analysis. Before concluding, we discuss the obtained results and provide some policy implications with respect to transboundary water conflicts in the region.

9.2 Water scarcity in the MENA region

The MENA region is variously defined but our study has taken the widest definition which includes 30 countries (Afghanistan, Algeria, Armenia, Bahrain, Cyprus, Egypt, Eritrea, Ethiopia, Djibouti, Iran, Iraq, Israel, Turkey, Jordan, Kuwait, Lebanon, Libya, Morocco, Mauritania, Oman, Palestine, Pakistan, Qatar, Saudi Arabia, Somalia, Sudan, Syria, Tunisia, the United Arab Emirates, and Yemen). This is recognised to be the most water-stressed area of the world, especially when considering the various types of scarcity as described by Molle and Mollinga (2003). Furthermore, water availability is extremely variable within the region with fewer than 50 m^3 per capita/year in Kuwait, United Arab Emirates, and Qatar and more than 2,600 m^3 per capita/year in Mauritania, Armenia, and Turkey (FAO-AQUASTAT, 2015). The region is home to about 6.3% of the world's population, but has only 1.4% of the world's renewable fresh water (Lipchin et al., 2006). This situation of water stress is further exacerbated by the fact that over 80% of the renewable water resources in several MENA countries originate from outside their borders. By comparing the global average water availability per capita of about 17,004 m^3 per capita/year with MENA's 1,670.84 m^3 per person per year in 2014, it is easy to see why more than half of the population of the region are facing extreme water stress (FAO-AQUASTAT, 2015).

In many countries of the MENA region, particularly in the southern part, water use regularly exceeds the theoretical available renewable amount. This is due to lack of data, and inaccurate hydrological estimations. These high levels of water stress have given rise to over 80% of the groundwater resources being depleted in these countries. In some cases, aquifer levels have dropped over the last 30 years by at least 60 meters. This situation of water stress has given rise to many problems in the region, not least on human health, with high consequent costs. Furthermore, many MENA countries have poor provision of sanitation which has led to contamination of both surface and groundwater, causing adverse effects on both ecosystem and public health. In several MENA countries, above-average infant mortality rates occur, along with significant environmental degradation estimated to be equivalent to some 0.5% of the region's GDP. In Iran, it is estimated that the economic consequences of this poor provision of sanitation may amount to as much as 0.3% of GDP (Hall & Lobina, 2008). There is clearly a need to develop better control over water resources and human impacts upon them, and a number of economic instruments appropriate to the MENA region can be used to support these (Russell et al., 2007). It must be noted, however, that the use of any economic instruments for water management must be matched by a concurrent strengthening of legislation and enforcement, to ensure equitable access to and distribution of water can be maintained.

As in almost all countries of the world, the agricultural sector in the MENA region is by far the biggest water user, accounting for as much as 90% of water use in several countries (FAO-

AQUASTAT, 2015). One of the reasons to include the efficiency of water use as one of the components of the WPI is to try and highlight the variation in economic returns to water use, to enable decision-makers to consider sectoral allocations of their scarce water resources. Recently, concern over the impact of climate change has risen, and it is anticipated that precipitation across the MENA region may be reduced by as much as 20% in coming decades. Coupled with rapid demographic growth in many of the MENA countries, and rising levels of economic development, there is no doubt that the levels of water stress are going to rise, especially in urban areas. In the Persian Gulf and North Africa physical water scarcity will increase, while in the Horn of Africa (Ethiopia, Somalia, Eritrea) economic water stress is likely to result due to lack of water infrastructure. In this latter region in particular, the situation is worsened by political constraints associated with institutional arrangements governing the waters of the Nile and other rivers of the region (Rached & Brooks, 2010). Some aspects of this current level of water stress across the region are illustrated through application of the Falkenmark index (see Figure 9.1).

Figure 9.1 shows that more than three-quarters of MENA countries experience water stress as annual water supplies are below 1,700 m^3/person/year. Some countries of the wider MENA region, including Mauritania and Turkey, have significant water supplies, but about 60% of the region faces conditions of water stress, with an average of fewer than 1,000 m^3/person/year. Notably, these are mostly located in North Africa and the Persian Gulf, with thirteen of these nations having even more severe conditions with available fresh water being fewer than 500 m^3/person/year. These highly water-stressed countries include Tunisia, Djibouti, Algeria, Israel, Palestine, Jordan, Bahrain, Libya, Yemen, Saudi Arabia, Qatar, UAE, and Kuwait.

9.3 Application of the restructured Water Poverty Index

Globally, the main data used in any current application of the WPI at the national scale are cross-country data collected and published by the FAO (AQUASTAT) and World Bank (World Development Indicators) over the relevant period (e.g. 2002–2012). The definition of variables and data used to calculate the different components of the WPI are given in detail in Table 9.1.

This section attempts to operationalise the concept of water poverty discussed above, by using the same structural framework of the WPI, developed initially by Sullivan (2001, 2002)

Figure 9.1 Water Crowding Index (Falkenmark Water Stress Index)

Table 9.1 Structure of the original Water Poverty Index

Components	*Sub-components (indicators)*	*Data sources*
Resources (RES)	Per capita internal renewable water resources Per capita external renewable water resources	FAO-AQUASTAT data
Access (ACC)	Percentage of population with access to water Percentage of population with access to sanitation services Percentage of population with access to irrigation	World Development Indicators (World Bank) World Development Indicators (World Bank) FAO-AQUASTAT data
Capacity (CAP)	Logarithm GDP per capita (adjusted by PPP)[1] Under-five mortality rate Education enrolment rate Gini coefficient	World Development Indicators (World Bank)
Use (USE)[2]	Domestic water use in litres per day Agricultural water use Industrial water use	FAO-AQUASTAT data
Environment (ENV)[3]	Water Quality Index Water Stress Index Regulation and management capacity Informational capacity Biodiversity based on threatened species	ESI data[3]

Source: Adapted from Sullivan et al. (2002).

Notes:

1) Purchasing power parity.
2) The Use component uses the ratio of water use by domestic, industrial, and agricultural sectors against the value of GDP generated by each sector.
3) Environmental integrity was based on water quality and water stress indices calculated from the environmental sustainability database.

and Sullivan et al. (2002). However, some sub-components used in the calculation of the *i*WPI, mentioned in Table 9.1, such as the irrigation index (Access component); Gini coefficient (Capacity component); industrial and agricultural indicators (Use component); regulation, management, and information capacity (Environment component); and biodiversity (Environment component) are omitted from the current study due to lack of data. For the purpose of the demonstration of the methodology proposed here, this omission is recognised, but, more importantly, this raises awareness of a serious gap in the collection of water management information in a number of countries.

As mentioned earlier, in the first stage of our analysis we discuss the relation between different variables and the appropriate weighting scheme using PCA. In the second stage, the multiplicative aggregation function is used for data combination, assuming the non-compensability among the different components. Before computing the five composite indices and the final *r*WPI, the sub-indices that are represented by different types of measurement, with different measurement units, are all normalised, to reduce incommensurability of information (Sullivan, 2001; Saisana & Tarantola, 2002). This transformation of data onto the same scale (0–100) is achieved by means of the following formula (Eq. 1a):

$$x_i^{\star} = \frac{x_i - x_{\min}}{\text{range}(x)} \times 100 \tag{1a}$$

where x_i^* is the current value of variable x for the country (i), with $\text{range}(x) = (x_{\max} - x_{\min})$ and x_{min} and x_{max} being the lowest and highest values of the considered variable in the region. The majority of indices are defined in such a way that the higher the value of the index, the better the country's water situation and vice versa. However, some components do not follow this pattern and have to be adjusted accordingly. For example, a high under-five mortality rate is not a good thing, and so this has to be calculated using the following formula (Eq. 1b):

$$x_i^* = \frac{x_{\max} - x_i}{\text{range}(x)} \times 100 \tag{1b}$$

Both equations, Eq. 1a and 1b, were used previously for normalisation of different variables in the original WPI calculation.

As first outlined by Sullivan et al. (2002, 2003), it was considered useful to adopt two thresholds for domestic water use, to account for basic human needs (50 litres/day), and for excessive water use by households (150 litres/day). This means that countries which have a daily domestic use below 50 litres/day (on that component) have higher levels of water poverty than those between 50 and 150 litres/day. For households where consumption is above 150 litres/day, this is considered wasteful. So their score is reduced to take account of this. Such an approach is illustrated in Eq. 2:

$$USE_i = \begin{cases} \frac{x_i}{50} \times 100, \; x_i \le 50 \\ 100 - \frac{x_i - 50}{x_{\max} - 50} \times 100, \; 50 \le x_i \le 150 \\ 100 - \frac{x_i - 50}{x_{\max} - 150} \times 100, \; 150 \le x_i \end{cases} \tag{2}$$

Once all the indicator values are calculated and re-scaled accordingly, the weighted average is calculated. In *r*WPI like other composite indices, the choice of weighting scheme is intended to reflect the relative magnitude given to different components of the index. Accordingly, greater weight would be assigned to the components that are regarded to be more significant in the water poverty context and vice versa. Various techniques used to find the adequate weights have been developed in the literature, including data-dependent statistical tools and judgment-based expert opinions. The classical practice is to determine subjectively the weighting scheme following consultation with experts. Nevertheless, this is a relatively skewed method of weighting, and it is frequently criticised for its arbitrariness (Booysen, 2002). Otherwise, multivariate techniques, such the PCA used in the current study, present an empirical and a more objective alternative for weighting different indicators (Giné-Garriga & Pérez-Foguet, 2010; Jemmali, 2013; Jemmali et al., 2013, 2014). This method is particularly useful for finding the best set of weights which explain the largest variation in the raw data (Slottje, 1991). Indeed, it is important to recognise that there may be some correlation between the various sub-components, and as indicated by Saisana et al. (2005), Nardo et al. (2005), and Hajkowicz (2006), but correlation between these sub-components should be evaluated before calculating the final component values. To this end, the PCA technique is performed at the sub-component level, to explore whether chosen indicators are statistically well-balanced or not.

Before applying PCA at the index and sub-index level, the overall significance of the correlation matrix should be examined using Bartlett's *Test of Sphericity*, with the factorability of indicators analysed collectively and individually, by applying the Kaiser-Meyer-Olkin *Measure of Sampling Adequacy* (MSA), as illustrated for instance by Hair et al. (2006). Based on the results and statistics of these tests, shown in Table 9.2, PCA can be performed only on the Capacity and Access components as both indices have an individual MSA above the threshold of 0.5 and a p-value less than 0.001. The remainder of component indices is calculated using the same weighting scheme as in the *i*WPI, including equal weights assigned to the two indicators for the Environment component (ENV1 and ENV2). Due to the greater uncertainty associated with waters flowing from other countries than those generated internally, a greater weight is assigned to external water inflows assessed by the RES2 indicator (Jemmali & Sullivan, 2014).

The main objective of this step is to reduce the number of correlated variables into a set of fewer and uncorrelated factors without losing too much information. Using the *variance explained criterion* to keep enough factors to account for 80% of the total variation (Nardo et al., 2005), only components with variance scores above 80% are retained. Applying this criterion, only the first components in both Capacity and Access are extracted (respectively, accounting for 81.81% and 91.58% of the total inertia). From this PCA, factor loading scores are used to determine the weights of various variables associated with each variable using the following formula in Eq. 3 (Jemmali et al., 2013, 2014):

$$w_i = \sum_{k=1\,K} PC_{k_i} \times \frac{\sqrt{\lambda_k}}{\sum_{j=1\ldots K}\sqrt{\lambda_j}} \tag{3}$$

where w_i is the calculated weight of the sub-index i and PC_{k_i} is the factor loading of such a sub-index belonging to one of the retained components (Capacity and Access) on the kth principal component, also called component loading. λ_j is the eigenvalue associated to the jth extracted principal component measuring its own variance.

The comparison between the two weighting approaches, applied at the sub-component level and referred to here as the *i*WPI (the weights are simply determined by the number of sub-components in each core component set) and the *r*WPI (the weights have been determined using PCA), reveals that the two approaches yield the same equal weighting scheme. The results of such a comparison are shown in Table 9.3. Notwithstanding this similarity in weighting strategies, it is obvious that while the first approach is simply the implicit weights,

Table 9.2 Factorability tests

Statistic	*RES*	*CAP*	*ACC*	*ENV*
Determinant of the correlation matrix	0.979	0.178	0.308	0.896
Overall MSA index	0.500	0.741	0.500	0.500
Bartlett test of sphericity				
- Chi-square	0.578	46.861	32.343	3.026
- DF	1	3	1	1
- p-value	0.447	< 0.001	< 0.001	0.082

Source: Authors' own calculation based on data set presented in Table 9.1.

Table 9.3 Weights of indicators at sub-component level

	Weights	
Sub-components	*Classic WPI*	*rWPI*
RES1: Internal water resources	0.66	0.66
RES2: External water resources	0.33	0.33
ACC1: Access to safe water	0.5	0.5
ACC2: Access to improved sanitation	0.5	0.5
CAP1: Economic capacity	0.33	0.33
CAP2: Under-five mortality rates	0.33	0.33
CAP3: Education enrolment rate	0.33	0.33
USE1: Domestic water consumption rate	1	1
ENV1: Water quality	0.5	0.5
ENV2: Water stress	0.5	0.5

Source: Authors' own calculation based on data set presented in Table 9.1.

Table 9.4 Kendall Correlations among the five rWPI components

	RES	*CAP*	*ACC*	*USE*	*ENV*
RES	1				
CAP	-0.55*	1			
ACC	-0.42*	0.89*	1		
USE	0.11	-0.10	0.02	1	
ENV	0.24	0.02	0.00	0.27	1

Source: Authors' own calculation based on data set presented in Table 9.1.
* Correlation is significant at the 0.05 level.

the second approach was based on a well-established robust statistical method. In terms of index interpretation, it is of primary importance to afford an appropriate and compelling justification for the specific weighting system adopted. Nevertheless, it is interesting to note the similarity between simple and more complex approaches.

As has been outlined above in the case of sub-components, the core components are then examined using PCA to determine the resultant weightings. Again, before applying the PCA to the data set, the degree of association among possible pairs of the five core components was analysed, using the Kendall *Correlation Coefficient* (*tau-B*) (Cho et al., 2010). There are three main outcomes of this analysis shown in the correlation matrix (see Table 9.4). Firstly, Access and Capacity exhibit the highest significant positive correlation (0.89) confirming that rich countries provide better access to water resources for their population. Secondly, when examining how the Resources component interacts with the Capacity and Access components, the significant negative correlations (-0.55, -0.42) of the two pairs, respectively, of Resources/Capacity and Resources/Access demonstrate that globally water-rich countries are generally low- and middle-income countries, where often large proportions of the population lack access to safe water and sanitation services. Thirdly, Environment and Access (0.0044) exhibit the lowest bivariate correlation, suggesting that there may be little relation between access and environmental impact. It must be noted however that the scores used here to reflect environmental impact are only proxies from available data rather than specific impact measures associated with water abstraction for human use. This relationship clearly needs further investigation to improve its representation.

After analysing the correlations between the components, Bartlett's *Test of Sphericity* is used to assess the overall significance of the correlation matrix shown above. The test indicates the presence of significant nonzero correlations at 1% significance level ($\chi^2 = 58.929$; p-value < 0.001). In addition, the recommended MSA is used to test for the factorability of the indices, both collectively and individually. By comparing the observed correlation coefficients with the partial correlations, the overall MSA determines if the data set has enough variance to make factor analysis relevant (Kaiser, 1974). Here, the overall MSA value is 0.5, which falls at the lower end of the useful range (i.e. between 0.5 and 0.7).

By examining the individual MSA values, variables that might be bringing the overall MSA value down could be determined more precisely. From this, it appears that the MSA values for both the Use and Environment components are low (0.28, 0.33), both being less than the threshold value (0.5). Thus, these two components are removed from further analysis. The removal of these two components however does weaken the original purpose of the WPI structure, which is to provide a holistic assessment methodology which captures the full range of human water use and its impacts. Once again, perhaps the challenge is to identify appropriate and effective ways of representing the Use and Environment components that can statistically, as well as conceptually, justify their inclusion. After discarding the Environment and Use components, the same process as above is repeated for the three remaining components (i.e. Resources, Access, and Capacity). Bartlett's *Test of Sphericity* indicates significant correlations at the 0.01 level ($\chi^2 = 53.25$; p-value < 0.001), and the overall MSA value is slightly higher than the value before discarding these two components, reaching 0.564, once again in the acceptable range. Similarly, the individual MSA values turn out to be 0.55 for Access, 0.54 for Capacity, and 0.68 for Resources, all of which lie in the somewhat useful range.

When just three components are considered, the first principal component explains the largest percentage of the variation in the three components (75.31%), with the two first dimensions in the component space accounting for approximately 97% of the global variance (see Table 9.5). When the *variance explained criteria* is applied to keep enough factors to account for 80% of the total variation, these two first components are retained. In such a case, to get the final weighting scheme, the extracted components should be weighted

Table 9.5 Results of the PCA of the selected components indices

	Principal component		
	Comp 1	*Comp 2*	*Comp 3*
Eigenvalues	2.26	0.64	0.1
Proportion of variance explained	75.31	21.46	3.23
Cumulative proportion of variance explained	75.31	96.77	100
Eigenvectors			
RES	-0.48	0.87	0.14
CAP	0.63	0.23	0.74
ACC	0.61	0.44	-0.66

Source: Authors' own calculation based on data set presented in Table 9.1.

with the proportion of variance measured by dividing the square root of the eigenvalue of each principal component by the sum of the square root of the eigenvalues of the two retained components; the greater the proportion, the higher the weight of the component (see Eq. 3).

At this point, the aggregation of the *r*WPI components can be carried out using the weights defined above, in order to re-assess the water poverty level for each country of the MENA region. The implications of using additive or multiplicative aggregation have been much discussed (Giné-Garriga & Pérez-Foguet, 2010; Pérez-Foguet & Giné-Garriga, 2011), but in the interests of simplicity, the additive approach is often recommended as the most appropriate method of aggregation. Nevertheless, as suggested by Pérez-Foguet and Giné-Garriga (2011), Manandhar et al. (2011), and Jemmali et al. (2013, 2014), the most appropriate aggregation function to calculate the *r*WPI is the weighted multiplicative function, as it does not allow compensability among the different components involved in the index formula. The same aggregation method is used in the current application. Numerically, the restructured Water Poverty Index can be formulated as follows (Eq. 4):

$$rWPI = \prod_{i=R,C,A} X_i^{w_i} = RES^{0.12} \times CAP^{0.4} \times ACC^{0.48} \tag{4}$$

where *r*WPI is the value of the restructured Water Poverty Index, X_i refers to the value of the component i which can be Resources (RES), Capacity (CAP) or Access (ACC), and w_i is the weight assigned to each considered component.

9.4 Results and discussion

The results of the *r*WPI application on the MENA countries is shown in Figure 9.2. On the basis of this analysis, the countries with the lowest *r*WPI score are the water-poorest, with the water-rich countries having higher scores in the *r*WPI ranking. This *r*WPI map can also be compared to those individual maps for Resources, Capacity, and Access indices (see, respectively, Figures 9.3, 9.4, and 9.5).

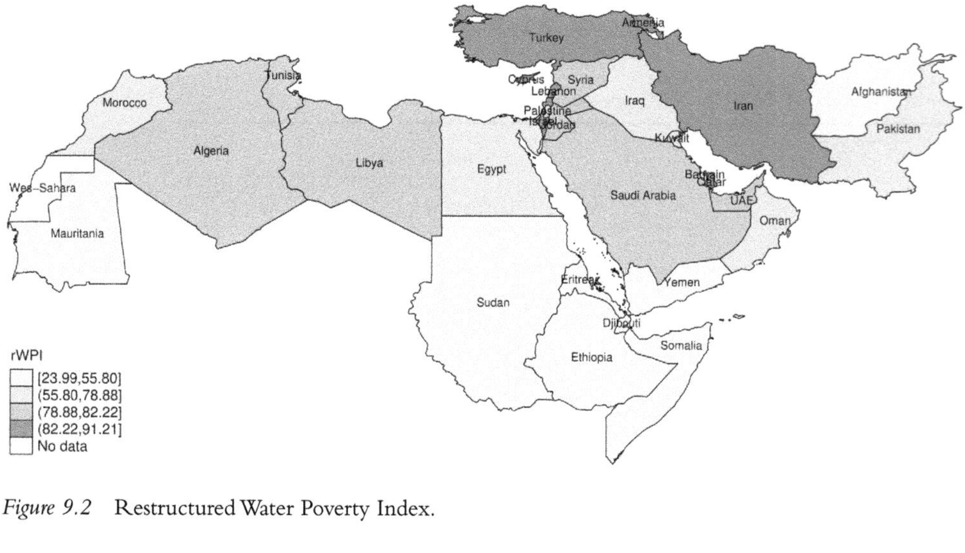

Figure 9.2 Restructured Water Poverty Index.

Figure 9.3 Resources Index.

Figure 9.4 Capacity Index.

9.4.1 Spatial variation of water poverty

Figure 9.2 reveals that countries in the Horn of Africa (Ethiopia, Eritrea, Djibouti, and Somalia) are the most water-poor with Afghanistan and Mauritania displaying properties of a lack of water infrastructures, which can be interpreted as lack of *institutional capacity*. On the other hand, the *r*WPI map shows that high- and middle-income countries such as Israel, Libya, Kuwait, United Arab Emirates, and other Gulf states are relatively water-rich, although they are technically facing serious water shortages. Thanks to their other natural resources such as natural gas and oil, Gulf states, particularly, have overcome these chronic shortages at least in the medium-term by using high-cost techniques such as desalination to satisfy the demands of their rapidly rising populations, and the increasing demand on water resources for economic development in industry and agriculture. Indeed, approximately 70% of water desalination projects in the world are located in the Gulf region.

Figure 9.5 Access Index.

According to many experts, water consumption per head in these natural resources-rich countries is among the highest in the world, and a better management system and a more sustainable strategy are urgently required to avoid dramatic effects of future water scarcity in this region. For example, more efficient use should be made of waste water through the development of modern sewerage treatment and water recycling at least for agricultural use. It is clear that under the present system, although the water situation of Gulf states is perhaps better than that of their neighbours at present, this cannot continue in the long run, where physical water scarcity will be an increasing problem and depletion of oil and gas resources will make desalination less attractive. On the other hand, those states whose populations may be more water-poor now (in spite of abundant water resources) will have a better prospect in the future if access and capacity can be further improved. In the case of Turkey, however, its good water resources and medium-income country status show promise for better water development in the future, as long as the political economy of the region can remain secure. This is increasingly uncertain with both internal and external conflicts occurring in that region.

9.4.2 Water conflicts in the Mena region

The hydro-political literature distinguishes between two types of water conflicts. The first one refers to the commonest of social and territorial disputes between different beneficiaries of water sources. It is well-known in the literature that water is not required only for consumptive use (e.g. drinking, sanitation, washing, agriculture, etc.) but is also required for other uses (e.g. fishing, drainage, navigation, industry, and ecology). Various groups of users on account of their strategic locations of changeable degrees of benefits will have opposite benefits which may conflict, particularly when the resource is scarce and access is limited. The second kind of conflict relates to transboundary water conflicts which occur usually between upstream and downstream countries sharing the same sources of water. The upstream denotes the geographical area where most water resources accumulate within the hydrological cycle, while the downstream refers to the area over which the water resources will flow (both above and below ground), within the limits of the river catchment area. Often the greatest beneficiaries are upstream water users, while downstream users may be deprived. This, however, is not the case in a number of important rivers in the MENA region. Unsurprisingly, the question of beneficiaries from water resource use is highly contested and has created centuries of social and political tension in many parts of this region of the world, and elsewhere.

In the MENA region, existing intergovernmental water conflicts take place where most countries share common water sources. The main conflicts currently arise from:

- the Euphrates and Tigris Rivers, between Turkey, Syria, and Iraq;
- the Jordan River between Israel, Lebanon, Jordan, and occupied Palestine; and
- the Nile River particularly between Egypt, Ethiopia, and Sudan, with additional tensions between some of the other Nile riparians.

Over two decades ago, it was suggested that due to the rapid rise of human water use in the region, water conflicts would be likely to become increasingly frequent and complex (Allan & Karshenas, 1995). Given the arbitrariness and uncertainty in the management of shared water resources, often subject to tensions or even conflict, the *external water resources* indicator has been assigned a weight (0.33) lower than the weight accorded to the *internal water resources* indicator (see Table 9.3). Accordingly, in this assessment of water availability for the countries in the MENA region, many of which share common resources with neighbours or other states, emphasis has been placed on sources of potential conflict over water and their resolution.

In the assessment of water poverty in the MENA region presented here, most countries which rely on the same water sources nevertheless have different rankings on the Resources, Capacity, and Access indices (see, respectively, Figures 9.3, 9.4, and 9.5). Particularly, when looking to the Access map (Figures 9.3), it is clear that some countries, in spite of limited internal water resources, manage to provide their populations with sufficient access to safe water and sanitation services. This is evident especially in Israel, while other neighbouring countries are unable to provide acceptable quality water to their populations at an affordable price (for example Jordan and Palestine).

To understand such disparate situations that characterise the Middle East region specifically, the Capacity component, which reflects the capability of people to manage their own water resources, is mapped for selected countries in Figures 9.4. Not surprisingly, this map shows that some water-scarce countries, such as Israel and Egypt, which rely primarily on external resources to provide adequate access for their growing populations, are better ranked according to the *r*WPI than their neighbours. A brief examination of these particular cases (the Jordan, Nile, and Tigris–Euphrates Rivers) demonstrates that the location of a country (upstream or downstream) added to its military and economic power are the main factors that influence transboundary water distribution in a region.

It is obvious from Figure 9.2 that countries of the Nile River Basin are characterised by different water poverty levels, ranging from the lowest *r*WPI value in the Horn of Africa to the highest score in Egypt. A look over the history of the basin shows that this remarkable disparity in water poverty levels coupled with outdated legacy legislation has given rise to inequality in the allocation of shared water resources, and today this situation provides the main driver of water conflict in the basin. For example, Ethiopia, the most water-poor of the basin, which is in fact the main upstream state where 85% of the Nile water originates, was excluded from any agreements and treaties in the past decades (Dumont et al., 2012). In April 2011, the Ethiopian government embarked upon the construction of one of the largest dams in the world, called the Grand Renaissance Dam in spite of potential objections from Egypt (Al Jazeera, 2010). Sudan also complains of its own allocation, amounting to only about 12% of the total Nile water although it contributes much more to the flow.

The Tigris–Euphrates river system is also an illustrative case of water conflict in the region as it is the only existing source of water between Turkey (as shown in Figure 9.2 as better ranked than its neighbours in the *r*WPI scale), Syria, and Iraq. The rivers are responsible for almost one-third of the Turkish population's water requirements. For this reason, Turkey has constructed three dams on the Euphrates and has just commissioned a $32 billion dam on the Tigris, while Syria has only built one dam on the Euphrates and is planning to build another to satisfy 85% of its population needs. Iraq, the last riparian state of these two rivers, has built dams both on the Tigris and the Euphrates to satisfy 1% of its population's needs. The potential for conflict between these riparian states came to the fore in the 1990s, when Turkey decided to cut off the flow of the Euphrates from Iraq and Syria to fill the Ataturk Dam Reservoir.

Given such a complicated water situation in these three highly stressed river basins, a robust assessment of the various types of water poverty could be a starting point in the development of fairer agreements and treaties on water allocation in the future. These agreements could be operationalised by the implementation of more effective institutional arrangements that strengthen political understanding of the reality of the water situation across the region. This will contribute to the alleviation of water conflicts, thus potentially improving water security in the region (Bruch et al., 2007), Both in the MENA region and beyond, there is clearly great merit in improving the range and quality of water-related data, along with more robust analytical frameworks, thus allowing greater transparency in any water resource allocation process.

9.5 Conclusion

The MENA region is one of the most highly water-stressed regions of the world, and one which is likely to be significantly impacted by climate change. Our research has enabled comparisons and contrasts to be made between countries, through the use of the *r*WPI. The challenges facing these countries with different natural capital endowments can be striking. Solutions available to oil-rich desert Gulf states are not always applicable in other locations, but it is clear from this work that there is much potential to reduce water conflicts across the MENA region, by countries implementing adequate water laws to recognise the international legal principles of the equitable and reasonable use of shared water resources (Bruch et al., 2007). In addition, through the implementation of integrated water resource management across the region, current water conflicts over transboundary basins could be reduced. The 2007 Cairo and the 2008 Marrakech International Conferences in the MENA region, and the agreement in Khartoum between Egypt, Sudan, and Ethiopia to end their long-running dispute over the sharing of Nile waters, were positive steps in this direction (Al Jazeera, 2010). Through agreements on benefit-sharing and recognition of national sovereignties, the building of Africa's biggest hydroelectric dam in Ethiopia is a good example of how cooperation and benefit-sharing can promote sustainable water management in the region.

Reaching such agreements is dependent on all parties having a good understanding of the conditions each is facing, especially in terms of water scarcity. The analytical framework provided by the *r*WPI facilitates examination of the various drivers of water scarcity found in countries in the MENA region. Analysis of component scores illustrates clear disparities between locations. Findings reveal that the key difference between oil-rich yet water-poor countries (Arabian Peninsula) and relatively water-rich yet money-poor countries (East Africa) is mainly the geographical availability of water resources, and the institutional capacity of the country. The Gulf region lacks sufficient water resources, while countries like Sudan, Somalia, Eritrea, and Ethiopia have relatively stable water abundance, shown for these latter countries by the higher

Resources score. As illustrated by the Capacity component, these same countries also lack institutional capacity to manage and exploit their own resources.

This chapter has provided an insight into the benefits of the use of a multidimensional assessment framework such as that afforded by the *r*WPI. Providing a rapid, consistent, and cost-effective appraisal methodology, a transparent process, and an easy-to-use indicator, this approach can be used by water managers, planners, and international organisations for country comparisons, or by individual countries to assess progress across their own diverse water landscapes. Indeed, this approach can provide a snapshot, serving as a baseline, with trends that can be observed both within and between countries, or regions, when the technique is repeated over time. For within country assessment, sub-national data, for example at the provincial or local government scale, can be used to generate local values of the *r*WPI.

From the current application of this approach to the MENA region, efforts to refine and simplify the calculation of the WPI are worthwhile. However, such refinement, based on the use of statistical techniques such as principal component analysis, should not be detrimental to the important holistic assessment made through the use of the conventional WPI framework. The analysis presented here demonstrates once again how important it is to have appropriate and reliable data by which important issues such as human water use and environmental impact can be represented. Without such data, water allocations are likely to tend towards a less sustainable outcome, so much more effort is needed to more effectively reflect the reality of water allocation between communities and uses. Through this revised assessment of water poverty, we have shown how diverse information can be robustly combined to shed light on complex and contentious water allocation problems.

References

Al Jazeera (2010). Ethiopia Rejects Egypt Nile Claims. *News Africa*, Thursday, May 20.

Allan, J.A. and Karshenas, M. (1995). Managing Environmental Capital: The Case of Water in Israel, Jordan, the West Bank and Gaza, 1947–1995. *Proceedings of the International Conference on water in the Jordan catchment countries*. SOAS: University of London.

Alterman, J.B. and Dziuban, M. (2010). *Clear Gold: Water as a Strategic Resource in the Middle East: A Report of the CSIS Middle East Program*. Centre for Strategic and International Studies.

Booysen, F. (2002). An Overview and Evaluation of Composite Indices of Development. *Social Indicators Research*, 59(2): 115–151.

Bruch, C., Altman, S., Al-Moumin, M., Troell, J. and Roffman, E. (2007). Legal Frameworks Governing Water in the Middle East and North Africa. *International Journal of Water Resources Development*, 23(4): 595–624.

Cho, D.I., Ogwang, T. and Opio, C. (2010). Simplifying the Water Poverty Index. *Social Indicators Research*, 97(2): 257–267.

Dumont, H.J., El Moghraby, A.I. and Desougi, L.A. (Eds.). (2012). *Limnology and Marine Biology in the Sudan* (Vol. 21). Springer Science & Business Media. The Hague, The Netherlands: Dr. W. Junk Publishers.

Falkenmark, M., Lundqvist, J. and Widstrand, C. (1989). Macro-Scale Water Scarcity Requires Micro-Scale Approaches. *Natural Resources Forum*, 13(4): 258–267.

FAO AQUASTAT. (2015). *AQUASTAT Database*. http://www.fao.org/nr/water/aquastat/data/query/index.html

Giné-Garriga, R. and Pérez-Foguet, A. (2010). Improved Method to Calculate a Water Poverty Index at Local Scale. *Journal of Environmental Engineering*, 136(11): 1287–1298.

Hair, J.F., Tatham, R.L., Anderson, R.E. and Black, W. (2006). *Multivariate Data Analysis (6)*. Upper Saddle River, NJ: Pearson Prentice Hall.

Hajkowicz, S. (2006). Multi-Attributed Environmental Index Construction. *Ecological Economics*, 57(1): 122–139.

Hall, D., & Lobina, E. (2008). Water Privatisation. *PSIRU Reports*.

Jemmali, H. (2013). Mesures de la pauvreté en eau: analyse comparative et développement de l'indice de pauvreté en eau. *VertigO - la revue électronique en sciences de l'environnement*, 13(2), doi:10.4000/vertigo.13982.

Jemmali, H. and Matoussi, M.S. (2013). A Multidimensional Analysis of Water Poverty at Local Scale: Application of Improved Water Poverty Index for Tunisia. *Water Policy*, 15(1): 98–115.

Jemmali, H. and Sullivan, C.A. (2014). Multidimensional Analysis of Water Poverty in MENA Region: An Empirical Comparison with Physical Indicators. *Social Indicators Research*, 115(1): 253–277.

Jonsson, A.C. and Wilk, J. (2014). Opening up the Water Poverty Index – Co-producing Knowledge on the Capacity for Community Water Management Using the Water Prosperity Index. *Society & Natural Resources*, 27(3): 265–280.

Kaiser, H.F. (1974). An Index of Factorial Simplicity. *Psychometrika*, 39(1): 31–36.

Lipchin, C., Eric, R., Danielle, S. and Allyson, A. (2006). *Integrated Water Resources Management and Security in the Middle East*. New York: Springer.

Manandhar, S., Pandey, V. and Kazama, F. (2011). Application of Water Poverty Index (wpi) in the Nepalese context: a case study of Kali Gandaki River Basin (KGRB). *Water Resources Management*, 26(1): 89-107.

Molle, F. and Mollinga, P. (2003). Water Poverty Indicators: Conceptual Problems and Policy Issues. *Water Policy*, 5(5): 529–544.

Nardo, M., Saisana, M., Saltelli, A., Tarantola, S., Hoffman, A. and Giovannini, E. (2005). *Handbook on Constructing Composite Indicators: Methodology and User Guide (No. 2005/3)*. OECD Statistics Working Papers.

Pérez-Foguet, A. and Garriga, R.G. (2011). Analyzing Water Poverty in Basins. *Water Resources Management*, 25(14): 3595–3612.

Rached, E. and Brooks, D.B. (2010). Water Governance in the Middle East and North Africa: An Unfinished Agenda. *International Journal of Water Resources Development*, 26(2): 141–155.

Russell, C.S., Clark, C.D. and Schuck, E.C. (2007). Economic Instruments for Water Management in the Middle East and North Africa. *International Journal of Water Resources Development*, 23(4): 659–677.

Saisana, M., Saltelli, A. and Tarantola, S. (2005). Uncertainty and Sensitivity Analysis Techniques as Tools for the Quality Assessment of Composite Indicators. *Journal of the Royal Statistical Society: Series A (Statistics in Society)*, 168(2): 307–323.

Saisana, M., & Tarantola, S. (2002). *State-of-the-Art Report on Current Methodologies and Practices for Composite Indicator Development*. European Commission, Joint Research Centre, Institute for the Protection and the Security of the Citizen, Technological and Economic Risk Management Unit.

Salameh, E. (2000). Redefining the Water Poverty Index. *Water International*, 25(3):469–473.

Slottje, D.J. (1991). Measuring the Quality of Life across Countries. *The Review of Economics and Statistics*, 73(4): 684–693.

Sullivan, C.A. (2000). *Constructing a Water Poverty Index: A feasibility study*. Wallingford: Institute of Hydrology, Centre for Ecology and Hydrology.

Sullivan, C.A. (2001). The Potential for Calculating a Meaningful Water Poverty Index. *Water International*, (26): 471–480.

Sullivan, C.A. (2002). Calculating a Water Poverty Index. *World Development*, 30(7): 1195–1210.

Sullivan, C.A., Meigh, J.R., Giacomello, A.M., Fediw, T., Lawrence, P., Samad, M., Mlote, S., Hutton, C., Allan, J.A., Schulze, R.E., Dlamini, D.J.M., Cosgrove, W., Delli Priscoli, J., Gleick, P., Smout, I., Cobbing, J., Calow, R., Hunt, C., Hussain, A., Acreman, M.C., King, J., Malomo, S., Tate, E.L., O'Regan, D., Milner, S. and Steyl, I. (2003). The Water Poverty Index: Development and Application at the Community Scale. *Natural Resources Forum*, 27(3): 189–199.

10

TRADE AND ECONOMIC GROWTH IN THE MENA REGION

Do trade in goods and trade in services differ in their impact on growth?[1]

Fida Karam and Chahir Zaki

10.1 Introduction

While the importance of services in the economy has received increasing attention, it is only recently that the international trade literature has started to investigate the linkages between trade in services and growth. Instead, the focus for a long time was on the relationship between goods trade and growth, albeit without reaching any empirical consensus. It does not seem unreasonable to assume that some services, just like certain goods, possess growth-generating characteristics. The fundamental function that many services perform in relation to overall economic growth is that they enhance the value of manufactured products and coordinate global value chains. Therefore, services trade barriers may spill over to other activities affecting the competitiveness of the entire supply chain. For this reason, services trade restrictions have caught the attention of services trade negotiators. A new strand of the literature shows that countries with open services markets tend to be more competitive in manufacturing (Francois and Woerz, 2008; Nordås, 2010), and that the reform of the service sector is associated with productivity gains in downstream manufacturing firms (Arnold et al., 2011).

This chapter explores the impact of trade in goods and trade in services on the growth performance of Middle East and North Africa (MENA) countries and suggests a decomposition of MENA GDP growth to disentangle the contributions of services trade and goods trade. Although the region has made some progress in liberalising goods trade, it is considered one of the most restrictive regions in services trade, with relatively high values for the Services Trade Restrictiveness Index (Borchert et al., 2012), revealing serious competitiveness issues. Indeed, inefficient services, provided mostly by the public sector, and the high cost of key backbone services such as transport, telecommunications, storage and distribution, are important factors that raise the cost of MENA exports (both services and manufacturing), while also impeding trade expansion in the region.[2]

The chapter is structured as follows: Section 10.1 depicts the evolution of MENA growth and trade over years; Section 10.2 sheds light on the literature on trade and growth; Section 10.3 extends the discussion of the empirical results of Karam and Zaki (2015) related to the effect of trade in services and goods on economic growth; Section 10.4 concludes.

Table 10.1 GDP growth, in percentage by country (2000–2017)

Country name	*2000–2007*	*2008*	*2009–2010*	*2011*	*2012–2016*
Region					
East Asia & Pacific	4.7	3.5	4.2	4.6	4.4
Europe & Central Asia	3.0	1.0	-0.9	2.4	1.4
Latin America & Carib.	3.5	3.9	2.0	4.4	1.2
MENA	4.8	4.5	2.8	3.7	3.3
Sub-Saharan Africa	6.0	5.4	4.1	4.5	3.6
North America	2.7	-0.2	-0.1	1.7	2.1
South Asia	6.7	3.9	8.3	6.3	6.6
Oil importers					
Egypt, Arab Rep.	4.6	7.2	4.9	1.8	3.2
Jordan	6.6	7.2	3.9	2.6	2.6
Lebanon	3.9	10.5	9.0	0.9	2.1
Morocco	4.7	5.9	4.0	5.2	3.2
Tunisia	4.5	4.2	3.3	-1.9	2.4
Israel	3.6	3.0	3.3	4.7	3.3
Malta	2.9	3.3	0.5	1.3	6.1
West Bank and Gaza	0.9	6.1	8.4	12.4	3.3
Oil exporters					
Algeria	4.4	2.4	2.6	2.9	3.4
Oman	2.5	8.2	5.5	-1.1	5.3
Bahrain	5.7	6.2	3.4	2.0	3.9
Kuwait	7.5	2.5	-4.7	9.6	2.5
Saudi Arabia	3.9	6.2	1.5	10.0	3.5
Iran, Islamic Rep.	5.4	0.3	3.4	2.6	1.8
Iraq	4.2	8.2	4.9	7.5	7.6
Libya	5.4	2.7	2.1	-62.1	14.8
Qatar	12.2	17.7	15.8	13.4	3.8
United Arab Emirates	6.4	3.2	-1.8	6.9	4.4
Yemen, Rep.	4.2	3.6	5.8	-12.7	-12.9

Source: Constructed by the authors using the World Development Indicators.

10.2 Stylised facts

10.2.1 Growth in the MENA region

Growth in the MENA region has been more volatile than the world economic growth (see Figure 10.1). This is mainly attributed to a high dependency on oil prices, on oil and non-oil exports and on imported intermediate inputs and equipment (that depend, in turn, on the developments of the world economy).

A more detailed analysis of the region shows that during 2000–2007, MENA's economic growth was increasing and was higher than other developing regions (such as Latin America and East Asia) but lower than sub-Saharan Africa and South Asia. In the wake of the financial crisis, with fewer exports and foreign direct investments (FDI), its average growth declined from 4.5% to 2.8% followed by a slight growth to reach 3.7% in 2011 (with lower figures for Egypt, Tunisia and Libya which experienced political turbulences). After a period of political instability, economic growth declined to 3.3% in the period 2012–2016.

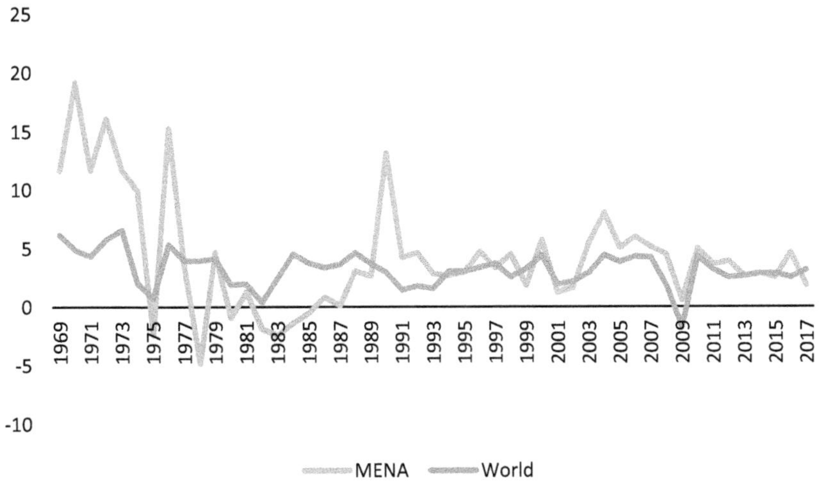

Figure 10.1 GDP growth in the MENA region (1969–2017). *Source*: World Development Indicators.

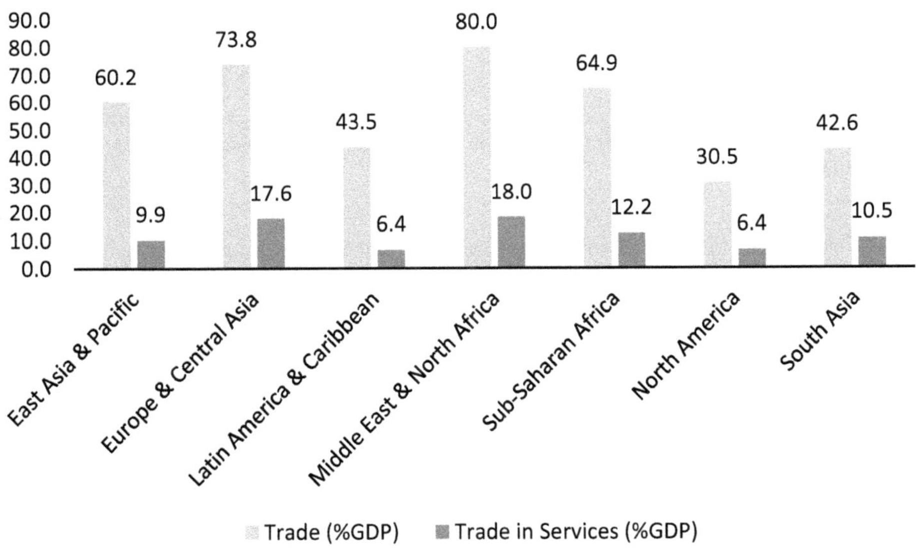

Figure 10.2 Trade and trade in services (%GDP). *Note*: These shares are averages over the period 2000–2016. *Source*: World Development Indicators.

Given this high dependence on oil and trade, the next section will provide a more detailed analysis of trade performance and trade policy.

10.2.2 Performance of trade in goods and services

Figure 10.2 shows that, over the period 2000–2016, with a share of trade in GDP reaching 80%, MENA exceeded other regions' share both in developed and developing regions (in North America the share was 30.5%; in sub-Saharan Africa 65%; and in Latin America 43.5%). Yet,

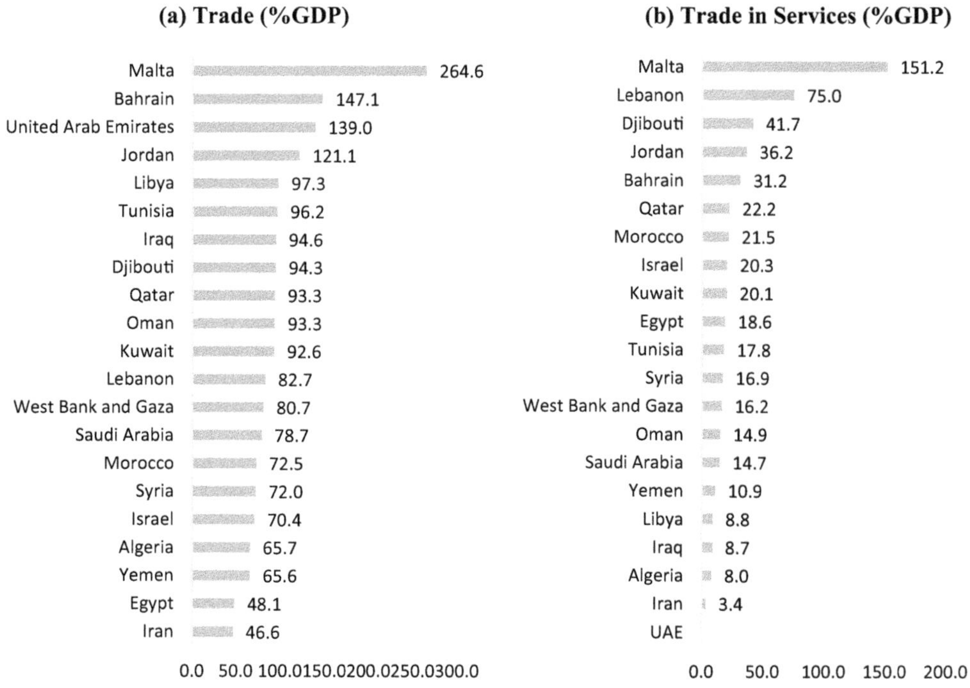

Figure 10.3 Trade and trade in services (by country): (a) trade (%GDP); (b) trade in services (%GDP). *Note*: These shares are averages over the period 2000–2016. *Source*: World Development Indicators.

Behar and Freund (2011) show that, if we take into account GDP, distance and a number of other factors, a typical MENA country under-trades with other countries: exports to the outside world are only a third of their potential (aggregate exports, non-natural exports and non-petroleum exports). The same analysis holds for services whose share is 18% of GDP (thanks to tourism, transportation, remittances and, to a lower extent, financial services, transportation and telecommunication).

At the country level (Figure 10.3a), oil-exporters (such as Bahrain, UAE or Libya) and moderately diversified economies (such as Jordan, Malta and Tunisia) have the highest share of trade to GDP. As for services (Figure 10.3b), Malta and Lebanon rank first due to tourism and financial services, respectively.

Regarding trade in goods, Figure 10.4 shows that the MENA region has the highest share of fuel exports and the lowest share of high-technology exports. Moreover, for countries that are moderately diversified (such as Egypt, Jordan and Tunisia as shown in Figure 10.5) exports consist mainly of traditional products (ready-made garments, processed food and chemicals).

10.2.3 An overview of protection measures on goods and services

One of the explanations behind this shy level of exports in non-oil products in general, and in products intensive in high technology in particular, points to impediments implied by non-tariff measures. Indeed, despite a significant decrease in tariffs (for all sectors and all countries between 2000 and 2016 as is shown in Table 10.2), trade in the MENA region is still facing a lot of obstacles in terms of non-tariff measures and administrative barriers to trade.

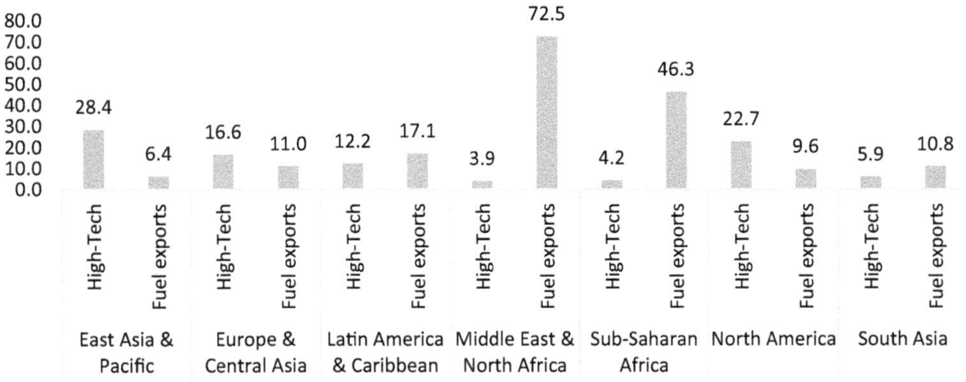

Figure 10.4 Fuel vs. high-technology exports. *Notes*: High technology exports as in % to manufactured exports. Fuel exports are in % to merchandise exports. These shares are averages over the period 2000–2016.*Source*: World Development Indicators.

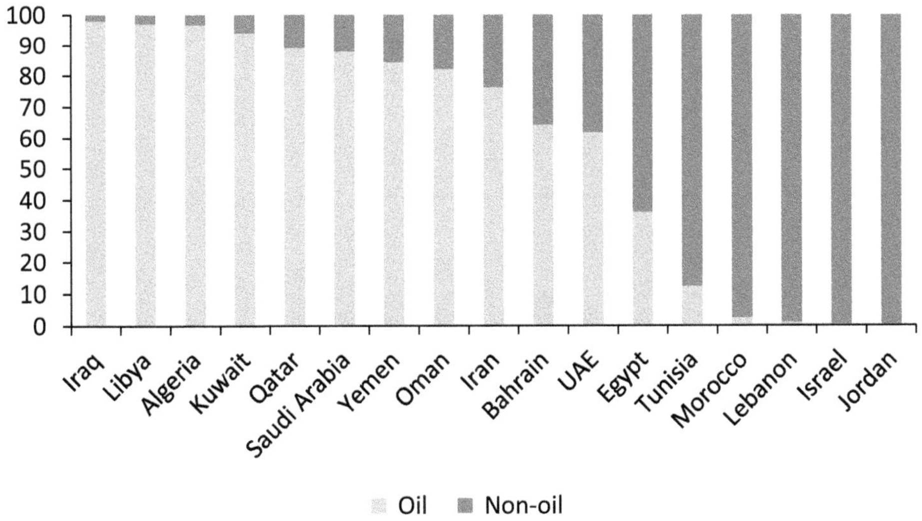

Figure 10.5 Oil vs. non-oil exports (by country). *Notes*: These shares are averages over the period 2000–2016. *Source*: World Development Indicators.

Indeed, Figure 10.6 shows that the administrative barriers to imports are much higher than those in comparator countries, such as lower-middle-income countries, on both procedural and cost sides. This in turn exerts a negative effect on exports, given the large reliance of domestic production on imported intermediate inputs.

As per other non-tariff measures, Figure 10.7 shows that the share of barriers faced domestically (21% for manufacturing and 22% for agriculture) and by Arab states (40% for manufacturing and 33% for agriculture) is larger than in non-Arab partners. In particular, labelling is associated with several problems, and is obviously easy to fix. Therefore, reforms have to be implemented in the home country.

A comparison of non-tariff measures applied by partner countries on manufacturing products is displayed in Figure 10.8. It shows that standards and conformity assessment procedures

Table 10.2 Applied tariffs by sector – simple mean (2000 and 2016)

	Primary		*Manufacturing*	
	2000	*2016*	*2000*	*2016*
Algeria	20.81	14.61	22.19	12
Bahrain	9.27	2.95	8.31	3.75
Djibouti	20.67	14.41	32.68	20.13
Egypt, Arab Rep.	52.34	29.55	21.63	5.34
Iran, Islamic Rep.	23.83	16.64	38.62	21.41
Israel	12.69	6.13	8.29	3.52
Jordan	27.86	9.27	23.26	5.08
Kuwait	1.2	3.22	3.99	3.97
Lebanon	23.26	12.18	18.98	4.16
Libya	48.24	..	19.53	..
Malta	7.76	5.32	2.24	1.88
Morocco	37.01	8.86	28.66	3.79
Oman	7.52	5.49	4.95	3.18
Qatar	4.51	3.09	4.01	3.8
Saudi Arabia	13.23	4.58	12.56	5.17
Syrian Arab Republic	14.42	15.29	14.71	15.14
Tunisia	41.38	19.53	27.09	9.32
United Arab Emirates	4.94	3.85	..	4.04
Yemen, Rep.	13.99	6.22	12.97	5.27

Source: World Development Indicators.

represent a serious obstacle for Arab countries. Furthermore, infrastructure is a major impediment to trade in the Arab world. Some studies argue that within the Arab states, the tax equivalent of non-tariff obstacles to trade (including customs procedures) represents 30–40% of the value of traded goods.

The same analysis holds for services. Indeed, Figure 10.9 shows that the MENA region is one of the most restrictive regions. Borchert et al. (2012) show that MENA countries, whether rich (such as GCC countries) or developing, are relatively closed to trade in services. Those trade barriers will not only have a negative impact on services trade, but also on the competitiveness of manufacturing, especially since some services such as transport and telecommunication services as well as financial services are complementary to the production and export of goods (Karam and Zaki, 2015).

At the multilateral level, the persistence of barriers to services trade in the region can also be illustrated by examining the state of WTO commitments.[3] Table 10.3 presents the number of "bound commitments without exceptions" by sector and by country in the MENA region. It is noteworthy that some countries such as Bahrain, Djibouti, Tunisia and Malta do not have bound commitments for many sectors. On the other hand, some countries like Jordan, Egypt, Oman, Morocco and Kuwait have committed their trade in services for several sectors at the WTO but this remains relatively limited.

In a nutshell, it is obvious that the MENA region is still suffering from several administrative barriers and non-tariff measures that hinder non-oil and high-value added exports, as well as standards that limit the liberalisation of services.

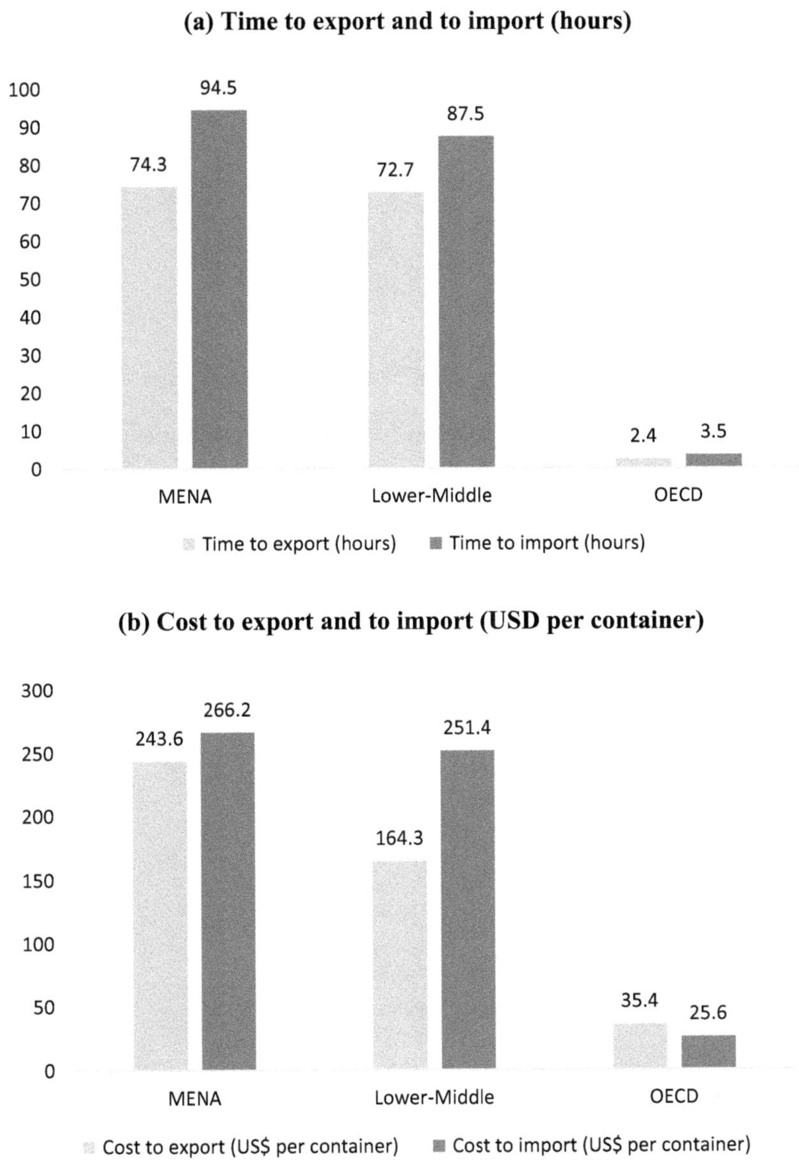

Figure 10.6 Time and cost to export and to import: (a) time to export and to import (hours); (b) cost to export and to import (USD per container). *Source:* World Bank – Doing Business dataset.

10.3 Literature review

10.3.1 Theoretical studies

The origin of the theoretical literature on trade and growth goes back to the Ricardian model of comparative advantage (David Ricardo, 1772–1823). In a world of two countries, two commodities and one factor of production, if each country specialises in commodities they can produce at the least comparative cost, both countries' welfare will improve as a result of trade

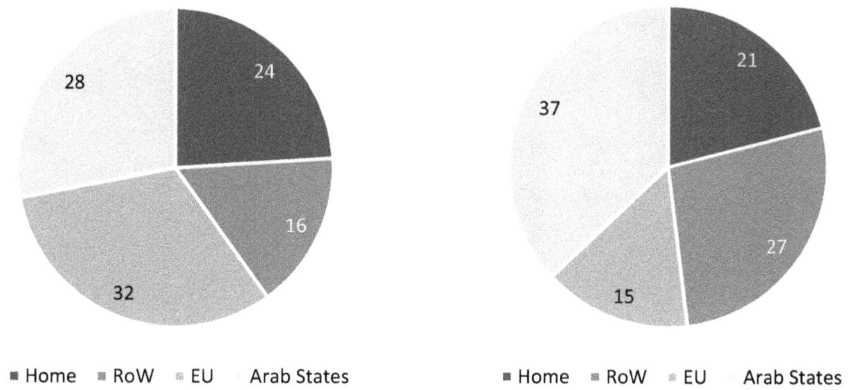

Figure 10.7 Breakdown of burdensome NTM cases reported by exporters in Arab states. *Note*: Non-tariff measures (NTM) are generally defined as policy measures other than ordinary customs tariffs that can potentially have an economic effect on international trade in goods, changing quantities traded, or prices or both (UNCTAD/DITC/ TAB/2009/3). *Source*: ITC (2015).

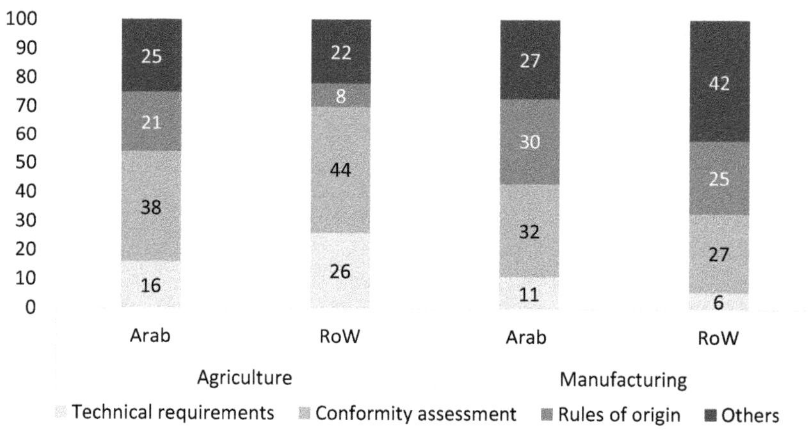

Figure 10.8 Burdensome NTMs applied by partner countries. *Note*: Non-tariff measures (NTM) are generally defined as policy measures other than ordinary customs tariffs that can potentially have an economic effect on international trade in goods, changing quantities traded, or prices or both (UNCTAD/DITC/ TAB/2009/3). *Source*: ITC (2015).

with each other. The Heckscher–Ohlin–Samuelson (HOS) model (Heckscher, 1950; Ohlin, 1933; Samuelson, 1949, 1953–1954) extends the Ricardian model to two factors of production and shows that comparative advantage arises from differences in factor endowments. Each country exports the commodity that uses the country's more abundant factor more intensively and international trade changes the income distribution of each economy in favour of their abundant factor, generating welfare gains for both countries. Although productivity efficiency and international competitiveness can be achieved through international trade – resulting thus in static welfare gains – it is not clear, under either theory, whether and how international trade determines economic growth in the long run.

Neoclassical trade models and their followers explain that gains from trade arise between countries that are different in their comparative advantage. They fail, however, to explain trade

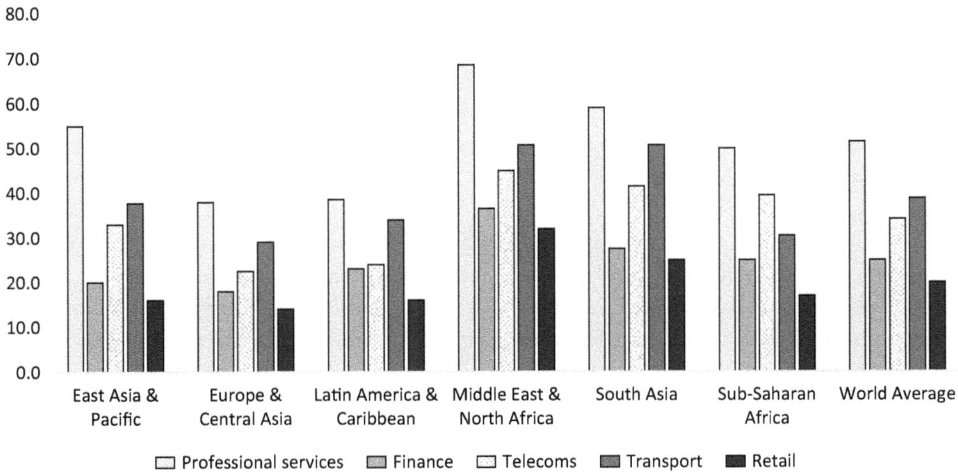

Figure 10.9 Services Trade Restrictiveness Index by sector and region. *Source*: Borchert et al. (2012: Figure 3).

Table 10.3 Number of commitments by country and by sector

	262	*268*	*245*	*249*	*253*	*260*	*291*	*236*	*287*	*205*
Bahrain					1	1				
Djibouti		1	3					1	1	
Egypt			1	3	1	2		4		1
Israel	1	2	4		1	1		3		
Jordan	1	5	3	5	1	1	8	2	4	7
Kuwait	1	3		4		1	3	3	2	3
Malta					1	1		2		1
Morocco	1	2	1	5	1	1		4		2
Oman	1	3	3	5	1	1	5	2		7
Qatar	1	3	1	4		2		1		0
Saudi Arabia	1	4	5	5		2	7	3	2	8
Tunisia			1		1	1		2		
UAE	1	3	1	5		1		2		

Source: Karam and Zaki (2013).
Notes: 205 = Transportation; 236 = Travel; 245 = Communication Services; 249 = Construction Services; 253 = Insurance Services; 260 = Financial Services; 262 = Computer and Information Services; 266 = Royalties and License Fees; 268 = Other Business Services; 287 = Personal, Cultural and Recreational Services; 291 = Government Services.

between similar countries (North–North; South–South). A new trade theory has emerged to highlight the limitations of the HOS model stemming from its strong assumptions to which results are sensitive (such as perfect competition, homogeneity of the production function implying constant returns to scale, labour market rigidity, fixed sectoral factor-intensities and fixed technology). The most important addition of the New Trade Theory (Krugman, 1979) is that it considers an imperfectly competitive market structure with economies of scale. But even under the new trade theory, free trade is better than autarky and interventionism.

Gains of trade mainly stem from the enlargement of the number of product varieties made accessible to consumers at a lower price. Indeed, prices of varieties fall because exposure to international markets allows the exploitation of increasing returns to scale, thus decreasing the per-unit cost of production. Competition in the industry, in turn, forces profit to zero for each firm, which implies that efficiency improvements are passed along to consumers in the form of lower prices. However, efforts to define a clear relationship between trade openness and growth remain limited.

The conclusion from trade models is basically that international trade, in the absence of market failures, leads to welfare gains relative to autarky. However, the neoclassical models' strong assumptions have been highlighted in subsequent works that show contrary results about trade and growth. For instance, in a dynamic version of the Ricardian model, Findlay (1984) shows that trade reduces the rate of growth relative to autarky, in a country exporting agricultural goods and importing industrial goods, because increased rents are absorbed by luxury consumption and the fall in the rate of profit reduces accumulation. Bhagwati (1958) shows that under certain conditions, national welfare may decline as a result of economic growth induced by technological progress. This is caused by a sufficient deterioration of the terms of trade – leading to overconsumption – that outweighs the beneficial effect of expansion at constant relative product prices.

Endogenous growth models identify a number of avenues through which free trade might affect long-run growth: first, the international exchange of high-tech goods facilitates the diffusion of knowledge and technology (Barro and Sala-i-Martin, 1997; Baldwin et al., 2005; Almeida and Fernandes, 2008). Grossman and Helpman (1991) show that trade openness eases the transfer of new technologies, thus contributing to productivity improvement through better resource allocation in the short run and technological development in the long run, and that these benefits depend on the degree of economic openness. Second, trade openness exposes countries to an increased market size, allowing them to better capture the benefits of increasing returns to scale (Romer, 1989; Ades and Glaeser, 1999; Alesina et al., 2000, 2005; Bond et al., 2005). Trade liberalisation can also force governments to commit to reform programmes that in turn enhance economic growth (Sachs and Warner, 1995a; Rajan and Zingales, 2003). However, the endogenous growth literature is far from being conclusive. Some models show that an asymmetric context of trading partners stemming from considerable differences in technology, research and development, capital accumulation and endowments may result in adverse effects of openness on countries with inferior technological progress (Grossmann and Helpman, 1990, 1991; Young, 1991; Lucas, 1988; Redding, 1999).

10.3.2 Empirical studies

The ambiguity of the relation between trade openness and growth raised in the theoretical literature has encouraged multiple attempts to identify the relationship empirically. Due to the difficulty in measuring openness, researchers have resorted to creative, sometimes complicated, indicators. Examples of such indicators include measures based on trade distortions (Edwards, 1998; Harrison, 1996; Pritchett, 1996; Yannikaya, 2003), qualitative indices classifying countries according to their trade and global policy regime (Sachs and Warner, 1995b; Wacziarg and Welch, 2003; Ulasan, 2015) or outcome-based measures based on trade flows (such as the trade dependency ratio, Frankel and Romer, 1999; Irwin and Tervio, 2002; Frankel and Rose, 2002; Dollar and Kraay, 2004; Squalli and Wilson, 2011; Ulasan, 2015).

While most empirical growth studies have provided an affirmative answer in favour of trade liberalisation (Dollar, 1992; Ben-David, 1993; Lee, 1993; Sachs and Warner, 1995b; Harrison, 1996;

Edwards, 1998; Wacziarg, 1998; Frankel and Romer, 1999; Frankel and Rose, 2002; Wacziarg and Welch, 2003; Dollar and Kraay, 2004; Lee et al., 2004), others have found mixed results including no association, or even a negative association between trade and growth. Rodriguez and Rodrik (2001) attribute the mixed effects of the empirical literature on trade and growth to two problems: first, the misspecification of the estimation method stemming mainly from poor data quality and inadequate control for the endogeneity of trade, also raised by Edwards (1993, 1998). Indeed, the causality between trade and growth may run in both directions: countries that trade more may have high income, while countries with higher income may be better able to afford the infrastructure conducive to trade, may have more resources with which to overcome the information search costs associated with trade or may demand more traded goods.[4] Second, the suggested openness indicators are proxies for other policy or institutional variables that have an independent effect on growth. Levine and Renelt (1992) discuss the fact that growth-related policy reforms, such as trade openness, macro stability, fiscal and monetary policies and legal quality, are in fact all highly correlated.

Therefore, subsequent works have adopted improved indices and robustness checks using multiple measures of trade liberalisation, as well as different econometric techniques that may fix the endogeneity problem raised in the literature. Some empirical studies show that the association between trade openness and growth depends on the trade openness measures used in the analysis (Yannikaya, 2003; Musila and Yiheyis, 2015). Yannikaya (2003) finds a positive association between trade openness and growth when measures of trade volumes are used, and a negative association between them when trade barriers are used. Musila and Yiheyis (2015) employ two measures of trade openness: aggregate trade openness and trade policy-induced openness. Controlling for a number of factors, aggregate trade openness is found to have a positive but statistically insignificant effect on the rate of economic growth, while trade policy-induced openness is found to have a negative and significant effect on the rate of economic growth in Kenya. Huchet-Bourbon et al. (2018) propose two outcome-based trade openness measures, following recent developments in international economics: the quality and the variety of the exported basket. They discuss the existence of a non-linear pattern between trade openness and growth when export quality is taken into account: the effect of trade on growth may have a negative effect when countries are specialised in low-quality products, and positive when countries are specialised in high-quality products. Similarly, their results also suggest a non-linear relationship between trade and growth when the variety of exports is taken into account. The impact of an increase in the export variety on growth seems positive for almost all countries, except for those with a low level of exports variety.

Other works highlight the importance of implementing complementary reforms, such as measures aimed at fostering macroeconomic stability and a favourable investment climate, to reap the growth benefits of trade openness (Bolaky and Freund, 2008; Chang et al., 2009; Zohonogo, 2016). Bolaky and Freund (2008) discuss how excessive regulations prevent resources from moving into the most productive sectors and to the most efficient firms within sectors, thus hampering economic growth in rigid economies. Zohonogo (2016) finds that the relation between trade openness and economic growth in sub-Saharan Africa is an inverted U curve, suggesting that trade openness has a positive effect on economic growth only up to a certain threshold, above which the effect declines. Since the growth effects of trade openness depend on the level of trade openness, he concludes that Sub-Saharan African countries must control the import of consumption goods and implement complementary policies that encourage investment, allow effective governance and promote human capital accumulation. These complementary policies would then allow resources to be reallocated away from less productive activities and toward more promising ones.

Another strand of the literature shows that the growth-enhancing effects of trade liberalisation vary according to the level of economic development (Kim and Lin, 2009; Kim, 2011; Herzer, 2013). Kim and Lin (2009) find that there exists an income threshold above which greater trade openness has positive effects on economic growth and below which trade liberalisation has detrimental consequences. Greater openness to international trade exerts a positive effect on economic growth for high-income economies and a negative effect on growth for low-income economies. Herzer (2013) shows that the cross-country heterogeneity in the impact of trade on income can be explained mainly by cross-country differences in primary export dependence and labour market regulation (being both negatively related to the income effect of trade), and property rights protection (being positively related to the income effect of trade).

While the state of the debate seems to be in ferment, comparable analysis depicting the impact of services trade liberalisation on economic growth is sparse and mainly to do with data constraints on services trade and service openness indicators, and often the best that can be done are cross-sectional analyses focusing on financial, transport and telecommunication services. The literature reveals a positive association between financial services openness and growth (Francois and Schuknecht, 1999; Eschenbach and Francois, 2006; Bayraktar and Wang, 2006), although the dependent variables and financial openness indicators vary between studies according to data availability. Mattoo et al. (2006) construct a policy-based measure of the openness of a country's services regime for two key service sectors: basic telecommunications and financial services. They show a statistically strong positive relation between openness in financial and telecommunication services and long-run growth performance. Eschenbach and Hoekman (2006) use three indicators of policy in banking, other financial services and infrastructure and show that measures of services policy reform are significantly positively related with the post-1990 performance of 20 transition economies. Another strand of the trade literature tackles the impact of transport, communication and distribution services on growth through their effects on trade costs that are incurred in getting goods from the point of production to the point of consumption. It shows that infrastructure is a significant determinant of export levels and the likelihood of exporting (Francois and Manchin, 2007) as well as the competitiveness of potential exporters (Djankov et al., 2006). A new strand of the literature investigates the effect of services liberalisation on the productivity of manufacturing firms. Arnold et al. (2011) show a strong positive relationship between FDI in services and total productivity growth of manufacturing firms in the Czech Republic. Arnold et al. (2012) show a significant positive relationship between Indian policy reforms in banking, telecommunications and transport and the productivity of manufacturing firms.

With a few exceptions, the MENA region has been widely neglected in the trade and growth literature (see Hakura, 2004; Nabli and Veganzones-Varoudakis, 2004; Jouini, 2015; and Makdisi et al., 2006). Hakura (2004) looks at the reasons behind the poor growth performance for a sample of 16 MENA countries during 1980–2000, differentiating between Gulf Cooperation Council (GCC) countries, other MENA oil-exporters and non-oil MENA exporters. She shows that the size of the government, poor institutional quality and political instability constitute the main impediments to growth in the region, while trade openness enters insignificantly in the regressions. Nabli and Veganzones-Varoudakis (2004) investigate the linkages between economic reforms (where the effect of trade openness enters implicitly in a composite indicator called "Structural Reforms"), human capital, physical infrastructure and growth for a panel of 44 developing countries over 1970–1980 to 1999. They find that the growth performance of the MENA region has been disappointing because these economies have lagged behind in terms of economic reforms. The results also show that, after human capital and physical infrastructure, macroeconomic and external stability are key variables for the reform process and for the growth prospects of the region. Jouini (2015) explores the relationship between trade openness and economic growth for the six GCC countries over the period 1980–2010. The results reveal that economic growth responds positively to trade openness over both the short run and long run. These results are robust to using various trade openness measures and alternative model specifications. Makdisi et al. (2006) study the growth pattern of the MENA region, averaging all variables over the period 1960–1998 and find that trade openness is less beneficial to growth and that the impact of adverse external shocks is more pronounced.

10.4 Trade in goods or trade in services for the MENA region?

While the empirical literature is inconclusive about the relation between trade and growth in the MENA region, studies have not made any attempt to differentiate between the impact on growth of goods trade liberalisation and services trade liberalisation. Exceptions are Karam and Zaki (2015) and Sandri et al. (2016). Sandri et al. (2016) investigate the growth contribution of goods trade and services trade in Jordan for the period 1980–2014 and find that trade in goods has a negative effect on GDP in Jordan, whereas trade in services positively affects economic performance.

We explore the macroeconomic and sectoral effects of goods and services trade on the economic performance of 21 MENA countries for the period 1960–2012 and offer a decomposition of MENA GDP growth in order to disentangle the contributions of both services and goods trade.

The following subsections summarise the results of Karam and Zaki (2015) for their macroeconomic, sectoral and country regressions, respectively, as well as the decomposition of MENA GDP growth.

10.4.1 An augmented growth model

Karam and Zaki (2015) use an augmented growth model (Mankiw et al., 1992) that takes into account, in addition to the traditional factors of production of the classical model (Solow, 1956), a host of variables such as human capital, trade in goods and trade in services.

$$\begin{aligned}\ln GDP_{it} &= \alpha_0 + \alpha_1 \ln GDP_{80} + \alpha_2 \ln INV_{it} + \alpha_3 \ln LAND_{it} \\ &+ \alpha_4 popgrowth_{it} + \alpha_5 school_{it} + \alpha_6 \ln GOODS_{it} \\ &+ \alpha_7 \ln SERVICES_{it} + \alpha_8 \ln GOODS_{it} * \ln SERVICES_{it} \\ &+ \alpha_9 Oil + \alpha_{10} Oil * \ln SERVICES_{it} + \alpha_{11} Oil * \ln GOODS_{it} + \epsilon_{it}\end{aligned}$$

The growth control variables include the initial GDP (*Ln(GDP80)*) to control for conditional convergence, real investment (*lnINV*) to measure physical capital, the population growth rate (*Popgrowth*) and the secondary enrolment rate (*School*) to measure human capital. Arable land (*lnLAND*) is added to have a comprehensive production function. Trade in goods (*lnGOODS*) and trade in services (*lnSERVICES*) are added to account for the impact of trade on growth, ϵ_{it} is the discrepancy term.

In the macroeconomic regressions, the interaction term between goods trade and services trade also enters in the specification (*lnGOODS*lnSERVICES*), to capture whether trade in goods and trade in services are complementary or substitutes in their effect on growth. Furthermore, because oil exports are the engine of economic growth for a number of MENA countries, a dummy variable (*Oil*) is added, which takes a value equal to 1 for oil-exporter countries, and 0 otherwise. The authors also distinguish between the effects of goods and services trade on growth for oil-exporter countries by including an interaction term between the *Oil* dummy and the natural lob of each type of trade (*Oil*lnGOODS* and *Oil*lnSERVICES*).

10.4.2 Data

Growth regressions are estimated for a sample of 21 countries from the MENA region for the period 1960–2012 using different econometric techniques namely panel estimations (both fixed effects FE and random effects RE) and dynamic panel (Arellano-Bond AB). All data are obtained from the World Development Indicators database at the World Bank and nominal values are deflated using the GDP deflator of 2005.

10.4.3 Empirical results

10.4.3.1 Macroeconomic results

The results of the macroeconomic regressions show, on the one hand, that trade in goods and trade in services both have a positive effect on economic growth, with the effect of goods trade being higher than the effect of services trade. This finding may be justified by the fact that the MENA region has significantly liberalised its trade in goods while trade in services is still facing several impediments, limiting its effect on growth. For this reason, the interaction term between trade in goods and trade in services is negative and statistically significant showing that the higher the trade in goods, the lower the marginal effect of trade in services on MENA growth (see Figure 10.10). This result is surprising given the well-documented complementarity between trade in goods and trade in services. However, as mentioned above, inefficient services, provided mostly by the public sector, and the high cost of key backbone services such as transport, telecommunications, storage and distribution, are important factors that raise the cost of MENA exports (both services and manufacturing), and impede trade expansion in the region.

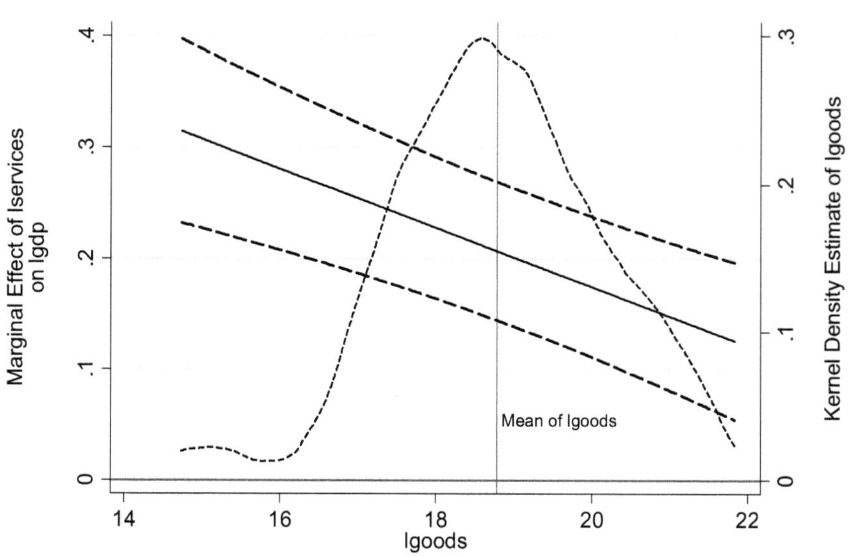

Figure 10.10 Interaction between the effects of trade in services and trade in goods on growth. *Source*: Karam and Zaki (2015).

On the other hand, the results show that oil-exporting countries do not perform better than non-oil countries. Moreover, while the effect of trade in goods on growth is expectedly positive for oil-exporting countries, the impact of trade in services is negative for those countries. This result is explained by the fact that trade of oil-exporters is highly concentrated in the oil sector and that non-oil trade – including services trade – is less diversified.

10.4.3.2 Sectoral results

Due to data deficiencies, the sectoral regressions can only be run for three aggregate sectors: agriculture, manufacturing and services. To assess the specific effect of services on growth, the authors add a dummy variable equal to 1 in case of services, and 0 otherwise, as well as its interaction with the trade variable. They also add an oil dummy and its interaction with the trade variable.

The conclusion drawn from the sectoral results regarding the relation between trade and growth are quite similar to the macroeconomic results. More specifically, the authors show that an increase in trade by 1% leads to an increase in GDP by 0.26%. In addition, while the service sector *per se* does not affect growth, the interaction term between trade and the service dummy is positive and significant suggesting that trade in services does have a positively significant impact on production.

10.4.3.3 Country regressions

Country regressions disentangle the growth determinants of MENA countries. The authors find that investment is a highly significant determinant of growth in these economies. Indeed, investment, especially foreign direct investment, can boost productivity, generate new employment opportunities and enhance technological progress. School enrolment is another important factor contributing to economic growth in MENA countries by improving the skills and the qualifications of human capital. More importantly, our results regarding the importance of both types of trade can be summarised as follows: first, trade in services has a positive and significant impact on growth in MENA economies relying heavily on tourism, finance activities and telecommunication in Bahrain, Jordan, Egypt, Tunisia, Malta and Morocco. Second, trade in goods has a significantly positive impact on growth in Bahrain, Djibouti, Oman and Palestine. Finally, in Algeria, Iran and Syria, neither trade in goods nor trade in services seem to have a significantly positive impact on growth. In fact, Algeria and Syria, being highly dependent on oil – and therefore not diversified – are vulnerable to external shocks and the negative impact of terms of trade in primary products. While Iran is highly dependent on oil, it is far more diversified than the other countries. However, our dataset for the period 1960–2012 includes a chronology of key events that explain our results such as the Iranian Revolution in 1979, the Iran–Iraq war from 1980 to 1988 and the oil and trade sanctions imposed by the United States since 1995.

10.4.3.4 Decomposition of GDP growth

Figures 10.11 and 10.12 present the contribution of trade in goods and trade in services to growth in the MENA region (by year and by country), as computed by Karam and Zaki (2015) by multiplying the share of trade in goods (in services) to GDP by its growth rate for a particular year. The authors find that trade in goods has substantially contributed to the MENA GDP growth more than trade in services, especially after 2000 due to significant tariff cuts. Moreover, GDP decreased significantly in 2009 due to a large decline in goods trade with the global financial crisis as shown in Figure 10.11. Similar findings can be found in Figure 10.12 which plots the contribution of trade in goods and services to GDP at the country level. Most of the

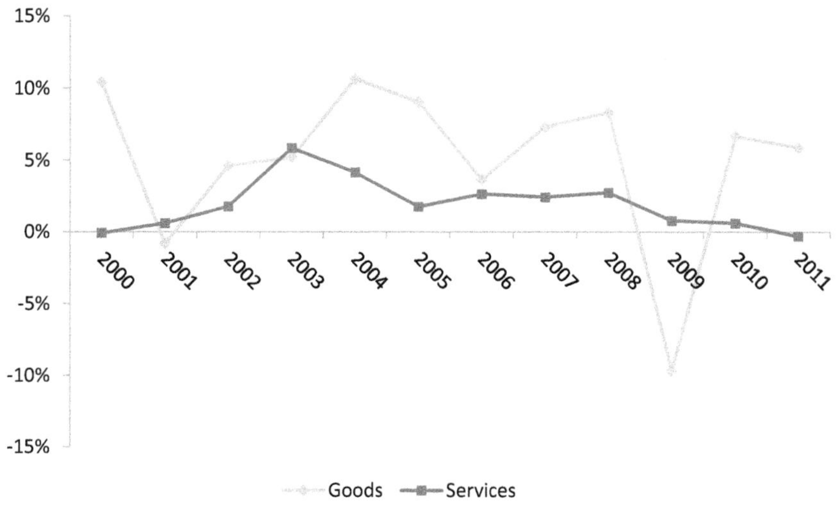

Figure 10.11 Contribution of trade in goods and trade in services to growth in the MENA region (by year). *Source*: Constructed by the authors using the World Development Indicators.

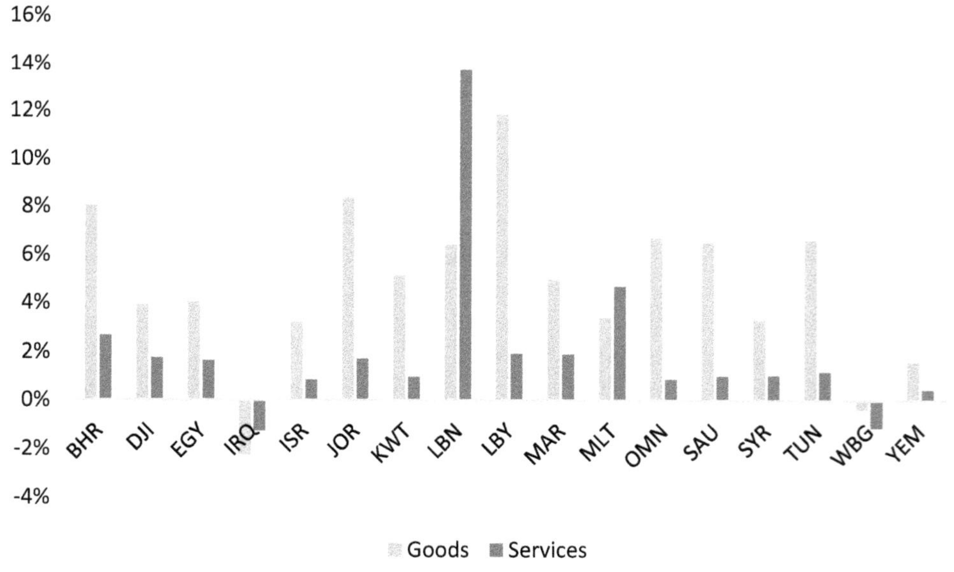

Figure 10.12 Contribution of trade in goods and trade in services to growth (average by country). *Source*: Constructed by the authors using the World Development Indicators.

MENA countries are characterised by a higher contribution of trade in goods to GDP growth. Exceptions to that are Lebanon and Malta for which services account for 70% of GDP.

Karam and Zaki (2015) split the analysis on the relative importance of different factors in the evolution of MENA GDP growth in two main sub-periods: 1980–1999 during which several MENA countries implemented economic reforms and structural adjustment programmes, and 2000–2010 where significant trade liberalisation efforts took place.

Table 10.4 shows that trade in goods explained around 45% of MENA GDP growth during the period 1980–1999 while the share of trade in services accounted for only 30.3%. The gap between the contribution of the two seems to have widened over the period 2000–2010 where the respective shares were 54% and 25%. The contribution of trade in goods to GDP growth is higher in the Arellano-Bond estimations relative to the fixed effect method: 58% during the first sub-period and 66.5% during the second one.

Karam and Zaki (2015) draw similar conclusions from the GDP growth decomposition at the country level (Table 10.5). First, goods trade contributed to GDP growth more than services trade for most countries. Second, this contribution increased in the second sub-period as compared to the first one for all countries except Algeria, Malta and Palestine. Furthermore, we find that countries like Egypt and Oman experienced a reversal in the contributions of goods and services: the contribution to growth of trade in goods increased from 31% to 64% in Egypt and from 32% to 43% in Oman between the two sub-periods, while the contribution of trade in services declined from 47% to 24% in Egypt and from 45% to 19% in Oman. For Egypt, the sharp drop in the contribution of services trade to growth is explained by the financial crisis that slowed down international trade and therefore affected negatively the revenues of the Suez Canal.

Table 10.4 Estimated contribution of trade in services and trade in goods to GDP growth for the MENA region (FE vs. AB)

		1980–1999					
		FE			*AB*		
	Growth rate (%)	*Coefficient*	*Multiplication (%)*	*Shares (%)*	*Coefficient*	*Multiplication (%)*	*Shares (%)*
Goods	3.4	0.744	2.6	44.8	0.322	1.1	57.9
Services	3.8	0.452	1.7	30.3	0.134	0.5	26.9
Inv.	4.0	0.312	1.2	21.7	0.068	0.3	14.2
Pop	2.9	0.000	0.0	0.0	0.000	0.0	0.0
School	10.2	0.018	0.2	3.2	0.002	0.0	1.1
Land	-0.4	0.000	0.0	0.0	0.000	0.0	0.0
		2000–2010					
		FE			*AB*		
	Growth rate (%)	*Coefficient*	*Multiplication (%)*	*Shares (%)*	*Coefficient*	*Multiplication (%)*	*Shares (%)*
Goods	8.5	0.744	6.3	54.3	0.322	2.7	66.5
Services	6.4	0.452	2.9	24.9	0.134	0.9	20.9
Inv.	7.4	0.312	2.3	19.9	0.068	0.5	12.3
Pop	1.9	0.000	0.0	0.0	0.000	0.0	0.0
School	6.4	0.018	0.1	1.0	0.002	0.0	0.3
Land	-0.5	0.000	0.0	0.0	0.000	0.0	0.0

Source: Karam and Zaki (2015).
Note: The coefficients of goods (services) are computed by adding the three coefficients: lnGood (lnService), the interaction between lnGood and lnService and the interaction between oil and lnGood (oil and lnService). This allows us to have the net effect of trade in goods and trade in services on growth.
FE: fixed effect estimation; AB: Arrelano-Bond dynamic panel estimation.

Table 10.5 Estimated contribution of trade in services and trade in goods to GDP growth for selected countries

	1980–1999				2000–2010			
	Goods	*(%)*	*Services*	*(%)*	*Goods*	*(%)*	*Services*	*(%)*
DJI	-3.8	66.2	-1.6	28.3	5.2	32.3	1.8	11.1
EGY	1.6	31.0	2.4	46.9	7.5	64.5	2.7	23.7
IRN	1.9	43.9	-1.7	-38.5	24.5	84.1	2.4	8.2
ISR	2.4	42.7	1.8	32.2	3.9	66.7	1.7	28.7
JOR	3.5	53.4	1.6	25.0	6.8	61.9	1.9	17.4
KWT	4.8	67.0	1.6	22.4	5.4	54.4	1.8	18.7
MAR	3.8	57.9	1.5	23.1	6.4	47.5	4.5	33.6
MLT	3.9	52.4	2.1	29.0	1.6	31.4	3.0	60.2
OMN	4.2	31.8	5.9	45.0	5.6	43.2	2.4	18.8
SAU	-0.2	-53.9	-0.2	-53.9	6.8	67.3	2.3	22.2
TUN	3.8	53.2	2.0	27.7	6.2	59.0	2.7	25.9
WBG	5.9	37.5	5.8	36.9	-0.7	13.1	-2.3	43.1
MENA (%)	**2.6**	**44.8**	**1.7**	**30.3**	**6.3**	**54.3**	**2.9**	**24.9**

Source: Karam and Zaki (2015).

10.5 Conclusion and policy recommendations

Karam and Zaki (2015) investigate a timely and critical question for the MENA region, the effects of services and goods trade on GDP growth. Their results reveal a positive association between GDP growth and both services and goods trade. Moreover, the results show that as goods trade increases, the marginal effect of services trade on real GDP decreases. However, the overall effect of services trade on real GDP is positive. The decomposition of GDP growth shows a greater impact of goods trade, although the contribution of services trade to growth is important, and for most countries, greater than the contribution of tertiary enrolment, being one of the most important growth determinants.

The policy implication is clear. Regulatory reforms that reduce trade barriers, including entry and operating costs for services exports providers, should stimulate investment and output, with positive employment effects. Growth volatility, high unemployment and debt and budget deficits across the region all point to the need for structural reforms of which trade liberalisation is a key element.

Appendix Table 10.1 List of MENA countries

Oil countries	*Non-oil countries*
Algeria	Djibouti
Bahrain	Egypt
Iran	Israel
Iraq	Jordan
Kuwait	Lebanon
Libya	Morocco
Oman	Malta
Qatar	Palestine
Saudi Arabia	Syria
UAE	Tunisia
	Yemen

Notes

1 This chapter draws from and builds on our earlier work in Karam and Zaki (2015). The authors would like to acknowledge the support of the Economic Research Forum (ERF) and of the African Development Bank.
2 For a list of MENA countries in this chapter, see Appendix Table 10.1.
3 "A specific commitment in a services schedule is an undertaking to provide market access and national treatment for the service activity in question on the terms and conditions specified in the schedule. When making a commitment a government therefore binds the specified level of market access and national treatment and undertakes not to impose any new measures that would restrict entry into the market or the operation of the service [...] Where there are no limitations on market access or national treatment in a given sector and mode of supply, the entry reads NONE. All commitments in a schedule are bound unless otherwise specified. In such a case, where a Member wishes to remain free in a given sector and mode of supply to introduce or maintain measures inconsistent with market access or national treatment, the Member has entered in the appropriate space the term UNBOUND [...]" (WTO website).
4 Zeren and Ari (2013) show positive bidirectional links between trade openness and economic growth for G7 countries.

References

Ades, A.F. and E. Glaeser (1999), "Evidence on Growth, Increasing Returns and the Extent of the Market", *Quarterly Journal of Economics*, 114(3): 1025–1046.
Alesina, A., Spolaore, E. and R. Wacziarg (2000), "Economic Integration and Political Disintegration", *American Economic Review*, 90(5): 1276–1296.
Alesina, A., Spolaore, E. and R. Wacziarg (2005), "Trade, Growth and the Size of Countries", *Handbook of Economic Growth*, 1(B): 1499–1542.
Almeida, R. and A. Fernandes (2008), "Openness and Technological Innovations in Developing Countries: Evidence from Firm-Level Surveys", *Journal of Development Studies*, 44(5): 701–727.
Arnold, J.M., Javorcik, B. and A. Mattoo (2011), "Does Services Liberalization Benefit Manufacturing Firms? Evidence from the Czech Republic", *Journal of International Economics*, 85: 136–146.
Arnold, J.M., Javorcik, B., Lipscomb, M. and A. Mattoo (2012), "Services Reform and Manufacturing Performance: Evidence from India", Policy Research Working Paper 5948, The World Bank, Washington, DC.
Baldwin, R.E., Braconier, H. and R. Forslid (2005), "Multinationals, Endogenous Growth, and Technological Spillovers: Theory and Evidence", *Review of International Economics*, 13(5): 945–963.
Barro, R.J. and X. Sala-i-Martin (1997), "Technological Diffusion, Convergence, and Growth", *Journal of Economic Growth*, 2(1): 2–26.
Bayraktar, N. and Y. Wang (2006), "Banking Sector Openness and Economic Growth", Policy Research Working Paper 4019, The World Bank, Washington, DC.
Behar, A. and C. Freund (2011), "The Trade Performance of the Middle East and North Africa", Middle East and North Africa Working Paper Series 53, The World Bank, Washington, DC.
Ben-David, D. (1993), "Equalizing Exchange: Trade Liberalization and Income Convergence", *Quarterly Journal of Economics*, 108(3): 653–679.
Bhagwati, J. (1958), "Immiserizing Growth: A Geometric Note", *Review of Economics Studies*, 25(3): 201–205.
Bolaky, B. and C. Freund (2008), "Trade, Regulations, and Income", *Journal of Development Economics*, 87: 309–321.
Bond, E.W., Jones, R.W. and W. Ping (2005), "Economic Take-offs in a Dynamic Process of Globalization", *Review of International Economics*, 13(1): 1–19.
Borchert, I., Gootiiz, B. and A. Mattoo (2012), "Policy Barriers to International Trade in Services: Evidence from a New Database", Policy Research Working Paper 6109, The World Bank, Washington, DC.
Chang, R., Kaltani, L. and N.V. Loayza, (2009), "Openness Can Be Good for Growth: The Role of Policy Complementarities", *Journal of Development Economics*, 90: 33–49.
Djankov, S., Freund, C. and C.S. Pham (2006), "Trading on Time", Policy Research Working Paper 3909, The World Bank, Washington, DC.
Dollar, D. (1992), "Outward-Oriented Developing Economies Really Do Grow More Rapidly: Evidence from 95 LDCs, 1976–1985", *Economic Development and Cultural Change*, 40: 523–544.

Dollar, D. and A. Kraay (2004), "Trade, Growth, and Poverty", *The Economic Journal*, 114: 22–49.

Edwards, S. (1993), "Openness, Trade Liberalization, and Growth in Developing Countries", *Journal of Economic Literature*, 31(3): 1358–1393.

Edwards, S. (1998), "Openness, Productivity and Growth: What Do We Really Know?", *Economic Journal*, 108: 383–398.

Eschenbach, F. and J. Francois (2006), "Capital Movement and Financial Services Trade", Sciences Po, Paris, mimeo.

Eschenbach, F. and B. Hoekman (2006), "Services Policy Reform and Economic Growth in Transition Economies, 1990–2004", *Review of World Economics*, 142(4): 746–764.

Findlay, R. (1984), "Growth and Development Trade Models", in: R.W. Jones and P.B. Kenen (eds.), *Handbook of International Economics*, North-Holland, Amsterdam.

Francois, J.F. and M. Manchin (2007), "Institutional Quality, Infrastructure, and the Propensity to Export", Policy Research Working Paper 4152, The World Bank, Washington, DC.

Francois, J.F. and L. Schuknecht (1999), "Trade in Financial Services: Procompetitive Effects and Growth Performance", CEPR Discussion Paper 2144.

Francois, J.F. and J. Woerz (2008), "Producer Services, Manufacturing Linkages, and Trade", *Journal of Industry Competition and Trade*, 8: 199–229.

Frankel, J.A. and D. Romer (1999), "Does Trade Cause Growth?", *American Economic Review*, 89(3): 379–399.

Frankel, J.A. and A. Rose (2002), "An Estimate of the Effect of Common Currencies on Trade and Income", *The Quarterly Journal of Economics*, 117(2): 437–466.

Grosman, G.M. and E. Helpman (1990), "Comparative Advantage and Long-Run Growth", *American Economic Review*, 80(4): 796–815.

Grossman, G.M. and E. Helpman (1991), *Innovation and Growth in the Global Economy*. MIT Press, Cambridge, MA.

Hakura, D.S. (2004), "Growth in the Middle East and North Africa", IMF Working Paper WP/04/56, International Monetary Fund.

Harrison, A. (1996), "Openness and Growth: A Time Series, Cross-Country Analysis for Developing Countries", *Journal of Development Economics*, 48: 419–447.

Heckscher, Eli F. (1950), "The Effect of Foreign Trade on the Distribution of Income", in: Howard S. Ellis and A. Lloyd (eds.), *Readings in the Theory of International Trade*. Metzler for the American Economic Association. Irwin, Homewood, IL: 272–300. Slightly abridged version translated from Ekonomisk Tidskrift (1919).

Herzer, D. (2013), "Cross-country Heterogeneity and the Trade-Income Relationship", *World Development*, 44: 194–211.

Huchet-Bourdon, M., Le Mouel, C. and M. Vigil (2018), "The Relationship between Trade Openness And Economic Growth: Some New Insights on the Openness Measurement Issue", *The World Economy*, 41: 59–76.

Irwin, D. and M. Tervio (2002), "Does Trade Raise Income? Evidence from the Twentieth Century", *Journal of International Economics*, 58(1): 1–18.

Jouini, J. (2015), "Linkage between International Trade and Economic Growth In GCC Countries: Empirical Evidence from PMG Estimation Approach", *Journal of International Trade and Economic Development*, 24(3): 341–372.

Karam, F. and C. Zaki (2013), "On the Determinants of Trade in Services: Evidence from the MENA Region?", *Applied Economics*, 45(33): 4662–4676.

Karam, F. and C. Zaki (2015), "Trade Volume and Economic Growth in the MENA Region: Goods or Services?", *Economic Modelling*, 45: 22–37.

Kim, D.-H. (2011), "Trade Growth and Income", *Journal of International Trade and Economic Development*, 20(5): 677–709.

Kim, D.-H. and S.-C. Lin (2009), "Trade and Growth at Different Stages of Economic Development", *Journal of Development Studies*, 45(8): 1211–1224.

Krugman, Paul R. (1979), "Increasing Returns, Monopolistic Competition, and International Trade", *Journal of International Economics*, 9(4): 469–479.

Lee, J.-W. (1993), "International Trade, Distortions, and Long-Run Economic Growth", *International Monetary Fund Staff Papers*, 40(2): 299–328.

Lee, H.Y., Ricci, L.A. and Rigobon, R. (2004), "Once Again, is Openness Good for Growth?", NBER Working Paper 10749, NBER, Cambridge, MA.

Levine, R. and D. Renelt (1992), "A Sensitivity Analysis of Cross-Country Growth Regressions", *American Economic Review*, 82(4): 942–963.

Lucas, R.E. (1988), "On the Mechanic of Economic Development", *Journal of Monetary Economics*, 46 (1): 167–182.

Makdisi, S., Fattah, Z. and Limam, I. (2006), "Determinants of Growth in the MENA Countries", in: J. Nugent and M. Hashem Pesaran (eds.), *Explaining Growth in the Middle East (Contributions to Economic Analysis, Vol. 278)*. Emerald Group Publishing Limited, Bingley: 32–60, https://doi.org/10.1016/S0573-8555(06)78002-6.

Mankiw, N.G., Romer, D. and D.N. Weil (1992), A Contribution to the Empirics of Economic Growth", *Quarterly Journal of Economics*, 107(2): 407–437.

Mattoo, A., Rathindran, R. and A. Subramanian (2006), "Measuring Services Trade Liberalisation and Its Impact on Economic Growth: An Illustration", *Journal of Economic Integration*, 21: 64–68.

Musila, J.W. and Z. Yiheyis (2015), "The Impact of Trade Openness on Growth: The Case of Kenya", *Journal of Policy Modelling*, 37: 342–354.

Nabli, M.K. and M.A. Veganzones-Varoudakis (2004), "Reforms and Growth in MENA Countries: New Empirical Evidence", World Bank Working Papers No. 36, The World Bank, Washington, DC.

Nordås, H.K. (2010), "Trade in Goods and Services: Two Sides of the Same Coin?", *Economic Modelling*, 27: 496–506.

Ohlin, B. (1933), *Interregional and International Trade*. Harvard University Press, Cambridge, MA.

Pritchett, L. (1996), "Measuring Outward Orientation in LDCs: Can it Be Done?", *Journal of Development Economics*, 49: 307–335.

Rajan, R.G. and L. Zingales (2003), "The Great Reversals: The Politics of Financial Development in the Twentieth Century", *Journal of Financial Economics*, 69 (1): 5–50.

Redding, S. (1999), "Dynamic Comparative Advantage and the Welfare Effects of Trade", *Oxford Economic Papers*, 51(1): 15–39.

Rodriguez, F. and D. Rodrik (2001), "Trade Policy and Economic Growth: A Skeptic's Guide to the Cross-National Evidence", in: Ben Bernanke and Kenneth S. Rogoff (eds.), *In NBER Macroeconomics Annual 2000*. MIT Press, Cambridge, MA: 261–388.

Romer, P.M. (1989), "Growth Based on Increasing Returns Due to Specialization", *American Economic Review*, 77(2): 56–62.

Sachs, J.D. and A.M. Warner (1995a), "Economic Reform and the Process of Global Integration", *Brookings Papers on Economic Activity*, 1: 1–118.

Sachs, J.D. and A.M. Warner (1995b), "Natural Resource Abundance and Economic Growth", NBER Working Papers 5398, NBER, Cambridge.

Samuelson, Paul A. (1949), "International Factor-Price Equalisation Once Again", *Economic Journal*, 59(234): 181–197.

Samuelson, Paul A. (1953–1954), "Prices of Goods and Factors in General Equilibrium", *Review of Economic Studies*, 21(1): 1–20.

Sandri, S., AlShyab, N. and A. Ghazo (2016), "Trade in Goods and Services and its Effect on Economic Growth – The Case of Jordan", *Applied Econometrics and International Development, Euro-American Association of Economic Development*, 16(2): 113–128.

Solow, Robert M. (1956), "A Contribution to the Theory of Economic Growth", *The Quarterly Journal of Economics*, 70(1): 65–94.

Squalli, J. and K. Wilson (2011), "A New Measure of Trade Openness", *The World Economy*, 34(10): 1745–1770.

Ulaşan, B. (2015), "Trade Openness and Economic Growth: Panel Evidence", *Applied Economics Letters*, 22(2):163–167.

Wacziarg, R. (1998), "Measuring the Dynamic Gains from Trade", World Bank Working Paper 2001, The World Bank, Washington, DC.

Wacziarg, R. and K.H. Welch (2003), "Trade Liberalisation and Growth: New Evidence", NBER Working Paper 10152, NBER, Cambridge.

Yannikaya, H. (2003), "Trade Openness and Economic Growth: A Cross-Country Empirical Investigation", *Journal of Development Economics*, 72: 57–89.

Young, A. (1991), "Learning by Doing and the Dynamic Effects of International Trade", *Quarterly Journal of Economics*, 106(2): 369–405.

Zeren, F. and Ari, A. (2013), "Trade Openness and Economic Growth: A Panel Causality Test", *International Journal of Business and Social Science*, 4(9): 317–24.

Zohonogo (2016), "Trade and Economic Growth in Developing Countries: Evidence from Sub-Saharan Africa", *Journal of African Trade*, 3: 41–56.

SECTION IV

Poverty, inequality and social policy

11

POVERTY AND VULNERABILITY IN THE MENA REGION

Khalid Abu-Ismail

11.1 Introduction

Poverty is traditionally thought of in money metric terms. From this angle, a household is defined as poor if its income or expenditure lies below a specific threshold, or a poverty line, equivalent to the cost of meeting its basic needs. The fundamental determinants of money metric poverty are the mean per capita consumption expenditure, the poverty line and the distribution of consumption expenditure (Kakwani and Son, 2006). Given this information, money metric poverty can be measured using various indices. The most common measure is the headcount ratio (the ratio of those with consumption expenditure below the poverty line to total population). The poverty ratio is expected, *ceteris paribus*, to decline (increase) as per capita consumption expenditure (poverty line) increases (decreases). Holding the growth in per capita consumption as constant, the poverty ratio is expected to increase as the degree of inequality increases and vice versa. It follows that any change in the headcount poverty ratio over time is due to net effects of the economic growth component and the distribution component.

Money metric poverty lines for a given society can be determined in absolute terms (the cost of basic needs) or in relative terms (such as one half of the median expenditure). Generally, absolute poverty measures are more suited to developing countries while relative poverty measures are more commonly applied in OECD economies. However, that does not mean that absolute poverty does not exist in richer countries. In the US, absolute poverty reached 12.7 percent of the population in 2016 according to the US Census Bureau (2017).

Absolute poverty lines can be divided into two groups: nationally defined poverty lines which vary depending on the cost of basic needs evaluated in local prices or fixed (in real terms) by holding its value constant over time and across countries using purchasing power parity exchange rates (PPPs), as in the literature on global poverty comparisons (see Illustration 1).[1] In principle, they test for the ability to purchase a minimum basket of goods and services that is roughly similar across the world. For example, the $1.9 a day poverty line which is commonly used as a threshold for extreme poverty comparisons corresponds to the value of the poverty lines used in some of the poorest countries.

Experts have questioned whether this approach produces consistent and comparable results for extreme poverty across countries and it remains a contentious academic issue (Deaton, 2008; Reddy, 2009). As argued by Deaton, a poverty line which is based on peoples' needs in the 15 poorest countries in the world, converted to PPP, doesn't adequately take into account levels of living in the middle-income countries of the region, particularly because the PPP conversions are often unreliable in comparing prevailing price levels across countries (Deaton, 2008). Critics of this approach to poverty measurement have also pointed to biases due to the choice of rock-bottom norms of expenditure unrealistically applied to the entire world and the fact that the data from which PPPs are derived were intended for comparing aggregates of national accounts and not the prices faced by the poor (Kakwani and Son, 2006; Reddy, 2009). Are these biases significant enough to change our regional and world view on poverty levels and trends? As argued in this chapter, it may very well be the case, particularly for the Middle East and North Africa (MENA) region (Abu-Ismail et al., 2012).

National poverty lines are superior to PPP-based poverty lines in three important respects. First, as they are household-specific, they tailor to the local food consumption patterns of the poor. Second, they consider the demographic and other characteristics of the household in determining minimum caloric requirements and basic non-food needs. Third, they evaluate the cost of these basic needs using prices at the local level. Moreover, countries have the flexibility to apply a variety of measurement techniques. In the US, it is calculated based on three times the inflation-adjusted cost of a minimum food diet (food poverty line) considering household size, composition and age.[2] In most Arab countries, national poverty lines are also calculated based on the cost of a minimum food diet, which itself is based on the recommended dietary requirements of calories and protein intake for normal functioning given the household's demographic and other characteristics. A minimum non-food expenditure share is determined using Engels Law and then added to this food poverty line to yield the national poverty line. In some countries a vulnerability line (or upper poverty line) is also estimated by awarding a more generous portion to the non-food expenditures.

This country-specific approach to poverty measurement is clearly of more use for the purposes of national policymaking, but its results are of little use in cross-country comparisons since the technique for setting the food and non-food components varies significantly across countries (and could be influenced by political reasons). For example, in the Arab region, the reference group for the food basket component of the poverty line is the lowest consumption quintile in Jordan and Morocco; the second lowest quintile in Egypt, Lebanon and Syria; the lowest two quintiles in Yemen and so on (Sarangi et al., 2015). In addition, the consumption/income expenditure surveys are not consistent across countries in terms of survey design, counting consumption expenditure itself, the periodicity of surveys and a number of other issues.

These factors make comparability difficult across countries or even over time within the same country, but provided that they are applied with methodological consistency over time, national poverty lines provide a robust basis for determining poverty levels and trends and as such their results serve as a 'reality check' for those derived from international poverty lines. This reality check is particularly important during periods of economic and political instability in which local prices and consequently consumption patterns may be altered significantly; hence, the earlier-noted weaknesses associated with the PPPs may be magnified to the point of yielding opposite trends to the ones derived from national sources, such as in the case in Egypt from 2000 to 2015 where indicators reveal $1.9 per day poverty had halved at the same time that poverty rates according to the national poverty line had increased by 50 percent.[3]

Given these and many other limitations of money metric poverty analysis,[4] recently there has been a growing appeal for the use of multidimensional poverty, or capability poverty, based on Nobel Laureate Amartya Sen's capability approach (Sen, 1980, 1984, 1985, 1987, 1992, 1999, 2009b). The approach suggests that the freedom people must have to achieve certain critical functioning is crucial in poverty measurement and analysis. According to this approach, poverty can be viewed as the inability (or lack of capability) to enjoy the basic rights and freedoms of life. In deciding the domains – or dimensions – of multidimensional poverty, several normative decisions are to be taken, based on contemporary theories and practice (Sen, 1985).

Progress in measuring multidimensional poverty has led to a variety of approaches and techniques (Tsui, 2002; Bourguignon and Chakravarty, 2003; Alkire and Santos, 2010; Alkire et al., 2015). Multidimensional poverty indices articulate nonmonetary deprivations across various dimensions, providing a more accurate depiction of the experience of the poor. The Global MPI (Multidimensional Poverty Index), based on the Alkire-Foster (AF) method, chooses three such domains – Education, Health and Living standards – with ten indicators (Alkire and Santos, 2014; UNDP, 2010). It helps in monitoring household deprivations in more than 100 developing countries and is regularly published by the Oxford Poverty and Human Development Initiative (OPHI) and the Human Development Report (HDR) of the United Nations Development Programme (UNDP).

These innovations in measuring multidimensional poverty are already influencing the mainstream poverty reduction perspectives, offering a significant complementary role to traditional money metric measurement. However, as its main function is to capture manifestations of extreme poverty, the MPI (as well as the $1.9 per day) will yield an incomplete picture on poverty levels and trends, especially in diversified regions such as the MENA and Arab states. It is important therefore to tailor money metric and multidimensional approaches to the specific conditions of the countries and/or regions under examination, especially their level of income per capita and human development.

To this end, this chapter has two main objectives. First, it provides a critical review of the main poverty stylised facts for MENA and other developing regions based on the commonly applied global indicators of money metric and multidimensional poverty. Second, it presents an alternative set of stylised facts based on nationally defined and regionally sensitive money metric and multidimensional poverty indicators. For the former the paper focuses on Egypt, using results from household income and expenditure surveys covering the period from 2005 to 2015. For multidimensional poverty, the paper relies on the recent Arab Multidimensional Poverty Report (LAS, ESCWA, UNICEF and OPHI, 2017) which presents two regionally tailored poverty measures: an acute poverty index with only minor adjustment from the global MPI suitable for Less Developed Countries such as Yemen, and a moderate poverty index which is more attuned to the conditions of middle-income countries such as Egypt and Tunisia. The chapter ends with a concluding section on how these findings may lead us to rethink the conventional wisdom on poverty and economic policy in the MENA region.

11.2 Poverty stylised facts using global measures

11.2.1 Money metric poverty

According to the $1.9 per day poverty line, the MENA region's headcount poverty ratio in 2015 was 5 percent, which is the third highest among developing regions (after Sub-Saharan Africa and South Asia) and half of the global average (Figure 11.1). The region has achieved only 19 percent poverty reduction since 1990, the lowest among developing regions and significantly lower than the global average of 72 percent led by the massive poverty reduction in East Asia and to a lesser extent in Latin America and South Asia. This has caused a phenomenal reduction in the world's total headcount ratio, from 35.8 percent in 1990 to 10 percent in 2015. Extrapolating these trends, it would appear that the developing world, with the exception of MENA and Sub-Saharan Africa, are on track to eradicate extreme poverty by 2030.

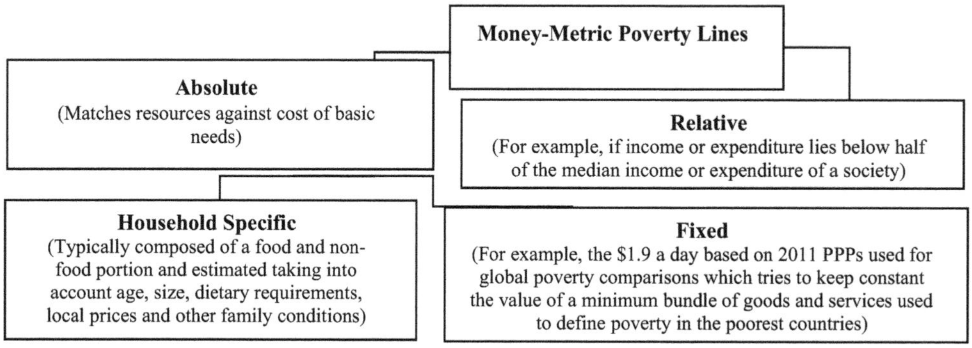

Illustration 11.1 Main approaches to money metric poverty measurement

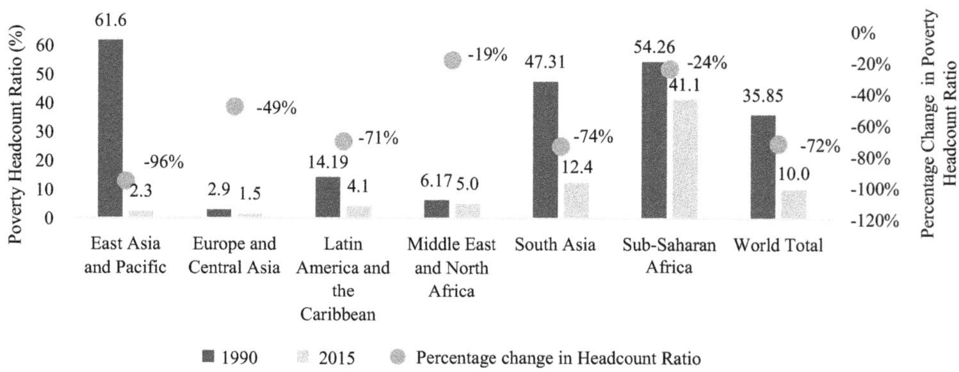

Figure 11.1 Poverty headcount ratio (percent) by region based on the $1.9 per day poverty line (in 2011 purchasing power parity), 1990–2015. *Note:* The countries included in the Middle East and North Africa are Algeria, Djibouti, Egypt, Iran, Iraq, Jordan, Lebanon, Morocco, Syria, Tunisia, West Bank and Gaza and Yemen. *Source:* Author's calculations based on data from PovcalNet, the online tool for poverty measurement developed by the Development Research Group of the World Bank; available from: http://iresearch.worldbank.org/PovcalNet/povOnDemand.aspx.

Figures 11.2A and 11.2B provide a snapshot of headcount poverty rates in 1990 and 2015 across a wide range of poverty lines starting from $0.5 per day and ending at $10 per day. Several stylised facts can be derived from the shape and shifting position of the lines in these figures. First, poverty reduction took place for MENA regardless of the choice of poverty line as indicated by the general downward shift of the red line in Figure 11.2B relative to its initial position in Figure 11.2A. Second, MENA has an 'S' shape poverty distribution curve. This implies poverty rates in MENA are quite low at poverty lines at or below $1.9 but they jump and continue to increase dramatically for poverty lines between $1.9 and $5.5, above which they continue to increase but at a slower pace. As shown in Figures 11.2 A and 11.2B, this distribution curve gives the region a unique property in global poverty comparisons: it is the only region whose poverty rate intersects with the global average (MENA is less poor than the global average or poorer than the global average depending on the choice of poverty line). Third, the area between the lines separating the lines for headcount poverty in the MENA region and the global average had shrunk significantly by 2015 compared to 1990. This implies poverty declined at a much slower pace in MENA relative to the global average regardless of the choice of poverty line.

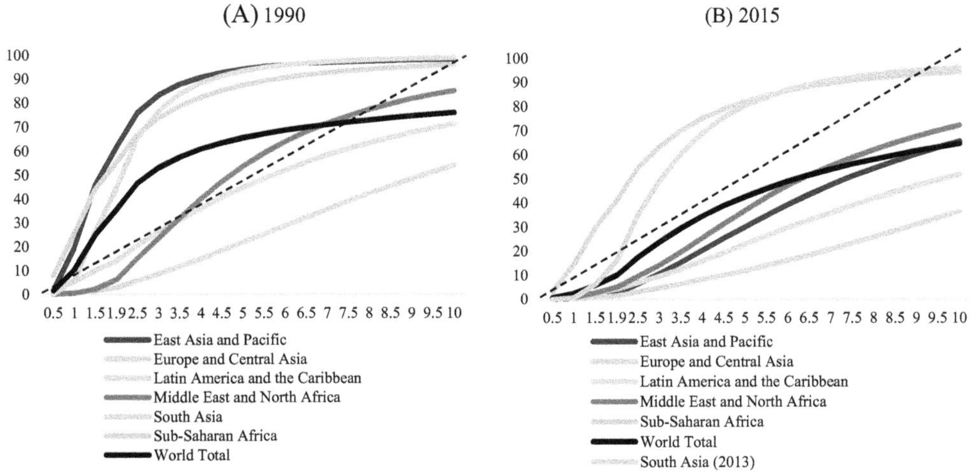

Figure 11.2 Poverty headcount ratio (percent) by region, \$0.5–\$10 poverty lines, 1990 and 2015. *Source*: Ibid.

Another stylised fact which can be intuitively derived from these results is that although a small share of the population lives below the \$1.9 line, a significantly higher share of the population in MENA are clustered between the \$1.9 and \$5.5 lines. In other words, extreme poverty is low in the MENA but vulnerability to it is high. To illustrate this point, consider this comparison between MENA and the global average. Global poverty rates increase by three folds from \$1.9 to \$3.5 and by more than four and a half folds from the \$1.9 to \$5.5 poverty lines. For MENA, the ratio increases by nearly four folds and nine folds, respectively. The implication is that the negative (or positive) poverty impact of any social and economic policies will be comparatively higher in MENA, a finding which has major political economy ramifications.

Given the large disparity in income per capita and conflict situations within the MENA region, these conclusions conceal some important country-level variations. These are shown in Figures 11.3 and 11.4. The first shows the level of poverty reduction in ten MENA countries according to the \$1.9 and \$3.5 per day lines from 1990 to 2015. The highest poverty reduction rates have been achieved by Iran, Jordan, Tunisia, Morocco, Egypt and Algeria and the lowest by Iraq (2 percent rise in poverty on the \$1.9 line and 14 percent reduction on the \$3.5 line). Three MENA countries, Syria, Yemen and Djibouti, witnessed significant increases in poverty mainly due to the impact of conflict. In Yemen extreme poverty increased by 272 percent from 1990 and an estimated 40 percent of the population were living under \$1.9 per day in 2015. In Syria the corresponding rate of increase was 170 percent.

Figures 11.4A and 11.4B show the combination of growth and distribution effects that have led to these poverty outcomes. In Algeria and Jordan, inequality reduction had a significant impact on poverty reduction. In Iran and Tunisia, the growth impact appears to have had a stronger hand in poverty reduction, but inequality reduction also helped. For Egypt and Morocco there was little change in inequality, but growth was fairly strong. Yemen appears to be in the worst possible location with a reduction in per capita expenditure along with a notable increase in inequality, hence its location in the upper left quadrant of Figure 11.4B. It is of course important to note that these figures do not include the impact of the conflict in Iraq, Yemen and Syria after 2015. The situation in those countries is likely to have deteriorated

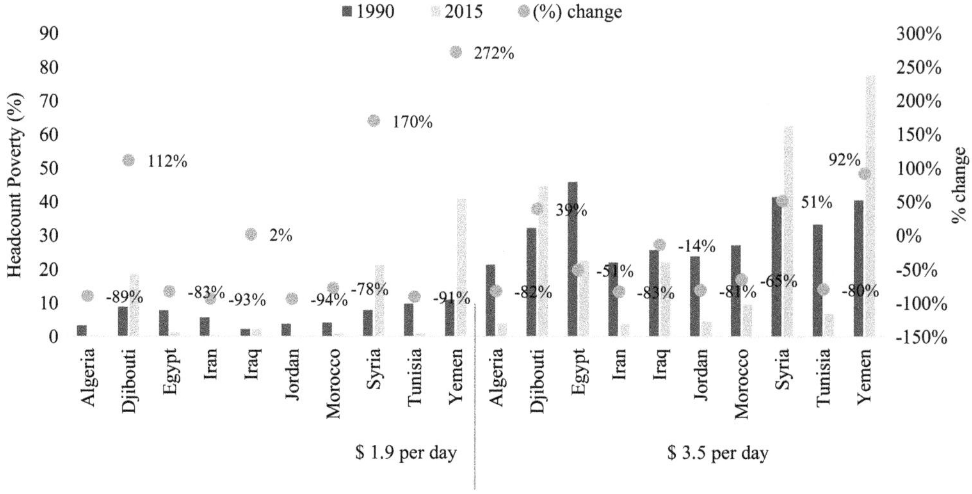

Figure 11.3 Headcount poverty ratio $1.9 and $3.5 and percentage change for selected MENA countries, 1990 and 2015. *Source*: Ibid.

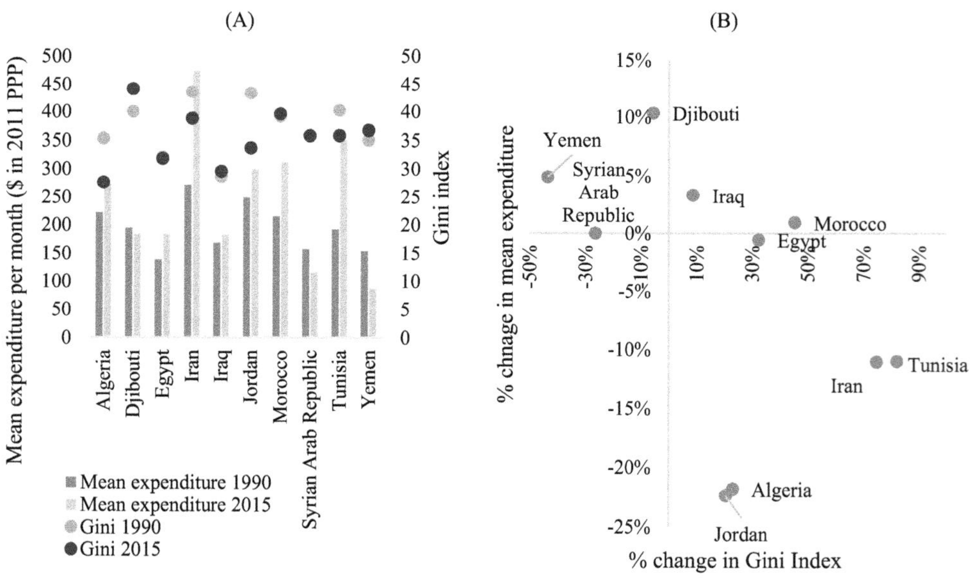

Figure 11.4 Mean per capita expenditure and Gini index (A) and percentage change (B), for MENA countries, 1990 and 2015. *Source*: Ibid.

further since then. The mean level of consumption expenditure in Yemen was already one of the lowest worldwide in 2015 (declining from $153 to $86 per capita per month in 2011 PPP as shown in Figure 11.4A).

Figure 11.4A also reveals that the overall level of inequality in MENA countries is moderate (hovering around 0.35) compared to other developing countries and that most countries have witnessed a reduction in their Gini scores. It is also worthy to note that these results are based on household income and expenditure surveys which systematically exclude the top earners and spenders. If the total earnings accrued to this top 1 percent of the population are taken into account, the inequality picture would change dramatically for all regions. This is particularly the case for MENA countries, which, according to the most recent World Inequality Report, become the highest in terms of inequality among developing regions once this adjustment is taken into account (World Inequality Report, 2018).

11.2.2 Multidimensional poverty

As noted in the introduction, Sen's development-as-freedom approach offers a broader conceptual framework for understanding poverty compared to the unidimensional money metric poverty approach. In this regard, 'poverty means that opportunities and choices most basic to human development are denied'.[5] The Multidimensional Poverty Index produced by the Oxford Poverty and Human Development Initiative and the United Nations Development Programme reflects an attempt to capture deprivation from 'instrumental freedoms' based on available comparable data sources (mainly demographic and health surveys). The MPI is composed of three dimensions and ten indicators. Each of these indicators has a weight and an associated deprivation cut-off. A household is considered poor if its total level of deprivation (sum of weighted deprivations in all indicators) is higher than one-third (33.3 percent) of the total possible deprivation. As shown in Table 11.1, the dimensions and their pertinent weights

Table 11.1 Dimensions, indicators, deprivation cut-offs and weights of the Global Multidimensional Poverty Index

Dimensions of poverty	*Indicator*	*Deprived if...*	*Weight*
Health	Nutrition	Any person under 70 years of age for whom there is nutritional information is undernourished.	1/6
	Child mortality	Any child has died in the family in the five-year period preceding the survey.	1/6
Education	Years of schooling	No household member aged ten years or older has completed six years of schooling.	1/6
	School attendance	Any school-aged child is not attending school up to the age at which he/she would complete class eight.	1/6
Living standards	Cooking fuel	A household cooks with dung, agricultural crop, shrubs, wood, charcoal or coal.	1/18
	Sanitation	The household's sanitation facility is not improved (according to SDG guidelines) or it is improved but shared with other households.	1/18
	Drinking water	The household does not have access to improved drinking water (according to SDG guidelines) or safe drinking water is at least a 30-minute walk from home, roundtrip.	1/18
	Electricity	The household has no electricity.	1/18
	Housing	The household has inadequate housing: the floor is of natural materials or the roof or walls are of rudimentary materials.	1/18
	Assets	The household does not own more than one of these assets: radio, TV, telephone, computer, animal cart, bicycle, motorbike or refrigerator, and does not own a car or truck.	1/18

Source: University of Oxford (OPHI), United Nations Development Programme (UNDP) (2018).

in the MPI are: health (child mortality and nutrition, each having 1/6 of the weight), education (years of schooling and child enrolment, each having 1/6 of the weight) and standard of living (electricity, drinking water, sanitation, housing, cooking fuel and possession of assets, each having 1/18 of the weight). The MPI is then calculated as the product of two numbers: the headcount ratio or proportion of people who are multidimensional poor and the average intensity of multidimensional deprivation, which reflects the proportion of dimensions in which households are deprived.

Table 11.2 provides summary headcount poverty aggregates, intensity of deprivations and the number of poor people for developing regions from applying the MPI based on the most recent available data. Multidimensional poverty is much higher for all developing regions compared to money metric poverty under the $1.9 poverty line and particularly for South Asia where multidimensional is nearly three times higher than money metric poverty. For MENA, it is slightly more than double the $1.9 poverty rate. These significant differences add another justification for the use of multidimensional poverty since it is often the case that households or individuals may not be income-poor but would be multidimensionally poor. However, this does not imply that both measures are not highly correlated. As shown in Figure 11.5, a positive correlation between both indicators is evident, but there are significant disparities around the mean indicating wide dissimilarities in money metric and multidimensional poverty profiles within many developing countries.

The multidimensional poverty approach based on the Alkire–Foster method also allows us to examine the share of the population living slightly above the poverty definition. People who are identified as non-poor according to the poverty cut-off could still be deprived in several

Table 11.2 Main multidimensional poverty indicators (%) for MENA and other developing regions

Developing regions	*MPI*[1]	*Headcount ratio (H)*[2] *(%)*	*Intensity (A)*[3] *(%)*	*Number of poor people (millions)*[4]	*Weighted population vulnerable to multidimensional poverty* (%)*	*Weighted population in severe multidimensional poverty* (%)*
Middle East and North Africa (MENA)*	0.047	11.50	40.40	33.1	8.68	3.85
East Asia and the Pacific	0.025	5.90	43.10	117.7	15.57	1.23
Eastern Europe and Central Asia	0.009	2.40	38.30	3.5	5.85	0.26
Latin America and the Caribbean	0.042	10.10	41.80	52.3	7.64	2.13
South Asia	0.143	31.30	45.80	545.9	19.28	11.71
Sub-Saharan Africa	0.317	57.80	54.90	559.6	17.89	36.52

Source: Author's calculations based on Global MPI Report, UNDP and OPHI September 2018.[5]

[1] The Multidimensional Poverty Index (MPI) ranges from 0 to 1.

[2] The headcount ratio is the percentage of the population with deprivation score of 1/3 or above.

[3] Intensity is the average percentage of weighted deprivations among the poor.

[4] The number of poor people uses 2016 population figures.

[5] Aggregates are population-weighted; the headcount ratio is multiplied by the 2016 population data from World Bank World Development Indicators online datasets.

Note: * The countries included in the Middle East and North Africa and survey years are: State of Palestine (MICS, 2014), Egypt (DHS, 2014), Morocco (PAPFAM, 2011), Djibouti (MICS, 2006), Iraq (MICS, 2011), Syrian Arab Republic (PAPFAM, 2009), Jordan (DHS, 2012), Algeria (MICS, 2013), Libya (PAPFAM, 2007), Yemen (DHS, 2013) and Tunisia (MICS, 2012).

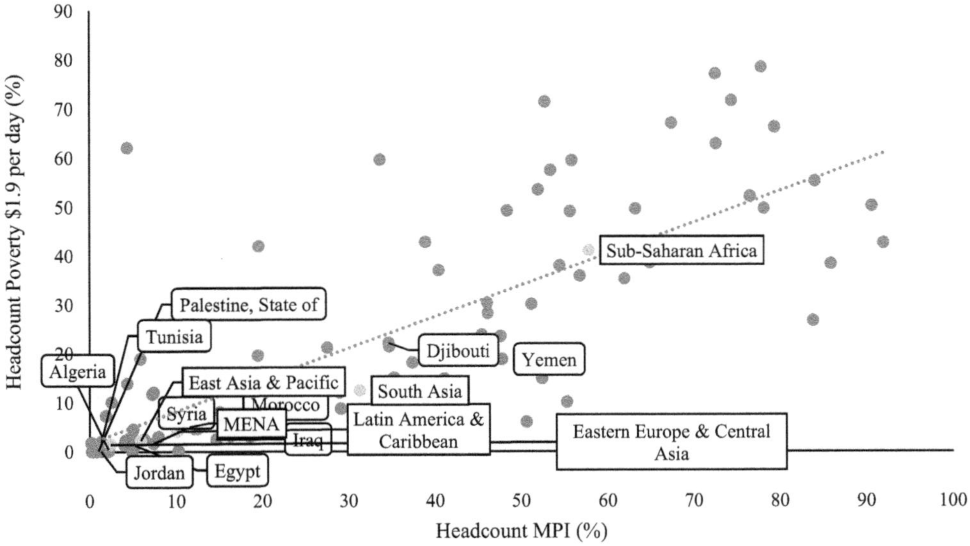

Figure 11.5 Headcount poverty $1.9 per day and multidimensional poverty based on most recent surveys.
Source: Author's calculations based on Alkire et al. (2018).

indicators. Accordingly, the share of the non-poor population who are deprived in 20–33.3 percent of the indicators are considered vulnerable to poverty. As mentioned above, people are identified as poor if their deprivations score is higher than the poverty cut-off of 33.3 percent. If poor people are deprived in over half of the indicators, i.e. the deprivation score is higher than 50 percent, they are considered severely poor. According to Table 11.2, vulnerability and severity of poverty do not appear to be significantly high for MENA in terms of the affected population share. However, the share of multidimensionally poor in the MENA countries who are severely poor is considerably higher than in Latin America and the Caribbean, although both regions have comparable headcount poverty ratios.

Country-level distribution of poverty shows a large disparity within MENA and more so within the Arab states between middle-income countries on the one hand and low-income countries on the other. Headcount poverty in Iraq and Morocco appears to be discernibly higher than the rest of the middle-income countries. While the intensity of poverty shows less variation, it is also notably higher in Djibouti and Yemen (Figure 11.6A).

In so far as poverty reduction trends are concerned, given it is more recent than money metric poverty analysis, there are few countries which have comparable trends for multidimensional poverty. Figure 11.6B, based on data produced by OPHI, provides such results. The relative annualised percentage change in the multidimensional headcount ratio is thus harmonised for comparisons across time for selected developing countries. Only two Arab countries were added to the list of 50 countries: Egypt, 2005–2008 and Jordan, 2007–2009. Despite the relatively short period between the surveys for Egypt and Jordan, both were among the top performers worldwide with 8–10 percent average annual headcount poverty reduction.

Finally, as shown in Figures 11.7A and 11.7B, deprivation from education appears to be the main source of poverty in the MENA, especially in middle- and upper-middle-income countries (with the exception of Jordan and the State of Palestine) while material deprivation affecting living conditions is the highest contributor to poverty in lower-income countries such as Yemen and Djibouti. Thus, a comparatively higher deprivation in MENA's education remains

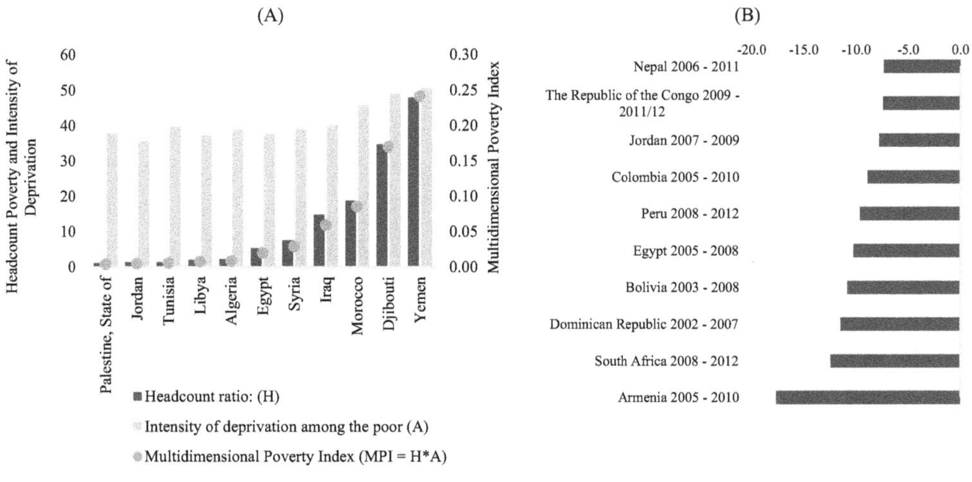

Figure 11.6 Multidimensional Poverty Index and its components for MENA (A) and annualised relative change in headcount poverty for the top ten performers among 50 developing countries (B). *Sources*: Figure 11.6 (A) is based on Alkire et al. (2018); Figure 11.6 (B) is from OPHI Update (2016). Comparisons over time obtained from Table 6 last updated in 2016; MPI resources on OPHI's webpage.

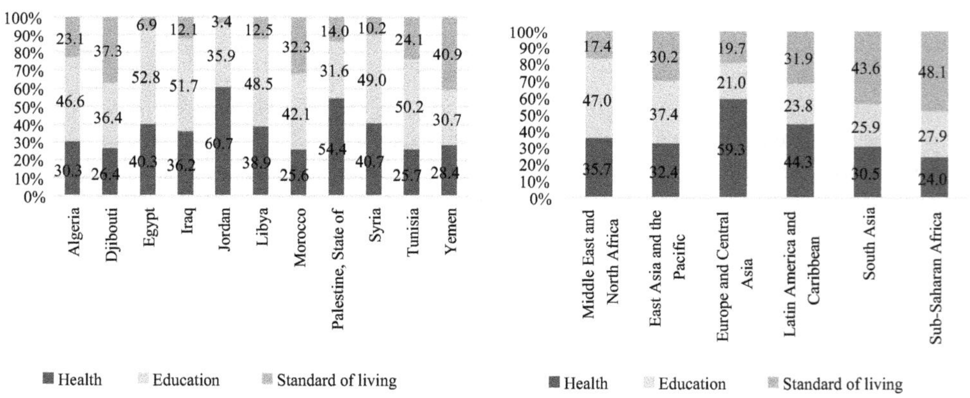

Figure 11.7 Contributions of deprivation dimensions to overall poverty for MENA (A) and for developing regions (weighted average) (B). *Sources*: Figure 11.7 (A) is based on Alkire et al. (2018); Figure 11.7 (B) is based on author's calculations based on Alkire et al. (2018).

as one of the main stylised facts to conclude from the cross-country analysis of multidimensional poverty between developing regions.

11.3 National and regional perspectives

11.3.1 Money metric poverty, vulnerability and the middle class

As they build on household-specific characteristics to estimate basic needs, national poverty lines have many advantages over fixed international poverty lines. However, their main limitation is the lack of comparability across countries due to the differences in poverty definitions, welfare measurement techniques, survey design, questionnaires, etc. To minimise these comparability problems, in 2015 the ESCWA led a research effort with a common measurement approach to examine the distribution of the population across four economically distinct household categories (poor, vulnerable, middle class and affluent) using household income and expenditure surveys in nine MENA countries (Sarangi et al., 2015). The question of what happened to the middle classes after the Arab Spring was pertinent at the time and hence a motivation behind this study.

To ensure consistency with national definitions, the report harmonised, to the extent possible, the poverty measurement techniques applied in national poverty assessments of these countries (which was made easier given that they were all conducted with technical support from the World Bank and the UN, and had already applied very similar poverty definitions and measurement procedures).[6] Accordingly, a household whose expenditure is less than the lower threshold for the cost of basic needs is considered 'poor' while a household whose expenditure lies between the lower and upper thresholds is considered 'vulnerable'. The middle class was correspondingly defined to consist of households whose expenditure lies above the upper poverty line and below the minimum line for affluence. The latter is defined as the level of expenditure on non-essential goods and services equivalent to the value of the lower poverty line (Abu-Ismail and Sarangi, 2013). This definition draws from the fact that poor households seldom have much choice in their expenditure decisions. Non-food expenditure choices, particularly non-essential ones (such as air conditioners, washing machines, cars, etc.), are a main feature of the expenditure of the middle class and affluent households (Abu-Ismail and Sarangi, 2013).

The results shown in Figure 11.8 confirm that, up to 2010, the middle class constituted nearly half of the population of the nine Arab countries (47.3 percent) (ESCWA, 2014). The (population weighted) regional average for poverty was 21 percent and except in Yemen and Egypt, headcount poverty did not exceed 13 percent. An additional 20 percent of the population were vulnerable. On average 12 percent of the population belonged to the affluent category but Jordan, Tunisia and Oman, given their higher expenditure per capita, recorded significantly higher shares.

Interestingly, the report indicated little change in poverty, vulnerability or the size of the middle class over the decade from 2000 to 2010, with the exception of Egypt, where economic

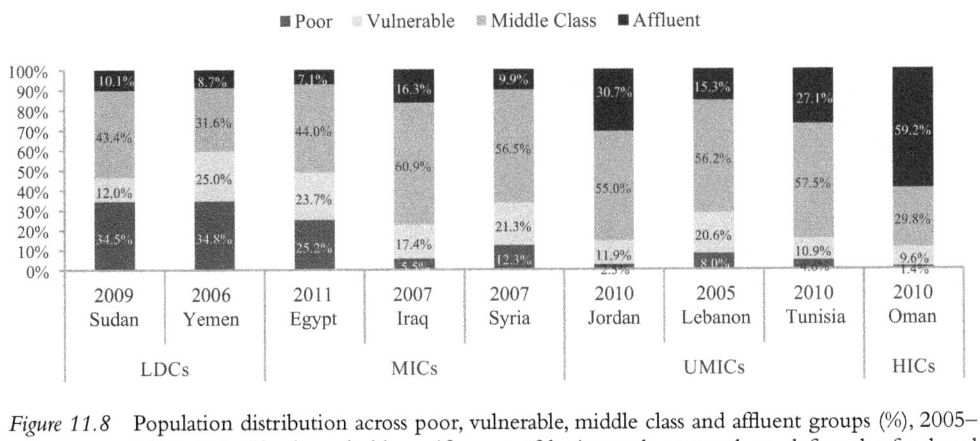

Figure 11.8 Population distribution across poor, vulnerable, middle class and affluent groups (%), 2005–2010. *Note*: The household-specific cost of basic needs approach to define the food and non-food components of the poverty line follow the methodology in El-Laithy et al. (2003). *Source*: ESCWA (2015).

pressure on the Egyptian middle class was clearly evident over the period from 2005 to 2010. These trends provide a basis to understand the economic concerns of the vulnerable and lower-middle-class groups in the period leading up to the Egyptian Revolution in 2011 (Abu-Ismail and Sarangi, 2013). It should be noted, however, that much has changed in the region since 2015. The conflicts in Syria, Iraq and Yemen are projected to have increased poverty to 45 percent and 55 percent, respectively, and in Syria vulnerability is assumed to affect another 40 percent of the population (ESCWA and St. Andrews University, 2016; and World Bank, 2018). As a consequence, there has been a significant decline in the size of the middle class to reach 8 percent in Yemen and 15 percent in Syria. Poverty and vulnerability are also expected to have increased in most other countries due to factors related to conflict (Iraq) and economic recession (Lebanon, Tunisia, Jordan and Egypt). Adjusting these estimates to reflect the impact of these, ESCWA (2014) estimated the regional average for poverty in the nine countries may have increased to 26 percent and the size of the middle class may have dropped to 42 percent of the population in 2014. Moreover, the poverty situation in 2018 is likely to have deteriorated even further for some countries, especially Egypt, after the impact of its currency devaluation as part of the economic reform program implemented in 2017.

To highlight the importance of the conceptual framework and measurement approach, international poverty measures give an opposite perspective on the economic welfare of Egyptian society during this period. As shown in Figure 11.9B, trends in poverty headcount rates at the PPP $3.8 per day line (equivalent to the value of the national poverty line 2015) indicate significant poverty reduction since 2005 (41 percent reduction in headcount poverty) while the ESCWA estimates using time-consistent national definitions indicate substantial increase in poverty (from 19.5 percent in 2005 to 28 percent in 2015 as shown in Figure 11.9A). Clearly, the narrative changes dramatically depending on the measurement approach.

11.3.2 Multidimensional poverty: a regional perspective

As noted earlier, multidimensional poverty measures avoid most of these comparability problems since they capture deprivations directly and thus have a major advantage over the money

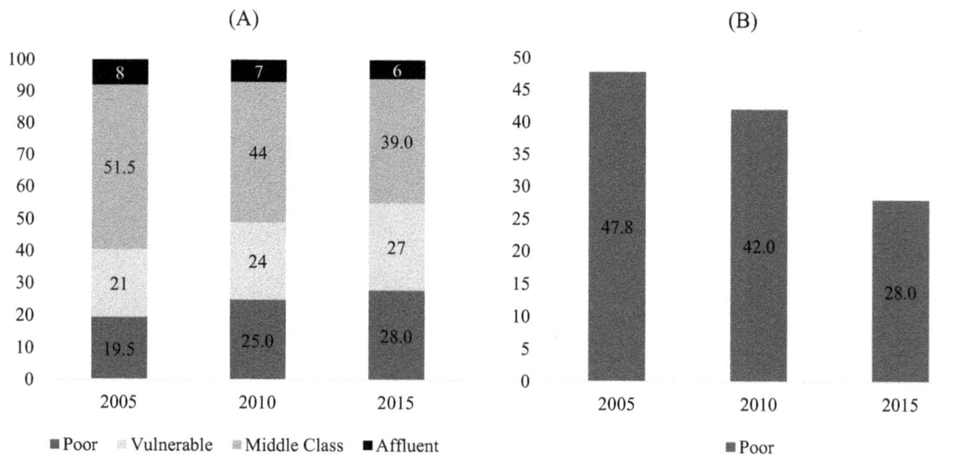

Figure 11.9 Population distribution across poor to affluent economic groups using national definitions (A) and poverty rates using PPP-based money metric lines (B) (%), Egypt 2005–2015. *Source*: Author's estimates based on World Bank Povcal.net accessed June 10, 2018, and Abu-Ismail and Sarangi (2013).

metric equivalents. However, by focusing on extreme and destitute poverty, the global MPI gives an incomplete picture on the spread of poverty since, by definition, it evades less severe deprivations that are widespread in middle-income countries. From the human development perspective, addressing these lower-level deprivations is crucial to the enhancement of capabilities, thus the formation and sustainability of the social middle class which forms the bedrock of socioeconomic structural transformation. For example, in the education dimension, the global MPI defines deprivation when none of the household members have attained a primary level education. For the majority of middle and upper-middle-income Arab countries, however, this threshold is too low particularly since the average expected years of schooling has already exceeded ten years in most countries. Hence, tailoring the global MPI to the region's specificities would require raising the deprivation threshold to secondary schooling.

Would such a regionally sensitive multidimensional poverty index alter the narrative on multidimensional poverty and vulnerability as in the case of money metric poverty? According to a recent report, it does and quite significantly so. The report, itself the result of a three-year joint effort and cooperation between the League of Arab States (LAS), the Economic and Social Commission for Western Asia (ESCWA), the United Nations Children's Fund (UNICEF) and the Oxford Poverty and Human Development Initiative (OPHI), examines household poverty using the global MPI but adapted to the Arab region which includes most of the MENA countries. The adapatation of the methodologies took place via an iterative consultative process with regional and global experts, as well as representatives of governments in the region, all to define poverty dimensions and indicators which are of relevance to the region's social and economic context and challenges. Thus, the regional MPI takes advantage of the academic rigour that went into building the global MPI and, at the same time, focuses on the priorities of the region. It follows the global MPI calculation methodology reviewed earlier, but adjusts the thresholds as in the above-mentioned example for education and adds two new indicators: one indicator on female genital mutulation and early pregnancy in the health dimension and an indicator of overcrowding in the living standard dimension. It also has a definition of acute poverty which is comparable to the global MPI.

There are four main results:

First, poverty is more widespread than previously believed: the estimated number of multidimensional poor stands at 116.1 million (40.6 percent of the total population of the ten countries included in the survey). This number includes the 38.2 million people (13.4 percent) that were identified as acutely poor. As shown in Figure 11.10, the ten countries are grouped into three clusters. Cluster 1 includes countries with poverty affecting less than one third of the population (Jordan, Tunisia, Algeria and Egypt). Cluster 2 includes Morocco and Iraq where poverty affects one third to one half of the population. Cluster 3 comprises the least developed countries (LDCs) – Comoros, Mauritania, Sudan and Yemen where more than half of the population are poor.

Second, vulnerability is quite high especially in Cluster 1 countries where it reaches 27.1 percent, following the pattern for poorer countries; and Cluster 3 countries have an extremely high share of severely deprived people (49.7 percent). On the aggregate level, one quarter of the population of the ten countries is vulnerable to poverty, while an additional 40.5 percent are poor or severely poor. This means that nearly two-thirds of the population are either poor or vulnerable to poverty.

Third, a staggeringly high share of households either do not have any member who has completed secondary school education and/or have children who are below the grade level for her/his age. In Algeria, Tunisia, Jordan, Morocco and Iraq, this indicator alone contributes

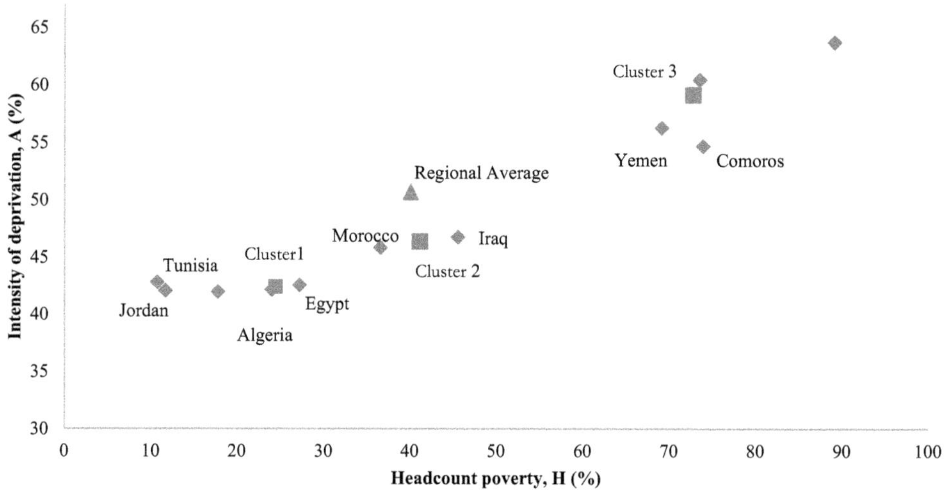

Figure 11.10 Headcount poverty and intensity of deprivation using the Arab MPI, 2011–2014. *Source*: LAS, ESCWA, UNICEF and OPHI (2017).

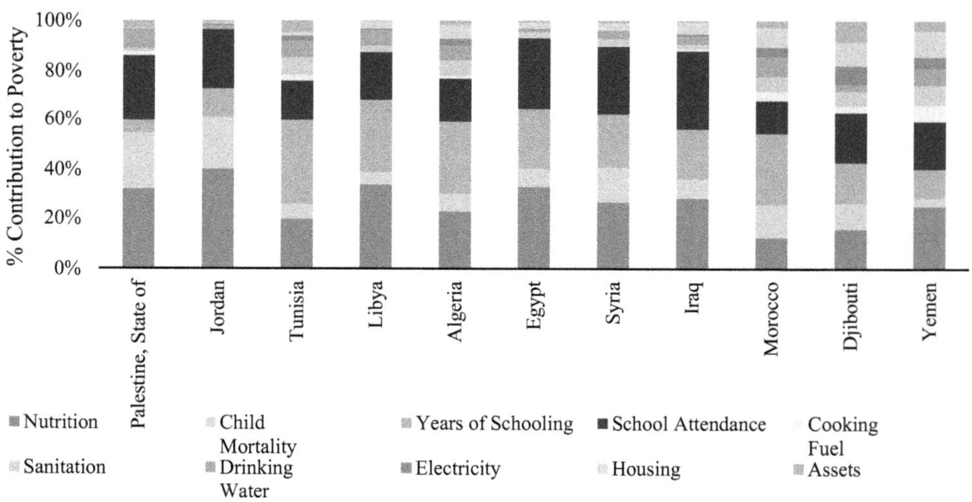

Figure 11.11 Contribution of indicators to multidimensional poverty (%) in twelve Arab states. *Source*: Based on Alkire et al. (2018).

25–30 percent to the total Multidimensional Poverty Index. The contribution of the living conditions dimension (housing conditions and asset ownership) for LDCs is much higher and nearly equivalent to that of education (Figure 11.11).

Fourth, inequalities both between and within countries are high. Rural areas are more than twice as poor as urban ones (for the headcount ratio it is 54 percent versus 24 percent, respectively). The poorest governorate in Egypt, Tunisia or Iraq is still by a stretch far better than the least deprived governorate in Yemen. Moreover, inequalities in deprivation across household characteristics are staggering. The lowest wealth quintiles are 50 times more likely to suffer from acute deprivations. Households with eight or more members have twice the poverty rate of households with one to four members. Educated heads of households are six times less poor than those with non-educated heads.

11.4 Conclusion

There are five relevant stylised facts related to poverty in the MENA that have been highlighted in this chapter.

First, according to the most common measure of extreme money metric poverty – the $1.9 per day poverty line – MENA's headcount poverty ratio in 2015 was 5 percent. This may seem low, but it is the third highest among developing regions (after Sub-Saharan Africa and South Asia). Just to put things in perspective, the global average was only 10 percent. Importantly, national poverty lines, though not designed for cross-country comparison, are more accurate for measuring poverty in the national context. When they are harmonised for cross-country comparison, national poverty lines can dramatically change the story on both the level and trend of poverty as in the case for Egypt over the period from 2000 to 2015. Multidimensional poverty measures are more superior to money metric ones in that they are better at capturing cross-country comparisons. Using the global MPI, the MENA region also shows a relatively lower incidence of multidimensional poverty (11.5 percent) in 2015 compared to other developing regions.

Second, the Arab region fell short of reducing extreme poverty by half from 1990 (the MDG goal) and it scored the lowest poverty reduction rate of 19 percent. Again, to give this figure a comparative basis, the global poverty reduction average was 72 percent. There is little evidence on trends in multidimensional poverty; however, the evidence available suggests rapid declines in Egypt and Jordan during the 2000s.

Third, as a result of conflict conditions in some countries, the MENA region is the only region that has witnessed an increase in extreme poverty since 2013. This is an alarming indicator as it signals a new trend of reversing poverty reduction gains. It is expected that multidimensional poverty may have been affected by the ongoing conflicts in many countries. However, there is no recent data to allow us to estimate the impact in these countries.

Fourth, the MENA ranking vis-à-vis the global average varies significantly depending on the choice of money metric poverty line. Money metric poverty is low using the $1.9 line but by no means so when we move beyond the $3.5 poverty line and the poverty headcount rate for the region is higher than the global average once we apply higher poverty lines above $5.5 per day. Thus, vulnerability to extreme poverty is high as a significantly higher share of the population in MENA countries is clustered right after the $1.9 per day line compared to other developing regions. Multidimensional poverty levels also change rather dramatically when a regionally sensitive measurement framework tailored to middle-income and medium-level human development countries is applied. Last year's Arab Multidimensional Poverty Report (LAS, ESCWA, UNICEF and OPHI, 2017) estimated the total number of multidimensional poor at 116.1 million (40 percent of the population). It also showed that vulnerability to multidimensional poverty is quite high, affecting one-quarter of the Arab population (which includes most of the MENA countries). This means that nearly two-thirds are either poor or vulnerable to multidimensional poverty using a regional definition with higher poverty lines.

Notes

1 For the vast literature on the calculation of the poverty line see, for example, Ravallion et al., (2008) and the references cited therein.

2 Center for Poverty Research, University of California Davis (https://poverty.ucdavis.edu/faq/what-current-poverty-rate-united-state).
3 Based on author's estimates from Povcal.Net and ESCWA (2014).
4 See for example Kanbur (2000: 791–841); Cornia and Kiiski (2001); and World Bank (2005).
5 See UNDP (2016) for the definition of human poverty.
6 See UNDP (2006c, 2009a) for Syria, UNDP (2008) for Lebanon, World Bank and UNDP (2007) for Yemen and World Bank (2005, 2007) for Egypt.

Bibliography

Abdel-Gadir, A. and K. Abu Ismail (2010). Pro-Poor Growth in Syria: Diagnosis and Policy Considerations. Syria: United Nations Development Programme.

Abu-Ismail, K. and N. Sarangi (2013). A New Approach to Measuring the Middle Class: Egypt. Symbol: E/ESCWA/EDGD/2013/WP.2. Beirut: ESCWA.

Abu-Ismail, K., Abou Taleb, G. and R. Ramadan (2012). Rethinking Global Poverty Measurement. IPC-IG (International Policy Centre for Inclusive Growth) Working Paper, No. 93. Brasilia: UNDP (United Nations Development Programme); available from: http://www.ipc-undp.org/pub/IPCWorkingPaper93.pdf.

Alkire, S. and G. Robles (2017). Multidimensional Poverty Index Summer 2017: Brief Methodological Note and Results. OPHI Methodological Note 44–45. University of Oxford.

Alkire, S. and M.E. Santos (2010). Acute Multidimensional Poverty: A New Index for Developing Countries. OPHI Working Paper No. 38.

Alkire, S. and M.E. Santos (2014). Measuring Acute Poverty in the Developing World: Robustness and Scope of the Multidimensional Poverty Index. World Development, 59, pp. 251–274.

Alkire, S., Conconi, A. and J.M. Roche (2013). Multidimensional Poverty Index 2013: Brief Methodological Note and Results. OPHI Briefing 12. Oxford University.

Alkire, S., Roche, J.M. and A. Vaz (2014). Multidimensional Poverty Dynamics: Methodology and Results for 34 Countries. Oxford, United Kingdom: Oxford Poverty and Human Development Initiative, Oxford University.

Alkire, S, Foster, J.E., Seth, S., Santos, M.E., Roche, J.M. and P. Ballon. (2015). Multidimensional Poverty Measurement and Analysis: A Counting Approach. Oxford, United Kingdom: Oxford University Press.

Alkire, S., Kanagaratnam, U. and N. Suppa (2018). Global Multidimensional Poverty Index 2018: Brief Methodological Note and Results. OPHI MPI Methodological Notes No. 46. Oxford Poverty and Human Development Initiative, University of Oxford.

Bourguignon, F. and S.R. Chakravarty (2003). The Measurement of Multidimensional Poverty. Journal of Economic Inequality, 1(1), pp. 25–19.

Cornia, G.A. and S. Kiiski (2001). Trends in Income Distribution in the Post World War II Period: Evidence and Interpretation. WIDER Discussion Paper 89. Helsinki: UNU/WIDER.

Deaton, A. (2008). Price Trends in India and Their Implications for Measuring Poverty. Economic and Political Weekly, 9 February, pp. 43–49.

Deaton, A. (2010). Price Indexes, Inequality, and the Measurement of World Poverty. *American Economic Review*, 100(1), pp. 5–34.

El Laithy, H., Lokshin, M. and A. Banerji (2003). Poverty and Economic Growth in Egypt, 1995–2000. Policy Research Working Paper, No. 3068. Washington, DC: World Bank.

ESCWA (2014). The Middle Class in Arab Countries: Measurement and Role in Driving Change. E/ESCWA/EDGD/2014/2.

ESCWA and St. Andrews University (2016). Syria at War: Five Years on. E/ESCWA/EDID/2016/2.

Government of Yemen, the World Bank, and the United Nations Development Programme (2007). Yemen Poverty Assessment. Main report No. 53076.

Kakwani, N. and H.H. Son (2006). Measuring the Impact of Price Changes on Poverty. UNDP International Poverty Centre, Working Paper No. 33, November 2006. Brasilia: UNDP.

Kanbur, R. (2000). Income Distribution and Development. In A.B. Atkinson and F. Bourguignon, Handbook of Income Distribution, Volume 1. Amsterdam: Elsevier, pp. 791–841.

LAS, ESCWA, UNICEF and OPHI (2017). Arab Multidimensional Poverty Report. E/ESCWA/EDID/2017/2.

Ravallion, M., Chen, S. and P. Sangraula (2008). Dollar a Day Revisited. Policy Research Working Paper 4620. World Bank; available from: http://documents.worldbank.org/curated/en/350401468157768465/pdf/wps4620.pdf

Reddy, S. (2009). The Emperor's New Suit: Global Poverty Estimates Reappraised. Working Paper, No. 79, United Nations Department of Economics and Social Affairs. New York: United Nations Department of Economics and Social Affairs.
Sarangi, N., et al. (2015). Towards Better Measurement of Poverty and Inequality in Arab Countries: A Proposed Pan-Arab Multipurpose Survey. ESCWA Working Paper. E/ESCWA/SD/2014/WP.1.
Sen, A. (1980). Equality of What? in McMurrin (ed.), Tanner Lectures on Human Values. Cambridge: Cambridge University Press, pp. 197–220.
Sen, A. (1984). Rights and Capabilities, in Resources, Values and Development. Cambridge, MA: Harvard University Press, pp. 307–324.
Sen, A. (1985). Commodities and Capabilities. Oxford: Elsevier Science Publishers.
Sen, A. (1987). The Standard of Living, in Sen, Muellbauer, Kanbur, Hart and Williams, (eds.), The Standard of Living: The Tanner Lectures on Human Values. Cambridge: Cambridge University Press, pp. 270–293.
Sen, A. (1992). Inequality Re-examined. Oxford: Clarendon Press.
Sen, A. (1999). Development as Freedom. New York: Knopf.
Sen, A. (2009a). The Idea of Justice. London: Allen Lane.
Sen, A. (2009b). Capability: Reach and Limit, in E. Chipper-Martinetti (ed.), Debating Global Society. Reach and Limit of the Capability Approach. Milan: Feltrinelli, pp. 15–28.
Tsui, K. (2002). Multidimensional Poverty Indices. Social Choice and Welfare, 19(1), pp. 69–93.
UNDP (United Nations Development Programme) (2005). Poverty in Syria; available from: https://www.arabstates.undp.org/content/rbas/en/home/library/Sustainable_development/poverty-in-syria--1996-2004.html
UNDP (United Nations Development Programme) (2006). Macroeconomic Policies for Poverty Reduction in Syria. Damascus: United Nations Development Programme.
UNDP (United Nations Development Programme) (2007). Poverty, Growth, Employment, and Income Distribution in Yemen 1998 – 2006. Sana'a: United Nations Development Programme (UNDP).
UNDP (United Nations Development Programme) (2008). Poverty, Growth and Income Distribution in Lebanon. Beirut; available from: https://www.undp.org/content/dam/lebanon/docs/Poverty/Publications/Poverty,%20Growth%20and%20Income%20Distribution%20in%20Lebanon.pdf
UNDP (United Nations Development Programme) (2009). Arab Human Development Report 2009: Challenges to Human Security in the Arab Countries. New York: UNDP.
UNDP (United Nations Development Programme) (2010). Human Development Report 2010. The Real Wealth of Nations: Pathways to Human Development. New York: UNDP.
UNDP (United Nations Development Programme) (2016). UNDP and The Concept and Measurement of Poverty, Issue Brief, October. New York: UNDP.
UNDP (United Nations Development Programme) (2018). Table 6a, accessed online June 8th 2018 UNDP Human Development Report online database.
University of Oxford (OPHI), United Nations Development Programme (UNDP) (2018). Global Multidimensional Poverty Index 2018. The Most Detailed Picture to Date of the World's Poorest People, Oxford, United Kingdom: Oxford Poverty and Human Development Initiative (OPHI) University of Oxford.
US Census Bureau (2017). Income and Poverty in the United States: 2016; available from: https://www.census.gov/content/dam/Census/library/publications/2017/demo/P60-259.pdf
World Bank (2005). The Growth Experience. What Have We Learned from the 1990s? A Background Note. Poverty Reduction & Economic Management Network. Washington, DC: World Bank, pp. 143–146.
World Bank (2007). Egypt – Poverty Assessment Update. Vols. 1–2, Washington, DC: The World Bank.
World Bank (2018). World Development Indicators Database. Available at https://databank.worldbank.org/source/world-development-indicators
World Inequality Lab (2017). World Inequality Report 2018. Washington, DC: World Bank, World Inequality Database; available from: https://wir2018.wid.world/files/download/wir2018-full-report-english.pdf

12

MEASURING INEQUALITY IN THE MIDDLE EAST

Facundo Alvaredo, Lydia Assouad and Thomas Piketty

12.1 Introduction

In recent decades, the Middle East has been the scene of dramatic political events: wars, invasions, revolutions and various attempts to redraw the regional political map. In this context, it is natural to ask whether the high level of political instability is related to the specific structure and level of socio-economic inequality in the region.[1]

Indeed, following the Arab Spring uprisings, there has been renewed interest in inequality measurements in Middle Eastern countries. Several papers have found that income inequality within these countries does not seem to be particularly high by international standards and that the source of dissatisfaction might lie elsewhere (World Bank, 2014; Bibi and Nabli, 2010). This somewhat surprising fact, coined "the Enigma of Inequality" (UNDP, 2012) or the "Arab Inequality Puzzle" (World Bank, 2015), has produced a rising rate of literature on inequality in the region (Ncube and Anyanwu, 2012; Hassine, 2015, Hlasny and Verme, 2015; Van der Weide et al., 2016; or Assaad et al., 2017).

We argue that the answer of the "enigma" lies in a measurement issue. In our research, we attempt to solve this puzzle in two ways. First, we collect all income and wealth data available in the region: household surveys, fiscal data, national accounts and rich lists. Using the methodology developed by Alvaredo et al. (2016) and used for other regions in the World Inequality Database (http://wid.world), we combine these different data sources in a systematic manner to correct upwards official survey-based inequality estimates for each country. Second, we aggregate the obtained within-country distributional data to estimate the distribution of income at the level of the entire Middle East.

These two contributions lead to novel estimates of the distribution of income in the region between 1990 and 2016: according to our benchmark series, the Middle East appears to be the most unequal region in the world, with a top decile income share as high as 64%, compared to 37% in Western Europe, 47% in the USA and 55% in Brazil (Alvaredo et al., 2018c). This is due to enormous inequality between countries (particularly between oil-rich and population-rich countries), as well as to very large inequality within countries, which we probably still underestimate given the data limitation.

Given the lack of fiscal data in the region, we are able to produce meaningful series at the regional level only and we leave within-country series for future research. For the moment, the only country in the region for which we can derive reliable income shares series is Lebanon, analysed in Assouad (2017). It is interesting to move the analysis to the regional level for 3 reasons. First, the concept of nation-state may not be the most meaningful lens through which one can analyse the concentration of income. National, regional and global inequality estimates give different insights on inequality dynamics and determinants (Milanovic, 2002; Bourguignon and Morrisson, 2002; Lakner and Milanovic, 2015; Alvaredo et al., 2018 on global and regional inequality estimates). Second, one can plausibly argue that perceptions about inequality and the fairness or unfairness of the distribution of income are determined not only by within-country inequality but also by inequality at the regional level, and even sometimes at the global level. This may be particularly the case for the Middle East where the population of the region, about 410 million in 2016, is comparable to Western Europe (420 million) or the United States (320 million) and is characterised by a relatively high degree of cultural, linguistic and religious homogeneity. Third, the final outcome of the aggregation of distributions is less straightforward than it may seem and requires an empirical examination *per se*. For example, when we integrate Eastern and Western European countries, thereby looking at a population of over 570 million, we find the top 10% income share rises moderately, from 37% in Western Europe to 39% for total Europe. When we put together Gulf countries with other Middle Eastern countries, the top 10% income share rises more drastically, from 55% to 64% (see Figure 12.9a). How much is due to the various institutional features of Europe, such as free mobility or regional development funds, and the lack thereof in the Middle East, is an interesting issue which falls beyond the scope of this chapter.

The extreme inequality level that characterises the region is not the only explanation for the regional political instability. Other factors – religious, historical, cultural and political – certainly play an important role as well. But we believe that inequality belongs to a set of background factors contributing to the generatation of political upheavals.

Finally, we still face important uncertainties regarding the measurement of income distribution in the region and stress the need to increase transparency on income and wealth. In particular, despite our best efforts, our ability to properly measure income inequality within individual countries is severely limited by the low data quality. The problem is particularly acute in the GGC states, for which there exist very few studies on income inequality (see, e.g., El Katiri et al., 2011 on Kuwait, and Naidu et al., 2016 on labour income in the UAE, using new administrative data for foreigners), and where the low-standard survey-based Gini coefficients seem to contradict important aspects of their political economy, namely the growing share of migrant population, a large majority of which is composed of low-paid workers living in difficult conditions (Human Rights Watch, 2013). Despite these uncertainties, our main conclusion – namely the fact that the Middle East is one of the most unequal regions in the world, if not the most unequal region – appears to be robust.

12.2 A measurement issue

Our research relies on four types of data sources: household surveys, income tax data, wealth rankings and national accounts. We define the Middle East as the region covering Egypt to Iran, and from Turkey to the Persian Gulf and Yemen, excluding Israel. We use the macroeconomic database with annual series of population and national income for each country between 1990 and 2016 available in the World Inequality Database.[2] Basic descriptive statistics for 2016 from this database are reported in Table 12.1.

In order to estimate the distribution of income in the Middle East, we proceed in three steps. We estimate survey income distribution for each country (step 1), which we correct using (i)

Table 12.1 Population and income in the Middle East (2016)

	Population (million)	*Adult population (aged 20 and more, in million)*	*Adult population (% of ME total)*	*National income (billion PPP Euro 2016)*	*% ME total income (PPP)*	*National income (billion MER Euro 2016)*	*% ME total income (MER)*
Turkey	**80**	**53**	**21%**	**1,073**	**19%**	**548**	**22%**
Iran	**80**	**56**	**22%**	**896**	**16%**	**330**	**13%**
Egypt	**93**	**54**	**22%**	**800**	**14%**	**234**	**9%**
Iraq–Syria–Other (non-Gulf)	**102**	**52**	**21%**	**570**	**10%**	**243**	**10%**
Iraq	*38*	*18*	*7%*	*354*	*6%*	*112*	*4%*
Syria	*19*	*10*	*4%*	*47*	*1%*	*28*	*1%*
Jordan	*8*	*4*	*2%*	*57*	*1%*	*30*	*1%*
Lebanon	*6*	*4*	*2%*	*57*	*1%*	*40*	*2%*
Palestine	*5*	*2*	*1%*	*16*	*0%*	*12*	*0%*
Yemen	*27*	*13*	*5%*	*39*	*1%*	*21*	*1%*
Gulf countries	**54**	**37**	**15%**	**2,394**	**42%**	**1,179**	**47%**
Saudi Arabia	*32*	*20*	*8%*	*1313*	*23%*	*575*	*23%*
Oman	*5*	*3*	*1%*	*118*	*2%*	*47*	*2%*
Bahrain	*1*	*1*	*0%*	*46*	*1%*	*26*	*1%*
UAE	*9*	*8*	*3%*	*430*	*7%*	*283*	*11%*
Kuwait	*4*	*3*	*1%*	*258*	*5%*	*122*	*5%*
Qatar	*2*	*2*	*1%*	*229*	*4%*	*126*	*5%*
Total Middle East	**409**	**252**	**100%**	**5,733**	**100%**	**2,534**	**100%**

personal income tax micro data available for Lebanon analysed in Assouad (2017) and generalised Pareto interpolation techniques developed by Blanchet, Fournier and Piketty (2017) (step 2). We then use national accounts and rich lists in order to impute tax exempt capital income (step 3). Our concepts and methods generally follow those described in the Distributional National Accounts guidelines used for the World Inequality Database (Alvaredo et al., 2016).

Step 1: Constructing a household income database for the Middle East

Income and inequality data are scarce in the Middle East, notably in the poorest and the richest countries. Even when national statistics offices do undertake household surveys on income or expenditures, the databases are often of poor quality and their access is very limited (Bibi and Nabli, 2010).[3] The first part of our work consists in gathering available survey data to create a Middle East income database and generate survey-based income distributions at the national and then the regional levels. Table 12.2 summarises the years for which household survey data are available.[4]

We faced three main issues in the data construction process. The first one refers to the definition of income. The data quality makes it impossible to harmonise the series in a completely satisfactory manner. Only the micro data for Turkey contain relatively detailed information on income categories. Other micro databases mostly provide the total disposable income and tabulated data generally do not distinguish between different income categories. Whenever possible, the survey income concept that we use attempts to approach pre-tax, post-replacement income

Table 12.2 Household surveys used in this paper (1990–2016)

	Survey years	*Average ratio (total survey income)/ (national income)*
Turkey	**1994, 2002–2016**	**43%**
Iran	**2010, 2013**	**49%**
Egypt	**1999, 2004, 2008, 2010, 2012, 2015**	**40%**
Iraq–Syria–Other (non-Gulf)	**1992–2013**	**53%**
Iraq	*2007*	*60%*
Syria	*2004*	*56%*
Jordan	*1992, 2002, 2006, 2008, 2010, 2013*	*70%*
Lebanon	*2007*	*37%*
Palestine	*1996–1998, 2004–2008, 2010–2011*	*65%*
Yemen	*2006*	*33%*
Gulf countries	**1995–2013**	**30%**
Saudi Arabia	*2008*	*30%*
Oman	*2010*	*29%*
Bahrain	*1995, 2005, 2015*	*37%*
UAE	*1998, 2009*	*39%*
Kuwait	*2007, 2013*	*21%*
Qatar	*2007, 2012*	*23%*

defined in the DINA guidelines.[5] Therefore, in the trade-off between harmonising our database (between years and/or countries) and approaching the pre-tax income concept we choose the latter. This is a substantial limitation that needs to be corrected in the future.

The second issue concerns the unit of observation. We take the adult individual (i.e. aged 20 and more) as the basic unit, and we assume that income is equally split between adult household members (Alvaredo et al., 2016).

The third issue is related to the years without data. As one can see from Table 12.2, household surveys are available only for a limited number of years. To infer the distribution of years with no data, we use the household surveys of the closest available year.[6] For a number of countries, we only have one household survey, which means that by construction we are forced to use the same inequality level over the period. This major limitation implies that we cannot draw robust conclusions on the *evolution* but only on the overall *level* of income inequality in the Middle East.

Additionally, to ensure maximal comparability across countries and years, we choose to anchor all country year level income distributions to the relevant per-adult national income. That is, for every country–year pair, we proportionally upgrade all income levels for all percentiles so that per-adult average income coincides always with per-adult average national income observed in our macroeconomic database (therefore keeping the income distribution and shares constant). By doing so, we certainly do not pretend that available national income series are perfectly comparable. We simply assume that these are the most comparable income series we have: national accounts at least attempt to apply the same definition of national income in all countries (as defined by the SNA Guidelines developed by the UN), which is not the case with survey income.

We also report on Table 12.2 the ratios between total survey income and national income. For most Middle East countries, the ratios lie between 40–50%, which is fairly small, but not unheard of by international standards. Note however that the ratios are substantially smaller in

Gulf countries – as low as 20–30%. That is, compared to other countries, a very large fraction of national income of Gulf countries is missing from self-reported household survey income. To the extent that nationals benefit from the excluded income components (which typically refer to the undistributed profits of oil corporations and the capital income from sovereign wealth funds) more than foreigners, this implies that we are likely to severely underestimate income inequality in Gulf countries. To correct for this, we proceed as follows: we impute a fraction of the missing income (the gap between national income and total survey income) to nationals only, so that the ratio between survey income (augmented by the imputation) and national income reaches 30%, 50%, 70% or 100%. We take as benchmark survey distributions for Gulf countries the series where this ratio equals 50%, except in Qatar where we take the series where the ratio is 30%.[7]

At the end of the first step, we obtain the full distribution of raw survey income separately for all countries and for the region as a whole between 1990 and 2016, using the generalised Pareto interpolation techniques (Blanchet et al., 2017) on tabulated data. We express the distributions in terms of generalised percentiles (or g-percentiles).[8]

Step 2: Fiscal data correction

Self-reported survey data is well known to underestimate incomes at the top, due to under-reporting, truncations and top coding problems. The strategy followed in the World Inequality Database to correct for this is to use income tax micro files. Unfortunately, fiscal data are extremely limited in Middle East countries. Lebanon is the only country for which we were able to access income tax micro files (see Assouad, 2017 for a detailed description of the data). This is unfortunate, because household surveys in the region appear to underestimate top incomes at least as much as in the rest of the world and possibly more (see Assouad et al., 2018 for a comparison with other extremely unequal regions). In particular, survey-based inverted Pareto coefficients (the ratio of the average income in a top group over the threshold to enter the group) are implausibly low for top incomes, generally around 1.5–1.7 (and sometime even less than 1.5) at the level of the top 10%.[9] In contrast, in all countries in the world with reliable income tax data, including Lebanon, inverted Pareto coefficients are typically between 2 and 3 (or even higher in extremely unequal country).

To construct our benchmark series, we choose to adopt correction factors for the top of the survey distribution of each country that are based upon the Lebanese fiscal data. More precisely, the income tax micro files enable us to compute correction coefficients for thresholds and upper average income by g-percentiles for each year with fiscal data (2005–2014).[10] To derive more precise estimates, we need to have access to income tax data for all Middle East countries. Our estimates must be improved in future research, if and when better sources become available.

Step 3: Missing capital income and wealth correction

Reallocating missing capital income based on wealth inequality estimates

Finally, we correct our fiscal income series to take into account non-reported and tax-exempt capital income, uncovered by fiscal data. These missing capital incomes typically include corporate retained earnings and imputed housing rental income. In the absence of detailed national accounts, we assume that this missing "non-fiscal" income y_{nf} equals 10% of national income in each country, a reasonable figure given what we observe in countries with good data.[11] Then, to estimate the distribution of personal income $y_p = y_f + y_{nf}$, i.e. the sum of fiscal and non-fiscal income, we need to make an assumption about the distribution of y_{nf} and the correlation between y_f and y_{nf}. We assume that y_{nf} follows the same distribution as wealth, which we estimate by applying generalised Pareto interpolation techniques to wealth rankings. As for the correlation structure between y_f and y_{nf}, on the basis of estimates obtained in countries with adequate micro files, we use the family of Gumbel copulas, with Gumbel parameter $\theta = 3$ (Piketty et al., 2017, and Novokmet et al., 2018).

Estimating wealth distributions

To estimate the wealth distributions necessary to reallocate the missing capital income and to derive our final estimates of the income distribution in our region (step 3), we face even greater problems, as wealth data are scarcer than income data in the region. Only billionaire lists, published by *Forbes* and the magazine *Arabian Business*, are available. To take advantage of this information, however, we proceed as follows. We first compute the ratio of billionaires' wealth to national income: for Saudi Arabia, Qatar, Bahrain and Lebanon, it is greater than 20% on average, while it varies between 5% and 15% in the United States, Germany and France over 2005–2015 (Figure 12.1). For each country, we take the average ratio over 1990–2016, as some years do not have information on billionaires. Second, we compute average standardised distributions of wealth for the US, France and China from the WID.world series.[12] We note that variations across countries and over time in these standardised wealth distributions mostly happen above $p_0=0.99$, i.e. below $p_0=0.99$ the ratios of the different percentile thresholds to average wealth are relatively stable over time and across countries, at least as a first approximation with most of the variation taking place within the top 1%. Therefore, we choose to use the same normalised distribution for Middle East countries below $p_0=0.99$ as the average US–France–China normalised distribution, hereby assuming that wealth is at least as concentrated as what we observe in other regions of the world with available data. To estimate the average wealth, necessary to derive the final wealth distribution, we compute an annual average wealth income ratio over all countries available in WID.world, and we apply this average to each country average income. The difficult

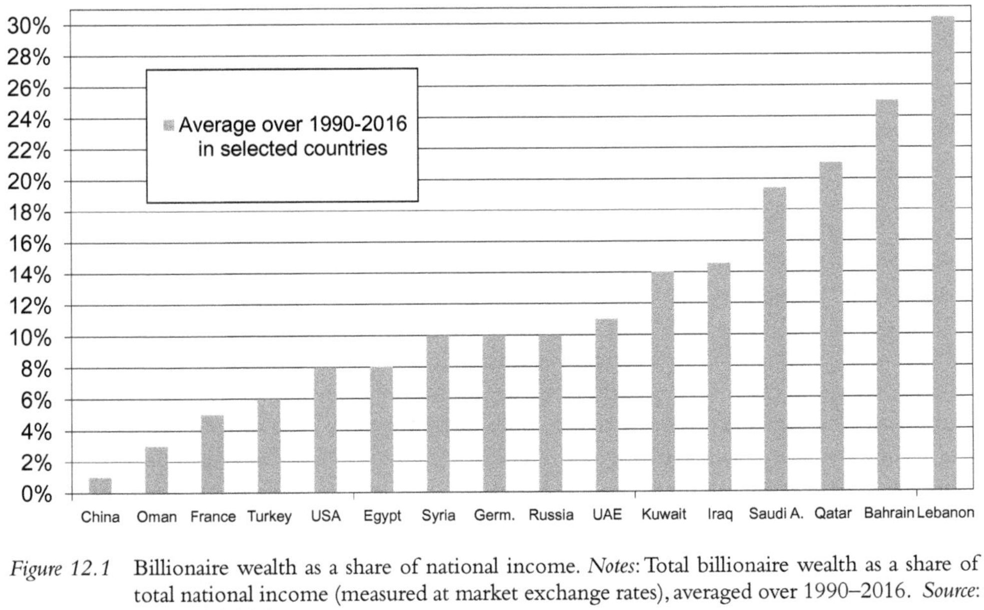

Figure 12.1 Billionaire wealth as a share of national income. *Notes*: Total billionaire wealth as a share of total national income (measured at market exchange rates), averaged over 1990–2016. *Source*: Assouad (2017).

question is to know how to link the distribution from p_0=0.99 to billionaire level and also to make an assumption about the average number of adults per billionaire family (sometime *Forbes* includes very large family groups in the same billionaire family; sometime it is just one individual or one married couple). We first estimate the 127 generalised percentile within the top 1% of the normalised distribution in order to reach billionaire level.[13]

Caveat on our wealth inequality estimates

Unfortunately, billionaire lists are particularly fragile and volatile in the region.[14] Using this data source to identify a trend in wealth concentration is impossible and our estimates of wealth inequality are extremely limited. Large amounts of wealth may be missing due to a pervasive use of tax havens and offshore bank accounts. The data leaked from HSBC Switzerland and Mossack Fonseca (the so-called "Swiss leaks" and "Panama Papers") show that Middle East countries are among the top clients of those offshore financial institutions. Andersen et al. (2017) show that "petroleum rich autocracies" in the Arab world tend to hide larger amounts of wealth and do so more easily than other countries with oil resources. In addition, rich lists do not include wealth owned by ruling families and heads of states. This may lead to a substantial downward bias in the region, where the line between public and private property is often blurred.[15]

Nevertheless, we believe that this method gives a good first approximation of the concentration of wealth in the region. Additionally, the wealth-based correction (step 3) has a smaller impact than the fiscal data correction (step 2), and therefore our assumptions on wealth inequality have a limited impact on the final income distribution and on our main conclusions regarding income inequality in the region.

12.3 Extreme concentration of income in the Middle East

12.3.1 Evolution of average incomes and population in the Middle East

The 1990–2016 period has seen a rapid population growth in the Middle East: total population rose by about 70%, from less than 240 million in 1990 to almost 410 million in 2016. The rise in average income has been much more modest. Using purchasing power parity estimates (PPP, expressed in 2016 euros), per-adult national income rose from about €20,000 in 1990 to €23,000 in 2016, i.e. by about 15%. Using market exchange rates (MER, in 2016 euros), per-adult national income rose from less than €9,000 in 1990 to about €10,000 in 2016 (Figure 12.2a).

The PPP and the MER viewpoints express valuable and complementary aspects of international inequality patterns. The PPP viewpoint should of course be preferred if we are interested in the living standards of the inhabitants living, working and spending their incomes in the various countries, which is the case for most people. However, the MER viewpoint is more relevant and meaningful if we are interested in external economic relations: e.g. the ability of tourists and visitors from Europe or from Gulf countries when they travel to other countries; or the ability of migrants or prospective migrants from Egypt or Syria to send part of their euro wages back home. It may also play an important role on the perceptions of inequality. Whatever the viewpoint, it is important to have in mind that per-adult average income benefited from very little growth over the 1990–2016 period: in effect, the vast majority of aggregate national income growth was absorbed by the rise of population (Figure 12.2b).

Next, there exists enormous and persistent between-country inequality behind the Middle East average (Table 12.1). To summarise the changing population and income structure of the

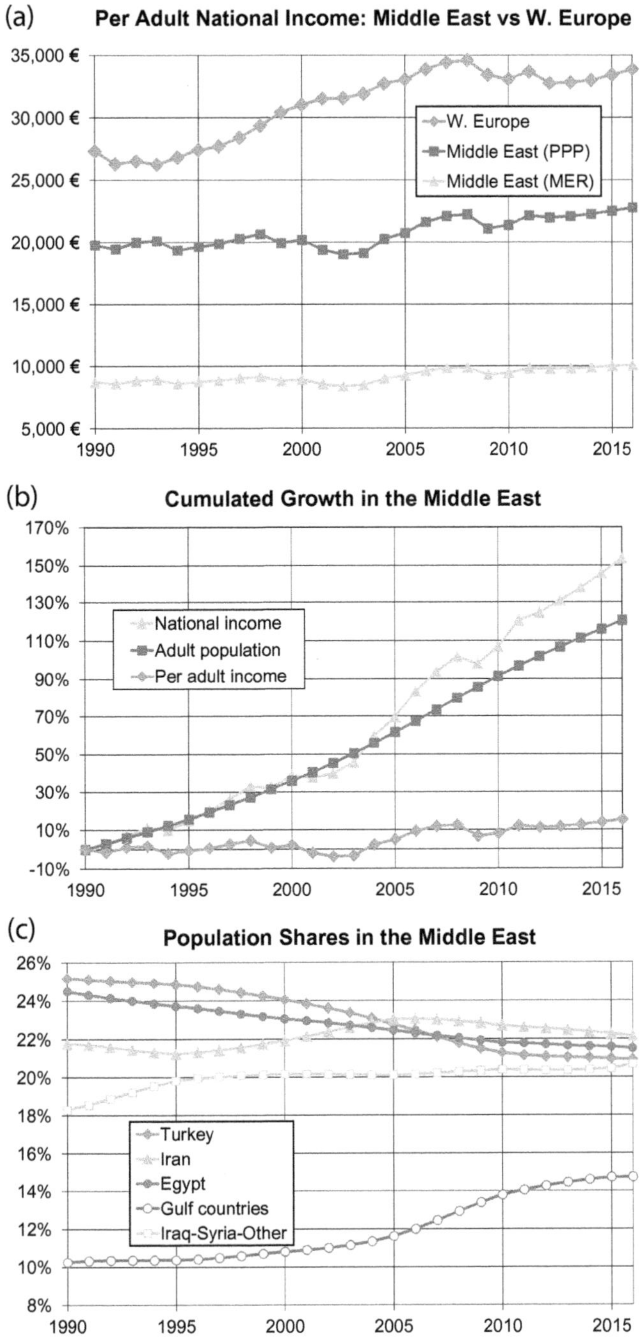

Figure 12.2 (a) Per-adult national income: Middle East vs. W. Europe. (b) Cumulated growth in the Middle East.

Middle East, it is helpful to decompose the region into five blocs: (i) Turkey; (ii) Iran; (iii) Egypt; (iv) Iraq, Syria and other non-Gulf countries: Jordan, Lebanon, Palestine, Yemen; and (v) the Gulf countries (Saudi Arabia, Oman, Bahrain, UAE, Qatar and Kuwait). Each of the first four blocs represents about 20–25% of the total population of the Middle East, with relatively little variation over the period. The main change in the structure of the Middle East population over the past quarter of a century is the rise of the population share of the Gulf countries, from about 10% in 1990 to 15% in 1996 (Figure 12.2c). This is almost entirely due to the rise of migrant workers in oil-rich countries.

Regarding the average income patterns in these five sub-regions, per-adult national income is substantially below average everywhere except in the Gulf countries (Figures 12.3a and 12.3b). One can distinguish between two groups: Turkey and Iran, where average incomes have generally been around 50–60% of the West European average in PPP terms (with a significant rise in Turkish incomes over the 2001–2015 period, in contrast to Iranian stagnation); and Egypt and Iraq–Syria–other, where average incomes have always stood at significantly lower levels (around 30–40% of West European average in PPP terms). Using MER, we find that Egypt–Iraq–Syria–other have stagnated at around 10–15% of the West European average.

Compared to the rest of the Middle East, Gulf countries belong to a different category. In PPP terms, their average per-adult national income was about three times that of Western Europe in 1990, and almost two times in 2016; in MER terms, their income was 40% higher than the West European level in 1990 and is currently about 10% lower (Figure 12.3c).

In brief: there exists an enormous gap in average incomes between Gulf countries and the more populated Middle East countries, which has, however, been trending downwards in the past 25 years. In 2016, Gulf countries represented only 15% of the Middle East population, but they received between 42% (in PPP terms) and 47% (in MER terms) of the total Middle East income (Table 12.1). The fall in the income gap between Gulf countries and the rest of the Middle East over the period is due to the evolution of oil prices and output levels, as well as to the relatively fast output growth in non-Gulf countries like Turkey. It is also due to the very large rise in the number of migrant workers, and the consequently migration-led reduction of per-adult national income in the Gulf countries: the massive inflow of foreign workers resulted in a bigger increase in the population denominator than in the income numerator of the Gulf countries. By putting together census and survey data for the various countries, we find that the overall rise of the population share of Gulf countries is almost entirely due to the massive rise in foreign workers, which increased from less than 50% in 1990 to almost 60% of the total population in 2016 (Figure 12.3d).

12.3.2 Enormous inequality between countries

According to our benchmark estimates, the share of total income going to the top 10% income earners is about 64% in the Middle East, compared to 37% in Western Europe and 47% in the USA (Figure 12.4a). Income inequality appears to be significantly higher in the Middle East than in Brazil, a country with a population of around 210 million and often described as one of the most unequal in the world, and where the top decile income share is about 55% (Morgan, 2017). The Middle East also displays slightly higher inequality estimates than South Africa, with about 63% for the top decile income share for the latest available years (Alvaredo and Atkinson, 2010, and series updated in WID.world). Finally, we can see in Figures 12.4b and 12.4c and 12.4d that the bottom 50% of the population receives about 9% of the total income in the Middle East (vs. 18% in Europe) As in other extremely unequal regions, the Middle East income

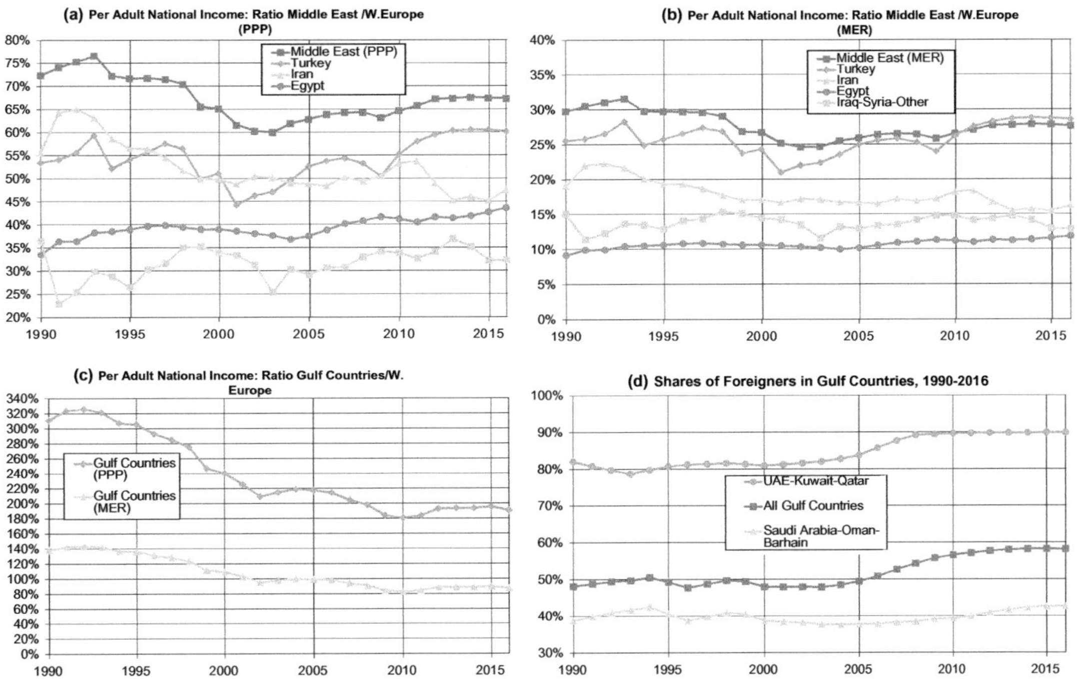

Figure 12.3 Evolution of average income in the Middle East, 1990–2016. *Notes*: Per-adult national income in € 2016 PPP (purchasing power parity) vs. MER (market exchange rate). Other Arab Middle East countries (Jordan, Lebanon, Palestine, Yemen) are included with Iraq–Syria. Western Europe = Germany–France–UK. Gulf countries include Saudi Arabia, UAE, Oman, Kuwait, Qatar, Barhein. Shares of foreigners in the adult population (20+) of Gulf countries (as measured by censuses, administrative sources and household surveys).(a) Per-adult national income: ratio Middle East / W. Europe (PPP). *Notes*: Per-adult national income in € 2016 PPP (purchasing power parity). Other Arab Middle East countries (Jordan, Lebanon, Palestine, Yemen) are included with Iraq–Syria. Western Europe = Germany–France–UK. (b) Per-adult national income: ratio Middle East / W. Europe (MER). *Notes*: Per adult national income in € 2016 MER (market exchange rate). Other Arab Middle East countries (Jordan, Lebanon, Palestine, Yemen) are included with Iraq–Syria. Western Europe = Germany–France–UK. (c) Per-adult national income: ratio Gulf countries / W. Europe. *Notes*: Per-adult national income in € 2016 PPP and MER. Gulf countries include Saudi Arabia, UAE, Oman, Kuwait, Qatar, Barhein. W. Europe = Germany–France–UK. (d) Shares of foreigners in Gulf Countries, 1990–2016. *Notes*: Shares of foreigners in the adult population (20+) of Gulf countries (as measured by censuses, administrative sources and household surveys).

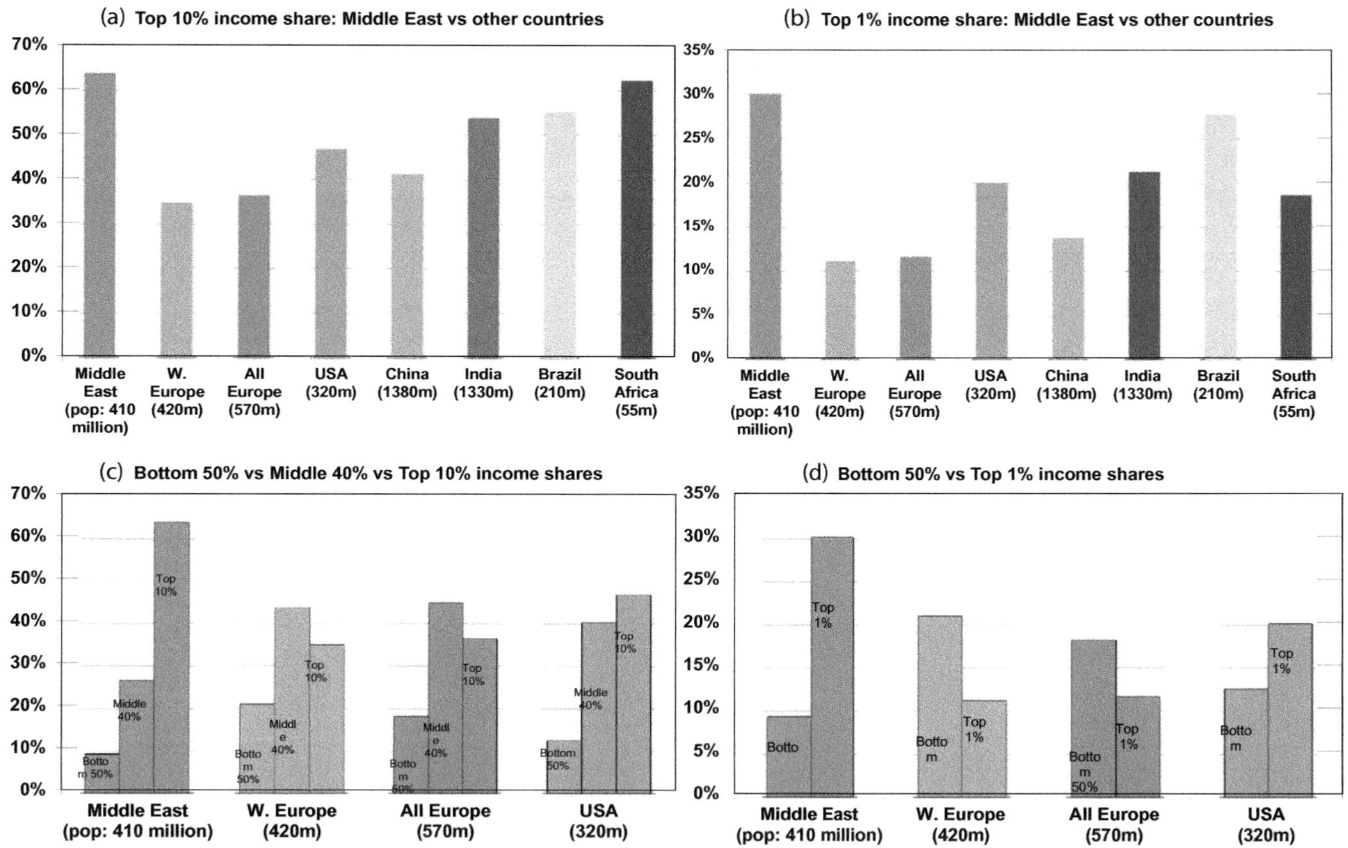

Figure 12.4 Income distribution in the Middle East and other countries and regions. *Notes*: Distribution of national income (before taxes and tranfers, except pensions and unempl. insurance) among adults. Corrected estimates combining survey, fiscal, wealth and national accounts data. Equal-split series (income of married couples divided by two). Latest years available (2012–2016). *Source*: WID.world.

distribution is extremely polarised, with a top 1% receiving more than three times as much as the bottom 50% (Figure 12.4d and Assouad et al., 2018).

The origins of inequality are very different in these different regions. In the Middle East, they are largely due to the geography of oil ownership and the transformation of oil revenues into permanent financial endowments. In contrast, extreme inequality in South Africa is intimately related to the legacy of the Apartheid system: until the early 1990s, only the white minority (about 10% of the population, which until today roughly corresponds to the top 10% income group) had full mobility and ownership rights. In Brazil, the legacy of racial inequality also plays an important role (it was the last major country to abolish slavery in 1887, at a time when slaves made up about 30% of the population), together with huge regional inequalities. It is striking to see that the Middle East, in spite of its much larger racial and ethno-cultural homogeneity, has reached income inequality levels that are comparable to – or even higher than – those observed in South Africa or Brazil.

Large within-country inequalities that are still underestimated

Our computations are based on extremely conservative estimates of within-country inequality, given the lack of fiscal data and the low quality of survey data. Our ability to measure income inequalities is particularly limited in oil-rich countries, where the data do not enable us to distinguish between nationals and foreigners. By exploiting available household surveys, we find that the ratio between average per-adult survey income between nationals and foreigners is particularly large in UAE–Kuwait–Qatar (which is not surprising, given the very small share of nationals), and most importantly that this ratio has increased over time, from 250% in 1990 to around 350% in 2016 (Figure 12.5). In those Gulf countries where the national–foreigner

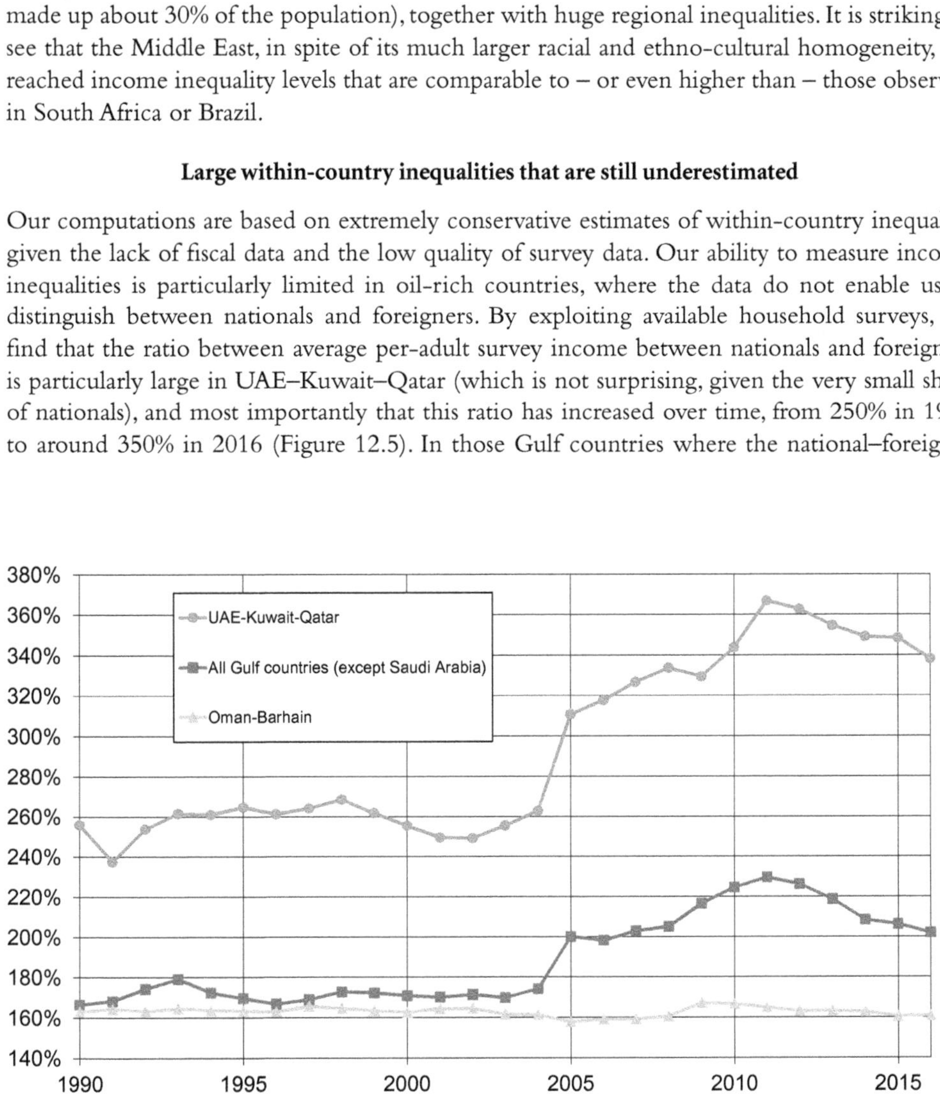

Figure 12.5 Income ratio nationals/foreigners in Gulf countries, 1990–2016. *Notes*: Ratios between average per-adult income of nationals and foreigners (as measured by household surveys). These ratios are likely to underestimate inequality between nationals and foreigners because top incomes are under-reported in surveys (no correction was made here). Detailed survey breakdown not available for Saudi Arabia.

population structure is closer to 50–50 (i.e. Oman–Bahrain), the average income ratio between nationals and foreigners appears to be less extreme but stays substantial at around 160%.[16]

Additionally, the gap between total survey income and national income in the Gulf countries is particularly high (see Table 12.2), that is why we attributed part of this missing income to nationals, in order to derive more reliable estimates (see the description of step 1). Figure 12.6 displays top income shares for each country in 2016, depending on different scenarios on the share of missing income attributed to nationals (so that the average income in the survey, augmented by the imputation, represents 30%, 50%, 70% or 100% of the average national income). Under these credible scenarios, we see that within-country inequality is probably higher than what we can presently observe.

Figure 12.7 shows how these different variants affect inequality at the regional levels.

Analysing the evolution of income inequality in the Middle East and other robustness checks

The data sources at our disposal are also insufficient to properly analyse trends in inequality. In our benchmark estimates, we find a declining inequality trend at the regional level between 1990 and 2010, followed by a rising trend between 2010 and 2016. However, these are trends of relatively small magnitude, and it is unclear whether these are robust findings.

The fact that inequality remains extreme for all years over the period provides further evidence for the robustness of our main result on the levels of inequality (Figure 12.8a). This holds in a large number of variant estimates: when we move from the MER estimates (our benchmark series) to the PPP estimates, or when we change the geographic definition (Figure 12.8b).[17]

It is worth noting that, as shown in Figure 12.9a, when we exclude the Gulf countries from our computations, inequality remains extreme, with a top decile receiving more than 50% of total regional income over the entire period.

To understand the origins of our high inequality estimates, Figure 12.9b displays the results obtained with our benchmark national income series (combining survey data, national accounts, income tax and wealth data), the results obtained with the fiscal income series (ignoring the wealth correction) and the results obtained with the survey data alone. The figures also display a hypothetical variant of the survey income series derived by assuming fixed country-level average incomes (thereby neutralising the impact of between-country inequality). As one can see, both the within-country inequality effect (fiscal data correction) and the between-country inequality drive our results.

Finally, we also simulate what the evolution of income inequality in the Middle East over 1990–2016 would have been if within-country inequality had remained fixed at the observed 1990 level. In Figure 12.9c, we see that the evolution of total inequality at the level of the Middle East taken as a whole would have been virtually the same. This shows that our estimates are mostly driven by the evolution of between-country inequality. This is partly due to the fact that we do not have survey data for all years so that for some countries our inequality estimates display very little time variations (and in some cases no time variation at all).[18] If we had access to adequate income tax data throughout the 1990–2016 period, we might have reached different conclusions and found a strong within-country rising inequality trend, as observed worldwide during this period. It is also possible that Middle East countries belong to a category of regions where inequality has always been very large historically. We leave the answers to these questions to future work.

12.4 Conclusion

In our research, we have combined household surveys, national accounts, income tax data and wealth data in order to estimate the level and evolution of income concentration in the Middle

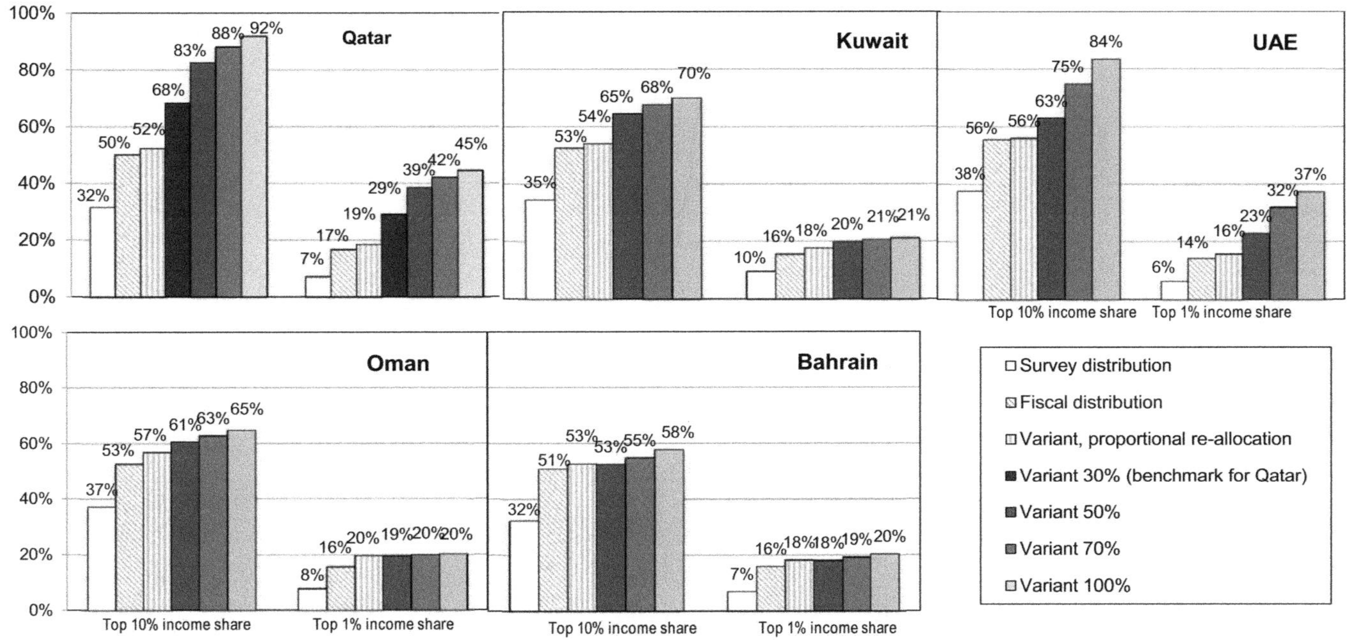

Figure 12.6 Inequality statistics in Gulf countries, 2016 (variants). *Notes*: Distribution of income (before taxes and transfers, except pensions and unemployment insurance) among equal-split adults (income of households divided equally among adult members). Survey income series solely use self-reported survey data (but anchors distributions to per-adult national income). Fiscal income estimates combine survey and income tax data (but do not use wealth data to allocate tax-exempt capital income). Final estimates (with variants) combine survey, fiscal, wealth and national accounts data. The same conclusion holds true when we look at other inequality indicators such as the bottom fiscal, wealth and national accounts data. Variants estimates are the result of imputing a fraction 50% income share or the Gini coefficient of missing income (the gap between national income and total survey income) so that the average income in the survey (augmented by the imputation) represents 30%, 50%, 70% or 100% of the average. Unfortunately, available series for the top 10 percent and top 1 percent share in South Africa do not cover all years, so it is difficult to make a complete comparison with the Middle East at this stage. We also consider a conservative variant where the missing income is proportionally attributed to both foreigners and nationals.

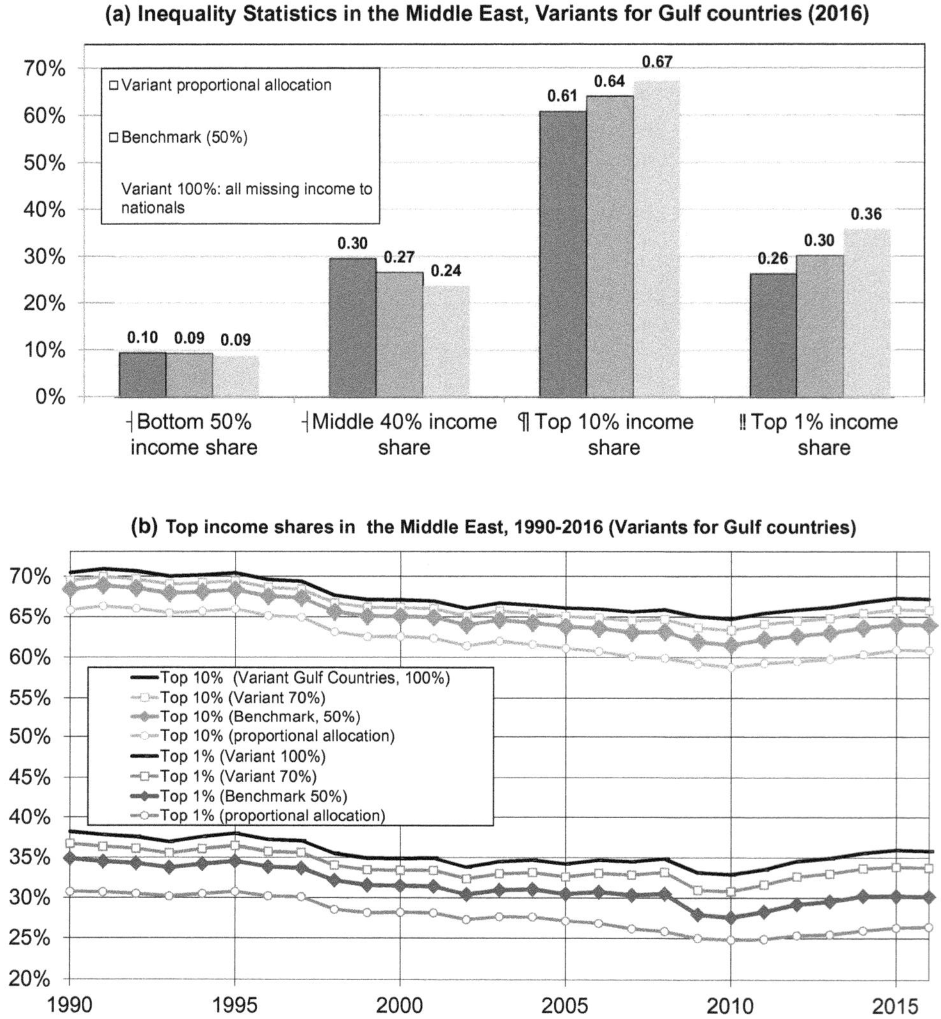

Figure 12.7 Top income shares in the Middle East, variant for Gulf countries. *Notes*: Distribution of income (before taxes and transfers, except pensions and unemployment insurance) among equal-split adults (income of households divided equally among adult members). Final estimates (with variants) combine survey, fiscal, wealth and national accounts data. Variants estimates are the result of imputing a fraction of missing income (the gap between national income and total survey income) so that the average income in the survey (augmented by the imputation) represents 50%, 70% or 100% of the average national income, and combines survey, fiscal, wealth and national accounts data. We also consider a conservative variant where the missing income is proportionally attributed to both foreigners and nationals.

East for the period 1990–2016. To our knowledge, this is the first attempt to measure income inequality at the level of the Middle East taken as a whole. The data at our disposal is highly imperfect and we still face considerable limitations in our ability to measure inequality in the Middle East. In particular, there is much uncertainty about inequality trends in the period under study. However, the general conclusion that the overall inequality level is one of the highest – if not the highest – in the world appears to be very robust.

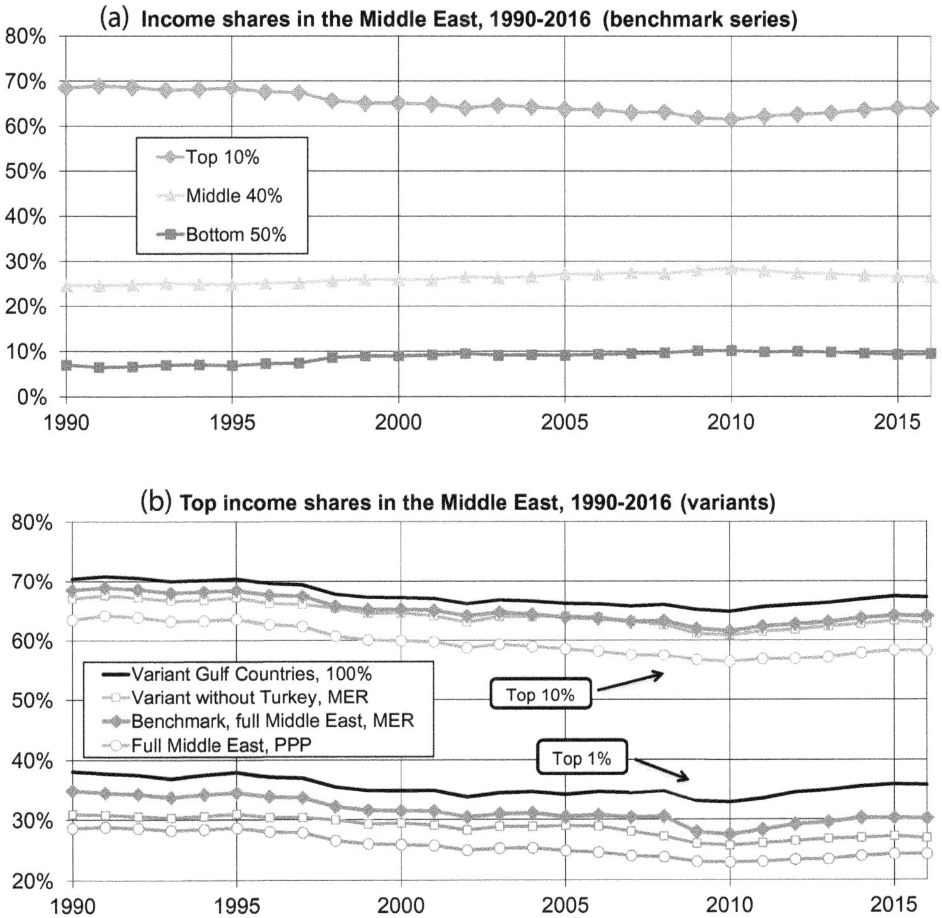

Figure 12.8 (a) Inequality statistics in the Middle East, variant for Gulf countries (2016). *Notes:* Distribution of income (before taxes and transfers, except pensions and unemployment insurance) among equal-split adults (income of households divided equally among adult members). Final estimates (with variants) combine survey, fiscal, wealth and national accounts data. Variants estimates are the result of imputing a fraction of missing income (the gap between national income and total survey income) so that the average income in the survey (augmented by the imputation) represents 50%, 70% or 100% of the average national income, and combine survey, fiscal, wealth and national accounts data. We also consider a conservative variant where the missing income is proportionally attributed to both foreigners and nationals. (b) Top income shares in the Middle East, 1990–2016 (variant for Gulf countries). *Notes:* Distribution of income (before taxes and transfers, except pensions and unemployment insurance) among equal-split adults (income of households divided equally among adult members). Final estimates (with variants) combine survey, fiscal, wealth and national accounts data. Variants estimates are the result of imputing a fraction of missing income (the gap between national income and total survey income) so that the average income in the survey (augmented by the imputation) represents 50%, 70% or 100% of the average national income, and combine survey, fiscal, wealth and national accounts data. We also consider a conservative variant where the missing income is proportionally attributed to both foreigners and nationals.

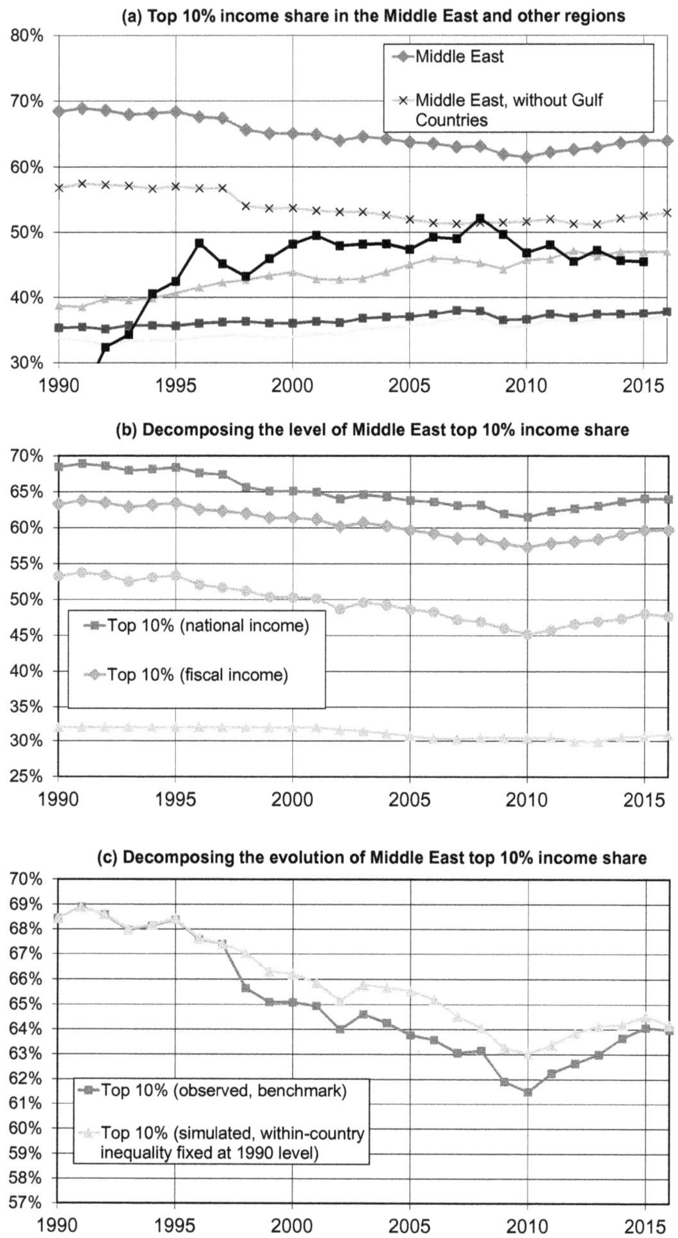

Figure 12.9 Top 10% income share in the Middle East: comparisons and decompositions. *Notes*: Distribution of income (before taxes and transfers, except pensions and unemployment insurance) among equal-split adults (income of households divided equally among adult members). Pre-tax national income estimates combine survey, fiscal, wealth and national accounts data. Fiscal income estimates combine survey and income tax data (but do not use wealth data to allocate tax-exempt capital income). Survey income series solely use self-reported survey data (but anchors national distributions to per-adult national income). Survey income with fixed-average-income series assumes same average income for all countries (thereby neutralising between-country inequality). In panel c, the simulated series assume within-country inequality fixed at 1990 level (so that evolution is entirely driven by trends in between-country inequality).

Our results regarding the enormous level of income inequality in the Middle East region naturally point toward the need to develop mechanisms of regional redistribution and investment. In a way, this is already happening, in the sense that oil-rich countries regularly make loans to poorer countries (e.g. Saudi Arabia to Egypt), and that these loans sometimes include implicit or explicit subsidies. However, such mechanisms are usually of limited magnitude, and tend to be highly unpredictable. Given the enormous concentration of gross domestic product and national income in the region, mechanisms of regional investment funds similar to those developed in the European Union (with permanent transfers between the richest and the poorest countries of the order of several percentage points of GDP) could make a large difference.

Finally, we stress the importance of increasing transparency on income and wealth in the Middle East. It is critical that Middle East countries provide access to household surveys' micro files and even more importantly that they provide access to income tax data, at least in the form of income tax tabulations. It is very difficult to have an informed public debate about inequality trends – and also about a large number of substantial policy issues such as taxation and public spending – without proper access to such data. While the lack of transparency on income and wealth is an important issue in many – if not most – areas of the world, it appears to be particularly extreme in the Middle East, and arguably raises in itself a problem of democratic accountability, quite independently from the actual level of inequality.

Notes

1 This chapter is based on our earlier research: Alvaredo and Piketty (2014), and Alvaredo, Assouad and Piketty (2017 and 2018).

2 See online, at http://wid.world, for the sources and method used to compile the macroeconomic data. In the rest of this chapter, "online sources" will refer to the WID.world online database and library, which includes the papers on which the chapter is based, as well as their appendices.

3 Until recently, with the launch of the "Open Access Micro Data Initiative" by the Economic Research Forum, it was almost impossible to obtain micro data.

4 In the online appendix, we provide a thorough description of the data and methodology used country by country.

5 Pension income (and other replacement income such as unemployment insurance) is included, while pension contributions (and other social contributions financing replacement income flows) are deducted.

6 We also constructed estimates based on the assumption of linear inequality trends between survey years. This made very little difference in both the level and trend of inequality in the Middle East as a whole, so in our benchmark series we simply use the closest available year for country-level data.

7 In Qatar, given that foreigners represent a large share of the total population (90%), and that the ratio between survey and national income is particularly low (22%), top income shares are very sensitive to the operation that reattributes part of the missing income to the nationals only. We therefore only attribute a share of missing income so that the ratio survey/national income equals 30% and not 50% as in other countries.

8 There are 127 g-percentiles: 99 for the bottom 99 percentiles, nine for the bottom nine tenths-of-percentile of the top percentile, nine for the bottom nine one-hundredths-of-percentile of the top tenth-of-percentile, and ten for the ten one-thousandths-of-percentile of the top one-hundredth-of-percentile.

9 See online technical appendix, Table A3.

10 By definition, the coefficients are the ratio of thresholds (resp. averages) between the raw survey and the corrected distributions. We apply no correction below p=0.8, i.e. we assume correction factors exactly equal to 1 below the top 20%, which is approximately the case in the Lebanese data. We apply the average correction coefficients per percentile over the 2005–2014 period in Lebanon to all other countries. We also compute variant coefficients (depending on the profile adopted) to link the bottom 80% to the top 1% covered by the fiscal data. The impact of variant estimations on the overall inequality level in the Middle East and the comparison with other world regions is relatively limited.

11 For Lebanon, however, we estimate it to be 20% of national income, by using available information from national accounts and government reports on tax revenues, published by the Ministry of Finance (Assouad, 2017).

12 That is, we divide all thresholds and bracket averages for all 127 generalised percentiles by average wealth, and we compute the arithmetic average for the three countries.

13 See online for variants with different assumptions on the billionaires' family size and the correction profiles. For countries without billionaire data (Iran, Jordan, Palestine, Yemen), we simply upgraded the average standardised distributions of wealth for the US, France and China to the country-specific average wealth.

14 There are relatively few billionaires and their number varies substantially from year to year and for many years we have no data. For instance, *Forbes* reports one or two billionaires in Bahrain and Qatar and only in three years between 1990–2016. For some years, billionaire wealth can represent a very high ratio to national income.

15 To partly overcome this problem, we included figures on state leaders' wealth when we could find some (in newspaper articles, *Forbes*' "Royals" and "Dictators" lists). Reliable information was still very scarce and we could not cover all ruling families. For an example, figures on the Assad family's wealth are only available for two years. We did not find figures on billionaires in Jordan.

16 These estimates are furthermore solely based upon self-reported survey data, with no correction for the underestimation of top incomes and should therefore be considered as a lower bound.

17 If both perspectives offer valuable and complementary insights, we tend to prefer MER estimates because they are in a way more comparable to those estimated for other world regions (i.e. we do not use price differentials when estimating income inequality within the USA, Brazil, China or India).

18 See Table 3 in Alvaredo, Assouad and Piketty (2017) for country specific trend.

References

Alvaredo, F. and A. Atkinson (2010). *Colonial Rule, Apartheid and Natural Resources.* London: CEPR DP 8155.

Alvaredo, F. and T. Piketty (2014). *Measuring Top Incomes and Inequality in the Middle East: Data Limitations and Illustration with the Case of Egypt.* London: CEPR DP 10068.

Alvaredo, F., Atkinson, A.B., Chancel, L., Piketty, T., Saez, E. and G. Zucman (2016). *Distributional National Accounts (DINA) Guidelines: Concepts and Methods Used in the World Wealth and Income Database.* WID.world Working Paper 2016/2.

Alvaredo, F., Assouad, L. and T. Piketty (2017). *Measuring Inequality in the Middle East 1990–2016: The World's Most Unequal Region?* WID.world Working Paper 2017/15.

Alvaredo, F., Assouad, L. and T. Piketty (2018a). Measuring Inequality in the Middle East 1990–2016: The World's Most Unequal Region? *Review of Income and Wealth*, Series 65, Number 4, December 2019; doi:10.1111/roiw.12385.

Alvaredo, F., Chancel, L., Piketty, T., Saez, E. and G. Zucman (2018b). *World Inequality Report.* 1st ed. Boston: Harvard University Press.

Alvaredo, F., Chancel, L., Piketty, T., Saez, E., & G. Zucman (2018c). *World Inequality Report 2018.* Boston: Harvard University Press.

Andersen, J., Johannesen, N., Lassen, D. and E. Paltseva (2017). Petro Rents, Political Institutions, and Hidden Wealth: Evidence from Offshore Bank Accounts. *Journal of the European Economic Association*, 15(4): 818–860.

Assaad, R., Krafft, C., Roemer, J. and D. Salehi-Isfahani (2017). Inequality of Opportunity in Wages and Consumption in Egypt. *Review of Income and Wealth*, 64(1): 26–54.

Assouad, L., (2017). *Rethinking the Lebanese Economic Miracle: The Extreme Concentration of Income and Wealth in Lebanon, 2005–2014.* WID.world Working Paper 2016/13.

Assouad, L., Chancel, L. and M. Morgan (2018). Extreme Inequality: Evidence from Brazil, India, the Middle East, and South Africa. *AEA Papers and Proceedings*, 108: 119–123.

Bibi, S. and M. Nabli (2010). *Equity and Inequality in the Arab Region.* Policy Research Reports, Economic Research Forum. http://erf.org.eg/publications/equity-and-inequality-in-the-arab-region/

Blanchet, T., Fournier, J. and P. Piketty, T. (2017). *Generalized Pareto Curves: Theory and Applications to Income and Wealth Tax Data for France and the United States, 1800–2014.* WID.world Working Paper 2017/3.

Bourguignon, F. and C. Morrisson (2002). Inequality among World Citizens: 1820–1992. *American Economic Review*, 92(4): 727–744.

El-Katiri, L., Fattouh, B. and P. Segal (2011). Anatomy of an oil-based Welfare State: Rent Distribution in Kuwait. Kuwait Programme on Development, Governance and Globalisation in the Gulf States. *London School of Economics*, 13.

Hassine, N. (2015). Economic Inequality in the Arab Region. *World Development*, 66: 532–556.

Hlasny, V. and P. Verme (2015). *Top Incomes and the Measurement of Inequality: A Comparative Analysis of Correction Methods Using Egyptian, EU, and US Survey Data*. Mimeo.

Human Rights Watch (2013). *South Asia: Protect Migrant Workers to Gulf Countries*. http://www.hrw.org/news/2013/12/18/south-asia-protect-migrant-workers-gulf-countries.

Lakner, C. and B. Milanovic (2015). Global Income Distribution: From the Fall of the Berlin Wall to the Great Recession. *The World Bank Economic Review*, 30(2): 203–232.

Milanovic, B. (2002). True World Income Distribution, 1988 and 1993: First Calculation Based on Household Surveys Alone. *The Economic Journal*, 112(476): 51–92.

Morgan, M. (2017). *Extreme and Persistent Inequality: New Evidence for Brazil Combining National Accounts, Surveys and Fiscal Data, 2001–2015*. WID.world Working Paper 2017/12.

Naidu, S., Nyarko, Y. and S. Wang (2016). Monopsony Power in Migrant Labor Markets: Evidence from the United Arab Emirates. *Journal of Political Economy*, 124(6): 1735–1792.

Ncube, M. and J.C. Anyanwu (2012). Inequality and Arab Spring Revolutions in North Africa and the Middle East. *Africa Economic Brief*, 3(7): 1–24. African Development Bank.

Novokmet, F., Piketty, T. and G. Zucman (2018). From Soviets to Oligarchs: Inequality and Property in Russia 1905–2016. *The Journal of Economic Inequality*, 16(2): 189–223.

Piketty, T., Yang, L. and G. Zucamn (2017). *Capital Accumulation, Private Property and Rising Inequality in China 1978–2015*. NBER Working Paper, Number 23368.

UNDP (2012). *Arab Development Challenges Report, Towards the Developmental State in the Arab Region*. Cairo: United Nations Development Programme, Regional Centre for Arab States, http://arabstates.undp.org/.

Van der Weide, R., Lakner, C. and E. Ianchovichina (2016). *Is Inequality Underestimated in Egypt? Evidence from House Prices*. World Bank Policy Research Working Paper 7727.

World Bank (2014). *Inside Inequality in the Arab Republic of Egypt: Facts and Perceptions Across People, Time and Space*, by Paolo Verme, Branko Milanovic, Sherine Al-Shawarby, Sahar El Tawila, May Gadallah, Enas Ali and A. El-Majeed. Washington, DC: The World Bank.

World Bank (2015). *Inequality, Uprisings, and Conflict in the Arab World, World Bank and Middle East and North Africa Region*. MENA Economic Monitor. Washington, DC: The World Bank.

13

INEQUALITIES IN EARLY CHILDHOOD DEVELOPMENT IN THE MIDDLE EAST AND NORTH AFRICA

Caroline Krafft and Safaa El-Kogali[1]

13.1 Introduction

That early childhood is the most important time for human development is now firmly established in the literature (Heckman 2006; Shonkoff & Phillips 2000; Black et al. 2017). The development of physical, cognitive, and socio-emotional skills begins before children are even born and rapidly evolves through the first years of life. The success – or faltering – of this early growth is critical to subsequent human development, including health and education outcomes, as well as economic outcomes. For instance, children who are stunted have poorer cognitive development (Glewwe & King 2001), perform worse in school (Glewwe et al. 2001), and ultimately earn lower wages (Hoddinott et al. 2008). Due to its developmental importance, early childhood also has a major role in the intergenerational transmission of poverty and inequality (Mayer-Foulkes 2008; Harper et al. 2003).

Despite the importance of early childhood development (ECD), it has received limited policy or research attention in the Middle East and North Africa (MENA) region. As a result, although the region is middle-income, ECD indicators in MENA more closely resemble those of Sub-Saharan Africa than other middle-income countries (UNESCO 2010; UNICEF 2008). This chapter reviews what we know about inequalities in ECD in MENA. The small but growing body of research on inequality in ECD in MENA suggests that there are substantial inequalities in this critical phase across multiple domains of human development. Deficits accumulating across different developmental domains throughout early childhood compound each other (Helmers & Patnam 2011) and position children for a lifetime of risk and diminished human capital.

The chapter examines multiple dimensions of ECD, including early health and nutrition, as well as cognitive and socio-emotional development. The focus of this work is on development from the prenatal period until school entry age (six in most MENA countries). The chapter begins with a discussion of the conceptual frameworks of ECD, human capital, and inequality of opportunity (IOp), which is inequality related to circumstances. A discussion of the measurement of IOp follows. The chapter then examines the existing data on ECD and literature on IOp and provides a case study of cross-country IOp, drawn from Krafft and El-Kogali (2014).

The chapter concludes with a discussion of constraints to research and action, as well as key directions for future work.

13.2 Conceptual frameworks

13.2.1 What is ECD?

ECD is a multi-dimensional process, encompassing health and nutrition as well as cognitive and non-cognitive (socio-emotional) development. These developmental processes peak early (Shonkoff & Phillips 2000). Deficits are difficult or impossible to reverse, conferring a fundamental biological importance to ECD.

There is ambiguity in the literature as to the start of ECD, specifically whether the prenatal period is included. At the other end, there is ambiguity in when early childhood ends, whether after the first 1,000 days (from conception through age two), at school entry age, or during early school years. The United Nations Committee on the Rights of the Child (CRC) recognised ECD as from birth until age eight (United Nations 2006). There may be different age emphases depending on what developmental domains are being considered. For example, the "First 1,000 Days" campaign focuses on nutrition from conception to age two, due to the fact that growth faltering occurs in this period before levelling off (Hoddinott et al. 2013). This chapter focuses on conception through pre-primary until school entry age (age six in MENA), since development, data, and potential interventions all shift substantially when children become school-aged.

13.2.2 ECD production functions

Conceptual frameworks for ECD generally rely on a human capital production function, in line with the health and education production function literature (Glewwe 2002; Strauss & Thomas 1998). For example, studies posit an ECD production function such as (Krafft & El-Kogali 2014):

$$ECD = f\left(N; I, H, C, \varepsilon\right) \tag{1}$$

where *ECD* is in the set of observed development outcomes. These are the output of an early childhood development production function, *f*, which is based on early childhood inputs, *N*. Both early childhood inputs and the technology that produces *ECD* depend on individual child characteristics, *I*, such as sex, and household socioeconomic characteristics, *H*, such as household wealth and parental education, as well as community and country characteristics, *C*. The ε term captures random genetic variation as well as luck. In estimating the determinants of ECD outcomes, this term will also capture measurement error and unobserved characteristics.

Development is a cumulative process, both in terms of the accumulation of development and the cumulative influence of inputs and the environment (Shonkoff & Phillips 2000). When considering multiple time periods, empirically, relatively earlier development has a greater impact (larger parameters in the production function) than later development (Leight et al. 2015; Christian et al. 2013; Almond & Currie 2011; Maccini & Yang 2009; Tanner et al. 2015). There can also be cross-productive development across different domains. For example, health at age one affects cognitive skills at age five (Helmers & Patnam 2011). The disproportionate importance of early development underpins arguments for investing in ECD as the highest-return phase of human development (Heckman 2006).

The cumulative nature of ECD means that the full history of inputs, circumstances, and even random variation has an impact on any particular outcome. Additionally, the subset of ECD outcomes, ECD^0, which has preceded any particular outcome *ECD'* may enter into the ECD production function (Helmers & Patnam 2011), acting as an input or shaping the technology of production, as in:

$$ECD' = f(N, ECD^0; I, H, C, ECD^0, \varepsilon) \quad (2)$$

This interplay between ECD outcomes has particularly important implications for inequality, which is likely to be compounded over the early life course. For instance, whether or not a child receives prenatal care can depend on their household's wealth and prenatal care may affect subsequent mortality, in addition to the direct effect of household wealth on mortality.

13.2.3 Inequality lenses

The critical nature of ECD contributes to its central role in inequality. Human development disparities related to risk factors such as poverty occur in foetal development (Currie & Moretti 2007). The accumulated impact of risk factors throughout early childhood generates differential developmental trajectories and leads to entrenched disparities by school age (Walker et al. 2011; Walker et al. 2007; Black et al. 2017). Early childhood is also when the transmission of poverty and inequality across generations begins; poverty traps are related to failures to invest in the early years (Mayer-Foulkes 2008; Harper et al. 2003).

Due, in part, to ECD's interdisciplinary nature, there is not a single unitary framework for considering inequality in ECD. However, much of the recent global literature on ECD and other human development inequalities draws on Roemer's (1998) concept of *inequality of opportunity* (IOp). Roemer makes the distinction between circumstances and effort in determining an individual's outcomes. *Effort* is under an individual's control, and therefore inequality due to effort is morally acceptable. *Circumstances* are factors that lie outside an individual's control, and inequality due to circumstances is not morally justifiable, and constitutes IOp.

In the case of early childhood development, no circumstances are within a child's control. Under Roemer's framework (2014), 'effort' is irrelevant and therefore all inequality in outcomes in early childhood is necessarily IOp. That equality of opportunity in ECD can be achieved only by perfect equality in outcomes is a problematic standard. Empirical researchers typically modify this framework and consider all inequality that is attributable to observable circumstances, such as sex or parents' education, to be IOp. Inequality not explained by observable circumstances is attributed to 'luck' and not considered to be IOp.

Both Roemer's original framework and the modified framework typical of empirical research have been critiqued (Kanbur & Wagstaff 2014). The circumstances researchers observe and measure are a lower bound on IOp, limited by what is within survey data (which varies by country) (Kanbur & Wagstaff 2014). Estimates suggest the bias from missing circumstances is substantial (Ibarra & Cruz 2015; Niehues & Peichl 2014; Balcázar 2015; Hufe & Peichl 2015). Particularly when such estimates are used to make policy decisions, their application is problematic (Kanbur & Wagstaff 2014). One advantage of assessing IOp in ECD is that children are usually in their natal households and thus more circumstances (particularly parental background, birth place, etc.) are directly observable than is typical for considering IOp. Although the critiques of IOp are considerable, even critics note that the fundamental exercise – empirically analysing inequality – is an important contribution (Kanbur & Wagstaff 2014).

13.3 Methods for quantifying inequality in ECD

Methods for quantifying IOp in ECD aim to decompose inequality: to assess the percentage of inequality in an outcome that is IOp (due to circumstances) and the role of specific circumstances in IOp. Methods vary in terms of: (1) addressing continuous or binary outcomes; (2) non-parametric or parametric methods; and (3) considering the entire distribution or the outcomes for those who are most (dis)advantaged. An important point in quantifying IOp is that structural and causal relationships are not needed (Niehues & Peichl 2014).

13.3.1 Continuous outcomes

Continuous ECD outcomes, such as height-for-age, require specific inequality measures. Although there are many continuous inequality measures, few are decomposable, a requirement for analysing IOp. The generalised entropy (GE) indices can decompose inequality in an outcome, y, into the part due to IOp versus luck. Underlying the GE indices is the idea of a cumulative distribution function, $F(y)$. From $F(y)$ we can determine $F(y)=p$, where p is the proportion of the population with outcome y or less than y. Likewise, we can consider a quantile function $Q(p)$, which denotes the outcome level below which we can find p fraction of the population. Comparing the quantile function (distribution) to the mean, μ, underlies GE measures. There are a number of different GE measures,[2] which are generally denoted GE(θ) (Duclos & Araar 2006):

$$GE_\theta(y) = \begin{cases} \int_0^1 ln\left(\frac{Q(p)}{\mu}\right) dp & if\, \theta = 0 \\ \int_0^1 \left(\frac{Q(p)}{\mu}\right) ln\left(\frac{Q(p)}{\mu}\right) dp & if\, \theta = 1 \\ \frac{1}{\theta(\theta-1)}\left(\int_0^1 \left(\frac{Q(p)}{\mu}\right)^\theta dp - 1\right) & if\, \theta \neq 0,1 \end{cases} \quad (3)$$

Lower values of θ, such as GE_0, will emphasise inequality in the lower end of the distribution, while higher values, such as GE_2, will emphasise inequality in the higher end of the distribution.

Assuming there are k groups, with each group having a unique combination of circumstances, IOp is the share of inequality that is between groups. Total inequality in y can be divided into within-group inequality and between-group inequality (Duclos & Araar 2006):

$$GE_\theta(y) = \underbrace{\sum_{k=1}^{K} \phi(k)\left(\frac{\mu_k}{\mu}\right)^\theta GE_{\theta,k}(y)}_{\text{Within}} + \underbrace{GE_\theta(\mu_k)}_{\text{Between}} \quad (4)$$

Here, $\phi(k)$ is the proportion of the population belonging to group k, μ_k is the mean outcome in group k, and $GE_{\theta,k}(y)$ is $GE_\theta(y)$ for group k. $GE_\theta(\mu_k)$ is a smoothed distribution that measures the inequality if each group member experienced their μ_k (Duclos & Araar 2006; Ferreira & Gignoux 2011). A further consideration is how inequality is decomposed, specifically whether the relative share of IOp, s, is calculated directly (s_d), as in:

$$s_d = \frac{GE_\theta\left(\mu_k\right)}{GE_\theta\left(y\right)} \tag{5}$$

or residually, with a standardised distribution where every y^k has been replaced with $y^k \frac{\mu}{\mu^k}$, so that each group has the population mean and only within-group inequality remains. This yields a residual (s_r) estimate of IOp as in:

$$s_r = 1 - \frac{GE_\theta\left(y^k \frac{\mu}{\mu^k}\right)}{GE_\theta\left(y\right)} \tag{6}$$

Only GE_0 will yield the same estimates regardless of decomposition, making it path-independent (along with a number of other desirable properties) (Ferreira & Gignoux 2011).

13.3.2 Binary outcomes

Binary outcomes, such as receiving immunisations, require different methods than continuous outcomes. IOp in binary outcomes is most commonly measured using the dissimilarity index (D-index) (de Barros et al. 2009; de Barros et al. 2008). The D-index for a particular ECD outcome is:

$$D = \frac{1}{2\overline{p}} \sum_{i=1}^{k} \alpha_i \left|p_i - \overline{p}\right| \tag{7}$$

where $\overline{p}$ is the population mean for that outcome and p_i is the mean for unique circumstance group i. The α_i are population shares or sampling weights (de Barros et al. 2009). The D-index essentially compares the difference between groups, as defined by circumstances, and the population mean. The D-index can be interpreted as the percentage of available opportunities that need to be reallocated from the children in groups that are better off to the children in groups that are worse off in order to achieve equality of opportunity (de Barros et al. 2009). Expressed as a percentage, the D-index ranges from 0 to 100. Studies also often report, either primarily or in addition to the D-index, the Human Opportunity Index (HOI). HOI multiplies the group mean for a (positive) outcome, such as freedom from stunting, by one minus the dissimilarity index. The measure thus mixes coverage of outcomes and inequality.

13.3.3 Non-parametric versus parametric methods

For both binary and continuous outcomes, either parametric or non-parametric methods can estimate IOp. Non-parametric methods are, in theory, quite straightforward; for the k groups that are unique combinations of circumstances, the group means (μ_k if continuous and p_i if binary) are directly observed. Estimating these group means is problematic when using survey data, particularly ensuring an adequate sample size for each group (Ferreira & Gignoux 2011). For example, for the circumstances of urban vs. rural (two categories), wealth quintiles (five categories), sex (two categories), and mother's education (five categories), already k would be 100 and unlikely to be reliably estimable for many groups. Non-parametric methods are thus limited to few circumstances in practice.

As a result of the limitations of non-parametric methods, most research relies on parametric (regression) methods. Either ordinary least squares (OLS) models for continuous outcomes or logit or probit models (for binary outcomes) can be used to estimate the relationship between an outcome, y or p, and circumstances, C (de Barros et al. 2008; Ferreira & Gignoux 2011). The predicted value from that regression can be used in the place of μ_k or p_i, since individuals with the same circumstances necessarily have the same predicted outcome. While this approach assumes a linear relationship for coefficients, which may not be an accurate assumption, it does allow for a much richer set of circumstances to be considered.

13.3.4 Contributions of particular circumstances or groups of circumstances

Analysing the contribution of a particular circumstance (e.g. sex) or group of circumstances (e.g. regions) is generally undertaken using parametric methods. For continuous outcomes, partial effects can be estimated using a regression model relating outcomes to J circumstances. A counter-factual standardised distribution, where predictions from the regression set certain J to their mean, is created. This counter-factual standardised distribution can be used to calculate the share of the certain subset of J in total inequality residually (Ferreira & Gignoux 2008).

Using the dissimilarity index for binary outcomes, a Shapley decomposition calculates the contribution of different circumstances (Shorrocks 2013; Deutsch & Silber 2008). The decomposition consists of calculating the marginal contributions of each circumstance as they are removed in sequence. The result is an exact, additive decomposition of the D-index into the contributions of each circumstance (Shorrocks 2013).

13.3.5 The most (dis)advantaged

While the methods discussed so far quantify inequality across the entire distribution, another approach is to consider how those with the most disadvantaged circumstances are faring (Roemer 2014). This approach is philosophically grounded in a commitment to public policy supporting the most vulnerable members of society. Those with the most disadvantaged circumstances are often compared to the most advantaged, with that distance being another operationalisation of inequality. Either parametric methods (simulations based on predictions) or non-parametric methods (group means for the most (dis)advantaged) can be used. The measures of the entire distribution and the most (dis)advantaged are often presented in combination.

One challenge in implementing the measurement of the most (dis)advantaged is determining what combination of circumstances is the relevant endpoint. This determination can be made empirically. Another challenge is that, particularly for comparisons across countries, these groups may not be very comparable in size or relative position in society: someone with an illiterate parent in Yemen is in a much different social position (and more common) than an individual with an illiterate parent in Jordan. Empirically identifying comparably sized groups (e.g. 5%) is important for cross-country comparison.

13.4 Measuring ECD in MENA

13.4.1 Microdata sources

Data availability is an enormous constraint on understanding IOp in ECD in MENA. The countries examined in this section are Algeria, Djibouti, Egypt, Iraq, Jordan, Lebanon, Libya, Morocco, Syria, Tunisia, Palestine,[3] and Yemen. This selection is primarily data driven; the

Table 13.1 Publicly available microdata on ECD in MENA

	DHS	*MICS*	*PAPFAM*
Algeria		2012–13	2002
Djibouti		2006	2002/3, 2012
Egypt	1988, 1992, 1995, 2000, 2003, 2005, 2008, 2014		
Iraq		2000, 2006, 2011	
Jordan	1990, 1997, 2002, 2007, 2009, 2012		
Lebanon			2004
Libya			2007, 2014
Morocco	1987, 1992, 1995, 2003–4		2011
Syria		2006	2001, 2009
Tunisia	1988	2011/12	2001
Palestine		2010, 2014	2006
Yemen	1991–2, 2013	2006	2003

Source: Authors' construction.
Note: Only nationally representative, publicly available surveys with ECD topics included.

authors know of no publicly available microdata on ECD for the Gulf Cooperation Council (GCC) states or Iran.

There are three main sources for publicly available microdata on ECD in MENA: the Demographic and Health Surveys (DHS), the Multiple Indicator Cluster Surveys (MICS), and the Pan-Arab Project for Family Health Surveys (PAPFAM). PAPFAM surveys are specific to MENA but other sources are global. Countries may also have country-specific surveys, usually health surveys, that include measures of ECD. Table 13.1 shows the surveys and years with publicly available ECD microdata in MENA. While countries tend to have at least one survey type (DHS, MICS, or PAPFAM) and sometimes multiple types, they do not necessarily have very recent or frequent data coverage. For example, Lebanon's last survey was a PAPFAM in 2004. Across countries and surveys, surveys are typically a decade (as in Tunisia) or five to six years apart (as in Iraq). Earlier surveys are likely to have a more limited (primarily health and nutrition) set of ECD indicators.

13.4.2 Common measures of ECD

The most common measures related to ECD, from in-utero through age five, in the publicly available data relate to health and nutrition, including:

- prenatal care
- having a skilled attendant at birth
- being fully immunised at age one
- neonatal mortality (mortality in the first month of life)
- infant mortality (mortality in the first year of life)
- height-for-age (and correspondingly stunting)
- weight-for-age (and correspondingly underweight)
- weight-for-height (and correspondingly wasting)
- access to adequately iodised salt (iodine being a type of micronutrient, key to brain development)

In terms of early learning, early cognitive and non-cognitive skills development, and early work, common measures include:

- whether a child was engaged in development activities
- whether a child was violently disciplined
- early childhood care and education (ECCE) attendance
- whether a child has engaged in domestic or paid work

Due to data availability, the indicators are a mix of early childhood inputs, such as iodised salt, which are important contributors to development, and early childhood outcomes, such as mortality. Although these are some of the most common measures, they provide particularly limited data on early development outside of health and nutrition.

13.5 Evidence on inequality of opportunity in ECD in MENA

13.5.1 Studies on inequality of opportunity in ECD

The literature on IOp in ECD in MENA is small but growing. Table 13.2 summarises the existing studies on IOp in ECD in MENA.[4,5] There are four comparative cross-country studies (Vladimir 2017; Krishnan et al. 2016; Krafft & El-Kogali 2014; Assaad et al. 2012). There are seven single-country studies, covering Algeria, Tunisia, Morocco, Jordan, and Egypt (Abdelkhalek & Lassassi 2018; Saidi & Hamdaoui 2017; Amara & Jemmali 2018; El-Kogali et al. 2016; Krafft 2015; Ersado & Aran 2014; Velez et al. 2012). The studies cover a variety of ECD outcomes as well as some basic housing services outcomes that are likely to affect ECD, such as access to safe water.[6] Health and nutrition outcomes are over-represented in the studies relative to other dimensions of early development.

All but two studies examine binary outcomes and therefore use the D-index and Shapley decomposition (often HOI as well). Two studies focusing on continuous anthropometric measures rely on various GE measures (Krafft 2015; Assaad et al. 2012). Around half the studies include simulations for the endpoints of advantage. Studies typically include as circumstances at least household wealth, parental education, geographic location, and child sex. Although this limited set of circumstances links to substantial IOp, Krafft (2015) demonstrates, using particularly rich circumstances available in the 2012 Jordan DHS, that examining IOp in height-for-age related solely to socioeconomic status circumstances yields only a quarter of the IOp estimated when early environment and prenatal environment variables are included. These circumstances are, however, rarely available in surveys.

Despite the limited circumstances the studies consider, they nonetheless find substantial IOp, particularly in comparison to school-age outcomes (Krafft & El-Kogali 2014). The studies that include trends (Abdelkhalek & Lassassi 2018; El-Kogali et al. 2016; Assaad et al. 2012; Ersado & Aran 2014; Vladimir 2017; Velez et al. 2012) show decreases in IOp in health (largely driven by increases in coverage), but other dimensions of ECD do not show such improvements. Decompositions indicate that while there are substantial inequalities related to parents' education, wealth, and geographic differences, children generally have equal opportunities for early development regardless of sex.

13.5.2 Case study: cross-country evidence on inequality in ECD

As an in-depth case study of IOp in ECD in MENA, this section presents the work of Krafft and El-Kogali (2014) examining inequality in ECD in the MENA countries in Table 13.1 using recent microdata.

Table 13.2 Studies of inequality of opportunity in ECD in MENA

Studies (authors, year)	*Countries*	*ECD outcomes*	*Circumstances*	*Methods*
Multi-country				
Hlasny (2017)	Algeria, Comoros, Djibouti, Egypt, Iraq, Jordan, Lebanon, Libya, Mauritania, Morocco, Palestine, Somalia, Sudan, Syria, Tunisia, Yemen	Prenatal, delivery, immunised, mortality, stunting, underweight, wasting, iodised salt, ECCE, development activities, violent discipline, (domestic) work	Wealth, mother's/father's/head's education, rural, governorates, child sex	HOI, D-index, Shapley, simulations
Krishnan et al. (2016)	Egypt, Iraq, Jordan, Morocco, Palestine, Tunisia	Prenatal, delivery, stunting, underweight, wasting, basic housing services	Consumption quintile, head education, head public worker, head age, single parent household, children in the household, elderly presence, location, region, child sex	HOI, D-index, Shapley
Krafft and El-Kogali (2014)	Algeria, Djibouti, Egypt, Iraq, Jordan, Lebanon, Libya, Morocco, Palestine, Syria, Tunisia, Yemen	Prenatal, delivery, immunised, mortality, stunting, iodised salt, development activities, violent discipline, ECCE, (domestic) work	Wealth, mother's/father's/head's education, rural, region, child sex, distance to health care	D-index, Shapley, simulations
Assaad et al. (2012)	Egypt, Jordan, Morocco, Tunisia, Turkey, Yemen	Height-for-age, weight-for-height	Mother's/father's education father's occupation, governorate, multiple birth, birth order, mother's age, mother's height, mother's BMI, toilet facilities, drinking water source, sewage/trash, cooking fuel, child sex	GE(1), simulations

Single-country				
Abdelkhalek and Lassassi (2018)	Algeria	Prenatal, delivery, immunised, stunting, underweight, wasting, iodised salt, ECE, development activities, violent discipline, (domestic) work	Wealth, mother's/father's education, location, region, child sex	D-index, Shapley, simulations
Saidi and Hamdaoui (2017)	Tunisia	Stunting, underweight, wasting, prenatal, postnatal	Wealth, head education, head age, head sex, children in the household, household size, location, region, child sex	HOI, D-index, Shapley
Amara and Jemmali (2018)	Tunisia	Prenatal, delivery, postnatal, immunised, safe water, toilet facilities, stunting, wasting, underweight	Wealth, mother's/father's education, number of children, number of household members, age of head, head sex, location, region, child sex	HOI, D-index, Shapley, simulations
El-Kogali et al. (2016)	Morocco	Prenatal, delivery, immunised, mortality, stunting, underweight, wasting, iodised salt, development activities, violent discipline, ECCE, (domestic) work	Wealth, mother's/father's/head's education, rural, region, child sex	D-index, Shapley, simulations
Krafft (2015)	Jordan	Height-for-age, Weight-for-age, Weight-for-height	Wealth, employment, mother's/father's education, geography, food, health knowledge, health conditions, health environment, mother's demographics, birth weight, child sex	GE(0)
Ersado and Aran (2014)	Egypt	Access to health care, nutrition, access to basic services, and composite indices	Wealth, mother's/father's education, number of siblings, location, child sex, imputed consumption	HOI, D-index, Shapley, simulations
Velez et al. (2012)	Egypt	Basic housing services, prenatal, delivery, postnatal, immunisation, stunting, underweight, wasting	Household income per capita/wealth quintile, mother's/father's education, presence of mother/father, number of household members of various ages, location, region, child sex	HOI, D-index, Shapley

Source: Authors' construction.

13.5.2.1 Comparing ECD outcomes across countries

An important and neglected point in the literature is that inequality within countries (the usual subject of research) often pales in comparison to inequality across countries. To illustrate this point, Table 13.3 presents the average level of eleven indicators for each country within MENA. Early health care, in terms of prenatal and delivery care, tends to be fairly high, although in Morocco in 2003–4 only 68% of births received prenatal care and 63% had a skilled delivery attendant, and Yemen in 2006 had a 47% rate of prenatal care and a 36% rate for skilled delivery. The pattern of full immunisations is bimodal; half of countries had rates around 90% or so, and half had rates around 50%. Infant mortality ranged from a low of 15 deaths per 1,000 births (Lebanon in 2004) to 71 deaths per 1,000 births (Yemen in 2006).

In terms of nutrition, only Jordan (in 2012) had stunting rates below 10% (8%). Yemen (in 2003) had the highest rate of stunting, with 53% of children zero to four years stunted. There was a very wide range of salt iodisation from less than 1% of children in Djibouti (in 2006) having iodised salt to 88% of children in Palestine (in 2006). Most countries have low rates of development activities. Jordan had the highest rate, with 82% of children experiencing development activities (in 2012). Djibouti (27% as of 2012) and Yemen (26% as of 2006) had the lowest rates. Violent child discipline is pervasive in MENA; 96% of children in Palestine (2006) were violently disciplined, and everywhere else with data, except for Djibouti (36% in 2012), had rates above 75%.

Few children attend early childhood care and education. In countries with data, Tunisia (2011–12) had the highest rate, with 45% of children three to four currently attending ECCE. Yemen (3% in 2006) and Iraq (4% in 2011) had some of the lowest rates of ECCE attendance. Overall, while most countries have fairly high coverage in terms of early health, MENA shows large deficits in ECD. The country a child is born into plays a critical role in their outcome.

13.5.2.2 Inequality in ECD by country

Ideally, a society would provide its youngest members with equal opportunities to develop and thrive, but in MENA, opportunities for children are not equal. Table 13.4 presents the dissimilarity index for the different ECD indicators and countries. There is a substantial amount of inequality starting early, in prenatal and delivery care. Yemen (2006) had the greatest inequality on these measures, with a D-index of 26 for skilled delivery. This means that 26% of the opportunities for skilled delivery would have to be reallocated for equality of opportunity to prevail. Morocco (2003–4) and Egypt (2008) also had relatively high inequality in early health, consistent with a common pattern that countries with lower rates of care have greater inequality (de Barros et al. 2009), as when countries approach universal care, inequality necessarily decreases.

In terms of children age one being fully immunised, a number of countries had low D-indices. Particularly notable are Egypt and Morocco, which did not have equitable access to prenatal or delivery care but had low D-indices for immunisations. Both Iraq (nine in 2011) and Yemen (21 in 2006) had high D-indices for early immunisations, meaning children have unequal opportunities to avoid the morbidity and potential mortality of common illnesses. Given the relative infrequency of early mortality, inequality on this measure must be interpreted with some caution; none of the D-indices for neonatal or infant mortality were statistically significant.

For stunting, the country with the lowest rate – Jordan – in fact had the highest inequality (24 in 2012), while the country with the highest rate – Yemen – in fact had the lowest inequality (five in 2003). In most countries, stunting is a pervasive problem that is exacerbated by circumstances. In the five countries with data, only Palestine demonstrated equality of opportunity for

Table 13.3 Percentage of children (or births) with ECD indicator

	Algeria (2002)	*Djibouti (2006/12)*	*Egypt (2008)*	*Iraq (2011)*	*Jordan (2012)*	*Lebanon (2004)*	*Libya (2007)*	*Morocco (2003/4)*	*Syria (2006/9)*	*Tunisia (2011)*	*Palestine (2006)*	*Yemen (2003/6)*
Prenatal care	79.2	87.9	73.6	77.7	99.1	95.4	93.8	67.9	87.7	98.1	98.5	47.0
Skilled delivery	94.4	87.4	79.0	90.8	99.6	98.2	98.7	62.9	96.3	98.6	97.7	35.7
Fully immunised	92.6	30.7	91.7	64.3	93.0	51.5	86.9	89.6	77.9	89.6		40.7
Neonatal mortality	2.0	3.6	1.6	2.0	1.5	1.0	1.1	2.5	1.2	1.2	2.1	4.0
Infant mortality	3.3	6.0	2.4	3.1	1.8	1.5	1.7	3.8	1.7	1.7	3.0	7.1
Stunted	19.3	33.5	28.9	21.7	7.6	10.7	21.0	23.1	25.8	10.1	11.8	53.1
Iodised salt		0.4	76.7	24.4			52.5		30.4		87.7	
Develop. activities		36.6		53.5	81.6				55.0	71.1	46.8	25.5
Violent discipline		36.2		77.2	91.3				85.0	94.9	95.5	93.2
ECCE		14.1	40.2	3.8	21.7		9.3		17.2	44.5	34.1	2.7
(Domes.) work		18.6		10.1			7.0		12.3	24.0		15.8

Source: Krafft and El-Kogali (2014).
Note: Year of survey(s) in parentheses. Number of observations and other details in Krafft and El-Kogali (2014).

Table 13.4 Dissimilarity indices for ECD outcomes

	Algeria	*Djibouti*	*Egypt*	*Iraq*	*Jordan*	*Lebanon*	*Libya*	*Morocco*	*Syria*	*Tunisia*	*Palestine*	*Yemen*
Prenatal care	7.7***	6.4**	9.0***	20.9	0.5	2.6	2.0*	14.3***	5.1***	high	0.5	16.8**
Skilled delivery	2.4*	9.6***	9.0***	2.9***	0.2	high	0.7*	19.6***	2.1***	high	0.8*	26.1***
Fully immunised	2.2	22.2	1.7	8.6***	2.3	18.4	2.7	3.6	6.2*	4.4		20.6*
Neonatal mortality	13.9	insig.	24.9	9.7	19.7	low	30.7	19.5	insig.	40.0	insig.	insig.
Infant mortality	14.7	insig.	20.3	6.1	20.3	low	25.8	19.8	insig.	33	insig.	15.5
Stunted	9.9	9.6	9.0**	7.1**	24.1*	insig.	6.3	16.1***	13.0***	20	13.4**	4.9*
Iodised salt		low	7.2***	20.3***			16.9***		32.3***		insig.	
Develop. activities		13.9*		12.6***	3.4				10.6***	12**	5.7**	19.3***
Violent discipline		11.6		2.6	4.5				1.7	insig.	0.8	high
ECCE		34.6	21.8***	43.5***	24.4***		23.7***		36.3***	26***	12.1**	low
(Domes.) work		23.2		17.0***			25.7		12.1	22		25.1

Source: Krafft and El-Kogali (2014).
Notes: Standard errors in Krafft and El-Kogali (2014).
*p<.05 ** p<.01 *** p<.001
"Insig." denotes a statistically insignificant model at the 5% level. When the model underlying the dissimilarity index was insignificant, the outcome was not modelled. "Low" denotes an outcome that was too infrequent to model while "high" denotes an outcome that was too close to universal to model. Blank cells indicate that outcomes were not available in the data.

iodised salt access and thus healthy brain development. In Egypt, Iraq, Libya, and Syria there was statistically significant and relatively substantial inequality of opportunity.

Children have unequal opportunities for social, emotional, and cognitive development. In every country with data except Jordan, the D-index was statistically significant for development activities. The D-index was relatively low in Palestine (2006), at six, and high in Yemen at 19 (2006). Yet, the D-index was consistently low and insignificant for violent discipline. Violent discipline rates are extremely high, and this is clearly a challenge to children's early development regardless of circumstances.

Early childhood care and education is the most unequal aspect of early childhood development. D-indices ranged from a high of 44 in Iraq (2011), to 12 in Palestine (2006). Inequality was high regardless of overall ECCE attendance rates, with a D-index of 26 in Tunisia (2011), which had a 45% attendance rate, as well as in Iraq (D-index of 44), which had 4% attendance.

To help contextualise the level of inequality in ECD in MENA as relatively high or low, we provide a few examples of other D-indices. In Egypt in 2008, the D-indices for a number of important services (household access to improved drinking water, electricity, and a non-shared toilet) ranged from one to three (World Bank 2012). In contrast, Egypt had statistically significant D-indices of seven to nine for prenatal care, delivery care, stunting, and salt iodisation, as well as a D-index of 22 for ECCE. As of 2005, the D-index for completing sixth grade on time in 19 Latin American and Caribbean countries averaged 11 and ranged from three to 27 (de Barros et al. 2009). Compared to these D-indices, the inequality of 12 to 44 in ECCE in MENA is very high.

Inequality in early childhood is likely to be compounded by the continued impact of children's circumstances. However, it may also be the case that inequality of opportunity is worse during early childhood than during the school years, but that early deficits still shape later outcomes. For instance, in Egypt, we found a D-index of 22 for ECCE. In contrast, a study using the same dataset and relatively similar circumstances found a D-index of two for school enrolment for ages six to 11 and a D-index of ten for school enrolment at ages 15 to 17 (World Bank 2012). Subsequent access to higher education is very unequal (Assaad 2013; Krafft et al. 2013), a D-index of 24 (Krafft & Alawode 2018). Inequality of opportunity in schooling access is high with ECCE, diminishes with primary enrolment, and then increases through secondary school and especially higher education. While children may have equal opportunities to enrol in primary school, they have unequal opportunities to succeed given the pattern of inequality in ECD.

13.5.2.3 Key drivers of inequality in ECD

Table 13.5 presents the Shapley decompositions, which show the contributions of different circumstances to IOp. There is substantial heterogeneity in the relationship between different ECD indicators and circumstances between and within countries. We therefore focus on patterns for countries with greater IOp in a particular measure.

Looking at early health care, particularly in countries with substantial inequality, wealth was an important determinant of inequality of opportunity. In Morocco and Yemen, which had the highest inequality in prenatal care, the contribution of wealth to inequality was slightly more than 25%. Mother's education also played a large role in early health care access, while father's education played a smaller but important role. Regional and rural/urban differences varied substantially, but regional differences were particularly large in Morocco for both prenatal and delivery care. For the countries with large inequality in immunisations, namely Iraq and Yemen, wealth had a large share in IOp (24–32%). Mother's education was associated with around a fifth

Table 13.5 Contributions of circumstances to inequality (D-Index) using Shapley decomposition (percentages)

	Wealth	*Mother's education*	*Father's education*	*Head's education*	*Rural*	*Region*	*Child sex*	*Distance to health care*
Prenatal care								
Algeria	21.3	37.0	26.4		15.4			
Djibouti	28.8	6.3	10.2		32.4	22.2		
Egypt	35.2	28.5	15.2			17.6		3.6
Iraq	30.6	23.6	16.7		23.7	5.4		
Jordan	45.6	23.6	22.0		0.6	2.2		5.9
Lebanon	24.0	46.3	29.7					
Libya	21.8	48.5	27.5			2.2		
Morocco	26.3	18.8	10.3		2.7	35.2		6.8
Palestine	21.5	23.9	17.5		21.6	15.6		
Syria	16.5	23.8	6.5		44.4	8.8		
Yemen	28.6	23.5	13.4		15.8	18.6		
Skilled delivery								
Algeria	17.9	36.8	22.3		23.0			
Djibouti	30.2	4.4	9.2		37.5	18.7		
Egypt	36.1	23.6	10.2			28.8		1.3
Iraq	37.4	18.1	15.2		25.6	3.6		
Jordan	46.7	21.8	27.1		1.9	0.6		2.0
Libya	2.3	17.7	12.6			67.3		
Morocco	28.1	16.4	12.4		3.5	32.6		7.1
Palestine	6.1	5.2	7.9		5.7	75.0		
Syria	21.4	25.1	7.2		32.1	14.2		
Yemen	42.2	12.1	3.3		20.5	21.9		
Fully immunised								
Algeria	44.5	36.2	16.3		3.0			
Djibouti	40.6	2.9	28.1		3.9	22.0	2.6	
Egypt	22.5	11.5	8.5			53.0	3.3	1.2
Iraq	23.8	17.2	12.9		23.2	22.5	0.5	
Jordan	28.5	29.7	9.7		17.1	2.4	1.1	11.6
Lebanon	50.4	14.8	34.8					
Libya	29.9	26.4	20.7			21.7	1.3	
Morocco	28.8	11.0	11.7		25.0	13.0	3.9	6.7
Tunisia	13.6	20.1	8.2		10.4	47.7	0.1	
Syria	10.3	29.1	11.1		46.5	2.2	0.8	
Yemen	32.4	28.6	6.8		19.4	12.7	0.2	
Neonatal mortality								
Algeria	28.9			19.0	2.2		2.2	
Egypt	15.8	28.8	3.2			25.0	27.2	
Iraq	3.7	11.7			6.9	3.3	74.4	
Jordan	41.5	15.5	20.0		0.4	0.7	21.1	0.8
Libya	15.6	11.7	17.6			31.9	23.2	
Morocco	20.9	14.6	11.2		28.9	18.7	5.7	
Tunisia	8.5	6.6	40.0		10.3	30.3	4.4	

(Continued)

Table 13.5 Continued

	Wealth	*Mother's education*	*Father's education*	*Head's education*	*Rural*	*Region*	*Child sex*	*Distance to health care*
Infant mortality								
Algeria	42.8			41.9	5.0		5.0	
Egypt	29.7	18.9	7.2			37.0	7.2	
Iraq	15.6	28.7			2.5	7.0	46.1	
Jordan	31.2	20.3	32.2		1.6	0.7	12.3	1.7
Libya	15.2	14.9	21.2			33.4	15.2	
Morocco	29.7	18.8	5.2		7.5	29.7	9.0	
Palestine	58.0			11.9	5.7	24.4	0.1	
Tunisia	19.5	7.0	43.7		10.2	19.3	0.2	
Yemen	29.7	3.5			3.3	60.0	3.4	
Stunted								
Algeria	56.4			32.0	4.2		4.2	
Djibouti	52.9	2.7	12.0		21.4	10.7	0.2	
Egypt	4.8	4.5	7.2			72.5	8.6	2.6
Iraq	10.6	10.8	15.5		7.8	49.9	5.4	
Jordan	28.9	24.3	13.1		17.7	2.0	13.2	0.8
Libya	20.9	35.0	16.9			12.6	14.6	
Morocco	38.1	8.3	9.5		16.1	17.3	2.2	8.5
Palestine	17.7	11.2	5.0		10.8	51.9	3.4	
Syria	12.9	18.1	5.4		60.0	2.6	0.9	
Tunisia	25.8	10.3	23.0		11.3	25.0	4.6	
Yemen	55.5			8.1	36.3		0.1	
Iodised salt								
Egypt	43.6	17.4	9.2			19.3	0.1	10.3
Iraq	22.5	9.7	4.0		16.0	47.8	0.1	
Libya	6.7	5.1	4.7			83.4	0.1	
Syria	15.1	12.9	2.7		57.7	11.6	0.0	
Development activities								
Djibouti	13.4	8.9	3.5		8.7	64.2	1.2	
Iraq	37.2	24.2	20.9		15.3	1.7	0.8	
Jordan	22.9	37.5	22.2		13.0	3.6	0.8	
Palestine	48.2	23.7	12.1		2.8	11.9	1.2	
Syria	17.5	23.0	12.5		40.6	6.4	0.0	
Tunisia	27.8	19.3	9.8		25.6	16.6	0.9	
Yemen	29.1	28.5	11.2		15.1	15.6	0.4	
Violent discipline								
Djibouti	36.7	11.7	13.8		10.6	27.0	0.3	
Iraq	22.9	8.9	20.3		4.2	28.9	14.9	
Jordan	25.0	13.2	26.8		11.9	18.6	4.5	
Palestine	23.7	17.8	6.7		8.3	40.9	2.7	
Syria	19.7	8.3	4.8		58.7	0.9	7.5	

(*Continued*)

Table 13.5 Continued

	Wealth	*Mother's education*	*Father's education*	*Head's education*	*Rural*	*Region*	*Child sex*	*Distance to health care*
ECCE								
Djibouti	21.3	21.3	32.4		3.5	20.9	0.5	
Egypt	36.8	26.0	13.2			23.3	0.8	
Iraq	33.5	21.1	17.0		25.5	2.7	0.3	
Jordan	38.2	39.6	14.5		7.3	0.4	0.0	
Libya	23.1	20.2	15.6			37.2	4.0	
Palestine	32.0	41.8	20.9		1.5	3.7	0.1	
Syria	23.4	31.3	14.4		26.1	4.7	0.1	
Tunisia	29.0	8.7	7.3		42.5	12.2	0.2	
(Domes.) work								
Djibouti	35.3	6.1	22.4	0.7	31.7	3.8	3.8	
Iraq	8.4	15.5	2.0		3.5	54.0	16.6	
Libya	7.8	12.7	11.5			67.9	0.1	
Syria	11.2	17.1	9.3		44.8	2.0	15.6	
Tunisia	16.3	12.7	6.2		8.7	49.5	6.6	
Yemen	11.3	22.6	20.0		1.1	39.3	5.7	

Source: Krafft and El-Kogali (2014).
Note: Cells are the percentage shares (contributions) of circumstances to inequality, with inequality measured by the D-index and circumstance contributions calculated by the Shapley decomposition. Blank cells indicate circumstances that were unavailable in the data or not applicable for the outcome.

or quarter share of inequality, and rural/urban differences around 20%. Regional differences were larger in Iraq (23%) than in Yemen (13%).

Examining the circumstances that contribute the most to IOp in stunting, two patterns emerge. Some countries (Egypt, Iraq, Syria) and Palestine had relatively low contributions to inequality from wealth, but high contributions from regional or urban/rural differences. The others tended to have a large share attributable to wealth and parents' education. For the countries where inequality is driven by geographic differences, pervasive public health issues may play a larger role than in the countries where inequality is driven by family circumstances. In Iraq, Libya, and Syria, most of the IOp in access to iodised salt was related to geographic differences, likely linked to iodine supply and iodisation enforcement, while in Egypt family wealth played a large role (44%).

Wealth usually played a large role in IOp for development activities (13–48%). Mother's education played a more important role than father's education, accounting for 9–38% of IOp in development activities. Geographic differences were generally smaller than for health outcomes. Notably, parents are investing equally in engagement with their sons and daughters. Violent discipline was pervasive, and relatively equitable, with widely varying contributors across different countries.

Early childhood care and education, one of the most inequitable outcomes, had inequality driven by multiple factors in all countries. Wealth played a particularly large role in Jordan (38%) and Egypt (37%), but was above a 20% share everywhere. Mother's education ranged from a 9% share in Tunisia to 42% in Palestine. There were appreciable urban/rural differences in Iraq,

Tunisia, and Syria. Regional differences were largest in Libya, Egypt, and Djibouti. Inequality related to sex was near zero for ECCE.

Overall, in addition to extensive IOp in ECD, there are a number of different contributors to inequality. Sex did not contribute substantially to IOp. While the share of inequality attributable to different circumstances varied by indicator and by country, wealth, parents' education, especially mother's education, and place of residence/region all contributed substantially to IOp. Addressing inequality for a particular indicator and in a particular country will require identifying the drivers of inequality of opportunity for that outcome and context.

13.6 Discussion

The early years of life are vital to the course of human development (Shonkoff & Phillips 2000). Deficits and inequality early in life tend to accumulate and compound (Helmers & Patnam 2011). Yet the MENA region is underinvesting in this critical phase of human development and there is considerable IOp in ECD. Interventions in early childhood, especially targeting disadvantaged children, are a case where there is no equity/efficiency tradeoff; both equity and economic efficiency are promoted by effective ECD programmes and policies (Heckman & Masterov 2007). Given the equity and efficiency arguments for ECD, why is this stage so neglected?

The underinvestment in ECD has links to both information issues and political economy challenges. Parents in MENA are not necessarily as aware of the value of ECD, or that their actions can affect early development (Zellman et al. 2014a, 2014b). At the same time, those most affected by ECD (under)investment, young children, lack political voice, particularly in contrast to competing constituencies, such as, in the education sector, university students. Public investment in, for example, free and public basic, secondary, and often even tertiary education in the MENA region is substantial, but countries do not necessarily offer free pre-primary education (Krafft & Alawode 2018; World Bank 2019). While free public services of education and health care were historically part of social contracts in the region, they did not yield equitable outcomes, nor did they include key aspects of ECD (Krishnan et al. 2016; Devarajan & Ianchovichina 2018).

A challenge to reducing inequality is that ECD takes place across a variety of sites, including in the home, where existing models of public services do not necessarily reach. Nor is it clear who is responsible for ECD or coordination, given its multi-sectoral nature. For example, in Egypt nurseries (intended for children under age four) are under the purview of the Ministry of Social Solidarity while pre-primary education is part of the Ministry of Education (UNDP & Institute of National Planning 2008). A strong multi-sectoral focus on ECD and particularly multi-dimensional interventions that promote nurturing care and reduce the constraints families face in providing that care is critically important (Britto et al. 2017). Given the evidence that ECD investments particularly benefit disadvantaged children, an important question, with implications for IOp, is whether countries provide universal benefits – as in Algeria's push for universal pre-primary (UNESCO 2014) – or more targeted programmes, such as cash transfers (Black et al. 2017; Richter et al. 2017).

13.6.1 Directions for future work

Future work on IOp in ECD in MENA has two key directions: (1) better data and therefore potential to understand IOp in ECD and (2) evaluating approaches to address IOp in ECD.

13.6.1.1 Data

A shortage of publicly available microdata on ECD in MENA has been a major constraint to research on IOp. Improvements in the ECD topical coverage of DHS, MICS, and PAPFAM have somewhat increased data availability. Indicators are largely easily measurable *inputs* to ECD, such as attending preschool or being immunised. Adding development assessments would allow for more direct measurement of ECD *outcomes* (Fernald et al. 2009). The Young Lives surveys provide an example of including direct development assessments, such as for early vocabulary development, in household surveys and at scale across countries. Such data can yield insight into, for example, the relationship between early cognitive skills and socioeconomic status, as well as mediators of that relationship (Lopez Boo 2016).

Administrative data on ECD is also limited. Implementing a model of kids-based budgeting (Isaacs et al. 2018), like gender-based budgeting (Rubin & Bartle 2005), could increase investment in ECD. Understanding spending across different life stages (for example, ECD, school-age, higher education, working years, and old age) can help identify equity issues. Comparing spending across countries can also be helpful. For example, work to identify the share of national budgets supporting ECD has been undertaken in 12 Latin American countries (Putcha & Van Der Gaag 2015).

13.6.1.2 Policies and Programmes

A critical area for future research in MENA is applying global best practices for promoting ECD (Richter et al. 2017; Britto et al. 2017; Black et al. 2017), especially piloting, scaling, and evaluating programmes and policies within MENA countries. Research on the effectiveness of different delivery models for ECD services, including, for example, the role of the private sector, or leveraging technology and media to promote ECD, can also help governments identify how best to address gaps in ECD. Globally, there are important lessons on how, for example, early childhood education can reduce learning gaps (Jung & Hasan 2014), but also lessons on how insufficient quality of early childhood programmes can preclude learning gains (Bouguen et al. 2013). An improved evidence base can be helpful to advocate for increases in funding to ECD over policies that are generally ineffective, such as active labour market programmes (Barsoum et al. 2016; Bausch et al. 2017; Groh et al. 2012, 2014; Blattman & Ralston 2015). Given the extent of conflict in the region, research on protecting ECD in conflict and displacement settings is particularly critical. With a better understanding of how circumstances contribute to inequality in ECD, as well as a better evidence base for what works to improve ECD and reduce inequalities, MENA countries could make effective investments in reducing IOp in ECD and promoting human development and equity.

Notes

1 The authors appreciate the research assistance of Morgan Weyrens-Welch. Parts of this work are derived from Krafft and El-Kogali (2014).

2 GE(0) is also known as the mean logarithmic deviation or the Theil-L. GE(1) is the Theil-T measure. GE(2) is half the square of the coefficient of variation (Duclos & Araar 2006; World Bank 2005).

3 Data are from the West Bank and Gaza.

4 Literature was searched using the terms 'inequality of opportunity' *and* 'early childhood' *and* ('MENA' *or* 'Arab') in Google Scholar.

5 Studies are those that use an IOp framework on nationally representative data. Other studies (not included) may look specifically at only one circumstance, for instance, regional disparities (e.g. Sharaf & Rashad 2016) or model inequalities in a non-IOp framework (e.g. Boutayeb & Helmert 2011; Khawaja et al. 2008; Sharaf & Rashad 2015).

6 Jemmali (2016) also examines inequality in access to basic housing services for all children (aged 0–18).

References

Abdelkhalek, T. & Lassassi, M., 2018. *Inequality of Opportunity in Early Childhood Development in Algeria Over Time*. Economic Research Forum Working Paper Series No. 1254.

Almond, D. & Currie, J., 2011. Killing Me Softly: The Fetal Origins Hypothesis. *Journal of Economic Perspectives*, 25(3), pp. 153–172.

Amara, M. & Jemmali, H., 2018. Do Tunisian Young Children Have Equal Chances in Access to Basic Services? A Special Focus on Opportunities in Healthcare and Nutrition. *Child Indicators Research*, 11(2), pp. 383–403.

Assaad, R., 2013. Equality for All? Egypt's Free Public Higher Education Policy Breeds Inequality of Opportunity. In A. Elbadawy, ed. *Is There Equality of Opportunity under Free Higher Education in Egypt? (Arabic)*. New York: Population Council, pp. 83–100.

Assaad, R., Krafft, C., Hassine, N.B., et al., 2012a. Inequality of Opportunity in Child Health in the Arab World and Turkey. *Middle East Development Journal*, 4(2), pp. 1250001–1250006.

Balcázar, C.F., 2015. *Lower Bounds on Inequality of Opportunity and Measurement Error*. World Bank Policy Research Working Paper Series No. 7379.

de Barros, R.P., et al., 2009. *Measuring Inequality of Opportunities in Latin America and the Caribbean*, Washington, DC: World Bank.

de Barros, R.P., Vega, J.R.M. & Saavedra, J., 2008. *Measuring Inequality of Opportunities for Children*. Washington, DC: World Bank.

Barsoum, G., et al., 2016. *Evaluating the Effects of Entrepreneurship Edutainment in Egypt*. Working Paper.

Bausch, J., et al., 2017. The Impact of Skills Training on Financial Behaviour, Employability, and Educational Choice of Youth: Evidence from a Randomized Controlled Trial in Morocco. In *ERF 23rd Annual Conference*. Amman, Jordan.

Black, M.M., et al., 2017. Early Childhood Development Coming of Age: Science Through the Life Course. *The Lancet*, 389(10064), pp. 77–90.

Blattman, C. & Ralston, L., 2015. *Generating Employment in Poor and Fragile States: Evidence from Labor Market and Entrepreneurship Programs*.

Bouguen, A., et al., 2013. *Impact Evaluation of Three Types of Early Childhood Development Interventions in Cambodia*. World Bank Policy Research Working Paper No. 6540.

Boutayeb, A. & Helmert, U., 2011. Social Inequalities, Regional Disparities and Health Inequity in North African Countries. *International Journal for Equity in Health*, 10(23), pp. 1–9.

Britto, P.R., et al., 2017. Nurturing Care: Promoting Early Childhood Development. *The Lancet*, 389(10064), pp. 91–102.

Christian, P., et al., 2013. Risk of Childhood Undernutrition Related to Small-For-Gestational Age and Preterm Birth in Low- and Middle-Income Countries. *International Journal of Epidemiology*, 42(5), pp. 1340–1355.

Currie, J. & Moretti, E., 2007. Biology as Destiny? Short- and Long-Run Determinants of Intergenerational Transmission of Birth Weight. *Journal of Labor Economics*, 25(2), pp. 231–264.

Deutsch, J. & Silber, J., 2008. On the Shapley Value and the Decomposition of Inequality by Population Subgroups with Special Emphasis on the Gini Index. In G. Betti & A. Lemmi, eds. *Advances on Income Inequality and Concentration Measures*. New York: Routledge, pp. 161–178.

Devarajan, S. & Ianchovichina, E., 2018. A Broken Social Contract, Not High Inequality, Led to the Arab Spring. *Review of Income and Wealth*, 64(s1), pp.S5–S25.

Duclos, J.-Y. & Araar, A., 2006. *Poverty and Equity: Measurement, Policy and Estimation with DAD*. New York: Springer International Development Research Centre.

El-Kogali, S., et al., 2016. *Inequality of Opportunity in Early Childhood Development in Morocco Over Time*. World Bank Policy Research Working Paper No. 7670.

Ersado, L. & Aran, M., 2014. *Inequality of Opportunity Among Egyptian Children*. World Bank Policy Research Paper No. 7026.

Fernald, L.C.H., et al., 2009. *Examining Early Child Development in Low-Income Countries*. Washington, DC: World Bank.

Ferreira, F.H.G. & Gignoux, J., 2008. *The Measurement of Inequality of Opportunity: Theory and an Application to Latin America*. World Bank Policy Research Working Paper No. 4659.

Ferreira, F.H.G. & Gignoux, J., 2011. The Measurement of Inequality of Opportunity: Theory and an Application to Latin America. *Review of Income and Wealth*, 57(4), pp. 622–657.

Glewwe, P., 2002. Schools and Skills in Developing Countries: Education Policies and Socioeconomic Outcomes. *Journal of Economic Literature*, 40(2), pp. 436–482.

Glewwe, P. & King, E.M., 2001. The Impact of Early Childhood Nutritional Status on Cognitive Development: Does the Timing of Malnutrition Matter? *The World Bank Economic Review*, 15(1), pp. 81–113.

Glewwe, P., Jacoby, H.G. & King, E.M., 2001. Early Childhood Nutrition and Academic Achievement: A Longitudinal Analysis. *Journal of Public Economics*, 81(3), pp. 345–368.

Groh, M., et al., 2012. *Soft Skills or Hard Cash? The Impact of Training and Wage Subsidy Programs on Female Youth Employment in Jordan.* World Bank Policy Research Working Paper No. 6141.

Groh, M., et al., 2014. *Testing the Importance of Search Frictions, Matching, and Reservation Prestige Through Randomized Experiments in Jordan.* World Bank Policy Research Working Paper No. 7030.

Harper, C., Marcus, R. & Moore, K., 2003. Enduring Poverty and the Conditions of Childhood: Lifecourse and Intergenerational Poverty Transmissions. *World Development*, 31(3), pp. 535–554.

Heckman, J.J., 2006. Skill Formation and the Economics of Investing in Disadvantaged Children. *Science*, 312, pp. 1900–1902.

Heckman, J.J. & Masterov, D.V., 2007. The Productivity Argument for Investing in Young Children. *Review of Agricultural Economics*, 29(3), pp. 446–493.

Helmers, C. & Patnam, M., 2011. The Formation and Evolution of Childhood Skill Acquisition: Evidence from India. *Journal of Development Economics*, 95(2), pp. 252–266.

Hoddinott, J., Maluccio, J.A., Behrman, J.R., Flores, R., and Martorell, R., 2008. Effect of a Nutrition Intervention during Early Childhood on Productivity in Guatemalan Adults. *Lancet*, 371(9610), pp. 411–416.

Hoddinott, J., Alderman, H., Behrman, J.R., Haddad, L., and Horton, S., 2013. The Economic Rationale for Investing in Stunting Reduction. *Maternal and Child Nutrition*, 9(S2), pp. 69–82.

Hufe, P. & Peichl, A., 2015. *Lower Bounds and the Linearity Assumption in Parametric Estimations of Inequality of Opportunity.* IZA Discussion Paper Series No. 9605.

Ibarra, G.L. & Cruz, A.L.M., 2015. *Exploring the Sources of Downward Bias in Measuring Inequality of Opportunity.* World Bank Policy Research Working Paper Series No. 7458.

Isaacs, J.B., et al., 2018. *Kids' Share 2018 Report on Federal Expenditures on Children Through 2017 and Future Projections.* Washington, DC: Urban Institute.

Jemmali, H., 2016. *Inequality of Opportunities among Tunisian Children Over Time and Space.* Economic Research Forum Working Paper Series No. 1048.

Jung, H. & Hasan, A., 2014. *The Impact of Early Childhood Education on Early Achievement Gaps: Evidence from the Indonesia Early Childhood Education and Development (ECED) Project.* World Bank Policy Research Working Paper No. 6794.

Kanbur, R. & Wagstaff, A., 2014. *How Useful is Inequality of Opportunity as a Policy Construct?* World Bank Policy Research Working Paper No. 6980.

Khawaja, M., et al., 2008. Disparities in Child Health in the Arab Region during the 1990s. *International Journal for Equity in Health*, 7(24), pp. 1–10.

Krafft, C., 2015. *The Determinants of Child Health Disparities in Jordan.* Economic Research Forum Working Paper Series No. 950.

Krafft, C. & Alawode, H., 2018. Inequality of Opportunity in Higher Education in the Middle East and North Africa. *International Journal of Educational Development*, 62, pp. 234–244.

Krafft, C. & El-Kogali, S., 2014. *Inequalities in Early Childhood Development in the Middle East and North Africa.* Economic Research Forum Working Paper Series No. 856.

Krafft, C., Elbadawy, A. & Assaad, R., 2013. Access Within the Higher Education System: Evidence for More Inequality of Opportunity. In A. Elbadawy, ed. *Is There Equality of Opportunity under Free Higher Education in Egypt? (Arabic).* New York: Population Council, pp. 101–134.

Krishnan, N., et al., 2016. *Uneven Odds, Unequal Outcomes: Inequality of Opportunity in the Middle East and North Africa.* Washington, DC: World Bank.

Leight, J., Glewwe, P. & Park, A., 2015. The Impact of Early Childhood Shocks on the Evolution of Cognitive and Non-Cognitive Skills. In *Allied Social Science Associations 2015 Annual Meeting.* Boston, MA.

Lopez Boo, F., 2016. Socio-economic Status and Early Childhood Cognitive Skills: A Mediation Analysis Using the Young Lives Panel. *International Journal of Behavioral Development*, 40(6), pp. 500–508.

Maccini, S. & Yang, D., 2009. Under the Weather: Health, Schooling, and Economic Consequences of Early-Life Rainfall. *American Economic Review*, 99(3), pp. 1006–1026.

Mayer-Foulkes, D., 2008. The Human Development Trap in Mexico. *World Development*, 36(5), pp. 775–796.

Niehues, J. & Peichl, A., 2014. Upper Bounds of Inequality of Opportunity: Theory and Evidence for Germany and the US. *Social Choice and Welfare*, 43(1), pp. 73–99.

Putcha, V. & Van Der Gaag, J., 2015. *Investing in Early Childhood Development: What is Being Spent, and What Does It Cost?* Global Economy & Development at Brookings Working Paper No. 81.

Richter, L.M., et al., 2017. Investing in the Foundation of Sustainable Development: Pathways to Scale Up for Early Childhood Development. *The Lancet*, 389(10064), pp. 103–118.

Roemer, J.E., 1998. *Equality of Opportunity*. Cambridge, MA: Harvard University Press.

Roemer, J.E., 2014. Economic Development as Opportunity Equalization. *The World Bank Economic Review*, 28(2), pp. 189–209.

Rubin, M.M. & Bartle, J.R., 2005. Integrating Gender into Government Budgets: A New Perspective. *Public Administration Review*, 65(3), pp. 259–272.

Saidi, A. & Hamdaoui, M., 2017. On Measuring and Decomposing Inequality of Opportunity in Access to Health Services Among Tunisian Children: A New Approach for Public Policy. *Health and Quality of Life Outcomes*, 15(213), pp. 1–29.

Sharaf, M.F. & Rashad, A.S., 2015. *Socioeconomic Inequalities in Infant Mortality in Egypt: Analyzing Trends between 1995 and 2014*. University of Alberta Faculty of Arts Department of Economics Working Paper No. 2015–17.

Sharaf, M.F. & Rashad, A.S., 2016. Regional Inequalities in Child Malnutrition in Egypt, Jordan, and Yemen: A Blinder-Oaxaca Decomposition Analysis. *Health Economics Review*, 6(23), pp. 1–11.

Shonkoff, J.P. & Phillips, D.A., 2000. *From Neurons to Neighborhoods: The Science of Early Childhood Development*, by J.P. Shonkoff & D.A. Phillips, eds. Washington, DC: National Academy of Sciences - National Research Council. Board on Children and Families. Institute of Medicine.

Shorrocks, A.F., 2013. Decomposition Procedures for Distributional Analysis: A Unified Framework Based on the Shapley Value. *Journal of Economic Inequality*, 11(1), pp. 99–126.

Strauss, J. & Thomas, D., 1998. Health, Nutrition, and Economic Development. *Journal of Economic Literature*, 36(2), pp. 766–817.

Tanner, J., Candland, T. & Odden, W.S., 2015. *Later Impacts of Early Childhood Interventions: A Systematic Review*. Washington, DC: Independent Evaluation Group, The World Bank Group.

UNDP & Institute of National Planning, 2008. *Egypt Human Development Report 2008: Egypt's Social Contract: The Role of Civil Society*. Cairo, Egypt: UNDP & Institute of National Planning.

UNESCO, 2010. *Education for All Global Monitoring Report 2011: The Hidden Crisis: Armed Conflict and Education*. Paris, France: UNESCO.

UNESCO, 2014. *Teaching and Learning: Achieving Quality for All: Education for All Global Monitoring Report 2013/4*. Paris, France: UNESCO

UNICEF, 2008. *The State of the World's Children 2009: Maternal and Newborn Health*.

United Nations, 2006. *Committee on the Rights of the Child, General Comment No. 7, Implementing Child Rights in Early Childhood (Fortieth Session, 2005), U.N. Doc. CRC/C/GC/7/Rev.1 (2006)*. http://hrlibrary.umn.edu/crc/comment7.html [Accessed August 18, 2018].

Velez, C.E., Al-Shawarby, S. & El-Laithy, H., 2012. *Equality of Opportunity for Children in Egypt, 2000 – 2009: Achievements and Challenges*. World Bank Policy Research Paper No. 6159.

Vladimir, H., 2017. Evolution of Opportunities for Early Childhood Development in Arab Countries. *International Journal of Human Rights in Healthcare*, 10(4), pp. 256–276.

Walker, S.P., et al., 2007. Child Development: Risk Factors for Adverse Outcomes in Developing Countries. *Lancet*, 369, pp. 145–157.

Walker, S.P., et al., 2011. Inequality in Early Childhood: Risk and Protective Factors for Early Child Development. *Lancet*, 378(9799), pp. 1325–1338.

World Bank, 2005. *World Development Report 2006: Equity and Development*.

World Bank, 2012. *Arab Republic of Egypt - Inequality of Opportunity in Access to Basic Services among Egyptian Children*. Washington, DC: World Bank.

World Bank, 2019. *Expectations and Aspirations: A New Framework for Education in the Middle East and North Africa: Overview*. Washington, DC: World Bank.

Zellman, G.L., Karam, R. & Perlman, M., 2014a. Predicting Child Development Knowledge and Engagement of Moroccan Parents. *Near and Middle Eastern Journal of Research in Education*, 5, pp. 1–17.

Zellman, G.L., Perlman, M. & Karam, R., 2014b. How Moroccan Mothers and Fathers View Child Development and Their Role in Their Children's Education. *International Journal of Early Years Education*, 22(2), pp. 197–209.

14

SOCIAL POLICY IN THE MENA REGION

Mahmood Messkoub

14.1 Introduction: from social welfare to social policy[1]

Historically, societies have witnessed a move from small-scale, largely faith-based, systems of mutual help based on reciprocity and charity to large-scale state-sponsored social support systems – a transition that has tracked closely the emergence of nation states. These developments are also reflected in the structure of social welfare provisioning in the MENA countries, where faith-based charitable social services are combined with extensive services provided by the state. Today, state-provided social services dominate the social policy agenda in the MENA region as elsewhere in the world (Mkandawire, 2004).

At the outset, it is necessary to distinguish between social welfare and social policy. Whilst social welfare refers to any kind of mutual help and socially organised activities – whether provided by the state or non-state actors – social policy is state-led and state-organised aiming to support individuals and households and forms part of the broad economic and development agenda of diversification of an economy that requires a healthy and educated labour force and a stable social environment. In this regard social policy can be viewed as a social contract between labour and capital – or even citizens and the state – in the development process of a nation state (Ghosh, 2004).

The distinction between social welfare and social policy would also draw attention to the role of non-state social actors in welfare provisioning. Examples of such social institutions are households that care for their members and non-state secular and religious charitable organisations that provide health and education services. In some MENA countries with a weakened central state such as Lebanon, these non-state providers play an important role in the delivery of basic health and education services (Cammett and Maclean, 2014).

Social policy is by definition societal in the sense that individuals and communities organise activities to achieve certain social objectives, with an implicit or explicit goal of achieving social justice. In the broadest and most positive sense, social policy is about improving human welfare and meeting human needs, as well as being concerned with the distribution of resources and assets that would enable individuals to realise their potential, develop their capabilities and contribute to the economic and social life of a country. Social policy thus not only covers the provision of health and education which are about *promotion* of human capability but also laws, rules and regulations that *protect* human capability.

There is also an important analytical difference between social provisioning organised by the state as part of its social policy agenda that is based on the principles of 'rights, regulation and redistribution' in the context of a social contract, and social provisioning provided by non-state actors (e.g. households, mutual and charitable organisations) that are based on 'reciprocity, inclusion and trust' as well as altruism. The premise of 'rights' has an important implication for entitlement, claim and access to various services as well as legal and regulatory provisions of social policies; that also provides the backdrop for political aspirations and claims on the state.

Rights also influence and contribute to what Fraser (1989) has called 'the political imaginary of social welfare,' an imaginary that may have originated in political promises on welfare provisioning. But rights put them on firmer footing which, combined with regulations of, for example, wages and labour relations will open up other areas to claim a fairer share of the fruits of labour from private and public employers.

In any welfare regime, the relative weights of different institutions (state, market, households and non-state organisations) critically depend on the balance of political forces and economic conditions in a country that over time sets the trajectory, achievements and vicissitude of social policies (Esping-Anderson, 1990; Kwan et al., 2009). Herein lies the path dependency of social policy and welfare regimes in the world.

In this context, like any other policy, social policy is a product of debates, arguments and conflicts over how to find solutions for the most pressing problems of a society (Blakemore, 1998). The process of policymaking itself also has an important bearing on its content and the success of implementation. Arguably, the more consensual and democratic the policy environment (with regard to formulation, implementation, monitoring and accountability), the more legitimised the policy and the more likely its chances of success.

However, the history of social policies around the world reveals that a Western-style parliamentary democracy is neither a necessary nor a sufficient condition for the implementation and success of specific policies. For evidence one should look at the achievements, *inter alia*, of countries as diverse as Cuba, Chile, China, the Republic of Korea, Sri Lanka, Taiwan and Vietnam in reducing infant and child mortalities, and increasing life expectancy, adult literacy and secondary school enrolment.

The MENA region is a complex set of heterogeneous countries with shared histories and culture. They have a varied record of human development and social policy that are directly related to the resource base and economic and political history of each country.[2] Studies of the achievements of social policies in MENA countries emphasise the importance of historical and cultural legacy, politics of social development as well as institutions and resources for delivering social services,[3] again drawing our attention to the path dependency of social policy.

The rest of this chapter is devoted to an overview of social policy developments in the MENA region with an emphasis on recent developments such as the narrowing down of social policy to social protection of the poor, and the reform of indirect/untargeted subsidy regimes to targeted social protection of the poor.

14.2 Social policy in MENA: a short history

Social policy, as discussed above, includes *inter alia* the provision of education and health services, development of social insurance, health and safety and other labour- and employment-related legislation to support nascent industries. In MENA, it has mainly emerged along with nation-building and state-building projects in Turkey and Iran, and in post-colonial countries like Egypt, Iraq, Jordan, Saudi Arabia, Algeria, Tunisia, Libya and Morocco. According to Karshenas and Moghadam, such developments had more to do 'with creating a social base of support for the emerging nation states and regimes than with any concept of citizens' rights' (2009: S53). However, one should not ignore references in manifestos and declarations of the anti-colonial and nationalist movements to citizens' entitlements to decent living standards. Such sentiments found their way into the constitutions, development plans and political declarations of some of the MENA nations, too.[4]

Despite its share of conflicts and wars, the MENA region has had impressive achievements in some areas of human development such as declines in both maternal mortality and infant and child mortality, an increase in life expectancy and improved educational outcomes such as increases in literacy, school attendance and gender parity.[5] These achievements have, to a large extent, benefited from the economic fortunes of the oil markets.

The oil income provided the region with resources to pay for health, education and extensive subsidies for food, fuel and power generation, with some of the most extensive social support packages of free health and education services provided to the citizens of the Persian Gulf oil-rich states. The non-oil producers have also benefited from oil bounties through worker remittances, foreign aid and investment by the oil-rich countries. After the oil boom of the early 1970s, the oil-exporting states had further opportunities to boost their spending on social policies and to increase the scale and scope of their various social programmes.

But the slow-down in economic growth and the decline in oil revenues in the 1980s put the finances of the MENA countries to the test, especially in the more populous oil-exporting countries like Iran, Algeria and Iraq, as well as countries that relied heavily on remittances and external finance like Egypt and Jordan. The region was ill-equipped in terms of a skilled labour force and social insurance policies to compete internationally and diversify its economy. This lack of flexibility has been inherent in the design and coverage of various social programmes in the region, the most striking of which is the extensive support offered to the military, police and other key state security services, as well as the civil servants and formal sector employees. Most of these schemes did not cover the vast number of informal sector workers, rural residents and agricultural workers. As Karshenas and Moghadam note:

> social benefits [...] were [...] regarded as the attributes of [the job] rather than social security safeguards [...] The lack of development of an adequate social insurance system has made labour markets in the region inflexible and rendered the task of economic reform in the post-oil-boom era difficult.
>
> *(2009: S58)*

Besides the lack of flexibility, the gap in coverage in this period left millions across the region with minimal access to health and education services as well as public health–related services like clean water and sanitation and support for the vulnerable groups of the elderly, people with disability and the poor. The excluded population had to rely on very poor publicly provided services or fall back on meagre family resources and charitable handouts of the non-state providers (NSPs) which is part of the so-called *informal security regime* (Cammett, 2014).

The NSPs in the MENA region have a long history dating back to charitable activities financed by Islamic religious endowments (*Waqf*) as well as other religious denominations. The scale and scope of NSPs have multiplied over the years and have been attributed to a multiplicity of sources such as (a) state failure, (b) market failure, (c) neo-liberal adjustment programmes resulting in retrenchment and downgrading of state services and decentralisation of service provisions,[6] and (d) conflict and wars such as in Lebanon, Iraq and more recently Yemen and Syria (Cammett, 2014; Jawad, 2009). It is important to note that in an era marked by 'less-state' and 'more-market' that encourages 'self-help,' NSPs would feed into social, ethnic and religious divisions and sectarianism in some of the MENA societies. In religiously more homogenous societies like Iran, NSPs that are primarily run by religious institutions and are financed by religious endowments of Waqf or through the state budget have become an instrument of social control promoting clientelism to strengthen and entrench power and political control of the religious establishment (Messkoub, 2006b).

The *informal security regime* based on family and NSPs have largely negative implications for the welfare of women in the context of the male-breadwinner/female-homemaker family model; that is further reinforced by the direct or indirect influence of Islamic Sharia law on the civil law of many MENA countries (Moghadam, 2006). The fact that health and education situations of women improved in the latter half of 20th century should not conceal the gender gap that still exists in terms of civil, social and economic rights. For example, access to family social welfare in Jordan and Saudi Arabia has been organised through male heads of households or male kin. Where no laws existed to discriminate against women, like in Egypt, it was the lack of a universal registration/identity card system that obliged women to access social services and subsidised goods through their spouses and male kin (*Ibid.*: 229).

Low labour force participation of women in the region has also meant a low presence in the formal sector and civil service which tend to offer better social support and benefits. Working women's concentration in the informal sector and rural areas has also limited their benefits from social protections and labour laws (*Ibid.*, and Karshenas and Moghadam, 2009). Add to these male disability due to conflict, the presence of young children in the workforce and male migration, it is hardly surprising that female-headed households are over-represented among poor households (FAO, 2007: 44).

What has been observed in relation to poverty and vulnerability in the region in normal times would be exacerbated with economic downturns and crises that hit the region, while social policy regimes have failed to respond appropriately to protect the population. Social policies should be designed in such a way as to provide socially *promotive* services like health and education, whilst also providing social insurance mechanisms to protect people against life contingencies such as accidents at work or unemployment due to an economic downturn. In other words, social policies should combine the *promotive* functions with the *protective* functions of social insurance in order to allow the individuals and the economy as a whole to be responsive to unforeseen contingencies and economic downturns. By using social policy principally as an instrument of patronage, the focus has been on its promotive aspects of improving health and education during the oil-boom periods, but failing to deliver its protective aspects when the economy is hit by oil-bust.[7]

14.3 From social policy to social protection in MENA

The existing social policy models in MENA combine *state support and subsidies* for a raft of health and education services with the supply of heavily *subsidised* staple foods and basic necessities (flour, bread and cooking oil as well as fuel and energy). These models have been severely criticised for their deficiencies in terms of their coverage of the population, entitlement to various social services, fragmentation of support for different groups and inadequacy of services provided, and above all for the *generalised subsidies* that favour the rich and the upper-middle classes (see, e.g., Karshenas et al., 2014; Loewe and Jawad, 2018; Loewe, 2019; Sdralevich et al., 2014; Silva et al., 2013).

The existing social protection policies in the MENA countries vary greatly in their scope, coverage and adequacy. The International Social Security Association (ISSA) collects data from member countries on their social security programmes. According to the latest ISSA country profiles, most MENA countries have programmes for some of the following categories: (a) old age, disability and survivors; (b) sickness and maternity; (c) work injury; (d) unemployment; and (e) family allowances (ISSA, 2019).

Appendix Table 14.1 provides a snapshot of the range of programmes available in each MENA country. It can be seen that whilst all countries do have social protection programmes, and in some cases extensive ones, coverage in most middle- and low-income MENA countries is limited to state employees in civil service, police and military as well as those in the modern regulated private sectors of manufacturing and services. But the majority of the population working in agriculture, the informal sector and other unregulated activities have very limited access, if any, to the state social protection programmes. To assess these programmes, we need to consider the nature of the *entitlements*, as well as their *coverage* of the population and the *adequacy* of services and financial compensations provided.

As far as entitlements are concerned, the majority of social protection programmes (except for 'family allowances' in some countries) require formal labour contracts – a requirement to enrol employees in the state social insurance programme. This raises important questions about the entitlement of those without a formal labour contract or those who are active and are self-employed in agriculture and in rural areas as well as those employed in sizeable 'informal sectors' in urban areas. There is also the case of migrant workers in major labour-importing GCC states, who are in general subject to different social protection rules compared with the nationals.

Loewe has estimated the effective coverage rates of several social protection schemes for the 2005–2010 period revealing a wide variation across MENA countries. Regarding social health insurance and non-contributory public health schemes, some of the middle-income countries (e.g. Algeria, Egypt, Iran, Jordan, Oman, Tunisia) offer basic health services to 75–90% of the population with other MENA countries dropping to below 50% (Loewe, 2019: Table 3.1). Whilst immunisation rates are high in the region and infant and mother and child mortalities have declined, the scope and quality of other health services vary greatly across countries. Out-of-pocket health expenses too could be substantial for middle- and low-income people in most MENA countries. In 2015 out-of-pocket expenses as a percentage of the total health expenditure could be as low as 6.2% in Qatar (resource rich with a small population) but as high as 81% in Yemen, 62% in Egypt and 76% in Iraq. In between lie countries like Iran and Tunisia with a figure of 39.4% and Morocco with 53% (WHO, 2019).

There are other important shortcomings in current health service provisions of the region. There is an urban–rural divide in favour of the former as well as poor inclusion and coverage for low-income/low-status migrants, displaced people, refugees and ethnic minorities, high spending on expensive diagnostic and curative health care and a general neglect of primary and preventive healthcare (WHO, 2010; Loewe, 2019).

Out-of-pocket expenditures and poor coverage of health services are reflections of the low spending on public health and inadequacy of public health services. Middle-income MENA countries spent 2.9% of their GDP on health in 2016; that showed an increase over the 2001 figure of 1.9%.[8] Despite such an increase, public expenditure only covered between 40–50% of the total health expenditure over the same period (World Bank, 2019). Inadequate spending on public health and general neglect of public health services has meant poor-quality health services for the great majority of people, which has pushed even the poor to seek private health services.[9]

Several policies have been suggested to improve the coverage and adequacy of health service provisions in MENA. An important policy is to extend the existing health insurance programmes to cover the poor and marginalised. In Morocco, for instance, such a scheme gave access to 8.5 million people at the cost of no more than a 1% tax on the earnings of private companies (Karshenas et al., 2014).

The fragmentation of health insurance and service provision is another major shortcoming that limits coverage and adequacy of social policy. In most MENA countries, there are different public and private health insurance programmes and health service providers. If these were integrated into a common national health insurance programme, the result could be increased coverage and an improvement of the services provided by reducing administrative costs and rationalising overlapping services. Loewe (2019) cites the case of the Egyptian public health system which in 2007–2008 spent 15% of its budget on administration. This was well above the average of 4.7% for OECD and EU countries in 2007 but in line for middle-income countries for which data is available: 16% in Mexico and 14.8% in Thailand in 2005. Administrative costs of private health insurance are three–four times higher than the public schemes in both high- and middle-income countries (Nicolle and Mathauer, 2010). This is an important finding considering that private health insurance is promoted in many countries to overcome the inadequate public health services. Other complementary public health measures that can improve social policy and should be placed on the agenda are: provision of clean water, improved sanitation and more emphasis on preventive health care (Karshenas et al., 2014).

Health as a foundation of human capital should be complemented with education in order to enhance capabilities of individuals and their societies in the development process. Moreover, education has important implications for poverty reduction and entitlement to social protection through employment, if the poor were to benefit from job creation – the so-called 'integrability' condition of the employment–poverty nexus.[10]

The region has been devoting a sizable share of its GDP (5%) and government expenditure (20%) to education in the past few decades and has made great strides in reducing illiteracy and increasing years of schooling. Yet it is lagging behind competitors in years of educational attainment, school dropout rates and scores on international tests (World Bank, 2008). By 2010 in all MENA countries (except Bahrain, Kuwait, Qatar and UAE) about 10% of those 15 years and over were not literate, with the average literacy rate for the MENA region being 85% (Karshenas et al., 2014: Table 4). In most MENA countries unemployment of educated youth has been higher than that of the same cohort in countries with similar levels of income per capita.

The problem of 'integrability' is more acute for the poor who pay an extra penalty if they are female and reside in rural areas. And finally, the quality and availability of public education have declined over the years because of the failure of public spending to keep up with the rising numbers of school-age children. Overcrowding and the resultant high students-to-teacher ratio and the poor quality of education have all contributed to the growth of private education in most MENA countries, which inevitably further widens the gap in educational achievements of the those who can afford private tuitions and private schools and the rest of the population (Karshenas et al., 2014; World Bank, 2008).

Besides health and education, improving welfare in old age is another important objective of social policy and social protection in the region. Here too we encounter great variations across different countries. The share of the employed population who are members of contributory and non-contributory public pension schemes varies from a low of 15% (Yemen) to a high of 80% (Libya). In a large number of MENA countries less than 50% of the *employed population* contributes to a public pension scheme, a figure that will be far lower if we consider the much larger figure of *working-age population* which includes women who have very low labour force participation rates (Loewe, 2019: 42; Robalino et al., 2005; ILO, 2014). The shortfall in coverage is most glaring when we note that only 27.4% of those who are above the statutory pensionable age benefit from old-age pensions in the region (ILO, 2017: Figure 6.20, p. 143).

Those who are covered by the formal pension schemes retire on pensions with large replacement rates (ratio of pension to final salary). The replacement rate in most MENA countries is around 80% compared to around 57% for the OECD countries and those in Latin America and the Caribbean, and Eastern and Central Asia (Robalino et al., 2005). It is not clear how over-time pensions are adjusted for inflation and average income in the MENA region. The same very detailed study of pensions in MENA does not provide, unfortunately, any information on indexation. High replacement rates and low coverage of the elderly population, however, raise important questions about the sustainability, efficiency and equity of the pension schemes especially when we factor in demographic transition, increase in the number of old people and their share in the population, and the speed of ageing of the population in some MENA countries (Robalino et al., 2005; Messkoub, 2017).

For example, Iran is projected to be the second fastest ageing population (after South Korea) judging by the increase in the share of 60-year-old-and-overs in the total population over the 2015–2050 period. The UAE, Oman, Bahrain and Lebanon are not far behind. Currently, these countries are in the top ten fastest ageing countries in the world. Demographers have suggested that the doubling of the share of 65-year-old-and-overs in the total population could be used as an indicator of the speed of ageing. It is remarkable that in France it took 115 years (1865 to 1980) for the percentage of those aged 65 and older to increase from 7% to 14%, whilst the same percentage increase in Iran will take 17 years only (Mehri et al., 2020). France and other high-income countries aged at a much slower pace. Over decades they developed legal, financial and institutional infrastructures such as social insurance, private pension funds for different professions, private insurance companies that provided life insurance policies and annuities, as well as health and social services to care for an ageing population (*Ibid.*).

The challenge for MENA countries – as elsewhere – is how to re-organise social policy in order to improve the scale and scope of social protection programmes by focusing on their coverage and range, efficacy and equity to align the social policy agenda more with the broad developmental goals and aspirations of people in MENA. These issues are taken up in the next section.

14.4 Reform of the subsidy structure and social programmes

One of the most important and pressing problems of financing social programmes is the re-organisation of the existing direct and indirect subsidy programmes in order to maximise their benefits to those in need. A simple comparison of different subsidy programmes reveals that in the MENA region, they are not targeted towards those in greatest need. Figure 14.1 shows the percentage of GDP spent in selected MENA countries on *indirect* subsidies for two main basic necessities: food and fuel. As we can see, only in Iraq are fuel subsidies above food subsidies. The latter mostly benefit the lower-income groups, whereas fuel subsidies benefit mostly the middle- and upper-income groups (Del Geranado et al., 2010). According to Silva et al. fuel subsidies account for nearly 75% of the total subsidy spending in MENA (2013: 111). They also demonstrate that spending on these indirect subsidies are much larger than spending on other social safety nets targeted at the poor.[11] The authors estimate that Egypt spent 20 times more on untargeted food and fuel subsidies in 2009 than on other social safety nets. They also quote Fattouh and El-Katiri (2012) who showed that in 2008 Egypt spent as much on fuel subsidies as on health and education combined. Likewise, prior to the subsidy reforms in 2010 Iran spent 30% of its GDP on various subsidy programmes (Messkoub, 2019). After nearly ten years of reforming indirect subsidies, these subsidies still account for 20% of Iran's GDP in 2019.[12]

Given the size and importance of indirect subsidies in MENA countries, there is a strong economic case to scale back these subsidies and to redirect them to health, education and other

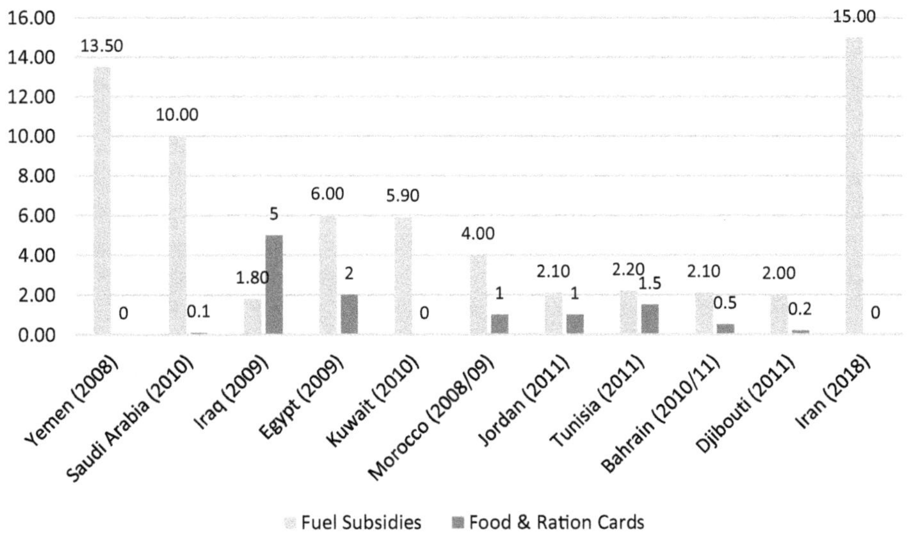

Figure 14.1 Fuel and food-ration card subsidies in selected MENA countries, various years (% GDP)
Note: A figure of zero in the case of Iran indicates non-availability of data. *Source*: *Financial Times* (2019) for Iran; Silva et al. (2013: Table 3.3, p. 112) for others.

social programmes and safety nets. As noted earlier, the current spending on health and education are inadequate and current social safety net programmes cover a small percentage of the total population, and more importantly, a small percentage of the poorest quintile of the population. Only 16% of the poorest quintile in the Arab MENA receive any social safety net transfers, compared with around 50% in East Asia and the Pacific, Latin America and the Caribbean, Europe and Central Asia (Silva et al., 2013: Figure 3.7, p. 118.).

Despite their low coverage, indirect fuel and other subsidies do contribute to the welfare of the poor. For example, over the 2004–2010 period, in Egypt and Iraq indirect food subsidies reduced the poverty rate by around 30%, whilst fuel subsidies in Egypt reduced poverty by around 18%, and in Jordan food, gas and water subsidies reduced poverty by just over 10% (*Ibid.*: Figure 3.17, p. 138). The reform of indirect subsidies therefore should take into account the differential impact of these subsidies on the poor and vulnerable and combine any reform with compensation to mitigate the impact of reforms.[13]

The most important social policy emerging from the debate on the reform of indirect subsidy in MENA is cash transfer (CT). CT is presented as a social protection policy, along with other non-subsidy social protection programmes, to compensate for the negative impact of increasing the price of major items of subsidised goods, such as fuel, energy and water as well as some food products that have been accessible to all.

Concerns with street protests and riots following the previous experiments of the removal of subsidies in Egypt, Morocco, Jordan and Iran (Walton and Seddon, 1994; Messkoub, 2019) have raised questions about the economic and political design and implementation of subsidy reform. A key question for the policy makers seems to be how to make the reforms more politically palatable rather than a governance approach that includes popular democratic participation, accountability of the policy makers and transparency of the process of policy making and implementation.[14] An interesting example is the World Bank's study of attitudes towards subsidies in four MENA countries (Egypt, Jordan, Lebanon and Tunisia), which found that the reform of indirect subsidies should be combined with non-subsidy social safety net programmes targeting the poor, paying benefits in cash rather than in kind, and interestingly, without any conditions attached (Silva et al., 2013: 170–177). It is interesting to note that only in Lebanon did respondents also include extra support for health and education as part of the compensation besides CT. The other major finding of the report is knowledge of the subsidy structure and cost and its impact on different groups. For example, in all surveyed countries there was more awareness of staple food subsidies than fuel subsidy, despite the fact that the latter costs much more as a percentage of the GDP than the former (e.g., in Egypt fuel subsidy costs 6.9% of GDP compared to 1.8% for food subsidies). Since food subsidies matter more to the majority of the population, its reform must therefore be treated with great care, which would also help with the public acceptance of subsidy reform policy in general (*Ibid*.: 177–181).

Notwithstanding the lack of discussion on the democratic governance of policy making in terms of participation, accountability and transparency, the literature attributes the success of any subsidy reform to the 'timing and pacing of the reform; appropriate communication strategy; broad coalition of support and compensation to short-term loser; technical capacity, leadership and commitment' (*Ibid*.: 185).

It is important to note that the cash transfer policy that emerged from the World Bank survey is put in the context of 'compensation to short-term loser' which seems to be envisaged as part of creating and maintaining a 'broad coalition of support' (*Ibid*.: 190–193). CT is not viewed as a long-term commitment, nor are there any ideas in the World Bank study on long-term social policy commitments beyond the development of social safety nets. This does not bode well for the future development of alternative progressive social policy regimes in MENA.

Given the economic imperatives of indirect subsidy reform and the social imperatives of reducing poverty and inequality, it is important that subsidy reforms are closely aligned with long-term social policy initiatives. Planning for these reforms is thus important for their success not simply to prepare the public for these changes, but also to factor in the patterns of consumption to minimise the adverse impact of any price rises on the poor and vulnerable groups in different countries.

There is support for such an approach judging by the responses in the survey countries in the World Bank report mentioned above (Egypt, Jordan, Lebanon and Tunisia). Respondents put various types of fuel subsidy on top of their list of subsidies that could be reduced, whilst bread and other staple foods were among the lowest on their list (*Ibid*.: Figure 4.2.3, p. 181). Regarding where any such savings from subsidy reform could be spent, targeting the poor (and the exclusion of wealthy) was the generally preferred method followed by a preference for investment in health and education with the strongest support for this coming in Lebanon (*Ibid*., 2013: Figure 4.2.5, p. 184).

Given the current emphasis on CT and targeting in social policy agendas, it is important that MENA countries draw on the experience of other countries to design targeting and CT programmes to ensure that errors of inclusion and exclusion associated with targeting are minimised. There is also a case for the monitoring and evaluation of targeted programmes to improve access, coverage and adequacy of support provided. Moreover, the cost of CT programmes relative to GDP and government budgets should also be taken into account to ensure that the programmes are financially sustainable. Controlling inflation and general macroeconomic stability are other important preconditions for the success of CT and other forms of cash compensation to different groups (including producers) for subsidy reform policies. And finally, MENA could learn from other countries (such as Mexico and Brazil) with successful CT programmes, especially those conditional on children's enrolment and attendance at schools and health clinics for vaccination and other preventive health check-ups.[15] Any savings from subsidy reforms should be used to improve health and education in general and especially those of children to improve the human capital of the country.

14.5 Conclusion

The Arab Spring and its counterparts in Turkey and Iran have been much more than a cry for freedom and democracy. It has also been a cry for social justice and against the corruption that has aggravated capitalist inequality. The use of and access to public office for private accumulation, lack of accountability and poor governance have all contributed to a sense of desperation and alienation of the population, especially the young. The region is in need of a new social contract. Social policy should play an important role in the design and implementation of this social contract.

The non-oil-exporting MENA countries face a substantial balance of payments and budget deficits that limit their policy space to continue with the current 'business as usual' approach of funding their social policy spending which in many cases does not benefit the majority of the population. This is due mainly to the neglect and under-spending of social policy programmes like health and education that claim to have a universal reach. At the same time the over-spending on social policies, such as pensions, has mainly benefited the better-off sections of the formal sector and government employees; and indirect subsidies to energy and fuel have mainly benefited the better-off sections of the population.

The existing generalised indirect subsidy-based social policy model has failed to provide a solution to increasing poverty and vulnerability in the region especially in periods of social and economic crisis. Yet certain subsidised goods like foodstuffs have been crucial in alleviating the severe pressure on household budgets for the poor. The reform of the subsidy structure not only should take note of the differential impact of indirect subsidies but also has to be part of a broad programme of social protection. The subsidy reform should not just be a component of orthodox structural adjustment programme that puts its emphasis on reducing the budget deficit by cutting back subsidies. Despite these caveats there has been a major shift in MENA social policy debate among the international financial institutions (the World Bank and the IMF), UN agencies (such as ESCWA) and MENA countries themselves towards a narrowing down of social policy to social protection, social safety nets and targeting.[16]

There is also the all-important concern with the role of households and families to support themselves. In the absence of adequate family resources, there is a need for social policy measures that would supplement family resources and support the broad developmental agenda and ensure societal and macro-level inter-generational support. In this context the most basic objective of any state intervention is to maintain and increase the resource base of households. This is particularly important if we take into account the changing demographics of the region: a trend towards lower fertility and ageing populations. MENA societies and families are ill-prepared for an ageing population. Yet families, and in particular women, will bear the brunt of coping with the care of their elderly, considering the absence of sufficient institutional support to care for the elderly in almost all MENA countries and the fact that most elderly will not be able to accumulate sufficient resources to care for themselves.

Questions remain as to whether state support to households should be based on targeting or rest on universal principles. Historical experience of MENA and other countries demonstrates that universal provision of health and education as well as public services of water and electricity and infrastructure have made the biggest impact on achieving human development goals. However, recent evidence of poor and inadequate public services and lack of meaningful and proper accountability by the politicians and civil servants has undermined universalist social policies. This has weakened the social contract between state and citizens further undermining the legitimacy of state-led social policy in the region (Brixi et al., 2015). In the low- and middle-income MENA countries, as elsewhere, this has laid the ground for scaling back the role of state in the economy and social provisioning, privatisation and cutting back on universal services whilst targeting social spending on the poor households. But social policy strategies that are concerned with targeting and poverty alleviation will fail to achieve the universal objectives of *promotion* and *protection* of human capability linked to a developmental strategy, because of the limited objectives of targeting. Moreover, a targeting strategy is usually promoted in the context of budgetary constraints and limited state financial capacity which are used to justify a reduction in social policy spending.

What MENA needs is a return to the universalist social policy ideals of a developmental state but within a democratic political environment that promotes genuine popular engagement and participation, as well as transparency and accountability, in order to arrive at an inclusive and new social contract. The details and boundaries of this new social contract would be country-specific and depend on the national political and economic developments.

Appendix Table 14.1 Key social protection programmes, MENA, in 2017, 2018

Country	*Old age pension* [(a,b)]	*Sickness, maternity* [(a,b)]	*Work injury* [(a,b)]	*Unemployment* [(a,b)]	*Family allowance* [(c)]
North Africa					
Algeria	+	+	+	+	+
Djibouti	+	+	+	-	+
Egypt	+	+	+	+	-
Libya	+	+	+	+	+
Mauritania	+	+	+	-	+
Morocco	+	+	+	+	+
Sudan	+	+	+	+	-
Tunisia	+	+	+	+	+
Middle East					
Bahrain	+	+	+	+	+
Iran	+	+	+	+	+
Iraq	+	NA	NA	NA	NA
Jordan	+	+	+	+	+
Kuwait	+	+	+	+	+
Lebanon	+	+	+	-	+
Oman	+	+	+	-	+
Palestinian Authority	+	NA	NA	NA	NA
Qatar	+	+	+	-	+
Saudi Arabia	+	+	+	-	+
Syria	+	+	+	-	-
Turkey	+	+	+	+	+

Source: Author's compilation based on ISSA Country Profiles (ISSA, 2019).

Notes:

(+) programme

(-) no programme

NA: not available in ISSA.

a. Type of programme: mostly social insurance contributions (funded by employees and employers), supplemented by other regulatory framework (e.g. unemployment lumpsum payment funded by employers and/or government) and social assistance programmes.

b. Coverage: mostly formal sector employees including state employees.

c. Family allowance is based on the number of children and dependant wives in some cases.

Notes

1 This chapter is partly based on my earlier works: Messkoub (2006a), and Jawad, Jones and Messkoub (2019). The latter provided me with inspiring ideas on social policy in MENA. I wish to thank my co-editors for their inspirations. I would also like to thank Hassan Hakimian for his judicious comments on earlier drafts of the chapter. His patience with my stretching the deadline has also been greatly appreciated! The remaining errors are, alas, mine.
2 For further details, see Cammett, Richards and Waterbury (2015), Karshenas and Moghadam (2006) and Karshenas and Moghadam (2009).
3 See for example Ghai (2000) and Mkandawire (2004).
4 See, for example, Article 19 in Iran's first constitution after the Constitutional Revolution of 1905–1911 (Messkoub, 2006b), Algeria's public provisioning of free health and education services to overcome decades of neglect under the French colonial rule (Layachi, 2006) and Egypt's provision of free public education under the National Charter of May 1962 – the *Al-Mithaq al-Watani* Charter (Bayat, 2006).
5 However, the region still lags behind East Asian countries with similar per capita income in areas such as female literacy rates and female tertiary enrolment (Karshenas and Moghadam, 2009).
6 For further details see Cammett and MacLean (2014: 11–14) and references therein.
7 For other assessment and details of different phases of social policy developments in the MENA see Yousef (2004) and Karshenas (2001).
8 This was on par with other middle-income countries, but below those of middle-income Latin American countries: 2.4% in 2001 and 3.9% in 2016.
9 For further discussion of social protection and health service provisions see Karshenas, Moghadam and Alami (2014) and Loewe and Jawad (2018).
10 For further discussion of the growth–employment nexus and in MENA see Messkoub (2008) and ILO (2015).
11 Social safety nets include cash transfers, workfare programmes, price subsidies (e.g., on food and energy) and fee waivers (e.g., gaining access to health and education; Silva et al. 2013: 45).
12 Estimate based on Iranian government information on subsidies (*Donya-e Eqtesad*, 12 Nov. 2019) and IMF figures on the GDP of Iran (IMF, 2018).
13 In the 1980s and 1990s, several MENA and Sub-Saharan African countries that suffered from high inflation and balance of payments deficits were advised by the international financial institutions to adopt orthodox structural adjustment programmes as a condition for balance of payments support. These led to sudden increases in prices of fuel, food and other basic goods. Strong resistance by the low-income groups who had to bear the brunt of price rises either led to the reforms being abandoned or to severe repression while pushing more people into poverty.
14 See references in Chapter 4 of Silva et al. (2013).
15 For a brief account of some subsidy reform programmes around the world see Silva et al. (2013: Chs. 4–5). For a detailed account of the reform of the indirect subsidy reform in Iran's energy sector and the use of compensatory CT and its comparison with other countries, see Messkoub (2019).
16 For a review of the state social policy and its reforms in MENA see, e.g., Silva et al. (2013), ESCWA (2019), Tzannatos (2000) and Sdralevich et al. (2014).

Bibiography

Barro, R. and J.W. Lee (2010), 'A New Data Set of Educational Attainment in the World 1950–2010', http://barrolee.com/data/dataexp.htm

Bayat, A. (2006), 'The Political Economy of Social Policy in Egypt', in Karshenas and Moghadam (2006), pp. 135–155.

Blakemore, K. (1998), *Social Policy: An Introduction*. Buckingham: Open University Press.

Brixi, H., Lust, E. and M. Woolcock (2015), *Trust, Voice and Incentives: Learning from Local Success Stories in Service Delivery in the Middle East and North Africa*. Washington, DC: World Bank.

Cammett, M. (2014), 'Secterian Politics and Social Welfare', in Cammett and MacLean, eds. (2014), pp. 137–156.

Cammett, M. and L.M. MacLean, eds. (2014), *The Politics of Non-state Social Welfare*. Ithaca: Cornell University Press.

Cammett, M., Richards, A. and J. Waterbury (2015), *A Political Economy of the Middle East: State, Class and Economic Development*. Fourth edition. Boulder, CO: Westview Press.
Del Geranado, J., Coady, A.D. and R. Gillingham (2010), 'The Unequal Benefits of Fuel Subsidies: A Review of Evidence for Developing Countries', Working Paper 10/202. Washington, DC: IMF.
Donya-e Eqtesad (2019), *Economic World, an Iranian Daily Paper Specializing on Iranian Economy*, 12 November.
ESCWA (2019), *Social Protection Reform in Arab Countries*. Beirut: UN, ESCWA.
Esping-Anderson, G. (1990), *The Three Worlds of Welfare Capitalism*. Princeton: Princeton University Press.
FAO (2007), *The Status of Rural Poverty in the Near East and North Africa*. Rome: FAO, 44p.
Fattouh, B. and L. El-Katiri (2012), *Energy Subsidies in the Arab World*. Arab Human Development Report Research Paper Series. New York: UNDP.
Financial Times (2019), 'Iran's Fuel Price Crisis Shows Economy Strangled under US Sanctions', 19 November.
Fraser, N. (1989), *Unruly Practices: Power, Discourse and Gender in Contemporary Social Theory*. Minneapolis: University of Minnesota Press.
Ghai, D. (2000), 'Social Development and Public Policy: Some Lessons from Successful Experiences', in Ghai, D. (ed.), *Social Development and Public Policy*. London: Palgrave Macmillan.
Ghosh, J. (2004), 'Social Policy in Indian Development', in Mkandawire, T. (ed.), *Social Policy in a Development Context*. Geneva: UNRISD; London: Palgrave-Macmillan.
Green, M. (2012), *Co-Producing Ineffective States: Social Knowledge, Social Policy and Social Citizenship in Africa and in Development*, ESID Working Paper No. 14.
Hakimian, H. and Z. Moshaver (eds.) (2001), *The State and Global Change: The Political Economy of Transition in the Middle East and North Africa*. London: Curzon Press.
IMF (2018), *Islamic Republic of Iran*. IMF Country Report No. 18/93.
ILO (2005), *World Employment Report 2004–05: Employment, Productivity and Poverty*. Geneva: ILO.
ILO (2006), *Employment Poverty Linkages and Policies for Pro-poor Growth in Jordan (1990–2003)*. Geneva: ILO. Second Draft. Mimeo (restricted document).
ILO (2014), *World Social Security Report 2014–15: Building Economic Recovery, Inclusive Development and Social Justice*. Geneva: ILO.
ILO (2015), *Key Indicators of the Labour Market (KILM)*. Ninth edition. Geneva: ILO.
ILO (2017), *World Social Security Report 2017–19: Universal Social Protection to Achieve the Sustainable Development Goals*. Geneva: ILO.
ISSA (International Social Security Association) (2019), *Country Profiles*. https://www.issa.int/en_GB/country-profiles. [Accessed August 2019].
Jawad, R. (2009), *Social Welfare and Religion in the Middle East: A Lebanese Perspective*. Bristol: Polity Press.
Jawad, R., Jones, N. and M. Messkoub (eds.) (2019), *Social Policy in the Middle East and North Africa: The New Social Protection Paradigm and Universal Coverage*. Cheltenham: Edward Elgar Publishers.
Karshenas, M. (2001), 'Structural Obstacles to Economic Adjustment in the MENA Region: The International Trade Aspects', in Hakimian and Moshaver (2001), pp. 59–80.
Karshenas, M. and V. Moghadam (eds.) (2006), *Social Policy in the Middle East and North Africa*. Basingsoke: Palgrave Macmillan; Geneva: UN Research Institute for Social Development.
Karshenas, M. and V. Moghadam (2009), 'Bringing Social Policy Back: A Look at the Middle East and North Africa', *International Journal of Social Welfare*, Vol. 18, pp. S52–S61.
Karshenas, M., Moghadam, V. and R. Alami (2014), 'Social Policy after the Arab Spring: States and Social Rights in the MENA Region', *World Development*, Vol. 64, No. C, pp. 726–739.
Kwan, H-J, Mkandawire, T. and J. Plame (2009), 'Introduction: Social Policy and Economic Development in Late Industrializers', *International Journal of Social Welfare*, Vol. 18, pp. S1–S11.
Layachi, A. (2006), 'Algeria: Crisis, Transition and Social Policy Outcomes', in Karshenas and Moghadam (2006), pp. 78–108.
Loewe, M. (2009), *Pension Schemes and Pension Reforms in the Middle East and North Africa*. Geneva: UNRISD.
Loewe, M. (2019), 'Social Protection Schemes in the Middle East and North Africa: Not Fair, Not Efficient, Not Effective', in Jawad, Jones and Messkoub (2019), pp. 35–60.
Loewe, M. and R. Jawad (2018), 'Introducing Social Protection in the Middle East and North Africa: Prospects for a New Social Contract', *International Social Security Review*, Vol. 71, pp. 3–18.
Mehri, N., Messkoub, M. and S. Kunkle (2020), 'Trends, Determinants and The Implications of Population Aging in Iran', *Ageing International*, Vol. 45, pp. 327–343.
Messkoub, M., (2006a) 'Social Policy in Iran in the 20th Century', *Iranian Studies*, Vol. 39, No. 2, pp. 227–252.

Messkoub, M. (2006b), 'Constitutionalism, Modernization and Islamization: A Political Economy of Social Policy in Iran', in Karshenas and Moghadam (2006), pp. 190–220.

Messkoub, M. (2008), *Economic Growth, Employment and Poverty in the Middle East and North Africa*. ILO Working Paper Series, No. 19, Geneva.

Messkoub, M. (2017), 'Population Ageing and Inter-generational Relation in the MENA: What Role for Social Policy?', *Population Horizons*, December.

Messkoub, M. (2019), 'Cash Transfer as a Social Policy Instrument or a Tool of Adjustment Policy: From Indirect Subsidies (to Energy and Utilities), to Cash Subsidies in Iran, 2010–2017', in Jawad, Jones and Messkoub (2019), pp. 116–133.

Mkandawire, T. (ed.) (2004), *Social Policy in a Development Context*. Basingstoke: Palgrave-Macmillan/ UNRISD.

Moghadam, V. (2006), 'Gender and Social Policy: Family Law and Women's Economic Citizenship in MENA Countries', in Karshenas and Moghadam (2006), pp. 221–253.

Nicolle, E. and I. Mathauer (2010), *Administrative Costs of Health Insurance Schemes: Exploring the Reasons for Their Variability*, Geneva: WHO.

Robalino, D.A. et al. (2005), *Pensions in the Middle East and North Africa Time for Change*. Washington, DC: World Bank.

Sdralevich, C., Sab, R., Zouhar, Y. and G. Albertin (2014), *Subsidy Reform in the Middle East and North Africa.: Recent Progress and Challenges Ahead*. Washington, DC: IMF.

Selwaness, I. and M. Messkoub (2019), 'The Egyptian Social Protection System: Coverage Gaps, Challenges and Opportunities', in Jawad, Jones and Messkoub, (2019).

Silva, J., Levin, V. and M. Morgandi (2013), *Inclusion and Resilience: The Way Forward for Social Safety Nets in the Middle East and North Africa*. Washington, DC: World Bank. doi:10.1596/978-0-8213-9771-8.

Tzannatos, Z. (2000), *Social Protection Middle East and North Africa Region*. Washington, DC: The World Bank.

Tzannatos, Z. (2009), *The Global Financial, Economic and Social Crisis and the Arab Countries: A Review of the Evidence and Policies for Employment Creation and Social Protection*. Beirut: ILO Regional Office for Arab States.

UNDP (2012), *Arab Development Report 2011*. Cairo: UNDP.

Walton, J.K. and D. Seddon (1994), *Free Markets and Food Riots: The Politics of Global Adjustment*. London: Wiley-Blackwell.

WHO (World Health Organisation) (2010), *World Health Report 2010*. Geneva: WHO.

WHO (World Health Organisation) (2019), Out-of-pocket Expenditure as Percentage of Current Health Expenditure (CHE), (%), Data by Country [2000–2015]. Geneva: WHO. http://apps.who.int/gho/data/node.main.GHEDOOPSCHESHA2011?lang=en [Accessed 15 August 2019].

World Bank (2008), The Road Not Traveled: Education Reform in the Middle East and North Africa. Washington, DC: IBRD.

World Bank (2009), *2008 Economic Development and Prospects: Regional Integration for Global Competitiveness. Middle East and North Africa Region*. Washington, DC: IBRD.

World Bank (2011), *World Development Report*. Washington, DC: IBRD.

World Bank (2018), *The State of Social Safety Nets*. Washington, DC: IBRD.

World Bank (2019), *Domestic General Government Health Expenditure (% of GDP), – Middle East & North Africa*. Washington, DC: World Bank. https://data.worldbank.org/indicator/SH.XPD.PVTD.CH.ZS?locations=ZQ [Accessed 21 October 2019].

Yousef, T.M. (2004), 'Development Growth and Policy Reform in the Middle East and North Africa since 1950', *Journal of Economic Perspectives*, Vol. 18, No. 3, pp. 91–116.

SECTION V

Institutions and transition to democracy

15

RELIGION AND POLITICS

Why the West got rich and the Middle East did not

Jared Rubin

15.1 Introduction

Understanding why the "West got rich" is one of the most important pursuits in economic history. The modern economy was born in northwestern Europe (England and the Dutch Republic) at some point in the 18th or 19th centuries, and has subsequently spread to many parts of the world. What was it about northwestern Europe at that particular point in time that allowed for such dramatic and rapid economic growth?

The converse of this question is equally interesting and important: why did the modern economy *not* first emerge in other parts of the world? As of the year 1000 C.E., parts of the Middle East, China, Eastern Europe and South Asia were much more likely candidates for an eventual economic fluorescence than northwestern Europe. The Middle East presents a particularly puzzling case. For centuries following the spread of Islam, the "Islamic world," which spread from Spain in the West to South Asia in the East, was much wealthier, technologically progressive, and more politically integrated than anywhere in Europe. Even when European economies started to revive in the 10th–13th centuries (a period known as the "Commercial Revolution"), Middle Eastern economies were hardly laggards. Moreover, there was much cross-cultural sharing of technology, institutions, and trade between Europe and the Middle East. Yet, by 1600, and likely before, many of the important pieces of northwestern Europe's eventual rise were already in place whereas nothing resembling the building blocks of the modern economy were present in the Middle East. What can explain this reversal of fortunes?

In this chapter, I provide an explanation for the reversal of fortunes which focuses on the role that *political legitimacy* plays in economic outcomes. Much of the framework I overview comes from my book *Rulers, Religion, and Riches: Why the West Got Rich and the Middle East Did Not*. This book builds a framework for understanding political legitimacy as an economic and political equilibrium. Rulers need legitimacy (and/or access to coercive power) to rule effectively, and there are individuals in society that can provide legitimacy. The outcome—economic policy—is thus a reflection of the bargaining power and the desires of the ruler and their various legitimating agents. This chapter proceeds to employ this framework on Middle Eastern and Western European history, drawing from my own work and the work of other economic historians who have worked on similar questions.

In short, we can answer the question "why did the modern economy first emerge in Western Europe, and not the Middle East?" (in part) by considering the role that *religious legitimacy* played in politics in the two regions. For historical reasons, Islam was better than Christianity at legitimating political rule. Although it ebbed and flowed by period and region, this tended to give Muslim religious authorities a greater seat at the political bargaining table than Christian religious authorities. This meant that policies tended to reflect the interests of religious authorities to a greater extent in the Middle East than in Western Europe. And while the desires of religious authorities in both religions were not necessarily antithetical to commerce, they were not exactly favourable to commerce either. On the other hand, in Western Europe the political power of religious authorities declined beginning around the 12th or 13th century—and this decline was exacerbated by the Reformation—and they were largely replaced by parliaments at the political bargaining table. Parliaments represented the economic elite (among others), and were more likely to bargain for the types of policies that favoured the economic elite. It happened that these types of policies, such as secure property rights, infrastructure investment, and the provision of certain types of public goods, also helped spur economic growth more generally. In this chapter, I will lay out how and why these historical processes unfolded when and where they did.

15.2 The framework

The game-theoretic framework formulated in Rubin (2017) considers the interactions between rulers and "legitimating agents." It is premised on the notion that rulers desire first and foremost to stay in power, and they have two (non-mutually exclusive) means to do so: coercion and legitimacy. Coercive power is the capability of forcing others to take actions via the threat of violence, and rulers derive coercive power from coercive agents such as militias, police, or warlords. Legitimacy is an intrinsic concept: people follow a ruler they view as legitimate because they believe that ruler has the right to rule and be obeyed. There are numerous individuals in any society that can contribute to a ruler's legitimacy. Tribal elders can support a national leader (as in parts of modern-day central Asia), landed elite can signify they follow a ruler and thus their subjects (i.e., those working their land) should do the same, and *religious elite* can credibly signal that a ruler is pious or just and thus should be followed.

The set of coercive and legitimating agents a ruler decides to negotiate with depends on the costs and benefits of what they can provide to the ruler. These costs and benefits differ across time and place, and thus different legitimating arrangements arise across time and place. The benefits of coercive power are reflective of the capacity of coercive agents to make people follow a ruler via the threat or use of violence. This depends on the state of military and information technology, a society's urbanisation level, and numerous other economic, social, and political features. Meanwhile, the benefits of legitimation depend on how effective legitimating agents are at affecting the beliefs of people regarding the ruler's right to rule. The efficacy of religious legitimation depends on the religiosity of society as well as the degree to which religious doctrine supports legitimation of rule.[1]

The costs of employing coercive and legitimating agents also affect how rulers use them. Gill (1998) pointed out that religious legitimation is *cheap*: historically, religious authorities would support political rulers, even those who acted contrary to religious doctrine, without expecting too much in return. This was true of both Muslim and Christian religious authorities, who often sought protection from rival religions (i.e., violent suppression of "heresy"), tax exemption, and the occasional policy concession (such as condemnation of usury). These costs paled in comparison to paying coercive agents—armies or policing units are not cheap—and were especially inexpensive relative to legitimation from the economic elite. Out of their own self-interest, the economic elite tend to desire the biggest prizes of all: protection of property rights (at least, their own property rights) and investment in large-scale projects (e.g., infrastructure). *De facto* property rights are particularly expensive for rulers to relinquish, since they are useful as a tool of political control and a source of emergency funds.

The benefits and costs of various forms of coercion and legitimacy determine both who rulers bring to the political bargaining table as well as the outcome of the bargain. Agents do not provide coercion and legitimacy free of charge; they expect something in return. The outcome of this bargain is the laws and policies enacted by the ruler, which reflect the interests and bargaining power of all the parties at the bargaining table. Hence, where religious legitimacy is particularly effective, the interests of religious authorities will be well-represented in the laws and policies of that society. The historical question to address is therefore why religious legitimation has been more effective in some societies than others, and why that changed—or stagnated—over time. Rubin (2011, 2017) contends that Muslim religious authorities were more effective at legitimating rule than Christian religious authorities due to the historical circumstances surrounding the births of the two religions. In short, Islam was formulated conterminously with an expanding empire in need of legitimation. As a result, numerous passages in the corpus of Islamic thought and law support the idea that Muslims should follow a ruler who acts in accordance with Islam but should overthrow a ruler who does not.[2] Of course, it is the religious establishment that has the capacity to interpret which actions are in accordance with Islamic dictates and which are not. To be clear, this is a more nuanced concept than the one proposed by Bernard Lewis (2002), which suggests that there was never a separation of "church and state" as there was in Christianity. While it is true that the lines between church and state were not as clear as they were in the Christian world, Muslim rulers rarely attempted to claim a monopoly on religious interpretation after the first few caliphs of the 7th century. Instead, the leading religious scholars formulated doctrine or fatwas that generally supported the ruler and their proposed policies, knowing they would receive concessions in return. This is the interaction at the heart of the proposed framework.

On the other hand, Christianity was born into the Roman Empire, which already had well-functioning political institutions and means of political legitimation. Indeed, for its first three centuries, Christians were persecuted and clearly in no position to legitimate the emperor. By the time that Constantine adopted Christianity in the early 4th century, there was a large corpus of Christian doctrine supporting the separate spheres of church and state. The most famous of these doctrines is attributed to Jesus: "Render unto Caesar the things which are Caesar's, and unto God the things that are God's" (Matthew 22:21). While it was hardly the case that Christianity was incapable of legitimating political rule—it clearly did during much of the medieval period, and it is a source of legitimacy in parts of the world today—the point is that it was not as effective at legitimating rule as was Islam.

Rubin (2017) proceeds to elaborate on some of the consequences of these differences in legitimating arrangements. First, building off the model laid out in Rubin (2011), the framework is employed to understand the divergent paths of usury (i.e., interest on loans) restrictions in the two religions. Both religions banned usury for over a millennium, but starting in the 13th century usury restrictions became greatly relaxed in Europe while they were still formally in place in parts of the Islamic world. The framework suggests why this outcome arose. In the Middle East, it was easy to evade interest restrictions through any number of costly ruses. While merchants and money-lenders would have had much to gain from being able to freely lend and borrow at interest without worry of their contracts being invalidated, the fact that they could lend via ruse meant that commerce flowed with only minimal impediments. Meanwhile, there was much to gain for political authorities from supporting and enforcing usury restrictions: it was part of the bargain in which in return for religious legitimacy, they permitted Islamic law (which forbade usury) to largely be the law of the land. Since the marginal benefit of further relaxations of usury laws (i.e., more commerce) would have been minimal relative to the loss of religious legitimacy, an equilibrium emerged in which rulers and religious authorities permitted ruses but forbade open lending at interest, and most people followed the law. On the other hand, in Europe the benefits to religious legitimacy were lower. Thus, when commerce began to revive in the 12th–13th centuries and thus the benefits of permitting lending at interest increased, there were similar benefits but *lower costs* for European rulers to relax usury restrictions. Indeed, in this period secular interest rate caps arose throughout Europe, providing a legal mechanism to lend at moderate interest.[3]

A more important consequence of religious legitimation was the differing responses to the printing press in Western Europe and the Middle East. While the press spread rapidly after its invention by Johannes Gutenberg in 1450—by 1500, most large cities in Europe had at least one press—the Ottoman Empire forbade printing in the Arabic script for almost *250 years* after learning of it. The framework, which draws heavily from Coşgel et al. (2012), sheds light on the Ottoman reaction to the press. The press would have been a significant threat to the Ottoman religious establishment, as it would have potentially undermined their monopoly over the transmission of knowledge. In the preceding centuries, the religious establishment—in the Ottoman Empire and elsewhere in the Islamic world—imposed increasingly large barriers to entry. To become a religious scholar, one had to memorise thousands of passages and be able to render interpretations based on these passages. The press could have undermined these barriers to entry by making access to religious knowledge available cheaply to anyone with the capacity to read. Thus, it is obvious why the religious establishment would want the press blocked. The framework is useful because it reveals why *secular* rulers would consent to the wishes of the religious establishment, despite the obvious benefits of permitting the press (both economic and propaganda). Even if there were significant benefits to permitting printing, the costs of undermining their key source of legitimation were too high to allow the technology to spread. This intuition *also* explains why the press spread so quickly in Europe. It is not as if similar pressures did not face the Church: indeed, the press was one of the key reasons the Reformation was able to succeed (Rubin, 2014, 2017, ch. 6). The key difference between Western Europe and the Middle East was that by the time of the invention of the printing press, the Church was no longer in a strong position to legitimate Christian rulers. Thus, the cost of permitting printing was much lower to European rulers, and as a result the press spread with little interference from political authorities.

There is much research outside of Rubin (2017) suggesting that religious legitimacy played a key role in determining political economy and economic outcomes in Western Europe and the Middle East. Chaney (2013) presents a fascinating study of political power and religion in medieval Egypt. He found that religious authorities were much less likely to be replaced following Nile floods or droughts. Although Chaney interprets this as evidence that religious authorities were more likely to coordinate revolt under these conditions, the framework presented above provides a more straight-forward (and complementary) explanation. During economic shocks, rulers were more vulnerable to mass discontent. Thus, religious legitimacy would have been particularly effective during these periods as a means of quelling the masses. In turn, this means that religious authorities would have had a stronger seat at the bargaining table, which would have resulted (among other things) in their staying in power.

Johnson and Koyama (2019) employ the framework in Rubin (2017) to argue that states with weak state capacity are more likely to persecute religious and ethnic minorities. The idea is straight-forward: rulers that have little capacity to provide rule of law or collect taxes are likely to rely more heavily on religious legitimacy to stay in power, since they have few other institutionalised sources of power. In times of crisis, one way to gain support of the elites and the population as a whole is to burnish one's religious credentials, which can take the form of persecuting minorities, whether real (Jews, Muslims) or imagined (witches). As European states matured and depended on alternative forms of legitimacy (such as parliaments and nationalism), such persecutions became much more infrequent.

Greif and Rubin (2021) extend the framework proposed in Rubin (2017) to argue that changes in how the English monarch was legitimated following the Wars of the Roses (1455–85) played a key role in the rise of the rule of law and limited governance in England in the period prior to industrialisation. The low legitimacy of the Tudors (Henry VII won the crown on the battlefield; it was not inherited) combined with the removal of the Church during the Reformation meant that the Crown had to turn elsewhere for legitimacy. Greif and Rubin contend that they turned to the English Parliament, whose source of power came from its capacity to create laws. This in turn increased the importance of following the law as a source of legitimacy in England.[4] Such processes never occurred in the Middle East, where religious legitimacy remained a potent source of power. This is perhaps one of the many reasons why the rule of law has been weak (if it exists at all) in most Middle Eastern societies in the 20th and 21st centuries.

15.3 Application: the Ottoman Empire

By 1500, the Ottoman Empire was one of the major players in both Europe and the Middle East. In 1453, the Ottomans conquered Constantinople, in the process finishing off the Byzantine Empire. In 1517, the Ottomans defeated the Egyptian Mamluk Empire, giving them purview over most of the north coast of Africa and, importantly, the holy cities of Mecca and Medina. For much of the century following the conquest of Constantinople, the Ottomans seemed unstoppable, approaching the gates of Vienna in the West and Persia in the East. Economically, the Ottomans rivalled the great European powers, and Istanbul was as important a cultural and economic centre as London, Amsterdam, or Paris. Yet, by 1600 a disparity began to emerge between the Ottomans and the leading European powers, and this disparity would widen over the following two centuries. By the 19th century, the Ottoman Empire was widely known as the "sick man of Europe." What happened? Why could the Ottomans not turn their early military and economic success into long-run, sustainable growth? Why did the modern economy emerge in northwestern Europe and not the Ottoman Empire?

The framework laid out above sheds light on the mechanisms that contributed to the Ottoman Empire's relative economic stagnation. Rubin (2017, ch. 8) notes that, especially after the defeat of the Mamluk Empire gave the Ottomans purview over Mecca and Medina, religious legitimacy became a key source of power to the sultanate. They brought the religious establishment into the state, creating the office of the Grand Mufti to issue important legal decisions. This gave the sultan the cover of religious legitimacy on what would have otherwise been controversial actions (such as attacking other Muslim powers, like the Egyptian Mamluks or the Persian Safavids). Moreover, key religious figures would frequently invoke the name of the sultan in the Friday prayers, thus appealing to the legitimating concept of the ruler acting like a "good Muslim."

The religious establishment did not legitimate the sultanate free of charge, of course. The most consequential concession made to the religious establishment, from an economic point of view, was that commercial law remained within the purview of Islamic courts. This had enormous unintended and unforeseeable consequences, many of which are detailed in Kuran

(2011). For one, the confluence of Islamic partnership law and Islamic inheritance law resulted in little demand for large, long-lasting business forms like the corporation. Kuran's insight is that Islamic inheritance law set strict, pre-ordained guidelines for how one's estate should be split upon death. Unlike primogeniture, which was common in some parts of Europe, the Islamic inheritance system typically specified many heirs receive a portion of the inheritance. This was an issue for potential partnerships because a partnership automatically ceased upon the death of one of its members, with the proceeds split among many heirs. These heirs could immediately reconstitute the partnership, but this would entail the cooperation of all (or most) of the heirs. These facets of Islamic law thus discouraged large partnerships: every partner added to the partnership increased the probability that some unforeseen event (i.e., a death of a partner) could prematurely dissolve the operation. This could result in a staggering loss to all partners. One way to reduce the odds of such a fate occurring were to keep partnerships small and of limited duration.

Meanwhile, precisely the opposite series of events occurred in Western Europe in the late medieval and early modern periods. Kuran (2005) notes that at the same time Middle Eastern business forms were stagnating, European ones progressively became more complex. Simple partnerships were replaced by family firms, which themselves were replaced by joint-stock companies. These incremental advancements solved problems associated with large-scale commerce, such as short life and unlimited liability. By the 17th century, the leading commercial centres of Europe had relatively advanced organisational forms that culminated in the corporation. Such an organisational form was far more advanced than anything available in the Middle East.

Islamic law stifled commerce for reasons well beyond disincentivising larger-scale business partnerships. Another key aspect of Islamic law which affected commerce was that it was *partial*. Certain groups (men, Muslims, elites) were *ceteris paribus* much more likely to win cases related to commerce in Islamic courts (Kuran and Lustig, 2012). This had an unintended, negative consequence for those favoured by the court system: they had to pay *higher* interest on loans than their unfavoured counterparts. This is contrary to the conventional relationship between elite status and credit cost. Since elites in most societies are viewed as better credit risks, they generally pay less for credit. However, Kuran and Rubin (2018) find that elites, men, and Muslims all paid more for credit than non-elites, women, and non-Muslims, respectively. The differences in credit cost were not trivial, ranging from 1.9–3.4 additional percentage points. The reason that those favoured by the courts paid more for credit is because of the courts' partiality, which allowed them to renege with relative impunity. In other words, the partiality of Ottoman courts made those favoured by the courts greater credit risks. This must have had a dampening effect on commerce, investment, and entrepreneurship in the Ottoman Empire. Those with the most resources and connections to invest in capital and business enterprises had to pay the *most* to do so.

15.4 Science and slave soldiers

Research by Eric Chaney and Lisa Blaydes has uncovered two phenomena regarding the economic and political divergence between Western Europe and the Middle East to which the framework described above applies. First, Chaney (2016) documents in great detail that Islamic science, as measured by publications and citations of Muslim authors, was far ahead of European science until the 12th century. By the end of the 15th century, European science had far surpassed that of the Muslim world. Second, Blaydes and Chaney (2013) show that around the 10th century the duration of European rulers' reigns became longer than those in the Islamic world, and this divergence grew throughout the remainder of the medieval period. This is an important metric, because longer tenure represents relative stability of political rule. Can the framework proposed above account for these phenomena?

Chaney (2016) argues that the rise of the madrassa system around the 11th–12th centuries was responsible for the decline in Islamic science. In this view, religious and (Islamic) legal texts became more important and attracted more patronage than scientific works, thus precipitating a decline in Islamic science. This interpretation is consistent with the framework proposed above. As the Sunni schools of jurisprudence consolidated in the 10th–11th centuries, the legitimating capacity of religious scholars—who gained independence from various Muslim states in the 9th–10th centuries—grew substantially. It follows from the framework that they would seek to institutionalise their position and the patronage they received from rulers. Madrassas were one of the important mechanisms through which this institutionalisation occurred. In the process, the academic elite placed more intellectual effort in religious interpretation, at the expense of science. This undoubtedly had an impact on the larger economic divergence between the two regions. As late as the 10th century—and likely as late as the 12th century—Europe was a technological laggard, and almost all scientific and technological breakthroughs flowed from East to West (i.e., from China, South Asia, or the Middle East to Europe) (Mokyr, 1990). However, by the onset of the early modern period (c. 1500) Europe had clearly caught up with the rest of the world. By 1750, on the eve of industrialisation, Europe was clearly ahead, and this advantage would increase by many orders of magnitude by the end of the 19th century.

Meanwhile, Blaydes and Chaney (2013) argue that the use of slave soldiers (*mamluks*) was responsible for the divergence in ruler tenure between the Christian West and the Muslim Middle East. The central idea they put forward is that European rulers were constrained by feudal lords, who doubled as their primary military units. Because European rulers were relatively weak militarily, they had to give concessions to their landed-*cum*-military elite. On the other hand, Muslim rulers were able to avoid bargaining with their economic elites because they did not need them for military service. Instead, Muslim rulers historically employed slave soldiers taken from conquered lands as the basis of their militaries. Slave soldiers could rise in the ranks and become quite powerful—indeed, the Egyptian Mamluk Empire was ruled by a caste of soldiers of slave origin—but because their positions were not hereditary, they held no real bargaining power vis-à-vis the ruler. In comparative terms, this means that European polities were more stable, since a larger share of the elite had some voice in politics. This meant fewer internal enemies for the kings and queens of Europe and thus longer dynastic tenure. Meanwhile, Muslim rulers were more easily able to rule with an iron fist and ignore other elites. While this gave them much more leverage to pursue any policy they desired, it also made them more enemies among their own citizens. As a result, Muslim rulers were more frequently murdered or overthrown, resulting in shorter average duration of rule.

These findings are consistent with a framework based on diverging legitimating arrangements in Western Europe and the Middle East. Indeed, a central implication of the framework proposed above is that European rulers ended up bargaining with their economic elites to a much greater extent than Middle Eastern rulers. While Blaydes and Chaney focus on feudal lords as the primary agents who constrained rulers, the mechanism through which they did so was parliament. These parliaments ultimately included urban, commercial leaders, whose economic interests coincided with those features that portend growth (e.g., property rights, public goods provision). Meanwhile, while Blaydes and Chaney focus on slave soldiers as a source of power for Middle Eastern rulers, this is not inconsistent with a framework that emphasises religious legitimacy. The framework suggests that rulers bargain with both coercive agents and legitimating agents. To the extent that neither of these types of agents has interests aligned with economic development—which was the case for slave soldiers and the Muslim religious establishment—it follows that the types of laws and policies enacted in those societies would not be consistent with economic development.

15.5 The institutional structure of Islam

In addition to having different capacities to legitimate political rule, (Sunni) Islam and (Catholic) Christianity also have different institutional structures. The Catholic Church is famously hierarchical, with the papacy and cardinals sitting at the top, followed by archbishops and bishops, all the way down to local parish priests. Meanwhile, Sunni Islam has a much more horizontal structure. Any learned scholar can produce fatwas and attract followers. Historically, there was no hierarchical structure in Sunni Islam: jurists attracted followers based on the quality of their opinions and interpretations, and there were no formal institutions determining one's place among other jurists.

Jean-Philippe Platteau argues that these differences in institutional structures resulted in different outcomes with respect to the manner in which Islam has been employed by Muslim rulers. His insight, laid out theoretically in Auriol and Platteau (2017) and in great historical detail in Platteau (2017), argues that the decentralised nature of Islam meant that in order to "seduce" the religious elite, Muslim rulers had to choose how much to cede to authorities in order to attract the support of a fraction of them. The remaining authorities, who disagreed with the ruler, served as potential enemies (or leaders of opposition movements), thus creating a source of instability. Meanwhile, Christian rulers only had to negotiate with one religious authority ("the Church"), and by gaining the support of this authority would gain the support of the entire religious establishment. This served as a source of relative stability: assuming that most of the church hierarchy would fall in line with the leaders, rulers only needed to negotiate with church leaders in order to secure the support of the entire establishment.

Platteau's (and Auriol's) theory complements the one presented above because it provides an additional reason why Muslim rulers depended on religious legitimacy to a greater extent than Christian rulers. According to Platteau, Muslim rulers had to "seduce" more of the religious establishment in order to provide insulation against revolt. While this theory does not do as good of a job at explaining why religious legitimacy ebbed and flowed with the rise and fall of commerce in Europe, it does provide additional insight into why the relationship between the political and religious elite was historically different in Europe and the Middle East. This, in turn, provides yet another mechanism for why the Middle Eastern political equilibrium was more self-enforcing than the European equilibrium. This is an important point to understand, since getting religion (mostly) out of politics was a key to Europe's eventual economic rise as well as the Middle East's long-run economic stagnation.

15.6 Conclusion

This chapter has overviewed the framework proposed in Rubin (2017), which attempts to shed light on the institutional mechanisms underlying the long-run economic divergence between Western Europe and the Middle East. We have argued that, for historical reasons, religious legitimacy played a more important role in Middle Eastern political bargains, and this was reflected in laws and policies. On the other hand, as commerce re-emerged in Europe in the 10th–13th centuries and the Reformation provided the death knell to the Church in parts of Europe, Christian rulers turned elsewhere for legitimacy. Specifically, they relied on legitimacy from the economic elites in their parliaments. These economic elites had interests that were more consistent with long-run economic success (e.g., property rights, public goods), and these interests were reflected in the grand political bargain. Economic elites rarely had a seat at the political bargaining table in Middle Eastern history (or, for that matter, in the present), and thus laws and policies favouring commerce were less frequently enacted.

In this chapter, these theoretical insights are applied to the historical divergence between the Middle East and Western Europe, but they also hold many implications for the 21st century. For instance, the house of Saud rules Saudi Arabia primarily via a mixture of oil revenues and religious legitimacy provided by the Wahhabi establishment. One of the big questions that will determine the fate of the Saudi royal family—and arguably the fate of the entire region—is what happens when the oil money starts to run dry. This is likely going to happen at some point in the 21st century, as additional sources of petroleum are found in the U.S. and Arctic or alternative energy sources decrease the demand for oil. The framework proposed above suggests the possibility that the Saudi leadership will rely all the more heavily on religious legitimacy, likely to the detriment of its economy and its people. Turkey provides another fascinating case. What was once a secular republic has fallen back into a religiously supported autocracy under Recep Tayyip Erdoğan. That Erdoğan was so effective in employing the old "Ottoman blueprint" for ruling suggests that religious legitimacy has a strong pull in the region for the wannabe autocrat. This is a sobering thought for the future prosperity and peace in the region, but it is unavoidable when studying the history of Middle Eastern religion and politics. Iran provides yet another important case. Since the 1979 Iranian Revolution, Iran has ostensibly been ruled as a theocracy. Meanwhile, its population is one of the most "Western-oriented" in the region, especially in the urban areas. This suggests that, in the long run, religious legitimacy may not be as potent in Iran as in other nations in the region. How the Iranian religious leadership responds to threats to its leadership may therefore take a different flavour than in Saudi Arabia (or even in Turkey). This will be one of the most important political phenomena in the region over the next few decades, and it is one of which Western observers should remain aware.

Notes

1 These points are fleshed out theoretically in Bisin et al. (2021), who study how a society's religiosity and religious legitimation co-evolve under various societal parameters.
2 See Rubin (2017, pp. 49–62) for numerous examples of Islamic doctrine supporting the right to rule of any ruler who "follows Islam."
3 Seror (2018) presents a similar theory of usury restrictions which focuses on how such restrictions can affect religious norms via cultural diffusion processes. This theory complements the one in Rubin (2017), which focuses on the interaction between "higher level" elites.
4 Similarly, Cantoni et al. (2018) find that sources of legitimacy became more secular following the Reformation in the German lands. This resulted in fewer university students majoring in theology and less construction of religious buildings.

References

Auriol, Emmanuelle, and Jean-Philippe Platteau. 2017. "Religious Co-option in Autocracy: A Theory Inspired by History." *Journal of Development Economics* 127: 395–412.

Bisin, Alberto, Jared Rubin, Avner Seror, and Thierry Verdier. 2021. "Culture, Institutions, and the Long Divergence." Working Paper.

Blaydes, Lisa, and Eric Chaney. 2013. "The Feudal Revolution and Europe's Rise: Political Divergence of the Christian West and the Muslim World before 1500 CE." *American Political Science Review* 107(1): 16–34.

Cantoni, Davide, Jeremiah Dittmar, and Noam Yuchtman. 2018. "Religious Competition and Reallocation: The Political Economy of Secularization in the Protestant Reformation." *Quarterly Journal of Economics* 133(4): 2037–2096.

Chaney, Eric. 2013. "Revolt on the Nile: Economic Shocks, Religion, and Political Power." *Econometrica* 81(5): 2033–2053.

Chaney, Eric. 2016. "Religion and the Rise and Fall of Islamic Science." Working Paper.

Coşgel, Metin M., Thomas J. Miceli, and Jared Rubin. 2012. "The Political Economy of Mass Printing: Legitimacy, Revolt, and Technology Change in the Ottoman Empire." *Journal of Comparative Economics* 40(3): 357–371.

Gill, Anthony. 1998. *Rendering unto Caesar: The Catholic Church and the State in Latin America*. Chicago: University of Chicago Press.

Greif, Avner, and Jared Rubin. 2021. "Political Legitimacy and the Institutional Foundations of Constitutional Government: The Case of England." Working Paper.

Johnson, Noel D., and Mark Koyama. 2019. *Persecution and Toleration: The Long Road to Religious Freedom*. New York: Cambridge University Press.

Kuran, Timur. 2005. "The Absence of the Corporation in Islamic Law: Origins and Persistence." *American Journal of Comparative Law* 53: 785–834.

Kuran, Timur. 2011. *The Long Divergence: How Islamic Law Held Back the Middle East*. Princeton: Princeton University Press.

Kuran, Timur, and Scott Lustig. 2012. "Judicial Biases in Ottoman Istanbul: Islamic Justice and its Compatibility with Modern Economic Life." *Journal of Law and Economics* 55(3): 631–666.

Kuran, Timur, and Jared Rubin. 2018. "The Financial Power of the Powerless: Socio-Economic Status and Interest Rates under Partial Rule of Law." *Economic Journal* 128(609): 758–796.

Lewis, Bernard. 2002. *What Went Wrong? The Clash between Islam and Modernity in the Middle East*. New York: Harper Collins.

Mokyr, Joel. 1990. *The Lever of Riches*. Oxford: Oxford University Press.

Platteau, Jean-Philippe. 2017. *Islam Instrumentalized: Religion and Politics in Historical Perspective*. Cambridge: Cambridge University Press.

Rubin, Jared. 2011. "Institutions, the Rise of Commerce, and the Persistence of Laws: Interest Restrictions in Islam & Christianity." *Economic Journal* 557: 1310–1339.

Rubin, Jared. 2014. "Printing and Protestants: An Empirical Test of the Role of Printing in the Reformation." *Review of Economics and Statistics* 96(2): 270–286.

Rubin, Jared. 2017. *Rulers, Religion, and Riches: Why the West Got Rich and the Middle East Did Not*. New York: Cambridge University Press.

Seror, Avner. 2018. "A Theory on the Evolution of Religious Norms and Economic Prohibition." *Journal of Development Economics* 134: 416–427.

16
ISLAM AND ECONOMIC DEVELOPMENT

David Cobham and Abdallah Zouache

16.1 Introduction

The relationship between Islam and economic development is not a new topic. Leaving aside the famous discussion in *Al Muqaddima* (Ibn Khaldûn, 1402), we can argue that the contemporary discussions on Islam and development arose in the aftermath of decolonisation (Rodinson, 1966). The main issue then was the identification of an appropriate economic system for the new independent countries in the Arab region and in Asia. Thus, De Bernis (1960) argued that Islam pushed the state to intervene in the economic and social areas; that under Islam the legal system was rather collectivist, property was often collective and attitudes were favourable to cooperatives. In practical terms, this means that the Arab independent states should choose socialism rather than capitalism. Many newly independent Arab states – Algeria, Syria, Egypt under Nasser, Iraq and Yemen – chose this path, combining socialism, Islam and authoritarianism, both to develop their countries and to make them independent from the former colonial power.

These discussions often referred to the works of the reformist authors of the Muslim doctrine – Jamal El Afghani, Mohamed Abduh, Rashid Rida, Malik Bennabi and Hassan El Banna (the leading figure of the Muslim Brotherhood) – who were active at the end of the nineteenth and the beginning of the twentieth centuries. These saw Islam as the building block of the newly independent Muslim states, from Morocco to Pakistan, believing that a reform based on Islamic principles could create institutions more sympathetic to economic development.

These Muslim reformists are still key figures in the tradition of Islamic economics. In the standard economic literature on growth and development, the Weberian thesis – that religion is a filter that creates an ethics, a morality, which produces a mentality more or less suitable for development – is very influential. Mainstream institutional economics, as well as old institutional economics (Zouache, 2017), holds that Christendom, especially in its Protestant expression, is favourable to economic and political development. In this literature, when it comes to discussions of Muslim countries, it appears that Islam is seen as an obstacle for development, in spite of empirical work indicating that there is no clear relationship between Islam and economic development, or that the effect is rather positive. Indeed, the empirical results show that the causal relationship between religion and economic growth is not clear, as in the key reference by Barro and McCleary (2003). They measure religiosity through two indicators: (1) active religious participation (attendance at religious services and prayers) and (2) beliefs that influence work ethics. Barro and McCleary conclude that religious beliefs, especially beliefs in heaven and hell, should have a positive impact on economic performance. On the contrary, growth should be negatively correlated with church attendance. In a re-examination of Barro and McCleary's seminal work (2003), Durlauf et al. (2012) find no evidence, using a Bayesian averaging methodology, that religiosity has a positive impact on growth. Concerning more specifically Islam, the key reference by Noland (2005) refutes the thesis that Islam is inimical to growth. Noland (2005) tests the relation between Islam and economic performance, using both cross-country (50 and 70 countries) and within-country regressions (for the cases of India, Malaysia and Ghana). His two main findings are first that the hypothesis that Islam harms growth should be rejected and, second, that Islam, at a certain level of development, is rather good for growth. These findings are not surprising in the light of the diversity among the members of the Organisation of Islamic Cooperation: Qatar, Kuwait and the United Arab Emirates are among the richest countries in the world; Yemen, Mali and the Union of the Comoros are among the poorest; and Indonesia and Turkey are countries in transition. In other words, the Muslim countries are extremely diverse, and it appears that the hypothesis that Islam is inimical to growth is not worth testing to explain economic development. Other hypotheses should also be tested, but this is not the object of this chapter.

The aim of this chapter is to provide a critical outline of the relationship between Islam and economic development as it is viewed in the two traditions that are the most influential both in the academic literature and in political agendas: Islamic economics and neo-institutional economics. The first research path, examined in the next section, considers that a return to Islamic principles is a condition for economic development in the Muslim countries. The second tradition, considered in the third section, argues that Islamic institutions and culture impede economic development in Muslim countries. The last section concludes on our personal view: it is time to go beyond these two research paths, and to propose alternatives that are able to offer serious policy proposals.

16.2 Islamic economics and development

The attempt to develop a distinctive Islamic economics goes back to the work of Sayyid Abul A'la Al-Mawdudi in Pakistan, where it was part of the effort to build distinctive Muslim social and political arrangements following the partition of India (see Warde, 2010: chapters 2 and 4). It was then taken up in the Arab world in the 1970s and later in Iran, Malaysia and other Muslim countries. One key element is the emphasis on the morally 'proper' behaviour of good Muslims, and its implications for the way the economy is organised; the effect is that there is often a tension between the ideal or desirable and the possible or probable behaviour, which is at odds with western-trained economists' starting-point (self-interest). Another key element is the proposition that the economy should be organised according to the principles of the *Shari'ah*, which is the corpus of Islamic law, as derived from the *Qur'an* (the holy book) and the *Sunnah* (the practice of the Prophet Muhammad).[1]

This corpus includes some rules about inheritance, and some rules about taxation, notably the concept of *zakat*, which is a tax – dating back to the time of Prophet Muhammad – levied on the better off to finance a range of good causes. The Qur'an specifies rates of tax on various tax bases, e.g. types of wealth or agricultural products; some modern governments have tried to implement these specifications or some modernised version of them. But the historical roots mean that there are a number of anomalies which arise here leading to debates around them. But the share of zakat revenues in overall tax revenue is not large now and is not likely ever to be large.[2]

The core element of Islamic economics, however, is clearly the prohibition of *riba*, which is interpreted as interest. There has been some dispute in the past about the precise meaning of the word *riba*, but the current consensus of Muslim scholars is that it refers to any lending at a fixed (predetermined) interest rate. There were a few early precursors such as the Mit Ghamr bank in the Nile delta in the mid-1960s, but Islamic banking in its modern form dates from the mid-1970s, when the Islamic Development Bank was established as a central institution with support from Saudi Arabia, Libya, Kuwait, the UAE and other countries in the then Organisation of the Islamic Conference (now the Organisation of Islamic Cooperation), and a range of separate Islamic banks began to operate (Warde, 2010: chapter 4). Among the most important of these, the Dubai Islamic Bank was set up in 1975, the Faisal Islamic Bank of Egypt and the Kuwait Finance House in 1977, the Bahrain Islamic Bank in 1978, the Islamic International Bank for Investment and Development (in Egypt) in 1980, the Dar al-Mal al-Islami group (registered in the Bahamas and Geneva, with shareholders from Saudi Arabia, other Gulf countries, Pakistan, Egypt, Sudan and elsewhere) in 1981, the Al Baraka Group and the Al Rajhi Group (both Saudi) in 1982 and 1983, and the Bank Islam Malaysia in 1983. Islamic banking continued to expand rapidly over the next three decades; by 2010 the aggregate balance sheets of Islamic banks had reached $1,300bn (Warde, 2010: 1), including the banks of the three Muslim countries where the whole banking system was 'Islamicised' during the 1980s: Iran (1983–6), Pakistan (1979–85) and Sudan (from 1983).[3]

The distinctive feature of Islamic banking, in principle and to some extent in practice during what Warde (2010) identifies as the first stage of Islamic finance (1975–91), is the ban on fixed interest payments. Instead, loans should be made on a profit and loss sharing (PLS) basis, with lender and borrower agreeing in advance how to share the profits which arise from an investment project. The two main types of contract involved are the *mudaraba*, in which the lender is a sleeping partner in the project, and the *musharaka*, in which the lender is an active partner. However, as Islamic banking grew, particularly in the second phase (1991–2000) identified by Warde (2010), the banks turned away from these PLS contracts towards sale-based or mark-up transactions, notably *murabaha* contracts, under which a bank buys raw materials or intermediate inputs for a company and the company pays the bank at a later date a higher price (agreed now). Such contracts look, to both western-trained economists and Muslim critics of the practice of Islamic banking, like fixed-interest contracts in (minimal) disguise. Whatever the reasons,[4] it is clear from the relatively small amounts of data available that Islamic banks simply did not do very much lending of the PLS type (even in the earlier years); that is, most of their activities were not significantly different from those of conventional western banks (Khan and Mirakhor, 1990; Aggarwal and Yousef, 2000). In the second phase and even more in Warde's third phase (2001–), Islamic banks moved further from PLS contracts and, as El-Gamal (2008) has discussed, came to focus more and more on finding ways to replicate conventional western bank contracts within an 'Islamic' format, so that they became even closer to western banks.

This tendency can be placed within an analytical perspective. The modern theory of financial intermediation, as developed in the 1980s on the basis of asymmetric information and incomplete financial markets, characterised banks as suppliers of 'liquidity insurance' and as 'delegated monitors'. On the liability side (Diamond and Dybvig, 1983), banks could be viewed as offering potential depositors a 'liquidity insurance' contract under which deposits held for a longer time would receive higher returns than those withdrawn earlier: this provides an incentive for depositors to deposit but allows them to withdraw earlier if they need to, and if the banks correctly estimate the rate of early withdrawals they can lend the remaining amounts on to firms with long-term investment projects.[5] On the asset side (Diamond, 1984), banks could be seen as offering to monitor loan contracts on behalf of a wide range of potential financiers (who become the banks' depositors) who would otherwise have each had to pay the fixed cost of monitoring: this minimises the overall cost of monitoring, while diversification plus the banks' own capital allow the banks to offer returns to the depositors which are fixed and independent of the return on any individual loans made by the banks.

The theory also argued (without any reference to Islamic banking) that the optimal financial contract for a bank is the standard debt contract, under which (1) the borrowing firm repays to the lending bank a fixed sum so long as the firm is solvent, (2) the firm is declared bankrupt if it cannot pay and (3) in that case the bank receives the firm's actual revenue and any remaining assets. The underlying argument (Gale and Hellwig, 1985) is that this arrangement minimises the monitoring costs which the bank has to undertake to protect its investment, because the borrower has no incentive to underreport his or her profits, the bank needs to monitor only in case of bankruptcy, and in such cases the bank receives the maximum return possible, which means that it requires (for the activity of lending to be worth undertaking) the lowest return in cases of solvency; this in turn implies that overall lending (and so welfare, investment and growth) is maximised. The implication for Islamic banking is that PLS lending requires additional costly monitoring and is therefore in some sense inefficient.[6]

On the other hand, as El-Gamal (2008) has shown clearly, the newer types of contract which became popular as Islamic banks turned away from PLS operations – including Islamic mortgages, asset-backed leasing bonds, synthesised forwards and *tawarruq* retail loans – inevitably involve excess transactions costs of other kinds (e.g. for the establishment of special purpose vehicles or for the purchase and sale of the intermediate commodities) compared to the conventional western bank equivalents. For example, El-Gamal (2008: 6–7) gives the example of an issue of sukuk (Islamic bonds) by the National Central Cooling Co. (Tabreed) of UAE: a special purpose vehicle (SPV) is set up in the Cayman Islands (tax haven) for the sole purpose of issuing these sukuk; it uses the finance from the issue to buy trust assets from Tabreed; it then leases the trust assets back to Tabreed (and will sell them to Tabreed on maturity) in return for lease payments (and an exercise price on dissolution); those lease payments are then used by the SPV to pay periodic and dissolution distribution amounts to sukuk holders. Thus the sukuk holders receive lease payments, not interest, while Tabreed gets funding for its investments and does not pay interest on the funding. The risk structure is the same as for conventional bonds, so issuers get the same credit ratings and sukuk-holders receive in effect the same interest rate, based on that credit rating. However, the setting up of the SPV involves significant additional transaction costs, and there are also jurist and legal fees to be paid. These costs constitute an alternative source of inefficiency to the higher monitoring costs involved in PLS contracts, so that the shift away from PLS to imitations of conventional contracts does not solve the basic problem which Islamic banking faces.

Tawarruq is an indirect way of providing an 'Islamic-compliant' loan which has recently been accepted by Gulf jurists: a bank buys $1,000 of some commodity then sells it on credit, with a mark-up, to a customer, who then immediately sells the commodity, for example back to the dealer who sold it to the bank in the first place: the dealer sells and buys back the commodity at once (presumably for a small fee), the bank pays out initially then gets (a larger amount of) repayment over time for a credit-sale, while the customer gets cash now and repays the bank (a larger amount) over time. This, it should be noted, is exactly the kind of stratagem used to get round the Catholic prohibition on usury in Europe in the Middle Ages. It had been in use for a while for Islamic bank loans to firms, but is now being used for retail loans as well. It involves additional costs, in the form of the fee received by the commodity dealer and the time and trouble involved in the transaction.

What all this suggests is that the most distinctive and developed element of Islamic economics turns out not to offer a serious alternative to the conventional paradigm. It is therefore not surprising that comparisons between Islamic and conventional banks reveal relatively few differences. Abedifar et al. (2015) survey a wide range of studies on the efficiency and performance of the two types of banks, and report that 'no strong consensus emerges from this literature, although a (small) majority of studies find no major difference between Islamic and conventional banks in terms of cost and profit efficiency' (pp. 641, 647).[7] They also find that small Islamic banks are less risky than conventional banks, which is related to the fact that they focus on small borrowers. It probably also reflects the fact that Islamic banks, like conventional banks in the MENA region, are not well integrated into the international financial system and typically have not, for example, held asset-backed securities originating in the US. In addition, there are some studies which compare the returns on deposits in Islamic banks with the interest rates paid on deposits by conventional banks. Cevik and Charap (2015), for example, using data from Turkey and Malaysia, find that Islamic bank deposit returns and conventional bank deposit interest rates are cointegrated, and that the latter Granger-cause the former (see also Chong and Liu, 2009).

In other areas Islamic economics has very little (distinctive or otherwise) to say on a wide range of the policy questions facing governments – overall demand management policy, exchange rate regimes, public expenditure and social security, anti-trust and competition policy, labour market regulation, health economics, education economics. El Hamiani Khatat (2016) and Hussain et al. (2015) also highlight other unresolved issues for the operation of monetary policy in the presence of Islamic banks (in the presence or the absence of conventional banks).

16.3 Neo-institutional economics: religion, culture and development

In this research tradition, the central message is that economic development is correlated with institutional change. Underdevelopment appears when a country is blocked at a low level of economic growth because of its weak institutions. Now, institutions do not evolve easily because of path-dependence, that is dependence on initial conditions: when an economy is located on an inefficient path that produces economic stagnation, it can remain blocked on it. The main question for development economics is thus to know why so few countries have succeeded in creating pro-growth rules and norms, that is a culture that promotes economic growth and social progress. The leading author of neo-institutional economics is Douglas North (1981, 1990, 2005, also North and Thomas, 1973), winner of the 1993 Nobel Prize in economics. As regards the application of the institutionalist ideas to the Muslim countries, the names that generally appear are those of Avner Greif (1994, 2008) and Timur Kuran (2004, 2011, 2018).

According to North (2005: 118), the 'most careful, and suggestive, study' of the creation of political institutions that create and enforce the necessary legal system has been made by Avner Greif (1994). Greif proposes a theory of endogenous change where institutions are produced and evolve over time as a function of the way merchants coordinate their exchanges. His historical work on the Maghrebi traders – Jewish merchants evolving in a Muslim culture – is fundamental as it provides the basis of his main thesis, which is that economic development necessitates the adoption of pro-growth cognitive rules that are built from a specific system of beliefs. Greif studied commerce in the mediaeval period, comparing the way international trade was implemented in the western and the Muslim countries. He defended the thesis that there existed strong differences in institutional arrangements as between Christian Europe – especially the Christian Italian merchants – and the Muslim world, whose functioning is derived from a careful study of Jewish merchants evolving in the Muslim Mediterranean space. According to Greif, the institutional foundations of markets in the western world were more solid in the sense that merchants were able to develop commerce with foreign countries since property rights were guaranteed: they were formal and impersonal rather than based on personal relationships. In particular, Greif compared how the structure of the political and economic institutions of Genoese traders evolved towards impersonal exchange, in contrast to the practices of Maghrebi traders who failed to make the necessary institutional adjustments and lost out in the competitive trade of the Mediterranean. According to Greif, multilateral reputation mechanisms governed the agency relations between the Maghrebi traders because they lacked a legal system that could provide the information and enforcement capacity necessary for the development of trade in the Mediterranean. To put it briefly, agency relationships between the western merchants were law-based, whereas the relationships between the Maghrebi traders and their overseas agents were personal and thus insecure. In a recent article Greif and Mokyr (2017) discuss the causal link North makes between the emergence of pro-growth institutions and the majoritarian cultural beliefs in a society. In their opinion, the emergence of modern growth followed an intellectual revolution that led the Occident to share a majoritarian mental model inside which the key components are the beliefs that economic progress depends on the progress of arts and science and that the control of natural phenomena are essential to human progress (Greif and Mokyr, 2017: 41). The concomitance of these cognitive foundations for economic growth and of the cognitive foundations of the European legal system led to the rise of a specific legal system whose main role was to protect new forms of property rights (copyright, patents) and to provide social safety nets to a larger population (food, poverty). This went along with the decline of the legal power of the Church and implied the increasing authority of the state over the law (*ibid.*: 44). On the contrary, in the 'Muslim Mediterranean area', the cognitive foundations evolved in a different way, leading to a weak, authoritarian, military state. In particular, in their view, one main weakness of the legal system is that it was in the hands of Muslim scholars. But the most important weakness comes from the lack of the cognitive changes needed in the Middle East because of the persistence of traditional Muslim religious beliefs that have been abandoned in the Christian world: fatalism, the belief in destiny, the role of God (Greif and Mokyr, 2017: 47).

Indeed, in North's interpretation of Greif's study, the difference between Maghrebi traders evolving in a Muslim culture and Genoese traders is a cultural difference. In other words, in North's view, the cultural differences between the Muslim environment and the Christian one explain the different beliefs and thus different institutional systems and, ultimately, different organisational structures that are positive or not for economic efficiency (North, 2005: 135–136). The crucial question is then the following: how have these cultural beliefs been formed? In other words, what ultimately explains the development of institutions that are good for growth in one case and the development of institutions that are bad for growth in the other case? The response seems to be clear in North's view: the cultural difference is ultimately a religious difference (North, 2005: 136–137). Timur Kuran (2004) implements this idea for the Muslim countries.

Kuran's main thesis is to relate the lack of development in the Middle East to inefficient institutions inherited from Islam. In the Middle East, according to Kuran (2011), the region became underdeveloped because of certain Islamic institutions that generated a mutually self-reinforcing set of institutional arrangements leading to economic inefficiency. Thus, the Islamic law of inheritance inhibited capital accumulation because it limited the concentration of wealth and tended to fragment the estates of successful businesses. This effect was amplified by polygamy which led to the dispersion of property among numerous claimants. In contrast, the inheritance system adopted in most western countries, primogeniture, permitted the creation of large commercial and financial enterprises.

Kuran especially denounces the Waqf institution. A waqf is a religious donation, in general for the benefit of the poor. It can take different forms: cash, a building, a piece of land, mosques, gardens or schools. Restated in current academic terms, a waqf could be interpreted as a public good given or produced by a private or a public donor. According to Kuran, the institution of the waqf has impeded the emergence of a state which would assume the development of public and semi-public goods, such as universities. The waqf system failed to provide the supply of public services in the Middle East while the West succeeded in providing them on a large scale. The waqf system also kept resources locked into uses decided centuries earlier. In Kuran's interpretation, the waqf, as a self-organising institution, even prevented the emergence of a strong civil society.

Furthermore, Kuran considers that Islamic law is too individualistic and thus impedes the emergence of large and impersonal corporations: 'Islamic law recognised only flesh-and-blood individuals' (Kuran, 2004: 73). The Islamic prohibition of *riba* not only retarded the emergence of a banking system but also reinforced the personal character of trade in the Middle East. Finally, by promoting legal pluralism, Islamic law offered substantive advantages to non-Muslim groups. In particular, Islamic law supported the transfer of economic power to the minorities, Christians and Jews, since they were able to choose the most efficient law: the western law. This choice was not permitted to Muslims who endured the allegedly inefficient Islamic law.

16.4 Concluding remarks: avoiding preconceptions in economics

The relationship between Islam and economic development in the current literature is subject to two contrasting perspectives. The first one argues in favour of more Islam in economics whereas the second postulates that Islam blocks economic development. Neither of these perspectives is satisfying from an analytical perspective, or helpful at the policy level.

Concerning Islamic economics, it seems that it has not achieved the expected success whether from a theoretical or an empirical perspective. At the theoretical level, Islamic economics has been *à la mode*, and is still very active, but in closed circles (El Karanshawy et al., 2015). This research tradition is getting more and more criticised at an internal level. Allard and Benchabane (2010) even consider that it is a *pastiche* of standard finance. The critique offered here might be seen as being too strong for Islamic scholars who still defend the idea that Islamic economics offers an alternative to conventional finance to achieve 'an inclusive and sustainable global economic and financial system' (El-Karanshawy, 2015:V). However, Islamic assets represent no more than 1% of the assets of the first thousand banks in the world; and the global value of sukuks represents no more than 0.1% of global debt assets (Allard and Benchabane, 2010). Even in the region where Islamic finance is active, that is mainly in the Arab states of the Gulf (Kuwait, Saudi Arabia, the UAE and Qatar) and in Asia (Malaysia, Indonesia, Brunei, Bangladesh), by 2015–16 the Islamic finance sector was experiencing growth which was both slower and below expectations (Islamic Financial Services Industry, 2017).

There is no consensus either over the nature of the relationship between Islam and economic development in neo-institutionalist economics among scholars working on the Middle East. The core of the argumentation, the historical scenario of the Maghrebi traders proposed by Greif, has been strongly challenged by Edwards and Ogilvie (2012, see also Shatzmiller, forthcoming). Working on the same historical sources as Greif (the Geniza papers),[8] they show that there is no historical evidence that the Maghrebi merchants did not trade using formal legal agreements. They did use informal mechanisms in their exchange, as other European traders did, but the economic relationships were not informal, as Greif argues. Furthermore, they provide historical arguments to confirm that not only the Genovese merchants, but also the Northern Europeans of the Hanseatic League, utilised informal institutions (like reputation as a collective sanction) to resolve conflicts. The consequence is of crucial importance for scholars working on the role of Islam in economic development: the story proposed by Greif on the lack of legal architecture, and on the role of backward cultural practices and beliefs in the Muslim world, appears to be inaccurate. Greif's (2008) reply to Edwards and Ogilvie's works could lead to polemical debates that are not interesting here. What is crucial is that Edwards and Ogilvie's article reveals that the recourse to history needs to be made with caution: different sources exist that are often omitted or underplayed in the neo-institutionalist approach to Islam. This point is key in a paper by Zouache (2017): an economic analysis of Islam that uses different historical sources has more chance of avoiding a culturalist and ethnocentrist interpretation of the relation between Islam and economic development.

Indeed, the vision promoted by neo-institutional economics should also be considered cautiously, given the culturalist bias of this approach. The main point of this tradition is that economic development has not occurred in the Muslim world because of the cultural beliefs conveyed in Islam. The argument is that the countries that have embraced Islam have not created complex institutional arrangements to deal with the increase of exchanges that came with the Industrial Revolution. Kuran goes even further and assumes an extremist position against Islam, judging this religion to be the main cause of underdevelopment in the Muslim countries and a cultural barrier against the import of western economic values. Alternative explanations are possible. A more balanced institutionalist perspective is provided by Platteau (2008, 2017): one can admit that culture or religion could be an obstacle to progress but that situation is often the result of its political instrumentalisation by political actors, local or external. This institutionalist perspective replaces politics at the centre of the political economy of development in Muslim countries. This is an interesting alternative but it seems also important to us to consider other historical sources and approaches which do not over-estimate the impact of Islamic principles in the economic development of Muslim countries. Historical lessons from 'the golden age of Islam' reveal that monetary factors as well as climatic and geographical considerations are crucial to understanding both the emergence and the decay of Muslim countries (Zouache, 2017). Let us give two examples.

On the monetary dimension, Braudel's view (1979a and 1979b) of the 'Muslim economy' is famous but yet not considered in the neo-institutionalist approach. Braudel argues that some economic and finance arrangements which impacted the development of the West came from the Muslim countries: it is known that the letter of exchange was imported from the East by the Italian merchants. Other contributions are less famous: Lombard (1947) highlighted the role of the monetary system in the process of economic growth in the Muslim world from the seventh to the eleventh century. Shatzmiller (2013) follows this hypothesis. She argues that monetary factors played a key role in the process of economic growth during the period of the Islamic Caliphate (650–1000), not only because of the quantitative factors raised by Lombard (positive money supply shocks) but also in terms of institutional innovations (credit and banking institutions) that occurred after the rise of the money stock in the Muslim world.

Secondly, as regards climatic and geographical factors, Bianquis (2005) emphasises that the Muslim world, despite its vastness, covered only a limited variety of climates. Therefore, the forests that existed covered only small areas and were scattered: wood and charcoal were rare and expensive until the invasion of the Balkans by the Ottomans, and were often imported from the West. This lack of natural resources had an impact on economic development. Bianquis argues that development was constrained by the scarcity of local natural resources, involving the persistence of a craft local production system instead of the development of an industrial global economy. Capitalism was thus commercial, artisanal, given that commerce was providing high incomes and industrial production was constrained by the limited availability of natural resources (Bianquis, 2005: 4).

Our final remark deals with the economic policy vacuum of Islamic economics and neo-institutionalism. Concerning Islamic economics, our other chapter in this book on the Arab Spring (Chapter 17) shows how Islamist movements did not have clear, alternative economic policies to the traditional ones. The policy messages of Islamic economics are vague: adopting Islamic principles and promoting Islamic finance. The neo-institutionalist approach also seems strangely silent on the economic policies that Muslim countries should adopt in order to converge on the level of rich countries. The only policy advice that can be deduced from neo-institutionalist economics is the following: forget your religion, or at least change your culture inherited from Islam, and adopt the western culture. One can imagine the reception of this policy message in Muslim countries.

Notes

1 Note, however, that there are different 'schools of law' in Islam which do not always agree on what is the 'correct' principle or action (El-Gamal, 2008).
2 Historically, different rates between 2.5% and 10% were to be applied to different products (agricultural and livestock); see Warde (2010: 186–188). In any case, it is not clear that the actual economy of the Muslim world was regulated in this way in the early years after the Prophet Muhammad (under the Umayyad caliphs) or in any later period.
3 Warde (2010, chapter 6). Pakistan has subsequently allowed the reintroduction of a substantial amount of conventional banking.
4 Other reasons suggested in the literature for the low level of PLS lending by Islamic banks include adverse selection (companies which apply for loans from Islamic banks are those which have been rejected by conventional banks), e.g. Kuran (2004: 12).
5 But if banks underestimated that rate, i.e. more depositors withdrew early for some reason, this could lead to a run on the bank and the possibility of a wider contagion-induced run on the banking system as a whole.
6 This argument is applied in the Islamic context by Khan (1985) and Cobham (1993). See also Aggarwal and Yousef (2000) for an argument which emphasises principal–agent problems for lenders but leads towards similar conclusions.
7 See in particular Beck et al. (2013), also Hussain et al. (2015) and di Mauro et al. (2013).
8 The Geniza papers are documents found in a synagogue located in a then merchant area of old Cairo – the Geniza – that record in particular the business activities of Jewish merchants in the Muslim Mediterranean space.

References

Abedifar, P., S. Ebrahim, P. Molyneux and A. Tarazi (2015), 'Islamic Banking and Finance: Recent Empirical Literature and Directions for Future Research', *Journal of Economic Surveys*, 29(4): 637–670.
Aggarwal, R. and T. Yousef (2000), 'Islamic Banks and Investment Financing', *Journal of Money, Credit and Banking*, 32(1): 93–120.
Allard, P. and D. Benchabane (2010), 'La Finance Islamique: Modèle Alternatif, Postiche ou Pastiche?', *Revue française d'économie*, 25(4): 11–38.
Barro, R. and R. McCleary (2003), 'Religion and Economic Growth across Countries', *American Journal of Sociology*, 68: 760–781.
Beck, T., A. Demirgüç-Kunt and O. Merrouche, (2013), 'Islamic vs. Conventional Banking Business Model, Efficiency and Stability', *Journal of Banking and Finance*, 37(2): 433–447.
Bianquis, T. (2005), 'La confrontation Est-Ouest en Méditerranée aux VIIE/XIIE et VIIIE/XIIIE S.', mimeo.
Braudel, F. (1979a), *Civilisation Matérielle, Economie et Capitalisme, XVe-XVIIIe siècle, Les Jeux de l'Echange*, tome 2. Paris: Armand Colin. English Translation, Civilisation and Capitalism, The Wheels of Commerce, New York: Harper & Row, 1982.
Braudel, F. (1979b), *Civilisation Matérielle, Economie et Capitalisme, XVe-XVIIIe siècle, Le Temps du Monde*, tome 3. Paris: Armand Colin. English Translation, Civilisation and Capitalism, The Perspective of the World, New York: Harper & Row, 1984.

Cevik, J. and J. Charap (2015), 'The Behavior of Conventional and Islamic Bank Deposit Returns in Malaysia and Turkey', *Journal of Economics and Financial Issues*, 5(1): 111–124.

Chong, B., and M.-H. Liu (2009), 'Islamic Banking: Interest-Free or Interest-Based?', *Pacific-Basin Finance Journal*, 17: 125–144.

Cobham, D. (1993), 'Islamic Banking: Perspectives from the Theory of Financial Intermediation', *Economia, Societa' e Istituzioni*, Gennaio-Aprile, 1–25.

De Bernis, Gérard Destanne, (1960), 'Islam et Développement Economique', *Cahiers de l'I.S.E.A*, série V, 106(2): 105–150.

Diamond, D. (1984), 'Financial Intermediation and Delegated Monitoring', *Review of Economic Studies*, 51: 393–414.

Diamond, D., and Dybvig, P. (1983), 'Bank Runs, Deposit Insurance and Liquidity', *Journal of Political Economy*, 91(3): 401–419.

di Mauro, F., P. Caristi, S. Couderc, A. Di Maria, L. Ho, B. Grewal, S. Masciantonio, S. Ongena and S. Zaher, (2013), 'Islamic Finance in Europe', Occasional Paper No. 146, European Central Bank.

Durlauf, S., A. Kourtellos and T.C. Ming (2012), 'Is God in the Details? A Reexamination of the Role of Religion in Economic Growth', *Journal of Applied Econometrics*, 27: 1059–1075.

Edwards, J. and S. Ogilvie (2012), 'Contract Enforcement, Institutions, and Social Capital: The Maghribi Traders Reappraised', *The Economic History Review*, 65(2): 421–444.

El-Gamal, M. (2008), *Islamic Finance: Law, Economics and Practice*. Cambridge: Cambridge University Press.

El Hamiani Khatat, M. (2016), 'Monetary Policy in the Presence of Islamic Banking', IMF Working Paper 16/72.

El-Karanshawy, H.A. et al. (eds.) (2015), *Islamic Economics: Theory, Policy and Social Justice*. Doha: Bloomsbury Qatar Foundation.

Gale, D. and M. Hellwig (1985), 'Incentive-Compatible Debt Contracts: The One-Period Problem", *Review of Economic Studies*, 52: 647–663.

Greif, A. (1994), 'Cultural Beliefs and the Organization of Society. A Historical and Theoretical Reflection on Collectivist and Individualist Societies', *The Journal of Political Economy*, 102(5): 912–950.

Greif, A. (2008), 'Contract Enforcement and Institutions among the Maghribi Traders: Refuting Edwards and Ogilvie', mimeo, 1–30.

Greif, A. and J. Mokyr (2017), 'Cognitive Rules, Institutions, and Economic Growth: Douglass North and Beyond', *Journal of Institutional Economics*, 13(1): 25–52.

Hussain, M., A. Shahmoradi and R. Turk (2015), 'An Overview of Islamic Finance', IMF Working Paper 15/120, also at Journal of International Commerce, Economics and Policy, 7(1).

Ibn Khaldûn (1402), *Al-Muqaddima, French Translation by Vincent Monteil, Discours sur l'histoire universelle*. Arles: Actes Sud.

Islamic Financial Services Industry (2017), *Stability Report, Islamic Financial Services Board*. Malaysia: Kuala Lumpur.

Khan, M.S. and A. Mirakhor (1990), 'Islamic Banking: Experiences in the Islamic Republic of Iran and in Pakistan', *Economic Development and Cultural Change*, University of Chicago Press, 38(2): 353–375.

Khan, W.M. (1985), *Towards an Interest-free Islamic Economic System*. Leicester: Islamic Foundation.

Kuran, T. (2004), *Islam and Mammon: The Economic Predicaments of Islamism*. Princeton: Princeton University Press.

Kuran, T. (2011), *The Long Divergence. How Islamic Law Held Back the Middle East*. Princeton: Princeton University Press.

Kuran, T. (2018), 'Islam and Economic Performance: Historical and Contemporary Links', *Journal of Economic Literature*, 56(4): 1292–1359. doi:10.1257/jel.20171243.

Lombard, M. (1947), 'Les bases monétaires d'une suprématie économique: l'or musulman du VIIe au XIe siècle', *Annales Economies, Sociétés, Civilisations.*, 2(2): 143–160.

Noland, M. (2005), 'Religion and Economic Performance', *World Development*, 38(8): 1215–1232.

North, D. (1981), *Structure and Change in Economic History*. New York: W.W. Norton.

North, D. (1990), *Institutions, Institutional Change and Economic Performance*. Cambridge: Cambridge University Press.

North, D. (2005), *Understanding the Process of Economic Change*. Princeton: Princeton University Press.

North, D., and R.P. Thomas (1973), *The Rise of the Western World. A New Economic History*. Cambridge: Cambridge University Press.

North, D. (1981), *Structure and Change in Economic History*, New York: W.W. Norton.

Platteau, J.P. (2008), 'Religion, Politics, and Development: Lessons from the Land of Islam', *Journal of Economic Behavior and Organization*, 68(2): 329. ff10.1016/j.jebo.2008.06.003ff. ffhal-00630790f
Platteau, J.P. (2017), *Islam Instrumentalised: Religion and Politics in Historical Perspective*. Cambridge: Cambridge University Press.
Rodinson, M. (1966), *Islam et Capitalisme*, Paris: Le Seuil. English Translation. Islam and Capitalism, New York: Pantheon, 1973.
Shatzmiller, A. (2013), 'The Role of Money in the Economic Growth of the Early Islamic Period (650-1000)', in Klemm V. et al. (eds.), *Sources and Approaches across Disciplines in Near Eastern Studies*, Proceedings of the 24th Congress, Union Européenne des Arabisants et Islamisants, Leipzig 2008, Orientalia Lovaniensia Analecta 215. Leuven- Paris-Walpole, MA: Peeters Publishers, pp. 271–305.
Shatzmiller, M. (forthcoming), 'Structural change and economic development in the Islamic Middle East 700-1500: population levels and property rights', forthcoming, *Scottish Journal of Political Economy*.
Warde, I. (2010), *Islamic Finance in the Global Economy*, 2nd edition. Edinburgh: Edinburgh University Press.
Zouache, A. (2017), 'Race, Competition, and Institutional Change in J.R. Commons', *European Journal of the History of Economic Thought*, 24(2): 341–368.

17

THE ARAB SPRING, AND AFTER

Economic features and policy challenges

David Cobham and Abdallah Zouache

17.1 Introduction

From one perspective the Arab Spring has come and gone. The dictators of Tunisia and Egypt were deposed in early 2011, and there were protests calling for change in many other countries. But while some countries (e.g. Morocco, Jordan) introduced limited reforms, the protests in others (e.g. Bahrain) were controlled or repressed or (as in Syria and Libya) turned into destructive civil wars, fuelled and financed in part by outsiders. In Egypt a new government was ejected in a bloody military coup in 2013, only a year after it had been elected. In Tunisia the Islamist party which dominated the first post-dictatorship government lost the next election to a more mainstream party with links to the old establishment, Nidaa Tounes. Judged by the results of the May 2018 election, post-Arab Spring Tunisians are sceptical about the changes caused by these political upheavals and, like other Arabs, appear to be mainly concerned by economic issues (Parent and Zouache, 2018).[1] Furthermore, in the Arab world as a whole, democracy appears to be an exception. Table 17.1 which gives the Polity IV index for the Arab countries in 2016 indicates that only Tunisia and Comoros, as well as, to a lesser extent, Lebanon and Iraq, could be considered democracies.[2]

From another perspective, however, the Arab Spring is likely to have more lasting effects. On the political level it showed that dictatorial regimes can be overthrown by democratic pressures. Such pressures are bound to recur at some point in the future. On the economic level, it raises a range of issues, which we seek to address here. First, how much did economic forces contribute to the eruption of the uprisings? Cobham and Zouache (2015) have argued that there were no obvious simple economic triggers: in particular, the Arab world was not strongly affected by the Global Financial Crisis (essentially because its degree of financial integration with the world economy was and remains low), GDP growth did not suffer particularly sharp falls and it is not clear whether real wages were badly hit, even with the 2008 spike in inflation.[3] Insofar as economic factors were important, then, it is necessary to examine the long-term failure of economic policies in the Arab world to generate significant domestically based growth. We do that in the next section.

Second, how might the Arab Spring, if it had not been so brutally repressed, have changed the unsuccessful economic policies of previous decades? In section 17.3 we analyse the economic programmes of three Islamist political parties in the immediate aftermath of the Spring.

Table 17.1 Economic and political indicators

Arab League members	*Polity IV (2016)*	*CIP Index*	*Share of export of merchandises in global trade (2016)*
Algeria	2	88	0.18731
Bahrain	-10	50	0.07976
Comoros	9		0.00019
Djibouti	3		0.00087
Egypt	-4	71	0.15888
Iraq	6	132	0.2738
Jordan	-3	74	0.04709
Kuwait	-7	52	0.28843
Lebanon	6	89	0.02452
Libya	0		0.03743
Mauritania	-2		0.00874
Morocco	-4	68	0,14248
Oman	-8	60	0.15256
Palestine		114	0.00498
Qatar	-10	64	0.35717
Saudi Arabia	-10	38	1.14525
Somalia	5		0.00274
Sudan	-4		
Syria	-9	104	0.01061
Tunisia	7	65	0.08467
United Arab Emirates	-8	41	1.86529
Yemen	0	130	
Total			1.96057

Sources: Polity IV 2016 (polity 2), CIP Index (UNIDO, 2017), UNCTAD statistics.

Third, given the failure of pre-Spring policies by authoritarian governments and the absence of ground-breaking new policies in the Islamist parties' programmes, how should economists who favour progress and democracy respond? In section 17.4 we discuss some key issues and call for wider research to develop appropriate economic policies. Section 17.5 concludes.

17.2 Economic failures and structural weaknesses of the Arab countries

This section will not present a detailed review of the vast literature on the Arab Spring which covers different sub-fields, from political science and sociology to history, economics and geo-politics. Inside the economics field, we will not address all the economic failures and the political economy explanations of the Arab Spring.[4] We will insist on what seems to have been decisive for us in the emergence of the Arab Spring: the poor performance of the Arab countries over a much longer period in terms of economic but also non-economic development. We highlight the following structural weaknesses of the Arab countries: weak economic performance over the long run, the lack of industrial competitiveness and participation in global trade, unemployment and inequality issues. We do not only examine the events at the moment of the Arab Spring since it is still being discussed and reconstructed with hindsight (Makdisi, 2017 and forthcoming) but also because these structural weaknesses have not disappeared, and have even sometimes worsened, so that, when possible, we use recent data and refer to post-Arab Spring analyses.

Concerning economic development, the performance of the Arab countries is disappointing. If we take GDP per capita as a standard indicator for economic performance, Arab countries have experienced slow economic performance over the long run (Cobham and Zouache, 2015). Figure 17.1 reproduces the evolution of the GDP per capita for the members of the Arab league, except Palestine, Syria and Somalia where there is a lack of data. It provides a basic but interesting feature of the Arab economies in a period that includes the Arab Spring uprisings (2000–2015). In 2016, the average GDP per capita for the Arab countries is $15,506, but this figure conceals a high diversity. In the graph the averages for three sub-groups are shown. The first one is what could be called the Gulf oil and gas club, that is the six GCC countries, of whom the richest are Qatar, Kuwait and the UAE, with an exceptional level of GDP per capita of $118,207 reached by Qatar. Commentators often associate the Arab world with natural resources but the richest countries of this first club (Qatar, Kuwait, the UAE) cover less than 4% of the total Arab population. Even when Saudi Arabia, Oman and Bahrain are included, no more than 17% of the population of the Arab countries benefit from high per capita GDP. The second sub-group in Figure 17.1 is the major club of Arab countries, which have a much lower average level of GDP per capita. This group includes the high-population countries of Egypt, Algeria, Iraq and Morocco and the low-population countries of Tunisia, Lebanon and Jordan. The final sub-group includes poor Arab countries: Yemen, Sudan, Mauritania, Comoros and Djibouti. In this group, the highest GDP per capita, in Sudan, does not exceed $4,300.

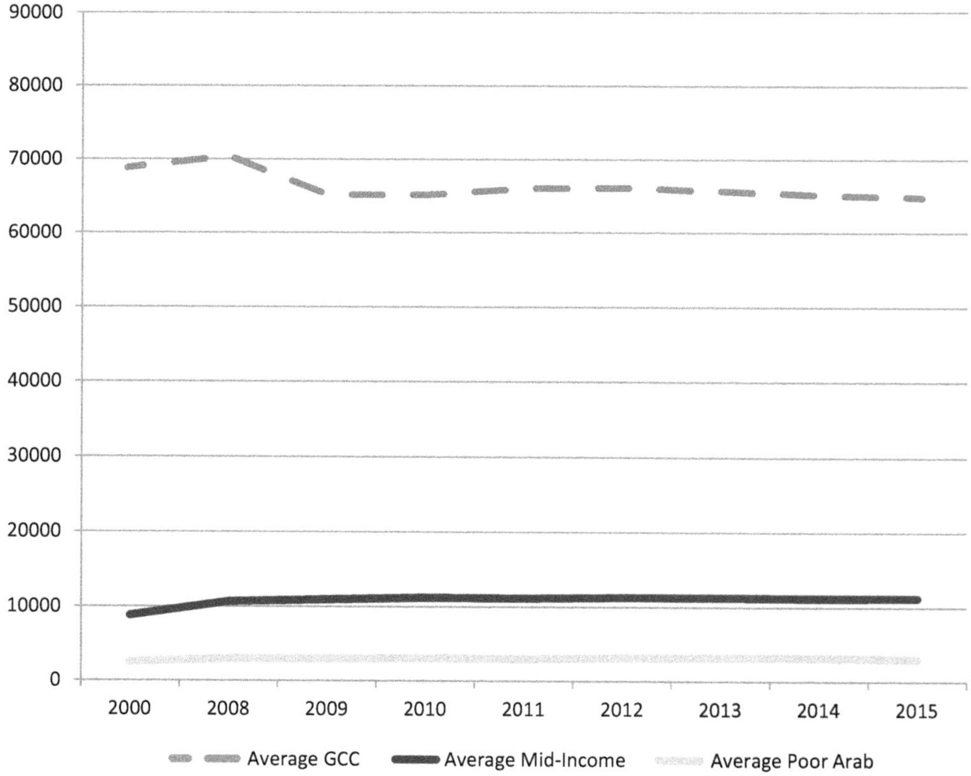

Figure 17.1 GDP per capita in the Arab countries (2000–2015). *Source*: World Development Indicators, World Bank.

If we focus on the countries that have been the most affected by the Arab Spring (Figure 17.2), Egypt, Yemen, Tunisia and Morocco are characterised by a low level of GDP per capita, the result of a long period of low and unstable growth (Cobham and Zouache, 2015), while Libya and above all Bahrain are on a different level. It seems that economic performance is less important in explaining the emergence of the Arab Spring in Libya and Bahrain. Political factors – tribalism in Libya (Brahimi, 2011), a confessional patrimonial power in Bahrain (Achcar, 2013, pp. 232–236) – were crucial to the uprisings in Libya and the protests in Bahrain. The Libyan revolution, which led to a continuing civil war, might be explained by the specificity of the regime, marked by an intense personalisation combined with the tribal nature of the 'stateless state' (Brahimi, 2011). This complex node of tribal alliances, regional divisions, family divisions inside the Qadhafi clan is often deployed by political scientists to analyse the uprisings in Libya, whereas they appeal to religious heterogeneity (the Shia/Sunni divide) and the geopolitical context (the Iran/Saudi Arabia 'cold war') to explain the protests in Bahrain (Pradhan, 2017).[5]

The structural weaknesses of the Arab countries also appear in the industrial and trade indicators. Table 17.1 reproduces the rank for each country in 2016 on the competitive industrial performance (CIP) index calculated by the United Nations Industrial Development Organisation (UNIDO)[6] and the shares of the Arab countries in global merchandise exports as they are reported by the United Nations Conference on Trade and Development (UNCTAD). These two figures are revealing in the sense that they reflect the competitiveness of Arab countries outside the natural resources effect. The share of merchandise exports also reveals the ability of Arab countries to export goods and thus their participation in global trade. From the CIP index we learn that the Arab countries are not strong industrial performers: the best score is obtained by Saudi Arabia which is ranked 38 among the 144 countries. This observation is confirmed by the participation of Arab countries in global exports: in 2016, the share of the Arab countries as a whole in global exports of merchandise is around 2%, close to the share of a much smaller

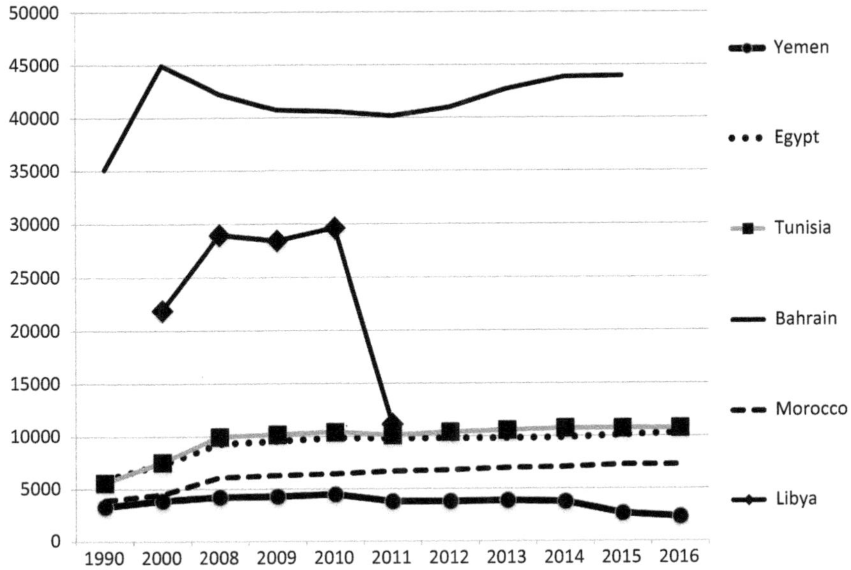

Figure 17.2 GDP per capita in the 'Arab Spring' countries (1990–2016). *Source*: World Development Indicators, World Bank, 2018.

single country like Spain (1.8%), and even below the share of a low-population country like the Netherlands (3.6%).

We should not be surprised that this very poor economic performance has had an adverse impact on socioeconomic indicators that directly affect the population. On the labour aspect, there have for many years been major issues in the Arab countries in the areas of employment, especially in female unemployment. The latest official figures (ILO Modelled Estimates, 2017) give an unemployment rate of 11.7% in the Middle East Arab states (9.3% for male and 19.8% for female) and 8.5% in North Africa (6.9% for male and 16.7% for female), compared to 5.7% worldwide. There is a disparity between countries where unemployment is quasi-nil, as in Bahrain (1.3%) or Kuwait (2.1%), and countries with huge unemployment like Palestine (27.9%) or Tunisia (15.2%). But official unemployment is not enough to characterise the situation in the Arab countries. Labour force participation rates are the lowest in the world at 48.6% in 2017 (Arab Development Portal, 2018) though higher in the Gulf countries (86.9% in Qatar, 79.7% in the UAE). Finally, labour markets in the Arab countries are marked by a high level of youth unemployment. According to the Arab Development Portal, the youth unemployment rate in the region was 26.7% in 2017, reaching the highest in Oman (48.2%) and Libya (46%) and the lowest in Qatar (0.5%). An interesting feature of Arab youth unemployment, as reported by the ILO in a (2017) study on North African countries, is that education does not protect against the risk of unemployment: on the contrary, unemployment is higher for individuals with secondary and tertiary levels of education than for individuals with primary education, except in Algeria where the rates are the same.

There is no agreement on the impact of inequality on the emergence of the Arab Spring. A World Bank report (2015) reviews the studies on the Arab inequality puzzle. It concludes that high and rising inequality had not been a key factor in triggering the Arab Spring events. However, the report confirms our preceding argumentation on the structural weaknesses of the Arab economies, pointing to the frustration of the middle classes with the deterioration of their standard of living, and to the lack of employment prospects, especially the shortage of formal sector jobs. Furthermore, the report mentions the role of wealth disparities in explaining the uprisings but stresses the difficulty of measuring them in this region. The recent contribution of the Piketty team is then crucial for assessing the role of the inequality factor in the Arab Spring. Alvaredo et al. (2018 and Chapter 12 in this volume) have produced a study of inequality in the Middle East that demonstrates that this region is one of the most (maybe the most) unequal regions in the world. According to their estimation, the top decile's income share is 64% for the Middle East, compared to 37% in Western Europe, 47% in USA and 55% in Brazil.

The economic performance of the Arab countries can be analysed through two approaches: the first is the growth accounting method which attributes to total factor productivity the residual growth rate of aggregate product that is not explained by the variations in the capital and labour inputs,[7] and the second involves a wider analysis of the empirics of economic growth that considers political and institutional factors.

One explanation of the weak economic performance of the Arab world is that their economies suffer from low levels of productivity growth. Pipitone (2009) estimates total factor productivity (TFP) for several Arab Mediterranean countries from 1971 to 2008.[8] The main result is that TFP growth has been low, with the 1980s being the decade with the worst average performance. In line with this result, Pipitone (2009) concludes that physical capital is the key factor driving actual economic growth in the Mediterranean area. Abu-Qarn and Abu-Bader (2007) confirm this result with a sample of ten MENA countries covering the period 1960–1998.[9] Accordingly, both of these papers conclude that investment, that is the accumulation of capital, seems to have been the major determinant of economic growth in the Arab countries. However,

Artadi and Sala-i-Martin (2002) did not find evidence that a low level of investment was the main source of low growth in the Arab world.[10] Instead they suggested that the decline in the investment rate since the 1980s was a consequence rather than a cause of the low economic performance. Accordingly, the main problem in the Arab world is not the quantity of investment – which has been relatively high by international and historical standards – but rather the quality of investment. They argue that the very high ratio of public to private investment in the Arab countries, together with the inefficiency of the financial system in allocating capital, has lowered the quality of investment. According to them, the development of private investment in the Arab economies has been impeded by hostile and unstable political environments. Given these results, many of the more recent studies have tried to estimate the impact of institutions in order to explain the poor economic performance in the Arab countries.

Using an empirical model of long-run growth, Hakura (2004) shows that the determinants of economic growth vary across the 16 MENA countries she considers.[11] For the GCC countries, the main factors that explain the weak growth performance are their initial level of income and the large size of the government sector. In the other MENA oil countries, the poor institutional environment (quality of the bureaucracy and rule of law) appears as a leading component in explaining the poor growth performance. With respect to the non-oil MENA countries, Hakura (2004) argues that one should add political instability to poor institutional quality and large size of governments. Makdisi, Fattah and Liman (2003) identify several factors which explain the growth performance of the MENA region in comparison with other regions: less efficient capital, a strong natural resource curse, a lower impact of trade openness, total factor productivity growth being low and a higher sensitivity to adverse external shocks. Elbadawi (2005) analyses the overall economic growth performance in the Arab world since the mid-1960s. The factors that he identifies as of first importance in explaining the weak performance of the Arab world in the long run are location and openness, demography and civil conflicts. The persistence of this weak performance can be explained by the combination of social conflicts and weak political institutions which may dampen the impact of external shocks.[12] The impact of conflicts is included in Parent and Zouache (2012) as a spatial transmission channel. These authors assume that conflicts spread between neighbouring countries and then examine how this spatial diffusion of political troubles influences the growth performance of the Arab countries.

17.3 Economic policy responses of Islamist political parties

We now turn to examine the policies put forward by three of the principal Islamist parties in the Arab world in the immediate aftermath of the Arab Spring: the Freedom and Justice Party (FJP, the party of the Muslim Brothers) in Egypt, the Ennahda Party in Tunisia (EP) and the Justice and Development Party in Morocco (JDP). Table 17.2 sets out the main elements of their economic programmes. We can identify a number of common points. First, these parties are neither very socialist nor highly pro-free market. They envisage some sort of balance between private and public sectors, with economic growth coming from private sector entrepreneurial activity in an enabling environment provided by the public sector, together with some sort of social safety net financed by a progressive taxation system. Secondly, they all aspire to high rates of economic growth in order to raise incomes and reduce unemployment. Thirdly, they all want to see corruption reduced and governance improved. Fourthly, they do not propose to ban conventional financial activities or even to shift the balance sharply in favour of Islamic banking. Fifthly, they all seem to be pragmatic about (foreign) tourism, that is, they do not intend to ban tourists from bathing or from consuming alcohol.[13] And finally, they are all relatively open to

Table 17.2 Economic programmes of Islamist parties: policies and targets

Policy area	*Freedom and Justice Party, Egypt*	*Ennahda Party, Tunisia*	*Justice and Development Party, Morocco*
Economic growth target	higher and more equitable growth	high: 7% 2012–2016, later revised down	high: 7% (later revised down), plus rise in human development index (especially literacy)
Unemployment and poverty	public services expansion; support for labour-intensive, import substitution and export industries; rises in minimum wages and pensions; introduction of unemployment benefits	reduce unemployment to 8.5% by 2016; free medical insurance and public transport for active job-seekers	employment and anti-poverty programmes to raise average income level by 40% in five years; raise pensions
Business taxes	n.s.	longer tax holiday for new firms	reduction of top rate from 30% to 25%
Business environment	pro-competition and anti-trust policies; support for SMEs; target raise investment as % of GDP	raise investment to 31% of GDP (from 25% 2011); more investment-friendly climate; encourage stock exchange listing of firms	new investment law, with Islamic finance providing cheaper loans, support to SMEs (including better access to public sector contracts)
Corruption and governance	corruption to be cut and governance to be improved via separation of powers, independent judiciary, free information, improved regulation	commission to combat corruption, disclosure of senior officials' assets	improvement in Corruption Perceptions Index to 40th from 85th in 2010; independent statistical agency
Household taxes	shift from sales and value-added taxes to progressive income taxes	lower tax burden on lower income groups	VAT reform; tax changes of progressive nature
Subsidies	to be targeted more on those who need them and/or phased out	n.s.	n.s.
Labour market	minimum and maximum wages for public sector, performance-related	vocational training especially for graduates, help for private sector to increase employment	raise minimum wage; employment incentives to firms; improved labour market monitoring and interventions; more technical training

(*Continued*)

Table 17.2 Continued

Policy area	*Freedom and Justice Party, Egypt*	*Ennahda Party, Tunisia*	*Justice and Development Party, Morocco*
Public services	improve health, education, housing, transportation; spend more on vocational training	n.s.	more social housing, better health and education
Financial sector	no specific policies but aim of gradual replacement of usurious institutions and transactions by Islamic ones	banking sector reform; adapt financial system to Islamic finance and micro-credit; make Tunis regional financial centre	facilitate Islamic finance
Tourism	support and development, no plans to ban alcohol or bathing	support and development, no plans to ban alcohol or bathing	support and development, no plans to ban alcohol or bathing
Foreign trade	amend agreements on oil/gas exports to Israel to raise prices; support for import substitution and exports; raise agricultural self-sufficiency	revive North African Union, get advanced partner status with EU	continued openness to EU, trade agreement with US, export diversification with rise in quality
Foreign investment	welcome insofar as it creates jobs and transfers technology	n.s.	welcome
Overall fiscal policy	no precise targets but ideas for raising taxes, cutting subsidies and other spending, getting better value out of past and future privatisations	n.s.	reduce deficit to within 3% of GDP
Monetary/ exchange rate policy	n.s.	support for central bank's independence; inflation target 3%	n.s.
Policies and aims not elsewhere specified	support for disabled; more R&D	reduce current account deficit; sectoral plans including alternative energy sources	encourage self-employment; environmental policies; sectoral growth policies including alternative energy sources; improve infant and natal mortality; more R&D

Sources: Constructed by authors from: Freedom and Justice Party's 2011 election programme; Ennahda's 2011 election programme; Justice and Development Party's 2011 election programme, see also their (2013) political report; Saif and Abu Rumman (2012).
Note: n.s. = nothing specific.

international economic flows, in both trade and investment. Of the three, the JDP reflects more influence from and connection to current debates in international economic policy circles, with its emphasis on the UNDP's Human Development Index and on certain types of labour market interventions. The EP's programme also has some echoes of such discussions, but the FJP rather less. The JDP also shows the most awareness of the constraints on economic policy, and the FJP the least.

We can also identify a number of common lacunae or gaps. First, while they have some limited ideas about both trade and fiscal policy, none of these parties' programmes address issues of monetary policy and exchange rate regimes, although these have been controversial in recent years, with talk (but no action) in Morocco, Tunisia and Egypt of the adoption of formal inflation targeting (IT). Secondly, they put forward no serious plans for the reform of education systems, although most observers regard failings in that area as key constraints on economic development (e.g. Muasher, 2014). Thirdly, they show little interest in issues concerning the remittances of overseas workers, which are of fundamental importance to all of these economies (should emigration be encouraged/discouraged, should the financial channels for remittances be of concern, should remittances be taxed, how might the investment of remittances in productive – as opposed to real estate – investment be encouraged, etc.). Fourthly, they do not set out any specific policies for increasing competition and reducing the power of oligopolies. And lastly, these programmes are typically light on numbers and precise commitments, from costings of public spending commitments to targets for the relative sizes of the public and private sectors. It should be said, however, that this lack of precision is no different from that found in the programmes of other parties in the region.

The relatively undistinctive nature of and the lacunae in these economic programmes are not surprising. These are the programmes of political parties which (at least in the Egyptian and Tunisian cases) had not previously expected to come to power in the near future, and therefore had little incentive to develop detailed economic programmes. But more importantly there was no obvious distinctive paradigm on which they could draw. As we explain in Chapter 16 of this book, most of the work on Islamic economics is concentrated on banking and finance – where there are considerable problems of theory and practice – and Islamic economics has very little if anything to say about core government functions such as fiscal policy, monetary and exchange rate policies, competition and anti-trust issues, labour market regulation and social security, health care management and education policy.

17.4 Alternative economic strategies and programmes

We can also pose the question, what policies might have been expected from a reformist government that emerged after the Arab Spring, that is, a government operating on the basis of conventional economic thinking in the interest of society as a whole rather than some narrow elite? Here there are few sources to draw on, but the kind of policies such a government could implement would surely include the following. First, such a government could act to limit corruption, within a framework of improved governance with an independent judiciary and a free press. Secondly, an improved social safety net could be created. Thirdly, revised labour laws, together with genuine (rather than government-controlled) trade unions and a substantial minimum wage, could allow a major shift in the balance of power in the labour market which would reduce inequality and poverty at the lower end of the income scale. Fourthly, additional state support for small businesses could be provided, notably in the form of access to finance. Fifthly, there is scope for public sector spending to improve the physical infrastructure in many cases, particularly transport but also telecommunications including internet access. Sixthly, major tax reforms are appropriate in many countries, including the introduction and/or reform of progressive income tax systems, in ways that would increase tax revenues and reduce existing inequalities. Seventhly, such a government could take action to improve competition and reduce monopoly elements in domestic production, which is particularly important in countries where liberalisation and privatisation under authoritarian regimes have produced an Arab version of crony capitalism (Owen, 2004; Chekir and Diwan, 2014; Hinnebusch, 2009). Eighthly, there is a clear need for a major improvement in the quality of the education system, particularly at primary and secondary levels. Lastly, monetary and exchange rate policies could be reformed in ways that give priority to price stability but allow the pursuit when appropriate of other objectives, as we suggest below.

Such policies, it should be noted, are in some cases not very different from those proposed, typically in less precise forms, by the Islamist parties. And in other cases where they cover gaps in the Islamists' proposals they could in many cases be adopted by them. This suggests that, at least insofar as the Islamist parties genuinely favour democratic practices, there is a middle ground where they and non-Islamist (but non-authoritarian) parties could hold constructive debates and even cooperate in coalitions. Acconcia (2018) shows that Tunisia's Arab Spring was more 'successful' than Egypt's because a consensus emerged between the political parties, notably between Ennahda and Nidaa Tounes, the civil society movements, and the main union UGTT (Union Générale Tunisienne du Travail).

However, it is not clear that either the Islamist policies discussed in section 17.3 or the reformist policies just mentioned are really able to address the reasons for the economic failures and structural weaknesses discussed in section 17.2. Given the gaps and the general nature of many of the policies discussed above, there is clearly a need for the development of more specific policies that could be implemented by reformist Arab governments in a range of areas and could address those failures with more chance of success. We consider as examples two sets of issues here, first the liberalisation process and the need to open the Arab economies to the private sector, and second the scope for improvements in monetary policy.

Firstly, it seems to us that we should be prudent on the adoption of liberalisation policies. Such policies should be clearly differentiated from those pursued over the previous decades by authoritarian governments which typically drew on elements of the 'neo-liberal' Washington consensus but operated in the interests of narrow government-connected elites. Malik and Awadallah (2013), who insist on the urgent need for Arab economies to generate independent and integrated private sectors in the Arab economies, remain vague on the mechanisms and policies which would facilitate this. Similarly, Rodrik (2009) discusses the need for industrial policies in the Middle East but fails to offer specific policy recommendations. Given the evidence that neo-liberal reforms by authoritarian governments have resulted in crony capitalism, how should a reformist government respond? Many writers (e.g. Chekir and Diwan, 2014; Malik and Awadallah, 2013) have argued that Arab crony capitalism is one of the main obstacles to faster economic growth (and greater employment and lower inequality). So should privatisations that involved sales of state firms at knockdown prices to the cronies of the then governments be unpicked? Or should policy aim to cut the oligopolies down to size by demolishing the tariff barriers that sustain them, introducing a strict anti-trust policy that imposes divestment and demerger, and/or providing help and encouragement to potential domestic competitors? And what, if anything, can and should be done about the concentration of industrial and commercial activity in the hands of the military, as in Egypt?

We agree with the recent literature on the political economy of reform in the Arab countries that points to the adverse effects of a prominent public sector and of public intervention in the Arab economies. Makdisi (2017) argues that the elite's capture of the public sector should be eliminated. In the same issue, Malik (2017) rightly insists on the diversity of rent sources in the Arab countries: foreign aid, remittances and government manipulation of the economy lead to similar adverse effects to those of the 'standard' hydrocarbon resource curse. He also appeals for reforms that could deal with the place of government in the economy. Indeed, a common theme in discussion of Arab countries' weak economic growth is the constraints on, and lack of, a dynamic private business sector.[14] Malik and Awadallah (2013) have taken up this theme in connection with the Arab Spring events. They relate the large role of the state, together with the weakness of private business which is not 'embedded' with or in the state, to the centralising tendencies of the Ottoman empire, the nature of the Arab successor states, the fragmentation of the Arab world[15] and the underdevelopment of infrastructure which could facilitate regional trade. There is a consensus between this academic literature and the opinions expressed by international institutions and Arab authorities. In a recent note based on the annual meeting of Arab finance ministers, the IMF (2016) insists on the private sector in pro-growth policies in the Arab countries and appeals for reforms that could 'boost' private investments in the region. Likewise, in a report on public employment in the Arab region, the World Bank (2016) argues that public sector employment in the Arab countries, one of the highest in the world, has adverse effects on growth; in particular, it lowers total factor productivity and causes a high public sector wage bill – the highest in the world – which dominates public spending. In principle, Arab authorities agree with this philosophy of diminishing the role of the public sector and increasing the place of the private one. For instance, Saudi Vision 2030 – a long-term economic strategy for the Kingdom of Saudi Arabia defended by the King of Saudi Arabia and promoted by the chairman of the Council of Economic and Development Affairs – clearly emphasises the role that the private sector should play in cooperation with the Saudi authorities: among the goals of Saudi Vision 2030, the authorities aim to 'increase the private sector's contribution from 45% to 65% of GDP' (Saudi Vision, 2030, p. 53).

However, would it be sufficient to diminish the size of the public sector and to reduce the place of the government in the economy, and thus to leave more space to the market and to private initiatives? Nepotism, corruption and collusion between private interests and politics are not the privilege of the state: a market-oriented economy can also work under these principles (e.g. Walras, 1897, part 2, p. 55). Thus, reforms and transition towards market-oriented economies should be treated with caution. Let us examine two examples of liberalisation, which occurred in Algeria and in Syria (Zouache, 2011), the two Arab countries which experienced and are experiencing a civil war.

In Syria and Algeria, the economic difficulties in the 1980s and the 1990s (low GDP, rising unemployment, high state expenditures leading to huge debt, etc.) created an urgent need for reforms. This need involved a transition from a heavily command economy towards more of a market economy. For instance, in Syria, the Baath party, in a meeting in 2005, recommended a programme of economic transition. Indeed, the tremendous amount of reforms that concerned Syria's financial system gave the impression that Syria had taken a new path towards the adoption of a market economy before the civil war started. But this was not the case: Syria had not really broken with its past, for at least two reasons. Firstly, Syria's banking system still presented the picture of a system in line with socialist principles where the economy is organised around a close relationship between public banks, public firms and the government. Secondly, Syria's authorities still had a direct control both over the new institutions created, such as the Council of Money and Credit, and older institutions such as the Central Bank of Syria. In Algeria, the Hamrouche government (1988–1991) promulgated a series of laws centred on the liberalisation of prices and the end of subsidies, the end of state monopolies on trade (imports) and the liberalisation of the labour market with the adoption of the principle of labour flexibility. But the most important reform was the law on money and credit of 10 April 1990, which, in addition to providing an institutional framework for the liberalisation of the banking and financial system, cut the state monopoly on foreign trade.

In practice, the reforms did not cause systemic change in the economic system in either country, mainly because the financial architecture in Algeria and Syria (central bank, banking and financial system) has not been developed and fiscal policies have been used to soften the budget constraints (Zouache, 2011). Furthermore, the political authorities have not accepted systemic change. Consequently, the selective economic liberalisation that Algeria and Syria chose to adopt from the beginning of the 1990s has not led to any systematic democratisation. On the contrary, the model of economic neo-liberalism accepted by the authorities has made political change more complex and more difficult since new actors have appeared on the scene, new actors who have adopted rent-seeking behaviour and now defend the status quo (Zouache, 2011). This all suggests that there is a great deal of work to be done in order to design effective policies to deal with the poor side-effects of past liberalisation and to organise a genuine and productive opening up of the Arab economies.

A second example of an area in which there is a need for good policy analysis is that of monetary and exchange rate policies.[16] Conventional arguments suggest that in monetary policy priority should be given to price stability, where inflation depends on inflation expectations as well as excess demand. 'Modern' central banks such as those in developed and in some emerging countries therefore typically put emphasis on transparency and accountability as ways to help them to influence inflation expectations (Blinder et al., 2008; Schmidt-Hebbel, 2010). In particular, (formal or informal) inflation-targeters usually publish regular monetary bulletins of some kind containing their forecasts for real income growth and inflation, indicate their likely reactions to possible shocks *ex ante* and try to explain their decisions *ex post*. These processes, which include the central bank answering and interacting with its financial sector, academic and political critics, are seen as fundamental to the operation of their monetary strategies.

Recent work on countries' monetary policy frameworks since the early 1970s (Cobham, 2021) has highlighted two main trends: the move towards inflation targeting, and the move towards more 'intensive' monetary policy frameworks that offer greater precision of monetary control (these include full inflation targeting but also a number of other frameworks such as full exchange rate targeting and well-structured discretion (see 2021). These trends are well-established among the 26 'advanced' economies covered by Cobham (2021), but they are also present among the 33 emerging economies considered, albeit the trends have not gone so far. However, in the Arab world the authoritarian regimes have always rejected this kind of engagement, and their central banks remain for the most part lacking in the transparency and accountability that are an important part of these trends. The basic reasons for the poor central bank governance, on the one hand, and for countries such as Egypt, Tunisia and Morocco not proceeding to inflation targeting (IT), on the other, would seem to lie not in carefully considered views about the costs and benefits of such changes,[17] but in the old regimes' preference for full control and their resistance to accountability and transparency (see, for example, Selim, 2011; Boughzala and Cobham, 2011; Boughzala and Moussa, 2011); in that sense monetary and exchange rate policy can be seen as a microcosm of the problems faced by these countries.[18]

But what should a reformist government which is willing to accept accountability and transparency do? Should it make its central bank independent, build up its technical expertise, develop the country's financial infrastructure (money and bond markets, payments systems), float the country's exchange rate and introduce standard inflation targeting? Should it opt for a more nuanced set of objectives so that the central bank can also respond, *in extremis*, to misalignments of exchange rates or asset prices? Or should it stick with the old policy of exchange rate targeting, which is inferior in several respects but has lower requirements in terms of technical capacity and the development of the financial infrastructure? These are the kind of issues which economists working on the region could usefully address.

17.5 Conclusion

In this chapter we have argued that there was a significant economic element to the Arab Spring, but this was more about the poor long-term economic (as well as non-economic) performance of Arab governments than any immediate short-term economic squeeze. We then examined the stated economic programmes of major Islamist parties and argued that they were not very different from the policies and strategies that might be pursued by non-Islamist reformist governments.

In our view it is time for economists to work on specific policy proposals in these and many other areas, proposals which reformist governments could implement, and which can be used to challenge authoritarian governments that are reluctant to reform. At the same time economists need themselves to take transparency and accountability seriously: reformist governments do not just need to implement good policies, they need to convince their peoples that they are good policies by explaining them and defending them, and economists should help to develop the arguments that are appropriate for this purpose.

Notes

1 In the May 2018 elections (ISIE, 2018), the independents obtained the highest share (32.9%), followed by Ennahda (29.68%) and Nidaa Tounes (22.7%). This was against a low participation rate of only 33.7%.
2 The Centre for Systemic Peace (the Polity IV project) proposes a 'Polity Score' that captures the spectrum of regimes on a 21-point scale ranging from -10 (hereditary monarchy) to +10 (consolidated democracy). The Polity scores can also be converted into regime categories in a suggested three-part categorisation of 'autocracies' (-10 to -6), 'anocracies' (-5 to +5) and 'democracies' (+6 to +10). 0 refers to the case of anarchy.
3 See Said (2015) for a discussion of the Egyptian case.
4 Malik and Awadallah (2013) give a broad perspective on the political economy of the Arab Spring. To them, the Arab model of preserving stability via social redistribution was no longer sustainable given the increase of population and the decrease of states' resources. The lack of a private sector that could furnish jobs is also emphasised. Makdisi (2017) offers an interesting reflection on the political dimension of the Arab Spring. Hertog's (2017) study of the political economy redistribution in the Middle East reveals how the Arab Spring testifies to the break-up of the Arab social contract previously based on the redistribution of resources, notably via government employment and energy and food subsidies.
5 See the special issue of *Arabian Humanities* on the Arab Spring in the Arabian Peninsula (Bonnefoy, 2015).
6 The CIP index measures the capacity of countries to produce and export manufactured goods and thus the situation of countries in the global division of labour. The CIP Index is composed of eight sub-indicators defined within the framework of three key dimensions that capture different aspects of a country's industrial competitive performance: the capacity to produce (manufactured value added per capita) and export (manufacturing export per capita), technological deepening and upgrading (industrial intensity and export quality) and the world impact (country-specific impact on world manufacturing value added and country-specific impact on world manufacturing exports).
7 Results using this method need to be treated with caution since TFP estimates depend heavily on the assumed form of the production function, and this caution is even more important in the light of the data issues in Arab countries.
8 The Arab countries examined are: Algeria, Egypt, Jordan, Lebanon, Libya, Morocco, Palestinian Territories, Syrian Arab Republic and Tunisia.

9 Algeria, Egypt, Iran, Israel, Jordan, Morocco, Sudan, Syria, Tunisia and Turkey. See Abu-Qarn and Abu-Bader (2007).

10 The authors constructed a measure of GDP per capita, by aggregating the World Bank or the Summers–Heston–Aten/Penn World Tables (2002) PPP-adjusted GDP data for each country and dividing it by aggregate population. The countries used to construct this measure of Arab World GDP were: Algeria, Egypt, Kuwait, Oman, Saudi Arabia, Mauritania, Morocco, Syria, Tunisia, Comoros and Jordan. Lebanon, Libya, the West Bank and Gaza Strip, Bahrain, Qatar, UAE, Iraq and Yemen were excluded because of data limitations.

11 In Hakura's (2004) study, the MENA countries are divided into three sub-groups: GCC countries (Bahrain, Kuwait, Oman, Qatar, Saudi Arabia, the United Arab Emirates); other oil-exporting countries (Algeria, Islamic Republic of Iran and Libya); and non-oil MENA countries (Egypt, Jordan, Lebanon, Morocco, Syrian Arab Republic, Tunisia and Yemen).

12 On the role of wars, see Elbadawi and Makdisi (2010).

13 It is less clear that such activities would be allowed for domestic citizens.

14 See Anderson and Martinez (1998).

15 Where, for example, intra-Arab trade is significantly below that predicted by a gravity model – see Al-Atrash and Yousef (2000).

16 There has been much more work on fiscal policy for the Arab countries, see for example ESCWA (2018), but monetary and exchange rate policies have often been neglected.

17 See Cobham (2011) for a discussion of these costs and benefits, against the background of an analysis of the relationship between countries' financial institutions and markets, on the one hand, and the monetary and exchange rate regime choices which they can reasonably make, on the other, with particular reference to the Arab countries. Cobham and Dibeh (2009, 2011) and Boughazala and Cobham (2011) each contain a range of papers on monetary policy issues in the Arab countries.

18 Arab governments have also failed to develop the statistical database for monetary policy decision-making: as of 1989 no Arab country had consistent quarterly data on real or nominal GDP published in *International Financial Statistics*, and several had no such data for inflation; even by 2015 only five had such data for real GDP and four for nominal.

References

Abu-Qarn, A.S. and Abu-Bader, S. (2007), 'Sources of Growth Revisited: Evidence from Selected MENA Countries', *World Development*, 35(5): 752–771.

Acconcia, G. (2018), 'The Uprisings in Egypt: Popular Committees and Independent Trade Unions', mimeo.

Achcar, G. (2013), *Le peuple veut. Une Exploration radicale du soulèvement arabe*, Arles: Actes Sud.

Al-Atrash, H. and Yousef, T. (2000), 'Intra-Arab Trade: Is it too Little?', Working Paper 00/10, Washington, DC: IMF.

Alvaredo, F., Assouad, L. and Piketty, T. (2018), 'Measuring Inequality in the Middle East 1990–2016: The World's Most Unequal Region?', WID.world Working Paper Series, 2017/15.

Anderson, R. and Martinez, A. (1998), 'Supporting Private Sector Development in the Middle East and North Africa', in N. Shafik (ed.), *Prospects for Middle Eastern and North African Economies*, London: Macmillan.

Arab Development Portal, 'Labour and Employment', http://www.arabdevelopmentportal.com/indicator/labor-and-employment (accessed May 2018).

Artadi, E.V. and Sala-i-Martin, X. (2002), 'Economic Growth and Investment in the Arab World', Economics Working Papers 683, Barcelona: Universitat Pompeu Fabra.

Blinder, A., Ehrmann, E., Fratzscher, M., De Haan, J. and Jansen, D-J. (2008), 'Central Bank Communication: A Survey of Theory and Evidence', *Journal of Economic Literature*, 46(4): 910–945.

Bonnefoy, L. (ed.) (2015), 'The Arab Spring in the Arabian Peninsula', *Arabian Humanities*, 4. https://journals.openedition.org/cy/2803

Boughzala, M. and Cobham, D. (2011), *Inflation Targeting in MENA Countries: An Unfinished Journey*, Basingstoke: Palgrave Macmillan.

Boughzala, M. and Moussa, H. (2011), 'The Uncertain Journey Towards Inflation Targeting in Tunisia', in Boughzala and Cobham (2011).

Brahimi, A. (2011), 'Libya's Revolution', *The Journal of North African Studies*, 16(4): 605–24.

Chekir, H. and Diwan, I. (2014), 'Crony Capitalism in Egypt', *Journal of Globalization and Development*, 5(2): 177–212.

Cobham, D. (2011), 'Monetary Policy Architecture, Financial Institutions and Financial Markets in the Middle East and North Africa: An Overview', in Cobham and Dibeh (2011).

Cobham, D. (2021), 'A Comprehensive Classification of Monetary Policy Frameworks for Advanced and Emerging Economies', *Oxford Economic Papers*, 73(1): 2–26.

Cobham, D. and Dibeh, G. (eds.) (2009), *Monetary Policy and Central Banking in the Middle East and North Africa*, London: Routledge.

Cobham, D. and Dibeh, G. (eds.) (2011), *Money in the Middle East and North Africa: Monetary Policy Frameworks and Strategies*, London: Routledge.

Cobham, D. and Zouache, A. (2015), 'Economic Features of the Arab Spring', Economic Research Forum, Working Paper No. 97.

Economic and Social Commission for Western Asia (2018), *Rethinking Fiscal Policy for the Arab Region*, Beirut: UNESCWA.

Elbadawi, I.A. (2005), 'Reviving Growth in the Arab World', *Economic Development and Cultural Change*, 53(2): 293–326.

Elbadawi, I.A. and Makdisi, S. (eds.) (2010), *Democracy in the Arab World: Explaining the Deficit*, London: Routledge.

Ennahda Party (Tunisia) (2011), *Election Programme 2011*, in Arabic, http://www.ennahdha.tn/%D8%A7%D9%84%D8%A8%D8%B1%D9%86%D8%A7%D9%85%D8%AC-%D8%A7%D9%84%D8%A7%D9%86%D8%AA%D8%AE%D8%A7%D8%A8%D9%8A-2011

Freedom and Justice Party (Egypt) (2011), *Election Program (for Parliamentary Elections 2011)*, Cairo: Freedom and Justice Party.

Hakura, D.S. (2004), 'Growth in the Middle East and North Africa', IMF Working Paper, 04/56.

Hertog, S. (2017), 'The Political Economy of Distribution in the Middle East: Is There a Scope for a New Social Contract?', *International Development Policy*, 7: 1–24.

Hinnebusch, R. (2009), 'Debates on Syrian Political Economy under the Ba'ath', in R. Hinnebusch and S. Schmidt (eds.), *The State and Political Economy of Reform in Syria*, St Andrews Papers on Contemporary Syria: University of St Andrews Centre for Syria Studies.

International Labour Organization (2017), *Youth and Unemployment in North Africa. A Regional Overview*, Geneva: ILO, 1–40.

International Monetary Fund (2016), *Investment and Growth in the Arab World. A Scoping Note*, Washington, DC: IMF, 1–40.

ISIE (2018), *Résultats des élections municipales*, Tunis: Instance Supérieure Indépendante pour les élections. http://www.isie.tn/elections/elections-municipales-2018/

Justice and Development Party (Morocco) (2011), *Election Programme 25 November 2011*, in Arabic, accessed online summer 2014 via www.pjd.ma (no longer available).

Justice and Development Party (Morocco) (2013), *Political Report to National Council 2013*, in Arabic, accessed online summer 2014 via www.pjd.ma (no longer available).

Makdisi, S. (2017), 'Reflections on the Arab Uprisings', *International Development Policy*, 7: 22–40.

Makdisi, S. (forthcoming), 'The Arab region: development without democracy', forthcoming, *Scottish Journal of Political Economy*.

Makdisi, S., Fattah, Z. and Liman, I. (2003), *Determinants of Growth in the MENA Countries*, Institute Working Paper, No. 39, Kuwait: Arab Planning.

Malik, A. (2017), 'Rethinking the Rentier Curse', *International Development Policy*, 7: 41–57.

Malik, A. and Awadallah, B. (2013), 'The Economics of the Arab Spring', *World Development*, 45: 296–313.

Muasher, M. (2014), *The Second Arab Awakening and the Battle for Pluralism*, New Haven, CT: Yale University Press

Owen, R. (2004), *State, Power and Politics in the Making of the Modern Middle East*, London: Routledge.

Parent, O. and Zouache, A. (2012), 'Geography versus Institutions: New Perspectives on the Growth of Africa and the Middle East', *Journal of Institutional and Theoretical Economics*, 168(3): 488–518.

Parent, O. and Zouache, A. (2018), 'Role of Peer Effects in Social Protests. Evidence from the Arab Spring', mimeo.

Pipitone, V. (2009), 'The Role of Total Factor Productivity in the Mediterranean Countries', *International Journal of Euro-Mediterranean Studies*, 2(1): 27–51.

Pradhan, P.K. (2017), *Arab Spring and Sectarian Faultlines in West Asia: Bahrain, Yemen and Syria*, New Delhi: Institute for Defence Studies and Analyses.

Rodrik, R. (2009), 'Industrial Policy: Don't ask Why? Ask How', *Middle East Development Journal*, 1(1): 1–29.

Said, M. (2015), 'Wages and Inequality in the Egyptian Labor Market in an Era of Financial Crisis and Revolution', Economic Research Forum Working Paper No. 912.

Saif, I. and Abu Rumman, M. (2012), *The Economic Agenda of the Islamist Parties*, Washington: Carnegie Middle East Center.

Schmidt-Hebbel, K. (2010), 'Inflation Targeting and Emerging Market Economies', in D. Cobham, O. Eitrheim, S. Gerlach and J. Qvigstad (eds), *Twenty Years of Inflation Targeting: Lessons Learned and Future Prospects*, Cambridge: Cambridge University Press.

Selim, H. (2011), 'The Evolution of the Monetary Framework in Egypt and the Elusive Goal of Price Stability', in Cobham and Dibeh (2011).

Vision 2030 (2016), Kingdom of Saudi Arabia, www.vision2030.gov.sa:1–85.

Walras, L. (1897), 'L'Etat et les chemins de fer', *Revue de Droit et Science Politique en France et à l'étranger*, tome 7: 417–436 and tome 8: 42-61, in Walras, Etudes d'Economie Appliquée.

World Bank (2015), 'Inequality, Uprisings, and Conflicts in the Arab World', MENA Economic Monitor, Washington, DC: The World Bank, 1–58.

World Bank (2016), 'Public Employment and Governance in MENA', Report No. ACS18501.

World Bank (2018), *World Development Indicators*, Washington: World Bank.

Zouache, A. (2011), 'Why Economic Liberalism Is Not Sufficient to Change the Arab World and Why Politics is Crucial. Lessons from Algeria and Syria', mimeo.

18

THE YOUTH BULGE

The mismeasured, misunderstood and mistreated Arab youth

Zafiris Tzannatos

18.1 Introduction

Industrialised countries complain about the "old age crisis": they already have too many and rising numbers of people past their working age. Developing countries have too many youths, the so called "youth bulge". The case of high-income countries is clear as ageing economies have increasingly fewer workers and face higher pension bills. Why the youth might be a problem is more complex, but a single explanation has gained prominence: "the presence of idle and unemployed young people in the developing world, or so-called 'youth bulge', is emerging as a catalyst for internal violence" (Beehner, 2007). This proposition has attracted significant support after 2001 following the September 11 events in the USA.

This belief is at face value supported by the empirical evidence. Following the claim that youth bulges above a certain "critical level" make countries especially prone to conflict (Huntington, 1996), an empirical study confirmed that "the ratio of the number of men ages 15 to 29 years of age versus men 30 and older in a population appears to be associated with the occurrence and severity of conflicts" (Mesquida and Wiener, 1999, Leahy et al., 2012). Others predicted that countries in Sub-Saharan Africa, the Middle East and South Asia face the highest demographic risk of civil conflict in the near future (Cincotta et al., 2003). Another study counted that "80 percent of civil conflicts between 1970 and the end of the millennium took place in nations where at least 60 percent of the population had not reached the age of 30 years."[1]

Not much has happened since in Africa or Asia. In fact, in many countries, notably in East Asia and to a lesser degree Latin America, the youth bulge passed without much fuss. However, the youth bulge in the Arab region had been noted before 2011: "the end of the youth bulge trend, for most states of the Arab world, will not occur until 2030 or, for states like Iraq, Oman, Qatar, the UAE, and Yemen that are further delayed in their youth bulges, until 2050" (World Bank, 2008).[2]

Then the Arab region exploded starting with Tunisia in 2011. This turned research on the youth bulge hypothesis from a cottage industry among demographers to a full-scale industrial scale production across the whole spectrum of social sciences from economics and politics to sociology and anthropology. Summarising early findings of the literature and fine-tuning the youth bulge hypothesis at the time of the uprisings, a study reported

> for years scholars have been warning about the youth bulge – that the disproportionately large population of young *men* in the Arab world is a ticking time bomb. This logic focused on young people's violent potential: young men with little access to jobs and whose grievances aren't addressed by good governance are more likely to join rebel movements.
>
> *(Schwartz, 2011)*

In the same year, a World Bank flagship publication on conflict, security and development confirmed that in North Africa "youth unemployment has been a severe problem" (World Bank, 2011). And the following year the World Bank's Chief Economist and Senior Vice President noted

> if a large cohort of young people cannot find employment and earn satisfactory income, the youth bulge will become a demographic bomb, because a large mass of frustrated youth is likely to become a potential source of social and political instability.
>
> *(Lin, 2012)*

By 2013, the list of problems associated with the youth bulge started rightly expanding beyond the youth bulge: "massive youth unemployment, increasing quantity but decreasing quality of education, large numbers of unemployed degree-holders, delayed marriage, and housing access concerns – translate into a massive societal problem not seen to this extreme elsewhere" (Mulderig, 2013).

Fast forward to 2017, and female unemployment was added to the picture: "Unemployment among the youth, especially *females*, was one of the most important causes behind the Arab Spring" (Ansani and Daniele, 2012; Korotayev et al., 2014; Qadir-Mushtaq and Afzal, 2017).[3]

This chapter examines these claims empirically. Have the youth bulge, youth (and female) unemployment and low quality and irrelevant education been mainly responsible for the uprisings? And how does this compare with other broader explanations?

The chapter adopts an economic perspective to which some political considerations are added. It argues that the uprisings cannot be credibly attributed mainly to the youth either demographically (due to "the bulge" that cannot be statistically confirmed) or economically (in terms of worsening prospects and also compared to those for adults). It concludes that the likely causes of the Arab Spring have been the many structural constraints Arab economies suffer from that affect both the youth *and* adults and also women *and* men.

While this chapter seeks to draw some empirical conclusions across the Arab region, their validity may be compromised by the huge diversity that exists between the Arab countries.[4] This issue is briefly covered in Section 18.2. Section 18.3 presents an overview of the situation of the youth, employment, education and gender. This is followed by putting these facts in economic and political contexts in Sections 18.4 and 18.5. The final section concludes.

18.2 Arab countries: diversity and measurement issues

Regional research makes interchangeable references to the Arab region and the "Middle East and North Africa" region (MENA). In some cases, regional profiles are constructed on the basis of only a handful of countries for which information is available, thus limiting their value for generalisations across the region. Moreover, a commonly used way to profile the region has been using population-weighted averages. The number of countries under consideration and the choice of metrics can affect the validity of conclusions as explained below.

There are several different ways of classifying the "MENA region".[5] This chapter encompasses all 22 Arab countries that are grouped into the Gulf Cooperation Council (GCC), North Africa (NA) and the Middle East (ME) and sub-Saharan countries (SSA).[6]

Second, there is a choice to be made between population-weighted averages and country averages. A common approach so far has been the use of weighted averages. Such an average refers to the "average Arab" which probably has some value in some cases. However, when assessing country economic performance, it is more appropriate to use country averages. This is not a trivial issue as Egypt accounts for 40 percent of the population in North Africa, and Saudi Arabia for 60 percent of the total population in GCC countries (and 80 percent of GCC nationals). Moreover, in the conventional classification of MENA, Iran accounts for 46 percent of the population in the Middle East.

Having defined the country groupings above and what kind of average is more appropriate, one remaining issue is the definition of the "youth". Regional analysts adopt at times a broad definition for the youth (persons between the ages of 15 and 29 – and some till the age of 35).[7] This chapter adopts the ILO and UN definitions that refer to persons between the ages of 15 and 24.

18.3 Facts or myths?

18.3.1 The youth bulge

Some analysts define the youth bulge relative to total rather than more appropriately to the adult population aged 25–64 as this chapter does. It is the adults that youth compete with for jobs, not the elderly or children who do not usually participate in the labour force or violent events. In the 1970s the youth-to-adult ratio was around 50 percent in all three Arab sub-regions. The decline in the GCC has been almost linear since then – partly because of the increase in the expatriate labour force. This has been followed by North African countries since the 1980s. In the Middle East the ratio peaked in 1990 and has declined significantly since (Figure 18.1). Taking the region as a whole, the ratio had already decreased by 22 percent between 1980 and 2010 – not an insignificant decline.

18.3.2 Youth unemployment

In addition to losing its share in the population, youth unemployment had declined more than that for adults over time. The overall ratio of unemployed youth to unemployed adults decreased from 1.4 in 1991 to near parity by 2010 and reached even lower levels in the Middle East (Figure 18.2). The overall decline has been of the order of a significant 30 percent. In fact, by 2010 there were 5 percent more unemployed adults than unemployed youth.

The decline in the importance of youth, both in terms of their shares in the population and unemployment, raises already the question: why did the youth revolt in 2010 after an apparently random event in Tunisia but not in 1990 when they were more numerous, more of them were unemployed, the economies had reached their rock bottom and the youth had an apparently obvious course to fight against, namely the introduction of structural adjustment and the roll-back of the state?

18.3.3 The structure of the youth population

It is worth putting the previous two demographic statistics in context. There does not seem to have been a deterioration in the structure of the youth population during the two decades

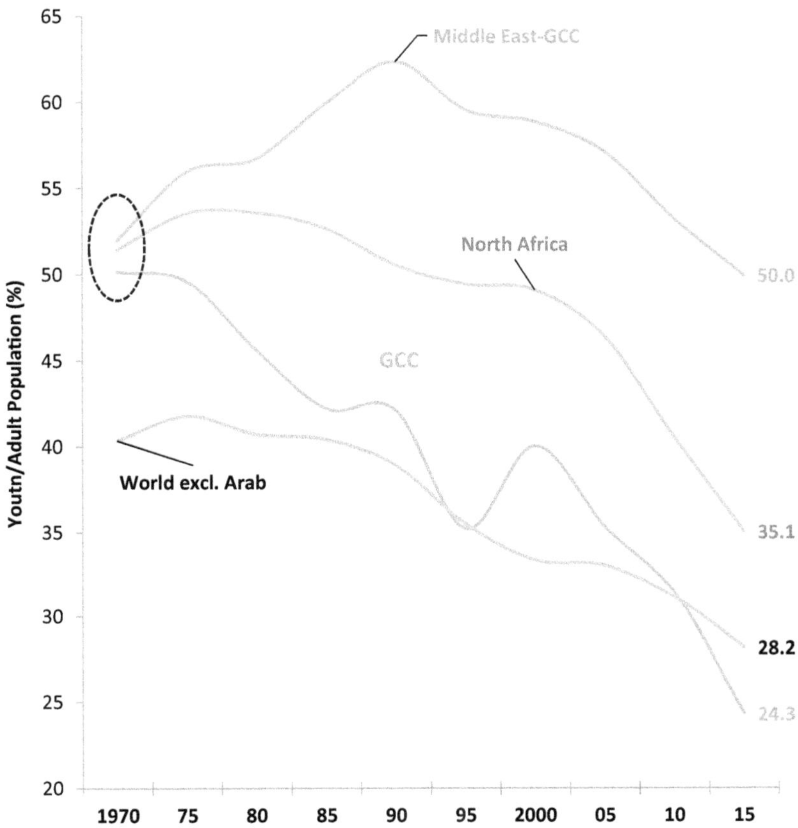

Figure 18.1 Ratio (%) of youth-to-adult population, 1970–2015. *Source*: Population Division of the Department of Economic and Social Affairs of the United Nations Secretariat, World Population Prospects: The 2010 Revision.

preceding the uprisings despite the fast increase in the population by 63 percent (Table 18.1). Most of the increase had been absorbed by the school system (56 percent) followed by employment (20 percent) (column 7). The share of inactive or not-in-school youth declined by 8 percent (column 6) and that for the unemployed by 2 percent and more for men (3 percent) than women (1 percent) (not shown in the table). Overall, the share of engaged youth (in school or employed) increased from below 50 percent (respectively, 17 percent and 32 percent) to almost 60 percent (32 percent and 27 percent) (columns 3 and 4). If anything, these changes suggest that the youth improved their position not only relatively to adults but also in terms of their own status.

18.3.4 Jobless growth

The fiscal consolidation and pro-market structural adjustment measures since the 1990s have often been charged with leading to a rise in unemployment, especially among the youth, the conclusion being that economic growth on the way to 2010 was jobless. This proposition has often been found to be correct as this type of reform is typically associated with austerity. However, following the reforms, there has been a vibrant employment response in the region.

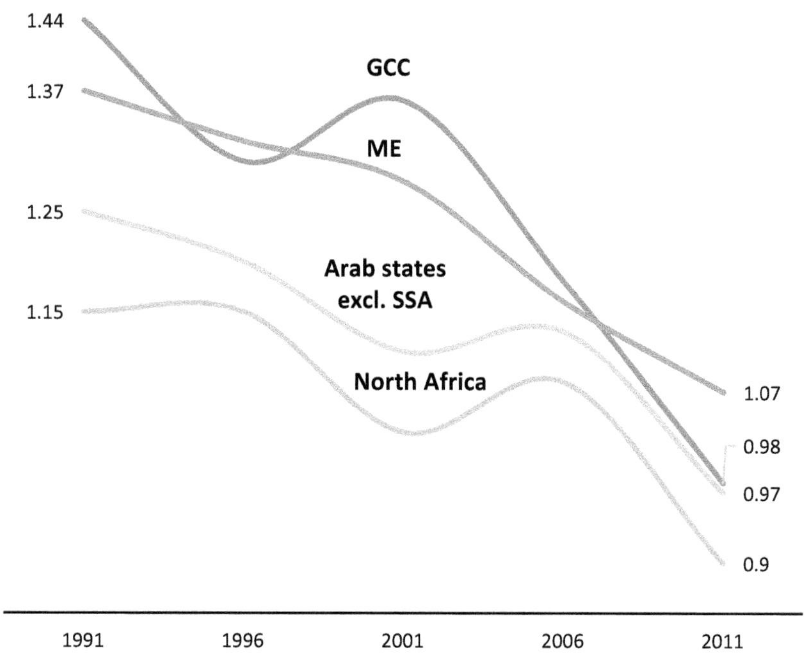

Figure 18.2 Ratio of unemployed youth to unemployed adults, 1991–2010 *Note*: For GCC earliest data are for 1994. *Source*: ILO/UNDP (2012).

Table 18.1 Structure of youth population, Arab countries* 1991–2010

	Number (,000)		*Rates (%)*		*Change in Number (,000)*	*Change in Rates (%)*	*% Contribution to change*
	(1)	*(2)*	*(3)*	*(4)*	*(5)*	*(6)*	*(7)*
Youth status	*1991*	*2010*	*1991*	*2010*	*1991–2010*	*1991–2010*	*1991–2010*
In school	6,300	19,169	17%	32%	12,869	15%	56%
Employed	11,775	16,365	32%	27%	4,590	-5%	20%
Unemployed	4,071	5,333	11%	9%	1,262	-2%	5%
Inactive *plus* NS	15,081	19,538	41%	32%	4,457	-8%	19%
TOTAL	37,227	60,405	100%	100%	23,178	..	100%
Unemployment rate	26%	25%	26%	25%	..	-1%	..
NS–NE	19,152	24,871	..	..	5,719	..	25%
(NS–NE)/Total	51%	41%	51%	41%	..	-10%	..
Total in million	37,227	60,405	37,227	60,405	23,178	..	..

Source: ILO/UNDP (2012): Statistical Appendix.
* Excluding the Sub-Saharan Arab countries
Note: NS: Not in School; NE: Not in Employment; figures subject to rounding.

Figure 18.3 shows the ratio of the percentage increase in employment to the percentage increase in economic growth (the so-called "employment elasticity"). A typical value of the elasticity is 0.5 plus/minus 0.1–0.2 points. The averages for the three Arab sub-regions are above this value and more than double that of their comparators. With respect to individual country

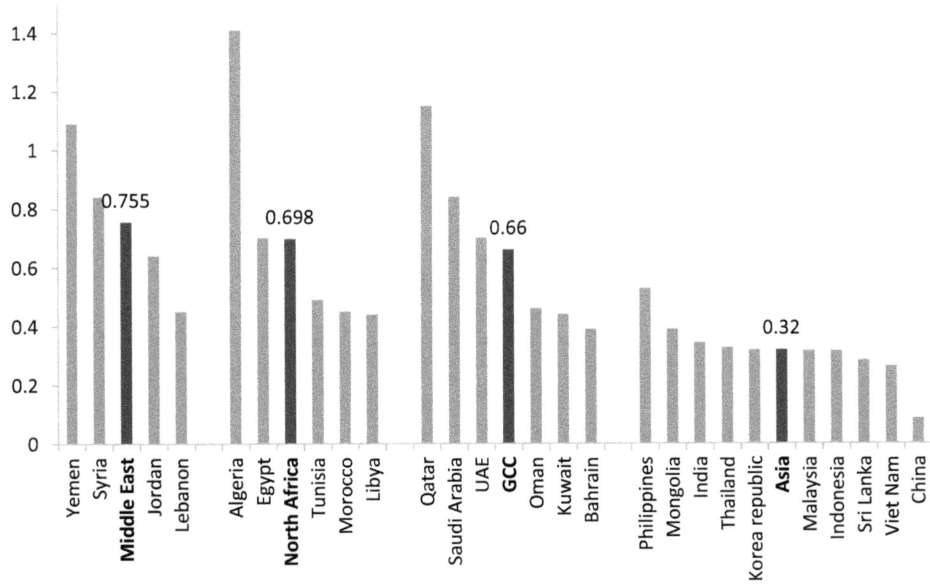

Figure 18.3 Employment output elasticity, Arab countries vs. comparators, 2000–2010. *Source*: ILO/UNDP (2012).

comparison, only the Philippines has a higher elasticity than one Middle East country, two North African countries and three GCC ones.

18.3.5 Low quality and irrelevant education

In practically all comparative international assessments (such as TIMSS, PISA and PIRLS),[8] the learning outcomes of students in participating Arab countries are found to be below the world average with respect to reading, mathematics, sciences and overall scholastic achievement. This is a fact that at face value may lead to the conclusion "The Middle East has today one of the highest rates of youth unemployment. Many of these young people are not only unemployed, they are also unemployable" (Malik, 2011). So far, the previous discussion showed that, if anything, the Arab youth have been more employable than adults. In any case, the issue is whether the low scholastic outcomes constitute a *binding* constraint to employment creation. For this to be so, first, the economy must be able to generate enough jobs and, second, these jobs should require more education than the job-seekers have (Tzannatos, 2014).

There are several reasons to take some of the heat away from education and argue that the binding constraint is the limited number of jobs the economy generates at the macro level and the low sophistication of production techniques used by companies (or required by the public sector). The latter refers to the low capital intensity that arises partly because of lack of competition and partly by low wages due to excess labour supply conditions in the labour market *for both youth and adults*. One indicator that suggests education is less of a constraint than is commonly perceived is that the Arab region has one of the highest skilled emigration rates. This raises the question, how come Arab job-seekers have the education that enables them to work in more sophisticated jobs abroad (e.g. in industrialised countries or the GCC) but their education is of little use in their own countries? The most credible answer to this is that employment growth has been biased towards low skills and, alternatively said, the demand for skills by the private sector has been low (Kawar and Tzannatos, 2012).

Two further indicators diluting the argument that education is of low quality and little relevance *compared to the requirements of production* are the low returns to education in the Arab region and the high unemployment rates of university graduates (Tzannatos et al., 2016). In combination, these two indicators suggest that employers are not prepared to pay high wages (a labour demand effect) while there is an excess supply of educated workers (a labour supply effect). Both suggest that the labour market is not clearing due to structural impediments (see below), though still academically education can and should be improved.

18.3.6 Lack of skills

A conclusion from this discussion is that, while learning outcomes among Arab students are low, they are still above those required by the number and type of jobs that the economy generates. This conclusion is reinforced by the results of surveys soliciting employers' views regarding skills shortages and mismatches as well as employers' willingness to train their workers or pay for higher skills. Recall the issue at stake is whether skills (and education) are a binding constraint to employment creation, or whether reasons should be sought in the functioning of the economy from macroeconomic policies all the way to private sector development and market competition.

Surveys of Arab employers' opinions place skills among their lowest concerns except in the GCC where answers are driven by requirements to employ nationals at times irrespective of merit and effort (ILO/UNDP, 2012: Table 1.1). Much more of concern to them are taxation, cost of finance, access to land, electricity supply, macroeconomic instability and corruption. It is true that still 30 percent of employers include skills as one of their concerns but this comes as a distant 9th among their other concerns (*ibid*: Figure 4.3).

Moreover, if Arab employers were constrained by skills they would train their workers rather than forfeit profits or even cease production. In this respect, Arab employers do not train much: the percentage of Arab companies offering training is only 25 percent. This is the lowest among all other regions (Almeida and Reyes, 2010). Finally, if lack of skills were real in economic terms, Arab companies would offer higher wages to poach them from other firms. As mentioned earlier, wage differentials are narrow in the Arab region and more so than in other regions (Tzannatos et al., op. cit.).

18.3.7 Unemployment and women

Female unemployment *rates* are much higher than those for men. This is another indisputable fact that can be coupled with another solid fact: Arab women face more restrictions in private and public life than women in most other countries. These restrictions can arise within the family or be driven by community norms, culture, religious practices or legal provisions. Though they vary across the Arab countries, legal barriers restrict women's ability to get employment without permission by a male member of the family, register a business, open a bank account, sign contracts, testify in the court, choose where to live/travel domestically or get a passport and, at a minimum, obtain a national identity card. Compared to other regions, these restrictions are much more commonly found in Arab countries and account in some cases for as many two-thirds of all countries where a specific restriction applies (World Bank, 2016). And while attitudes against women's work outside the home appear to be a widespread phenomenon among worldwide Muslim-majority countries, highly patriarchal values are particularly pronounced in Arab countries especially in the Middle East and the oil-producing countries though less so in North Africa (Diwan and Vartanova, 2017).

Still, like in the case of education, the issue is whether these restrictions are the main constraint to female employment or the general state of the economy. Looking at the composition of unemployment, one would expect to find that, compared to the rest of the world, Arab women (and youth) would account for a much higher share of *total* unemployment given their high *rates* of unemployment. Rather unexpectedly, the share of female Arab youth is on par with the rest of the world at 14 percent, and that for Arab women lower than women in other regions at 38 percent vs. 43 percent (Table 18.2). This is driven in part by the low female participation of adult women but this is precisely the point: the economy does not generate jobs for adult women, either.

Taken together, the previous discussion does not provide much evidence for the various youth bulge hypotheses posed in the introduction of this chapter. Instead of attempting to summarise the individual findings mentioned above, one can save space and conclude that, by the time of the uprisings, the Arab countries had significant structural constraints as discussed next.

18.4 So, what led to the Arab Spring?

The post-colonial period in the Arab region was followed by one dominated by state-led development and import-substitution policies. The independent states that emerged can in general be described as authoritarian and their economies as closed, that is, immune to international pressures and, more recently, largely isolated from the globalisation process.

Initially this produced relatively good results till the early 1980s in terms of economic growth and social improvements, for example, in education and health. Underlying this has been a social contract under which the state provided various economic benefits (such as public sector jobs, free social services, low taxes and subsidies for energy, water, transportation, housing and food) to a relatively sufficient number of citizens but denied most of them political participation. This arrangement has been aptly called a "democratic–authoritarian bargain" (or simply "authoritarian bargain") whereby the citizens and state join in a promise to produce material advantage "in quantities hardly available hitherto even for a restricted minority" on the condition that society demands only what the regime is capable and willing to offer. Alternatively said, this arrangement constitutes "a magnificent bribe ... on the condition that one must not merely ask for nothing that the system does not provide" (Mumford, 1964: 8–9).

Table 18.2 Unemployment composition by region, 2016

	Arab	*World*
Female adult	24%	28%
Female youth	14%	14%
Male adult	34%	37%
Male youth	28%	20%
Adults	58%	65%
Youth	43%	35%
Male	62%	57%
Female	38%	43%
All	100%	100%
All (million)	14.8	197.7

Source: ILOSTAT.

As long as the Arab economies had been growing and could fund increasing public expenditures, social protection was administered through employment in the public sector, subsidies, benefits and expanding education and health services. Over time increasing public expenditures supported the emergence and rise of middle and especially richer classes in which the educated accounted for an increasing share. They identified their interests with those of the regime and thus became its defender against more open political alternatives that they perceived would hurt their interests (Diwan and Vartanova, 2018). A final boost to this social contract came from the increase in oil prices that quadrupled in 1973–1974. The resulting benefits accrued directly to oil exporters and indirectly to the other Arab countries through emigration and transfers. By the 1980s government expenditures peaked on average at over 50 percent of GDP (Diwan and Akin, 2015).

However, the ability of Arab states to maintain high public expenditures was curtailed after 1980 with the collapse of oil prices. This resulted in rising deficits and debts that unmasked the limitations of the state-led closed-economy model. The old social contract could no longer be sustained and a series of pro-market reforms were introduced from the beginning of the 1990s. The reforms were supported by the international financial institutions and followed the conventional policies of fiscal stabilisation and structural adjustment. They aimed to reduce expenditures and increase revenues; enhance market competition by removing restrictions in the operations of the private sector and reducing state ownership; and increase flexibility in the labour market by downsizing government employment and reducing worker protection. They also provided for limited political liberalisation (for example, through elections) that nevertheless rarely resulted in broader citizen participation or significant leadership changes. While the relationship between the rulers and their citizens remained to a large extent the same, the reforms were accompanied both by economic and social changes.

Fiscal consolidation largely achieved its macro objectives: the public deficits and debts were significantly reduced and by the 2000s government expenditures had been reduced to 25 percent of GDP (Diwan and Akin, 2015). This had, however, implications for the labour market as it lessened the ability of the governments to act as "employer of last resort" that also provided higher wages, better employment conditions and adequate pensions. On the social side, the rolling back of the state from social services reduced the protection afforded to many from publicly provided social services or subsidised goods and services thereby increasing insecurity among the citizens. In fairness, public expenditures needed to be rationalised. For example, social security systems generally failed to protect the poorest and benefited mostly the better off. Their replacement should have been accompanied by accommodating provisions by the private sector but generally this did not happen.

Pro-market measures aiming to increase economic growth had also some success. After the lost decade of the 1980s when growth rates had collapsed, growth was revived. However, economic growth in Arab countries has not been commensurate to that in the rest of the world. In short, the region failed to join the global frenzy that ended with the financial crisis of 2008. The reason for this is that there is a difference between "markets" and "*competitive* markets". The switch from state-led to pro-market growth had been associated with a preferential treatment of politically connected families and firms.

The privatisation that took place can be better described as "denationalisation" whose returns accrued to a small group of political insiders. These establishment elites ended up controlling larger firms and off-shore businesses that took advantage of concessionary low taxation (on the logic that this would boost exports – a key ingredient for economic growth). In reality, however, the growth of exports was constrained by the low competitiveness of on-shore production and was unable to upgrade over time (Cammett et al., 2015: Chapter 9). In the absence of domestic competition, the few (but dominant) politically connected "crony" firms proved to be less dynamic than if they faced competition. Their owners were contented with the large profits they reaped but did not create as many jobs compared to more competitive firms in the economy. One study of Egypt estimated that these privileges resulted in a loss of annual economic growth of one percent and a reduction in employment of 20 percent over a decade (Diwan et al., 2015). And in Tunisia the year before the uprisings, just 0.2 percent of firms accounted for 5.3 percent of output but as much as 16 percent of *net* profits (Rijkers et al., 2017).

On the way to the uprisings, the results from macroeconomic stabilisation and structural adjustment, albeit more limited, were appreciated by the then governments and praised by many practitioners including international organisations. Citizens' sentiments had, however, been moving in the opposite direction. Opinion surveys revealed that prior to 2008 the rest of the world was facing the future with optimism but the perceptions of Arab citizens regarding their future were negative.[9] This is not unexpected. The decline in total unemployment had come from job creation mostly in the informal economy fetching low wages under poor employment conditions (while the education attainment of job-seekers had been rising). While unemployment is generally found among lower socio-economic groups, in Arab countries it affected households across all income deciles more or less equally (Montenegro and Hirn, 2009). Two "grand ratios" in economics that show how workers and households fare had declined since the reforms were initiated: both the wage share and also the share of household consumption in GDP in the Arab region had been declining (ILO/UNDP, 2012; Tzannatos, 2015).

In addition to economic sentiments, adverse sentiments regarding governance had been piling up. Public accountability in the eyes of citizens had been declining over time. A combined economic and political picture of Arab countries is shown in Figure 18.4. All Arab countries are contained in the wrong south-west quadrant. And all Arab countries but one (Saudi Arabia) in that quadrant that had the lowest voice and accountability exploded in 2011, namely: Libya, Syria, Yemen, Tunisia and Egypt. This five-out-of-six (83 percent) "success" rate of accountability as an indicator for unrest can be compared to the usual predictive power of regressions (the R-squared) that rarely reaches more than 30 percent in cross-country analyses.

Protests started to emerge. Citizens demanded a move away from a rentier state towards a different and transformative productive state and "a new social contract with radically different 'rules of the game': the constitutions, laws and regulations, and the underlying public discourse on political and economic freedoms, social and economic justice, and the future role of the state" (Razzaz, 2013). The protests were initially contained but kept coming with increasing force. They were supressed until Tunisia provided the spark and the youth took to the streets.

If the youth have been more visible in demonstrations (and in social media), this was because they are youth: more warm-blooded and ideological, fitter and tech-savvier. However, a survey that monitored the evolving popular opinion across 18 Arab countries throughout 2011 showed that those aged over 35 were more likely to take part in protests than younger people.[10] Another survey found the percentage of unemployed who participated in protests was lower than that of the fully employed while the protests did not come from aggressive unemployed male youth but "from a diverse group of mostly young people who were middle class or affluent and had a wider set of grievances, not just labour market concerns" (Ianchovichina, 2018, 118–119).

18.5 Summary, prospects and policies

The previous section showed that rising dissatisfaction from lack of inclusive growth has been more or less universal: among youth *and* adults and also women *and* men. And the earlier discus-

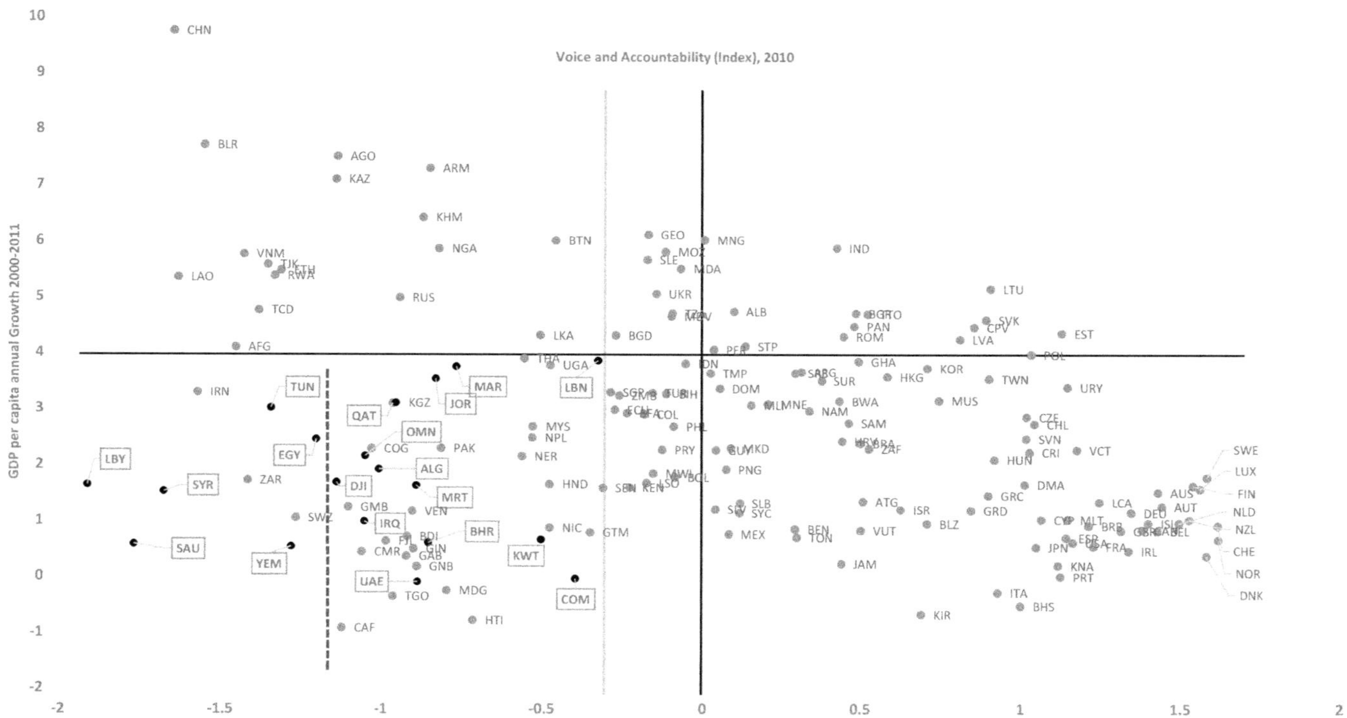

Figure 18.4 Per capita income growth and voice and accountability in the Arab states, voice and accountability index, 2010. *Source*: The Worldwide Governance Indicators, World Bank (2011); World Economic Outlook Database, IMF (2018).

sion argued that, though the labour market has been underperforming, this was not mainly due to specific youth issues.

These conclusions are in line with the empirical findings of this chapter that are, first, the youth bulge had largely gone by the 2000s – and most notably so in Tunisia where it all started from. Second, by 2010 the region had experienced fast employment growth both in historical terms and also compared to other regions – thus the alleged competition for jobs arising from the bulge weakened. Third, unemployment had become less of a youth issue and more a problem among adults. Finally, new employment had been mostly informal – something that renders immaterial the proposition about the low quality and irrelevance of education.

While one can argue that youth bulges increase the risk of conflict under conditions of economic stagnation (Urdal, 2004), the Arab economies had not been stagnating and employment was growing. However, their economic growth had not been inclusive. The unequal distributional outcomes of the reforms were felt by most citizens and not just the youth but also the adults. Thus the uprisings were not totally unanticipated. A report on the effects of the global financial crisis in the MENA region had already noted in 2009 that social tensions "*may be higher when governments in the [MENA] region pursue economic liberalization*" (emphasis added: Tzannatos, 2009, 28).

Thus, the uprisings cannot be credibly attributed to the youth either demographically (due to the bulge) or economically (in terms of worsening prospects compared to those for adults). Instead, this chapter argued that the causes of the Arab Spring can be more credibly linked to the pro-market reforms adopted from the 1990s that did not lead to *competitive* markets. Being politically controlled, the reforms preserved the political regimes. It is indisputable that the state-led quasi-paternalistic model of development favouring the establishments' insiders that formed the basis of the old social contract (till the 1990s) had to be replaced in the face of rising deficits, debts and inflation. And indeed, the reforms reduced all three and accelerated growth and employment albeit at low wages. However, the new social contract was replaced by one that recycled economic rents among the elites with little "trickle down" to the increasingly educated and higher aspiring masses. The rolling back of the state from public services and social protection had been followed by an increase in insecurity and decline in social mobility.

As quoted in the introduction of this chapter, there was indeed a "ticking time bomb" lurking in the Arab region. However, this was less due to the youth bulge and more because of "bad politics *and* bad economics" with the latter being the result of the former as "the revolutionaries came to the conclusion that it is bad politics that produced undesirable outcomes, not bad economics *per se*" (Galal and Selim, 2012). The way the reforms had been implemented exposed the assumed trade-off between economic rights and political rights.

Why, then, has the youth bulge hypothesis been initially so appealing for the Arab region? Perhaps because, first, quantities are easier to be measured and modelled than causal behavioural relationships. Second, it somehow let policy makers off the hook by arguing that high fertility reflects family, social and cultural (if not untouchable religious) values and arrangements while the youth do not like studying, are lazy consumerists and are picky as to what work they want to do. Third, the blame does not stop at the youth but extends to the low quality *and* relevance of education thus bringing into the discussion the lack of commitment and underperformance of teachers, who are mainly civil servants enjoying job security. This reasoning downplays another duty of policy makers, that is, to administer and manage education through meritocratic hiring and the modernisation both of curricula and pedagogical methods while paving the way to privatisation whose proceeds are usually appropriated by the regime's insiders.

It is therefore not surprising that references to (fictitious) *rising youth* unemployment as an important cause for the Arab Spring are still being made: "Youth unemployment rising to very high levels and the persistence of deep economic inequality were important factors contributing to the uprisings" (Makdisi, 2017). The Arab youth bulge still finds its way into many publications also with reference to the fact that the youth unemployment rate is double the global youth unemployment rate (Arab Human Development Report, 2016). This misses that the Arab unemployment rate is also double the global one.

New myths have kept being added. An impressive one is that after the uprisings, the Arab world would have needed to create 100m jobs by 2020 (Dhillon and Yousef, 2007; WEF, 2012 articles by Kuran; Al-Ississ; Al Oraibi and Jarrar). This is more a case of "groupthink" as the Arab labour force at that time was smaller than 100m. The additional 100m new jobs would have required annual increases in employment of 10 percent. This is an economic impossibility. To put this figure into perspective the increase in the Arab population between the mid-2010s and 2035 is forecast to increase by 125m. Of that increase 71 percent would come from adults (25–64) and another 19 percent from the elderly (65+). This means that adult employment creation and old age security will be a much more challenging policy issue than addressing just youth unemployment.

Looking forward, like in many other regions, Arab countries need to do more of everything and do it better. A precondition for this is to get the facts right before the facts get them (again). For example, the structural adjustment policies from the 1990s were premised on the belief that citizens would prefer private services in education and health more than public ones – something that has anecdotally been summarised in the case of Egypt as "you can go to the private clinic and lose all your money, or go to the public clinic and lose your life" (Devarajan, 2016). However, in Egypt only 11 percent of one survey's respondents stated that the private sector provides better services.[11] Even services provided by charities were found to be appreciated twice as much (20 percent) compared to those offered in the private sector. It is worth noting that the survey question was not which provider is more cost effective or which provider you would visit: the question was "*who* provides *better* health services". And with respect to education, 41 percent of respondents stated that private services were "not good" compared to only 18 percent for public services.

Future policies should also avoid the mistakes of the past. For example, the reaction of Arab governments to the Arab Spring was similar to that in previous crises, such as the food crisis of 2003 and financial crisis of 2008 (Saif and Choucair, 2009). In fact, unlike in those previous two cases, even those countries that were not directly affected by the uprisings took extensive precautionary measures to avert protests, apparently with little consideration to their long-term economic implications. In none of the three crises have the responses been coherent, being instead concentrated on quick and sizeable disbursements that were expected to produce results in the short-run. Most countries expanded public sector employment and raised salaries therein, increased minimum wages, expanded or introduced unemployment benefits and cash transfers, raised or reintroduced subsidies and (probably least necessary) raised pensions. The result has been that GDP growth has stalled, budget deficits and public debt have increased while employment creation has slowed down and unemployment has increased both for youth and adults and women and men (Galal et al., 2017).

The issue is not just to adopt sound economic fundamentals but to also address their relationship to political constraints and their impact on governance. The Arab reforms appear to have followed the logic "economic reforms first, political later". The result has been that political forces derailed the creation of *competitive* markets and prevented the emergence of inclusive economic growth while they preserved the existing structures through a combination of repression and redistribution.

The Arab countries still rank at the bottom of the world league with respect to various indices measuring citizen participation, voice and accountability, governance and democratic institutions. The latest complied *Democracy Index 2017* ranks the Arab region lowest among the rest.[12] All in all, "the Arab Spring suggests that improved economic performance cannot be viewed as an insurance policy against political instability" as "it is not straightforward economic hardship, but rather frustration with the disparity between expectation and reality that awakens the masses ... And autocrats are not exactly known for placing a high priority on social justice" (Hakimian, 2017).

Improving institutions is a bigger challenge than blaming the youth and education or claiming that Islamic values predispose citizens of Arab countries to be in favour of redistribution (compared to working harder) or against the workings of a market economy (Diwan et al., 2018a). The main value that is inimical to the workings of a market economy in the region is a low trust in state institutions, combined with a perception of high levels of corruption both in government and business (Diwan et al., 2018b).

18.6 Concluding remarks

Empirical evidence presented in this chapter and the discussion based on it have highlighted mismeasurements and misunderstandings regarding youth dynamics in Arab countries. A more factually supported conclusion is that causation runs from the mismanagement of the economy to the youth *and adults*, not from the youth bulge to the economy (and conflict). The Arab youth are not unemployable. They are more educated than their parents but there are too few jobs around not only for them but also for their parents (Kawar and Tzannatos, 2017). Unemployment in the Arab region is mainly structural rather than just a school-to-work transition issue.

Mismeasurement and misunderstandings aside, at least half of the Arab youth seem to be mistreated if only from dominant patriarchal values. Compared to their counterparts in other regions, Arab female youth are facing the future with severe cultural, legal and institutional constraints. And young Arabs, both females and males, face one of the highest "intergenerational persistence" (low upward mobility) (Krishnan et al., 2016) while inequality of opportunity in education between students from rich and poor Arab families is even higher than in Latin America which is known for its high and persistent inequalities (Salehi-Isfahani et al., 2012).

Education attainment has increased and education is certain to expand further as is also the persistence of weak labour market conditions (for adults, too). It is the combination of these two factors that has driven the uprisings as the rising aspirations of citizens are met with limited opportunities. If this combination continues for much longer, then it might be followed by another Spring that, together with that of 2011, might simply add to a recurrent pattern in the region whereby

> the interests of governing coalitions have proved more enduring than the force of ideology. Neither the socialism of the 1960s and 1970s nor the neo-liberal economic reforms of the 1990s have been able to dismantle this system of centralised control, discretion and privilege.
>
> *(Malik, 2011)*

The road to creating decent employment for youths and adults and women and men and to also unblocking societies through systems that can process competing social demands to satisfy rising expectations is much longer than the school-to-work transitions.

Notes

1 Study conducted by Population Action International and quoted from the Council of Foreign Relations: https://www.cfr.org/backgrounder/effects-youth-bulge-civil-conflicts.
2 However, earlier World Bank studies did not support the youth bulge hypothesis (Collier, 2000; Collier and Hoeffler, 1998 and 2001).
3 Some authors have even gone on to argue that "in 'youth bulge' countries, young men tend to eliminate each other or get killed in aggressive wars until a balance is reached between their ambitions and the number of acceptable positions available in their society". Algeria and Lebanon, where civil wars killed hundreds of thousands in the 1980s and 1990s, have been associated with declining fertility rates and "the warring stopped because no more warriors were being born" (Gunnar Heinsohn quoted in Kingsley, 2014).
4 Representing any region through averages can be misleading, if the countries within it differ significantly. Perhaps the within-region diversity is greater in the Arab region than in other world regions. This is so in terms of per capita income and resources, especially energy endowments, institutions, dependence on agriculture and water, population size and composition by age, religion, nationality and, in some cases, tribal origins.
5 MENA, which includes the six GCC states (Bahrain, Kuwait, Oman, Qatar, Saudi Arabia and United Arab Emirates), Algeria, Djibouti, Egypt, Iraq, Jordan, Lebanon, Libya, Morocco, occupied Palestinian territories (*aka* West Bank and Gaza), Syria, Tunisia, Yemen plus Iran. The excluded countries are those classified by the World Bank as Sub-Saharan Africa (SSA) countries: Comoros, Mauritania, Somalia and Sudan. The IMF groups the Middle East with Central Asia together (e.g. the latter includes Afghanistan, Armenia, Azerbaijan, Georgia, Iran, the Kyrgyz Republic and Pakistan). The UN (Economic and Social Commission for West Asia – ESCWA) includes more or less the same countries as MENA except Algeria and Iran.
6 This classification typically groups Iraq, Jordan, Lebanon, Syria, occupied Palestinian territories and Yemen in the ME; Algeria, Egypt, Libya, Morocco, Sudan and Tunisia in NA; and Comoros, Djibouti, Mauritania and Somalia in SSA. See ILO/UNDP (2012). SSA is at times excluded from the statistics and this is indicated accordingly.
7 See the *African Youth Charter* definition that "youth" includes those between the ages of 15 and 35 years; http://www.unesco.org/new/en/social-and-human-sciences/themes/youth/youth-definition/.
8 The three assessments are TIMSS (Trends in International Mathematics and Science Study), PIRLS (Progress in International Reading Literacy Study) and PISA (Programme for International Student Assessment).
9 Gallup World Poll Database quoted in International Institute for Labour Studies (2011).
10 The survey was conducted by the Department of Politics and International Studies at the University of Cambridge (POLIS); https://www.cam.ac.uk/research/news/the-myth-of-the-arab-spring.
11 The Egyptian Center for Public Opinion Research (Baseera, 2015).
12 The Economist presented in: https://en.wikipedia.org/wiki/Democracy_Index#Democracy_Index_by_region.

References

Adeel, Malik (2011). The Economics ofThe Arab Spring: The Region's Dependence on Natural Resources Has Prevented the Emergence of A Strong Private Sector. *Al Jazeera*, 13 October; available from: https://www.aljazeera.com/indepth/opinion/2011/10/20111010142425419849.html.

Al-Ississ, Mohamad (2012). The Access to Credit Dichotomy: Arab Financial Markets between the Pull of the Disenfranchised and Push of the Entrenched. In WEF (2012).

Almeida, Rita K. and Reyes Aterido (2010). *Investment in Job Training: Why Are SMEs Lagging so Much Behind?* Policy Research Working Paper, No. WPS 5358. The World Bank, Washington, DC.

Al Oraibi, Mina (Al-Awsat Newspaper) and Yasar Jarrar (2012). A Paradigm Shift in Government – From 'Creating' Jobs to 'Enabling' Job Creation. In WEF (2012).

Ansani, Andrea and Vittorio Danielle (2012). About a Revolution: The Economic Motivations of the Arab Spring, *International Journal of Development and Conflict*, Gokhale Institute of Politics and Economics, 2(3): 1250013–125.

Baseera (2015). *The Role of the Egyptian State in Basic Services Provision*. The Egyptian Center for Public Opinion Research (Baseera), Egypt; available from: http://baseera.com.eg/InfoGallery.aspx?ID=10

Beehner, Lionel (2007). The Effects of 'Youth Bulge' on Civil Conflicts. *Council of Foreign Relations*, 13 April.
Cammett, Melanie C., I. Diwan, A. Richards and J. Waterbury (2015). *A Political Economy of the Middle East*, Fourth Edition. Westview Press, Boulder, Colorado.
Cincotta, R., R. Engelman and D. Anastasion. (2003). *The Security Demographic: Population and Civil Conflict after the Cold War*. Population Action International, Washington, DC.
Collier, Paul. (2000). Doing Well Out of War: An Economic Perspective. In Mats Berdal and David M. Malone, eds., *Greed and Grievance: Economic Agendas in Civil Wars*. Lynne Rienner, Boulder, CO, 91–111.
Collier, Paul and Anke Hoeffler, (1998). On Economic Causes of Civil War. *Oxford Economic Papers* 50(4): 563–573.
Collier, Paul and Anke Hoeffler, (2001). *Greed and Grievance in Civil War*. World Bank, Washington, DC.
Devarajan, S. (2016). *What is the Social Contract and Why Does the Arab World Need a New One?* World Bank; available from: https://blogs.worldbank.org/arabvoices/what-social-contract-and-why-does-arab-world-need-new-one.
Dhillon, Navtej and Tarik Yousef (2007). *Inclusion: Meeting the 100 Million Youth Challenge*. Middle East Youth Initiative at Brookings Wolfensohn Center for Development and Dubai School of Government.
Diwan, Ishac and Tarik Akin (2015). *Fifty Years of Fiscal Policy in the Arab Region*. Economic Research Forum, Working Paper No. 914. Cairo.
Diwan, Ishac and Irina Vartanova (2017). The Effect of Patriarchal Culture on Women's Labor Force Participation, Working Papers 1101, Economic Research Forum, revised 06 Jan 2017.
Diwan, Ishac and Irina Vartanova (2018). *Does Education Indoctrinate? The Effect of Education on Political Preferences in Democracies and Autocracies*. Economic Research Forum, Working Paper No. 1178. Cairo.
Diwan, Ishac, P. Keefer and M. Schiffbauer (2015). *Pyramid Capitalism: Political Connections, Regulation, and Firm Productivity in Egypt*. World Bank, Policy Research Working Paper No. 7354.
Diwan, Ishac, Zafiris Tzannatos and Tarek Akin (2018a). *Economic Values in the Arab World Favor Capitalism*. Economic Research Forum Policy Perspective No. 25. Cairo.
Diwan, Ishac, Zafiris Tzannatos and Tarik Akin (2018). Debunking Myth: Economic Values in the Arab World through the Prism of Opinion Polls, *Middle East Development Journal*, 10(1), 31–63, January.
Galal', Ahmed and Hoda Selim (2012). *The Elusive Quest for Arab Economic Development*. Economic Research Forum Working Paper 722. Cairo.
Galal, Ahmed, Ishac Diwan, Ibrahim Elbadawi, Hoda Selim, Zafiris Tzannatos and Jala Youssef (2017). *Economic Management under Fire*. FEMISE Euromed Report. Economic Research Forum and FEMISE.
Hakimian, Hassan (2017). Why Economists Missed the Arab Spring. *EDITOR'S CHOICE in Online Journal Strategic Culture*, 24 March; available from: https://www.strategic-culture.org/news/2017/03/24/why-economists-missed-arab-spring/
Huntington, Samuel P. (1996). *The Clash of Civilizations and the Remaking of World Order*. Simon & Schuster, New York.
Ianchovichina, Elena (2018). *Eruptions of Popular Anger: The Economics of the Arab Spring and Its Aftermath*. World Bank, Washington, DC.
International Institute for Labour Studies (IILS) (2011). *World of Work Report 2011: Making Markets Work for Jobs*. International Labour Office, Geneva.
International Labour Organisation/United Nations Development Program (ILO/UNDP) (2012). *Rethinking Economic Growth: Towards Productive and Inclusive Arab Societies*. ILO Regional Office for the Arab States, Beirut.
International Monetary Fund (2018). *World Economic Outlook Database*. April. International Monetary Fund, Washington, DC.
Kawar, M. and Z. Tzannatos (2012). *Private Sector Does Not Demand Enough Skilled Labour*. Lebanese Center for Policy Studies, Beirut.
Kawar, M. and Z. Tzannatos (2017). Young People Need Jobs, and So Do Their Parents. *Venture*, September. Amman.
Kingsley, Patrick (2014). Does a Growing Global Youth Population Fuel Political Unrest? *The Guardian*, 19 March.
Korotayev, Andrey V.; Leonid M. Issaev, Sergey Yu. Malkov and Alisa R. Shishkina (2014). The Arab Spring: A Quantitative Analysis. *Arab Studies Quarterly* 36(2): 149–169 (Spring). Oxford.
Kuran, Timur (2012). Building Arab Civil Society to Promote Economic Growth. In WEF (2012).
Leahy, Elizabeth, Robert Engelman, Carolyn Gibb Vogel, Sarah Haddock and Tod Preston (2012). *The Shape of Things to Come: Why Age Structure Matters to a Safer, More Equitable World*. Population Action International, Washington, D.C.

Lin, Justin Yifu (2012). Youth Bulge: A Demographic Dividend or a Demographic Bomb in Developing Countries?; available from: http://blogs.worldbank.org/developmenttalk/youth-bulge-a-demographic-dividend-or-a-demographic-bomb-in-developing-countries.
Mesquida, Christian G. and Neil I. Wiener (1999). Male Age Composition and Severity of Conflicts. *Politics and the Life Sciences*, September.
Montenegro, Claudio and L. Hirn (2009). *A New Disaggregated Set of Labour Market Indicators Using Standardized Household Surveys from Around the World*. Background Paper for the World Bank's World Development Report 2009: Reshaping Economic Geography. World Bank, Washington, DC.
Mulderig, M. Chloe (2013). *An Uncertain Future: Youth Frustration and the Arab Spring*. THE PARDEE PAPERS / No. 16 / April 2013. Boston University.
Mumford, L. (1964). Authoritarian and Democratic Technics. *Technology and Culture* 5: 1–8. University of Chicago Press, Chicago, IL.
Nandini, Krishnan, Gabriel Lara Ibarra, Ambar Narayan, Sailesh Tiwari and Tara Vishwanath (2016). *Uneven Odds, Unequal Outcomes: Inequality of Opportunity in the Middle East and North Africa*. World Bank, Washington, DC.
Qadir-Mushtaq, Abdul and Muhammad Afzal (2017). Arab Spring: Its Causes and Consequences. *Journal of the Punjab University Historical Society* 30(1): 1–10 (January–June).
Razzaz, O. (2013). *The Treacherous Path Towards a New Arab Social Contract*. , Issam Fares Institute for Public Policy and International Affairs. Beirut.
Rijkers, B., C. Freund and A. Nucifora (2017). All in the Family: State Capture in Tunisia. *Journal of Development Economics* 124(C): 41–59.
Saif, Ibrahim and Farah Choucair (2009). *Arab Countries Stumble in the Face of Crisis*. Carnegie Middle East Center, Beirut.
Salehi-Isfahani, D., N. Belhaj Hassine and R. Assaad (2012). *Equality of Opportunity in Education in the Middle East and North Africa*. Economic Research Forum Working Paper No. 689. Cairo.
Samir, Makdisi (2017). Reflections on the Arab Uprisings. In G. Luciani (ed.), *Combining Economic and Political Development: The Experience of MENA*. International Development Policy series 7. Graduate Institute Publications, Geneva; Brill-Nijhoff, Boston, 22–40.
Schwartz, Stephanie (2011). Youth and the 'Arab Spring'. *USA Institute for Peace*, 28 April.
Tzannatos, Zafiris (2009). *The Impact of the Financial Crisis on the Labour Market and Social Sectors in the ESCWA Region*. ILO/ESCWA, Beirut.
Tzannatos, Zafiris (2014). *Labour Demand and Social Dialogue: Two Binding Constraints for Creating Decent Employment and Ensuring Effective Utilization of Human Resources in the Arab Region*. Employment Policy Department Working Paper No. 164. ILO, Geneva.
Tzannatos, Zafiris (2015). *Employment Creation, Poverty Reduction and Social Integration in The Arab World: The Unfinished Agenda*. International Institute of Social Studies, Erasmus University, Rotterdam, Netherlands.
Tzannatos, Zafiris, Ishac Diwan and Joanna Abdel-Ahad (2016). *Rates of Return to Education in Twenty Two Arab Countries: An Update and Comparison between MENA and the Rest of the World*. Economic Research Forum Working Paper No. 1007. Cairo.
UNDP (2016). *Arab Human Development Report*. United Nations Development Programme. New York.
Urdal, Henrik (2004). *The Devil in the Demographics: The Effect of Youth Bulges on Domestic Armed Conflict, 1950–2000*. World Bank, Social Development Paper on Conflict Prevention and Reconstruction, No. 14.
World Bank (2008). *The Road Not Traveled: Education Reform in the Middle East and North Africa*. The World Bank, Washington, DC.
World Bank (2011). *World Development Report 2011: Conflict, Security, and Development*. The World Bank, Washington, DC.
World Bank (2016). *Women Business and the Law*. The World Bank, Washington, DC.
World Economic Forum (WEF) (2012). *Addressing the 100 Million Youth Challenge: Perspectives on Youth Employment in the Arab World in 2012*. World Economic Forum. Geneva.

19

ARAB DEVELOPMENT AND THE TRANSITION TO DEMOCRACY[1]

Samir Makdisi

19.1 Introduction

The concept of development to which this chapter refers is a broad one embodying both the socio-economic as well as the political domains. It encompasses a transition from exclusive or inequitable growth to an equitable and healthy path of economic growth accompanied by a growing space of freedom and democratic governance.

Following the Second World War, the Arab countries, most of which had been under colonial rule, attained independence, though at different times, the latest being in 1971 when the Gulf emirates gained their political freedom. A good time earlier, in 1945, the Arab League was established, initially comprising only the then independent Arab states, with the major objective of defending the sovereignty of its members and forging close economic and political bonds among them. Economic integration was one of the goals the League subsequently attempted but failed to achieve. With the exception of Lebanon, political independence did not bring with it any substantive advancement towards genuine democratic governance: controlled parliamentary systems came into being in non-oil countries, while absolute monarchies prevailed in the Gulf oil countries. Tunisia moved to democratic rule following the 2011 uprisings. Of the other four countries where uprisings took place (Egypt, Libya, Syria, Yemen), Egypt reverted to an autocratic form of governance. The rest have been mired in civil conflicts with as yet unclear outcomes.

Looking at developments in the Arab region in this period, three major features emerge: (a) overall, a socio-economic record that shows the Arab countries to be generally in line with other developing regions; (b) the prevalence of a highly conflictual environment: major manifestations include the still unresolved 1948 Palestinian (Arab/Israeli) conflict with all its tragic Palestinian and regional consequences, as well as multiple civil conflicts in the region, notably the dramatic 2011 uprisings in five Arab countries and the ensuing brutal civil wars in three of them; and (c) as noted, the overall persistence of varying forms of autocracies or what has been referred to as the democracy deficit, in contrast with the experience of other developing regions which have generally moved ahead along the path towards democratic governance.

These three features of Arab development are interconnected and the aim of this chapter is to explore this interconnectedness. It comprises four sections: (a) a brief background discussion of the relationship between democracy and development; (b) the non-correlation between development and democracy in the Arab region; (c) the factors that explain the region's lagging steps towards democracy; and (d) the uprisings and the transition to peace-building and inclusive development.

19.2 The relationship between democracy and development[2]

The literature on democratic transition is vast, spanning varied hypotheses explaining this phenomenon. Foremost is the influential modernisation hypothesis advanced by Lipset correlating democracy and development (1959 and 1960); alternative hypotheses have focused, among other factors, on institutional and cultural factors, negotiated transitions by political elites and the instrumentalisation of identity cleavages or ideology.[3]

Briefly, the modernisation hypothesis argues that economic development (reflected in growth in real per capita income, rising levels of education, technological advances, etc.) tends to weaken dictatorial controls and pave the way towards democratic forms of governance, i.e. there is positive correlation between development and democracy. Whether it translates into a causative relationship has, however, been a contested issue.[4] For example, Przeworski (2004), investigating a probability model for political regime transition over the period 1950–90, concludes that the modernisation theory does not offer convincing empirical support for democratic transitions: development makes democracies endure, but it does not make them more likely to emerge.[5]

However, in defence of the modernisation hypothesis, and in response to Przeworski's critique, Boix and Stokes (2003) argue that one needs to 'push back' his entire sample (1950–90) to a point in time when no country was democratic, that is, 1850–1950. They then show that the endogenous effect (i.e. the positive impact of development on democracy) applies not only to the 1950–90 periods Przeworski and others analysed, but that it is even stronger for the pre-1950 period. For their part, Epstein et al. (2006) argue that higher per capita incomes significantly increase the likelihood of democratic regimes, both by enhancing the consolidation of existing democracies and by promoting transitions from authoritarian to democratic systems.

Another critical perspective of the modernisation hypothesis is put forward by Acemoglu et al. (2008, 2009), who take a long historical view and focus on the relationships between economic, political and historical factors. They argue that, although income and democracy are positively correlated (over long periods of time), no evidence emerges of a causal effect. Instead, omitted factors – most probably historical – appear to have shaped the divergent political and economic development paths of various societies, leading to the positive association between democracy and economic performance. Thus, they call for a revaluation of the modernisation hypothesis with much greater emphasis on the underlying factors that influence the political and economic paths which developing societies have followed.[6]

On the other hand, Barro (2015) challenges Acemoglu et al.'s critique and argues that, at the empirical level, their rejection of the modernisation theory hinges on the insignificance of income and education as determinants of democracy in fixed-effects panel regression systems with a moderate time dimension. Instead, he contends that estimating fixed-effects regressions for a smaller number of countries for which data are available throughout a century lends strong support to the modernisation hypothesis. Similarly, taking a long historical view going back to 1870, and employing modern dynamic panel data methods, Murtin and Wacziarg (2014) provide empirical support for the modernisation hypothesis.

The modernisation hypothesis has also met with further wide-ranging critiques from some strands of the political science literature. For example, Gleditsch and Choung (2004) argue that economic factors influence the stability of autocracies and the likelihood of crises in general, but do not make transitions to democracy more likely; and Gleditsch and Ward (2006) stress the importance of the geographic neighbourhood and argue that there is a tendency for transitions to democracy to cluster regionally. In a similar vein, Ulfelder and Lustik (2005) emphasise the role of past experiences with democracy in such transitions, for both resource-rich and other countries, while saying that economic recessions increase its likelihood. Furthermore, they argue that in countries where they prevail, higher levels of civil liberties and non-violent collective action help to initiate such transitions. Therborn (1977) argues that European countries became democratic as a result of wars rather than modernisation.

Finally, Inglehart and Welzel (2009) emphasise differentiating between two distinct phases of modernisation: industrialisation and post-industrialisation. Whereas industrialisation is accompanied by bureaucratisation, centralisation, rationalisation and secularisation, people in post-industrial societies display an increasing emphasis on autonomy, choice, creativity and self-expression. Both processes have changed the way people relate to authority. Emancipation from authority takes place only during the post-industrialisation phase, when the focus shifts from external authority to greater individual autonomy and human choice.

This brings up, in particular, the question of religious practices in the transition to democracy, specifically as they concern the Arab region. Rothstein and Broms (2011) have focused on how these practices are financed. In the Christian West, they argue, religion has been financed from below, which has followed semi-democratic representation, transparency and accountability. They claim that in the Arab-Muslim countries religion has been financed from above instead, thereby hindering the development of semi-democratic representation as well as systems for transparency and accountability in public affairs. Chaney (2012) makes a similar claim in that this links Arab autocracy to the long-running influence of a 'control structure' that evolved under the Islamic empires in the pre-modern era. Of course earlier writers (e.g. Huntington, 1993; Kedourie, 1994) have invoked Islamic religious practices and/or traditions as being conducive to non-democratic governance.

However, others, for example Maseland and van Hoorn (2013), Kuru (2014) and Elbadawi and Makdisi (2011), do not find that religion is a significant element in this regard. In rejecting religion (specifically Islam) as an explanatory factor for the lack of democracy, Kuru instead focuses on the influences of the rentier state as a region-wide phenomenon. This, in his view, should help to explain the persistence of authoritarianism in Muslim-majority countries in MENA and Central Asia, in contrast to the democratic experience of Muslim-majority countries in other regions where the democratisation process has taken place. But, as Aldashev et al. (2013) have pointed out, religion can be employed as an instrument to promote authoritarian rule: clerics beholden to the ruler, especially in oil-rich countries, have and continue to present themselves as defenders of the status quo. Indeed, it can be said today's fundamentalist groups have advanced the instrumentalisation of religion to much higher (not to say brutal) levels in an attempt to achieve their political (autocratic) goals.

Regarding the Arab world, while religion may have been instrumentalised by the ruling authorities to foster authoritarianism, this does not account in any major way for its general endurance. Other fundamental factors explain the overall persistence of Arab autocracy despite the region's socio-economic development, in contrast with the modernisation hypothesis and the experiences of other regions (Section 19.3 below). The uprisings of 2011 ushered a new but so far an uncertain phase (Section 19.4). In spite of existing obstacles, they could still usher a move towards a democratic Arab world (Section 19.5).

First a word on broad developmental outcomes.

19.3 Developmental outcomes

Figure 19.1 shows the trends of weighted average per capita income for various developing regions from 1960 up to 2017. The Arab region ranks in the middle, increasingly outpacing sub-Saharan Africa and South Asia but falling behind East Asia and Latin America. Indeed, the Arab world and the East Asia and Pacific region had roughly the same levels of per capita income in the 1970s. By 2017 the latter's per capita income was roughly two-thirds higher than that of the former. It might be argued that given the Arab region's immense oil resources a more advanced level could have been achieved. However, failed efforts at region-wide economic integration, the prevalence of a conflictual environment and often misguided or ineffective economic policies all combined to prevent the region from attaining higher levels of broad-based growth. Only the oil-rich countries, and in particular the smaller ones, were able to attain comparatively high per capita income levels, though with fluctuations in oil prices their growth path has been uneven. As would be expected, the per capita levels of individual countries have come to differ widely. For 2017, Qatar's per capita income (at constant 2010 US $) stood at over $65,000 compared to Mauritania's $1,305. Of the non-oil countries, Lebanon's per capita income levels have continuously been the highest standing for the same year at over $7,000 followed by Tunisia's at over $4,000.

Income averages, of course, conceal variations in the quality of development. Figure 19.2 includes the broader Human Development Index (average of health, education and per capita income indicators) beginning in 1990. Again, the Arab world outperforms sub-Saharan Africa and South Asia but falls behind East Asia and Latin America. But rates of HDI growth give a different picture. Over the period 1990–2017, the average annual growth rate for the Arab states was about 0.8 percent, a little higher than that for Latin America (0.7 percent) but lower than the rates of growth for the other three developing regions (1.1 for sub-Saharan Africa, 1.3 for East Asia and 1.4 for South Asia). Also, there are wide variations in HDI rankings among the Arab states ranging for 2017 from 37 for Qatar to 178 (one of the lowest) for Yemen; for the non-oil-rich Arab countries, their rank ranged from 80 for Lebanon to 123 for Morocco. HDI improvements seem to be related more to a rise in the levels of per capita income and education (school years) than to health conditions (life expectancy to birth).

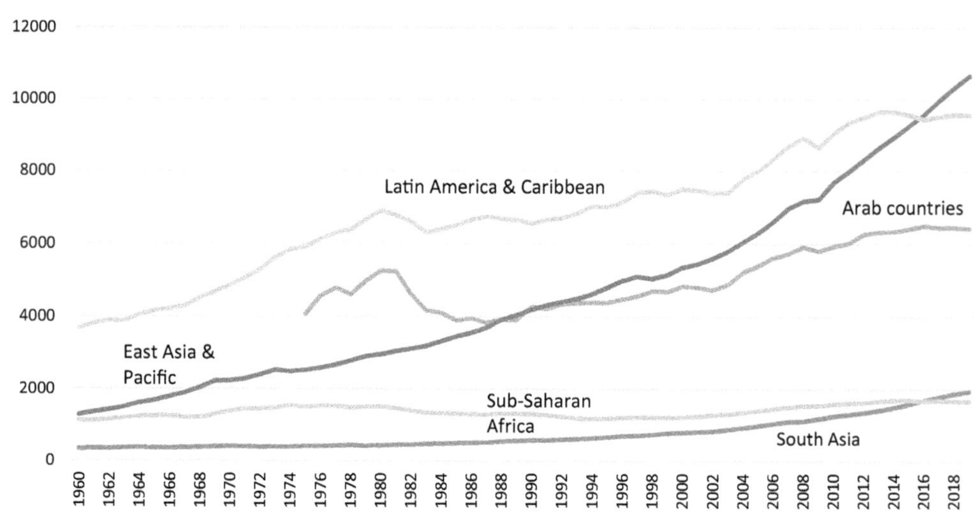

Figure 19.1 GDP per capita levels by region, 1960–2019 (constant 2010 US Dollars). *Source:* World Bank Development Indicators.

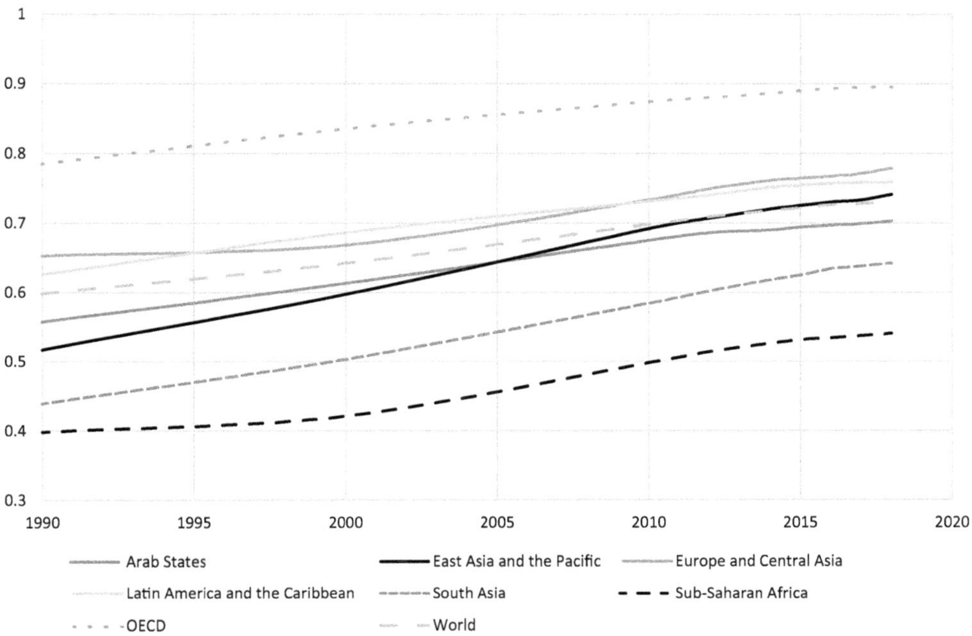

Figure 19.2 Human development classification (Human Development Index value). *Source*: UNDP, Human Development Indices and Indicators (2018).

More recently (2010) income inequality has been added to the HDI. When factored in, the comparative ranking of the Arab world among developing regions remains basically the same except that the adjusted HDI for the Arab region, along with that for sub-Saharan Africa and South Asia, consequently suffers greater overall losses (25, 37 and 26 percent, respectively, for 2017) than those for Latin America or East Asia (22 and 15.6 percent, respectively, for the same year) (UNDP, 2018). Within the Arab region, according to available estimates (bearing in mind uncertain degrees of reliability), Saudi Arabia had the highest degree of income inequality (a Gini index of 45.9 for 2013) and Algeria the lowest (27.5 for 2011).

A gender inequality index (GII) has also been introduced for the year 2017. It presents a composite measure of gender inequality using three dimensions: reproductive health, empowerment and economic status.[7] It has its own rank separate from the HDI that indicates the percentage of potential human development lost due to gender inequality. A low GII value points to low inequality between women and men, and vice-versa. Among developing regions, the GII value ranges from 0.312 for East Asia and the Pacific to 0.531 for the Arab states and 0.569 for sub-Saharan Africa. By comparison the value for OECD countries is 0.186. In particular, the lag of the Arab region is in the areas of female participation in the labour market and parliamentary representations, standing in 2017 at 21 percent (lowest rate) for the first and 18 percent (second lowest rate) for the second (UNDP, 2018).

The above development picture seems to be line with the findings of certain studies that when the HDI is adjusted for inequality, on the whole, countries with lesser human development tend to suffer greater losses due to inequality than those with more advanced human development thus widening the gap between the two groups (Daniele and Malanima, 2013; Amendola and Dell'Anno, 2014).

By contrast, it is the very limited evolution of genuine democratic institutions in the Arab region which is the most striking comparative feature. Various democracy measurements capture this picture. We reproduce here the widely used Polity IV index of democracy for the period

1975–2017 (the index goes back to 1946) and the more recent and comprehensive Economist Intelligence Unit Democracy Index, which begins with 2006.

According to Polity IV (see Table 19.1), as of 2018 only Lebanon, Iraq and Tunisia fall into the democracy category. While since independence in 1943 Lebanon has continually maintained its consociational form of democracy, the latter two countries have managed to move from an autocratic to a democratic order only as of 2014. The democratic transformation of Tunisia after its 2011 uprising stands in sharp contrast with the civil wars that have raged in three of the countries where uprisings also broke out that year, i.e. Libya, Syria and Yemen.

The classifications of the other Arab countries range from hereditary autocracy in some of the Gulf countries to varying forms of anocracies in non-oil-rich countries. Thus Lebanon, Iraq and Tunisia apart, the region, as a whole, has continually been non-democratic though over time with a lessening of the overall severity of the prevailing autocracy. This evolving picture contrasts with the Polity IV trends in other regions of the world, especially since the 1970s, of a significantly expanding number of democracies and the retreat of autocracies.

A similar picture is also portrayed by the EIU index of democracy (Figure 19.3). Among all regions, the Arab world has maintained since 2006 the lowest scores being the only region classified as authoritarian. Again, there are marked variations with respect to individual countries. For 2017 the index classifies most of the Arab countries as autocracies though with varying scores, three as hybrid regimes (Iraq, Morocco and Lebanon) and one as a flawed democracy (Tunisia). By contrast, for 2006 only two countries (Iraq and Lebanon) were classified as hybrid while the rest fell in the authoritarian category.[8]

To sum up this section, the Arab region has kept in step with other developing regions in the broad domains of economic and social development, but it has fallen behind in the political domain, i.e. specifically in moving towards democratic governance. In other words, while other developing regions have generally moved up the ladder from the category of authoritarianism, the Arab region, as a whole, has continued to be classified as authoritarian.

This apparent non-correlation between Arab development and democracy is taken up next.

19.4 Understanding the non-correlation of development and democracy in the Arab region[9]

Numerous past and more recent analyses have addressed the question of lagging democracy in the Arab region compared to other regions, i.e. its weak correlation with economic development. These vary from a broad, historical viewpoint to more focused analyses of specific underlying factors. Various historical, religious, social, ethnic, political, economic and colonial explanations of this phenomenon have been posited.[10]

Taking the modernisation hypothesis as a framework a recent work by Elbadawi and Makdisi (2017) tests a benchmark model for analysing the Arab democracy deficit relative to the counterfactual level of democracy consistent with its level of development. The findings show that for the Arab region as a whole, while the traditional 'modernisation' variables remain important determinants of democracy in the long run, they fail to explain the Arab democracy deficit relative to other regions. Rather, oil and conflicts and their interactions appear to explain this persistent deficit and more generally the politico-economic trajectory of the Arab region, at least in the post-Second World War period.

The 'oil curse' effect – the trade-off between economic welfare and political rights, associated with the relative abundance of oil resources – is well established in the literature (for a review, see Ross, 2015) though it is not necessarily a matter of universal agreement (Haber and Menaldo, 2011). Nonetheless, at the political level its negative political impact on governance specifically

Table 19.1 Polity IV index, 1975–2017

	1975	*1980*	*1985*	*1990*	*1995*	*2000*	*2005*	*2010*
Algeria	-9	-9	-9	-2	-3	-3	2	2
Bahrain	-10	-10	-10	-10	-9	-9	-7	-5
Egypt	-7	-6	-6	-6	-6	-6	-3	-3
Iraq	-7	-9	-9	-9	-9	-9	3	3
Jordan	-10	-10	-9	-4	-2	-2	-2	-3
Kuwait	-8	-10	-8	-9	-7	-7	-7	-7
Lebanon							6	6
Libya	-7	-7	-7	-7	-7	-7	-7	-7
Mauritania	-7	-7	-7	-7	-6	-6	-5	-2
Morocco	-9	-8	-8	-8	-7	-6	-6	-6
Oman	-10	-10	-10	-10	-9	-9	-8	-8
Qatar	-10	-10	-10	-10	-10	-10	-10	-10
Saudi Arabia	-10	-10	-10	-10	-10	-10	-10	-10
Sudan (South)								0
Syria	-9	-9	-9	-9	-9	-7	-7	-7
Tunisia	-9	-9	-8	-5	-3	-3	-4	-4
UAE	-8	-8	-8	-8	-8	-8	-8	-8
Yemen	-6	-7	-7	-5	-2	-2	-2	-2
	2011	2012	2013	2014	2015	2016	2017	2018
Algeria	2	2	2	2	2	2	2	
Bahrain	-8	-10	-10	-10	-10	-10	-10	-10
Egypt	-2	-88	-4	-4	-4	-4	-4	-4
Iraq	3	3	3	6	6	6	6	6
Jordan	-3	-3	-3	-3	-3	-3	-3	-3
Kuwait	-7	-7	-7	-7	-7	-7	-7	-7
Lebanon	6	6	6	6	6	6	6	6
Libya	-77	-77	-77	-77	0	0	0	-77
Mauritania	-2	-2	-2	-2	-2	-2	-2	-2
Morocco	-4	-4	-4	-4	-4	-4	-4	-4
Oman	-8	-8	-8	-8	-8	-8	-8	-8
Qatar	-10	-10	-10	-10	-10	-10	-10	-10
Saudi Arabia	-10	-10	-10	-10	-10	-10	-10	-10
Sudan (South)	-2				-7	-7	-7	
Syria	-7	-9	-9	-9	-9	-9	-9	-9
Tunisia	-88	-88	-88	7	7	7	7	8
UAE	-8	-8	-8	-8	-8	-8	-8	-8
Yemen	-2	3	3	-77	0	0	-7	-77

Source: Polity IV Data Series.
Note: The Polity IV scheme consists of six component measures that record the key qualities of executive recruitment, constraints on executive authority and political competition. The 'Polity score' captures this regime authority spectrum on a 21-point scale ranging from -10 (hereditary monarchy) to +10 (consolidated democracy). They can also be converted to regime categories, for which a three-part categorisation is recommended: 'autocracies' (-10 to -6), 'anocracies' (-5 to +5) and 'democracies' (+6 to +10). The Polity IV data include information only on the institutions of the central government and on political groups acting, or reacting, within the scope of that authority. It does not include a consideration of groups and territories that are actively removed from that authority (i.e. separatists or 'fragments'; these are considered to be separate, though not independent, polities) or segments of the population that are not yet effectively politicised in relation to central state politics.

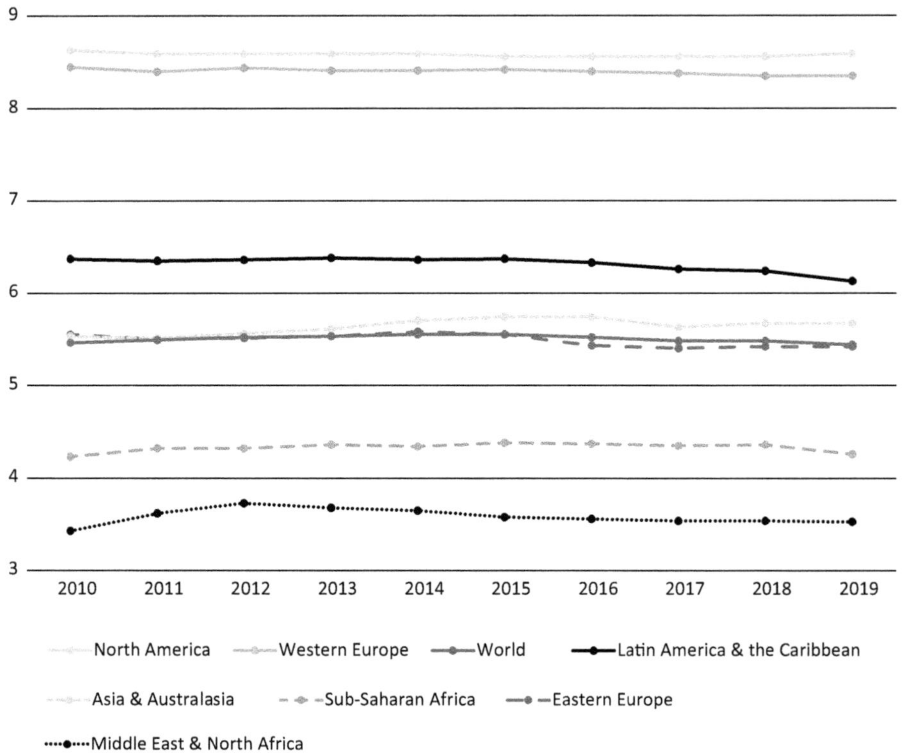

Figure 19.3 EUI index of democracy. *Note*: The EIU index is a weighted average of 60 indicators grouped into five different categories: electoral process and pluralism, civil liberties, functioning of government, political participation and political culture. In addition to a numeric score and a ranking, the index categorises countries as one of four regime types: full democracies (a score of 8–10), flawed democracies (6–7.9), hybrid regimes (4–5.9) or authoritarian regimes (0–3.9). *Source*: Economist Intelligence Unit (EIU), Democracy Index.

in the oil-rich countries is perhaps widely recognised. But at the economic level the influence of abundant oil wealth is more varied. While various beneficial effects on development can rightly be pointed out (Luciani, 2012), recent empirical work has drawn attention to the required role of fiscal and monetary policies in countering its negative impact (e.g. the hindrance of economic diversification) thereby ensuring that oil resources are efficiently used for developmental purposes. This outcome, it is argued, would in large measure hinge on the efficacy and accountability of the institutions in place, notably fiscal institutions, keeping in mind that Arab fiscal institutions remain wanting in this regard (El Anshasy et al., 2015).

Equally important, and perhaps more so, is the persistence of a conflictual regional environment in the Middle East. According to the Uppsala Conflict Data Program (UCDP, 2018) data for the period 1990–2017, the region accounted for about 23 percent of world conflicts; and for the period 2011–17 by far for the largest number of the world's battle-related deaths.[11] Of course, at the centre of the region's conflictual environment is the unsettled but simmering Arab–Israeli conflict, which goes back to 1948 and does not have a parallel in other regions, at least in recent history; and in more recent years we have the emergence of major civil conflicts fed by multifaceted international interventions.

Indeed, conflicts are found to have a uniquely negative effect on the democratisation process in the Arab region (keeping in mind that this effect can vary significantly from one country to another) partly because these conflicts have been exploited by incumbent autocratic regimes to justify their rule and to escape the consequences of their national failures (for a detailed analysis of the conflict effect, see Elbadawi and Makdisi, 2017). The Palestinian question remains unresolved while the settlement of civil wars in the pre-2010 period did not lead to a significant change in the political regimes of the war-torn countries involved. And the outcome of the post-uprising civil conflicts is yet to be determined.

To all that we have to add the huge impact of the rise in recent years of fundamentalist groups in the region (especially in Syria and Iraq) and the consequent additional vicious conflicts their emergence has caused. While the dominance of the fundamentalist groups has of late been on the wane, the outcome of the post-uprising civil conflicts is yet to be decided. By contrast, in other regions of the contemporary world civil conflicts have mostly been followed by a move towards democracy, noted reversals notwithstanding (Jai Kwan, 2008), a contrast that is often alluded to in support of the arguments in favour of the Arab region's exceptionalism.

But we should keep in mind that as useful as cross-country research may be, it remains that a study of individual country experiences would afford a deeper and more nuanced understanding of the oil and conflict thesis, e.g. how its various manifestations are affected by the specific socio-economic and political history of the country concerned (for a review see Makdisi, 2018).

19.5 The uprisings and the transition to peace-building and inclusive development

Whatever the immediate circumstances that led to the Tunisian uprisings, a combination of economic, political and other underlying factors has been building up over the years for a push towards a democratic space in the region with the successful overthrow of the Tunisian autocracy acting as a spur for the subsequent uprisings. They include, among others, rising unemployment to high levels, especially youth unemployment; persistence of deep economic inequalities and related declining levels of subjective wellbeing; loss of faith in the role of traditionalist reformist political parties; growing openness of national economies; and rising aspirations for greater freedom and political participation on the part of large segments of the populace that have felt disenfranchised and largely excluded from the benefits of economic development.[12]

Our concern here is that whereas the uprisings may have shaken the foundations of autocracy in the Arab region the initial glimmer of hope for a democratic change in the countries concerned (and by extension of the region as whole) has so far failed to materialize save for in Tunisia. The civil conflicts that have subsequently emerged, fed by emerging sectarian divisiveness, including the intensification of identity politics and the rise of fundamentalist groups, have further strengthened the region's conflictual environment, posing threats of democratic reversals for countries that managed to break out of the grip of entrenched autocracies (Makdisi, 2018).[13]

The region's resistance to democracy is not unique or specific, and can be ascribed to the same elements that have, to varying degrees, helped maintain different forms of autocracy in other regions of the world as well as the Arab region (i.e. oil, conflicts, neighbourhood effects and external interventions by both regional and international powers). However, perhaps due to the intensity of these factors, what is special about the Arab region is the almost immediate emergence of what appears to be a wide authoritarian counter-revolution in response to the uprisings.

Shortly after the collapse of the regimes in Tunisia, Egypt and Libya, potentially vulnerable authoritarian regimes in the region responded by deploying a massive degree of violence that has so far either stifled incipient or nascent uprisings or transformed essentially peaceful mass movements into armed conflicts or outright civil war, as in the cases of Libya, Yemen and Syria.

Especially the struggle for Syria has become a violent and tragic contest between radical fundamentalist Sunni groups and the regime supported by transnational Shi'a militias, intertwined with regional and external interventions in support of opposing sides of the conflict.

The rise of strict fundamentalist groups in the Arab regions has commonly been attributed to a variety of factors, including their promotion by the so-called deep state which uses them as a pretext for its counter-revolution (Filiu, 2015); a response on the part of the poorer segments of the population to political and economic exclusion; the desire of certain fundamentalist regimes and/or foreign powers to use them for their own political ends; a response to past Western colonialism and continued interventions in the affairs of the region; the failure to build a nation-state; or the breakdown of the central concept of Arab nationalism. However, the rising sectarian divide fuelled by regional power-plays and of the direct military involvement of external powers, primarily the United States and Russia, must be the most alarming underlying cause or catalyst behind the prominence of the fundamentalist-sponsored violence that engulfed the region. This divide has been manifested in the emergence of factional sectarian democracy as in Iraq, as well as in the violent response of the essentially sectarian minority regime in Syria to the initially peaceful democratic movement that swept through the country for almost six months before turning into a militarised opposition dominated by fundamentalist groups though their influence has recently considerably waned.

Even if the question of fundamentalism in the region had not arisen, it remains a fact that some countries will still experience a difficult and/or violent transition process, if not an authoritarian counteroffensive that may take hold at least temporarily. The respective experiences of the countries where uprisings have taken place demonstrate clearly how transition experiences can vary. The eventual outcome of the ensuing brutal civil conflicts in Syria, Yemen and Libya will determine the nature of the political regimes to follow, and to what extent, if any, these future regimes will come to reflect the attributes of democratic governance rather than those of new autocratic orders. The delay so far of a substantive democratic move in Egypt is associated with the persisting political dominance of the military elite and the continued political divisions in the country, not to mention the persisting if not expanding conflicts in the region with all their corrosive effects on the transition process. Thus, save for Tunisia, a region-wide transition to genuine democracy following the initial uprisings remains more an aspiration than a concrete reality.

What about the prospects for transition towards democracy in the Arab region?

As long as the multi-dimensional civil conflicts in Syria, Yemen and Libya continue to rage, the prospects for democratic transitions in the region remain dim. These conflicts are manifestations of a counter-revolution (partly linked to foreign interventions) intended to stifle transitions towards democratic forms of governance. But eventually they will be resolved and the prospects for establishing accountable democratic political institutions will in turn strengthen.

Pushing in that direction are evolving socio-economic and political processes in various countries of the region that will yet help pave the way for a democratic change, with some being much more gradual than others. They include the building up of modernising influences which admittedly the civil conflicts have slowed down or disrupted at least temporarily (e.g. a growing middle class, improving levels of education and growing female participation in the economic and political domains); an increasing incompatibility between exclusive political institutions and the increasing openness of economic institutions; and an expanding popular demand for freedom, equal political rights and social justice reinforced by decreasing fundamentalist influences.

Furthermore, the corrosive political effects of relatively abundant oil resources will, in the passage of time, be countered by the influences forcing change, such as mounting socio-economic inequities and growing popular dissatisfaction, the weakening rentier effect due in part to changing internal economic conditions and a growing democratic neighbourhood as more and more countries move to partial if not full democracies. Moreover, the seeming structural changes in the global oil market and the potential long-term deceleration of prices towards low 'equilibrium' prices will likely further threaten the sustainability of the authoritarian bargain, even in the highly endowed Arab Gulf societies (Elbadawi and Makdisi, 2020). It is noteworthy that the more countries succeed in moving towards a consolidated democracy the less the potential threat of reversal is (e.g. see Poast and Urpelainen, 2015).

19.6 Concluding observations

The raging Arab conflicts will hopefully be settled sooner rather than later. Looking at post-conflict transition the question that follows these settlements is their nature, i.e. whether they would lead to democratic governance or simply return to a re-defined autocratic order. If the latter, then we will be back to a renewed struggle for democratic change.

But if the outcome is the establishment of accountable democratic political institutions then the daunting task of delivering the required public goods and implementing socio-economic policies which promote and sustain a broad based and equitable development will begin. This would minimise, if not eliminate, the prospects for a potential democratic reversal. It follows that economic liberalism, understood as the mainstay of purely and minimally regulated market-oriented economic policies, is not really the model for transition. Such a model could allow for inappropriate dominance of the economy by elites and big business that could frustrate the objectives of a balanced and inclusive post-conflict recovery and threaten the prospects for a sustained democratic process (El Ouardani and Makdisi, 2018).

Economic reconstruction is necessarily more encompassing than postwar stabilisation. It would include not only the rehabilitation of basic services and infrastructure destroyed during the war, but also the creation of a basic macro- and microeconomic institutional and policy framework necessary for the emergence of a viable economy, one that would provide employment opportunities allowing citizens to make a decent and licit living (del Castillo, 2015). Equally importantly, it should lead to wider economic inclusion and less inequality; in other words, to the creation of new institutions that would no longer permit a privileged few to capture the benefits of natural resources, economic growth and overall development but would allow their spread to the populace at large.

Notes

1 The author is grateful to Razan Amine for excellent research assistance.
2 This section draws on a recent work by Elbadawi and Makdisi (2017).
3 For useful reviews, see Brumberg, 2014 and Munck, 1994.
4 The contrasting empirical outcomes, it should be added, may be related to the differing empirical methodologies that have been employed: countries selected, statistical methods applied, selection of socio-economic indicators, democracy measure chosen and the form of the relationship being tested.
5 This is in line with the transitions paradigm, which holds that no level of economic, social or cultural development constitutes a necessary prerequisite for the initiation of a transition. Instead, transitions are governed by political 'pacts' through which opposition forces or parties guarantee the property rights of regimes in return for formal political rights, thereby mitigating social tensions that otherwise could prevail (for example, see Brumberg, 2014).
6 Certain writings have referred to the particular features or identities of the region as illustrating the limitations of the global approach of the modernisation hypothesis or transition theory in identifying the factors that underlie the transition process of any given country or region. It is contended there is a need to focus on endogenous forces that shape political preferences or dictate a particular transition course – see Brumberg (2014) for a critique of transition and post-transition theories.

7 Reproductive health is measured by maternal mortality ratio and adolescent birth rates; empowerment is measured by the proportion of parliamentary seats occupied by females and proportion of adult females and males aged 25 years and older with at least some secondary education; economic status is expressed as labour market participation and measured by labour force participation rates of female and male populations aged 15 years and older (UNDP, 2018).

8 We should, however, keep in mind that democracy indices have their own limitations. Empirical measurements do not necessarily succeed in fully reflecting the true democratic status in any given country; debatably more so in developing than in developed countries. In part this may be attributable to methodological flaws of the measurements, but also to their coding rules, which do not always capture accurately the abuses of the governing classes and/or of special interest groups. This might explain, for example, why Kuwait, with its relatively freely elected and active national assembly, remains classified as highly autocratic (Polity score for 2017: -7). Indeed, a full appreciation of the attributes of the political system of any country can be achieved only through an in-depth study of the country concerned (for an assessment of select Arab countries see Elbadawi and Makdisi, 2017).

9 This section also draws on Elbadawi and Makdisi (2017).

10 Earlier studies, notably by Beblawi and Luciani (1987), have analysed the impact of oil revenues on the nature and functions of oil-exporting countries such as the Gulf countries. They describe them as allocation states or rentier economies, i.e. states that derive their income from abroad and can spend without having to collect domestic taxes. Importantly, with no taxation, citizens are far less demanding in terms of political participation, let alone the negative impact of the rentier nature of the state on work ethics. Also see Waterbury (1994) for an early analysis of specific features of Arab regimes that accounted for the lag in their democratic development.

11 The UCDP defines conflict as 'a contested incompatibility that concerns government and/or territory where the use of armed force between two parties, of which at least one is the government of a state, results in at least 25 battle-related deaths over one calendar year.'

12 There is an extensive literature on the causes of the uzprisings which lie outside the purview of this chapter; for a review see, for example, Amin et al., 2012; Bibi and Nabli, 2010; Devarajan and Elena Ianchovichina, 2017; Elbadawi and Makdisi, 2017; Hakimian et al., 2013; Makdisi, 2018.

13 In the early part of 2019 massive popular demonstrations broke out in Algeria and Sudan demanding the dismantling of their entrenched autocracies; as of this writing (April 2019) their outcome remains uncertain.

References

Acemoglu, D. and J. Robinson (2008), "The Role of Institutions in Growth and Development, Commission on Growth and Development". Working paper No.10. Washington, DC: World Bank.

Acemoglu, D., S. Johnson, J. Robinson and P. Yared (2009), "Reevaluating the Modernization Hypothesis". *Journal of Monetary Economics*, 56(8): 1043–1058.

Aldashev, G, J.-P. Platteau and P. Sekeris (2013), *Seduction of Religious Clerics and Violence in Autocratic Regimes with Special Emphasis on Islam*, unpublished manuscript.

Amendola, Adalgiso and Roberto Dell'Anno (2014), "Income Inequality and Economic Growth: An Empirical Investigation in Mediterranean Countries". *Rivista Italiana di Economia Demografia e Statistica*, LXVIII(2).

Amin, M., R. Assaad, N. al-Baharna, K. Dervis, R.M. Desai, N.S. Dhillon, A. Galal, Hafez Ghanem, C. Graham and D. Kaufmann (2012), *After the Spring: Economic Transitions in the Arab World*, Oxford: Oxford University Press.

Barro, R. (2015), "Convergence and Modernization". *Economic Journal*, 125(585), doi:10.1111/ecoj.12247.

Beblawi, H. and G. Luciani (eds.) (1987), *The Rentier State*, London: Routledge.

Bibi, S. and M.K. Nabli (2009), "Income Inequality in the Arab Region: Data and Measurement, Patterns and Trends". *Middle East Development Journal*, 1(2), doi:10.1142.

Boix, C. and S. Stoke (2003), "Endogenous Democratization". *World Politics*, 55, July.

Brumberg, Daniel (2014), "Reconsidering 'Theories of Transition". In Marc Lynch (ed.), *The Arab Uprisings Explained: New Contentious Politics in the Middle East*, Columbia Studies in Middle East Politics.

Chaney, E. (2012), *Democratic Change in the Arab World, Past and Present*, unpublished mimeo, Department of Economics, Cambridge, MA: Harvard University.

Daniele, V. and P. Malanima (2013), *Le economie del Mediterraneo fra divergenza e convergenza 1950–2011, Rapporto sulle economie del Mediterraneo*, Edizione 2013, Bologna: Il Mulino, 13–31.
del Castillo, Graciana (2015), "Economic Reconstruction and Reforms in Post Conflict Countries". Working Paper No. 25 2015, Centre for Research on Peace and Development (CRPD), KU Leuven.
Devarajan, S. and E. Ianchovichina (2017), "A Broken Social Contract, Not High Inequality, Led to the Arab Spring". *Review of Income and Wealth*, Washington, DC: The World Bank.
Economist Intelligence Unit, *Democracy Index*; available from: https://www.eiu.com/topic/democracy-index
El Anshasy, A., K. Mohaddes and J.B. Nugent (2015), "Fiscal Institutions and Macro-Economic Management in Resource-Rich Arab Countries". Paper presented at a conference of the Economic Research Forum on 'Monetary and Fiscal Institutions in Resource-Rich Arab Economies', Kuwait, November 4–6.
Elbadawi, I. and S. Makdisi (2011), *Democracy in the Arab World, Explaining the Deficit*, London: Routledge.
Elbadawi, I. and S. Makdisi (eds.) (2017), *Democratic Transitions in the Arab World*, Cambridge: Cambridge University Press.
Elbadawi, I. and S. Makdisi (2020), "The Sustainability of GCC Development under the New Global Oil Order". In G. Luciani and T. Moerenhout (eds.), *When Can Oil Economies be Deemed Sustainable?* London: Palgrave Macmillan.
El Ouardani, H. and S. Makdisi (2018), "Autocracy, Democracy and Populism". *ORIENT, IV.*
Epstein, D., R. Bates, J. Goldstone, I. Kristensen and Sharyn O'Halloran (2006), "Democratic Transitions". *American Journal of Political Science*, 50(3).
Fabrice, Murtin and Romain Wacziarg (2014), "The Democratic Transition". *Journal of Economic Growth*, 19(2).
Filiu, Jean-Pierre (2015), *From Deep State to Islamic State*, Oxford: Oxford University Press.
Gleditsch, K. and M. Ward (2006), "Diffusion and the International Context of Democratization". *International Organization*, 60, Fall.
Haber, Stephen and Victor Menaldo (2011), "Do Natural Resources Fuel Authoritarianism, A Reappraisal of the Resource Curse". *American Political Science Review*, 105(1).
Hakimian, H. (ed.) (2013), *Inclusive Growth in MENA: Employment and Poverty Dimensions in a Comparative Context*, Femise Research Programme Research No. FEM 35.
Huntington, S. (1993), "The Clash of Civilization?". *Foreign Affairs*, Summer Issue, https://www.foreignaffairs.com/articles/united-states/1993-06-01/clash-civilizations.
Inglehart, R. and C. Welzel (2009), "How Development Leads to Democracy: What We Know About Modernization Today?". *Foreign Affairs*, 88(2).
International Labour Organization, *World Employment Social Outlook, Trends 2016 and 2017* Geneva: International Labor Office.
Jai Kwan, J. (2008), *Mission Impossible? Democracy Building in Post-Civil War Societies*, Chicago: Midwest Political Science Association Annual Meeting.
Kedourie, E. (1994), *Democracy and Arab Political Culture*, London: Frank Cass.
Kristian Skrede, Gleditsch and Jinhee Lee Choung (2004), "Autocratic Transitions and Democratization". Paper presented at the annual meeting of the International Studies Association, Quebec, Canada, Mar 17.
Kuru, A.T. (2014), "Authoritarianism and Democracy in Muslim Countries: Rentier States and Regional Diffusion". *Political Science Quarterly*, 129(3).
Lipset, S.M. (1959), "Some Social Requisites of Democracy: Economic Development and Political Legitimacy". *American Political Science Review*, 53(1).
Lipset, S.M. (1960), *Political Man: The Social Bases of Politics*, New York: Doubleday.
Luciani, G. (ed.) (2012), *Resources Blessed, Diversification and the Gulf Development Model*, Berlin: Gerlach Press.
Makdisi, S. (2018), "Sulle disparità economiche e politiche e sulle prospettive di integrazione nella regione euro-mediterranea". In E. Ferragina (ed.), *Rapporto sulle economie del Mediterraneo. Edizione2018*, Naples: Institute of Studies on the Mediterranean Society.
Maseland, R. and A. Van Hoorn (2013), "Does Democracy Deliver in Islamic Societies?". American Political Science Association 2013 Annual Meeting Paper.
Munck, Gerardo L. (1994), "Democratic Transitions in Comparative Perspective". *Comparative Politics*, 26(3).
Murtin, Fabrice and Romain Wacziarg (2014), "The Democratic Transition". *Journal of Economic Growth*, 19(2).

Poast, Paul and Johannes Urpelainen (2015), "How International Organizations Support Democratization: Preventing Authoritarian Reversals or Promoting Consolidation?". *World Politics*, 67(1).
Przeworski, A. (2004), "Economic Development and Transitions to Democracy". March, (ms), https://as.nyu.edu/content/dam/nyu-as/faculty/documents/transwp.pdf.
Ross, M. (2015), "What Have *We* Learned about the Resource Curse?" *Annual Review of Political Science*, 18.
Rothstein, B. and R. Broms (2011), "Why No Democracy in the Arab-Muslim World? The Importance of Temple Financing". Presentation at Seattle: American Political Science Association, Annual Meeting.
Therborn, G. (1977), "The Rule of Capital and the Rise of Democracy". *New Left Review*, i/103, May-June.
Ulfelder, J. and M. Lustik (2005), "Modeling Transitions to and from Democracy". Paper prepared for the Annual Meeting of the American Political Science Association, September 1–4.
UNDP (2018), *Human Development Indices and Indicators*, 2018 Statistical Update.
Uppsala Conflict Data Program (2018), Department of Peace and Conflict Research, Department of Peace and Conflict Research, Upssala: Upssala University.
Waterbury, J. (1994), "Democracy Without Democrats? The Potential for Political Liberalization in the Middle East". In G. Salameh (ed.) *Democracy Without Democrats? The Renewal of Politics in Muslim World*, London: I.B. Tauris.
World Bank, *World Development Indicators*, Washington, DC: The World Bank.

SECTION VI

Corruption, conflict and refugees

20

A PYRAMID OF PRIVILEGE

How cronyism shapes business–state relations in the Middle East

Izak Atiyas, Ishac Diwan and Adeel Malik[1]

20.1 Introduction

The popular Arab uprisings in 2011 that overthrew dictators in North Africa were both a revolt against dictatorships and a rebuke to crony capitalism, targeted against insider businessmen who were connected to the ruling circle and ended up monopolising all economic opportunities. As the curtain of authoritarianism fell, stories of insider privilege became public knowledge. In Egypt leading businessmen closely connected with the rulers became the object of public resentment. In Tunisia, it became clear that President Ben Ali, his wife, and extended family owned a multitude of firms in some of the most lucrative sectors of the economy.

For the lay citizen this was hardly a surprise. In the Arab public imagination businessmen and rulers are often treated as the same. The Arab private sector is typically a handmaiden of the state, surviving and thriving in the comforts of the ruling circle. It is therefore unsurprising to find a stark overlap in public perceptions of corruption in government versus corruption in business. The mutually constitutive relationship between economic and political power has long been recognised by Middle East specialists, but it became a particularly important concern after the initiation of economic reforms in several Arab states in 1990s. Unlike Latin America or Eastern Europe, Arab countries liberalised their economies without liberalising their polities, and autocrats remained in place across the region. To stay in power in the face of rising social grievances, they reverted to repression—not only of people, but also of markets. Arab states increasingly intervened in financial, product, and labour markets to advance their political interests.

The political economy literature on the region has described the management of the private sector as a security issue (Henry and Springborg 2010). Autocrats survived by empowering firms that they considered politically trustworthy and closing off business opportunities for firms that they suspected of supporting the opposition. As a result, even though the reforms of the 1990s rolled back the state's direct economic role (public spending in Egypt and Tunisia declined to less than 35% of GDP in 2010 from about 60% in Egypt and 45% in Tunisia in the early 1980s), political expediency continued to shape interaction with the market. As a result, favoured firms acquired near-monopoly power over entire sectors of the economy. For example, in Egypt, they were dominant in real estate, tourism, construction, wholesale and retail trade, mining, finance, business services, and information technology (Diwan et al. 2015, 2019a).

Economic reform afforded new opportunities for reconfiguring economic and political power in many Arab societies. This point was best illustrated through a series of influential papers put together by Steven Heydemann in an edited volume, *Networks of Privilege: The Politics of Economic Reform Revisited* (Heydemann 2004). The Arab Spring provided an impetus for a better empirical understanding of these "networks of privilege". The Economic Research Forum (ERF) launched a major new initiative on the political economy of private sector dynamism in the Middle East. The main objective of this project was to empirically map the nature of political connections among the private sector in key Middle Eastern states, and to probe its impact on prosperity through such outcomes as the growth and productivity of firms, employment generation, reliance on subsidies and credit, and sectorial exposure to trade protection, to name a few. Papers were commissioned for key Arab states in the Middle East and North Africa (MENA), along with special comparative studies on Turkey and Iran. The project was unique both in its focus and comparative scale. Capturing variation across countries, firms, and sectors, it looked at several dimensions of crony capitalism in the Middle East.

Different papers in this project, which were recently published in an edited volume (Diwan et al. 2019b), offer fresh insights on the conceptualisation, measurement, and impact of cronyism. A key challenge in any such endeavour is to identify politically connected firms (PCFs). In the scholarly tradition of Faccio (2006), most papers considered a company as politically connected if one of the company's shareholders or management was a member of parliament, held a ministerial position, or was closely related to the regime through ties of kinship. In some cases—such as Egypt and Tunisia—such information was more easily available after the Arab Spring when companies owned by the Ben Ali family were confiscated and insider links in Egypt came under public spotlight. In others, such as Lebanon and Turkey, the identification of politically connected firms or sectors had to rely on more indirect procedures. Although this empirical exercise is both preliminary and imperfect, it can allow scholars to gain a better understanding of the exposure of different sectors to crony activities and its possible impact on performance characteristics.

In terms of temporal focus, most studies in this project focused on the post-liberalisation period (late 1990s and beyond). During this period many countries in North Africa and the Levant embarked on a process of selective economic reform that included deregulation, privatisation, and partial trade liberalisation. Economic reforms generated new possibilities for elites to strike deals and receive preferential treatment. Although the boundaries between private and public have always remained blurred in the region, cronyism became a more prominent feature of the liberalisation era and fed into larger public disenchantment about corruption and governance.

The evidence presented in this chapter is based on a plurality of empirical approaches, both qualitative and quantitative. Typically, we compiled qualitative data on the presence and numerical strength of politically connected businesses in different sectors of the economy and matched it with publicly available information on firm-level or sector-level outcomes. Our objective is not to establish causal relationships but to establish robust stylised patterns to identify the impact of political connections on outcomes (firm profitability, growth, credit, trade policy, etc.). Occasionally, we were able to leverage relatively exogenous and discrete events in our research design, such as the revolutionary overthrow of regimes, the EU trade agreement with Egypt, and elections in Lebanon (see Malik et al., 2019).

20.2 Character of connected firms

The findings from various papers sponsored by this project point to some very interesting empirical patterns, hypotheses, and explanations. The underlying research provides a much better sense of the number, presence, and characteristics of politically connected firms in several MENA countries. In their work on Egypt, Diwan et al. (2015) identified 469 firms that were either directly or indirectly connected with one of the politically connected businessmen. Overall, about 50% of the sectors were exposed to politically connected firms. In Tunisia, this ratio was about 40%, and in Lebanon only 22% (Rijkers et al. 2017, Diwan and Haidar 2019). In Turkey religious network-affiliated firms constituted about 20% of the total firms (Gürakar and Bircan 2019). These differences partly reflect the differential reach of the state in these countries, and thus its ability to create regulatory rents. In Lebanon, for example, elected governments are weak relative to oligarchs from sectarian communities. This limits the scope of government intervention to a handful of sectors with traditional state influence (zoning laws, regulation of schools and hospitals, and procurement).

In general, cronies tend to conglomerate in sectors that are sheltered from competition and susceptible to policy manipulation through the use of regulatory barriers and selective enforcement. There is a visible tendency of PCFs to conglomerate in the non-tradable sectors. In particular, service sectors oriented towards domestic markets remain a preferred home for political cronies in the post-liberalisation era. Across the region, PCFs tend to cluster in the banking, real estate, tourism, distribution, natural resources, and telecommunications sectors. Standing out in terms of growth and profitability, these sectors were often selectively opened in the wake of liberalisation through discretionary licences, which were typically awarded to political insiders. Apart from the need to obtain explicit state permission to operate in these sectors, politically connected actors were also afforded favourable access to complimentary inputs, such as land, capital, water, and related infrastructure. In Egypt for example, crony firms led the expansion of tourism in the Sinai, the construction of large and prospering real estate projects, the modernisation of the distribution system, and the take-off of modern telecoms, thanks to their access to privileged land, licences, and credit. Foreign-owned banks and firms seeking entry in domestic MENA markets were only allowed if they were willing to partner with one of the regime cronies. In many instances, this was a result of highly centralised brokerage involving the most trusted confidants of the regime: in Morocco's case the King and his two closest advisors approved all major real estate ventures. Politically connected entrepreneurs also acquired important stakes in media outlets. The Sawiris family in Egypt, AKP-affiliated business groups in Turkey, and the sectarian oligarchs in Lebanon made major inroads in the media and entertainment industry.

PCFs tend to be large. In Egypt, they included eight of the top 20 firms traded on the stock exchange, and they tend to also be capital- and energy-intensive. In Tunisia the Ben Ali firms were over-represented at the top end of the firm-size and -output distributions, especially in highly regulated sectors. Similarly, in Lebanon connected firms tend to be larger than their unconnected competitors in the same sector. PCFs are often organised around pyramidal structures, as is common around the world, in an attempt to leverage control over cash flow as much as possible in order to improve the returns on connections. This is a characteristic of many of the PCFs in Egypt, which tend to have several layers of ownership.

Some evidence points to the intensification of cronyism during the liberalisation era. Since the late 1990s Egyptian manufacturing saw a growing exposure to cronyism. While, in 1996, there was, on average, less than one crony operating in a typical sector this number had doubled by the late 2000s. Morocco witnessed a similarly upward shift. Since 1993 there has been a steady shift away from sectors facing international competition to sectors primarily subjected to domestic regulations.

20.3 Impact on job creation and growth

Using micro data on political connections and corporate performance, several recent papers have examined the relative performance of PCFs and have probed the effect of unfair competition on the dynamism of unconnected firms.

Diwan et al. (2015) show that connected firms in Egypt tend to be larger in size as well as more indebted, capital-intensive, and reliant on subsidies. In 2010 such firms derived 60% of net corporate profits but generated only 11% of employment. Sectors where PCFs entered became more skewed in terms of employment distribution and had relatively fewer middle-sized firms. Importantly, employment growth *declined* after the entry of these firms into sectors previously unexposed to cronies. The decline is attributable to the negative impact of the entry of politically connected firms on their unconnected competitors, whose incentives to invest and innovate shrink in the face of unfair competition. The overall estimated effects are quantitatively large: employment in the formal sector could have been 25% larger in the idealised scenario of perfect competition. There is thus a tangible cost of cronyism in terms of lost growth. In the absence of cronyism, job creation in the Egyptian formal sectors could have been higher by 25 percentage points over a ten-year period.

In Tunisia, Baghdadi et al. (2019) show that firms owned by the Ben Ali clan produced around 5% of all private sector output and derived 15% of all net private sector profits, the very large firms being hugely profitable. For instance, the top ten Ben Ali firms accounted for approximately 4% of economy-wide output and 10% of gross profits in the economy. Strikingly, these firms dominated sectors that were protected by regulatory restrictions. Connected firms represented a paltry 0.1% of all firms in these protected sectors but accounted for 10% of all jobs, 39% of output, and 53% of net profits.

The analysis of Lebanon by Diwan and Haidar (2019) presents an interesting parallel. The bulk of job creation in Lebanon takes place through large firms who employ around 16% of the total labour force. When excluding self-employed firms, large firms actually accounted for 55% of net job creation in Lebanon. This stands in stark comparison to Egypt and Tunisia where 90% of the new jobs were created by small firms. Importantly, in Lebanon, connected firms, which tend to be larger in size, employed more workers per unit of output produced and were less productive. The PCFs created 20.32% more jobs each year on average than unconnected firms operating within the same sector, but their output per employee was 20.4% lower.

Diwan and Haidar show that, on a net basis, job creation has been constrained by the dominance of political connections. For every additional PCF in a sector, 6.8% fewer jobs are created each year, on average, in this sector. These patterns of job creation are not attributable to PCFs conglomerating in sectors that have low growth potential. Neither are these sectors capital-intensive and thus dominated in low job growth. These findings need to be situated in the specific Lebanese political economy where oligarchic business interests are nested within a broader clientelistic system that exchanges privileges with jobs for political constituents.

While the findings on Morocco are less fine-grained, Saadi (2019) furnishes broad illustrative patterns on the monarchy's commercial interests, locating its presence in different sectors and offering broad comparisons across connected and unconnected sectors. Preliminary evidence suggests that the PCFs in Morocco enjoyed a greater market share, higher net and gross margins, and greater value-added per worker. While more definitive evidence is yet unavailable, there is a suggestion that Morocco has managed to achieve moderate levels of growth despite pervasive cronyism, possibly because connected individuals were under more pressure by the Palace to manage their firms efficiently in the service of national economy.

Turkey adds a crucial source of variation. Atiyas et al. (2019) offer more unambiguous evidence. The authors show that the gap between the labour productivity of new growth centres in Anatolia, the AKP heartland where the country's emergent devout bourgeoisie is based, and that in traditional industrial centres (such as Istanbul, Ankara, Izmir, and Kocaeli) was reduced, especially in the 2000s. This productivity catch-up was accompanied with an increase in the share of Anatolian provinces in total exports of the country. Importantly, the number of firms associated with religious networks among the top manufacturing firms in Turkey increased significantly, again in the 2000s. Thus, here it is the process of increased inclusion of a rising tide of SMEs in the national economy that led to a solid growth performance.

The preferential treatment of AKP-affiliated regions ended up including firms that were previously excluded and on the margins of economy. Culling evidence from the 1,000 largest industrial firms, Atiyas et al. demonstrates that a growing share of Turkey's largest firms are now affiliated with the religious network. Still, however, these firms are comparatively smaller in size than their secular counterparts and are predominantly active in traditional labour-intensive industries. In manufacturing sectors, an affiliation with the religious network generated additional entry of firms and increased exports. These favourable effects of political affiliation are, however, conditional on the sector where these firms operate. Focusing on the construction sector, Gürakar and Bircan (2019) show that AKP-affiliated companies won more contracts when less competitive tender procedures were used.

With the exception of Turkey and Morocco, the evidence marshalled in the literature so far suggests that cronyism has imposed significant costs on Middle Eastern economies. Extending prior analysis of this subject (World Bank 2014), this conclusion underscores a perverse trade-off between privileges and jobs: while connected firms receive a disproportionate share of privileges, employment is largely concentrated among informal firms (Malik 2014). This disconnect represents a key paradox of private sector development in the Middle East. Politically connected sectors are generally less competitive and have fewer medium-sized firms than sectors with less crony exposure. The cost advantages derived by crony firms are usually a result of state patronage, which can kill their incentives to innovate or compete on a global scale. In Egypt, the probability that a PCF invests in product innovation is a meagre 1% compared to over 7% for unconnected firms (Francis et al. 2018). At the same time, unfair competition drives their competitors to shrink and reduce their investments as well.

This evidence fits well in the analytical characterisation of an Arab variety of capitalism offered by Steffen Hertog (2019). Hertog argues that privileges distributed by expansive and "over-ambitious" Arab states create deep divisions, both among workers and businesses, between insiders who have access to those privileges and outsiders who do not. These divisions destroy incentives for productivity, enhancing investments on the one hand and creating vested interests that block any attempt to reform on the other. The result is a deep segmentation between a relatively small and generally uncompetitive formal business sector and a relatively large informal sector that lacks the resources and capacity to grow and become more competitive.

While this evidence opens a new window into a relatively understudied subject, we have only begun to scratch the surface of a complex phenomenon. The form and function of cronyism and its consequences remain poorly understood. Cronyism is a differentiated tapestry whose effects are often subtle and highly context-specific. While for Egypt's political cronies employment creation did not seem to be a first-order political concern, it is a central function of politically connected sectors in Lebanon's fractured and clientelistic milieu. In both Egypt and Tunisia cronyism deploys the sort of blunt instruments that can exclude competitors and hurt private sector development (Diwan 2019).

While cronyism can be clearly viewed as a barrier to prosperity in some countries, it can be entirely consistent with economic growth in others (e.g., Morocco and Turkey). In Turkey the rise of new economic players, popularly described as Anatolian tigers, supports not just export-oriented growth but also a new brand of popular politics. While there are many instances of insider privileges, including advantages in the bidding of construction contracts, Turkey's emergent private sector is supporting export-oriented growth with favourable effects for domestic job creation. The more recent period that saw the closure of hundreds of Gulenist firms illustrates a different political phenomenon that may be economically destructive. Iran presents a distinct intertwining of economics and politics where organisational interests, rather than private sector firms, control the commanding heights of the economy. Again, this should be understood in the context of Iran's peculiar political economy where parastatal organisations that were vanguards of the 1979 Revolution acted as key distributional nodes for supporters of the Revolution (Hariss 2019). Such heterogeneity across MENA cases suggests that each context is unique and needs to be studied in its relevant milieu.

20.4 Mechanisms of privilege

Although there is some variation in their nature, there is a common reliance on an array of mechanisms of privilege used. These include: preferential access to subsidies, regulatory capture, preferential access to finance, privatisation, non-tariff measures, and public procurement, among others. These are briefly discussed below.

Subsidies. Evidence suggests that, in Egypt, PCFs disproportionately benefited from energy subsidies. In turn, such subsidies incentivise these firms to become more capital-intensive. Anecdotal evidence from Tunisia and Morocco also point to a greater reliance of connected firms on energy subsidies.

Regulatory capture. Connected firms also receive better regulatory treatment in ways that make them inherently more profitable. Ben Ali firms had a disproportionately greater presence in sectors that were closed to foreign direct investment and required licences to operate. These firms were more profitable, and the gap in profitability was higher in sectors subjected to greater entry regulations. Such profitability was clearly a result of protection from market competition. Connected firms were also more likely to evade taxes.

Access to credit. Another important mechanism used to privilege insider firms is favourable access to credit. This is fairly widespread across the Middle East, where PCFs tend to have a much higher capital intensity than the rest of the economy. Diwan and Schiffbauer (2018) showed that 92% of the overall loans extended to the private sector in Egypt in 2010 went to PCFs. This extraordinary concentration of loans in capital-intensive—and typically energy-intensive firms—contributes to the inefficient deployment of capital, starving the rest of the economy from capital, and forcing firms to remain self-sufficient and to give up growth opportunities. The advantage of PCFs in accessing credit is largely due to the implicit guarantees from the state. Indeed, using an event study around the time of the revolution in Egypt in 2011, Chekir and Diwan (2014) measure those advantages to be around 20% of the value of PCFs.

In Lebanon the ruling class directly controls the ownership of local commercial banks. Compiling detailed ownership and political affiliation data on the major 20 commercial banks in 2014, Chabaan (2019) has shown that the shareholders of 18 out of the 20 Lebanese banks are linked to political elites. Nearly 43% of assets in the sector are attributable to political control. "Crony capital" within the banking sector is also shown to affect the quality of banks' loans, and their exposure to public debt.

By contrast, the control of banking system is more indirect in Morocco where the regime uses indirect corporate governance instruments such as board membership to appoint members close to the ruling circle. To demonstrate the centrality of finance in Moroccan cronyism, Oubenal (2019) conducted a detailed network analysis of board members of key bank and non-bank financial institutions and found the growing presence of board members linked to the royal family.

In Turkey, Birkan and Saka (2019) present evidence of co-movement of electoral and credit cycles. They show that, in the run-up to local elections, the lending behaviour of private and state-owned banks differs markedly in provinces controlled by the ruling AK Party and the opposition. Evidence suggests that state banks comparatively scaled up their lending in politically competitive provinces under AKP rule even as they decreased such lending in competitive provinces headed by an opposition mayor. Part of the financial sector has therefore emerged as an important instrument in contentious politics.

Privatisation. Connected actors were also able to capture the privatisation process. Several public companies went into private hands closely tied with political regimes. This was most evident in Tunisia where eight out of 84 privatised firms ended up in the hands of Ben Ali family. Importantly, it was mainly these newly acquired firms whose profits witnessed a huge increase after privatisation; the non-Ben Ali privatised firms did not enjoy similar profitability. The greater profitability of Ben Ali firms was largely attributable to their privileged and protected status after privatisation. While privatisations in many other MENA contexts are known to have favoured politically entrenched businessmen, there are some important differences between the Arab and Iranian experiences. In Iran, assets were privatised to organisations rather than families, which highlights the importance of the underlying political context. These Iranian organisations sit at the fluid boundary between the public and private sectors and enjoy the commanding heights of both economy and polity. As guardians of the Revolution in 1979, they cater to its key social constituencies.

Trade policy. Connected firms are shielded from global competition through conventional instruments of trade protection. In Tunisia firms owned by the Ben Ali clan tended to operate in sectors that are shielded through higher tariff barriers. Selective and politically brokered trade liberalisation provides a fascinating instance of how trade policy gets captured even in the process of trade reform. Eibl and Malik (2016) document how in the wake of the Egypt–EU trade agreement in 2004 which entailed substantial tariff liberalisation, non-tariff barriers went up for nearly all sectors. About 75% of the total manufacturing sub-sectors that faced a tariff reduction in 2004 witnessed an increase in NTMs in 2005. This increase in compensatory non-tariff protection was systematically higher for sectors previously exposed to crony presence. Connected sectors had 50% higher probability of an NTM being applied. Replicating this exercise in Morocco, the authors find similar evidence on trade policy substitution in the wake of an EU agreement whereby tariff reductions were followed by increases in NTMs (Malik and Eibl 2019).

The politics of trade protection assumes a distinct ethnic undertone in Jordan where historically embedded cleavages exist between the two main ethnic groups, the local Jordanian tribes described as East bankers that control the public sector and the Palestinians who, as mercantile elites, dominate the private sector. Jordan's political settlement is maintained by appeasing the two ethnic groups through different economic policy instruments. As Steve Monroe (2019) shows the nature of compensation that import-competing industrialists received in the wake of liberalisation depended on their ethnic affiliation. Specifically, the politically included co-ethnic groups were compensated through informal protectionist deals, such as a lighter tax and regulatory enforcement, uncompetitive government contracts, access to policymakers, and insider information. By contrast, private sector elites belonging to the politically excluded ethnic groups—namely Palestinians—were compensated through formal instruments of protection such as tariffs, regulatory barriers, and subsidies.

Procurement. Another arena where connected firms are privileged is procurement, especially in relation to construction contracts. This has acquired particular salience in Turkey where public procurement contracts are awarded to more than 50,000 firms annually. Such contracts can serve as an important form of rent distribution. Studying 18,000 procurement contracts in Turkey, Gürakar and Bircan (2016) offer systemic evidence of favouritism for firms that are connected to the religious business networks associated with AKP. The majority of the firms receiving these contracts were established in the 1990s, the period that coincided with the rise of the Anatolian tigers. Such preferential arrangements were especially rife when competitive procedures were more relaxed. Much like Iran, these rents seem to be directed towards a social constituency that supports the political order dominated by AKP. However, the consequences of these arrangements on investment climate and growth remain unclear.

20.5 Other countries in MENA

The discussion above has focused on the cases of countries where good enough data has allowed for the production of solid empirical analysis. But so far, data limitation has restricted the ability of researchers to analyse cronyism in Syria, Iraq, Algeria, and the GCC. Here, we add comparative insights on these missing cases, drawing on existing qualitative research.

Like many other MENA countries, the Syrian regime was compelled to partially liberalise its economy in the face of falling external rents from oil and aid in the late 1990s. The private sector that gained strength after Syria's partial reform efforts was cultivated through informal networks managed by the regime's bureaucratic and security elites along with their extended families. Privatisation benefited selected families of regime-connected businessmen and bureaucrats. Regulation and its selective enforcement provided an important source of privilege. Syria's Investment Law No 10, introduced in early 1990s, offered tax and tariff exemptions to encourage investment. However, given that private investors were required to obtain official permission, enforcement became an arena for the negotiation of privileges as the regime could arbitrarily reward cronies.

In Algeria the business–state relationship operates in murky and opaque ways. The private sector is both weak and depoliticised. The country's substantial oil riches and its adverse historical legacy, defined by the mass exodus of French capital and skilled labour at the time of independence, meant that the Algerian state came to play a more domineering role in the economy. Algeria stands out for its extreme resistance to economic reform. Even when reform became unavoidable in the face of plunging oil prices in the mid-1980s, mounting debt, and civil war, the regime undertook only partial steps, some of which were quickly revoked. The restricted space for reform is partly rooted in a factionalised system, which makes elite consensus difficult, and the regime's extreme risk aversion towards the emergence of independent business actors. While stories of corruption and cronyism are rife in public circles, oligarchic interests tend to operate under a garb of secrecy that makes it difficult to identify the nature and scale of cronyism. After Bouteflika's recent "retirement", business tycoons tied to the presidency have been officially accused of corruption. They were rumoured to have controlled the heights of Algerian economy through questionable business practices. Since the government and its allied departments hold a firm grip on the economy, procurement, contracts, and licenses remain key arenas of patronage. Exchange rate restrictions have given rise to a huge black-market premium. Cronies also tend to operate through a variety of import and distribution companies that depend on preferential access to foreign exchange and tag onto the state's extensive subsidy and procurement regime.

The entanglement between business and politics takes a slightly different turn in the GCC where oil riches mean that there is little need to close off economic access to generate additional rents. Although the GCC private sector has shown greater dynamism and strength in recent decades it still lacks "structural independence" from the state and is unable to act as an organised class with strong bargaining power. Despite a more open door and less intrusive economic policy, the business climate for smaller firms is poor with limited access to finance, high barriers to entry, and weak bankruptcy rules. The private sector is typically made up of large established firms operating in refining, construction, and trade and that enjoy preferential access to the state and its subsidies. Importantly, access to these sectors is restricted to business conglomerates that are connected to the royal circle through regime fixers, favoured clan groups, members of the royalty, and their trusted intermediaries.

Like elsewhere in the Middle East, it is impossible to gain economic influence without the regime's endorsement. State contracts and licenses are, once again, important means of rewarding business cronies. While the GCC private sector has a weak presence in manufacturing, connected families tend to operate in sectors oriented towards domestic consumption and services. Leading families have won exclusive rights to the distribution of foreign brands, such as cars, electronics, food products, and the like. Ownership patterns are organised around familial lines intersecting with ethnic and royal kinship bonds. In this milieu, there are very thin dividing lines between public and private interests.

Traces of cronyism can also be found in the Palestinian territories in the post-Oslo period, which saw a distinct intertwining of business and politics that was manifested in the emergence of powerful business conglomerates in the West Bank controlling prized sectors, such as telecommunications, real estate, and retail trade (Dana 2015). This coincided with the emergence of a new class of political entrepreneurs who enjoyed both close connections with the Palestinian Authority and Israeli business counterparts (and security establishment). Embedded in the larger geo-political settlement, these crony capitalist relations provide binding elite commitments for a project of state-building under occupation.

Iraq offers another peculiar case where the private sector has historically operated under the state's thumb, enjoying very limited autonomy and depending mostly on public contracts in an oil-driven economy. The US occupation brought a major shift in the country's political economy. In its wake, Iraq made an abrupt transition from an economy of centralised control to an economy of decentralised corruption. Political fragmentation along ethnic and sectarian lines has institutionalised clientelism by creating a competition for spoils, as in Lebanon where sectarian competition for political office has blurred the boundaries between clientelism and cronyism. However, a key difference is the sheer scale of the resources available to the public sector in Iraq. While Iraq's private sector is particularly anaemic—the majority of manufacturing firms have either closed down or are working well below capacity—the few companies that became successful are essentially suppliers and importers whose survival remains tightly linked with government procurement contracts. One region within Iraq where some private sector activity has taken off since Saddam's overthrow is Kurdistan, which has witnessed growing foreign investment activity in real estate, banking, and telecom. Even here, owners of telecom operators that received exclusive rights to operate were deemed close to the political leadership of the Kurdistan Regional Government.

20.6 The politics of private sector development

The above evidence confirms the conventional academic wisdom on crony capitalism where those in close proximity to power win "favours that allow them to earn returns far above market returns" (Haber 2002). There is often some exchange behind these favours. Apart from enriching those close to the ruling circles, preferential treatment of cronies can serve as a "binding commitment" for elites that ensures their support for the prevailing political order (North et al. 2009). The business–state relationship is therefore central to understanding the genesis and persistence of political power. Our evidence supports the time-tested wisdom that economic and political power are co-constituted in the process of development. Half-baked attempts at economic liberalisation are therefore unlikely to succeed without having due regard for its attendant consequences in the political domain.

Dissatisfaction with cronyism, and the resultant economic stagnation and lack of jobs and opportunities, was a major impetus for the Arab Spring. Eight years later, very little has changed in the Middle East: corruption and cronyism still remain rampant. A fresh wave of protests are raging from Iraq to Lebanon. These protests are directed against pervasive corruption in the system, which distributes spoils to sectarian and ethnic oligarchs in both countries. It is not just the state that remains captured in Iraq and Lebanon, but also the business–state relationship. In the former, the private sector remains dependent on state contracts; in the latter, it is beholden to oligarchic interests that pretty much monopolise the market. The protests in Algeria have problematised the business–state relationship in an even more significant manner, forcing the regime to put key businessmen in jail (e.g. Ali Haddad and Rabrab).

While the political control of markets is a central variable in Middle Eastern political economy, no country arising out of the Arab Spring has made a serious effort to eliminate economic privileges for special interests and to institute pro-competition reforms. In Egypt, the Sissi regime is wary of the political clout of an autonomous private sector. So, it has built up friendly cronies that can be trusted—a small group of army-owned corporations and firms previously connected to the Mubarak regime. In Tunisia, corruption flourished after the revolution partly due to a breakdown in bureaucratic discipline. In both countries, public dissatisfaction with economic performance is growing. But over time, this is likely to help the economy in Tunisia and hurt it in Egypt. In Tunisia, greater inclusion fosters dialogue and the search for solutions. Ex-union leaders now sit in the cabinet, and they can influence broad economic policies, not just wages. The debate has become more constructive, focusing on how labour and business can fairly share the burden of a necessary adjustment. The country has stronger bargaining structures to negotiate conflict over the distribution of economic resources. But economic reform still appears distant.

Note

1 This Chapter draws on results and messages from our edited volume, Diwan et al. (2019b), and its introductory chapter, Malik et al. (2019).

References

Atiyas, Izak, Ozan Bakış, and Esra Çeviker Gürakar (2019), "Anatolian Tigers and the Emergence of the Devout Bourgeoisie in the Turkish Manufacturing Industry", in Diwan, Malik and Atiyas (2019).

Baghdadi, Leila, Hassan Arouri, and Bob Rijkers (2019), "How Do Dictators Get Rich? State Capture in Ben Ali's Tunisia", in Diwan, Malik and Atiyas (2019).

Birkan, Cagatay, and Orkun Saka (2019), "Elections and Economic Cycles: What Can We Learn from the Recent Turkish Experience?", in Diwan, Malik and Atiyas (2019).

Chaaban, Jad (2019), "I've Got the Power: Mapping Connections between Lebanon's Banking Sector and the Ruling Class", in Diwan, Malik and Atiyas (2019).

Chekir, Hamouda, and Ishac Diwan (2014), "Crony Capitalism in Egypt", *Journal of Globalization and Development*, 5(2): 177–211.

Dana, T. (2015), "The Symbiosis between Palestinian 'Fayyadism' And Israeli 'Economic Peace': The Political Economy Of Capitalist Peace In The Context Of Colonisation", *Conflict, Security and Development*, 15(5): 455–477.

Diwan, Ishac (2019), "The Future of the Private Sector in an Age of Uncertainty", in Diwan, Malik and Atiyas (2019).

Diwan, Ishac, and Jamal Ibrahim Haidar (2019), "Do Political Connections Reduce Job Creation? Evidence from Lebanon", in Diwan, Malik and Atiyas (2019).

Diwan, Ishac, and Marc Schiffbauer (2018), "Private Banking and Crony Capitalism in Egypt", *Business and Politics*, 20(3): 390–409.
Diwan, Ishac, Philip Keefer, and Marc Schiffbauer (2015), "Pyramid Capitalism: Cronyism, Regulation, and Firm Productivity in Egypt", *The Review of International Organizations*, (1): 1–36.
Diwan, Ishac, Philip Keefer, and Marc Schiffbauer (2019a), "Pyramid Capitalism: Evidence from Egypt", in Diwan, Malik and Atiyas (2019).
Diwan, Ishac, Adeel Malik, and Izak Atiyas (eds.) (2019b), *Crony Capitalism in the Middle East: Business and Politics from Liberalization to the Arab Spring*, Oxford: Oxford University Press.
Eibl, Ferdinand, and Adeel Malik (2016), "The Politics of Partial Liberalization: Non-Tariff Protection in Mubarak's Egypt", CSAE Working Paper 27, Department of Economics, University of Oxford.
Faccio, Mara (2006), "Politically Connected Firms", *American Economic Review*, 96(1): 369–386.
Francis, David, Sahar Hussain, and Marc Schiffbauer (2018), "Do Politically Connected Firms Innovate, Contributing to Long-Term Economic Growth?", Policy Research Working Paper, No. WPS 8502; Washington, DC: World Bank.
Gürakar, Esra and Tuba Bircan (2019), "Political Connections and Public Procurement in Turkey", in Diwan, Malik and Atiyas (2019).
Haber, Stephen (2002), *Crony Capitalism in Latin America: Theory and Evidence*, Paolo Alto: Stanford University Press.
Harris, Kevan (2019), "Iran's Commanding Heights: Conglomerate Ownership in the Islamic Republic", in Diwan, Malik and Atiyas (2019).
Henry, Clement Moore, and Robert Springborg (2010), *Globalization and the Politics of Development in the Middle East*, Cambridge: Cambridge University Press.
Hertog, Steffen (2019), "Is There an Arab Variety of Capitalism?", in Diwan, Malik and Atiyas (2019).
Heydemann, S. (ed.) (2004), *Networks of Privilege in the Middle East*, New York: Palgrave Macmillan US.
Malik, Adeel (2014), "A Requiem for the Arab Development Model", *Journal of International Affairs*, 68(1): 95–115.
Malik, Adeel, and Ferdinand Eibl (2019), "The Politics of Trade Protection in North Africa", in Diwan, Malik and Atiyas (2019).
Malik, Adeel, Izak Atiyas, and Ishac Diwan (2019), "Introduction: Crony Capitalism in the Middle East—What Do We Know and Why Does it Matter?", in Diwan, Malik and Atiyas (2019).
Monroe, Steve (2019), "Boundaries of Protectionism: Ethnic Politics and Crony Capitalism in Jordan", in Diwan, Malik and Atiyas (2019).
North, Douglass, John Wallis, and Barry Weingast (2009), *Violence and Social Orders*, Cambridge: Cambridge University Press.
Oubenal, Mohamed (2019), "Crony Interlockers and the Centrality of Banks in Morocco", in Diwan, Malik and Atiyas (2019).
Rijkers, B., C. Freund, and A. Nucifora (2017), "All in the Family: State Capture in Tunisia", *Journal of Development Economics*, 124: 41–59.
Saadi, Said Mohamed (2019), "Moroccan Cronyism: Facts, Mechanisms and Impact", in Diwan, Malik and Atiyas (2019).
World Bank (2014), *Jobs or Privileges: Unleashing the Employment Potential of the Middle East and North Africa*, Washington, DC: World Bank.

21

REFUGEES IN THE MENA REGION

Historical overview, effects and challenges

Jeffrey B. Nugent

21.1 Background and outline

The UNHCR (2018a) has estimated that MENA is the source for over two-thirds of the world's refugees and a large portion of its internally displaced persons (IDPs).[1] These record numbers of displaced human beings are the result of numerous conflicts in MENA over the last 60 years. Because the vast majority of refugees from these conflicts have fled to neighbouring countries, and countries in Europe and North America have been reluctant to share the refugee burden, this has imposed increasingly serious burdens on the refugee-hosting countries and assistance agencies in the MENA region.

The availability of detailed information on the socio-economic conditions of refugees and IDPs has only recently begun to improve. Since the conflict in Syria from 2011 to the present has displaced the most people (6 million refugees and 6.5 million IDPs according to UNHCR, 2018a), much of the present analysis focuses on the Syrian crisis and its refugee problems, though not ignoring the experience of other refugee populations.

The chapter consists of the following sections: after this introduction, Section 21.2 provides an historical overview of the main conflicts and refugee crises in the region since the end of WWII and points to the increasingly long duration of such crises. Section 21.3 identifies the geographic patterns of the refugee migrations from origin to destination. Section 21.4 focuses on the employment, health and education condition of Syrian refugees and their children. Section 21.5 turns to the various economic, socio-political, security and environmental burdens that these refugees impose on host country populations. Section 21.6 draws on the preceding sections by identifying the major challenges posed by refugees in the region and points to some policy initiatives which could mitigate some of the unfortunate effects on both refugees and host countries in recent years.

21.2 Historical overview of the main conflicts and refugee crises in MENA since WWII

Although MENA boasts a rich history of civilisations and dynasties, not surprisingly, it has also played host over the last four thousand years to major conflicts among tribes or religious or regional groups, or between states and empires, often on multiple occasions. This chapter is, however, restricted to those conflicts that have occurred since WWII.

The three most important sets of conflicts have been: (a) the Israeli–Palestinian conflicts of 1947–1948, 1956, 1967; the two Intifadas (1987–1991 and 2000–2005); and the Gaza War of 2008–2009; (b) conflicts involving Iraq (the Iran–Iraq War, 1980–1988; the Gulf War with Kuwait, 1990–1991; and the Iraq War, 2003–2011); and (c) the Syrian Civil War (2011–present).

Each of these conflicts has given rise to large numbers of refugees and IDPs. For example, the Israeli–Palestinian conflict of 1947–1948 forced several millions, indeed over half of the total population of Palestine, to flee to virtually everywhere in the region. Similarly, at its worst, in 2008 the Iraq War generated 2.5 million IDPs and about the same number of refugees. By 2018, however, Iraq had come to host 0.25 million Syrians, and Jordan, Lebanon and Turkey together to host almost 6 million Syrians.

Other important conflicts occurring either in the region or close enough to it to have important effects on it have been the civil wars in Libya (2011 and on and off again 2014–2018); various wars in Sudan and South Sudan between 1990 and 2017; conflicts in Eritrea and Ethiopia; Algeria's long-lasting war for independence (1954–1962) and its civil war (1991–1998); Lebanon's civil war (1975–1980) followed by Israel's occupation of part of its territory in 1982; and war in Afghanistan from 1972 to about 2000 and, off and on again, since then.

With respect to the refugees and IDPs emanating from these conflicts, in the case of Libya, while most of the displacements were IDPs, there were also over 1 million Egyptians who returned to Egypt and many Palestinians who had arrived in Libya after being forced out of Kuwait by Iraq in its 1990 invasion. Because of its large population size and localised character of hostilities, the number of IDPs was also more than 3.2 million in Sudan (Edwards, 2007).

Algeria's War of Independence was especially traumatic and deadly, with perhaps 1.5 million killed and 3 million uprooted (Home, 1978). The viciousness of that war may have contributed to how a disputed election outcome in 1991 managed to trigger Algeria's long-lasting civil war (1991–1998), which gave rise to perhaps 200,000 IDPs (Pack, 2013).

Yemen, too, has had civil and other wars for many years, the most recent being between the Houthis of the Hodeida Port region and the others from the south. At a peak in violence in 2015, the UNHCR asserted that 100,000 Yemenis had fled the country as refugees (to Djibouti, Somalia, Oman, Saudi Arabia and elsewhere) and that there were 2.4 million IDPs. Worse yet, the UN and its agencies have declared that Yemen is in imminent danger of becoming a major humanitarian disaster. Over 80% of its population lives below the poverty line, diseases (especially cholera) are being spread and fighting (including airstrikes from Saudi Arabia in the port of Hodeida) has been preventing the delivery of desperately needed food and medicines from reaching its millions of starving and diseased people.

Even relatively peaceful Jordan was witness to bloody confrontations between its military and the Palestinian Liberation Organization (PLO) (under Yasser Arafat) which had relocated to Jordan in 1970. This onslaught against the PLO forced it and many other Palestinians to relocate to Southern Lebanon, where they participated to some extent in the Lebanese Civil War and precipitated Israel's occupation of Southern Lebanon in 1982.

Although officially just outside the MENA region, Afghanistan's wars (with the Soviets 1979–1989, civil war 1989–1992 and off and on again with the Taliban) have given rise to over 6 million refugees and had enormous effects on MENA countries (Colville, 1997). The long-term character of Afghan refugees in other countries and increasing opposition to hosting them highlight the fact that hosting refugees is becoming an increasingly long-run burden, undermining willingness to accept them.[2]

21.3 The geographic pattern of refugee displacement and settlement and its dynamics

After the 1947–1948 Israeli–Palestinian conflict, approximately one-third of the Palestinian refugees fled to the West Bank and Gaza, which would then be occupied by Israel in 1967. Almost another third of them fled to Jordan, and most of the others to Lebanon, Syria and Egypt. They have never been allowed to return to Israel and, as a result, there are currently over 4 million officially registered Palestinian refugees and at least another million unregistered ones in the region (American Friends Service Committee). In some cases, many such refugees have been forced to flee again as subsequent conflicts displaced them from their locations in Lebanon, Syria and Iraq.

Compared to all these earlier episodes of violence that have given rise to large numbers of refugees, the still on-going surge of refugees from Syria has become even more voluminous and has had very serious impacts on host countries. Lebanon's small population (slightly over 6 million in 2018) is host to almost 2.3 million refugees from Palestine, Syria, Iraq and elsewhere, making the country the largest recipient of refugees per capita in the world (UNHCR, 2018a). Since well over 70 percent of the Syrians in Lebanon had less than primary education, not surprisingly a large percentage of Syrian refugees (including child workers) in the country were in 2013 employed in Lebanon's agricultural sector, constituting perhaps 85 percent of its agricultural labour force. Hence, refugees are not only highly over-represented in Lebanon, but also in a single sector of its economy.

Despite a larger population of about 9.6 million, with at least a million refugees from Palestine, hundreds of thousands from Iraq and Yemen, and now another 0.8 million from Syria (Assaad, 2018), Jordan, too, has a large number of refugees per capita. Even though many of the Syrian refugees in Jordan are located in large camps outside of towns, more of them are located in urban areas than in Lebanon and that proportion is growing. Although only a minority of these refugees are employed, those employed are more spread across industries (construction, trade and other services) than in Lebanon (Kumar et al., 2018).

In the case of Turkey, its population is much larger (over 80 million and growing) but it is hosting over 3.9 million Syrian refugees (again not all officially registered). While large percentages of these refugees have been settled in provinces near the Syrian border, refugees are located in every one of Turkey's 81 provinces. Although as in Lebanon and Jordan, large percentages of the refugees are children, up to 1 million refugees (including children) have managed to find employment of some kind in Turkey. Here too, large percentages of those found not working indicated in focus group interviews that they would like to work if they could find a job (Kumar et al., 2018).

The three countries which host the most Syrian refugees (Jordan, Lebanon and Turkey) are not poor. Yet, the fact that they hold such a large share of all Syrian refugees makes it clear that burden-sharing of these refugees is far short of the "fair burden-sharing rule" suggested in the 1970s whereby refugees should be shared among all countries in the world according to their wealth and population density (Suhrke, 1998).

21.4 Consequences of conflict and refugee status for Syrian refugees

One might think that refugees in Lebanon would be better off than in those Jordan or Turkey because of its proximity to Syria and its many border crossings (which made travel and work in Lebanon much easier to access before the crisis in Syria). Yet, according to Kumar et al. (2018: Ch. 13) all interviewed firms in Lebanon said that they either were employing Syrians at present or had recently, whereas much lower percentages of firms in Jordan and especially Turkey indicated this. Another favourable indicator for Syrian refugees in Lebanon from the same source is that larger percentages of refugee workers there said that they were working in the same sectors and occupations as they had previously been in Syria. Yet, since there were far more Syrian refugees per host country national in Lebanon and Jordan than in Turkey, these findings should not be surprising. According to other responses from Syrian refugee workers to questions posed in the same study, in Jordan they were better educated, employed in jobs requiring somewhat greater skills and were more confident of getting training and education for the skills needed than in the other countries. Higher percentages of refugee workers in Turkey also reported that, if mistreated at work, they would feel comfortable going to public authorities, and lower percentages of such workers said they would be afraid of getting into trouble with the government or police for working than in Lebanon. Syrian women in Lebanon, meanwhile, worried more about harassment at work and about safely getting to work.

The fact that over half of the Syrian refugees in Lebanon, Jordan and Turkey are young (below 16) indicates that, in assessing the consequences of both conflict in Syria and treatment as refugees in the receiving countries, considerable attention should also be given to their access to health care and education for both themselves and their children.

By virtually every measure in questionnaires and focus group interviews with refugees across these countries undertaken by Kumar et al. (2018) for both Lebanon and Jordan, and by Yahya et al. (2018) for Jordan, it would seem that refugees and their children have benefitted far less in these respects in Lebanon than in Jordan and especially Turkey. Contributing to the inferior situation of refugees in Lebanon are (a) that both before and after the beginning of the crisis, political relations between Syria and Lebanon were more adverse; (b) that more segments of Lebanon's population were more worried about political and terrorism threats from Syrians than in Jordan and Turkey; (c) that for much of the period, Lebanon was without an effective government following the assassination of its prime minister (possibly by a Syrian) and thus without a well-coordinated national policy for dealing with refugees; (d) that larger percentages of the refugees in Lebanon came in unofficially and thus without all the services provided to official refugees and without the same proportional funding from the refugee support organisations like the UNHCR; and (e) that the financial and administrative support for refugees by such agencies was subject to longer and more frequent delays in Lebanon.

Thanks to the report on Lebanon of the UNHCR, UNICEF and the World Food Program (2018), by taking advantage of the results of comparable surveys of Syrian refugees in all parts of the country over time, one can also point to some changes that have contributed to this somewhat inferior situation of refugees in Lebanon. First, while in Lebanon, legal residency documents are required to secure access to support, education and health services and employment, the percentage of Syrian refugee households in Lebanon with such documents for all family members declined quite sharply from 58% in 2011 to 19% in 2017. Much of that decline has been attributed to the complicated four-step procedure insisted upon by the Lebanese government for registering new births of non-Lebanese and the high costs of renewing these residency documents each year.[3] Service provision in Lebanon may also have been impeded by the fact that Lebanon has never ratified either the 1951 Refugee Convention or subsequent Protocols on Refugees, and requires non-Lebanese to get work permits, which are costly to employers. Based on its comparison of the economic and health situation of the Syrian refugees in Lebanon over time, the UNHCR (2018b) concluded that by 2017 Syrian refugees in Lebanon had become poorer and more vulnerable than in earlier years, indeed with 76% of them living below the poverty line. While its refugee care suppliers apparently became more efficient in identifying the neediest refugees and in expanding access to both health and education services over time (raising school enrolment rates of children aged 6–14 to 70% in 2017), several shortcomings were said to have gotten worse.[4]

Because of impressive pledges made by the Jordanian government to expand its schooling system to include refugee children, refugee school enrolments in Jordan expanded rapidly, although even there a detailed study (UNICEF, 2015) found that far fewer refugees were enrolled than expected. Explanations offered were (a) that many of the Syrian refugees had been IDPs for some time within Syria, so that on arriving in Jordan, many young refugees considered themselves too old to start attending school; (b) that the long distances between refugee housing and schools in Jordan subjected them to greater harassment from Jordanians while going to school; (c) the relatively high and unsubsidised costs of books and materials; (d) that many children with disabilities chose not to attend school; and (e) that parental needs for the children to earn money outweighed the importance of going to school.[5] Access to health care for Syrian refugees in Jordan also declined due to increasing funding shortfalls for the refugee agencies as well as the rising costs of health services and medicines caused by increasing demand (International Medical Corps, 2015). Access to jobs for the refugees in Jordan also became increasingly difficult due to the worsening situation of Jordan's economy (with foreign and domestic sources of investment being curtailed by the increasing political and economic insecurity emanating from the continuing conflicts in neighbouring Syria and Iraq). This was despite the impressive proposals identified in the "Jordan Compact" of February 2016, which were designed to allow Jordanian industry to take advantage of skills and experience of some Syrian refugees.[6] Three other important obstacles to these efforts in Jordan to hire Syrian workers were (a) (as in Lebanon) the adverse effect of the conflict in Syria on Jordan's export channels; (b) the declining access by firms to finance; and (c) the lack of adequate systems for linking refugees with the skills needed by firms.

Because of language differences between Syrians (Arabic) and Turks (Turkish), the challenges of handling Syrian refugees in Turkey have been greater than in Lebanon and Jordan where Arabic was the common language. Nevertheless, Turkey has done quite well in facing those challenges for the following reasons: (a) shortly before the Syrian Civil War, Syria and Turkey had formed a high-level Strategic Council which implemented a series of cooperation agreements including one on bilateral mobility (Betts et al., 2018); (b) Turkey already had an agency with considerable prior experience in handling environmental disasters (AFAD); (c) Turkey adopted in 2013 a Law on Foreigners and International Protection which put greater emphasis on the integration of migrants in general (as opposed to its earlier focus on only migrants of Turkish descent) (Icduygu, 2015); (d) in 2015 and 2016, Turkey and the European Union came to an agreement in which Turkey agreed to re-admit all Syrian refugees and to prevent additional refugees from leaving for Europe in return for some 6 billion Euros of support for their Syrian refugees; (e) some cities and governorates within Turkey began to foster integration between locals and refugees or encourage the local chamber of commerce to establish new businesses aiming to take advantage of Syrian workers or entrepreneurs (Betts et al., 2018).

On the educational front, at first the emphasis in Turkey was on setting up Temporary Education Centres teaching an approved curriculum in Arabic, but over time the emphasis has shifted to attendance to Turkish public schools. Public education in Turkish schools is free, not only for regular grades but (unlike in Jordan) also for kindergarten. Again, thanks to EU and other support, subsidies are also provided to Syrian refugees who attend 80% of their classes, and even larger ones for those deemed most likely to drop out like female high-schoolers. As a result, enrolment of school-age Syrian refugees in schools had risen to about 75% by 2018, and increasingly in Turkish public schools that better integrated them into Turkish society and employment than the Temporary Educational Centres. Indeed, the plans at the time of writing (2019) are to phase out all the Temporary Education Centres in favour of Turkish Public Schools (Borgen Project, 2018). The access of Syrians to health care in Turkey also seems to have been high and the services evaluated quite highly. Yet even there, there seems to have been insufficient attention to depression among both the youth and the elderly given the high percentages of Syrians who have lost a loved one, had their house bombed or suffered conflict-related injuries (World Bank, 2017: 41).

Yet, despite considerable progress in Turkey on meeting its special challenges in handling its refugees, three factors point to why continued progress for Syrian refugees in Turkey may be difficult: (a) most such refugees are employed at low wages in the informal sector with little job protection; (b) Turkey's unemployment rate has been rising; and (c) inflation and financial crises hit Turkey in late 2018.

21.5 Economic, political and other challenges posed by Syrian refugees on host countries

Any assessment of the effect of refugee presence on host country economies may well depend heavily on who is making these assessments and the scope of analysis. Host country governments may often be inclined to emphasise and perhaps exaggerate the costs to solicit compensation from aid agencies and other nations. While it has been common for such assessments to include direct effects on the health, education and employment of host country populations, over time and with greater accumulated experience with refugees, quite appropriately the scope of analysis has broadened to incorporate political, security and environmental effects that had seldom been included earlier (Zetter, 2012).

Some very commonly observed economic challenges for the host economy attributable to the large numbers of refugees are those on the prices of food, medicine and housing in the vicinity of the refugees. In almost all cases where these prices have been tracked over time, the impact of refugee presence has been to raise these prices quite substantially, thereby hurting local consumers of these items, though quite naturally also benefitting some local suppliers of these items. Rozo and Sviatschi (forthcoming) have shown precisely these effects by comparing the expenditures of Jordanian households in Syrian refugee-receiving locations both before and after the arrival of the refugees, indeed going so far as to show that the actual expenditures on food and health care of those Jordanian households located near these refugees was lowered. However, they found no evidence that these effects actually lowered either access to health care or child health. Likewise, neither these authors nor Assad (2018) has identified any negative effects of refugee presence on educational outcomes of Jordanian children. However, the inflows of these generally impoverished and often less-educated refugees have also been found to lower the wage rates of nationals in the same kinds of jobs because refugees are so often needy of employment as to force them to work in the informal sector and at wage rates well below previously set minimum wage rates.

Especially in the rather depressed economic conditions that Lebanon, Jordan and Turkey have been experiencing since taking in so many Syrian refugees, it has become common for nationals to place much of the blame for their own sometimes deteriorating job prospects and wage rates on the refugees, giving rise to resentment against them. Language and cultural differences, as in the case of the Syrians in Turkey, can make mutual discussion as a means of reducing such frictions more difficult. Shortcomings in the health treatment of refugees or in the quality of housing provided to them can also have important externalities for nationals living near or working with these underserved refugees. The location of refugees in crowded parts of cities and towns, moreover, can make for traffic and other congestion problems and can increase environmental pollution.

In some cases, the presence and composition of the refugees can also be threatening to the personal safety of nationals and to political stability in the host country, thereby not only scaring local residents but also undermining the confidence in them of employers, investors and governments of these host countries, thus lowering investment and employment growth. This was especially so in the case of Lebanon, where both of its principal refugee groups, Palestinians and Syrians, have had these effects.[7] Turkey also has felt a security threat from the refugees, both because they viewed Kurds located just across their borders in Syria and Iraq as threats to the Turkish nation, and because many Turks seem to view the refugees as criminals.[8]

While all these complaints against refugees, especially the economic ones, are legitimate and may underscore the large cost burden of the refugees on the host countries, often overlooked are some more subtle and indirect effects, some of which may be positive. For example, refugees increase the sizes of various markets, which could, in turn, raise the potential for efficiency-increasing benefits in the form of increasing specialisation. Such effects can benefit both nationals and refugees by raising complementarities not only between local and refugee workers and consumers but also with firm owners and managers. Kumar et al. (2018) repeatedly point to the importance of job-matching in taking advantage of the potential benefits of these effects.

Ruiz and Vargas-Silva (2015) and Ozden and Wagner (2014) have produced empirical results along these lines in other regions of the world showing that the effects of forced migration on labour markets for host country nationals may not be as negative as often believed. While exogenous inflows of refugee workers have the effect of lowering wage rates, the lower labour costs to employers may lower product prices in labour-intensive activities, thereby encouraging consumer demand for such products and raising income and employment.

In the context of Turkey, several studies have demonstrated the applicability of these effects. Del Carpio and Wagner (2015), e.g., examined this issue using distance from Syrian location of origin to the largest city in each of these subregions in Turkey as an instrument to help them identify causal effects on Turkish labour markets. They show that, while the influx of Syrians has led to considerable displacement of poorly educated, low-skilled, female part-time Turkish workers, especially in agriculture, it has encouraged additional production and income and occupational upgrading of Turkish workers. So, too, have Altindag et al. (2020) and Akgunduz et al. (2018), also using instrumental variables, shown that the locations in Turkey with larger percentages of Syrian refugees have been ones in which local firms (some foreign-owned) have managed to raise profits and increase employment for both Turks and Syrian refugees.

Kumar et al. (2018) have gone to great lengths through both questionnaires and focus group interviews of both refugees and local firms and workers to identify the grievances of nationals with the Syrian refugees in Lebanon, Jordan and Turkey. However, they have also identified the existence and nature of the corresponding complaints against the attitudes and behaviour of nationals on the part of Syrian refugees. Out of this analysis come some suggestions (to be drawn upon in Section 21.6) of policy changes that could improve refugee–national relations and provide better "opportunities for all".

Clearly, however, another important factor affecting the receptivity of hosts to refugees and the kinds of effects deemed most harmful is the duration of refugee stay. This has major implications for whether the respective parties will find it in their interest to make suitable adjustments in their dealings with each other to maintain better relations and a mutual sense of well-being.[9] Often they will only want to change their attitudes and behaviour if the expected duration of refugee stay will be long enough to justify the investments needed to make these adjustments.

In the case of Syrian refugees, of critical importance to their willingness to return to Syria is the status of the political, economic and safety situation back in Syria. Yet, given the prospects for resolving the political conflict between the incumbent Bashar al-Assad regime and its opponents, or for diminishing the Syrian government's rather severe repression of its opponents, there is little reason to believe that Syrian refugees will be willing to leave the countries hosting them now anytime soon (Kirisci and Ferris, 2015). Evidence on this score comes from not only political and military pundits but also from attitudinal measures of Syrian refugees themselves. In particular, Balcilar and Nugent (forthcoming) take advantage of a successive series of surveys of Syrian refugees in Turkey, using their survey responses to show that there are several very important factors lowering the interest and willingness of Syrian refugees to return to Syria. These are (a) the number of family members back in Syria who have been killed or wounded, and damage to their homes; (b) the accumulating duration of their stay in Turkey; and (c) the relatively high and rising quantity and quality of services that they are receiving in Turkey. The first two of these can only rise over time and the last seems to have been rising as refugees have become increasingly located outside of the camps, in cities with improved access to public education, health care and employment. These authors showed these results to be robust to the use of alternative measures of the relevant variables and estimation procedures. Thus, it would seem that Syrian refugees, even if often still poor and with very low-paying jobs in Turkey, Jordan and Lebanon, are still unlikely to return to Syria anytime soon.

Also overlooked, even in the detailed surveys of Syrian refugees in Jordan, Lebanon and Turkey cited above, are environmental issues. Because it is the fourth poorest country in the world with respect to water resources per capita, Jordan is of special concern in this respect. Based on their reading of press articles and other studies in Jordan, Alshoubaki and Harris (2018, pp. 172–173) point to two serious environmental consequences that have arisen from the massive inflows of refugees into Jordan. First, because 70% of the Syrian refugees in Jordan have been concentrated in the generally dry areas of Jordan's north, this has led to excess demand for water in that region, lowering the supply of water to Syrians and Jordanians in that region to only 70% of the national standard. Second, since this area is also rather high in altitude, is windy and has been subject to the cutting of trees for firewood, it has also induced degradation of land. Still another adverse environmental effect of refugees is the continuing effect of rising temperatures and greenhouse gases which have been especially prominent in MENA, and at least partly attributable to refugees and the need for expanding agricultural land use and non-renewable energy use in cities. Yet, as with some of the economic effects, there may be reasons why the adverse effects identified may be overstated. For example, Muller et al. (2018) show that an offset to the harmful impacts on increasing water use in the dry areas of Northern Jordan is that the outflow of the large numbers of Syrians from Syria sharply reduced the use in Syria itself of irrigation water from the Yarmouk River that descends into Jordan and Israel, thereby leaving these countries with much more river water for irrigation.

21.6 Matching challenges with policy responses

Drawing on the findings in the previous section, Table 21.1 provides a list of factors deemed essential to reducing the costs of meeting the most important challenges confronting the agencies and countries hosting the refugees. As indicated in the different sections of the table, these consist of timing issues, actions to reduce costs to the host country and actions to take advantage of complementarities among refugees and nationals without aggravating frictions between them. While providing detailed policy proposals is beyond the scope of this chapter and would

Table 21.1 Factors affecting costs and benefits of hosting refugees to host country by type

A. Timing factors

1 Encourage temporary seasonal labour mobility before conflict and refugees
  - Example: Lebanon's long-term use of seasonal Syrian workers on farms

2 Initiation and design of services
  - Preparation for accommodating refugees will ensure appropriate services supplied

3 Relocations over time
  - Costly reallocations and rebuilding over time can be reduced by planning for long-term duration

4 Duration and termination of refugee services
  - But unnecessary continuation can be avoided by appropriate coordination for return to country of origin or to new country of destination in part taking advantage of refugees' preferences and needs of alternative host countries

B. Actions that can reduce costs to host country

1 Importance of sufficient international support to reduce host country burden
  - As EU support to Turkey has shown, generous support can reduce many frictions and increase market development

2 Programs sufficiently well-designed and -funded to be effective and comprehensive
  - Specific and high-quality programs of health, education and training
  - Programs may need to be diverse and gender-specific

3 Monetary costs reduced by allowing refugees to work with little friction

C. Actions to take advantage of complementary skills of refugees

1 Need to assess skills and experience of refugees and foster their efficient allocation to firms and locations

2 Foster market development
  - Export industries
    - By developing export industries, international balances could be increased, and these industries could have complementary linkages to other existing or new industries
  - Domestic market development
    - Use the higher spending of refugees, especially employed ones, to stimulate development of new markets and growth of new and existing firms
  - Facilitate trade and collaborative investment with country of origin

3 Avoid or mitigate frictions and conflicts between refugees and host population
  - Mitigate conflicts in labour market
  - Mitigate adverse effects of price increases (housing and other services) in areas where refugees are living
  - Avoid harmful environmental externalities
  - Promote social capital between refugees and host citizens

need to be specific to every pair of refugee origin and host countries, the following paragraphs provide some general suggestions.

First, with respect to timing, the host country should be as prepared as possible to have the relevant services ready when the refugees arrive and in suitable locations. Given that experience has shown that refugees are unlikely to be able to return to their country of origin anytime soon, the planning should be for a relatively long term. Yet, to the extent possible efforts should be made to explore efficient means of repatriating them when possible and to explore alternative destination countries where refugees could be better absorbed and refugee preferences might be respected to a larger extent (Jones and Teytelboym, 2017).

Second, to reduce the costs relative to the benefits of hosting refugees, refugee location and services should be designed to emphasise market creation by facilitating access to employment, especially in exporting and domestic activities aimed at taking advantage of complementarities between nationals and refugees through improved means of job-searching and training.

Third, and most importantly, host government policies should be designed to mitigate the adverse effects of refugees on host populations, e.g., by (a) avoiding inflationary consequences arising from the increased demands for housing, food and other services in areas where refugees are concentrated; (b) enforcing rules needed to avoid crime, corruption and environmental degradation; (c) encouraging cooperation among refugee groups and nationals at the local level by connecting local refugee administrators with national ones and both with civil society institutions; (d) facilitating cooperation at the international level by encouraging all MENA countries to sign the International Refugee Convention or related protocols, and more non-MENA countries to share the burden of hosting refugees, either by hosting more refugees themselves or by contributing to their support in host countries; and (e) for refugee origin countries by re-establishing the rule of law, justice and security for all returning refugees, including the rights to the property that they once had, greatly improving governance institutions and tolerance of different religions, so that refugees will be willing to return.

Notes

1 The MENA region is defined to include Afghanistan and Turkey in this chapter.

2 Indeed, while soon after the Soviet invasion of Afghanistan, and with assistance from the UNHCR, Iran and Pakistan welcomed those refugees, a decade later as conflict inside Afghanistan continued these countries refused to accept additional refugees and forced over 1.3 million of them to be repatriated. While by 2004 over 3 million had returned, the return experience highlighted two difficult problems: (a) the rapidity of their return challenged the ability of the underfunded UNHCR and International Organization for Migration to relocate them efficiently (Willner-Reid, 2017); and (b) the extremely low take-up of Afghan asylum seekers by countries outside the region.

3 According to Kumar et al. (2018: 96), however, some of these restrictions may have been eased in 2018.

4 For example, only 11% of children aged 3–5 are enrolled in pre-primary education, and only 12% of those aged 17–19 had completed grade 9, an outcome attributed to the costs of books, transportation and uniforms. Also since elderly refugees were insufficiently integrated with other family members, depression of the elderly was said to be a major problem (Chemali et al., 2018). Even more importantly, between 2015 and 2017 the percentage of refugees with inadequate food consumption increased from 2% to 11% and those with "borderline" consumption from 14% to 27% (UNHCR, 2018b).

5 Indeed, 47% of households surveyed said that a portion of their income was earned by a child (UNICEF, 2015).

6 As pointed out by Kumar et al. (2018: 59), these export workplaces for hiring Syrian workers were in special zones which were not easily accessible from the locations where Syrians were living.

7 As noted above, Palestinians have been associated with the Hezbollah militants in South Lebanon, seen by many as a divisive force and which had triggered an invasion by Israel. Also, since the Syrians in Lebanon are mostly Sunni, this has made their presence uncomfortable for the Shia Hezbollah in Lebanon, some of whom have been fighting against the Syrian Sunni opposition on behalf of the incumbent al-Assad regime.

8 While both these suspicions may linger, local authorities in Turkey have said criminality is surprisingly low among the Syrian refugees (Kirisci and Ferris, 2015).

9 Numerous studies of social well-being around the world have shown that the nearby presence of persons of different religion, nationality and language has the effect of lowering individual sense of happiness or well-being.

Biblography

Akgunduz, Y.E., M. van den Berg and W. Hassink (2018). *The Impact of the Syrian Refugee Crisis on Firm Entry and Performance in Turkey*, World Bank Policy Research Working Paper 8323.

Alshoubaki, W. and M. Harris (2018). The Impact of Syrian Refugees on Jordan: A Framework for Analysis, *Journal of International Studies* 11(2): 154–179.

Altindag, O, O. Bakis and S. Rozo (2020). Blessing or Burden? The Impact of Refugees on Businesses and the Informal Economy, *Journal of Development Economics*, 146, Article 102490.

American Friends Service Committee, *Palestinian Refugees and the Right to Return*, https://afsc.org/resource/palestinian-refugees-and-right-return

Assaad, R. (2018). *The Impact of the Syrian Refugee Influx on the Education and Housing Outcomes of Jordanians*, Economic Research Forum Policy Brief No. 33, Economic Research Forum, May.

Balcilar, M. and J.B. Nugent (2019). The Migration of Fear: An Analysis of Migration Choices among Syrian Refugees, *Quarterly Review of Economics and Finance*, 73: 95–110.

Betts, A., A. Ali and F. Memisoglu (2018). *Local Politics and the Syrian Refugee Crisis: Exploring Responses in Turkey*, Lebanon: University of Oxford: Refugee Studies Center.

Borgen Project (2018). *Efforts to Expand Education for Syrian Refugees in Turkey*, https://borgenproject.org/expanding-education-for-syrian-refugees-in-turkey/

Chaaban, J., N. Salti, H. Ghattas, A. Irani, T. Ismail and L. Batlouni (2016). *Survey on the Socioeconomic Status of Palestinian Refugees in Lebanon 2015*, https://www.unrwa.org/sites/default/files/content/resources/survey_on_the_economic_status_of_palestine_refugees_in_lebanon_2015.pdf

Chemali, Z.C., P.C. Borba, K. Johnson, S. Khair and G.L. Fricchione (2018). Needs Assessment with Elder Syrian Refugees in Lebanon: Implication for Services and Interventions, *Global Public Health* 13(8): 1216–1228.

Colville, R. (1997). Afghanistan: The Unending Crisis: The Biggest Caseload in the World, *Refugees Magazine*, 108, UNHCR.

Del Carpio, X. and M. Wagner (2015). *The Impact of Syrian Refugees on the Turkish Labor Market*, World Bank Group Policy Research Working Paper 7401.

Edwards, J.K. (2007). *Sudanese Women Refugees: Transformations and Future Imaginings*, New York: Palgrave Macmillan.

Esen, O. and A.O. Binatli (2017). The Impact of Syrian Refugees on the Turkish Economy: Regional Labour Market Effects, *Social Science* 6(129): 1–12.

Fallah, B., C. Krafft and J. Wahba (2018). *The Impact of Refugees on Employment and Wages in Jordan, Economic Research Forum*, Working Paper 1189 April 2018.

Ferris, E. (2008). *On the Record: Internal Displacement and International Law*; available from: https://www.brookings.edu/on-the-record/iraqi-internal-displacement-and-international-law/.

Home, Alistair (1978). *A Savage War of Peace: Algeria 1954–1962*, New York: Viking Press.

Icduygu, A. (2015). *Syrian Refugees in Turkey: The Long Road Ahead*, Washington, DC: Migration Policy Institute.

International Medical Corps (2015). Health Care Assessment of Syrian and Iraqi Urban Refugees in Jordan, *Ipsos*, October 5, Jordan.

Jones, W. and A. Teytelboym (2017). The International Refugee Match: A System That Respects Refugees' Preferences and the Priorities of States, *Refugee Survey Quarterly* 36(2): 84–109.

Kirisci, K. and E. Ferris (2015). *Not Likely to Go Home: Syrian Refugees and the Challenges to Turkey- and the International Community*, Brookings: Center on the United States and Europe at Brookings, Turkey Project Policy Paper No 7.

Kumar, K.B., S. Culbertson, L. Constant, S. Nabaj, F. Urlu, K.E. Bouskill, J.S. Maini, K. Costello, G.R. Aliyev and F. Afashe (2018). *Opportunities for All: Mutually Beneficial Opportunities for Syrian Refugees and Host Countries in Middle Eastern Labor Markets*, Santa Monica: RAND Corporation.

Martinez, Luis (2000). *The Algerian Civil War 1990–1998*. New York: Columbia University Press.

Muller, M.F., J. Yoon, S.M. Gorelick, N Avise and A. Tilmant (2018). Impact of Syrian Refugee Crisis on Land Use and Transborder Freshwater Resources, *PNAS* 113(52): 4932.

Office for the Coordination of Humanitarian Affairs (OCHA) (2018). Humanitarian, *Bulletin Iraq*, 20 November. OCHA.

Olmstead, J. (2020). *Gendered Socioeconomic Impacts of Conflict in the Middle East*, Chapter 22 in this volume.

Ozden, C. and M. Wagner (2014). *Immigrants Versus Natives?: Displacement and Job Creation*, World Bank Working Paper Series, WPS6900.

Pack, J. (ed., 2013). *The 2011 Libyan Uprisings and the Struggle for the Post-Qadhafi Future*, New York: Palgrave Macmillan.
Roussi, A. (2018). Despite the Peace Deal with Ethiopia, Eritrean Refugees Are Still Afraid to Return Home, *Global Post*, September 13.
Rozo, S. and M.M. Sviatschi (forthcoming). Is a Refugee Crisis a Housing Crisis? Only if Supply is Unresponsive? , *Journal of Development Economics*.
Ruiz, I. and C. Vargas-Silva (2015). The Labour Market Consquences of Hosting Refugeees, *Journal of Economic Geography* 16(3): 667–694.
Salehyan, I. and K.S. Gleditsch (2006). Refugees and the Spread of Civil War, *International Organization* 60(02): 335–366.
Salti, N., J. Chaaban, A. Irani and R. Al Mokdiad (2018). *A Multidimensional Measure of Well-being among Youth: The Case of Palestinian Refugee Youth in Lebanon*, Economic Research Forum Working Paper 1268.
Suhrke, A. (1998). Burden-Sharing during Refugee Emergencies: The Logic of Collective versus National Action, *Journal of Refugee Studies* 11(4): 396–415.
The American Team for Displaced Eritreans (2018). *Some Recent Statistics Regarding Refugees and Asylum Seekers*, https:// Eritrean-refugee-stats.
Trapp, A.C., A. Teytelboym, A. Martinello, T. Andersson and N. Ahani (2018). *Placement Optimization in Refugee Resettlement*, Working Paper 2018, Lund University, 23.
UNHCR, UNICEF and World Food Program (2018). *Vulnerability Assessment of Syrian Refugees in Lebanon; VASyR 2018*; available from: https://data2.unhcr.org/en/documents/download/67380.
UNHCR (United Nations High Commission for Refugees) (2018a). *Mid-Year Trends June 2017 Technical Report*; available from: https://www.unhcr.org/5aaa4fd27.pdf
UNHCR (United Nations High Commission for Refugees) (2018b). *Iraq Factsheet*, January; available from: https://reliefweb.int/report/iraq/unhcr-iraq-factsheet-january-2018.
UNICEF (2015). *Syria Crisis April 2015 Humanitarian Situation Report*; available from: https://www.unicef.org/appeals/files/UNICEF_Syria_Crisis_SitRep_April_2015.pdf
Willner-Reid, M. (2017). Afghanistan: Displacement Challenges in a Country on the Move, *Migration Policy Institute*, November 16.
World Bank (2017). *The Toll of War: The Economic and Social Consequences of the Conflict in Syria*, Washington, DC: World Bank.
Yahya, M., J. Kassir and K. el-Harriri (2018). *Unheard Voices: What Syrian Refugees Need to Return Home*, Washington, DC: Carnegie Endowment for International Peace.
Zetter, R. (2012). Are Refugees an Economic Burden or Benefit? *Forced Migration Review* 41: 50–52.

22
GENDERED COPING STRATEGIES AND ARMED CONFLICT IN THE MIDDLE EAST

Jennifer C. Olmsted

22.1 Introduction – macroeconomic context

In its 2019 Global Peace Index (GPI) report, the Institute for Economics and Peace identified the Middle East as "the world's least peaceful region," pointing out that the situation in the region has been critical for a number of years (Institute for Economics and Peace, 2019: 4).[1] Among the list of the ten least peaceful countries in that report, five were in the Middle East (Iraq, Libya, Somalia, Syria and Yemen) and Sudan was ranked in the bottom fifteen. On a more positive note, the same report stated that the region became "marginally more peaceful" between 2018 and 2019 (*Ibid.*: 6).

UNHCR (2019) data also indicate that among the top refugee-generating countries, Syria topped the list, with Somalia and Sudan ranking fifth and seventh globally (and Afghanistan – while not technically in the region – ranking second, which is worthy of note, since many of those refugees have been hosted by Iran). Although no longer in the top ten, refugees from Iraq remain a concern as well. Even among countries that are relatively stable, spillover effects from other countries are in evidence. Iran, Jordan, Lebanon, Sudan and Turkey in particular have borne the brunt of regional conflicts, with these five countries being among the top ten refugee-hosting countries globally (UNHCR, 2019).

Taking a more historic view, in the post-colonial period the vast majority of countries in the region, including Algeria, Bahrain, Egypt, Iran, Iraq, Israel/Palestine, Jordan, Kuwait, Lebanon, Libya, Mauritania, Morocco, Somalia, Syria, Sudan, Tunisia, Turkey and Yemen have all experienced some form of armed conflict. A number of countries appear to have emerged from and been able to resume their development after considerable civil conflicts (for instance, Algeria and Lebanon) and in some cases while political tensions remain, periods of widespread violence have been relatively short in duration (such as in Bahrain, Egypt, Iran, Kuwait and Tunisia). In general, it is clear that the region has suffered considerable and long-term economic damage because of prolonged and ongoing conflict. The Middle East also has some of the highest rates of military spending globally.[2] High military spending and militarism more generally can have various gender implications, as noted by Midgley (2005), Segal (2008) and others. These can include government spending patterns that prioritise military over social services, normalisation of various forms of violence, etc.

Also important to note is that the Middle East has been particularly vulnerable to sanctions. Although often defined by those who impose them as an alternative to conflict, sanctions are in fact a form of aggression with serious (and gendered) economic implications (Olmsted, 2007; Hakimian, 2019). Most recently, Iran has been reeling under some of the harshest economic sanctions since the Trump administration walked away from the Iran Nuclear Deal in May 2018 (Hakimian, 2018). Another recent example is Qatar, which has been subjected to economic blockade by Saudi Arabia, the United Arab Emirates (UAE), Bahrain and Egypt since June 2017. This led to an earlier GPI report (2018: 2) identifying Qatar as having had "the region's biggest deterioration" in its index score between 2017 and 2018. Other Middle Eastern countries that have had sanctions imposed on them include Iraq, Lebanon, Libya, Somalia, Sudan and Yemen. Additionally the West Bank and Gaza Strip have been economically isolated by Israel, with Gaza subject to particularly severe economic and political isolation since the election of the Hamas government (Olmsted, 2009).

The consequences of these various forms of conflict include increased exposure to violence, as well as worsening macroeconomic conditions, which in turn have contributed to worsening well-being.

The following are some of the consequences of conflict, which impact both micro- and macroeconomic conditions. Obviously, violence related to armed conflict raises death and injury rates directly. But, even in cases of particularly brutal conflicts, death rates tend to underestimate the hardship inflicted on the general population who survive direct violence. They can, for instance, conceal rising infant mortality rates and shortened general life expectancy. In Syria, for example, it is estimated that about half a million people have died, which is just over 2% of the Syrian population (Specia, 2018). But the tragedy does not end there as survivors face increased economic hardship, including loss of food systems and livelihoods, which in turn leads to lower consumption levels and often worsening nutrition, education and health outcomes. Some choose to flee and this in turn creates its own set of challenges with the creation of large numbers of internally displaced persons (IDPs) and refugees. Not only does death lead to loss of human capital, but so too does displacement. In addition, future generations of workers are often unable to pursue their education in the context of armed conflict. The ability to pursue education may be curtailed due to infrastructural damage and/or the dislocation of both students and/or instructors, if not the physical destruction of educational facilities. Worsening economic conditions also may lead to rising rates of criminal activity, both as a coping strategy and in a context of increased lawlessness and lax enforcement.

All these factors in turn contribute to worsening economic outcomes with gendered implications. The next section elaborates on the link between conflict and gender.

22.2 Gendered consequences of armed conflict: theoretical and empirical aspects

Gender differences in outcomes are due to both biological and social factors. Pregnancy for example creates particular risks for women, which may be exacerbated by conflict. At the same time, differences in social norms and expectations also affect how men, women, girls and boys experience conflict differently. Gender intersects with other individual and group traits such as age, education, (dis)ability, class, etc., with the result that the degree to which, and how, individuals are vulnerable in conflict contexts can vary.

Aside from the negative short- and long-term macroeconomic impacts of armed conflict, the breakdown in the social fabric has important gender consequences. This fraying of social cohesion results from both increased violence itself as well as the physical and mental health challenges associated with such conflict. With the breakdown of the social fabric can also come changes in norms, a particularly important point when it comes to assessing the longer-term gendered effects of conflict on societies.

Unfortunately, in many conflict contexts data are limited and sex-disaggregated data in particular may be lacking. Governments are not likely to prioritise data collection in situations when their power is challenged internally or externally. Even if they have the capacity to collect data, they may not have the will to highlight economic hardships and human rights abuses. This may be particularly true of politically sensitive data focusing on issues such as sexual violence. Additionally, a number of the countries in the region that are suffering from conflict are among the least developed in the region (for instance, Yemen, Sudan and Somalia), a factor that has also contributed to emerging data gaps.

One of the most obvious impacts of armed conflict is mortality. Life expectancy in armed conflict declines both due to the direct impact of war and because of worsening infrastructure. Data on mortality rates in the context of armed conflict can be a challenge to obtain and those that are sex-disaggregated are even more difficult to find (Ormhaug, 2009). Given their more active and direct participation in fighting, combat-related mortality rates are generally higher for males, but much of the increased mortality in the context of armed conflict is due to indirect consequences of violence. As stated on a Brown University webpage (2015), "Death can happen weeks or months after a battle. Many times more civilians have died as a result of battered infrastructure and poor health conditions arising from the wars than directly from its violence." Worsening infrastructure for example can reduce access to medical care, as well as clean water, sanitation and food. A cross-country macroeconomic analysis of the impact of armed conflict (Plümper and Neumayer, 2006) suggests that while men are more likely to die directly from conflict, females are more at risk of dying from indirect factors. These authors focused on life expectancy to arrive at these conclusions, and other studies have confirmed this to be the case as well, using different methods (Ormhaug, 2009).

Shifts in educational attainment as well as health and nutrition outcomes also occur in conflict contexts (UNICEF, 2010). Concerning the issue of nutrition, some of the most tragic recent cases include the widespread starvation that has occurred in Yemen, as well as Sudan and Somalia. UNDP (2012) estimated that tens of thousands died in Somalia as a result of hunger that was in turn linked to the ongoing conflict, both due to a breakdown of infrastructure needed to distribute food as well as various factions deliberately withholding food from vulnerable populations (BBC, 2010). In 2017, Somalia was again in crisis with an estimated six million individuals "facing acute food insecurity" (McVeigh, 2017). Areas of Syria have also seen food used as a weapon to control populations with devastating results (UNICEF, 2017). More recently, reports of widespread famine have been reported in Yemen directly linked to the ongoing conflict and particularly to the Saudi-supported blockade (Ferguson, 2018).

Even in contexts where extensive armed combat is not a factor, the imposition of sanctions can cause malnutrition rates to rise significantly, as happened in the case of Iraq, during the imposition of some of the harshest sanctions after 2003. More recently in the Gaza Strip, malnutrition rates have risen considerably in the face of economic restrictions imposed on the Palestinian population by Israel. Garfield (1999) estimates that rates of malnutrition in Iraq rose from 3% to 11% with the introduction of sanctions. A UNDP report (2005a) suggests that malnutrition rates then continued to rise, with the rate among children aged 5 and under estimated at 23% by 2003. Acute malnutrition rates were highest in the south where they reached as high as 17%. In Palestine, food insecurity and chronic malnutrition have also been linked to the ongoing conflict with Israel, particularly in Gaza (Kanafani and Al-Botmeh, 2008; Tsigga and Grammatikopoulou, 2012). Since the siege of Gaza began in 2006, in particular, food insecurity has worsened with anaemia and stunting rates rising among children (Radi et al., 2013). Unfortunately, most studies carried out in conflict contexts do not evaluate gender differences in terms of malnutrition outcomes. One exception is the UNDP (2005a) report mentioned above that examines data for Iraq and does not find differences in malnutrition between boys and girls.

The data on malnutrition are inconclusive, but when it comes to child mortality more generally, data from Bahrain, Egypt, Iran and Jordan, which are relatively conflict-free countries in the region, suggest a gender bias that disadvantages girls (Alkema, 2014). The same study interestingly does not find a similar bias in Lebanon, the Palestinian Territories and Yemen, which have all suffered from considerable conflict. This analysis, as well as an examination of recent World Bank data, suggests that conflict puts both boys and girls at risk of higher mortality and therefore may unfortunately be a downward equaliser in terms of the gender gap. Again the particularly tragic example of this is Iraq which is, as noted by Tabutin et al. (2005), the only country in the region that did not reduce its infant mortality rates between the 1960s and 2000s, a finding they link to Iraq's multiple wars and the imposition of harsh sanctions. This contrasts sharply with the fact that in the region as a whole, infant mortality declined from 192 to about 39 per 1,000 between 1952 and 2002.

The Tabutin et al. study does not provide sex-disaggregated figures on child mortality for Iraq, but does find consistent biases against girls in a number of other Middle Eastern countries. This study also separates Yemen and Iraq from the rest of the data[3] for some of its analysis, because of "their particularly poor health situation" (Tabutin et al., 2005: 558). In Yemen and Iraq they indicate that the probability of dying between the age of zero and five is 105 per 1000, which is three and a half times the average of 30 deaths per thousand in the 18 other countries in the region. Similar patterns are found for infants. In Iraq and Yemen long-term conflict has clearly played an adverse role in preventing progress in health improvements for both boys and girls.

Another unfortunate consequence of armed conflict, discussed by Rehn and Sirleaf (2002), is the "lost generation," which the authors mention in the context of Somali women talking about their children's lack of access to education. Similar to child mortality rates, in the general development literature there is evidence that boys are favoured over girls when it comes to access to education, particularly in countries at lower levels of development. As in the case of malnutrition, data broken down by sex are not always available in conflict contexts, and where data are available, the gender impacts are not entirely clear. A cross-country analysis of the impact of conflict on education found that not only do education levels decline, but often gender gaps are also exacerbated, although considerable variation exists across countries (UNESCO, 2011).

In Yemen and Somalia levels of illiteracy have remained persistently high, particularly for females. UNESCO (2015) reports an out of school rate of 21% for girls and 5% for boys of primary school age in Yemen. By secondary school the rate for girls had risen to 49% and for boys to 26%. In Somalia, as UNICEF (nd) points out, the literacy rates are among the lowest globally. Only 30% of children are in primary school and girls make up only 40% of that group, suggesting a rate well below 30% among females although they make up about half the population.

In extreme cases, children may have lower educational achievements than their parents. In Iraq education was downwardly affected by both sanctions and war and at the same time the gap between the males and females narrowed as overall rates of literacy declined (Olmsted, 2007). Unfortunately, later data suggest the gender gap has re-emerged in Iraq (UNESCO and UNICEF, 2015). The Syrian conflict has also had a devastating impact on children's education. According to a recent report by Teschendorff (2017), "[t]he net enrolment rate [among Syrians] for primary education dropped from 92% in 2004 to 61% by 2013 (61.1% for female and 62.4% for male) and, for secondary education, from around 72% in 2009 to 44% in 2013 (43.8% for female and 44.3% for male)."

There are also more general health risks directly related to the violence that surrounds conflict, which we should consider (for instance, disability rates increase, as injuries lead to amputations). Other health-related complications also rise. But as in the case of mortality, many health challenges are linked only indirectly to armed conflict and are instead a function of worsening infrastructure, and other challenges related to service delivery. Women of child-bearing age face a particular set of risks related to pregnancy and birth. While the correlation is not perfect, a number of the countries in the Middle East that have high maternal mortality rates are also those that have experienced extensive conflict. These include Somalia, Sudan and Yemen where the rates in 2017 were 829, 295 and 164, respectively, per 100,000 live births (World Bank, n.d.a). More generally UNICEF (2010: 29) discusses the link between higher rates of maternal mortality and armed conflict, noting that "half of the 33 conflict-affected countries [globally, not just in the region] have maternal mortality rates of 550 or more," while the world average for the same year was 400 per 100,000 live births (since then the global average has declined to 211).

Again examining Iraq provides particular insights into this challenge – Iraq had maternal mortality rates that were between those for Egypt and Tunisia in 1990, but while in the latter countries maternal mortality rates continued to decline, in Iraq maternal declines in mortality rates stagnated and even rose in some periods, due to sanctions and war.

A 2014 report by Family Care International (FCI), International Center for Research on Women (ICRW) and the KEMRI/CDC Research and Public Health Collaboration provides grim insights into the long-term negative impact that mothers dying in childbirth has on their families. This study found that not only are infants – if they survive their mother's death – more likely to be trapped in a cycle of poverty, but so too are their older siblings. In other words, preventable maternal death is not only a human rights violation, it is a contributor to the intergenerational cycle of poverty as well.

Apart from maternal death and its intergenerational consequences, maternal health can be compromised in other ways too. In the Palestinian territories, for example, access to antenatal care declined between 2000 and 2002 after Israel's tightening control over the West Bank and Gaza Strip (UNDP, 2005b) leading to women facing particular mental and physical health challenges (Aswad, 2007). Periods of intense conflict in Gaza have also been linked to lower birth weights (Mansour and Rees, 2011).

22.3 Gendered coping strategies

As households experience increased economic hardship and are exposed to various forms of violence, they respond in innumerable ways. One coping strategy that individuals or families may pursue is fleeing from areas where they are threatened by violence or can no longer sustain themselves. The Middle East has a long history of tragic refugee populations, with the Palestinians being the largest long-standing displaced group globally, while more recent refugee communities include Iraqis and Syrians among others. Massive numbers of IDPs have also been an issue in Iraq, Somalia, Sudan, Syria and Yemen. One gendered reason why fleeing occurs relates to the threat of sexual violence, but becoming displaced itself can create considerable physical and economic vulnerability as well.

Whether they flee or not, households experiencing economic hardship or loss of access to resources and/or services often need to make difficult decisions. The process of decision-making may be gendered as may be the outcomes. Women in particular are often tasked with budgeting and food procurement. Work by Cainkar (1993) and Al-Ali (2005) illustrates some of the challenging decisions women were forced to make around food allocation in the context of increased hardship in Iraq. Similar decisions are also being made around education and health care, as evidenced by the declining enrolment rates.

Households may also have to make difficult decisions about income generation and asset liquidation in the context of armed conflict. Women's and men's access to paid employment differ due to a variety of reasons. In the Middle East, in particular women's labour force participation rates have generally been considerably lower than men's (Olmsted, 2005, 2020), which has resulted in women being dependent on male breadwinners. Theory is not clear on whether women are more or less likely to engage in paid employment in conflict contexts since the fact that men are more likely to be conscripted can open up opportunities for women. Macroeconomic hardship may also put pressure on women to seek employment in contexts where men are not able to find work. On the other hand, if jobs are scarce, prevailing gender norms can put pressure on women to stay at home and increased street violence may further exacerbate caution in venturing out.

The United Nations has made a concerted effort to incorporate women refugees into labour markets in the context of the Syrian crisis, but has faced political, cultural and economic challenges in doing so (Olmsted and Killian, 2021). Data provided by Kumar et al. (2018) indicate though that Syrian refugee women's labour force participation rates have risen in the context of the Syrian displacement. Whether these patterns are an indication that women are gaining social and economic power, or instead an indication of their extreme vulnerability, remains a question. Certainly various qualitative studies such as the one by Knappert, Kornau and Figengül (2017) suggest that exploitation is a concern.

At the same time, the imposition of sanctions in various Middle Eastern countries has put downward pressure on women's employment. In the cases of Iran and Palestine, women with lower levels of education were particularly affected (Olmsted, 2007, 2011). In Iraq, the class implications were somewhat different, because Iraq had a very large state section that employed large numbers of educated women, and that system was eroded after sanctions were imposed (Olmsted, 2007).

One of the more tragic outcomes of war is that families facing economic hardship may need to resort to a number of labour market strategies that they would not have chosen in the absence of crisis. This can include making use of child labour or child marriage (both of which also involve curtailment of education). In Arab contexts, boys are more likely to be expected to work (Olmsted and Killian, 2021), whereas girls are more likely to be vulnerable to child marriage, a point elaborated on below (UN ESCWA and UNFPA, 2015). Both have long-term implications for the cycle of poverty and macroeconomic productivity.

Another often-gendered employment response involves participation in criminal activity. While men are more likely to be involved in looting and smuggling rings (antiquities, arms, drugs, human trafficking, oil, etc.) women are more likely to end up involved in sex-related criminal activity. During the Iraq war, for example, both smuggling and sex-related crime rose (Women's Commission for Refugee Women and Children, 2007). Criminal activity has also risen in Syria since the war (Steenkamp, 2017). Sex work often comes with very particular sexual and reproductive health challenges (sexually transmitted diseases and the risk of pregnancy). And in cultural contexts where honour is emphasised, the risks can be even greater for women and girls.

Another gendered labour impact relates to unpaid work. Data on unpaid work is a challenge to obtain for the region and there have been no consistent studies of this phenomenon for the region, but qualitative studies suggest that given prevailing gender norms, unpaid work stresses may weigh particularly heavy on women (Maassarani and Olmsted, 2004; Olmsted, 2007).

Little is known about the gendering of asset liquidation in the context of conflict. One of the more mobile forms of wealth in the region is gold, which is often an asset owned by women. In the context of Lebanon, Iraq and Palestine, analysts (Hijab, 1988; Cainkar, 1993; UN Women, 2013) have noted that one strategy that households may resort to during conflict is selling gold, which in turn can have longer-term implications for women in particular (Olmsted, 2007).

This is not to say that men also do not suffer from wealth depletion in the context of war. Property and other assets are often under male control and may be lost or damaged during conflict. To date, though, few if any studies have looked at asset control and loss in conflict contexts through a gender lens. However, such questions are certainly relevant both for post-conflict redevelopment and in terms of understanding vulnerability among the aging in conflict contexts.

Aside from consumption and wealth management decisions, households may also either make the decision to change the household structure in the context of conflict or have that decision imposed upon them. Whether due to increased deaths or other causes, changing household structure is often linked to increased rates of female headship, which in turn are often an indication of increased economic vulnerability, as has been observed in the context of the Syrian crisis (Olmsted and Killian, 2021).

Recruitment of soldiers is another clear way in which armed conflict is shaped by dominant gender norms. Boys and men are more likely to be expected to serve in active combat and therefore may be more at risk of death. Additionally, in cases where forced conscription is in place, sexual violence may be used as a way to control both conscripts and their families. Cohen (2011) argues that within the region this has particularly been the case in Somalia and Sudan. The use of this type of sexual violence in turn has serious long-term gendered economic consequences for communities, in the context of post-conflict reconstruction. Reintegrating former soldiers who have on the one hand been traumatised by recruitment tactics and their combat experiences, but at the same time may have been perpetrators of sexual violence, creates challenges in contexts where survivors are expected to welcome perpetrators back into the community.

For child-bearing females an added complication is the fact that where sexual violence does occur, pregnancy and birth can also follow, leading not only to the increased burden of caring for another life, but also to stigma and trauma. Even when no pregnancy occurs, rape can have long- term consequences, including stigma, mental and physical health consequences in contexts, as sexual violence is linked to fistula and other reproductive health implications. And as a recent RAND study points out (Tanielian and Jaycox, 2008), post-traumatic stress disorder (PTSD) can have far-reaching effects not just for individuals but also their families. That study argued that the ability to parent effectively is negatively impacted by PTSD for example, which in turn is likely to have intergenerational impacts on the ability to thrive.

Another way that household composition shifts involves decisions about marriage and divorce. Theoretically, the impact of armed conflict on age of marriage is ambiguous. Finding marriage partners may be a challenge in the context of war, as is the cost of marrying and this can increase the age of marriage as a result. At the same time, marriage may be viewed by some as a coping strategy to protect girls and this can cause the average age of marriage to decline. Whereas there is no empirical evidence that child marriage rose in the context of the Lebanese or Algerian wars, in a number of recent Middle Eastern conflicts child marriage has been a serious concern. In Yemen, Somalia, Palestine, Iraq and Syria, there is evidence that one strategy that parents have used to survive during difficult social and economic conditions brought about by prolonged conflict has been to marry their daughters off earlier than they might have done. Child marriage may occur because families are struggling to feed large households and think that marrying their daughters will not only reduce the burden on their natal homes, but also improve their child's economic situation. Child marriage may also be seen as a strategy for protecting both a child's and her parents' honour in contexts where sex outside of marriage is perceived as shameful and the threat of sexual violence is perceived to be high (UN ESCWA and UNFPA, 2015).

Child marriage, like sexual violence, can have a number of hidden economic costs. For one thing, early marriage is often linked to earlier and higher fertility rates, which in turn can be linked to economic hardship. Girls may also have their education terminated when married off young, although in conflict contexts – as discussed above – education may be terminated for other reasons too. Low education in turn is linked to worse nutritional outcomes, which in turn can lead to an intergenerational cycle of poverty.

Many of the other impacts discussed above are also intergenerational. The inability to pursue education, whether in a context of child marriage, child labour, both or neither, has consequences for individuals' earnings and decision-making prospects later in life (parents' lack of education for example has been tied to children's malnutrition). This can in turn contribute to a cycle of poverty and persistent underdevelopment.

In addition to the impact conflict has on individuals' and communities' abilities to thrive, more subtle changes can also take place in the context of armed conflict related to social norms. Gender norm change in particular can have long-term consequences, both positively and negatively. Fear of violence can cause parents to restrict their children's mobility, which has implications in terms of access to health and education. Patriarchal norms also can lead to particularly harsh restrictions being imposed on female household members, although in contexts where forced conscription is in place the opposite may occur. There is considerable empirical evidence that in contexts of armed conflicts and militarism more generally, gender-based violence increases (Al-Ali and Pratt, 2009; Sharoni, 2016). At the same time, feminists have argued that post-conflict situations in particular may be ideal times to push for increased women's involvement in the economic and political spheres, given that norms are in flux and women often take on more and different types of responsibilities given the circumstances.

22.4 Conclusion

Clearly, war and military conflicts lead to death, infrastructure destruction and economic stagnation negatively affecting economies and societies. Vulnerability is conditioned by age, location, class and (dis)ability, in addition to gender. Sadly, war can be a downward equaliser in terms of various developmental yardsticks. Since the nutritional, educational and health status of both males and females decline in the context of war, gender gaps may close under such conditions. This does not mean greater gender equality, but rather that the tragedy of war has a downward equalising tendency creating substantial hardship for all.

At the same time, the impact of war is highly gendered in many ways. This includes, for instance, forced conscription and child labour, which are more likely to affect boys, and child marriage and the threat of sexual violence more generally, which are more likely to affect girls. Female headship also often increases in the context of war, and yet females' access to paid employment remains much lower than males'. This in turn indicates the particular economic vulnerability of female household heads, the dependants they care for as well as women more generally. Gender norms are also often in flux in the context of armed conflict, which can lead to increased challenges and opportunities related to addressing gender norms.

Given these realities, numerous gender-related challenges can be identified both in the context of humanitarian responses and post-conflict redevelopment. Concerning the former, the development community has increasingly been attempting to ensure that humanitarian responses are gender-sensitive, although the results of these efforts are mixed (Olmsted and Killian, 2021). Feminists have also been vocal about the need to make sure women are at the table when post-conflict negotiations take place, but success in achieving this remains mixed.

One of the key takeaways from this analysis is that conflict is not only bad for short-term development prospects, but that it also has intergenerational gendered impacts that require more attention in thinking about post-conflict reconstruction. Breaking the intergenerational cycle of poverty that is often linked to conflict contexts requires particular attention to be given to gendered vulnerabilities, as well as to understanding how deprivation of girls and women affects the well-being of entire families, not just individuals.

Notes

1 Both external and internal factors have played a role in creating the present-day tragic outcomes but the aim of this chapter is not to focus on the causes of these conflicts. The region for example has a long history of external intervention going back to the colonial period (such as the creation of Israel by the UN as well as the drawing of other contested borders by colonial powers, election interventions, arms sales, etc.). The presence of oil and the scarcity of water have also contributed to current tensions and conflicts. We should also note that while a number of the region's conflicts are categorised as civil wars, interstate conflicts as well as foreign interventions also have played a role in regional instability. As analysis by the Heidelberg Institute (2015) indicates, in most countries multiple conflicts are occurring simultaneously with both internal and external actors contributing to the deaths and destruction that emanate from them.

2 An examination of World Bank data for which 2019 data were available indicated that of the top ten countries in terms of military spending as a percent of GDP, seven were in the Middle East, with Oman and Saudi Arabia topping the list followed by Algeria, Kuwait, Jordan, Israel, and Lebanon.

3 Tabutin et al. (2005) do not include Somalia or Sudan in their study and the conflicts in Libya and Syria had not yet begun.

References

Al-Ali, Nadje (2005), "Reconstructing Gender: Iraqi Women between Dictatorship, War, Sanctions and Occupation", *Third World Quarterly*, 26(4/5): 739–758.

Al-Ali, Nadje and Pratt Nicola (2009), *What Kind of Liberation? Women and the Occupation in Iraq*, Berkeley: University of California Press.

Alkema, Leontine, Fengqing Chao, Danzhen You, Jon Pedersen and Cheryl C Sawyer (2014), "National, Regional, and Global Sex Ratios of Infant, Child, and Under-5 Mortality and Identification of Countries with Outlying Ratios: A Systematic Assessment", *Lancet*, 2, September, 521–530.

Aswad, Henrietta (2007), "Checkpoints Compound the Risks of Childbirth for Palestinian Women", United Nations Population Fund *(UNPFA)*, 15 May; available from: http://www.unfpa.org/news/checkpoints-compound-risks-childbirth-palestinian-women

BBC (2010), "Somali Militants 'Block UN Food Aid'", 28 February; available from: http://news.bbc.co.uk/2/hi/africa/8541315.stm

Brown University (2015), "The Costs of War"; available from: https://watson.brown.edu/costsofwar/costs/human/civilians

Cainkar, Louise (1993), "The Gulf War, Sanctions and the Lives of Iraqi Women", *Arab Studies Quarterly*, 15(2): 15–51.

Cohen Dara Kay (2011), "Causes of Sexual Violence During Civil War: Cross-National Evidence (1980–2009)", Working Paper, Humphrey School of Public Affairs University of Minnesota Prepared for the Minnesota International Relations Colloquium 28 March 2011; available from: https://www.researchgate.net/publication/268416822_Causes_of_Sexual_Violence_During_Civil_War_Cross-National_Evidence_1980-2009

Family Care International (FCI), International Center for Research on Women (ICRW), and the KEMRI/CDC Research and Public Health Collaboration (2014), *A Price Too High to Bear: The Costs of Maternal*

Mortality; available from: https://www.icrw.org/publications/a-price-too-high-to-bear-the-costs-of-maternal-mortality-to-families-and-communities/

Ferguson, Jane (2018), "Is Intentional Starvation the Future of War?", *The New Yorker Magazine*, 11 July; available from: https://www.newyorker.com/news/news-desk/is-yemen-intentional-starvation-the-future-of-war

Garfield, Richard (1999), *The Impact of Economic Sanctions on Health and Well-Being*, London: Overseas Development Institute.

Hakimian, Hassan (2018), "Can Trump's Sanctions Break Iran?", *Project Syndicate*, September; available from: https://www.project-syndicate.org/commentary/will-trump-sanctions-break-iran-by-hassan-hakimian-2018-09

Hakimian, Hassan (2019), "Seven Fallacies of Economic Sanctions", Project Syndicate, May; available from: https://www.project-syndicate.org/commentary/economic-sanctions-seven-fallacies-by-hassan-hakimian-2019-05

Heidelberg Institute for International Conflict Research (2015), "Conflict Barometer 2014"; available from: https://hiik.de/conflict-barometer/bisherige-ausgaben/?lang=en

Hijab, Nadia (1988), *Womanpower: The Arab Debate on Women at Work*, Cambridge: Cambridge University Press.

Institute for Economics and Peace (2019), "Global Peace Index 2019: Measuring Peace in a Complex World", Sydney, June; available from: https://www.visionofhumanity.org/wp-content/uploads/2020/10/GPI-2019web.pdf.

Kanafani, Numan and Samia Al-Botmeh (2008), "The Political Economy of Food Aid in Palestine", *Economics of Peace and Security Journal*, 3(2): 39–46.

Knappert, Lena, Angela Kornau and Meltem Figengül (2017), "Refugees' Exclusion at Work and the Intersection with Gender: Insights from the Turkish-Syrian Border", *Journal of Vocational Behavior*, April, 105: 62–82.

Kumar, Krishna B., Shelly Culbertson, Louay Constant, Shanthi Nataraj, Fatih Unlu, Kathryn E. Bouskill, Joy S. Moini, Katherine Costello, Gursel Rafig oglu Aliyev and Fadia Afashe (2018), *Opportunities for All: Mutually Beneficial Opportunities for Syrians and Host Countries in Middle Eastern Labor Markets*, Santa Monica, CA: RAND Corporation; available from: https://www.rand.org/pubs/research_reports/RR2653.html. Also available in print form.

Maassarani, Tarek and Jennifer Olmsted (2004), "Gendered Occupation and Resistance in Palestine", *Middle East Women's Studies Review*, Spring/Summer, 19(1/2): 1–4.

Mansour, H. and D.I. Rees (2011), "Armed Conflict and Birth Weight: Evidence from the al-Aqsa Intifada", *Journal of Development Economics*, 99: 190–199.

McVeigh, Karen (2017), "Somalia Famine Fears Prompt UN Call for 'Immediate and Massive' Reaction", *The Guardian*, 3 February; available from: https://www.theguardian.com/global-development/2017/feb/03/somalia-famine-fears-un-call-immediate-massive-reaction

Midgley, Jane (2005), *Gender Budgeting and the U.S.: Creating New Economic Priorities for 2010 and beyond*; available from: http://exhibitions.globalfundforwomen.org/economica/new-visions/gender-budgeting

Olmsted, Jennifer (2005), "Is Paid Work the (Only) Answer? Neoliberalism, Arab Women's Well-Being, and the Social Contract", *Journal of Middle East Women's Studies*, 2(1): 112–139.

Olmsted, Jennifer (2007), "'Globalization' Denied: Gender and Poverty in Iraq and Palestine", in Cabezas, Amalia, Ellen Reese and Marguerite Waller (eds.), *The Wages of Empire: Neoliberal Policies, Armed Repression, and Women's Poverty*, Boulder, CO: Paradigm: 178–233.

Olmsted, Jennifer (2009), "The Physical and Economic Devastation of Gaza", *Dollars and Sense*, July; available from: http://dollarsandsense.org/archives/2009/0609olmsted.html

Olmsted, Jennifer (2011), "Gender and Globalization: The Iranian Experience", in Bahramitash, R. and H. Esfahani (eds.) *Globalization, Islamism and Women in Iran*, Syracuse: Syracuse University Press: 25–52.

Olmsted, Jennifer (2020), *Feminist Critique of Neoliberalism in the MENA Region*, Friedrich Ebert Stiftung; available from: http://library.fes.de/pdf-files/bueros/beirut/16019-20200422.pdf

Olmsted, Jennifer and Caitlin Killian (2021), *Women and Work: Improving Gender Integration in the Livelihoods Response to the Syrian Crisis*, United Nations Development Programme (UNDP); available from: https://www.arabstates.undp.org/content/rbas/en/home/library/crisis-response0/women-and-work--improving-gender-integration-in-the-livelihoods-.html?cq_ck=1613472188873

Ormhaug, Christin, in collaboration with Patrick Meier and Helga Hernes (2009), "Armed Conflict Deaths Disaggregated by Gender", PRIO Papers; available from: https://www.prio.org/Publications/Publication/?x=7207

Plümper, T and E. Neumayer (2006), "The Unequal Burden of War: The Effect of Armed Conflict on the Gender Gap in Life Expectancy", *International Organization*, 60(3): 723–754.

Radi, S.M., N.A. El-Sayed, L.M. Nofal and Z.A. Abdeen (2013), "Ongoing Deterioration Of The Nutritional Status of Palestinian Preschool Children in Gaza under the Israeli Siege", *Eastern Mediterranean Health Journal*, 19(3): 234–241; available from: http://www.emro.who.int/emhj-vol-19-2013/3/ongoing-deterioration-of-the-nutritional-status-of-palestinian.html

Rehn, Elisabeth and Ellen Johnson Sirleaf (2002), *Women, War and Peace: The Independent Experts' Assessment on the Impact of Armed Conflict on Women and Women's Role in Peace-building*; available from: http://www.unfpa.org/sites/default/files/pub-pdf/3F71081FF391653DC1256C69003170E9-unicef-WomenWarPeace.pdf

Segal, Lynne (2008), "Gender, War and Militarism: Making and Questioning the Links", *Feminist Review*, 88: 21–35.

Sharoni, Simona (2016), "Militarism and Gender-Based Violence", in *The Wiley Blackwell Encyclopedia of Gender and Sexuality Studies*, edited by Nancy Naples, Wiley.

Specia, Megan (2018), "How Syria's Death Toll is Lost in the Fog of War", *New York Times*, 13 April; available from: https://www.nytimes.com/2018/04/13/world/middleeast/syria-death-toll.html

Steenkamp, Christina (2017), "The Crime-Conflict Nexus and the Civil War in Syria", *Stability: International Journal of Security and Development*, 6(1): 11; available from: https://www.stabilityjournal.org/articles/10.5334/sta.522/

Tabutin, Dominique, Bruno Schoumaker, Godfrey Rogers, Jonathan Mandelbaum and Catriona Dutreuilh (2005), "The Demography of the Arab World and the Middle East from the 1950s to the 2000s. A Survey of Changes and a Statistical Assessment", *Population*, 60(5/6): 505–591, 593–615.

Tanielian, Terri L. and Lisa H. Jaycox (eds.) (2008), *Invisible Wounds of War: Psychological and Cognitive Injuries, Their Consequences, and Services to Assist Recovery*, Santa Monica, CA: RAND; available from: http://www.rand.org/pubs/monographs/MG720.html

Teschendorff, Marta Guasp (2017), *Loss of Access to Education Puts Well-being of Syrian Girls at Risk*, United Nations University; available from: https://ourworld.unu.edu/en/loss-of-access-to-education-puts-well-being-of-syrian-girls-at-risk

Tsigga, M. and M.G. Grammatikopoulou (2012), "Assessing the Silent Epidemic of Malnutrition in Palestinian Preschool Children", *Journal of Epidemiological Global Health*, 2(4): 181–191.

UNESCO (2011), *The Hidden Crisis: Armed Conflict and Education - Education for All Global Monitoring Report 2011*, United Nations Educational, Scientific and Cultural Organization; available from: https://unesdoc.unesco.org/ark:/48223/pf0000190743

UNESCO Institute for Statistics (UIS) and UNICEF (2015). *Fixing the Broken Promise of Education for All: Findings from the Global Initiative on Out-of-School Children*. Montreal: UIS. http://uis.unesco.org/sites/default/files/documents/fixing-broken-promise-efa-findings-global-initiative-oosc-education-2015-en_2.pdf

UNICEF (2010), *Machel Study 10-Year Strategic Review: Children and Conflict in a Changing World*; United Nations International Children's Emergency Fund; available from: https://www.un.org/ruleoflaw/blog/document/machel-study-10-year-strategic-review-children-and-conflict-in-a-changing-world/

UNICEF (2017), "Child Malnutrition Levels Increase Sharply in Besieged Syrian Town of East Ghouta"; available from: https://www.unicef.org/media/media_101732.html

UNICEF (n.d.), "Education in Somalia"; available from: https://www.unicef.org/somalia/education.html

United Nations Development Programme (UNDP) (2005a), *Iraq Living Conditions Survey 2004, Volume II: Analytical Report*, United Nations Development Programme in cooperation with the Ministry of Planning and Development Cooperation of Iraq, Baghdad; available from: https://reliefweb.int/report/iraq/iraq-living-conditions-survey-2004

UNDP (2005b), *Human Development Report*; available from: http://hdr.undp.org/sites/default/files/reports/266/hdr05_complete.pdf

UNDP (2012), *Somalia Human Development Report*, Nairobi; available from: http://hdr.undp.org/en/content/2012-somalia-human-development-report

UN ESCWA and UNFPA (2015), *Child Marriage in Humanitarian Settings in the Arab Region: Dynamics, Challenges and Policy Options*; United Nations Economic and Social Commission for West Asia and United Nations Population Fund; available from: https://www.unescwa.org/ar/file/43807/download?token=rex65Qcz

UNHCR (2019), Mid-Year Trends United Nations High Commissioner for Refugees; available from: https://www.unhcr.org/en-us/statistics/unhcrstats/5e57d0c57/mid-year-trends-2019.html

UN Women (2013), *Building Ties: Towards Integrated Strategies & Policies for Empowering Palestinian Women*, May; available from: http://palestine.unwomen.org/en/digital-library/publications/2014/6/building-ties
Women's Commission for Refugee Women and Children (2007), *Iraqi Refugee Women and Youth in Jordan: Reproductive Health Findings*; available from: https://reliefweb.int/report/iraq/iraqi-refugee-women-and-youth-jordan-reproductive-health-findings
World Bank (n.d.a), Maternal Mortality ratio. Available from: https://data.worldbank.org/indicator/sh.sta.mmrt?year_high_desc=true
World Bank (n.d.b), Military expenditure (% of GDP). https://data.worldbank.org /indicator/MS.MIL.XPND.GD.ZS?end=2017&start=2017&view=map&year_high_desc=true

INDEX

Page numbers in *italics* represent figures, while page numbers in **bold** mark tables.

Taylor & Francis eBooks

www.taylorfrancis.com

A single destination for eBooks from Taylor & Francis with increased functionality and an improved user experience to meet the needs of our customers.

90,000+ eBooks of award-winning academic content in Humanities, Social Science, Science, Technology, Engineering, and Medical written by a global network of editors and authors.

TAYLOR & FRANCIS EBOOKS OFFERS:

- A streamlined experience for our library customers
- A single point of discovery for all of our eBook content
- Improved search and discovery of content at both book and chapter level

REQUEST A FREE TRIAL

support@taylorfrancis.com

Routledge
Taylor & Francis Group

CRC Press
Taylor & Francis Group

For Product Safety Concerns and Information please contact our EU
representative GPSR@taylorandfrancis.com
Taylor & Francis Verlag GmbH, Kaufingerstraße 24, 80331 München, Germany

www.ingramcontent.com/pod-product-compliance
Ingram Content Group UK Ltd.
Pitfield, Milton Keynes, MK11 3LW, UK
UKHW050232200926
475702UK00020B/2982
9781032021379